ACCOUNTABILITY IN THE CONTEMPORARY CONSTITUTION

Accountability in the Contemporary Constitution

Edited by
NICHOLAS BAMFORTH
and
PETER LEYLAND

OXFORD
UNIVERSITY PRESS

OXFORD
UNIVERSITY PRESS

Great Clarendon Street, Oxford, OX2 6DP,
United Kingdom

Oxford University Press is a department of the University of Oxford.
It furthers the University's objective of excellence in research, scholarship,
and education by publishing worldwide. Oxford is a registered trade mark of
Oxford University Press in the UK and in certain other countries

Published in the United States of America by Oxford University Press
198 Madison Avenue, New York, NY 10016, United States of America

British Library Cataloguing in Publication Data
Data available

Library of Congress Control Number: 2013937733

ISBN 978–0–19–967002–4

Printed and bound in Great Britain by
CPI Group (UK) Ltd, Croydon, CR0 4YY

Preface

For many years, 'accountability' has been a central term in public and academic debate about the constitutional arrangements of the United Kingdom and other comparable democratic societies. While many high quality academic analyses of the notion of accountability have appeared in particular contexts, the genesis of the present collection of essays lay in a view that the time was ripe to set out a range of informed contributions to debate about the role played by accountability-related ideas in contemporary constitutional law.

Apart from thanking our contributors, we owe a debt of thanks to many people for their support for this project. At OUP, we extend our thanks to Alex Flach, Natasha Fleming, Clare Kennedy, John Britto Stephen and those involved in editorial and production tasks associated with the book. Thanks are also due to Breony Allen and Jack Bradley-Seddon for their work on the indexing. Gordon Anthony, Carol Harlow, Rick Rawlings and Andrew Harding generously offered helpful advice at many points during work on the project, and Aileen Kavanagh and Cheryl Saunders made useful contributions at an early stage. We would also like to acknowledge the help of Sebastian Payne and Colin Scott.

Thanks are also due to Professor Robert McKeever, Claire Keefe and Lucy Hall for their assistance with a workshop involving many of those associated with the project and held at London Metropolitan University in September 2010. We would also like to acknowledge the support provided by the Oxford University Law faculty in relation to the production of the book.

Finally, both of us would like to extend special thanks to Putachad who interpreted our arguments and debates about the project to create her wonderfully evocative cover design for this volume.

Nicholas Bamforth and Peter Leyland
August 2013

Contents

PART V

List of Contributors

T R S Allan is Professor of Jurisprudence and Public Law at the University of Cambridge, and a Fellow of Pembroke College, Cambridge.

J W F Allison is a University Senior Lecturer in Law at the University of Cambridge, and a Fellow of Queens' College, Cambridge.

Nicholas Bamforth is a Fellow in Law at The Queen's College, Oxford.

Julia Black is Professor of Law at the London School of Economics and Political Science.

Paul Craig is Professor of English Law at the University of Oxford, and a Fellow of St John's College, Oxford.

A C L Davies is Garrick Fellow and Tutor in Law at Brasenose College, Oxford and Professor of Law and Public Policy at the University of Oxford.

Mark Elliott is a Reader in Public Law at the University of Cambridge and a Fellow of St Catharine's College, Cambridge.

Sandra Fredman is the Rhodes Professor of the Laws of the British Commonwealth and the United States at the University of Oxford, and a Fellow of Pembroke College, Oxford.

Jeff King is a Senior Lecturer in Law at University College, London.

Andrew Le Sueur is Professor of Constitutional Justice at the University of Essex.

Peter Leyland is Professor of Public Law at London Metropolitan University.

Colm O'Cinneide is a Reader in Law at University College, London.

Dawn Oliver is Emeritus Professor of Constitutional Law at University College, London.

Mark Tushnet is the William Nelson Cromwell Professor of Law at Harvard Law School.

Alison L Young is a Fellow in Law at Hertford College, Oxford.

1

Introduction: Accountability in the Contemporary Constitution

*Nicholas Bamforth and Peter Leyland**

'Accountability' is one of the more frequently used terms in today's constitutional vocabulary, whether in the United Kingdom, the European Union more broadly, the United States, or other liberal democracies. Interestingly, at least when it is deployed as a normative end-goal, the term seems to find equal favour with those who, in considering arrangements for policing the exercise of governmental power in a democracy, would prioritize the role of elected authorities (in particular the legislature) and those who would prioritize the role of courts. Despite their differences, members of each camp can easily designate their own favoured approach as one which directly relates to accountability, even if they understand that term rather differently when it is explored at a more detailed level. More generally, the term 'accountability', however defined, has come to assume a particular prominence in official, academic and popular discourse concerning matters of constitutional law. As such, a re-examination of ideas of accountability in a constitutional law setting, conducted from a variety of perspectives, seems entirely appropriate. This introductory chapter seeks to sketch out some of the themes relating to debates about accountability in general, and to tie these to some of the specific issues raised and debated in the present collection of essays.

A. Concepts of accountability in the constitution

Ideas of accountability play a prominent role in contemporary discussions of constitutional law and practice, and politicians, judges and other actors tend frequently to claim, whatever the substantive viewpoint or proposal which they advocate, that more or better accountability is their end-goal. Mark Bovens notes that 'what started as an instrument to enhance the effectiveness and efficiency of public governance, has gradually become a goal in itself', and 'an icon for good governance' on both

* Fellow in Law, The Queen's College, Oxford, and Professor of Public Law, London Metropolitan University.

sides of the Atlantic.[1] According to Elizabeth Fisher, 'Accountability has become a cherished principle and its importance is [nowadays] being stressed in everything from the provision of public services to criminal justice to transnational governance regimes. It is the ultimate principle for the new age of governance in which the exercise of power has transcended the boundaries of the nation state. It is a pliable concept that can seemingly adapt to novel modes of governing while at the same time ensuring such modes are legitimate'.[2] Anne Davies is clear that 'Accountability is a central value of modern constitutions'.[3] In relation specifically to the United Kingdom, Dawn Oliver has suggested that concerns about securing accountability 'became an issue in politics' in the 1970s, focusing in particular on the government's accountability both to Parliament and to the electorate, and have maintained a central role since then.[4] Colin Scott suggests that from the mid-1980s, 'public lawyers have paid more attention to accountability mechanisms going beyond the parliament and the courts, including grievance-handling, audit and internal review', but have subsequently been faced with greater challenges due to the impact on public administration of New Public Management, with its focus on strategy and economic impetus rather than constitutional constraints.[5] Carol Harlow takes this further, arguing that in the United Kingdom, 'with its current reliance on regulation as a technique of administration, accountability has become something of a fetish'.[6] The most recent sense of accountability is dominated by ideas of audit (associated with New Public Management) and punishment: 'the essential features of every administrative programme are reduced to numbers and evaluated, and every administrative action scrutinized with a view to allocating blame and censure. Transparency has been taken to extreme lengths, and has become a weapon with which the media presses incursions into private life, howling for punitive action and seeking exaggerated redress for the simplest of errors. With this has come a change in public-service values: from public service to management, economy, and efficiency, from trust and discretion to rules and regulation, and above all to quantifiable criteria'.[7]

Against this background, Fisher's reference to 'novel modes' could be felt to have particular resonance. Calls for greater or better accountability have seemingly been fuelled by the expanding opportunities presented by the development of the internet for rapid governmental responses to events, for inter-governmental cooperation, and for public discussion of politicians and government (a point related to the development—in the

[1] M Bovens, 'Analysing and Assessing Accountability: A Conceptual Framework' (2007) 13 *European LJ* 447, 449.

[2] E Fisher, 'The European Union in the Age of Accountability' (2004) 23 *OJLS* 495, 495; note also C Scott, 'Accountability in the Regulatory State' (2000) 27 *JLS* 38, 39.

[3] A C L Davies *The Public Law of Government Contracts* (Oxford: Oxford University. Press, 2008), 92.

[4] D Oliver *Government in the United Kingdom: The Search for Accountability, Effectiveness and Citizenship* (Milton Keynes: Open University Press, 1991), 12.

[5] Scott, 'Accountability', n 2 above, 40. See also Bovens, 'Analysing and Assessing', n1 above, 449.

[6] C Harlow *Accountability in the European Union* (Oxford: Oxford University Press, 2002), 189; note also her assertion, at 6, that 'the terminology of accountability may be a relatively recent arrival'.

[7] Harlow, *Accountability*, n 6 above, 189; see also 18–24. Harlow associates this with what Michael Power describes as the 'audit explosion' (*The Audit Explosion* (London: Demos, 1994), 37–9). As she makes clear at 190–1, she believes the shift towards audit-based accountability in the United Kingdom has gone too far, although she also draws attention at 109–10 to connections between the perceived efficacy of political accountability and national traditions of audit. Elizabeth Fisher has also noted

United Kingdom, at least until very recently—of an increasingly close relationship between politicians and other public servants and the broadcast and print media, coupled with occasional disquiet as to the actions and approaches of journalists[8]). Alongside the rise of New Public Management, the period since the late 1980s has seen the 'hollowing out' of government activity in the United States and the United Kingdom, with central government focusing increasingly on overall policy formation while agencies or privately-owned contractors take responsibility for areas of its execution, sparking debate about how the emerging arrangements can operate in a properly accountable fashion.[9] As Carol Harlow has observed, 'The public wants to know how it is governed; it wants in particular to know how public money is spent and to receive assurances that it has been well spent'.[10] This observation might be applied with equal force, in the contemporary constitutional landscape, to any level of government.

The notion that at least some constitutional actors should be accountable for their decisions and actions is nonetheless an old one. While it may have been assumed, in an age of inherited headships of government, that individuals were accountable to the overlord or dynastic ruler currently in power, the Enlightenment brought with it the idea that legitimate government was conducted, even if not directly by the people, then nonetheless in their interest and ultimately for their benefit.[11] The loose idea that government should properly be conducted in a fashion that was accountable to the general population emerged alongside the gradual extension of the franchise in northern and western countries, and it is hardly novel to employ accountability-related ideas in constitutional law, as well as in relation to the administrative and other legal liability of public bodies and to processes of political and public scrutiny of office-holders. As commentators note, however, ambiguity and uncertainty have long surrounded the meaning and reach of the term.[12] Discussion of accountability begs the question concerning what it means to be 'accountable', which parties an accountability relationship might or must exist between and in relation to which issues, and the sanctions which should be attached to an actor's failure to behave in an appropriate fashion, however this is defined.[13] Furthermore, whether accountability should be policed through the law, through political channels, or through some combination of the two, can be a matter for debate both generally and from situation to situation.

---

the incursion of accountability concerns into the private sphere: Fisher 'European Union', n 2 above, 499–500, 504; see also Scott, 'Accountability', n 2 above, 39–41.

[8] Most recently in the United Kingdom, see *An inquiry into the culture, practices and ethics of the press: report* (London: The Stationery Office, 2012), chaired by Lord Justice Leveson.

[9] See eg. D Oliver and G Drewry *Public Service Reforms: Issues of Accountability and Public Law* (London: Pinter, 1996), ch 1; Scott, 'Accountability', n 2 above, esp. 44–60; D Woodhouse, 'The Reconstruction of Constitutional Accountability' [2002] 73 *Public Law*.

[10] Harlow, *Accountability* n 6 above, 2. Note also Scott's critique of arrangements at domestic level: 'Accountability', n.2 above, 44–8.

[11] See, generally, Bovens, 'Analysing and Assessing', n 1 above, 448–9; Scott, 'Accountability', n 2 above, 39; Harlow, *Accountability*, n 6 above, 14–15.

[12] Eg. Oliver and Drewry, *Public Service Reforms*, n 9 above, 3; Bovens, 'Analysing and Assessing', n 1 above, 448, 449.

[13] See esp. Scott, 'Accountability', n 2 above, 41–2 ff; Bovens, 'Analysing and Assessing', n 1 above, 450–5; Fisher, 'European Union', n 2 above, 497–8.

At a conceptual level, Oliver has suggested that accountability is associated with responsibility, transparency, answerability and responsiveness, that it is 'explanatory and amendatory' insofar as it is associated with 'being liable to be required to give an account or explanation of actions and, where appropriate, to suffer the consequences, take the blame or undertake to put matters right if it should appear that errors have been made',[14] and that it is an ingredient of good governance.[15] Since decision-makers are not infallible, they are required in a liberal democratic polity to justify their acts, provision being made for redress when things go wrong. Oliver argues that accountability 'furthers important objectives. It is supposed to promote openness, effectiveness, and public participation, and it is part of the system for safeguarding an uncorrupt system from corruption'.[16] Accountability mechanisms are central to such concerns,[17] and Oliver distinguishes between four types of mechanism in constitutional terms.[18] First, political accountability is owed to politicians, encompassing ministerial accountability to Parliament (in the United Kingdom) or local authority accountability to central government and Parliament. Under this mechanism, accountable actors and bodies are exposed to possible political censure and electoral risk, with political costs sometimes being exacted at a personal level (for example, via the forced resignation of a minister) if performance falls below the expected standard.[19] Secondly, public accountability is owed to the general public or interested sections of it. Most obviously, elected national and local politicians are politically obliged to explain and justify their actions to electors, with political penalties to be paid at the ballot box if an adequate account is not offered (indeed, the widest sense of accountability might be thought to be linked to the electoral process).[20] Thirdly, public bodies are legally accountable to the courts as an

---

[14] Oliver, *Government in the United Kingdom*, n 4 above, 22. See also Scott, 'Accountability', n 2 above, 39–40; Bovens, 'Analysing and Assessing', n 1 above, 450–9; A C L Davies *Accountability: A Public Law Analysis of Government by Contract* (Oxford: Oxford University Press, 2001), 75–6 and *The Public Law of Government Contracts*, n 3 above, 67. Oliver and Drewry suggest that accountability is 'the duty to explain or justify and then the duty to make amends to anyone who has suffered loss or injustice if something has gone wrong' whereas responsibility means 'having a job to do, and being liable to take the blame when things go wrong' (*Public Service Reforms* n 9 above, 134), but draw attention to the political and administrative debate concerning the relationship between the two (*Public Service Reforms*, ch.1). Harlow equates Oliver's definition with the rule of law: *Accountability* n 6 above, 144 (see also her broader analysis of Oliver's approach in ch.1).

[15] D Oliver *Constitutional Reform in the United Kingdom* (Oxford: Oxford University Press, 2003), 47; note also the definition advanced by R Mulgan: ' "Accountability": An Ever Expanding Concept?' (2000) 78 *Public Administration* 555, 555–6.

[16] Oliver, *Constitutional Reform* n 15 above, 48. See also the association drawn with liberal constitutionalism by Fisher: 'European Union', n 2 above, 496, 500–1, 504. Davies describes accountability in seemingly broader terms, namely as 'a core value in *a democracy* [emphasis added]' (*Public Law Analysis*, n 14 above, 76).

[17] Oliver, *Government in the United Kingdom*, n 4 above, 22–3, *Constitutional Reform*, n 15 above, 48–9; Oliver notes that the range of things for which it is deemed appropriate to designate particular decision-makers as accountable will depend upon one's political philosophy.

[18] See also Bovens, 'Analysing and Assessing', n 1 above, 455–62; Fisher, 'European Union', n 2 above, 501–8; Davies, *Public Law Analysis*, n 14 above, esp. 76–87.

[19] Oliver, *Government in the United Kingdom*, n 4 above, 23–5; *Constitutional Reform*, n 15 above, 49–50. See also Harlow, *Accountability*, n 6 above, 47–52.

[20] Oliver, *Government in the United Kingdom*, n 4 above, 25–6; *Constitutional Reform*, n 15 above, 50–1. See also Harlow, *Accountability*, n 6 above, 168–9.

aspect of the rule of law, being obliged to demonstrate a legal justification for their actions if sued and to make amends if they are found to have acted unlawfully.[21] Carol Harlow has also associated legal accountability, in the European Union context, with proportionality review (given that it requires administrative measures to be appropriate as well as necessary to achieve the desired objectives) and, within limits, with requirements of due process (given that these encourage transparency in decision-making).[22] Fourthly, public bodies are sometimes accountable to non-political governmental bodies such as ombudsmen and public sector auditors, to whom explanations must be provided for their conduct.[23] As Elizabeth Fisher perhaps unsurprisingly notes, a 'resulting impression from reading these categories... is that accountability is a series of tools and to make any governing system "better" requires identifying and utilizing the right types of accountability'.[24]

Although Anne Davies has suggested that the fact that government acts on behalf of others 'is closely linked to the particular emphasis placed in public law on the concept of accountability',[25] Colin Scott argues that public lawyers have generally drawn ideas of accountability somewhat narrowly, relating them to the duties formally owed by one specific set of public bodies/actors to another specific set.[26] Whether or not this is correct, Richard Mulgan, a specialist in public policy rather than public law, has advanced the most visibly narrow definition of relationships which concern accountability, warning that 'accountability threatens to extend its reach over the entire field of constitutional design' if its ambit is not properly controlled.[27] Mulgan characterises the 'central sense' of accountability as 'external scrutiny', this being 'only one type of institutional mechanism for controlling governments and government officials'.[28] Other types of control exist—constitutional constraints and legal regulations—but these should not be described as accountability-related. In logic, 'being accountable for alleged breaches of the law does not mean that compliance with the law is also an act of accountability or that the law itself is an accountability mechanism... in the core sense. The main body of the law, which most public servants follow as a matter of normal practice' is, according to Mulgan, 'an instrument for controlling their behaviour but not for holding them accountable'.[29] Accountability need not include every mechanism—for example, judicial review, the separation of powers, federalism or the rule of law—which helps control government power. Instead, legal accountability 'is confined

---

[21] Oliver, *Government in the United Kingdom*, n 4 above, 26–7; *Constitutional Reform*, n 15 above, 51–2. Harlow associates Oliver's definition with procedural constraints as well as remedies (*Accountability*, n 6 above, 146) and contrasts it with Mulgan's approach as articulated in ' "Accountability": An Ever-Expanding Concept', n 15 above.

[22] Harlow, *Accountability*, n 6 above, 164–5.

[23] Oliver, *Government in the United Kingdom*, n 4 above, 27–8; *Constitutional Reform*, n 15 above, 52–4.

[24] Fisher, 'European Union', n 2 above, 497.

[25] Davies, *Public Law of Government Contracts*, n 3 above, 67.

[26] Scott, 'Accountability', n 2 above, 40.

[27] Mulgan, 'Ever-Expanding Concept', n 15 above, 563.

[28] Mulgan, 'Ever-Expanding Concept', n 15 above, 563.

[29] Mulgan, 'Ever-Expanding Concept', n 15 above, 564.

to that part of the law which lays down enforcement procedures', with the main body of law serving as an instrument for controlling the behaviour of public servants rather than for holding them accountable.[30] On Mulgan's narrow view, only institutions such as audit offices, ombudsmen and administrative tribunals are properly described as institutions of accountability, given that their 'primary function is to call public officials to account'.[31] Other institutions, including legislatures, may adopt an accountability role, but it is not their *exclusive or primary* purpose (within a legislature, accountability is associated with Select Committee inquiries and the questioning of ministers, but legislatures also perform other central functions, including passing legislation). Similarly, while holding government officials to account for their actions is one important function of courts, it is not necessarily a *defining* role of the legal system or of courts in general.

Debate thus exists about the range of relationships which should properly be categorised as concerning accountability. A separate but related issue concerns which form(s) of accountability should be prioritized. Dawn Oliver notes that '[t]he question of to whom accountability is owed is often crucial, as is the design of the mechanisms of accountability, to the good working of the constitution. Choices have to be made about the balance between the different forms of account-ability—whether legal accountability is to be preferred to political accountability, or whether a number of forms of accountability can operate in parallel'.[32] Anne Davies associates political accountability with the government's accountability to Parliament for the merits of decisions, and legal accountability with the standards applied by courts to test the legality of such decisions. She also emphasizes the importance, in the constitutional setting, of accountability to the public, whether through the ballot box or participation in the decision-making process.[33] Different forms of accountability—accountability being tied (on this view) to the promo-tion of the public interest and the justification by public bodies of their actions, to the modification of policies which turn out not to have been well-conceived, and to the making of amends where there have been mistakes or misjudgements—may have advantages and disadvantages in different contexts,[34] even if the term 'accountability' might at the most general level be associated with matters of insti-tutional design relating to the 'rule of law' values involved in democratic govern-ment. Debates about the meaning of accountability are crucial to furthering such values at both macro- and micro-levels and thus play a large role in many of the essays in the present collection, as does the distinction between different forms of accountability.

---

[30] Mulgan, 'Ever-Expanding Concept', n 15 above, 564.

[31] Mulgan, 'Ever-Expanding Concept', n 15 above, 565. Accountability is also to be distinguished from 'responsiveness' and 'dialogue': n 15 above, 566–72.

[32] Oliver, *Government in the United Kingdom*, n 4 above, 28. See also *Constitutional Reform*, n 15 above, 54–6. Note also Bovens's bases for assessing accountability: 'Analysing and Assessing', n 1 above, 462–7.

[33] Davies, *Public Law of Government Contracts*, n 3 above, 67 and ch.4.

[34] Oliver, *Government in the United Kingdom*, n 4 above, 30; see also *Constitutional Reform*, n 15 above, 55–6. Compare Harlow, *Accountability*, n 6 above, 165–7.

Nonetheless, as is evident from Richard Mulgan's arguments, some theorists are concerned about the potential looseness of accountability language, and have called for proper controls to be imposed upon its usage. Mulgan himself notes that it is 'now a commonplace' that ' "accountability" is a complex and chameleon-like term' which 'crops up everywhere performing all manner of analytical and rhetorical tasks and carrying most of the major burdens of democratic "governance" (itself another conceptual newcomer)'.[35] Mark Bovens suggests that accountability 'is one of those golden concepts that no one can be against', while being 'a very elusive concept because it can mean many different things to different people'.[36] It is 'one of those evocative political words that can be used to patch up a rambling argument, to evoke an image of trustworthiness, fidelity and justice, or to hold critics at bay.... As an icon, the concept has become less useful for analytical purposes, and today resembles a dustbin filled with good intentions, loosely defined concepts and vague images of good governance'.[37] Carol Harlow talks of its 'current catch-all meaning',[38] the practical implication being that accountability might be seen, alternatively, in an all-things-to-all-people sense, in narrowly audit-focused terms, or by prioritizing the political.[39]

Given the range of contexts in which the term 'accountability' is now used, concerns of the type just articulated may to some extent be inevitable. Nonetheless, it is clearly important—in order to avoid undue ambiguity in constitutional analysis—to keep them fully in mind when considering how ideas of accountability are defined and applied, and when asking whether they play a valuable role. This point certainly applies when considering the essays in the present collection.

B. Accountability in the contemporary constitution

Turning now to the individual contributions, it should be stressed that the concern in this collection is not to investigate accountability from the perspective of political science, but rather to develop the idea in the context of constitutional and public law (UK constitutional and public law in particular). As noted earlier, for public lawyers one of the deeper arguments about the proper or best understanding of accountability lies between those who advocate the prioritization of accountability through political mechanisms and those who would prioritize legal accountability. This sometimes feeds through into the many key questions concerning the contemporary constitution which can be seen through the lens of accountability: or, more

[35] Mulgan, 'Ever-Expanding Concept', n 15 above, 555.
[36] Bovens, 'Analysing and Assessing', n 1 above, 448.
[37] Bovens, 'Analysing and Assessing', n 1 above, 449; see also 467. Although the definition of accountability proposed by Bovens seems in practice to be akin to Oliver's, he also argues against *equating* accountability with transparency, equity, democracy, efficiency, responsiveness, responsibility and integrity, perhaps leading to ambiguity given that Oliver *associates* the concept with responsibility, transparency and answerability (alongside the public interest).
[38] Harlow, *Accountability*, n 6 above, 23.
[39] Fisher, in 'European Union', n 2 above, 499–500, also notes the broad and fluid nature of the term.

exactly, via debates about its meaning. Many of these questions were highlighted in the previous section, and include in particular the definition of accountability (if an exact definition is possible), its role in relation to institutions and values, and whether accountability is better promoted in the constitutional context through the courts, political institutions or a combination of the two. The collection thus opens in Part I with arguments from a variety of theoretical perspectives: historical, comparative, constitutional and philosophical. In Part II, the focus shifts more specifically to courts, and in Part III to the legislative and executive branches of the state. In Part IV, the interplay between the legislature, executive and judiciary in contemporary constitutional arrangements is considered, and in Part V other specific areas are analysed from an accountability standpoint. In each part of the collection, though, the contributors seek to tie discussion to general views of accountability. Of course, it is inevitable that there are considerable overlaps between the material in the different Parts, in particular given the extent to which theoretical and practical analyses interact. The Parts are intended merely to provide a loose ordering so as to assist with navigation around the diverse ideas which arise in the course of the discussion.

In Part I, John Allison revisits the work of the nineteenth and early twentieth century theorist A V Dicey, presenting new arguments about Dicey's perspective concerning legal accountability, while Mark Tushnet explores accountability and the nature of judicial decision-making from the standpoint of a political conception of law.

Allison[40] seeks to explore the dichotomy between legal and political accountability by focusing in particular on Dicey's historically neglected focus on the legal spirit of the constitution, by which he meant the way in which the persons of the time looked on their institutions and expected them to work (Dicey thus believed the spirit of the English constitution to be legal rather than military or civil administrative). Allison suggests that each possible spirit corresponded to a different idea of accountability. Legal accountability, corresponding to the legal spirit, was owed by officials to independent judicial authorities (rather than a specialist administrative court) acting according to due process and established rules and principles. While Dicey anticipated political accountability through constitutional conventions, its role was sidelined in his account, helping to entrench the legal/political dichotomy taken up by later scholars. Allison also suggests, though, that it is important to view Dicey's arguments in context. When Dicey was writing, university-level legal education was only just emerging in the United Kingdom, helping to explain what might nowadays be seen as his undue focus on the purely legal. Furthermore, his characterization of the spirits of different constitutions seems to involve understandings of the idea of national character which would nowadays be seen as artificial. Allison argues that over time, Dicey was forced to acknowledge the existence of certain civil administrative elements in the English constitution, but that the role of those elements was broader and far stronger than he was prepared openly to acknowledge. Military elements also emerged with the two world wars

---

[40] JWF Allison, 'The Spirits of the Constitution'.

and the courts' reactions to challenges to government actions related to those wars. In reality, Allison concludes, the twentieth century witnessed the emergence of a trichronic constitution—that is, with all three elements characterised by Dicey as belonging to different constitutions—and it is appropriate to think in a more balanced fashion about the accountability arrangements in play. With this in mind, he details at length the gradual move among public law scholars away from paying lip-service to Dicey's account through to moving wholly beyond it or rejecting it. Analysis of ideas of accountability, on this view, clearly plays an important part in our understanding of the development of public law thought.

Mark Tushnet's essay[41] engages with accountability from a comparative and political rather than directly historical perspective. Tushnet's central question concerns how judges on the highest (apex) courts are made accountable as part of a constitutional system. The question is posed on the assumption that such judges wield political power, particularly when exercising discretion. This point in itself raises accountability issues which cannot easily be answered, because it is recognised that to make judges directly accountable might threaten to undermine their independence. As a result, Tushnet's essay not only provides an assessment of the effect on accountability of institutional features, including the control of judicial salaries, judicial tenure and the mechanisms for judicial appointment (including the case for election), but also analyses from a comparative standpoint how judges in the United States and other jurisdictions are made directly accountable to the law. Tushnet contributes to the debate concerning approaches to the judicial reasoning process with reference to recent decisions of the Supreme Court in order to better understand what legally restrains judges from making entirely personal judgments. Is it, for example, because there are 'right' answers in the law, or is it merely because a decision is simply in an abstract sense palpably legal? Tushnet reasons that there are too many potentially 'correct' decisions for 'correctness' to be the criterion for accountability to law, except in the weak sense that a judge is accountable to law where his or her decision falls within the (often wide) range of reasonably defensible legal interpretations. It goes without saying that constitutional theory and legal theory are heavily intertwined. With this in mind, Tushnet's arguments might be said to be deploying a particular account of the nature of law in order to explain a theory of constitutional accountability.

In this regard, there are direct links between Tushnet's account and the essays found in Part II—although in these latter essays, by Trevor Allan, Sandra Fredman and Jeff King, it might be suggested that arguments concerning the nature of law are slightly more implicit, the foreground concern being to offer an analysis of judicial accountability within the context of constitutional theory (in the essays found in Part III, in turn, a theoretical dimension is still important, but attention is concentrated still more visibly on the consequences of theory for judicial accountability in practice).

---

[41] M Tushnet, 'Judicial Accountability in Comparative Perspective'.

Allan[42] seeks to defend a legal constitutionalist view of accountability and legitimacy. He characterises the rival political constitutionalist view (associated with, among others, Mark Tushnet), which he rejects, as associating administrative legality with conformity to statutory standards. Legal constitutionalists, by contrast, understand administrative legality or accountability to law as entailing the judicial enforcement of rule of law-based values of fair or just treatment. The debate between these schools, and between rival legal constitutionalist views, depends on our understanding of the concept of law, and in turn of executive accountability to law. Allan suggests that whereas political constitutionalism sees law as a tool for the execution of political goals, common law constitutionalism promotes accountability to law as a moral vision of law related to liberty and justice. Similarly, in enforcing principles of legality through judicial review, the courts are seeking to identify the boundaries of legitimate state power, rather than to usurp other institutions.

If, as Allan suggests, law is always an interpretation of the demands of legality, positivist concerns about the sources of law are superfluous. From Allan's non-positivist perspective, accountability to law entails conformity to the constitution of a free society, different types of legal power being read in the light of that tradition. In supervising the legality of administrative action, a court must construct the character of the jurisdiction under review by reference to independent standards of legality as well as legitimate public purposes. Courts seek to find coherence within legislation and judicial precedent. Allan seeks, against this background, to interpret debate about the rule of law and about the role of the common law as opposed to legislative intent as the basis for judicial review of executive action. He suggests that the demands of legality are met by bringing common law principle to bear (via interpretation) on statutory functions, avoiding an unhelpful competition between competing sources of law.

For Allan, judicial review of executive action is thus based on the principle of legality, which is closely linked to the political values of freedom and justice. Accountability to law means more than compliance with positive law: it informs and guides interpretation of the law, amounting ultimately to respect for law and legal process. Allan is thus seeking to tie his approach to judicial review and (more theoretically) accountability to law to his rejection of a positivist conception of the nature of law. This is connected in turn to the idea that government (and implicitly Parliament) is being made accountable to the idea and the ideal of legality, linked to the rule of law, and that the standards of judicial review reflect this. His account is thus normative and interpretive, tying accountability to the nature of public law and of law more generally.

The background to Sandra Fredman's essay[43] lies in the debate between legal and political constitutionalists. Some commentators have tried to move beyond the sharply-delineated boundaries in this debate: for example, 'dialogue theorists' have characterised certain pieces of legislation, including the Human Rights Act 1998 in the United Kingdom, as dividing the protection of individual rights between the

---

[42] T Allan, 'Accountabilty to Law'.
[43] S Fredman, 'Adjudication as Accountability: A Deliberative Approach'.

legislature and the judiciary, each institution being offered opportunities to arrive at 'inter-institutional comity designed to' safeguard such rights.[44] Fredman seeks to move beyond pure dialogue theory, instead defending a 'bounded deliberation' approach to decision-making and in turn accountability in human rights cases. In this regard, she seeks to use constitutional theory to explain her desired role for courts. Fredman begins by asking what unique contribution courts can make to the protection of human rights, and argues that majoritarian institutions such as legislatures do not fully encompass all models of democracy. In interest-governed decision-making, parties come to the table with fixed interests, their aim being to induce the other party to accept their claim rather than seeking to reason with them; deliberative decision-making, by contrast, requires that the parties articulate persuasive reasons and display a willingness to revise their own preferences and convictions. Fredman argues that while there is room for both approaches in a democracy, interest-based decision-making—more typically associated with legislatures—is not suitable for human rights. Nonetheless, she aims to move beyond charges of promoting any form of 'judicial supremacism' by noting that courts must operate within the bounds of human rights viewed as the product of prior deliberative consensus.

Fredman suggests that both legislatures and courts should give deliberative accounts of their decisions concerning human rights. Judges should not substitute their opinion for that of the legislature, but neither should they defer. Decisions should be based on principle rather than the strength of the interests in play, and it is in this regard that courts can make a unique contribution to the democratic resolution of disputes concerning human rights. On this view, a Bill of Rights could make judges more rather than less accountable given that, like legislators, they too would have to justify their decisions against a background of values reached by a process of prior consensus. Litigation, under a deliberative approach, might encourage greater public participation. Fredman is not inflexible in her argument, however, accepting that where the judicial process is inaccessible or reinforces existing inequalities, reforms will be needed (indeed, one might argue that in practice aspects of her argument rely on the progressive experience of the South African Constitutional Court in opening up litigation to a wide range of citizens and interest groups, as well as a range of cases in which courts have dealt with claims involving socio-economic rights). She thus proposes that since a key aim of protecting human rights is to grant everyone a voice in society, litigation can often offer a better vehicle than the political process for wide-ranging participation in decision-making, not least when the latter process is dominated by interest groups. Deliberative judgments by courts are binding for the dispute in front of them, but the subject-matter may be revisited later via the legislative process. While Fredman acknowledges that the 'bounded deliberation' approach begs certain questions, her argument can be seen as an attempt to strike a middle path between approaches which prioritize the

---

[44] A L Young *Parliamentary Sovereignty and the Human Rights Act* (Oxford: Hart, 2009), 174. One of the most prominent examples relates to the Canadian Charter of Rights and Freedoms: J Hiebert *Charter Conflicts: What is Parliament's Role?* (Montreal: MacGill-Queen's University Press, 2002).

roles—and thus the accountability obligations imposed upon—the legislature and the courts considered in wholly distinct terms.

Jeff King[45] returns the focus to legal accountability by attempting to clarify the nature of the instrumental benefits—if any—which it offers. In possible contradistinction to Trevor Allan, he suggests that it is insufficiently precise merely to argue that legal accountability protects the rule of law, prevents the abuse of powers, or safeguards individual rights. When evaluating legal accountability, a focused definition must be used. King thus categorizes legal accountability as an institutional process involving an individual right of petition to an independent adjudicator for a remedy, the adjudicator being required to give a transparent and well-reasoned judgment and a final remedy for breach of the applicable standards.[46] While a set of prima facie instrumental benefits can be identified as resulting from such a process, King argues, they must inevitably be weighed alongside more context-specific factors in determining whether expanded legal accountability is appropriate in an individual case. Furthermore, any instrumentalist argument about the benefits of legal accountability is necessarily context-dependent.

King goes on to suggest that to count as a prima facie benefit, something needs to be specific and concrete enough that it can be evaluated empirically and serve as a reference point that supporters and opponents of legal accountability can use as a measuring device. On this basis, prima facie benefits of legal accountability are that it prompts focus on the narratives of individuals, on a policy's effects on them, and on the distinct legal issues involved; that it entails the use of principled reasoning; that courts have a special form of constitutional authority; that judges are independent and impartial; that legal adjudicators are good at rule-interpretation, and courts have real competence in respect of procedural fairness; that litigation can encourage the participation of the otherwise excluded; and that legal accountability can express key principles, policies or other values in judicial decisions, and generate publicity or a political response for a cause, and can encourage the legislature, executive and judiciary to work together to some extent. King also articulates a range of criteria which can be employed in practice by the courts in this context: something which may help illustrate how far support for legal accountability is associated with any theorist's basic vision of the ideal constitution. However, King's concern to find factors which all sides can recognize may also allow for a connection between theory and practical methodology when considering any defence of legal or political accountability.

Each of the essays found in Part III focuses on a specific practically-focused aspect of constitutional accountability, but in doing so engages theoretical approaches to accountability. Alison Young focuses on the nature of the judicial role when considering deference and accountability in United Kingdom Human Rights Act 1998 case law, while Paul Craig relates debate about the constitutional role of courts to specific questions in European Union and English domestic law, building analogies

---

[45] J King, 'The Instrumental Value of Legal Accountability'.
[46] King follows Bovens' definition of legal accountability, as articulated in 'Analysing and Assessing', n 1 above.

between the two. Meanwhile, Andrew Le Sueur seeks to investigate the evolving accountability of the judicial system in the United Kingdom before Parliament.

Alison Young[47] draws on Mark Bovens' definition of accountability (discussed above) and on a broader view of accountability as incorporating a normative dimension via the notions that a body which can be held to account for its actions is more legitimate than one which cannot and that any practice which enhances accountability enhances legitimacy. She claims that both senses are applicable within human rights adjudication. Young is concerned to explore—in relation to the interpretation and application of the Human Rights Act 1998—the implications of judicial deference for transparency and the facilitation of a 'culture of justification', an idea associated with accountability's normative dimension in the human rights context. Young contrasts legal and political accountability mechanisms at both national and European levels, which she argues create 'chains of accountability'. In particular, she considers the assessments of the Westminster Parliament's Joint Committee on Human Rights as to the compatibility of proposed legislation with European Convention rights—a form of political accountability—and the determinations of domestic United Kingdom courts concerning the compatibility of enacted legislation.

Young argues that problems may arise where courts defer too generally to the legislature when Convention-compatibility has been discussed during the passage of legislation, for this may gloss over context-specific issues relating to enacted legislation of the type ideally suited for judicial determination. Furthermore, courts have not been coherent in their understandings of deference, failing as a result properly to promote accountability. For example, courts have elided constitutional issues focusing on authority and legitimacy (in relation to which deference may be owed to a legislature because it is democratically elected and democratically accountable) with institutional issues focusing on relative expertise and knowledge; have failed to understand the appropriate parameters of deference on a case-by-case basis; and have confused deference with justiciability. Young argues that these problems reflect uncertainties concerning the roles of the legislature and the courts in relation to the protection of and accountability concerning human rights. By contrast, the ideal of a 'culture of justification' stipulates that restrictions of human rights must be proportionate and that deference should not exclude judicial assessment of the reasons offered for the decision under scrutiny, promoting transparency and accountability. However, this would entail a greater focus than is currently the case on holding the legislature and the executive to account for the way in which they reach conclusions regarding the restriction of human rights. At a theoretical level, Young therefore offers a clear demonstration of the inter-relationship between judicial and political accountability in relation to human rights adjudication. A significant aspect of her argument would appear to be the suggestion that the real issue in relation to accountability is the need to require justification for the decisions of *both* the legislature and the executive (in this sense there may be commonalities

---

[47] A Young, 'Accountability, Human Rights Adjudication and the Human Rights Act'.

with the arguments concerning the importance and role of justification advanced by Fredman and King).

Adopting a clearly comparative approach between domestic English domestic law and European Union law, Paul Craig's focus[48] is on the role and legitimacy of judicial review as one among a range of accountability mechanisms. He seeks to compare, as devices for understanding and assessing judicial review within each system (insofar as the two may be viewed as distinct), debates concerning the conceptual foundations and legitimacy of, as well as the hierarchy of norms and the role of rights within, the review jurisdiction as a basis for facilitating accountability.

In relation to conceptual foundations, Craig argues that judicial review in both systems has been fashioned pursuant to the rule of law, notwithstanding express authorization for judicial review at European Union level in the original Treaty of Rome. He also suggests that any particular accountability mechanism must be analysed with reference to the legitimacy of the detailed precepts which it uses when holding others to account, but refutes the view that review of executive action at either European Union or domestic level rests on an unduly general/normative and illegitimate basis. Craig argues that judicial intervention, whether in public or private law, has instead rested on the identification of a particular reason for intervention, the fashioning of general categories of liability to be applied within the area involved (something which may be associated with more general values within the law), and the determination of more detailed aspects such as the standard of liability and the availability of justifications or defences. The most basic rationale for judicial review, viewed historically, was the need to render public power accountable. While this idea was associated with legitimacy, the development of legal liability at both domestic and European Union levels has occurred in accordance with the general pattern and by analogy with other areas of law. In relation to the hierarchy of norms, Craig notes that divergent choices have been made in national and European Union law concerning the permissible objects of review, something which is significant when assessing judicial review as an accountability mechanism within each system. This affects, in turn, the ambit of judicial power when it comes to the protection of rights, a field of review which is nonetheless developing within each system.

As Craig acknowledges, assessment of the efficacy of judicial review as an accountability mechanism in the systems he considers is very much a work in progress. When considered in terms of accountability mechanisms in general, however, the importance of his essay may lie in its articulation of concrete criteria by reference to which efficacy can be measured, and its deployment of those criteria on a comparative basis in relation to judicial review in domestic English and European Union law.

While Mark Tushnet's study (see above) explored the relationship between accountability and independence of the judiciary in more general and theoretical terms, Andrew Le Sueur discusses[49] judicial accountability specifically in the

---

[48] P Craig, 'Accountability and Judicial Review in the UK and EU: Central Precepts'.
[49] A Le Sueur, 'Parliamentary Accountability and the Judicial System'.

United Kingdom context. The replacement of the Appellate Committee of the House of Lords with a United Kingdom Supreme Court, together with a radical overhaul of the system of judicial appointments in England and Wales, were among the most significant constitutional reforms undertaken by the Labour government in office between 1997 and 2010. The Supreme Court, while envisaged as a national institution of and for the whole of the United Kingdom—with jurisdiction over devolution issues as a key aspect of this—was not given authority to strike down primary legislation passed by the Westminster Parliament (save, of course, where directly effective rules of European Union law are in play). Nevertheless, Le Sueur recognises that there has been a significant increase of judicial power and refers to an 'accountability toolkit' covering the variety of mechanisms at Parliament's disposal to provide oversight. For example, one of the more controversial issues in recent years has concerned the frequent appearance of judges before Parliamentary committees (particularly Departmental Select Committees whose primary function it is to provide executive oversight) and whether there should be an element of Parliamentary oversight of senior judicial appointments. Benefits of greater Parliamentary scrutiny of the administration of justice have included greater transparency concerning administrative performance, with the publication of information about conviction rates, sentencing decisions and spending in general.

Le Sueur concentrates on the lines of demarcation between Parliament and the courts in relation to accountability, including which aspects of the judicial system members of the legislature should be able to inquire into and the effectiveness of such inquiries. Clearly, judges are accountable for their decisions through the appellate process, Parliamentary standing orders discourage intervention by MPs in the core aspects of the judicial system, and *in extremis* judges may be removed by Parliament. At a general level, Le Sueur nonetheless reiterates the special importance of provisions concerning the governance of the judiciary. The Constitutional Reform Act 2005 imposed a statutory duty upon the Lord Chancellor and other Ministers of the Crown to uphold the independence of the judiciary, modifying the pre-existing constitutional position. At the same time, under the 'soft law' concordat agreed by the then office-holders in 2004, the Lord Chief Justice stepped into the shoes of the Lord Chancellor as the head of the judiciary, with responsibility for representing judicial views to Parliament and to the government. This change, coupled with the reconfiguration in departmental responsibility for the administration of justice, has impacted directly on accountability to Parliament under the convention of individual ministerial responsibility. Not only did the formation of the Ministry of Justice in 2007 involve responsibility for prisons and the courts being combined under the same departmental heading for the first time, but the Lord Chief Justice now has responsibility for maintaining an adequate annual funding settlement for the courts and the judicial system. Le Sueur argues that the lack of a proper legislative footing for the position of Lord Chief Justice has led to uncertainty about the office-holder's performance before Parliament. Issues of this type have added to the appearance of uncertainty surrounding the accountability arrangements for the judiciary in the United Kingdom, perhaps begging the question how far such arrangements can be free from political intervention in a system based only upon statute and common law.

The essays in Part IV, by Mark Elliott, Nicholas Bamforth, Dawn Oliver and Peter Leyland, consider the interplay between the legislature, executive and (where relevant) judiciary in contemporary constitutional accountability arrangements. In focusing on ombudsmen, tribunals and inquiries, Mark Elliott engages in an analysis of accountability mechanisms which fall outside the remit of the courts, even while they possess an investigative or quasi-judicial function and are in no sense party political. Nicholas Bamforth contrasts political and non-political mechanisms for holding legislators and legislatures to account, as well as justifications for excluding legislatures from the ordinary scope of legal review: something which serves to underpin arguments for a zone of political-only accountability, even if such accountability is in practice tinged with legal elements. Dawn Oliver investigates the public service principle in relation to government, Parliament and the separation of powers. Peter Leyland focuses in particular on financial accountability in the context of devolution and the relationships, legal and political, between the various 'layers' within the domestic constitution.

By way of background, a key aspect of the development of political accountability in the United Kingdom is reflected in the evolution of the constitutional convention of ministerial responsibility in response to changes in the shape and functions of the state. Sir Ivor Jennings arguably captured the post-war consensus when he described the administrative machine as exercising three sorts of function: 'the police functions and general external functions of the old "executive"; the regulatory functions of the Board of Trade, the Home Office, and the Ministry of Transport; and the public services provided by a collection of Ministries now too numerous to mention specifically, and the subordinate authorities connected to them'.[50] Having explained that the law and practice of the civil service existed outside the jurisdiction of the courts, Jennings was able to state that the system as a whole rarely led to serious political difficulties because of the overriding, accountability-driven constitutional convention of ministerial responsibility, which regulated the whole of the civil service. The point was that 'Each minister is responsible to Parliament for the conduct of his department. The act of every civil servant is by convention regarded as the act of his minister'.[51] By the start of the twenty-first century, by contrast, Geoffrey Marshall pointed out that 'Certainly any future Dicey, recording the progress of the rule of law in twentieth-century Britain would be bound to conclude that the constitution underwent significant and accelerating change in the period from 1960 onwards. At the midway point British constitutional arrangements could still be described as embodying a bundle of traditional doctrines. They could be summed up as parliamentary sovereignty, crown prerogative, legislative privilege and administrative discretion. At the close of the century all of

---

[50] I Jennings *The Law and the Constitution* (London: University of London Press, 1959), 196. See also R H S Crossman, 'Introduction', in W Bagehot *The English Constitution* (London: Fontana, 1963 edn).

[51] Jennings, 207.

these had been subjected to a prolonged process of questioning based on the principle that no power can be absolute or unreviewable or immune from challenge in the light of rights-based principles such as fairness, equality, rationality, proportionality and perhaps some form of separation of powers'.[52] More specifically, there has been a significant ideological shift towards economic liberalism in the period following the election of Margaret Thatcher's government in May 1979, which has resulted—whatever the official political ideology of subsequent governments—in 'The market creed [being] extended deep into public administrations as the collectivist welfare state was remodelled as a market in democratic goods and the notion of choice became a fetish'.[53] The consequences have been dramatic in relation to the structure of government, with important implications for notions of accountability. Some of these points are captured in the essays in Part IV.[54]

The starting point for Mark Elliott[55] in exploring accountability beyond the courts is to recognise that there needs to be an appropriate balance between legal and political control of government. He thus focuses on what might be seen as bodies which are charged with filling a particular 'gap' in the accountability 'market' in the United Kingdom. When it reported in 1932, the Donoughmore Committee rejected the idea of a system of administrative courts for England and Wales but rather sought to lay down principles for the allocation of 'judicial' and 'quasi-judicial' functions between courts, administrative tribunals and ministers.[56] Further, as Sir John Whyatt put it some thirty years later in envisaging a role for a Parliamentary Ombudsman,[57] the office holder was intended neither as a watchdog for the public nor as an apologist of the administration, but rather as an independent upholder of the highest standards of efficient and fair administration and as a guardian of good practice rather than a mere judicial combatant.[58] It follows inexorably that any definition of accountability in relation to such an office-holder must be broad, reflecting the diversity of accountability institutions, with tribunals, ombudsmen and inquiries all performing important but somewhat different functions. In so far as it is possible to reach a definition of accountability, Elliott recognizes that it must be calibrated and its different senses identified by considering three sets of

---

[52] G Marshall, 'The Constitution: Its Theory and Interpretation', ch 2 in V Bogdanor (ed) *The British Constitution in the Twentieth Century* (Oxford: Oxford University Press, 2003), 61–2.

[53] C Harlow and R Rawlings *Law and Administration* (Cambridge: Cambridge University Press, 3rd edn, 2009), 57. See also I Harden *The Contracting State* (Buckingham: Open University Press, 1992).

[54] Obvious examples might include those relating to the alleged distinction between ministerial 'responsibility' and 'accountability' for functions respectively performed directly by central government departments and for those which have been 'contracted-out' (particularly, in the latter case, when issues of 'commercial confidentiality' come into play): see, eg., A Tomkins *The Constitution after Scott: Government Unwrapped* (Oxford: Oxford University Press, 1998), Woodhouse, 'Reconstruction', n 9 above, and 'Ministerial Responsibility', ch 8 in Bogdanor, *British Constitution*, n.52 above.

[55] 'Ombudsmen, tribunals, inquiries: re-fashioning accountability beyond the courts'.

[56] P Cane, 'Understanding Administrative Adjudication', in L Pearson, C Harlow and M Taggart (eds.) *Administrative Law in a Changing State* (Oxford: Hart, 2008), 285.

[57] *The Citizen and Administration: The Redress of Grievances* (London: JUSTICE, 1961).

[58] A Abraham 'The Parliamentary Ombudsman and Administrative Justice: Shaping the next 50 years' (JUSTICE: Tom Sargant memorial annual lecture, October 2011; <http://www.justice.org.uk/resources.php/304/the-parliamentary-ombudsman-and-administrative-justice)(accessed 23 April 2013)>, 4.

related issues which connect back to the nature of accountability: namely, the *subjects* that may form the focus of an accountability inquiry, the *criteria* or *standards* by reference to which such an inquiry may proceed, and the *purposes* that might be served by such an inquiry.

Elliott evaluates the contribution of tribunals in providing accountability in the light of the Leggatt reforms,[59] which since their implementation have strongly emphasized the independence of tribunals. The tribunal service is now system-atized and self-contained as part of an executive agency falling under the Ministry of Justice operating at some distance from (in nearly every case) the department being held to account. It is also significant that the tribunal service, as a two-tier appellate body presided over by tribunal judges, has become more judicial in character despite being less subject to external judicial oversight. Notwithstanding this change in emphasis towards judicialization, tribunals remain distinct from ordinary courts (and the administrative court) as oversight bodies because they must deliver mass administrative justice and are capable of routinely dealing with the merits of cases as they arise. By contrast, ombudsman systems have been designed to deliver a distinct form of accountability, involving as they do an independent 'outsider' with investigative powers capable of uncovering routine maladministration as well as systemic failures. Elliott argues that the Parliamentary Commissioner for Administration (or 'Parliamentary Ombudsman'), now supported by the Public Administration Select Committee, makes an important contribution to accountable government and that the non-enforceable nature of its recommendations has generally not undermined its effectiveness. Indeed, the findings of the Parliamentary Ombudsman have generally been accepted as a matter of course. Finally, the special role of inquiries (in particular judicial inquiries) is examined both in relation to their contribution to the public decision-making process and as mechanisms capable of investigating events in depth after they have taken place.

Nicholas Bamforth focuses[60] specifically on the role of Parliament (within the United Kingdom system) and legislatures more generally. Underpinning his ana-lysis is the argument that theories concerning the roles of courts and legislatures, and more specifically legal and political constitutionalist accounts, entail certain assumptions about or explicit views concerning accountability within a democratic constitution. While public attention has recently focused on the accountability of Members of Parliament to their electors, this is only one of a range of important accountability relationships in play in connection with the legislature, and the priority one accords to each of these different relationships will tie directly to one's background approach to legal and/or political accountability. A traditional political constitutionalist would thus prioritize accountability of the United Kingdom government to the Westminster Parliament over judicial review, whereas a legal constitutionalist would focus pre-eminently on the role of the courts.

---

[59] *Tribunals for Users: One Service, One System* (London: Department for Constitutional Affairs, 2001). See also the Tribunals, Courts and Enforcement Act 2007.

[60] N Bamforth, 'Accountability of and to the legislature'.

Nonetheless, all theories about accountability rest on certain assumptions. Jeremy Waldron's work explicitly demonstrates the role of assumptions about the efficacy of legislative scrutiny when asserting the priority of the legislature over courts as an agent of accountability; once questions are raised about Waldron's assumptions, his argument looks more vulnerable to challenge.[61] Equally, though, Ronald Dworkin's notion of (judicially-protected) 'rights as trumps' over the actions of the legislature expressly presupposes a commitment to an anti-majoritarian conception of democracy and rights.[62] If such presuppositions are challenged, the prioritization of judicial accountability appears more open to question. To take some practical examples, arguments supporting the placing of prerogative powers and constitutional conventions on a statutory footing presuppose the efficacy of formal rules (sometimes formal rules alone) as agents for guiding the executive, legislators and courts, whereas other theories assume that more informal techniques of guidance and 'correction', where there has been an error, will work more effectively and/or desirably.[63] Other theorists have become committed to 'dialogue' theories of accountability. Bamforth favours such a stance, and seeks to explain debate about the accountability arrangements prevailing in relation to the Westminster Parliament—that is, arrangements surrounding ministerial responsibility and/or accountability, constitutional conventions more generally, the role of Members of Parliament in relation to their constituents, and scrutiny of executive power exercised via the prerogative and statute—by reference to it. In particular, he argues that the combination of judicial and political scrutiny of legislative proposals and executive action in the anti-terrorism context provides a key—and centrally-focused—illustration of the correlation between the promotion of effective accountability and the existence of judicial and political methods working in tandem.

Dawn Oliver[64] is concerned to examine a set of foundational principles relating to public service which underpin important aspects of constitutional conduct and which at the same time promote accountability. She defines accountability in similar terms to those used in her previous work (and discussed above), an approach which supports the idea that there is more than one single mechanism for promoting accountability and that there needs to be an appropriate balance between different mechanisms. Oliver argues that at one level, what most accountability arrangements in the United Kingdom have in common is a recognition of the need to promote a general or public interest which is seen firstly in a public interest principle and secondly in a public service principle. The latter proposes that public officials and politicians should altruistically serve the public, rather than their own interests.

---

[61] J Waldron *Law and Disagreement* (Oxford: Oxford University Press, 1999) and 'The Core of the Case Against Judicial Review' (2006) 115 *Yale LJ* 1346.

[62] R Dworkin *Taking Rights Seriously* (London: Duckworth, 1977),85 and *A Matter of Principle* (Oxford: Oxford University Press, 1985), 70–1.

[63] Note here Craig's connection between Dicey's account of Parliamentary sovereignty and the rule of law with a particular idea of democracy: 'Dicey: Unitary, Self-Correcting Democracy and Public Law' (1990) 106 *LQR* 105.

[64] D Oliver, 'Accountability and the foundations of British Democracy—the Public Interest and Public Service Principles'.

A crucial point is that this form of accountability is understood as something distinct from partisan standards. One question might be how relevant public service standards are to be defined, and how they might be reconciled with the underlying political considerations which inevitably are of concern to politicians. Oliver believes that these are largely consensual standards which might be regarded as extending across governmental organisations and other public bodies. For example, the public service principles first set out by the Nolan Committee amounted to a commitment to certain values that have since been reinterpreted in codes of practice which have come to be applied in many areas of public life.[65] The application includes recognizing the importance of 'soft law' codes in setting out standards which might be enforced through political means (for example, by requiring the resignation of political actors). Equally, it is possible to find common law decisions where the courts have been prepared to uphold general duties on public decision-makers to act fairly and impartially rather than through favouring any sectional political interest. Such principles might be thought to have something akin to a constitutional flavour in so far as they promise to transcend a narrow conception of the rule of law and can come to be recognized as a set of positive principles containing the liberal democratic values of a morally unified collectivity, thereby restraining the processes by which governmental powers are exercised by constitutional actors.[66]

While there are many accountability-related issues posed by and associated with the constitutional arrangements governing devolution to Scotland, Wales and Northern Ireland (most obviously, in relation to Scotland, the so-called 'West Lothian Question'), one often-overlooked aspect is the tension between the general formulae applied to the allocation of funds to all devolved parts of the United Kingdom and the fund-raising powers which may now be granted to Scotland under the Scotland Act 2012. Peter Leyland investigates[67] what this development means in terms of accountability both in regard to the functioning of traditional mechanisms for constitutional oversight at Westminster and devolved levels, and more specifically in relation to the financial relationship between sub-national government and Westminster. It is suggested that the financing of sub-national government reveals an important and somewhat contradictory meta-narrative. When viewed from the standpoint of financial allocation the devolved governments have been granted a relatively high degree of autonomy as the block grant system has guaranteed funding levels above those in England and allowed each devolved administration to spend in accordance with its own priorities in policy-making. English local government, on the other hand, has been heavily constrained in its spending by repeated central government intervention through statutory rate-capping regimes and more

---

[65] See P Leopold 'Standards in Public Life', ch 13 in J Jowell and D Oliver (eds) *The Changing Constitution* (Oxford: Oxford University Press, 7th edn, 2011).

[66] J Murkens, 'The Quest for Constitutionalism in UK Public Law Discourse' (2009) 29 *OJLS* 427, 451.

[67] P Leyland, 'Multi-layered constitutional accountability and the refinancing of territorial governance in the UK'.

recently under provisions requiring referendums to control rises in council tax under the Localism Act 2011.

Leyland argues that notwithstanding the 'asymmetry' of devolution and the absence of an 'English' level of democratically elected government, each sub-national system has been relatively successful in creating new forms of political and legal accountability which apply to the devolved parts of the United Kingdom. In particular, the devolved institutions have developed increased emphasis on access and participation in relation to law-making and have introduced mechanisms of rigorous executive oversight at sub-national level. At the same time, the secure funding parameters for devolution have not only provided an adequate base for its introduction, but the so-called 'Barnett Formula' for the block grant system has (although maligned in other respects) largely prevented the kind of haggling which remains a feature of many systems of federal, devolved and regional government around the world. Nevertheless, in the absence of both an explicit needs-based element and special oversight procedure at Westminster to provide scrutiny there have been many calls for the replacement of the current system. The Scotland Act 2012 promises to partly address such concerns by introducing a significant element of locally-raised income tax in Scotland. However, Leyland argues that a fundamental weakness of the financing of both devolution and English local government has been a failure to provide a clear relationship between the raising of revenue and the spending of revenue at sub-national levels of government.

While the three essays in Part V are focused on distinct topics—'New Public Management' in the case of Anne Davies, regulatory accountability in the case of Julia Black, and accountability mechanisms in relation to socio-economic rights in the case of Colm O'Cinneide—each takes earlier, more general, debates further and makes its own contribution to them. In particular, each essay deals with how accountability issues have arisen in identifiable areas of public affairs involving an interaction between established institutions and the implementation of particular policy agendas.

Anne Davies investigates[68] accountability issues posed by 'New Public Management', applied by the Thatcher, Major, Blair, Brown and Cameron governments to issues demarcated as concerning 'governance' (a term itself linked to the mindset concerned). Officially, this initiative was concerned with minimizing the direct role of government by the use of private law contracts as a tool for policy delivery across the public sector, alongside the provision of efficiency and value for money for the taxpayer. In this regard, it has consequences for accountability-related arrangements such as ministerial responsibility, albeit from a different perspective from that provided by traditional defences of those arrangements. Davies agrees with the view that accountability entails an actor taking account for his or her activities, not least when these are conducted on behalf of another. From this standpoint, an accountability mechanism in the context of New Public Management normally has to set standards against which performance can be judged, collect information about that performance, and apply

---

[68] A Davies, 'Beyond new public management: Problems of accountability in the modern administrative state'.

incentives for good performance or sanctions for poor performance. A potential problem from the outset of New Public Management was that the contracting-out of services to the private sector severed the direct link in the chain of account-ability as it had previously existed between the department, governmental agency or local authority responsible for commissioning a service and the private/inde-pendent sector organization under a contractual duty to deliver it. The division of roles and blurring of boundaries created scope for the shifting of blame from one party to the other: something which has been highly important in terms of accountability.

Davies argues that New Public Management has continued to evolve into what she terms 'deep NPM' and 'post NPM' forms, and that as it has done so its var-ieties (particularly under the post-May 2010 coalition government) are becoming more complex and present a distinct set of accountability problems. Against the current background of budget cuts, New Public Management in its revised forms has involved attempts to meet objectives in innovative ways at lower cost. Davies illustrates the transition to 'deep NPM' in the contracting-out of govern-ment purchasing tasks through a case study focusing on the use of management consultants in the National Health Service as Clinical Commissioning Groups assume a purchasing role. She suggests that accountability problems may arise here because private sector firms will be involved at all stages of the process and may end up deciding what services are going to be provided to patients. Further, potential conflicts of interest arise because the same firm that provides commis-sioning support might already be providing health care services. Davies illustrates 'post NPM' with a case study focusing on the Localism Act 2011 and attempts to progressively remove services from local authorities and transfer them to citizens, community groups and businesses so as to provide more responsiveness. This, she argues, promises to have equally far-reaching implications for accountability, for it is likely to transform the traditional role of elected local government while simultaneously consolidating the position of central government in relation to the allocation of local government finance for such services as remain. Davies's essay thus demonstrates the importance of empirical analysis to conceptual argument concerning ideas of accountability in a jurisdiction's practices of government.

Regulation might be thought to provide a particular illustration of a tension relating to accountability seen in many areas of constitutional study: namely, how the possibility of conflict between accountability as something designed to protect and serve the individual citizen or other actor and as a vehicle for implementing controls over them is to be managed. Governments of different political complexions have argued that regulation is bad for business and that progressive deregulation should be promoted, while also believing that the enforcement of regulation in a positive sense will help to protect consumers, businesses, workers and the environ-ment. Regulation has been identified as the target of some policy objectives by contemporary government and as a key instrument for achieving others. In what Carol Harlow and Richard Rawlings have identified as the rise of a 'regulatory state', regulation is regarded as being of first importance in the functioning of the economy, and with the economic failings of recent years regulatory failure has become a topic of contentious political debate.[69] Julia Black's essay[70] thus considers accountability against the background of shifting priorities within the regulatory landscape. She focuses on the political mechanisms for calling independent regulatory agencies to account in order to assess regulatory accountability—or what she calls the conflicting logics of different accountability demands—more generally. She suggests that accountability is now embedded in a multi-stage process involving day-to-day interactions between regulators and those subject to regulation, but also with scope for Parliamentary involvement. The picture relating to regimes of regulation is often one of considerable complexity. Not only has the core executive established overlapping regulatory bodies, incidentally begging the question of who regulates the relevant regulators, but also, given the European Union dimension in the domain of regulation, the framework of accountability has to contend with the demands of multi-level governance.[71]

Colm O'Cinneide[72] is concerned with the role of law in promoting social justice, and more particularly with the limited extent to which legal accountability mechanisms currently make it possible for individuals and groups to seek social justice through public law. In common with Allison, O'Cinneide traces the growth of legal accountability in the twentieth century, and furthermore draws attention to difficulties now facing classic political accountability mechanisms due to phenomena such as globalization and privatization. While legal accountability does not compensate for the deficiencies in political accountability, he suggests that there is at least now an expectation that public bodies will be subject to a range of legal controls.

O'Cinneide concentrates on the 'corrective' rather than the 'distributive' function of legal accountability. He suggests that its reach is thought to be curtailed in the area of social justice, being concerned to ensure that existing rules are adhered to rather than a fair outcome secured. In practice, courts and tribunals play a considerable role in relation to social welfare, housing and education, but such interventions tend to focus much more on matters of procedure than on those of substance. There is considerable evidence, seen in the drafting of primary and secondary legislation, of Parliamentary concern to limit judicial involvement. The courts themselves have also been deferential in cases involving socio-economic issues, including in relation to defining the scope of any rights recognized as being in play in an individual case. As O'Cinneide points out, however, there have been limited counter-examples in which litigation has proceeded successfully, one area in which legislation has made provision for legal challenges being in relation to the positive equality duty imposed on public bodies.

O'Cinneide concludes by suggesting that current public law orthodoxy fails to offer convincing reasons for the general exclusion of scrutiny by courts of resource-allocation decisions. Courts are regularly and inevitably involved with

---

[69] Harlow and Rawlings, *Law and Administration*, n 45 above, 234.

[70] J Black, 'Regulatory Accountability: Capacities, Challenges and Prospects'.

[71] See, eg., N Bamforth and P Leyland, 'Public Law in a Multi-Layered Constitution', ch 1 in N Bamforth and. Leyland (eds) *Public Law in a Multi-Layered Constitution* (Oxford: Hart, 2003), 1–9.

[72] C O'Cinneide, 'Legal Accountability and Social Justice'.

such decisions across a range of areas, making it impossible convincingly to argue that they should aim to steer clear of these within public law. The wholesale judicial determination of budgetary questions may be illegitimate, but that is a different matter from questions of individual rights where resource implications are relatively well-defined. The argument that such issues are polycentric and thus unsuitable for judicial resolution is also undermined by judicial intervention in polycentric issues in areas such as tax law. In addition, the general exclusion of social justice issues leaves members of marginalized groups, generally those who are most in need of support, without a means of resolution in complex cases or without a remedy in the face of bureaucratic wrongdoing. The arguments in favour of retaining the official *status quo*—that is, in maintaining political rather than legal accountability in decisions affecting social justice matters—is thus increasingly questionable, and may come under still greater pressure due to the influence of the European Union Charter of Fundamental Rights.

In discussing these issues, O'Cinneide returns us to many of the questions considered by Fredman and by Allan, among other contributors to this collection. At a more general level, all three essays in Part V raise questions about the proper role of law in relation to accountability: answers to which, as noted earlier, must depend upon one's underpinning theories of democracy and rights.

C. Conclusion

The essays in this collection do not seek to offer a comprehensive survey of accountability issues, but instead to open up questions at a range of levels and to provide fresh insights informed by contemporary constitutional debates. As noted in this introduction, accountability issues have assumed a particular prominence in recent years, even though they have always been present in constitutional discourse. This is perhaps unsurprising given the many substantive constitutional changes which have occurred during this time in the United Kingdom and the European Union, as well as the growth in comparative analysis of constitutional law. Given the apparent elusiveness of the term 'accountability', it may perhaps be fair to suggest that a central question we are left with is whether it is better seen as possessing an unvarying core meaning (however that is defined in relation to its form, the relationships involved and the contexts in which it applies), or whether it is better regarded in looser terms, simply as a mechanism of good government practice the details of which are constantly shifting in response to practical constitutional developments or the context in which particular accountability-related questions arise. The essays presented here are likely to offer foundations for a variety of possible conclusions.

PART I

2

The Spirits of the Constitution

*J W F Allison**

Concern about accountability is the outcome of dissatisfaction, whether with the actual working of mechanisms of accountability, or with the way accountability is being understood or misunderstood. In the understanding of accountability in the English context, the objects of dissatisfaction include legal academic or common lawyerly preoccupation with legal accountability, one-sided polemical promotion of political accountability, and a basic legal/political dichotomy, which those advocating the priority of the legal or that of the political have both struggled to transcend.

This chapter's concern is the dichotomy between legal and political accountability, and its approach is historical. The approach taken here differs from modern conventional historical approaches in its use of history, which is express for the sake of transparency. My intention is not to put forward a historical account of the dichotomy so as to describe, record, and explain twentieth-century constitutional developments in all their complexity and nuanced detail. It is also not to use history so as to promote or venerate some or other aspect of the constitution or one or other of its leading authorities, as it was used on occasion in bygone periods, expressing nationalist sentiment and stimulating collective self-confidence. Rather, apart from using history in a conventional way to help clarify context and recall what might otherwise be forgotten or ignored, my intention here is to use history so as to help facilitate change or reorientation—through sensitivity to wrong turns taken, or perhaps to the right turns taken but towards destinations that no longer exist or no longer matter.

In the late-nineteenth century and for much of the twentieth century, Albert Venn Dicey was the leading influence upon English constitutional thought and thus acquired great authority and the status of orthodoxy towards which the constitution's critics oriented their criticism or critical alternatives.[1] Dicey's differentiation of three views—the legal, the historical, and the political—in outlining

* University Senior Lecturer in Law, University of Cambridge, and Fellow of Queens' College, Cambridge. For many helpful comments, I would like to thank the editors Nick Bamforth and Peter Leyland, the other contributors, and especially Trevor Allan, John Bell, Colin Campbell, Peter Cane, Paul Daly, Christopher Forsyth, Chris Knight, Martin Loughlin, Abda Sharif, and Mark Walters.

[1] On Dicey's pre-eminent authority, see M Foley's comparative survey of references to Dicey and other authorities, *The Politics of the British Constitution* (Manchester: Manchester University Press, 1999), 34ff.

his subject at the start of *Law of the Constitution* is well known, as is his prioritization of the legal view. According to Dicey, solely the *law* of the constitution was to be the subject of constitutional legal study.[2] Much less well known or remembered is Dicey's now seemingly quaint notion of what he generalized to be a constitution's spirit and particularized as the legal spirit of the English constitution. It is alluded to here and there in *Law of the Constitution* but received sustained attention in his long forgotten comparative constitutional lectures delivered to students at Oxford, the LSE, and in the United States in the late-nineteenth, and the early-twentieth, century.[3]

A. The spirit of a constitution

In one of his early comparative constitutional lectures, Dicey cited Montesquieu's famous *Spirit of the Laws* but distinguished the meaning he attributed to the term 'spirit' from Montesquieu's meaning.[4] Montesquieu had there made an initial concession to the natural lawyers by declaring that '[l]aw in general is human reason insofar as it governs all the peoples of the earth'[5] but had immediately particularized that reason—'the political and civil laws of each nation should be only the particular cases to which human reason is applied'.[6] According to Montesquieu, those laws should be related to the various factors affecting a people, such as 'the nature and the principle of the government', 'the climate, be it freezing, torrid, or temperate', 'the properties of the terrain', and 'the way of life of the peoples', so as to give rise to relations all of which together form what Montesquieu had called 'the spirit of the laws'.[7]

Dicey's notion of a constitution's spirit in his comparative constitutional lectures was expressly differentiated from Montesquieu's. For Dicey, the term 'spirit' did not mean 'the end or final cause for which a constitution, or law, or institutions generally exist or may be supposed to exist',[8] which is the meaning he wrongly supposed

---

[2] A V Dicey *An Introduction to the Study of the Law of the Constitution* (London: Macmillan, 10th edn, 1959), 1–35.

[3] See *The Oxford Edition of Dicey* (Allison (ed.)) (Oxford: Oxford University Press, forthcoming in 2013), ii, *Comparative Constitutionalism*, Pt I, ch 3. Dicey's comparative constitutional lectures in *The Oxford Edition of Dicey*, ii, are in two parts: 'The Comparative Study of the Constitution' (Pt I); 'The Comparative Study of Constitutions' (Pt II). The original manuscripts are in All Souls College, Oxford, Codrington Library, MS 323, and, where cited below, the page number originally written on each is provided as an MS p. For scattered allusions to spirit in Dicey, *Law of the Constitution* (10th edn), n 2 above, see, eg., 179, 252, 265–7, 283, 331f, 410, 414.

[4] Dicey, 'English Constitutionalism under George III' (undated), *Comparative Constitutionalism*, n 3 above, Pt I, ch 3, MS p. 31. But see Dicey, 'Introduction' (dated 16 November 1894), *Comparative Constitutionalism*, MS pp 8f, where, in an earlier lecture, he identified his meaning with Montesquieu's.

[5] Montesquieu, *The Spirit of the Laws* (A M Cohler, B C Miller, and H S Stone (trs and eds)) (Cambridge: Cambridge University Press, 1989), bk 1, ch 3, 8.

[6] Montesquieu, *The Spirit of the Laws*, 8.

[7] Montesquieu, *The Spirit of the Laws*, 8–9.

[8] Dicey, 'English Constitutionalism', n 4 above, MS p. 31.

Montesquieu had attributed to it.[9] Nor did it mean 'something very near to the working of a constitution'.[10] Rather, with the term 'spirit of a constitution', Dicey referred 'to the way in which the persons of a given time look upon their institutions, the way in which they expect them to work or assume that they will work'.[11] In short, for Dicey, the spirit of institutions was 'the subjective side of their working'.[12] He admitted that the term 'spirit' was 'an extremely vague one' but stressed that it was one which conveyed 'a notion as indefinite as it is important'.[13]

Dicey's notion of a constitution's spirit might now seem quaintly metaphysical but was similar, at least in function, to common modern notions of legal/constitutional culture. These notions remain current however problematic[14] many of their uses—whether assuming uniformity and continuity, pretending to explain but invoking a notion of culture that is itself in need of explanation, or suggesting an environment of attitudes that may be most influential when unnoticed and barely open to enquiry. Their continuing currency is reason to reconsider Dicey's very early attempts to articulate and make sense of something similar.

Dicey identified the spirit of the institutions of the English constitution, commonly looked upon 'from a legal point of view', as legal and contrasted it, on the one hand, with the military spirit of the institutions of Prussian constitutionalism, looked upon 'from the point of view of soldiers' and, on the other, with the civil administrative spirit of the institutions of French constitutionalism.[15] For Dicey, the English constitution was viewed from the perspective of a people with 'a legal turn of mind', 'imbued with legalism and who import into their political arrangements that love of precedent and acquiescence in fictions which is proper to the law courts.'[16] Through 'a love for forms and precedents', the English constitution is characterized by formal, often fictitious, continuities.[17] Dicey characterized the Prussian constitutionalism in the reign of King Wilhelm I by its unified, hierarchical, and disciplined administrative *corps* of soldier citizens who, as citizens, were subject to compulsory military service, and were headed by the King as a real,

---

[9] Dicey, 'English Constitutionalism', MS p. 31. Through his emphasis upon the relations between a people's laws and the factors affecting a people, Montesquieu seems to have envisaged what we might call the spirit of a society.

[10] Dicey, 'English Constitutionalism', MS p. 31.

[11] Dicey, 'English Constitutionalism', MS p. 31.

[12] Dicey, 'English Constitutionalism', MS p. 31. In its emphasis upon the subjective—the attitudes of people towards their institutions—Dicey's notion of spirit was closer to the nineteenth-century Germanic notion of the *Volksgeist* than it was to Montesquieu's notion.

[13] Dicey, 'English Constitutionalism', MS p. 32.

[14] See, generally, R Cotterrell, *Law, Culture and Society: Legal Ideas in the Mirror of Social Theory* (Aldershot: Ashgate, 2006), especially ch 5; R Cotterrell, 'The Concept of Legal Culture' in D Nelken (ed.), *Comparing Legal Cultures* (Aldershot: Dartmouth, 1997), 13–31.

[15] Dicey, 'English Constitutionalism', n 4 above, MS pp 31f.

[16] Dicey, 'Historical Constitutions and Non-historical Constitutions' (dated 26 May 1900), Dicey, *Comparative Constitutionalism*, n 3 above, Pt II, ch 1, MS pp 36A, 36.

[17] Dicey, 'Historical Constitutions and Non-historical Constitutions', MS p. 36A. Dicey's main example was 'the fiction that in 1649 Charles II immediately succeeded Charles I', thus 'blott[ing] out from popular tradition the very memory of the Interregnum', Dicey, 'Historical Constitutions and Non-historical Constitutions', MS p. 26. In *Law of the Constitution* (10th edn), Dicey similarly presented 'the mystery and formalism of English constitutionalism' as characteristic, n 2 above, 462.

militarily-trained, Commander-in-Chief to whom they were subservient by oath of allegiance.[18] In contrast, Dicey characterized French constitutionalism by its 'administration carried on by civilians in a civil spirit and not an administration modelled on the principles of an army'.[19] He distinguished it by reference to the civil, 'authoritative and centralized' character of its administration and the width of that administration's executive, legislative, and judicial powers, through the exercise of the last of which administrative courts developed a *droit administratif*.[20]

B. Legal, military, and civil administrative forms of accountability

Forms of accountability can readily be identified that correspond to the forms of constitutionalism Dicey typified with his notions of the legal, military, and civil administrative spirits of a constitution. What is expected of each form becomes clearer through consideration of the following three basic questions—about the kind of superior authority, the process, and the applicable standards in the working of that form of accountability. First, to what superior authority is the official, politician, or other actor to be held to account? Secondly, by what process/procedures (also in interpretive practice) is accountability to be achieved? And, thirdly, according to what standards is the outcome of accountability to be determined?

In considering the questions about the authority, the process, and the applicable standards, one would expect legal accountability in its pure form to be to independent judicial authorities by due process and according to established legal rules and principles. In contrast, one would expect strictly military mechanisms of accountability in the disciplining, for example, of service personnel, to be adapted to a context of military threats, exigencies, intelligence concerns, strategic imperatives, such as discipline, unity, and morale, etc. One would anticipate adaptation of the superior authority to which accountability is required,[21] of the process[22] (especially of its speed and transparency), and of the standards to be applied[23] or as they are applied.

---

[18] Dicey, 'Prussian Constitutionalism' (dated 15 May 1897), *Comparative Constitutionalism*, n 3 above, Pt I, ch 6, esp. MS pp 16ff.

[19] Dicey, 'French Constitutionalism' (dated 13 May 1897), *Comparative Constitutionalism*, n 3 above, Pt I, ch 5, esp. MS pp 9f.

[20] Dicey, 'French Constitutionalism', MS pp 9f.

[21] Such as provision for the role of a commanding officer in summary hearings and of other military officers in the Summary Appeal Court and the Court Martial, Armed Forces Act 2006, ss 131, 142–4, 155–7.

[22] Such as summary hearings before a commanding officer, Armed Forces Act 2006, ss 131ff.

[23] Such as 'misconduct on operations' in failing to use 'utmost exertions' to carry out lawful commands or in communicating with a person where 'the communication is likely to cause that person to become despondent or alarmed', Armed Forces Act 2006, s 2(3), (5). For committing the offence of misconduct on operations, a serviceman might be imprisoned for life, s 2(7). 'Misconduct in action' was previously widened to cover using 'words likely to cause despondency or unnecessary alarm', Armed Forces Act 1971, s 2(2).

Civil administrative accountability can similarly be differentiated from legal and military accountability by considering the questions about the authority, the process, and the applicable standards. One would expect civil administrative accountability to be to higher administrative or governing authority, according to more flexible administrative procedures, and by reference to what might be rules of policy, principles of good administration, or conventions of official conduct. The political accountability of democratic parliamentary executives indirectly to the electorate would then be a form of civil administrative accountability to higher and, ultimately, the highest governing authority (as would the more direct political accountability of the democratic non-parliamentary executive).

As distinguished by Dicey, the legal, the military, and the civil administrative spirits of English, Prussian, and French constitutionalism respectively can be translated into the common language of accountability. As translated, English constitutionalism would be characterized by accountability in a legal form, Prussian constitutionalism by accountability in a military form, and French constitutionalism by accountability in a civil administrative form.

C. Dicey—legal or political views of the constitution

Dicey's view of the English constitution was doubly legal. First, in *Law of the Constitution*, he differentiated the legal view from the political view, which was pre-eminently that of the classic political theorist Walter Bagehot.[24] For Dicey, solely the *law* of the constitution was to be the subject of constitutional legal study.[25] Secondly, in his comparative constitutional lectures, he characterized the very spirit of the constitution as legal. In short, Dicey promoted a legal perspective on a constitution with a legal spirit. From that perspective, legal accountability of individuals and officials alike before the ordinary courts enjoyed constitutional centrality.[26] Political accountability through the working of conventions, he clearly envisaged[27]but juxtaposed and thus marginalized as the object of the differentiated political view of political theorists.

By differentiating and promoting the legal view of the constitution, Dicey marginalized the political view. At least from a political perspective, he left political accountability and political understandings of the constitution in need of polemical, even dichotomous, advocacy, which they duly received. Leading reactions were that of W Ivor Jennings in his book *The Law and the Constitution*,[28] which was pointedly entitled to differ from Dicey's *The Law of the Constitution*, and that of J A G Griffith in his famous Chorley Lecture 'The Political Constitution'.[29]

---

[24] Dicey, *Law of the Constitution* (10th edn), n 2 above, 19ff.
[25] Dicey, *Law of the Constitution* (10th edn), 30.
[26] As in Dicey's rule of law, Dicey, *Law of the Constitution* (10th edn), 193ff.
[27] Dicey, *Law of the Constitution* (10th edn), 19ff. See 34f below.
[28] London: University of London Press, 1933.
[29] J A G Griffith, 'The Political Constitution' 42 *MLR* (1979) 1. See also the priority given to political, not legal, controls over the administration in J A G Griffith and H Street, *Principles of*

The advocacy of political accountability and political constitutionalism has been maintained by others[30] in opposition to the dominant or common legal perspective on a legal constitution inherited from Dicey.

By differentiating and marginalizing the political view in *Law of the Constitution* and then identifying the constitution's spirit as legal in his comparative constitutional lectures, Dicey not only expressed but also popularized and entrenched a legal/ political dichotomy, which has long been maintained by the many he influenced or provoked. Dicey's legal view of a legally-spirited constitution, however, was, I will argue, elaborated on for a purpose at a time and in a way such as to disclose the means with which to help address the dichotomy in Dicey's own terms.

D. Transforming point of view and the spirit of the constitution

The potential to transform Dicey's legal view of a legal constitution is threefold. First, Dicey's promotion of the legal view was at a time when the study of constitutional law in its own right—as distinct from constitutional history and political thought—was not well established. Dicey was lecturing and writing shortly after the Oxford Law School had been institutionally detached from its former School of Law and Modern History,[31] that is, at a time when he had reason to distinguish the legal view from other views so as to consolidate the study of constitutional law in its own right as distinct from other disciplines. Dicey was clearly preoccupied with the teaching of law at university rather than in practice, and elaborated on his preoccupation in his inaugural lecture 'Can English Law be Taught at the Universities?'[32] In outlining his legal subject at the start of *Law of the Constitution*, he was staking out his teaching terrain. His purpose has long since lost relevance, in part through his success and that of other pioneering teachers of law at the universities. For decades, the situation has been quite different from that which Dicey faced. Constitutional law as a core subject is well established, as are law faculties or law schools and the teaching of law typically at university. Our law students now need at university, arguably, the opposite of a narrow, strictly legal, focus so as to enrich their legal understanding and later careers with insight into

---

Administrative Law (London: Pitman, 1952). See, generally, M Loughlin, *Public Law and Political Theory* (Oxford: Oxford University Press, 1992), 165–8, 197–201; Foley, *Politics of the Constitution*, n 1 above, ch 2, especially 30ff; G Gee, 'The Political Constitutionalism of JAG Griffith' 28 *LS* (2008) 20.

[30] See, eg., Foley, *Politics of the Constitution*, n 1 above; R Bellamy, *Political Constitutionalism: A Republican Defence of the Constitutionality of Democracy* (Cambridge: Cambridge University Press, 2007); A Tomkins, *Public Law* (Oxford: Oxford University Press, 2003); A Tomkins, *Our Republican Constitution* (Oxford: Hart, 2005). See generally G Gee and G C N Webber, 'What is a Political Constitution?' 30 *OJLS* (2010) 273; J W F Allison, *The English Historical Constitution: Continuity, Change and European Effects* (Cambridge: Cambridge University Press, 2007), 33ff.

[31] F H Lawson, *The Oxford Law School, 1850–1965* (Oxford: Oxford University Press, 1968), chs 1–3; R W Blackburn, 'Dicey and the Teaching of Public Law' *PL* [1985] 679.

[32] London: Macmillan, 1883; republished in *The Oxford Edition of Dicey* i, *The Law of the Constitution*, App I.

subjects, such as history, philosophy, and political theory, which are readily taught and learnt at university.

Secondly, the views of the constitution—legal, historical, and political—were expressly only views in Dicey's *Law of the Constitution*. Although, for legal educational reasons, Dicey declared[33] the exclusivity of the legal view in the study of constitutional law, the legal, historical, and political views were, as views, not mutually exclusive and have the potential[34] to be fully complementary.

Thirdly, the object of the legal view—a supposedly legal constitution—was legal because it had, according to Dicey, a legal spirit understood by him as the subjective side of the working of its institutions. The constitution was legal in the sense meant by Dicey only because he saw it as so viewed by the people through their real or presumed love of legal forms, fictions, and precedents.[35] If their presumed views were in fact more complex or became more complex, the constitution was not, or ceased to be, simply legal with legal accountability simply central.

That the supposed legal, military, and civil administrative views of entire peoples, which Dicey used to distinguish English, Prussian, and French constitutionalism, were in fact more complex, and became increasingly so, is now to be expected. Dicey's stark monolithic national contrast of the constitutionalism of England with that of nineteenth-century Prussia and that of France now appears oversimplified and overstated. Suspect and unconvincing, it would seem to illustrate a late-nineteenth or early-twentieth century nationalist outlook and is contradicted by the extensive interaction of legal systems recognized in more recent comparative scholarship. If so, the scope of the change and its implications need to be considered.

To determine quite how much has changed through developments in the century after Dicey penned his lectures[36] and to suggest implications for the legal/political dichotomy in common assumptions about the constitution and accountability under it, the inverse of the three spirits Dicey attributed to English, Prussian, and French constitutionalism respectively will be considered. In issue here is therefore the relative significance with which all three spirits—the legal, the military, and the civil administrative—were together manifest in English legal and constitutional thought during the twentieth century, whether by way of domestic development or external influence/impact. What will be offered below is an overview of what I will suggest is a considerably more complex and changing constitutional terrain than that elaborated upon by Dicey from what was then known and understood in accordance with his own concerns or preoccupations. On the one hand, it is an

[33] But Dicey's comparative constitutional lectures, *Comparative Constitutionalism*, n 3 above, were, in fact, particularly wide-ranging and went well beyond 'solely law of the constitution', Dicey, *Law of the Constitution* (10th edn), n 2 above, 30.

[34] See generally, eg., the role of complementary and competing points of view in English constitutional formation, Allison, *English Historical Constitution*, n 30 above, esp. 39. See also Gee and Webber's argument for political and legal constitutions both to be embraced as models by which 'they present themselves as essential facets of our constitutional self-understandings', Gee and Webber, 'What is a Political Constitution?', n 30 above, esp. 299.

[35] See p 29f above.

[36] Twenty-first century developments, such as the coming into force of the Human Rights Act 1998 in October 2000, are beyond the scope of this chapter.

overview of initial manifestations of the constitution's civil administrative spirit and of further shifts of the constitution and its legal spirit in a civil administrative direction. On the other hand, it is an overview of legal manifestations of a military spirit in administrative cases at a time of world war and well beyond its aftermath.

E. Initial manifestations of the constitution's civil administrative spirit

Despite Dicey's promotion of a legal view of a legal constitution, the polemical reaction it provoked, and Dicey's presentation of French constitutionalism as fundamentally different from English constitutionalism—indeed, through its *droit administratif*, 'fundamentally inconsistent'[37] with the English rule of law—Dicey's legal starting point for the shifts of the constitution in a civil administrative direction should not be exaggerated. What might be called civil administrative advantages of the English, and even of the French, constitution, it will be shown, were variously emphasized or acknowledged by Dicey (particularly in his comparative constitutional lectures) in his own treatment of each of the following: constitutional conventions; the executive's parliamentary character; the constitution's responsiveness to public opinion; the administrative expertise provided by a permanent and expert civil service; and, even *droit administratif*.

First, one of Dicey's greatest contributions in *Law of the Constitution* was to bring constitutional conventions to the forefront of constitutional thought and practice, albeit solely as the object of the political view of the constitution that he differentiated from the legal view and thus marginalized.[38] Important constitutional conventions, however, as standards of political accountability, such as the individual and collective responsibility of ministers to the higher governing authority of Parliament and, through Parliament's representatives, ultimately to the electorate in civil society, are civil administrative in form.

Secondly, in *Law of the Constitution*, Dicey explained that the responsibility of ministers to Parliament was dependent on constitutional conventions 'with which the law has no direct concern', but, in his comparative constitutional lectures, he did emphasize the 'vital importance' to a constitution's character of whether its executive was parliamentary in that the 'ability to appoint or dismiss the executive' was that of Parliament.[39] For Dicey, this ability was the basis of the 'practical power' of Parliament, and 'possession of this right [was] the source of more than half the authority' that had then accrued to the English House of Commons in

---

[37] Dicey, *Law of the Constitution* (10th edn), n 2 above, 332.
[38] Dicey, *Law of the Constitution*, 19ff (see p 31 above). See also Dicey, *Law of the Constitution*, chs 14 and 15.
[39] Dicey, *Law of the Constitution* (10th edn), n 2 above, 325; 'Divisions of Constitutions' (dated 27 June 1900), Dicey, *Comparative Constitutionalism*, n 3 above, Pt II, ch 5, MS pp 35, 24. See generally Dicey 'Comparison between English Executive and other Executives' (undated), Dicey, *Comparative Constitutionalism*, n 3 above, App II; Dicey, *Law of the Constitution* (London: Macmillan, 4th edn, 1893), App, Note III (retained as such in the next four editions).

reality although not in name.[40] This ability was thus more important as a source of authority than Parliament's legal sovereignty 'in the technical sense' of being able to 'make and repeal any law whatever'.[41] Dicey thus recognized, in other words, that the executive's political accountability to the higher authority of a representative Parliament—here conceived as a form of civil administrative accountability ultimately to the electorate—was more fundamental to Parliament's authority than its legal sovereignty.

Thirdly, in part because of its parliamentary executive, Dicey classified the English constitution as a responsive constitution, that is, responsive to public opinion or popular feeling, and described it as exemplary:

> The best example in existence and perhaps which has ever existed of a 'responsive constitution' is the modern constitution of England. It is...an instrument which responds easily and immediately to the wishes of Englishmen. The Houses of Parliament, and especially the House of Commons, can constitutionally and do in fact give effect to the real or supposed wishes, one might even say, to the whims of the electorate. This is so in matters of legislation, in matters of policy, in matters of administration [where 'in nothing whatever is the responsiveness...better seen'].[42]

Dicey's belief in the constitution's responsiveness is vulnerable to criticism[43] but nonetheless shows the extent to which Dicey regarded Parliament as the vehicle of civil society in its responsiveness to 'the wishes, feelings, or opinions of the citizens...or rather of those citizens who as a class enjoy full political rights'.[44]

Fourthly, Dicey complemented his emphasis on the responsiveness of the constitution with appreciation of the administrative expertise of experts in a modern state. In comparing modern constitutionalism with the ancient constitutionalism of city-states (originally motivated by the ideal of an 'intensely active civil life'), Dicey described how in large modern states 'the art of administration' had become 'a highly technical art which must be entrusted to experts'.[45] He pointed out that therefore in a modern state 'the most that a citizen can do is to take some indirect part, generally a very indirect part indeed, in appointing the persons who, to use

---

[40] Dicey, 'Divisions of Constitutions', n 39 above, MS pp 24f. Dicey also made the claim in *Law of the Constitution* (4th edn), n 39 above, Note III, 412.

[41] Dicey, 'Divisions of Constitutions', MS p. 25.

[42] Dicey, 'Divisions of Constitutions', MS pp 36f, 38.

[43] See, generally, A V Dicey, *Lectures on the Relation between Law and Public Opinion in England during the Nineteenth Century* (London: Macmillan, 2nd edn, 1914); P P Craig, 'Dicey: Unitary, Self-Correcting Democracy and Public Law' 106 *LQR* (1990) 105; Allison, *English Historical Constitution*, n 30 above, 164f. Dicey himself became increasingly concerned with the growing threat of the party system to both Parliament's responsiveness and its executive's responsibility: 'Memorandum on English Party System of Government' (dated 6 August 1889), Dicey, *Comparative Constitutionalism*, n 3 above, App I; Dicey, 'Party Government' (dated July 1898), Dicey, *Comparative Constitutionalism*, Pt I, ch 7; Introduction, Dicey, *Law of the Constitution* (London: Macmillan, 8th edn, 1915), pp xcviiff; Dicey, 'The Development of Administrative Law in England' 31 *LQR* (1915) 148: 152.

[44] Dicey, 'Division of Constitutions', n 39 above, MS p 36.

[45] Dicey, 'Ancient Constitutionalism and Modern Constitutionalism' (dated 29 March 1900 and 18 April 1900 on the manuscript's 1st and 2nd pages respectively), Dicey, *Comparative Constitutionalism*, n 3 above, Pt II, ch 2, MS pp 67, 66.

modern expressions, are the civil or military servants of the state'.[46] Accordingly, Dicey regarded the longstanding refusal in the United States to create and maintain a permanent, special, and skilled civil service as the outcome of distinct prejudice— a prejudice due to ignorance although born out of democratic feeling.[47]

Fifthly, contradicting or qualifying his well-known rejection of French administrative law as contrary to the English rule of law in *Law of the Constitution*,[48] Dicey also expressed a high degree of admiration for the remedies of developed French administrative law. In a to-date unpublished and unnoticed manuscript Note, Dicey elaborated on the remedial merits of French administrative law relative to certain deficiencies in English law and concluded with the following: 'On the whole it appears to be true that if administrative law is to exist it is seen at its best as French *droit administratif*.'[49] The stated remedial reasons for his admiration, it will be shown, were crucial to the second of three later basic shifts of the constitution and particularly of its legal spirit in a civil administrative direction.

F. The constitution's civil administrative direction

The constitution's basic shifts in a civil administrative direction were threefold— institutional, legal remedial, and political constitutionalist. The first shift was reflected in Dicey's later revisionist writings where he begrudgingly recognized the growth of what he called official law and its conceivably beneficial extension through the use of expert and independent administrative tribunals. The second shift was necessitated by Dicey's neglect of the English prerogative remedies and occurred in the development of English administrative law through their recognition and further evolution. The third shift was through the political constitutional understanding of that development as ancillary to the exercise of political controls over the administration.

The constitution's first basic, institutional, shift in a civil administrative direction was through the proliferation of administrative tribunals, variously associated with state departments. It was minimized by Dicey in later editions of *Law of the Constitution* as 'a slight approximation to *droit administratif*',[50] which he fundamentally rejected as contrary to the English rule of law. It has since been the subject of controversy.

---

[46] Dicey, 'Ancient Constitutionalism and Modern Constitutionalism', MS pp 66f.

[47] Dicey, 'Ancient Constitutionalism and Modern Constitutionalism', MS p 67, note.

[48] Dicey, *Law of the Constitution* (10th edn), n 2 above, ch 12.

[49] Dicey, 'Note 17: Conclusions as to French Droit Administratif', *Comparative Constitutionalism*, n 3 above, App VI, MS pp 44–66, esp. p 66. The Note itself was not dated but is related to the previous Note, which was dated 25 May 1899. It may have been preparatory work for his new Notes on *droit administratif* in the Appendix of the French edition of *Law of the Constitution* (Paris: Giard & Brière, 1902) and of its 6th English edition (London: Macmillan, 1902), which he incorporated in ch 12 of later editions.

[50] Dicey, *Law of the Constitution* (6th edn), n 49 above, Note X, 489 (incorporated in ch 12 of later editions, eg 10th edn, n 2 above, 390).

In 1902, Dicey first noted the perplexity caused by the very inquiry into whether *droit administratif* had in any sense recently been introduced into English law.[51] Dicey sought to allay concerns by asserting that the legislative innovations giving to officials something like judicial authority were 'rare', 'suggested merely by considerations of practical convenience', and did not 'betray the least intention on the part of English statesmen to modify the essential principles of English law'.[52] Although he later acknowledged that the approximation of English official law and French *droit administratif* was 'very noticeable though comparatively slight' and that it was 'at least conceivable that modern England would be benefited by the extension of official law',[53] his conclusion in the main text of *Law of the Constitution* remained that there 'exists in England no true *droit administratif*'.[54] But while edition after edition of Dicey's *Law of the Constitution* reiterated that those principles of English law required the unitary application of the ordinary law of the ordinary courts, officials were increasingly exercising judicial authority in administrative tribunals that were proliferating to deal with the disputes arising from the expanding social services of the developing welfare state.[55]

By the late 1920s, the perplexity caused by the proliferation of administrative tribunals, noted by Dicey almost thirty years earlier, had turned to fervent denunciation from within the legal profession. Lord Chief Justice Hewart famously advocated their abolition and attributed what he called their administrative lawlessness, inter alia, to the irregularity of their procedures and a lack of impartiality.[56] At about the same time, others, such as W A Robson and F J Port, defended the tribunals and proposed their refinement. Robson defended them, inter alia, because of their flexibility, expertise in particular fields, and sympathy for the ideal of social justice inspiring the expanding administration.[57] He praised the development of an English administrative law and proposed that a uniform system of administrative appeal tribunals be established. In 1929, in what was the first English administrative law textbook, Port focused on the administrative tribunals and, for guidance, looked to France (and America) where 'Administrative Law has been the subject of long and careful study' and where a uniform system of administrative courts had been established that has been 'altogether admirable' with 'much to admire if not to imitate'.[58] In view of the 'bewildering variety of characteristics' of the English tribunals, 'many of which cannot rightly be called Courts', Port also proposed that

---

[51] Dicey, *Law of the Constitution* (6th edn), 488.

[52] Dicey, *Law of the Constitution* (6th edn), 489.

[53] Introduction, Dicey, *Law of the Constitution* (8th edn), n 43 above, pp xliii–xlviii, esp. xliii, xlviii. See also A V Dicey, '*Droit Administratif* in Modern French Law' 18 *LQR* (1901) 302; Dicey, 'Administrative Law in England', n 43 above.

[54] Dicey, *Law of the Constitution* (10th edn), n 2 above, 390. See generally J W F Allison *A Continental Distinction in the Common Law: A Historical and Comparative Perspective on English Public Law* (Oxford: Oxford University Press, rev. pbk. edn, 2000), 18ff.

[55] Allison, *Continental Distinction*, 81ff, 158f.

[56] Lord Hewart, *The New Despotism* (London: Ernest Benn, 1929), 43–58. See generally Allison, *Continental Distinction*, 158ff.

[57] W A Robson, *Justice and Administrative Law: A Study of the British Constitution* (London: Macmillan, 1928).

[58] F J Port, *Administrative Law* (London: Longmans, 1929), esp pp xii, 21.

a uniform system of administrative tribunals headed by an 'Administrative Court of Appeal' be established.[59]

Two Committees of Inquiry—the Donoughmore Committee and the Franks Committee—considered the opposing views and the pressing issues they raised. The Donoughmore Committee[60] adopted neither Hewart's position nor that of Robson and Port. On the one hand, it accepted that the tribunals under the supervisory jurisdiction and an appellate jurisdiction of the ordinary courts had advantages such as administrative expertise, and, on the other, mindful of Dicey's rule of law, it rejected the proposal for administrative appeal tribunals and declared that establishing a system of administrative law was inexpedient. The Franks Committee similarly rejected that proposal but decisively approved of the permanence of tribunals as machinery for adjudication under the supervisory and an appellate jurisdiction of the ordinary courts.[61] Through the implementation of many of the Committee's recommendations in the Tribunals and Inquiries Act 1958, the administrative tribunals were significantly judicialized and decisively subordinated[62] to the ordinary courts. The proliferation of administrative tribunals was a significant constitutional shift in a civil administrative direction but one that provoked a decisive Diceyan assertion of the supremacy of the ordinary English courts and rejection of a separate French-styled expert civil administrative jurisdiction.

The constitution's second basic, legal remedial, shift in a civil administrative direction had as its starting point Dicey's puzzling neglect in *Law of the Constitution* of the ancient prerogative writs of certiorari, mandamus, and prohibition issued by English courts.[63] In his treatment of remedies, Dicey had two preoccupations—one

---

[59] Port, *Administrative Law,* ch 8, esp. 347, 358.

[60] *Report of the Committee on Ministers' Powers* (1932), (Cmd 4060).

[61] *Report of the Committee on Administrative Tribunals and Enquiries* (1957), (Cmnd 218). See generally Allison, *Continental Distinction,* n 54 above, 158–64; P Cane's illuminating historical and comparative analysis, *Administrative Tribunals and Adjudication* (Oxford: Hart, 2009), esp. 23–48, 69–72.

[62] See now the Tribunals, Courts and Enforcement Act 2007, which implemented many of the recommendations in the Report of the Leggatt Review of Tribunals, *Tribunals for Users: One System, One Service* (London: TSO, 2001). Further significant judicialization and subordination of the tribunals system recently seemed likely when, on 16 September 2010, Mr Kenneth Clarke as Lord Chancellor and Secretary of State for Justice 'announced . . . proposals to bring the tribunals judiciary in England and Wales under the overall leadership of the Lord Chief Justice' in furtherance of a vision shared with the Lord Chief Justice and Senior President of Tribunals 'to work towards a unified judiciary encompassing both courts and tribunals', Written Ministerial Statement, 16 September 2010. HM Courts and Tribunals Service was accordingly created on 1 April 2011 but on the basis of an agreed partnership between the Lord Chancellor, the Lord Chief Justice, and the Senior President of Tribunals 'in relation to the effective governance, financing and operation of the HM Courts and Tribunals Service', *Her Majesty's Courts and Tribunals Service Framework Document,* 2011, (Cm 8043), para 1.5.

[63] The references in *Law of the Constitution* are occasional, and either indirect or largely unexplained. In the 1st edition, Dicey made only a passing reference to another's suggestion—the worth of which 'has never been, and possibly never will be, tested'—that mandamus might be available to coerce the Comptroller to fulfil his duties in the issuing of public money, London, 1885, 329 (see also 200). Elsewhere, with respect to ultra vires action of a Court-martial, in the 3rd and later editions, Dicey supplemented what had been a reference only to habeas corpus with a lengthy quotation from a military law manual referring to the availability of prohibition and certiorari as well, 3rd edn, London, 1889, 283f (cf. 1st edn, 313). On Dicey's assumption that it was 'not the function of any court or judge to declare void or directly annul' an ultra vires by-law, see Dicey, *Law of the Constitution* (10th edn), n 2 above, 95ff, 100ff, esp. 96. On the historical origins of the prerogative writs and on the development

with the personal liability of officials for official wrongdoing and the other with the writ of habeas corpus. In the one, he celebrated the personal liability of officials as exemplifying the second meaning he attributed to the English rule of law—'that here every man, whatever be his rank or condition, is subject to the ordinary law of the realm and amenable to the jurisdiction of the ordinary tribunals'.[64] In the other, he celebrated the writ of habeas corpus as determinative of 'the whole relation of the judicial body towards the executive': 'The judges therefore [through their power to release anyone imprisoned unlawfully] are in truth, though not in name, invested with the means of hampering or supervising the whole administrative action of the government, and of at once putting a veto upon any proceeding not authorised by the letter of the law'.[65]

E C S Wade, the editor of the 9th and 10th editions of *Law of the Constitution*, observed that Dicey's failure to discuss the prerogative writs apart from that of habeas corpus seemed strange.[66] He suggested three possible explanations: first, that the writ of habeas corpus was naturally Dicey's primary concern because it is the ultimate guarantee of personal liberty; secondly, that Dicey had not been concerned to discuss administration as such and thus not the various remedies by which it was supervized; and, thirdly, that Dicey had been preoccupied with deterring the official who was a wrongdoer and who, at least when Dicey first wrote, did wrong mainly by interfering with liberty and property.[67] One might similarly speculate that, because habeas corpus had become a symbol of liberty and a source of educational inspiration, Dicey focused upon it, as did the whig historians[68] who influenced him and similarly emphasized habeas corpus and neglected the other more mundane and technical writs. One might also speculate that the intensity of Dicey's aversion to an English approximation to *droit administratif* resulted in remedial myopia, but it was not such as to preclude his belated and begrudging recognition of an official law in England.

Past speculation should now be reconsidered in the light of Dicey's as yet unpublished and unnoticed manuscript Note, mentioned above,[69] in which he expressed a high degree of admiration for French *droit administratif* in comparing it with English law. His stated reasons for that admiration were remedial. After citing the availability of a remedy against the French state for compensation as a general rule (ie. not limited to the exceptional circumstances in which a petition of right lies against the Crown), Dicey cited proceedings for the annulment of official acts:

Then too[,] what is a valuable part of the French system, a person has in many cases it would appear a right to get administrative or official acts annulled which are *ultra vires* even

---

of certiorari's quashing function from the 17th to the 18th century, see A Rubinstein, 'On the Origins of Judicial Review' 2 *UBC LRev* (1964) 1; S A de Smith, 'The Prerogative Writs: Historical Origins', *Judicial Review of Administrative Action* (J M Evans (ed.)) (London: Stevens, 4th edn, 1980), App I.

[64] Dicey, *Law of the Constitution* (10th edn), n 2 above, 193.
[65] Dicey, *Law of the Constitution* (10th edn), 222.
[66] Dicey, *Law of the Constitution* (10th edn), cxxxvi.
[67] Dicey, *Law of the Constitution* (10th edn), cxxxvi, xif. See also F H Lawson, 'Dicey Revisited I' *Political Studies* [1959] 109: 120f.
[68] See generally Allison, *English Historical Constitution*, n 30 above,165ff.
[69] Dicey, 'Conclusions as to French *Droit Administratif*', n 49 above.

where they have not caused him actual pecuniary damage. As far as I can discover no similar power exists under English law. If for example, the Home Office were to issue an order or notice which was *ultra vires*, i.e. which went beyond any right possessed by the Secretary of State either in virtue of the prerogative of the Crown or under a statute, any man might, if he chose to risk doing so, treat the notice as a nullity. But there does not appear to be any way in which he could get it withdrawn or nullified.[70]

Beneath Dicey's neglect was not merely a preoccupation with habeas corpus, disregard for the administration as such, and an aversion to an English administrative law. At its root was a real ignorance or lost memory of the writ of certiorari by which an administrative act might be quashed. His sketchy knowledge of the prerogative writs of certiorari, mandamus, and prohibition still needs to be explained, whether with reference to Dicey's shortcomings or our own expectations. Dicey may well not have had 'a good memory for cases', the lack of which he lamented.[71] In any event, Dicey's knowledge of remedies and their case law was certainly not as thorough and systematic as is now expected of a leading textbook writer.

The textbook corrective to Dicey's neglect of the prerogative writs as the remedial source for an English administrative law was initiated by E C S Wade in the editing of the 9th and 10th editions of *Law of the Constitution* and carried out by J A G Griffith and H Street, S A de Smith, and H W R Wade in their writing of new administrative law textbooks.[72] It was brought about in clear view, it will be shown, of the French civil administrative jurisdiction to which more than merely passing references were made.

In the 9th edition of *Law of the Constitution*, E C S Wade recognized Dicey's responsibility for much misunderstanding about administrative law both in England and in France, recorded Dicey's reluctant recognition of an English administrative law in his later writings and authored a lengthy section on it in the Appendix.[73] There he recognized the centrality of the prerogative orders or writs of mandamus, certiorari, and prohibition alongside the increasingly important ordinary remedies of the injunction and declaration in English administrative law and included a section entitled '*Droit Administratif* in France', authored by René David and ending with the full table of contents of Hauriou's French administrative law

---

[70] Dicey, 'Conclusions as to French *Droit Administratif*, MS pp 64f. Dicey's manuscript includes this footnote: 'It is in several ways a defect of English law that it affords very little means of testing the legality of any one's action until actual damage has been caused by it', Dicey, 'Conclusions as to French *Droit Administratif*, MS p. 65. In Dicey, *Law of the Constitution* (London: Macmillan, 7th edn,1908), 393f, Dicey added praise for the annulment jurisdiction of the *Conseil d'État* (retained in later editions) but did not specify the supposed comparative defect in English law.

[71] Dicey, letter to James Bryce, 28 September 1895, James Bryce Papers, Bodleian Library, Oxford, Bryce 2: fols 218–20. In the letter Dicey added that 'no one has read so many [cases] & remembers so few'.

[72] Dicey, *Law of the Constitution* (London: Macmillan, 9th edn,1939); Dicey, *Law of the Constitution* (10th edn), n 2 above; Griffith and Street, *Principles of Administrative Law*, n 29 above; S A de Smith, *Judicial Review of Administrative Action* (London: Stevens, 1959); H W R Wade, *Administrative Law* (Oxford: Oxford University Press, 1961).

[73] Dicey, *Law of the Constitution* (9th edn), xiv, 1xxviff, 475ff.

textbook.[74] In his Introduction to the 10th edition of *Law of the Constitution*, E C S Wade incorporated an account of English administrative law centred on the available prerogative and other remedies and, in the Appendix, an account of French administrative law by P M Gaudemet followed by Dicey's 1915 revisionist article on the development of administrative law in England.[75]

In his Introduction to the 10th edition, for further detail on the remedial methods of judicial control, E C S Wade cited *Principles of Administrative Law* by Griffith and Street, first published in 1952 and the second English administrative law textbook after Port's.[76] Griffith and Street in turn acknowledged their considerable debt to 'the pioneers of the subject' and particularly to Robson and E C S Wade.[77] In their treatment of administrative law, however, Griffith and Street differed significantly from Port, Robson, and E C S Wade. Unlike Port and Robson in the constitution's first shift in a civil administrative direction, Griffith and Street were not focused on administrative tribunals as the institutional means to administrative law. Their work was distinctive from earlier work, it will be shown, in two other ways: first, in its domestic orientation and, secondly, in its measure of political constitutionalism.

First, Griffith and Street made far fewer references to French administrative law than did Port and E C S Wade. Apart from briefly mentioning Dicey's misunderstanding of French administrative law and his damaging denial of the existence of an English administrative law in consequence and occasionally referring, for example, to French innovations in the curtailment of administrative immunity,[78] they elaborated on various domestic political and legal controls over the administration. Secondly, they expressed their textbook's political constitutionalism in their substantive argument at the outset and in their formal presentation of the book's contents thereafter. They opened their introductory chapter in direct opposition to nineteenth-century individualism and *laissez-faire* thinking. For Griffith and Street, the 'very success of *laissez-faire* was its undoing':

Concentrations of large sections of the population in overcrowded cities brought problems of housing, disease, and smoke that could not be ignored. The Administration had to intervene in the interests of public safety and health, an interference necessarily inconsistent with an unlimited freedom of property and of the person.[79]

They therefore centred their analysis on the administration, which was to be accountable, subject to parliamentary and judicial controls. They gave much attention to judicial controls over the administration's legislative, administrative, and judicial powers through legal remedies[80] but formally presented them in relation to each

---

[74] Dicey, *Law of the Constitution* (9th edn), 487, 495ff, 518ff; M Hauriou, *Précis Élémentaire de Droit Administratif* (Paris: Sirey, 14th edn (4th edn rev. A Hauriou), 1938).

[75] Dicey, *Law of the Constitution* (10th edn), n 2 above, pp cxxxvff, 475ff; Dicey, 'Administrative Law in England', n 43 above.

[76] Dicey, *Law of the Constitution* (10th edn), n 2 above, p. cxli.

[77] Griffith and Street, *Principles of Administrative Law*, n 29 above, p. vi.

[78] Griffith and Street, *Principles of Administrative Law*, 3f, 240.

[79] Griffith and Street, *Principles of Administrative Law*, 1.

[80] See, eg., Griffith and Street, *Principles of Administrative Law*, 225ff, 239ff.

power only after[81] parliamentary controls (and their limitations) and in addition to controls in administrative practice rather than in law or established convention.[82] Their formal presentation of political controls as pre-eminent although limited in practical reality[83] was true to their essentially political understanding of the constitution in which accountability was first and foremost to Parliament, and thus ultimately to the higher governing authority of the electorate in civil society, as well as to groups beyond Parliament and to the people in other ways yet to be developed:

The Administration is responsible and accountable for its actions. Finally its responsibility is to the people. In theory, and practice, its responsibility is to Parliament. But the Administration must listen to voices other than those of elected representatives or noble lords. It must listen to the voice of organised groups in the State and the pressure on the Administration outside Parliament is very strong... Responsibility to Parliament is not the only kind of responsibility to the people; but so far the other kinds have not been developed.[84]

Griffith and Street furthered the third basic, political constitutionalist, shift of the constitution in a civil administrative direction. Parliamentary controls of the administration were paramount but limited in practice and complemented by judicial controls. Accountability according to their political constitutional understanding was, in other words, to be civil and administrative as well as judicial.

Griffith's domestic focus was again evident in his famous and much later Chorley Lecture 'The Political Constitution',[85] but, it will be shown, did not preclude a significant, although indirect, French influence upon him. One leading influence, inter alia, was that of Jennings, under whom Griffith studied, particularly in the reaction of Jennings to Dicey's legal view of the constitution mentioned above, and in Jennings' orienting of public law to the development of the state and the powers of public authorities.[86] Another such influence upon Griffith, as upon Robson, Port, and Jennings, was that of Harold Laski.[87] Consider Griffith's basic tenets. He expressed them more polemically in his famous Chorley Lecture than in the textbook he authored with Street. One example in that lecture was his categorical assertion that the remedies to authoritarianism in government are political, not legal, so that 'the responsibility and accountability of our rulers should be real and not fictitious'.[88] Another was his insistence upon the centrality and power of the governments of the United Kingdom. For him in that lecture, the very

---

[81] See, eg., Griffith and Street, *Principles of Administrative Law*, 18ff, 99ff, 205ff, 288ff.
[82] Griffith and Street, *Principles of Administrative Law*, 6.
[83] See, eg., Griffith and Street, *Principles of Administrative Law*, 196–205, 284–8.
[84] Griffith and Street, *Principles of Administrative Law*, 23, 25.
[85] Note 29 above.
[86] Jennings, *Law and the Constitution*, n 28 above. See above p. 31f. See, generally, Loughlin, *Public Law and Political Theory*, n 29 above, 167ff; Allison, *Continental Distinction*, n 54 above, 82, 87ff; Foley, *Politics of British Constitution*, n 1 above, 30ff.
[87] Port fully recognized that influence in thanking Laski for his 'unfailing help and encouragement', Port, *Administrative Law*, n 58 above, p. xiv. See generally Loughlin, *Public Law and Political Theory*, n 29 above, 169ff.
[88] Griffith, 'Political Constitution', n 29 above, 16.

heart of the constitution was that they 'may take any action necessary for the proper government of the United Kingdom, as they see it', limited (in the absence of express authority under statute or the prerogative) only by the legal rights of others and the requirement that Parliament assent to changing the law.[89] Both these tenets were already prominent in Laski's writings. Laski expressed a similar distrust in legal controls of government. He emphasized parliamentary controls and citizen participation through advisory committees rather than law as answers to administrative problems.[90] Laski's basic orientation was also towards government or the state administration and the needs to which it gave rise. Laski's influence upon Griffith brings into question the various influences upon Laski's legal and political thought. A leading influence was French. Laski initially derived ideas about the state from Léon Duguit, one of whose main works Laski jointly translated and thus made readily accessible.[91] Duguit, who claimed that France 'holds open the gate through which the sister nations pass', Laski presented as a source of 'enlightenment and inspiration'.[92]

Both the constitution's first, institutional, shift in a civil administrative direction through the proliferation of administrative tribunals, central to the work of Robson and Port, and its third, political constitutionalist, shift through the increased emphasis on parliamentary and other non-legal controls of the administration were within what is now commonly known as the functionalist tradition or style of public law thought.[93] That tradition, centred on the LSE, involved, inter alia, the orientation of public law so as to facilitate the functioning of the state administration. Within that tradition, Duguit's influence directly upon Laski, and indirectly upon those influenced by Laski, was an enduring effect of French constitutional thought upon English constitutionalism.

The constitution's second, remedial, shift in a civil administrative direction focused increasingly on the prerogative and other remedies as domestic sources for the development of an English administrative law. Griffith and Street's textbook made a significant early contribution to that development, inter alia, by clearly recognizing judicial controls through the prerogative and other remedies.[94] In 1959, in his first edition of *Judicial Review of Administrative Action*, De Smith went much further than did Griffith and Street in focusing on the available remedies. De Smith briefly dismissed Dicey's account of the French administrative jurisdiction

---

[89] Griffith, 'Political Constitution', 15.

[90] See, eg., H J Laski, *Parliamentary Government in England: A Commentary* (London: Allen & Unwin, 1938), 147ff, 211f, 344ff, 360ff.

[91] See, eg., H J Laski, 'A Note on M. Duguit', 31 *Harvard Law Review* (1917/18) 186; H J Laski, 'M. Duguit's Conception of the State' in W I Jennings et al, *Modern Theories of Law* (London: Oxford University Press, 1933) 52–67, esp. 65–6; L Duguit, *Law in the Modern State* (F and H Laski (trs)) (New York: Howard Fertig, 1970).

[92] Duguit, *Law in the Modern State*, p. xxxvi; Laski in Duguit, *Law in the Modern State*, xxxiv.

[93] See Loughlin's leading account, *Public Law and Political Theory*, n 29 above,165ff. On the various influences upon Laski and on what Loughlin calls the 'major influence over the British functionalists' of Duguit's work, see also M Loughlin, 'The Functionalist Style in Public Law' 55 *University of Toronto Law Journal* (2005) 361: 392ff, 368ff, esp. 373f.

[94] Griffith and Street, *Principles of Administrative Law*, n 29 above, 225ff.

as misconceived and misleading but corrected, in effect, through the influence of the recent comparative studies of Jack Hamson and Bernard Schwartz inter alia; and De Smith added that English 'imitation is precluded by three centuries of tradition and myth'.[95] He also dismissed the related controversies about the propriety of English administrative tribunals as 'mainly sterile' and stated that his textbook aimed 'to expound the rules comprised within a single sector of English administrative law that has taken shape in a peculiarly insular manner.'[96] Devoting half his book to the available remedies, he had a clear sense of their fundamental importance to judicial review in England. His spin on Maitland's famous remark was that '[i]n private law the forms of action may still rule us from their graves; in administrative law they retain a conspicuous vitality and a long expectation of life'.[97] His book's success helped make of Dicey's puzzling neglect of the prerogative remedies a distant memory, as did that of H W R Wade's a couple of years later.

In the first edition of his textbook, H W R Wade asserted that Dicey's account of French administrative law had long been recognized to be wrong and reduced Dicey's denunciation of administrative law as contrary to the English rule of law to a mere verbal misunderstanding of 'administrative law' to mean a special system of administrative courts.[98] With equanimity and without expressing any inclination either towards rejection or imitation, he recognized great advantages both of the French method of control by administrative courts within the administration, thus with 'deep official experience', and of the English method of external judicial control by the 'entirely different' ordinary courts.[99] Only in one place, did he suggest that the English method was 'more logical' than the French.[100] His reason seems to have been that to entrust all judicial decisions to the ordinary courts, as in England (apart from the administrative tribunals[101] to which Wade devoted a brief critical chapter), was to distinguish powers by their nature. In contrast, to prohibit the civil courts from interfering with the administration under the French separation of powers was to distinguish powers by the persons who happened to exercise them. Apart from his brief introductory comparison of the English and French methods of control, Wade devoted the bulk of his textbook to the prerogative and other remedies available to English courts and the various areas of substantive administrative law they had developed in granting them.

The textbooks of De Smith and Wade were influential products of the constitution's second basic shift in a civil administrative direction that had begun with Dicey's neglect of the ancient prerogative writs and rejection of administrative law.

---

[95] De Smith, *Judicial Review*, n 72 above, 6; C J Hamson, *Executive Discretion and Judicial Control: An Aspect of the French Conseil d'État* (London: Stevens, 1954); B Schwartz, *French Administrative Law and the Common-Law World* (New York: New York University Press, 1954).

[96] De Smith, *Judicial Review*, n 72 above, 10.

[97] De Smith, *Judicial Review* 17. See F W Maitland *The Forms of Action at Common Law: A Course of Lectures* (Cambridge: Cambridge University Press, 1936), 2.

[98] Wade, *Administrative Law*, n 72 above, 7f.

[99] Wade, *Administrative Law*, 8.

[100] Wade, *Administrative Law*, 37.

[101] For Wade, the tribunals were still in 'the no man's land between the legal and administrative worlds', Wade, *Administrative Law*, ch 7, esp. 209.

They recognized, refined, and thus strengthened a domestic English administrative law inspired, to adapt Dicey's words, by the constitution's ordinary legal spirit.

De Smith used features of French administrative law to provide a few points of comparison with English law, as did Wade in presenting the English method of judicial control by the ordinary courts.[102] French administrative law has since remained a measure or source of comparison by which to assess the significance of later developments in English administrative law, whether in relation to procedure, the proportionality principle, or the renaming of the Crown Office List of ordinary judges hearing judicial review cases as the Administrative Court.[103]

All three of the constitution's shifts in a civil administrative direction took place in view of the French administrative jurisdiction but were variously affected by it. In the first, institutional, shift, it was a source of inspiration to those advocating the refinement of the proliferating administrative tribunals into a uniform system. It was, however, a source that provoked official rejection of anything approximating to an English imitation. In the second, legal remedial, shift, it provided a measure or points of comparison by which to assess developments in English administrative law. In the third, political constitutionalist, shift, Duguit's theory of law and the state provided an early but enduring French influence on the functionalist approach to English public law.

G. Manifestations of the constitution's military spirit

Shortly after the outbreak of the First World War, Dicey completed his new Introduction to the last edition of *Law of the Constitution* that would appear in his lifetime. In its conclusion, he depicted the day as having come 'when the solemn call to the performance of a grave national duty has united every man and every class of our common country in the determination to defy the strength, the delusions, and the arrogance of a militarised nation, and at all costs to secure for the civilised world the triumph of freedom, of humanity, and of justice.'[104] The military spirit to which Dicey then gave voice reflected the build-up to war and its outbreak. Facets of a similar spirit, it will be argued, were, first, already evident although less prominent in Dicey's own earlier lectures and did, secondly, profoundly affect the constitution's later development by way of leading administrative cases decided under the shadows of the First and Second World Wars.

---

[102] See, eg, Wade, *Administrative Law*, 37; De Smith, *Judicial Review*, n 72 above, 12f (n 23), 190, 196, 240.

[103] The Civil Procedure (Amendment No. 4) Rules 2000, No 2092, r 22, Sch; Civil Procedure Rules 1998, r 54.4. See, generally, J W F Allison, 'Variation of View on English Legal Distinctions between Public and Private' *CLJ* [2007] 698, esp. 707–9

[104] Dicey, *Law of the Constitution* (8th edn 1915), p. cv. Cf., generally, George Custance's exhortations a century before in response to the Napoleonic threat. For him, cultivation of knowledge in all of equal rights under the constitution was to ensure that 'England would not be disappointed in "*expecting every man to do his duty*"', *A Concise View of the Constitution of England* (London: the Author, 1808), p. xxiii. See, generally, Allison, *English Historical Constitution*, n 30 above, 174.

Dicey's lecture on Prussian constitutionalism was penned in 1897, long before the threat of war with Germany had been realized. In that lecture, Dicey expressed a realistic appreciation and even some admiration for its military spirit, which he attributed to military necessities.[105] That appreciation was particularly evident in his support for Otto von Bismarck's position in the constitutional conflict between the Prussian Crown and Parliament of 1862-66.[106] He described how, as leading minister, Bismarck had effectively governed for five years in defiance of Parliament and its constitutional refusal to settle the budget for implementing a scheme of military reorganization. He added that 'constitutional conflicts are at bottom contests decided by policy and power rather than by argument or law'.[107] In Dicey's view, Prussia owed 'its greatness and its existence to the maintenance of its armed power' in the Prussian army upon the reorganization of which German political unity was founded.[108] Although Dicey presented Prussian constitutionalism as essentially different from English constitutionalism, his appreciation of military realities and necessities, it will be shown, was not confined to it.

In the third and later editions of *Law of the Constitution*, Dicey devoted one chapter to martial law but made clear that it was unknown to English law in the proper sense of 'the suspension of ordinary law and the temporary government of a country or parts of it by military tribunals' as meant in many other countries.[109] What was, however, for Dicey part of the law of England was martial law in the sense of the power of the government 'at whatever cost of blood or property may be necessary' to maintain public order or resist with force invasion, insurrection, riot, etc.[110] English martial law was thus the ordinary law of parliamentary statute and of judicial decisions, under which Dicey envisaged a wide-ranging freedom of officials to take whatever action be necessary in the circumstances subject to limited judicial control. Apart from countenancing in another chapter the 'arbitrary powers' with which the executive might be armed by a Habeas Corpus Suspension Act 'coupled with the prospect of an Indemnity Act',[111] he described, for example, the effect of the enactment of the Riot Act 1714 in straightforward terms. If the Act's conditions were met, mainly of notice and necessity, he stated that the magistrate might 'command the troops to fire upon the rioters or charge them sword in hand'.[112]

---

[105] Dicey, 'Prussian Constitutionalism', n 18 above, MS p. 48.

[106] Dicey, 'Prussian Constitutionalism', MS pp 35ff.

[107] Dicey, 'Prussian Constitutionalism', MS p. 38. The gist is repeated, Dicey, 'Prussian Constitutionalism', MS p. 39.

[108] Dicey, 'Prussian Constitutionalism', MS p. 48. See also Dicey, 'Prussian Constitutionalism', MS p. 38.

[109] Dicey, *Law of the Constitution* (10th edn), n 2 above, ch 8, 287 (see also 291ff).

[110] Dicey, *Law of the Constitution* (10th edn), 288ff, esp. 290. Without changing the chapter on martial law, Dicey added a Note emphasizing the requirement of necessity, *Law of the Constitution* (6th edn), n 49 above, App, Note XII (Note X, 7th and 8th edns), 503–4, 506–8. He also considered 'that the conditions of modern warfare, such as the existence of the telegraph, . . . greatly extend the area of necessity' and may at least conceivably justify summary interference with individual freedom, Dicey, *Law of the Constitution* (6th edn), 506.

[111] Dicey, *Law of the Constitution* (10th edn), n 2 above, ch 5, 236.

[112] Dicey, *Law of the Constitution* (10th edn), ch 8, 290. See, generally, Dicey, *Law of the Constitution* (London: Macmillan, 5th edn, 1897), App, Note VI (retained as such in the next three editions).

Under martial law, Dicey envisaged judicial control, but its limited scope is apparent from the chapter's concluding reference to *Wolfe Tone's Case*.[113] Dicey concluded his chapter with the claim that 'no more splendid assertion of the supremacy of the law can be found' than in the Irish King's Bench's protection of Wolfe Tone by writ of habeas corpus.[114] Wolfe Tone, who had participated in the French invasion of Ireland of 1798, was captured and court-martialed by the English army (although he was commissioned as an officer in the French army, not the English), and was about to be executed by public hanging. The Irish King's Bench did eventually order that a rule suspending the execution be made and served, but only after Wolfe Tone had already slit his own throat (so as to prevent, as some supposed, his being paraded through the streets prior to execution) and only after the sheriff of court had repeatedly been refused admittance to the army barracks. Behind Dicey's celebration, despite the obvious obstacles and an appalling outcome (of which he made no mention), was realistic or pragmatic acceptance of the limitations upon judicial control in a military context.

That the ordinary law of parliamentary statute and of judicial decision was seriously affected during and immediately after the two world wars is indisputable and well recognized.[115] To allow executive detention and other emergency measures, the earlier practice of passing a Habeas Corpus Suspension Act gave way to the passing of primary and secondary legislation that granted wide-ranging powers to the executive and attempted to exclude judicial supervision.[116] The submissive or deferential judicial response in *Liversidge v Anderson*[117]is common knowledge. In the early 1970s, with reference to leading cases such as *Duncan v Cammell, Laird, & Co Ltd*,[118]B Schwartz and H W R Wade called the 1940s and 1950s 'the great depression' when 'administrative law was at its lowest ebb for perhaps a century'.[119] They suggested it was a 'lingering effect' of the 'spirit of abnegation and sacrifice' at time of war that had necessarily reconciled the country to much government by executive decree.[120] Judicial review's development in the 1960s was, for them, a recovery from its 'post-war relapse'.[121]

Comprehensive treatment of the effect of the world wars upon English constitutional law is beyond the scope of this chapter. Its modest aim in this section is to show that it went well beyond a few wartime statutes and cases and that it

---

[113] (1798) 27 St Tr 614. See generally Marianne Elliott, *Wolfe Tone* (Liverpool: Liverpool University Press, 2nd edn, 2012), ch 29, esp. 378–87; Allison, *English Historical Constitution*, n 30 above, 160f.

[114] Dicey, *Law of the Constitution* (10th edn), n 2 above, 294.

[115] See, eg., Lord Woolf, J Jowell, A P Le Sueur, C Donnelly, and I Hare, *De Smith's Judicial Review* (London: Sweet & Maxwell, 7th edn, 2013), 5–014; C Harlow and R Rawlings *Law and Administration* (Cambridge: Cambridge University Press, 3rd edn, 2009), 96f.

[116] On the change of practice, see *R v Halliday, ex p Zadig* [1917] AC 260; A W B Simpson *In the Highest Degree Odious: Detention without Trial in Wartime Britain* (Oxford: Oxford University Press, 1992), esp. 2ff,, 15ff, 44ff, 379f.

[117] *Liversidge v Anderson* [1942] AC 206. See pp 48 below.

[118] *Duncan v Cammell, Laird, & Co Ltd* [1942] AC 624. See pp 51 below.

[119] B Schwartz and H W R Wade *Legal Control of Government: Administrative Law in Britain and the United States* (Oxford: Oxford University Press, 1972), 319, 320.

[120] Schwartz and Wade, *Legal Control of Government*, 320.

[121] Schwartz and Wade, *Legal Control of Government*, 327.

needs renewed attention. Its hypothesis is that judicial decision-making in wartime administrative cases was often such as to have an extraordinary longevity in the common law. It is that wartime judicial decisions gave rise to enduring difficulties when overstated and under-explained, as they often were by the judges who made them in a common executive-minded spirit at time of war. Their curtailment of the judicial role and of common law process and principle was often overstated so as to reduce the legal restrictions upon a massively overstretched government and the likelihood of further litigation. They were also often under-explained in supporting an executive-minded outcome that appeared obvious amidst wartime executive necessities, which were themselves often barely-mentioned, whether because they too were obvious and spelling out their implications risked creating 'alarm or despondency'[122] or whether because of a judicial preference for the generality and legitimacy of common law precept over the specificity and changeability of bare executive necessity. The enduring difficulty for later courts and counsel was that the context of the wartime decision was then no longer appreciated or no longer fully appreciated. To the extent it was appreciated by them, the wartime decision's precedential effect in peacetime was weak and uncertain; to the extent it was not appreciated, its precedential effect appeared strong and certain but might be wholly or readily mistaken.

This chapter's hypothesis on wartime judicial decision-making and its enduring legacy depends for plausibility upon the effect of war on legal accountability in leading administrative cases. How accountability was affected shall be presented below by considering each of the three basic accountability questions described above[123]— questions about the authority, the process, and the applicable standards.

Under the first question, probably the best-known wartime case, excluding in effect the supervisory role of the court as the authority to which accountability was owed, has been *Liversidge v Anderson*.[124] It has been for that reason, it will be argued, the least problematic as a precedent in peacetime. In issue, for the purpose of executive detention, was the interpretation of the phrase '[i]f the Secretary of State has reasonable cause to believe any person to be of hostile origin or associations' in Regulation 18B of the Defence (General) Regulations 1939, made under the Emergency Powers (Defence) Act 1939. The majority in the House of Lords interpreted 'reasonable cause to believe' to require not that there in fact be reasonable cause in the view of the court but that it be thought by the court that there

---

[122] Under Defence (General) Regulations 1939, Reg. 39BA, 'a person who publishes any report or statement relating to matters connected with the war which is likely to cause alarm or despondency' was liable on summary conviction to be imprisoned and/or fined. In distinguishing wartime cases on natural justice in which courts had inferred from wartime legislation, in the absence of express words, that Parliament had intended to exclude the principles of natural justice, Lord Reid argued that 'it was not to be expected that anyone would state in so many words that a temporary abandonment of the rules of natural justice was one of the sacrifices which war conditions required—that would have been almost calculated to create the alarm and despondency against which one of the regulations was specifically directed', *Ridge v Baldwin* [1964] AC 40, 73. Cf. generally Armed Forces Act 2006, s 2 (see n 23 above).

[123] Pages 30f.

[124] Note 117 above.

be reasonable cause in the view in good faith of the Home Secretary account-able to Parliament.[125] *Liversidge* has long been controversial,[126] in part because of Lord Atkin's strong dissent, rejecting the majority's interpretation for importing a novel and unnatural meaning into the common law and making the celebrated claim: 'In this country, amid the clash of arms, the laws are not silent. They may be changed, but they speak the same language in war as in peace'.[127] As much in Lord Atkin's rhetoric as in the speeches of the majority, the war context was unmistakable and fully recognized.[128] *Liversidge*'s precedential authority was accordingly short-lived after the war. Apart from the abolition of Regulation 18B by an Order in Council on VE Day,[129] *Liversidge* was distinguished shortly after the war by the Privy Council in *Nakkuda Ali* as only applicable in that particular regulation's 'context and attendant circumstances' to which the majority of the House had then given 'elaborate consideration'.[130] Its 'very peculiar decision' was simply left 'out of account' by Lord Reid in *Ridge v Baldwin* and, with reference to its wartime context, rejected as authority by Lord Diplock in *Rossminster*: 'For my part I think the time has come to acknowledge openly that the majority of this House in *Liversidge* v. *Anderson* were expediently and, at that time, perhaps, excusably, wrong'.[131] What authority *Liversidge* has retained, save in comparably extraordinary circumstances, is that of Lord Atkin's dissent.[132]

Far more enduring than *Liversidge*, and in that respect more problematic, has been the requisitioning case of *Carltona*[133] decided the following year. The court cursorily dismissed the appeal against the lower court's refusal to grant a declaration in regard to the requisitioning of a factory under Reg. 51(1) of the Defence (General) Regulations 1939. In his judgment, citing only the relevant legislation and no case law, and expressing barely-concealed impatience, for example, with the 'complete misapprehension as to the facts' regarding the competent authority in the appellant's argument, with the 'waste of time' to which the authority's specification of

---

[125] See, eg., 220, 222 (Viscount Maugham).

[126] Cf. generally G W Keeton, 'Liversidge *v.* Anderson' 5 *MLR* (1942) 162; R F V Heuston, 'Liversidge v. Anderson in Retrospect' 86 *LQR* (1970) 33, 87 *LQR* (1971) 161; A Denning *Freedom under the Law* (London: Stevens, 1949), 15f.; A W B Simpson, 'The Judges and the Vigilant State' 4 *Denning Law Journal* (1989) 145; *In the Highest Degree Odious*, n 116 above; F A R Bennion, 'Defending *Liversidge v Anderson*', http://www.francisbennion.com/pdfs/fb/1988/1988–007-liversidge-v-anderson.pdf (accessed 7 May 2013); H Heuzenroeder, 'A Response to Francis Bennion's Defence of *Liversidge v Anderson*', Bennion, 'Defending *Liversidge v Anderson*'; Lord Bingham, 'Mr Perlzweig, Mr Liversidge, and Lord Atkin', Lecture, Reform Club, 16 October 1997, in T H Bingham, *The Business of Judging: Selected Essays and Speeches* (Oxford: Oxford University Press, 2000), 211–21.

[127] Note 117 above, 226, 228, esp. 244. Although the speeches of the majority and the court's decision afford much evidence to the contrary, Lord Atkin's claim has long been celebrated. See, eg., Heuston, 'Liversidge in Retrospect', n 126 above, 66f.; Bingham, 'Mr Perlzweig', n 126 above, 220f.

[128] See, eg., *Liversidge*, n 117 above, 251, 265, 281.

[129] Simpson, *In the Highest Degree Odious*, n 116 above, 408.

[130] *Nakkuda Ali v Jayaratne* [1951] AC 66, 77.

[131] *Ridge v Baldwin*, n 122 above, 73; *R v IRC, ex p Rossminster* [1980] AC 952,1011.

[132] See, eg., *Ridge v Baldwin*, 73; *Rossminster*, 1011; Woolf, Jowell, Le Sueur, Donnelly, and Hare, *Judicial Review*, n 115 above, 5–012, 5–013, 5–042; H W R Wade and C F Forsyth, *Administrative Law* (Oxford: Oxford University Press, 10th edn, 2009), 249, 356, 363ff.

[133] *Carltona Ltd v Commissioner of Works* [1943] 2 All ER 560.

a particular ground for the requisition would give rise, and with the denial of any judicial competence 'to investigate the grounds or the reasonableness of the decision in the absence of an allegation of bad faith', Lord Greene gave the appellant's objections short shrift.[134] The case's obvious war context was barely mentioned in Lord Greene's argument for what is now commonly understood as the *Carltona* exception (to the rule against delegation) according to which Ministers are constitutionally accountable to Parliament, not the courts, for delegations within a department. Only in exemplifying its then practical necessity did Lord Greene mention the 'thousands of requisitions in this country by individual ministers' to which they could not have been expected to attend to personally.[135] Lord Greene's ill-considered, overstated, and under-explained wartime exception excluding any judicial supervision of departmental delegations was eventually—half a century later—qualified (without any reference to *Carltona*'s war context) in a dictum requiring that delegated decisions be suitable to the 'grading and experience' of civil servants.[136] The qualification's scope and the exception's reach, basis/character, and administrative suitability have long been the disputed outcome[137] of a case insufficiently recognized as a product of its war context.

Under the second basic accountability question—about adaptation of the process or the procedures—*R v Halliday, ex p Zadig*[138] may be compared with *Duncan v Cammell, Laird, & Co Ltd*.[139] In *Halliday*, Zadig was interned as a person 'of hostile origin or associations' under Reg.14B of the Defence of the Realm (Consolidated) Regulations 1914, made under the Defence of the Realm Consolidation Act 1914. In habeas corpus proceedings, Zadig's counsel argued that the detention order was invalid because the regulation was ultra vires the Act, which only provided for the issuing of regulations 'for securing the public safety and the defence of the realm'.[140] They urged the House to follow the usual rule that penal statutes be strictly construed—that 'an Act which infringes the liberty of the subject should be construed as far as possible in favour of the subject and against the Crown'—and argued that, had Parliament intended habeas corpus to be suspended, it would have followed its past practice of expressly enacting a Habeas Corpus Suspension Act.[141] The majority decided, in the words of Lord Finlay, that the rule had 'no relevance in dealing with an executive measure by way of preventing a public danger'.[142] In place of a presumption to secure strict construction that Parliament did

---

[134] *Carltona*, 562, 564.
[135] *Carltona*, 563.
[136] *R v Secretary of State for the Home Department, ex p Oladehinde* [1991] 1 AC 254, 300–1, esp. 303.
[137] See, eg., *Re Golden Chemical Products Ltd* [1976] 1 Ch 300, esp. 307, 310; *Bushell v Secretary of State for the Environment* [1981] AC 75, esp. 95–6; *R v Secretary of State for Social Services, ex p Sherwin* [1996] BMLR 1; *R (Chief Constable of West Midlands Police) v Birmingham Justices* [2002] All ER 502; *Director of Public Prosecutions v Haw* [2008] 1 WLR 379; D Lanham, 'Delegation and the Alter Ego Principle' 100 *LQR* (1984) 587; M Freedland, 'The Rule against Delegation and the *Carltona* doctrine in an agency context' *PL* [1996] 19; P P Craig, *Administrative Law* (London: Sweet & Maxwell, 7th edn, 2012), 18-006ff; Harlow and Rawlings, *Law and Administration*, n 115 above, 195f; Wade and Forsyth, *Administrative Law*, n 132 above, 266ff.
[138] Note 116 above.   [139] Note 118 above.   [140] Section 1(1).
[141] *Halliday*, n 116 above, 261–2, esp. 261.
[142] *Halliday*, 270. See also *Halliday*, 270–1 (Lord Dunedin).

not intend to interfere with individual liberty, there was acknowledgment from the outset by Lord Atkinson that '[h]owever precious the personal liberty of the subject may be, there is something for which it may well be, to some extent, sacrificed by legal enactment, namely national success in the war, or escape from national plunder or enslavement'.[143] In full recognition of the 'supreme national danger' and 'the circumstances of a war', the majority did not apply the presumption, and its inapplicability in similar circumstances was confirmed in *Liversidge v Anderson*.[144] The majority's alteration of strict construction and of the presumption's application, thus also of process in interpretive practice, was overt and purposeful, thus clearly limited as a precedent to the context of war or a comparably grave national emergency.

In stark contrast with the clearly limited precedent in *Halliday* was that set in *Duncan*. On an objection to discovery made by the First Lord of the Admiralty in civil proceedings, the House of Lords unanimously concurred with Viscount Simon in ruling that the 'principle to be applied in every case is that documents otherwise relevant and liable to production must not be produced if the public interest requires that they should be withheld'.[145] Although facing conflicting lines of authority, the House of Lords held further that an objection to production by the head of a government department, whether in respect of a particular document or a class of documents, should be treated by the court as conclusive.[146] That the relevant documents related to the hull, machinery, and other parts of the *Thetis* submarine, which had been sunk shortly before the outbreak of the Second World War, could barely be identified from Viscount Simon's speech. He made only a brief tangential reference in his treatment of the limited prior publication of certain of the documents before the tribunal of inquiry into the loss of the *Thetis*, about which he remarked 'some portion of the tribunal's sittings may have been secret'.[147] At most, the war context of the case was implicit in his speech's sweeping conclusion: 'the public interest is also the interest of every subject of the realm, and while, in these exceptional cases, the private citizen may seem to be denied what is to his immediate advantage, *he, like the rest of us, would suffer if the needs of protecting the interests of the country as a whole* were not ranked as a prior obligation'.[148]

Duncan remained authoritative for twenty years after the war,[149] until in the mid-1960s it was belatedly restricted to its war context. In *Re Grosvenor Hotel*, Lord Denning MR stated that the decision in *Duncan* 'can be well explained on its own special [wartime] facts', and, in *Merricks*, Salmon LJ argued that its authority was limited in that the House Lords had been dealing 'only with documents the

---

[143] *Halliday*, 271; cited with approval in *Liversidge*, n 117 above, 257 (Lord Macmillan).
[144] *Halliday*, 270, 271; *Liversidge*, 219–20 (Viscount Maugham); 262–3 (Lord Wright). Cf. generally the judicial claims to be simply determining statutory meaning rather than varying rules of construction: *Halliday*, 274 (Lord Atkinson); *Liversidge*, 251–2, 257 (Lord Macmillan).
[145] *Duncan*, n 118 above, 636.
[146] *Duncan*, 636, 638ff.
[147] *Duncan*, 629–30, esp. 630.
[148] *Duncan*, 643 (my emphasis).
[149] See, eg., *Ellis v Home Office* [1953] 2 QB 135; *Conway v Rimmer* [1967] 1 WLR 1031 (CA).

production of which would manifestly have been injurious to national defence'
and had decided the case 'in the darkest days of the war...before the Battle of
Alamein'.[150] In *Conway v Rimmer*, the House of Lords did eventually reassert that
public interest immunity to discovery was for judicial determination, and Lord
Reid effectively distinguished *Duncan*:

> I have no doubt that the case of *Duncan v. Cammell, Laird & Co. Ltd.* was rightly decided.
> The plaintiff sought discovery of documents relating to the submarine *Thetis* including a
> contract for the hull and machinery and plans and specifications...Any of these documents
> might well have given valuable information, or at least clues, to the skilled eye of an agent
> of a foreign power. But Lord Simon L.C. took the opportunity to deal with the whole
> question of the right of the Crown to prevent production of documents in a litigation. Yet
> a study of his speech leaves me with the strong impression that throughout he had primarily
> in mind cases where discovery or disclosure would involve a danger of real prejudice to the
> national interest. I find it difficult to believe that his speech would have been the same if the
> case had related, as the present case does, to discovery of routine reports on a probationer
> constable.[151]

Lord Reid thus emphasized the context that the court in *Duncan* had barely
mentioned.

The difficulties, however, created by *Duncan*, persisted until the House of
Lords delivered its judgment in *Conway v Rimmer*. The Court of Appeal (Lord
Denning dissenting) had followed the authority of *Duncan* and could find nothing
in Viscount Simon's speech with which to justify a restrictive interpretation.[152]
After its decision, in his critical analysis of the use of authority in *Duncan*, because
the judgment contained 'not one word about the existence of a state of war', D
H Clarke had reason to claim that Lord Denning's earlier statement in *Grosvenor
Hotel* had exceeded 'the bounds of judicial license' and to dismiss Salmon LJ's
argument in *Merricks* as 'apocryphal and unsupportable'.[153] Apart from *Duncan*'s
longevity, that its judges could be said by David Lanham there to have 'delegated
to the Minister their own power to control the administration of evidence'[154] suggests the irregularity and extreme executive-minded breadth of their obviously but
incognito wartime decision on the production of evidence crucial to due process.

Under the third basic accountability question—about the applicable standards—*Amphitrite* and *Harman v Butt* (particularly as followed immediately after the
Second World War by Lord Greene in *Wednesbury*) are illustrative.[155] In *Amphitrite*,
a Swedish ship-owning company sued the Crown by petition of right for damages
for breach of contract where the Crown had not abided by its undertaking during the
First World War not to detain the *S.S. Amphitrite* when it entered a British port.

---

[150] *Re Grosvenor Hotel, London (No. 2)* [1965] Ch 1210, 1244; *Merricks v Nott-Bower* [1965] 1 QB
57, 75.
[151] *Conway v Rimmer* [1968] AC 910, 938–9 (HL).
[152] *Conway v Rimmer*, n 149 above, 1046, 1050f (CA).
[153] D H Clarke, 'Administrative Control of Judicial Action: the Authority of *Duncan* v. *Cammell
Laird*' 30 *MLR* (1967) 489: 510.
[154] Lanham, 'Delegation', n 137 above, 599.
[155] *Rederiaktiebolaget Amphitrite v The King* [1921] 3 KB 500; *Harman v Butt* [1944] KB 491.

In finding for the Crown, Rowlatt J's restrictive application of common law principle was a perfect illustration of overstatement and under-explanation:

I am of the opinion that there was not [an enforceable contract]. No doubt the Government can bind itself... by a commercial contract... But this was not a commercial contract... It was merely an expression of intention to act in a particular way. My main reason for so thinking is that it is not competent for the Government to fetter its future executive action, which must necessarily be determined by the needs of the community when the question arises. It cannot by contract hamper its freedom of action in matters which concern the welfare of the State.[156]

Rowlatt J provided no case law in support of his no-fettering rule, only an analogy with the then rule of the dismissibility of Crown servants at the Crown's pleasure, itself a highly questionable[157] earlier extension of the rule of the dismissibility of military officers. Rowlatt J's 'very sweeping proposition', its 'slender foundation',[158] and the 'uncertainties of its principle, and of its scope', especially its inapplicability to ordinary commercial contracts have long been objects of criticism and sources of difficulty.[159] *Amphitrite* could not easily be judicially restricted to its war context. Although it had been argued for the Crown that the 'granting of clearance to a ship cannot be made the subject of a contract' because it 'must depend upon the military exigencies at the time that it is applied for',[160] Rowlatt J made no mention of those exigencies in laying down his sweeping general rule. That it 'arose out of the exigencies of war' was at least once, after more than half a century, given as a judicial reason for it not to be followed in a peacetime case.[161]

Wednesbury review has been described as 'shorthand for that constitutional school of thought which advocates judicial self-restraint in public law matters'— a shorthand which the 'vast majority of lawyers would still acknowledge to be the guiding principle of our system of judicial review'.[162] Lord Greene's famous formulation is said to be 'the most frequently cited passage... in administrative law'.[163] His main authority, described by him as 'unassailable',[164] was the wartime case of *Harman v Butt*, which has seldom been cited and, if cited, only alongside *Wednesbury*.

---

[156] *Amphitrite*, 503.
[157] See J D B Mitchell, 'Limitations on the Contractual Liability of Public Authorities' 13 *MLR* (1950) 318, 455: 321ff, esp. 325, 334; J D B Mitchell, *The Contracts of Public Authorities: A Comparative Survey* (London: Bell, 1954), 32ff.
[158] W S Holdsworth, 'A Case Book on Constitutional Law' 45 *LQR* (1929) 162: 166.
[159] Mitchell, 'Contractual Liability of Public Authorities', n 157 above, 320; Mitchell, *Contracts of Public Authorities*, n 157 above, 29. For disparate judicial treatment, see, eg., *Robertson v Minister of Pensions* [1949] 1 KB 227, 231; *Commissioner of Crown Lands v Page* [1960] 2 QB 274, esp. 291, 293; *Ansett v Commonwealth* (1977) 17 ALR 513, 530, 533, 562. See also, eg., Woolf, Jowell, Le Sueur, Donnelly, and Hare, *Judicial Review*, n 115 above, 9–022; Wade and Forsyth, *Administrative Law*, n 132 above, 716f.
[160] *Amphitrite*, n 155 above, 502.
[161] Mason J in *Ansett*, n 159 above, 533.
[162] Lord Irvine, 'Judges and Decision-Makers: The Theory and Practice of *Wednesbury Review*' PL [1996] 59: 62–3.
[163] Wade and Forsyth, *Administrative Law*, n 132 above, 303.
[164] *Associated Provincial Picture Houses Ltd v Wednesbury Corporation* [1948] 1 KB 223, 231.

In *Harman* v *Butt*, on representations being made by the commanding officer of forces stationed in the neighbourhood under Reg. 42B of the Defence (General) Regulations 1939, that a cinema should be open on Sundays for the benefit of those forces, the licensing justices had granted a license under the Sunday Entertainments Act 1932 subject to the condition that no child under the age of sixteen should be admitted. In deciding that the condition was neither ultra vires nor unreasonable, Atkinson J disapproved and distinguished, as counsel for the licensing justices had argued, the conflicting authority of the majority judgment in *Theatre de Luxe* as applicable only to licenses granted under the Cinematograph Act 1909, not to licenses granted where the application had been made for the benefit of the armed forces.[165] He stated broadly that the licensing justices have 'a very free hand in the matter of imposing conditions', 'as long as those conditions are not unreasonable', and that 'the court will be slow to interfere' with the exercise of their powers.[166] In his judgment, Atkinson J gave careful consideration[167] to various matters rendering the condition not unreasonable. They included community reverence for Sunday and for church attendance by children, the availability of cheap seats for servicemen, and, most importantly, the undesirability of admitting children below the age of consent where the licence was being granted on the ground that members of the armed forces were in the vicinity in large numbers. Atkinson J did not quite spell out the implications of the age of consent, but concluded as follows:

Sunday audiences at this cinema consist almost entirely of men of the forces. The environment is not one suitable for girls under the age of sixteen. I cannot shut my eyes to the distressing facts with which no judge of assize nor any magistrate can fail to be familiar.[168]

His own concern and appreciation for what must have concerned the licensing justices above all else was unmistakeable.

In *Wednesbury*, the Court of Appeal held that the local authority had not acted ultra vires in granting a licence to open on Sundays subject to the condition that no children under the age of fifteen be admitted, and similarly disapproved the contrary authority of *Theatre de Luxe*.[169] In comparison with Atkinson's J's ruling in *Harman v Butt*, Lord Greene's restrictive ruling on review for unreasonableness— only where the decision is 'so unreasonable that no reasonable authority could ever have come to it'—was similarly broad but with additional embellishment (as well as tautology and ambiguity or inconsistency)[170] and without any attention to the war context of the case upon which he principally relied. For Lord Greene, the decision in *Harman v Butt* was simply 'unassailable' with the only difference from the

---

[165] *Harman v Butt*, n 155 above, 493–4, 496, 498–9; *Theatre de Luxe (Halifax) Ltd v Gledhill* [1915] 2 KB 49, which was decided very early in the First World War and seems to have lacked any war aspect.
[166] *Harman v Butt*, 498, 494, 495.
[167] Cf. the limited justification in *Wednesbury*, n. 164 above, emphasized by M Taggart, 'Reinventing Administrative Law' in N Bamforth and P Leyland (eds), *Public Law in a Multi-Layered Constitution* (Oxford: Hart, 2003), 311–35, esp. 324ff.
[168] *Harman v Butt*, n 155 above, 501.
[169] *Wednesbury*, n 164 above; *Theatre de Luxe*, n 165 above.
[170] *Wednesbury*, 230. See J Jowell and A Lester, 'Beyond *Wednesbury*: Substantive Principles of Administrative Law' *PL* [1987] 368.

case before him being that the licence there 'originated in a representation by the commanding officer of forces stationed in the neighbourhood.'[171] Lord Greene did not recognize any significance in that difference or mention any related difference despite their centrality to the reasoning[172] of counsel for the licensing justices and to that of the court in *Harman v Butt*. In his use of precedent, Lord Greene yielded to a temptation—'to take a statement of principle out of its context of fact'—about which he had warned extra-judicially before the war[173] and of which he seems to have been all too aware.

For judicial review, the outcome of *Harman v Butt*, as followed by Lord Greene in *Wednesbury*, was a guiding principle that was overstated and under-explained on being abstracted from the war context in which it originated. It has long remained authoritative despite substantial and wide-ranging criticism.[174]

The wartime administrative cases described above varied in overstatement, under-explanation, and recognition of context, hence in the certainty and desirability of their precedential effect. To the extent that '[in] law context is everything',[175] they varied for that reason in quality. What is clear is that their effect was not limited to judicial review's 'great depression'[176] of the 1940s and 1950s. Decided in a realistic and highly pragmatic wartime spirit amidst the extraordinary necessities of war, they profoundly affected how the basic questions of accountability—about the authority, the process, and the applicable standards—were, in effect, answered for years to come. They necessitated continuing correction or civilianization in the common law's development in the aftermath of the world wars and thereafter. Their problematic and enduring outcome is an additional legal reason to avoid loose talk of a war on terror since the attacks of 11 September 2001 and later atrocities. Extraordinary necessities in the context of real war brought into acute, but often later barely recognizable, tension two basic features of the common law—attention to context in the treatment of precedent and claims to its continuity, that its laws, for example, 'speak the same language in war as in peace'.[177]

---

[171] *Wednesbury*, 231.

[172] *Harman v Butt*, n 155 above, 493–4, 500–1.

[173] 'The desire for simplification is a perennial weakness of the human mind, even the mind of judges; and the temptation to take a statement of principle out of its context of fact is one which is not always resisted, particularly if the recital of facts fills many dreary pages in the report and the principle is concisely stated in the head-note. But it is a temptation that must be resisted and it can be resisted by those who fully understand the proper use of precedent in the judicial method', Sir Wilfrid Greene, 'The Judicial Office', Presidential Address to the Holdsworth Club, Faculty of Law, University of Birmingham, 13 May 1938, 10–12, esp. 12. See also, Greene, 'The Judicial Office', 6f.

[174] See generally Lord Cooke's dicta in *R (Daly) v Secretary of State for the Home Department* [2001] 2 AC 532, 549, and in *R v Chief Constable of Sussex, ex p International Trader's Ferry Ltd* [1999] 2 AC 418, 452. See also, eg, Jowell and Lester, 'Beyond *Wednesbury*', n 170 above; Irvine, 'Judges and Decision-Makers', n 162 above.

[175] Lord Steyn in *Daly*, n 174 above, 548.

[176] Schwartz and Wade, *Legal Control of Government*, n 119 above, 319.

[177] Lord Atkin, *Liversidge*, n 117 above, 244.

H. A trichroic constitution

Much has changed since Dicey attributed a legal spirit to the institutions of the English constitution because they were commonly looked upon from a legal point of view, and contrasted it with the civil administrative spirit of French constitutionalism and the military spirit of Prussian constitutionalism. From a historical perspective on changes of the last century, coming into common view has been a complex trichroic constitution—legal, developing further in a civil administrative direction, both internally and under French influence, and showing lasting military manifestations in response to the extraordinary necessities of world war. It has been the outcome of internal domestic development and European interaction, varying from influence and imitation to reaction and war.

From a late-modern historical perspective, the trichroic constitution's basic forms of accountability have not been dichotomous or trichotomous because they have not been mutually exclusive, but complementary and mutually interactive. Throughout the period with which this chapter is concerned, insistence upon legal accountability has been complemented with emphasis upon political or, more generally, civil administrative accountability, the importance and advantages of which Dicey himself for his part both recognized and emphasized, particularly in his treatment of conventions and the executive's parliamentary character. Griffith and Street for their part, in their leading early-1950s administrative law textbook, treated accountability through political and other civil administrative controls of the administration as primary and treated legal accountability through the prerogative remedies and other judicial controls as secondary, but both nonetheless as clearly complementary. Through their treatment and the constitution's various other institutional, legal remedial, and political constitutionalist shifts in a civil administrative direction, administrative law has been developed and complemented with emphasis on political accountability. The extent to which administrative legal accountability in the common law has been both necessarily affected by the extraordinary military necessities of world war and thus mistakenly distorted thereafter has been considerable. It deserves greater recognition and warrants further research.

From a strictly legal perspective, the military manifestations of the constitution's trichroic spirit may remain difficult to discern in the continuity of the common law. If so, the legal spirit Dicey attributed to 'a love for forms and precedents' and 'acquiescence in fictions'[178] within 'the mystery and formalism of English constitutionalism'[179] would have lost its claim to exclusivity, but little of its significance.

---

[178] 'Historical and Non-historical constitutions', n 16 above, MS pp 36A, 36.
[179] Dicey, *Law of the Constitution* (10th edn), n 2 above, 462.

3

Judicial Accountability in Comparative Perspective

*Mark Tushnet**

A. Introduction

Judicial accountability is one desideratum in institutional design; judicial independence is another.[1] Put another way, in examining judicial accountability we must ask: accountability to whom, and how much? One answer is that judges in modern democracies are to be accountable to the people roughly contemporaneously, just as other wielders of public power are. Judges wield public power, and they ought to be accountable to the people to the extent that they exercise discretion. Call this political accountability. Yet, 'too much' political accountability is troublesome, because it conflicts with the independence we seek in judges. And, it might be thought, judges do not make discretionary choices, or at least the same kinds of discretionary choices that others who exercise public power do. They 'merely' interpret and enforce the law.

Another answer, then, is that judges are to be accountable to 'the law', and somehow 'the law' is accountable to the people as they were constituted at some earlier time. Law intervenes between the people and judges, allowing judges to be what I will call *derivatively* accountable while maintaining independence. Yet, 'too much' judicial independence can also be troublesome, if the mechanisms of indirect accountability are so weak that judges are in practice politically unaccountable except in some quite loose, even metaphorical sense: 'Too much' independence, and judges wield power in the service of their own aims, mediated only by their own understanding of what 'the law' requires of them, which may not be much, or which may be what they would try to accomplish were they merely private citizens.

---

* William Nelson Cromwell Professor of Law, Harvard Law School.

[1] There is a very large body of literature on judicial accountability and independence, focused both on specific national judiciaries and on comparing the methods by which accountability and independence are secured. A recent collection is HP Lee (ed.) *Judiciaries in Comparative Perspective* (Cambridge: Cambridge University Press, 2011). I have drawn from this literature in many places, but think it would be both superfluous and misleading to cite specific works for quite general propositions common within the literature.

The tension between accountability and independence is not unique to judges. Whenever we design institutions to commit some substantial amount of public power to professionals—scientists or social workers, no less than lawyers and judges—we do so because we want to combine accountability to the profession's norms with accountability to the people. Consider for example a system in which the government makes grants to scientists to pursue their inquiries. We could sensibly assign authority to select grantees to committees of scientists, which we hope will decide among applicants in substantial part with reference to the scientific merits of their proposals. The grant agency should be accountable to 'science', the norms of its enterprise. But, we might also want the grant agency's scientists to decide with reference to public preferences—to make progress on some scientific inquiries relevant to pressing problems of public policy before examining more esoteric ('basic' or 'pure') scientific questions, for example. Here, too, political accountability occurs through mechanisms of indirect responsibility: some elected officials will in the end examine the agency's decisions and decide whether to increase, maintain, or decrease the agency's budget for grants by evaluating its performance.

In both settings we seek some balance between accountability to professional norms and accountability to the public. Too much of either will generate undesirable outcomes. I limit the discussion hereafter to the legal setting (though parallel issues arise in the scientific one). Too much political accountability, and some litigants who ought to prevail under concededly applicable legal norms will lose. We can readily describe that as a violation of the litigant's fundamental right to a decision 'according to law'. Too much accountability to an impersonal law, and judges will be able to pursue their personal projects by describing their decisions as consistent with, or even compelled by, the law. Perhaps because of their own professional commitment to 'the law', legal theorists tend to emphasize the risks of too much accountability to the people, defending judicial independence and supporting mechanisms of indirect political accountability with relatively little concern about the extent to which those mechanisms in fact promote such accountability.

This chapter offers an overview of mechanisms of accountability, both to 'the law' and to the people. It focuses on the accountability of judges on apex courts,[2] those whose decisions are not subject to review by (judges on) other courts.[3] The reason is two-fold. First, subordinate judges might be subject to accountability mechanisms common to them and to apex courts – scrutiny of their decisions by the profession, for example. But, subordinate judges are *also* subject to review by hierarchically superior judges, whereas judges on apex courts are not. Review by hierarchical superiors is a common phenomenon in every complex institution. In this, courts are no different from any other complex bureaucracy. Superiors in the judicial bureaucracy

---

[2] I use the term 'apex courts' to indicate that my discussion deals with legal systems in which some courts—in some systems, a labour or commercial court, for example—are final with respect to their subject matters. In modern constitutional democracies, even specialized apex courts are typically subject to review for constitutional error by a superior 'constitutional' court.

[3] I will typically refer to 'courts' rather than 'judges' simply for ease of exposition, but it is important to remember that the relevant decision-makers are all individuals, sometimes making individual decisions that are aggregated to produce an institutional one.

face problems of securing the accountability of inferiors to the norms the superiors hold (be they norms of adherence to 'the law' or any other norms). These problems, generically described as principal-agent problems or agency slack, are pervasive. The superiors may not have the capacity to review every decision by subordinates with enough attention to ensure compliance with the superiors' norms. The superiors' directives may not be precise enough to ensure routine compliance even by the best motivated subordinates. Considered as bureaucracies, courts do not raise distinctive accountability questions, and I do not consider them in detail here. The mechanisms of accountability I describe are relevant to subordinate judges to the extent that such judges are independent, either because of agency slack or because they and their hierarchical superiors hold a view of the law's requirements under which individual judges are fully responsible to 'the law' alone.

Second, and more important, it is difficult to defend the proposition that judges on apex courts, and in particular on constitutional courts, exercise no discretion at all in deciding cases. Further, under most views judges on apex courts properly take into account the policy aspects of their actions, either as a component of the justifications they offer for their decisions or as a constraint on how far specific legal principles should extend. To that extent judges on apex courts ought to be accountable politically, though not necessarily to the extent that other policy-makers are.

Finally, although the discussion is framed in terms of judicial accountability generally, issues of accountability and independence are most pressing with respect to decisions about constitutional law. Legislatures and executive officials can revise decisions on non-constitutional matters through their ordinary policy-making processes. Issues of accountability and independence are not entirely irrelevant even here, because revising decisions thought to be mistaken consumes political time and energy that could be devoted to other matters that the policy-makers on their own would have given higher priority. 'Inertia,' in short, may allow 'mistaken' decisions to remain on the books. The extent to which constitutional questions are different depends on issues of constitutional structure. Constitutional decisions thought to be mistaken can be revised directly by amending the constitution.[4] The ease with which that can be done depends on the decision-rule of constitutional amendments. A relatively easy amendment rule means that there might be few systemic concerns about excessive judicial independence, and the issue of *judicial* accountability might be largely irrelevant. Systems of weak-form constitutional review, which authorize revision of constitutional decisions through the ordinary legislative process, similarly can promote the compatibility of constitutional law with current policy preferences, and do so without trenching on judicial

---

[4] I exclude from detailed consideration statutory and constitutional amendments made as a response to judicial decisions with which the public disagrees. In the first instance, such amendments do nothing to promote judicial *accountability*; they merely revise the law, which is an aspect of accountability to law. To the extent that judges dislike amendments that respond to their decisions, such amendments might be a form of indirect political responsibility, and judges might shape their decisions to avoid responsive amendments. I note that it is unclear to me what that extent is, or even why judges should dislike such amendments at all.

independence.[5] The discussion in this chapter puts these structural issues to one side, and deals with the issue of judicial accountability in systems with strong-form constitutional review.

B. Political accountability

Indirect political accountability comes in many forms. One perhaps obvious comment applies to many, if not all: the less indirect the political accountability is—and even if indirect, the stronger it is—the more controversial will be its exercise. The more direct and the stronger, the greater the incursion political accountability makes on judicial independence. This observation underlies the common distinction between individual accountability and independence, and institutional accountability and independence. The distinction rests on the judgment that mechanisms focusing on individuals are likely to raise more serious concerns than mechanisms dealing with the court (or a specific court), in terms of achieving the proper balance between accountability and independence. So, for example, using some obviously political process to remove a judge from office because of her rulings is perhaps the strongest possible form of direct political accountability, and is, I believe, widely thought to be fundamentally incompatible with judicial independence and the rule of law. Indirect political accountability with a relatively narrow target—for example, removal of an entire bench because of disagreement with one or more of its rulings—is more controversial than broader forms of indirect political accountability, such as a political role in judicial appointments.[6] For these reasons, protections of judicial independence are typically embedded in constitutions or entrenched organic laws, which are themselves interpreted to limit the grounds properly invoked to remove judges from office to matters like physical or mental disability, corruption, and administrative malfeasance.[7]

The preceding paragraph suggests an additional point that should be made explicit. System designers seek an acceptable balance between independence and accountability in judicial systems that are quite complex. Although some mechanisms may tend more than others to advance accountability relative to independence, other features of the specific institutional design being employed might offset that tendency. Put perhaps a bit crudely: a system designer constrained to choose one particular mechanism of indirect political accountability can achieve any desired balance between accountability and independence by coupling that mechanism with a set

---

[5] For a discussion of weak-form systems, see Mark Tushnet *Weak Courts, Strong Rights: Social Welfare Rights in Comparative Constitutional Law* (Princeton: Princeton University Press, 2008). Some defenders of Canada's system of weak-form review suggest that it empowers judges by providing a mechanism for correcting 'mistaken' decisions in a way that preserves the judges' independence.

[6] Precisely targeted interventions, such as removals of individual judges because of their rulings, are forms of direct political accountability. See Section B3 below.

[7] Of course, to the extent that the bodies charged with determining whether a judge was corrupt are themselves under political control, or even influence, the possibility always exists that these grounds will be invoked improperly where the 'true' motivation for removal is disagreement with the judge's rulings.

of other mechanisms as to which choice is unconstrained.[8] As a consequence, the normative implications of using any one mechanism are generally indeterminate, and normative recommendations focusing on only one or a few mechanisms are likely to be otiose.

1. Budget control and judicial salaries

Indirect political accountability occurs when political officials exercise substantial control over judicial budgets, including salaries. Not surprisingly, judges typically seek to establish as large a degree of fiscal autonomy as they can. They object to lodging responsibility for judicial budgets in a political ministry, for example, rather than in the judicial hierarchy itself. An international norm regarding judicial salary protections may be emerging: judicial salaries may be reduced only as part of a more broadly applicable austerity program, whereas reductions applicable solely to judges are inconsistent with judicial independence.[9] Or, to put it in the terms I have been using, indirect political accountability by means of salary adjustments targeted at the judiciary are too strong, posing too great a risk that they will be used to create more political accountability than is compatible with the rule of law.

2. Judicial appointment

Assuming that judges will be independent and relatively unaccountable *during* their tenure, system-designers can promote indirect political accountability at the front end, that is, at the point of selection (and, perhaps, promotion). There are many variables subject to manipulation. The length of tenure is one. Judges of apex courts can have relatively short terms, through longer terms, up to tenure for life, subject to removal for disability or misconduct. The shorter the term, the easier it is for the public and its political leaders simply to wait out judges whose decisions they dislike and replace them with others.[10] The United States may lie at the 'long terms' extreme of the continuum, with judges on the Supreme Court serving during good behavior, essentially for life, with no mandatory retirement age.

---

[8] Vicki Jackson refers to this as the phenomenon of constitutional 'packages', Vicki C Jackson, 'Packages of Judicial Independence: The Selection and Tenure of Article III Judges', *Georgetown Law Journal* (2007) 95: 965–1039.

[9] See, eg. Peter H Russell, 'Towards a General Theory of Judicial Independence', in Peter H Russell and David M O'Brien (eds.) *Judicial Independence in the Age of Democracy: Critical Perspectives from Around the World* (University of Virginia Press, 2001), 18. The jurisprudence of the Canadian Supreme Court is probably the most detailed on this matter, and contains one feature that goes beyond what I have described as the consensus. According to the Canadian Supreme Court, judicial salary reductions that are part of a comprehensive austerity program are impermissible unless they are endorsed by a commission that focuses solely on judicial salaries. See *Reference re Remuneration of Judges of the Provincial Court of Prince Edward Island* [1997] 3 SCR 3 (Sup Ct Canada). Russell notes that 'Canadian judges appear to be at the cutting edge' on these issues, ibid.

[10] Here too there are incentive effects to worry about: if reappointment is possible, judges may shape their decisions with an eye to reappointment, thereby being subject to indirect political accountability; if reappointment is precluded, judges may shape their decisions with an eye to their prospects for post-service employment, which may promote indirect accountability to someone, though not

As with judicial salary adjustments, there may be an emerging norm of constitutional design here—convergence on the judgment that judges on apex courts should serve non-renewable terms lasting somewhere between nine and fourteen years.[11]

The mechanisms of appointment, on the one hand, and of discipline and removal, on the other, provide useful illustrations of indirect political accountability for courts as institutions and for judges as individuals respectively. Again at the risk of introducing some distortion, I suggest something like a continuum of mechanisms for achieving indirect political accountability through appointments. At one end is the system, typical in the state judicial systems within the United States, of popular election of judges.[12] Variations exist within this category, of course: judicial terms can be short or long; the elections can be partisan or nominally nonpartisan; the issue in an election might be whether a specific candidate should be retained as a judge, rather than which of several candidates should be elected. Each variant provides a different balance between political accountability and independence. Further, because the structure of the judiciary is complex and multidimensional, the metaphor of a single dimension might be inapt: a system that has judicial elections for quite long terms might have less popular accountability than a system of appointments by political figures for renewable, relatively short terms.[13]

a. Elections

Judicial elections provide today's people with a means of holding individual judges accountable reasonably directly—and, to the extent that other judges take the results of judicial elections as providing information that they use in reaching their own decisions, also promote the accountability of courts as institutions. Between elections, of course, judges are not accountable for specific decisions, but in this they do not differ from purely political representatives during *their* terms.[14] Yet, some additional qualifications need to be mentioned. Political leaders may play a large role in selecting judges as candidates. In the United States, typically a judge in a retention election holds her seat because of a previous appointment by a

necessarily the public. And, for obvious reasons, these effects may differ depending on the age at which judges take their positions on apex courts, and whether they are subject to rules requiring or norms encouraging retirement at a specific age or restrictions on post-service employment.

[11] The precise numbers may depend on other design variables, such as the size of the apex court. System designers appear to try to calibrate the length of terms with size, to ensure a regular replacement process: courts with nine members have nine-year terms, allowing—if all goes well—one replacement a year; courts with seven members have fourteen-year terms. (For obvious reasons, system designers prefer that apex courts have an odd number of members, and preferably a relatively small number so that the entire court can sit on particularly controversial cases, thereby eliminating the risk that a decision will be rendered by a panel whose composition is skewed.)

[12] There are scattered examples of judicial elections elsewhere in the world. The judges of the Japanese Supreme Court face retention elections every ten years. Constitution of Japan, art. 79, ¶ 2, available at <http://www.solon.org/Constitutions/Japan/English/english-Constitution.html.>

[13] I owe the point and the example to Vicki Jackson.

[14] *Cf* Jean-Jacques Rousseau, *The Social Contract* (Wordsworths Classics, Chatham, 1998), bk 3, ch 15 ('The people of England thinks itself free; but it is free only during the parliamentary elections. As soon as they are over, slavery overtakes them, and they are nothing'.).

governor. And, in contested elections and even in nominally nonpartisan ones, political leaders may have a strong influence in determining whose names appear on the ballot.[15] Perhaps more important, and introducing an idea that will play a more prominent role as we proceed, the norms voters believe appropriate in judicial elections may be distinctive. In voting for legislators, I believe, voters typically focus almost exclusively on the policy positions candidates take or on how those who are seeking re-election have performed as legislators. Voting for judges may be different because pure policy considerations, while never absent, may be supplemented by a sense among voters that they should also consider the extent to which a judge or candidate has or is likely to conform to professional norms, including compliance with 'the law.'

b. Purely political processes and the role of norms

The next category includes systems in which judicial appointments are made by elected officials, for example in the national courts of the United States, by the President with the advice and consent of the Senate, and in Canada and Australia by the Prime Minister acting alone. It is commonplace in studies of US national judicial appointments that presidents often make rough predictions of how prospective nominees might cast their votes if appointed, in selecting who among the list should be nominated. Predictions may be inaccurate even in the short run, and presidents understandably are more likely to focus on the issues of more immediate concern than on issues that might arise over the often long tenure of the judge. Predictions about future decisions are rarely the sole consideration presidents have in mind when selecting nominees. In the end, presidents (and senators) use the appointment process to make a rough but generally accurate judgment about how a nominee's approach to adjudication will play out over her career. This is a prime example of indirect political accountability.[16]

What might be called professional norms play some role in the US process. References to a nominee's professional qualifications and to her character and judicial temperament recur, although my judgment is that these references have become boiler-plate over the past few decades. Strikingly, though, the appointment processes in Canada and Australia, while seemingly unconstrained because appointments lie in the hands of the Prime Minister alone, might well be more constrained—and therefore achieve less indirect political accountability. The reason is that appointments to the apex courts in both nations appear to be strongly constrained by professional norms. For example, Helen Irving, an Australian academic, described

---

[15] For a discussion of the role of party leaders in the judicial election system in New York state, see *New York State Board of Elections v Lopez Torres*, 552 US 196 (2008).

[16] As Vicki Jackson suggested to me, this form of accountability might better be called 'input' or 'prospective judgment' rather than 'accountability'. A comparison to legislators in their first term and second term, and during their last term in a system with term limits, is suggestive: the people have input or influence on the selection of the legislator in the first and last election, and hold the legislator accountable at the second and later elections (for her actions during the preceding term of office).

a call in Australia for the appointment of a 'capital-C Conservative' a 'barely disguised attack on the Court's "character."'[17] As a matter of near-constitutional convention, geographic considerations matter in Canada and, to a lesser extent, in Australia. More importantly, for each vacancy there will be only a handful of prospective nominees thought in the relevant circles to be qualified for appointment. In both nations the subset of lawyers and sitting judges who are generally thought to be qualified for judicial appointment is quite small, and the potentially appointable women and men are generally well known within the profession. The judgment that a person is qualified for the highest courts tends to rest on the political classes' judgment that the person has performed well, according to professional rather than political norms, in a person's prior position as a judge or high-level practising lawyer. There is no real 'system' in this, only a set of norms that might amount to a convention, and, like all conventions, it has the potential for displacement by simple departure from prior practice.

The important role professional norms play in appointments processes that are nominally purely political raises new questions which I can do no more than mention here. Professional norms are rooted in the profession itself. Roughly, leaders of the bar make judgments about whether a person's views are 'sound' or 'unsound'. Precisely what will seem 'sound' or 'unsound' will of course vary as the profession changes.[18] The precise relation between changes in the profession and changes in the norms relevant to judicial selection deserves further exploration. For example, the American Bar Association (ABA), the organized national bar in the United States,[19] used to be politically conservative and has now become relatively more liberal. Prior to the 1990s, presidents consulted with the ABA prior to selecting nominees for national judicial office, and deferred substantially though not completely to the ABA's judgments about potential nominees' professional qualifications. As the ABA became more liberal, Republican presidents and their advisers became increasingly uncomfortable with giving the organized bar this role, and the administration of George W Bush abandoned the practice. President Obama revived it.

Again roughly, there will almost certainly be some loose correlation between how society generally changes and how the legal profession changes. The change in the ABA's political orientation, for example, almost certainly resulted from a dramatic increase in the number of women lawyers. The role of professional norms in the appointment process thereby becomes a mechanism for an attenuated form of indirect political responsibility.

---

[17] Helen Irving, 'A True Conservative,' in Robert Manne, *The Howard Years* (Melbourne: Black Inc. Agenda, 2004), 105-6.

[18] In my judgment, the most dramatic example is the change in the United States about what constitutes a 'sound' view on gender equality—and, elsewhere, probably a similar change with respect to views about the rights of gays and lesbians.

[19] Membership in the ABA is voluntary.

c. Judicial nominating commissions

A final set of appointment mechanisms may attenuate political responsibility even more. These mechanisms are judicial nominating commissions, which take various forms but whose general characteristic is limiting the role elected officials play in selecting judges. A nominating commission's composition matters a great deal. Typically, such commissions include some elected officials, some representatives of the bar, some members of the public, and—importantly—some judges.[20] Norms matter a great deal in nominating commissions' deliberations, and here too professional norms are likely to dominate.[21] Judges may vote as a bloc, the bar's representatives are likely to take professional norms to be their primary concern, and the representatives of the public may be co-opted by the professionals into accepting professional norms.[22] Sometimes judges can take control of the selection process either informally, by dominating commission deliberations, or formally through the commission's composition, or, unusually, through constitutional interpretations that give the judiciary a controlling role.[23] Further, nominating commissions may be charged with specific tasks, such as seeking to achieve diversity on the bench, with diversity measured in demographic terms rather than ideological ones. To the extent that commissions are charged to take some things into account and there is silence about others such as ideology or 'judicial philosophy', the latter concerns are likely to be pushed down on the commission's agenda. Often the nominating commission presents a short list of candidates for appointment to a political authority such as the Prime Minister. The list constrains the political authority's choice, though the commission might anticipate that authority's reaction to the list and take its anticipated reaction (meaning, its policy preferences) into account along with professional norms in developing the list.

d. Conclusion

Political accountability is unlikely to disappear as mechanisms move from popular elections to judicial nominating commissions dominated by judges, but it seems

---

[20] Eg. the Judicial Appointments Commission created by the Constitutional Reform Act 2005 in the UK must have five judges (plus one 'lay justice' or magistrate and one tribunal judge), two lawyers, and six nonlawyers.

[21] This too is a topic crying out for more research.

[22] Concerned about cooptation and related policy questions, in 2007 Canadian Prime Minister Stephen Harper added a person he regarded as a representative of the law enforcement community to the committee that advised him on the appointment of judges to courts other than the Supreme Court. For a discussion, see Rainier Knopff, 'The Politics of Reforming Judicial Appointments' *University of New Brunswick Law Journal* (2008) 58: 44–51. Discussions of modifications in the selection process for the Supreme Court of Israel, to reduce the extent to which the process is dominated by judges and their allies in the bar, are continuing. Of the current lay members of the UK Judicial Appointments Commission, one served as director of human resources for Linklaters, a large law firm, and another served as a lay member of a commission on legal education.

[23] The Supreme Court of India has interpreted a constitutional provision requiring that the nation's President consult with its Chief Justice on appointments to the Supreme Court as giving the Chief Justice an effective veto over the President's choice. See *Supreme Court Advocates on Record Ass'n v Union of India*, AIR 1994 SC 268 (S Ct India).

quite likely that it will weaken. Which mechanism achieves the appropriate balance between accountability and independence is a normative question that different liberal democracies may properly resolve differently.

3. Judicial discipline and removal

Appointment mechanisms affect the indirect political accountability of courts as institutions. Mechanisms of judicial discipline and removal typically deal with judges as individuals.[24] In doing so, they raise pointed questions about the appropriate balance between accountability and independence.[25] A judge would be maximally and directly political accountable were she to know that she could be removed from her position relatively easily, simply because political actors disagreed with her rulings on the merits of cases that came before her. Such a judge would also be minimally independent. Emerging international norms of constitutional design strongly disapprove of removal mechanisms of this sort.[26]

The difficulty lies in designing mechanisms of discipline and removal that are not readily subject to 'capture' for these mean purposes; that is, mechanisms whose operators will find it difficult to use some pretext for discipline or removal actually predicated on disagreement with rulings on the merits. There are two generic solutions. The first is to specify relatively precise grounds for discipline or removal; the second is to place the decision within the control of the judiciary itself.

The United States has chosen the first mechanism for removal. A judge on the national courts can be removed from office—'impeachment and conviction' is the appropriate term, generally reduced to 'impeached'—if he fails to display 'good behavior', which has come to mean only if he is guilty of a serious criminal

---

[24] Adopted by a new Jeffersonian majority in Congress, the 1801 Judiciary Act in the United States abolished a set of courts created by a Federalist. Congress abolished the Commerce Court in 1913 because of its controversial rulings. On both incidents, see Roger C Cramton, 'Reforming the Supreme Court' *California Law Review* (2007) 95: 1313–34. The Russian Constitutional Court was 'suspended' in 1993 as part of a conflict between President Boris Yeltsin and the Russian legislature. For a discussion, see Alexei Trochev *Judging Russia: Constitutional Court in Russian Politics, 1990–2006* (New York: Cambridge University Press, 2008) 191–205.

[25] A recent extreme example is the reduction in the age of mandatory retirement for judges in Hungary, which had the effect of removing a large number of individual judges instantaneously. It is generally thought that this was done to alter the composition of the nation's constitutional court by allowing the sitting government to name new justices. The reduction has recently been held unconstitutional by the constitutional court (by an equally divided vote setting the new appointees against the holdovers). The outcome remains undetermined at this writing. For an early and understandably incomplete discussion, see Kim Lane Scheppele, 'How to Evade the Constitution: The Case of the Hungarian Constitutional Court's Decision on the Judicial Retirement Age,' available at <http://www.comparativeconstitutions.org/2012/08/how-to-evade-constitution-case-of.html?utm_source=feedburner&utm_medium=feed&utm_campaign=Feed%3A+ComparativeConstitutions+%28ComparativeConstitutions.org%29&utm_content=Google+Reader>.

[26] For an overview, see Stephen J Schnably, 'Emerging International Law Constraints on Constitutional Structure and Revision: A Preliminary Appraisal' *University of Miami Law Review* (2007–8) 62: 417–89. I should note that there may be isolated situations in which a judge could appropriately be removed on the basis of her rulings on the merits. The example of a judge who simply refuses to acknowledge the large-scale legal transformations attendant upon a transition to democracy comes to mind.

offence.[27] This has led to an administrative problem, posed by judges who become disabled, typically mentally, and refuse to acknowledge their disability. The first national judge removed from office was indeed removed for mental disability,[28] but the next case raised questions about the suitability of that mechanism for disability. In 1804, the House of Representatives sought the removal of Justice Samuel Chase, charging him with having made several rulings that the House believed to reach grossly erroneous results for merely political reasons, and with lacking an appropriate judicial temperament. The Senate narrowly refused to remove Chase, establishing a convention that the merits of a judge's rulings should play no part in the decision to remove him from office. It was the combination of the charge of failures of judicial temperament with charges of erroneous rulings that created the enduring difficulty. The Chase impeachment showed that removal for alleged disability might be a pretext for removal based on disagreement with rulings. It took more than a century, but eventually the United States solved the problem by placing authority to impose discipline for injudicious behavior, and effectively to remove a disabled but recalcitrant judge, in the hands of the judiciary itself.[29]

These two solutions—narrow criteria for discipline and removal administered outside or inside the judiciary, and broader criteria administered within the judiciary—are widely used. Neither is particularly well-designed to achieve political accountability, which may well be normatively desirable. Focusing on individual judges, removal and discipline proceedings pose a greater threat to judicial independence—or, obversely, make direct political accountability more potent—than the indirect political accountability associated with appointment processes.

4. Political accountability through the threat of noncompliance

In the end, judges must call upon the state's coercive apparatus to ensure that their decisions are complied with. The strength of traditions of compliance varies widely. In well-functioning liberal democracies, traditions of compliance are typically quite strong, which may mean only that the nation's people have had enough experience to have concluded that the benefits of 'voluntary' compliance are worth it even in cases where they as individuals happen to have lost. Sometimes in such democracies and perhaps more often in nations with less experience in the practices of liberal democracy, noncompliance occurs merely because the state's coercive apparatus is itself too weak. Officials would ensure compliance if they

---

[27] Former judge Alcee Hastings was charged in criminal proceedings with bribery and related corruption offences. Impeachment proceedings were begun after the criminal jury acquitted him. He was impeached and removed for the same corruption offences, along with a charge that he had perjured himself in the criminal proceedings. *See* David Johnston, 'Hastings Ousted as Senate Vote Convicts Judge', *New York Times*, 21 October 1989 p.1. The restriction of 'good behavior' to compliance with the general criminal law has evolved into what I believe to be a constitutional convention, and the Hastings impeachment is not inconsistent with that assessment.

[28] The judge was John Pickering of New Hampshire.

[29] For the background and later developments, see Lynn A Baker, 'Unnecessary and Improper: The Judicial Councils Reform and Judicial Conduct and Disability Act of 1980' *Yale Law Journal* 94: (1985) 1117–43.

could, but lack the capacity to do so. Sometimes, though, those in charge of the coercive apparatus could deploy it to ensure compliance, but choose not to do so because they disagree with a judge's decision.

More common than wilful noncompliance are evasion and erosion over time, which occur even in well-established liberal democracies when judges issue rulings that are deeply unpopular; which is to say, when judges act too independently.[30] Officials will claim that their practices are distinguishable from the ones the courts condemned, for example. Sometimes evasion is so widespread that even those who agree with the courts' decisions refrain from challenging the evasions because of the social stigma attached to doing so. As evasion persists, the underlying decision can lose whatever normative hold it initially had.

Judges may describe wilful noncompliance by officials as lawlessness, and many would agree that at the least there is a strong normative presumption against the propriety of wilful official noncompliance. Yet, norms are one thing; practices another. Noncompliance where compliance is possible is another mechanism of judicial accountability. It can operate after the event, of course, in cases of actual noncompliance. In addition, the mere possibility of noncompliance may have ex ante effects on the decisions judges make, though, as I have suggested, we need additional explication of the psychological processes that lead judges to alter the conclusions they would otherwise reach because they anticipate noncompliance, a behavior they will almost necessarily think normatively unjustified.

C. Accountability to 'the law'

Strong political accountability might be worrisome because it increases the risk that we will have a government of 'men', not laws, and in the extreme, a system of so-called telephone justice in which decisions are determined entirely by political considerations and not at all with reference to the supposedly applicable law. We want judges to be accountable to the law, but spelling out precisely what we mean by that phrase is perhaps surprisingly difficult. Judges in subordinate positions in judicial hierarchies might be said to be accountable to law because, and to the extent that, their decisions are subject to review by hierarchical superiors. Even here the conceptual issue is not simple: why should we say that lower-court judges are accountable 'to law' rather than 'to their superiors', just as subordinates in any bureaucracy are? But this apparently simple solution is unavailable when we consider judges on apex courts whose decisions are, by definition, not subject to hierarchical supervision by some other judges.

---

[30] Perhaps the clearest example is that of the US Supreme Court's decisions holding unconstitutional the practice of school-organized prayer in the nation's public schools. For decades those decisions were simply ignored in many rural school districts, and legislators and school officials continue to seek ways of encouraging prayer within the contours of the court's decisions as they interpret them. On the widespread refusal to comply with the decisions, see Kenneth M Dolbeare and Phillip E Hammond *The School Prayer Decisions from Court Policy to Local Practice* (Chicago: University of Chicago Press, 1971); on continuing efforts to evade the decision, see, eg. *Santa Fe Independent School District v Doe* (2000) 530 US 290.

An additional preliminary point is that the distinction between political accountability and accountability to law has an important temporal dimension. Under prevailing understandings in liberal democracies, law is a human artifact, so accountability 'to law' must involve accountability to *someone*.[31] Roughly, 'political accountability' refers to accountability to contemporaneous power-holders as representatives of today's people, whereas 'accountability to law' refers to accountability to the people and their representatives in the more distant past. Accountability to law is a form of indirect accountability to the people in the past, taking its route through their enactments of law.

1. Accountability as correctness, method, and orientation

Too much political accountability and too much independence pose similar risks – rule by 'men' rather than according to law. A judge completely free to act may implement her personal judgments about good public policy, or about what the law should be, or about what would make her life easier. Accountability to law limits those risks, but exactly how?

It is tempting to say a judge is accountable to law when her decisions are correct; that is, when she does what the law at issue in the case at hand requires of her. Ronald Dworkin might be taken as advocating for a standard of correctness in his argument that there are always right answers in the law.[32] The temptation to do so, and the more general temptation to adopt a standard of correctness, must be resisted. Dworkin's argument is that there *are* right answers; that an all-knowing and perfectly competent judge Hercules would arrive at those answers; that ordinary judges seeking to understand their own decisions must conclude that they have reached the right answer even if that answer differs from Hercules's; and that ordinary judges and people evaluating their work cannot know whether there are such differences between the judges' answers and Hercules'. This means, though, that specific decisions cannot be assessed according to a criterion of Herculean 'correctness'.

Put more mundanely, judges in apex courts, and especially in apex courts with some discretionary control over their dockets, will inevitably face difficult legal questions, in which there can be reasonable disagreement over what the law at issue requires.[33] There are too many potentially correct decisions for 'correctness' to be the criterion for accountability to law, except in the weak sense that a judge is

---

[31] The restriction to liberal democracies is designed to rule out systems in which judges treat some legal rules as flowing directly from one or more gods, unmediated by human intervention. I believe that my formulations do not commit me to a position on the question mooted in the literature on legal positivism, Do some legal rules necessarily have non-legal, that is, moral, content? But, I am willing to be corrected on this.

[32] Ronald Dworkin *A Matter of Principle* (Oxford: Oxford University Press, 1985), ch 5.

[33] Public expression of that disagreement can be suppressed by rules against publication of dissenting views, but the analytic point—that reasonable disagreement is inevitable—remains true. On dissents, see Section C2 below.

accountable to law when her decision falls within the (often wide) range of reasonably defensible legal interpretations.

We can make more progress by moving to a more abstract level, where we are concerned not with the particular decision at hand and the specific law, about which there is controversy, but rather with the body of law taken as a whole. A judge is accountable to law, understood at this level of abstraction, when her decision is in some sense palpably legal. Here too we may not be ruling out a great deal, although, importantly, we would be able to say that a judge is not accountable to law when the *only* justification for a decision we can come up with takes the form, 'this decision would promote the material interests of a person important to the judge (a class that can include the judge himself and no one else)'.

A related issue is this: at the heart of accountability to law is accountability to the historical public. But, does accountability to law give some place to accountability to the contemporaneous public? Consider here the US Supreme Court's decision finding the Affordable Care Act constitutional.[34] The deciding vote was cast by Chief Justice John Roberts, who held, to the surprise of many observers, that the Act was constitutional as an exercise of congress's power to tax and spend for the general welfare. The Chief Justice's action was praised *and* criticized as an act of judicial statesmanship. The praise took the form of saying that the decision preserved the Supreme Court's legitimacy in the public's eyes; it was, in this chapter's terms, a decision promoting accountability to the contemporaneous public through the form of law. The criticism took the form of saying that the Chief Justice departed from accountability to law precisely because he inserted the non-legal factor of 'statesmanship' into his decision-making process. The dispute turns on whether accountability to law licenses direct consideration of the contribution a decision makes to accountability to the contemporaneous public rather than the historical public that created the Constitution. That dispute cannot be resolved within a framework dealing only with accountability and independence.

The jurisprudence associated with American Legal Realism suggests that accountability as 'palpable legality' is a quite weak constraint, again especially in apex courts. A core proposition of Legal Realism, widely though not universally accepted, is that in many contexts judges properly take into account considerations of public policy in determining what the law is. The proposition implies that a judge who invokes her personal judgments about good public policy is making a palpably legal decision, and so is accountable to law.[35]

But, perhaps the Legal Realists were wrong, normatively if not descriptively, and judges should not advert to their judgments about good public policy in their decisions. This raises another possibility: that a judge makes a palpably legal decision when she uses acceptable methods to arrive at her conclusion. In liberal

---

[34] *National Federation of Independent Business v Sibelius*, 132 Sct 2566 (2012).

[35] See, eg. Benjamin Cardozo *The Nature of the Judicial Process* (New Haven: Yale University Press, 1921), 94 ('There are some rules of private law which have been shaped in their creation by public policy, and this, not merely silently or in conjunction with other forces, but avowedly, and almost, if not quite, exclusively.'). Though Cardozo refers here to private law, the Legal Realists took his argument to be applicable, perhaps even more strongly, to constitutional law.

democracies, for example, a decision relying on the revealed word of God would not be palpably legal (even if it were correct on other grounds). To some in the United States, a constitutional decision invoking anything other than original meanings directly or derivatively through precedents themselves resting on original understandings is not palpably legal. That example, though, shows that treating the use of acceptable methods as necessary for accountability to law may not do much more than using correctness as the criterion, and for the same reason: There is reasonable disagreement over which methods of legal analysis are acceptable. So, a judge who uses any of the methods within a range of reasonable ones would be accountable to law on this understanding.[36]

A more controversial proposition of legal realism is that the materials generally accepted as available for use in coming to a decision are usually so comprehensive that essentially any decision—including a decision that benefits the judge or an important sponsor personally, the paradigm of government by 'men'—can be explained with reference to materials in that corpus. It will be almost impossible to find a decision that we can explain only with reference to the judge's personal material interests. It bears emphasizing that I am dealing here with an 'existence' proposition: almost every possible outcome will be defensible through the careful use of materials within the body of law, even if the judge making the decision fails to offer a credible defence. So, finding an outcome that the judge fails adequately to defend, we will almost always be uncertain about whether we are dealing with venality, and so with a failure of accountability to law, or mere incompetence, which is not a failure of that sort. In modern US discussions, *Bush v Gore* is the case that poses these questions most dramatically.[37] Many analysts believe it a failure of accountability to law because it is explicable only with reference to the majority Justices' desire to see George W Bush become President; others believe the court opinion to be nearly incompetent but the result defensible on other grounds; and a few believe it to be correct in its own terms.[38]

A final candidate for determining accountability to law is what I call an appropriate orientation or mindset. A judge is accountable to law if and to the extent that she orients her thinking to legal materials and thinks of herself as a judge rather than, for example, a bureaucrat or politician. This is a mental disposition. It is impossible to discern directly, and the materials that might be used to infer the mental disposition—what the judge says in her opinions and extrajudicial statements, her temperament in court and elsewhere—may be misleading.

Accountability to law as using acceptable methods or having an appropriate disposition necessarily has an important, perhaps dominant, and perhaps even exclusive, sociological component. Who determines which methods are acceptable ones; what

---

[36] Perhaps the best articulation of this proposition, though focusing on private law, is Karl Llewellyn *The Common Law Tradition: Deciding Appeals* (Boston: Little Brown & Co. 1960). The leading modern exposition of the proposition that there is irreducible reasonable disagreement on questions of constitutional law is Jeremy Waldron *Law and Disagreement* (Oxford: Oxford University Press, 1999).

[37] (2000) 531 US 98.

[38] See Howard Gillman, 'Judicial Independence Through the Lens of *Bush v Gore*: Four Lessons from Political Science' *Ohio State Law Journal* (2003) 64: 249–64.

disposition is appropriate? The obvious answer is the legal profession, or the elites within the profession who pay special attention to the judiciary.[39] This answer inserts a contemporaneous, though perhaps narrow, public into an analysis that at its core deals with accountability to a historical public. The earlier comments on 'soundness' and its social determinants are relevant here, but take on a slightly different normative cast. That judges should be accountable to the law seems beyond question, yet to the extent that accountability to law is a form of accountability to legal elites, one might reasonably question its normative value—or at least raise questions about the extent to which accountability to law is compatible with norms of democratic self-government that one hopes characterize liberal democracies. One might think that *if* accountability to law can or must include some degree of accountability to the contemporaneous public, that public should be wide rather than narrow.

2. Transparency: writing opinions, publishing dissents

Scholars from the common-law tradition are likely to think that accountability to law requires some degree of transparency in judicial behavior. How can we know whether judges actually have the requisite orientation to the law unless they inform us about their decisions? Yet, the civil law tradition allows judges to generate quite terse and, on their face, uninformative judgments. The awkward place judicial precedent holds in civilian legal theory demonstrates civil law's commitment to accountability to law. Today's judges should be the 'mouths of the law' as enacted in the past, not parrots repeating what some other judges have said.[40] The same thought underlies the practice in some nations of prohibiting the publication of dissents. That practice contributes to, or reflects, an ideology in which 'the law' so tightly constrains judgment that open disagreement about the law's requirements seems indefensible. Can these practices—uninformative judgments, no dissents, and little precedential effect to decisions—be reconciled with the ideal of accountability to law?

The 'no dissent' tradition appears to be under some pressure in apex *constitutional* courts.[41] One reason may be a recognition that constitutional law is different from 'ordinary' law. Constitutional law, it might be said, distinctively combines aspects of law with judgments about sound long-term social and political policy. For example, it seems difficult to defend the proposition that the widespread invocation of a proportionality test for constitutionality is a matter of purely legal judgment, if

---

[39] Perhaps continuing competence is another requirement for accountability to law. Again, the legal profession will determine the criteria for assessing competence. The discussion of mechanisms for judicial discipline above is relevant here, particularly its observation that such mechanisms typically give members of the profession the dominant role.

[40] The role of precedent is awkward because most civilian legal theorists agree that a cumulation of similar rulings on a specific question can come to have jurisprudential weight equal to that of the enacted law. As I understand it, in some Latin American nations, when the constitutional court has reached the same conclusion five times on a specific question, that conclusion becomes a precedent binding lower court judges.

[41] The German Constitutional Court began issuing dissents in 1971, after two decades in operation, after a reform law had been adopted a year earlier.

only because it seems impossible to divorce policy assessment entirely from the judgment that some regulation, narrowly drawn to conform to the requirement that regulations restrict liberty no more than necessary, nonetheless imposes a burden on liberty disproportionate to the accomplishment of concededly permissible social goals. Judges on constitutional apex courts may find it difficult to think that they are merely the 'mouths of the law' when they enforce constitutional law understood in this way.

The legal realist tradition suggests that one cannot easily defend the claim that constitutional law is distinctive in its combination of legal and policy judgment. Yet, whatever pressure there is for more discursive opinions in apex courts dealing with 'ordinary' law seems much weaker than the pressure for such opinions in constitutional courts.[42] Another feature of civilian legal discourse may reconcile terse or opaque decisions with the ideal of accountability to law. Mitchel Lasser argues that the opinions of the apex courts in France dealing with administrative and ordinary civil law may be opaque but that the jurisprudence of those courts is not.[43] They achieve transparency, and thereby accountability to law, because the opinions are accompanied by, and are integrated with, published material laying out the arguments made to the court and offering scholarly comment on the decisions.

Notably, the existence of scholarly commentary introduces into the discussion of transparency in civilian legal systems precisely the same constraint that professionalism imposes in the common law world. That is, in both systems professional norms ultimately determine whether an opinion is appropriately oriented to 'the law' and so whether judges are indeed accountable to the law.

D. Conclusion

Many social institutions require some accommodation of accountability and independence. Typically, though, the institutions are accountable to and independent from the same entity. So, for example, legislators are accountable to their constituents by means of elections, but are on the Burkean conception to be independent from the constituents as well; the media are accountable to, but independent from, the public. In these settings it is natural to speak of a trade-off between independence and accountability. The situation may be different for judges and courts. As I have argued, there is a trade-off between accountability to and independence from the public, instantiated in methods of judicial selection and removal. Yet, courts and judges are also, or perhaps even primarily, accountable to the law. There is no direct trade-off here with independence: a judge who acted independently

---

[42] Discursiveness is of course more difficult to achieve when caseloads are high, which may account in part for the continuing strength of the civil law tradition of terse opinions in apex courts dealing with 'ordinary' law.

[43] Mitchel De S-O-I'E Lasser *Judicial Deliberations: A Comparative Analysis of Judicial Transparency and Legitimacy* (New York: Oxford University Press, 2004).

of the law would be corrupt or lawless. Yet, under contemporary understandings 'the law' is ultimately grounded in human choice, and so accountability to law is accountability to someone. Ultimately it is accountability to the past authors of the law, but proximately, I have argued, it is accountability to contemporaries in the legal profession, who identify the modes of reasoning they take as defining what acting according to law is.

Judicial accountability and its obverse judicial independence are important components of constitutional design. Their relationship is complex, with numerous variants in design that all can achieve any specified accommodation of accountability and independence. In addition, it seems unlikely that the general principles of liberal democracy dictate one, or even a few, basic versions of appropriate accommodations. Those who are concerned about judicial accountability and independence probably must be satisfied with judgments that systems have 'enough' or 'not enough' accountability and independence.

PART II

4

Accountability to Law

T R S Allan*

A. Introduction

Contemporary constitutional theory in the United Kingdom is marked by a series of debates that have deeper roots in legal and political theory. Competing theories of legal and political constitutionalism place rather different emphases on the central-ity of legal or political accountability. Political constitutionalists tend to associate administrative legality with conformity to the limits of a jurisdiction conferred (for the most part) by statute: judicial review exists to enforce the legislative will against plain transgressions by public authorities. A legal constitutionalist, by contrast, will understand administrative legality more broadly: accountability to law entails the judicial enforcement of constitutional standards of fair or just treatment. A public agency exercises power within the framework of a legal tradition which Parliament itself is assumed to honour: common law rights as well as European Convention rights form part of the interpretative background, features of the landscape that the courts must defend in their role as guardians of liberty. I shall argue for the superiority of this latter conception of law and liberty. Accountability means, above all, com-pliance with the rule of law—an ideal of governance closely bound up with our very conception of the United Kingdom as a liberal democracy.

Within the legal constitutionalist fold there has been a vibrant debate about the constitutional foundations of judicial review; accepting the present scope and legitimacy of judicial review, opinions have differed, nonetheless, over the best char-acterization of its place within the larger constitutional order.[1] That debate, however, has exhibited a rather uncertain relationship with more immediate questions of legality: the connection, if any, between preferred conceptual foundation and public law doctrine has been hard to discern. Nor have the conceptual assumptions of the rival theories been clearly distinguished from those of political constitutionalist

* Professor of Jurisprudence & Public Law, University of Cambridge; Fellow of Pembroke College, Cambridge. The helpful comments made by Nicholas Bamforth, David Dyzenhaus, and Peter Leyland on earlier drafts are gratefully acknowledged.

[1] See, generally, Christopher Forsyth, (ed.) *Judicial Review and the Constitution* (Oxford: Hart Publishing, 2000).

thinkers, leaving the relationship between the different debates obscure.[2] We need
to dig a little deeper into legal theory to make sense of these various debates—to
see how they depend, at root, on jurisprudential questions about the nature of law.
At the heart of the matter is our ideal of the rule of law, and hence our understanding
of executive accountability to law; and that ideal is itself dependent (or so I shall
argue) on a proper grasp of the concept of law.

For the most part, controversy over the constitutional role of the courts vis-à-vis
other branches of government takes the nature of law for granted: law is treated,
implicitly, mainly as a tool for the translation of political initiatives into law. On
that view, the 'rule of law' is a value related to the supposed instrumental nature
of law: it makes a demand for published, prospective general rules, sufficiently
clear and consistent to serve as a guide for people to follow, thereby making the
law's prescriptions more effective. Compliance with the rule of law enhances the
law's efficiency, as sharp blades improve the instrumental value of knives; if such
compliance enhances human dignity, it is only in the 'negative' sense that the rule
of law is a safeguard against the law itself, which may be deployed in high-handed
or oppressive ways.[3] The rule of law, on that account, should not 'be confused
with democracy, justice, equality (before the law or otherwise), human rights
of any kind or respect for persons or for the dignity of man'.[4] If, then, English
law embraces fundamental rights, preserving a sphere of individual autonomy
grounded in respect for human dignity, such rights depend on continuing parliamentary support; and their judicial protection and enforcement similarly depend
on whatever remedies are for the time being approved by current legislation, which
is always subject to repeal.

Common law constitutionalism, which accords the courts a place of honour
alongside the legislature in the distribution or exercise of sovereignty, is best
understood as repudiating that instrumental conception of law. The common law
practice of judicial review is rooted in an avowedly moral concept of law, related
to fundamental ideas about liberty and justice. On this approach, the values of individual autonomy and human dignity are *internal* to law, basic assumptions critical
to its meaning and application in specific cases. And so far from the rule of law
being merely a safeguard against the abuse of law itself—a shield against a political
oppression imposed by assertion of law—it is, on the contrary, a basic protection
against arbitrary power from whatever quarter it appears.[5] The rule of law is the
ideal of government according to *law*, insulating the individual citizen against
the unfettered discretion of officials, on one hand, and the depredations of other
persons or private organizations, on the other. The familiar distinction between the
concept of law and the ideal of the rule of law—between law as a tool and legality

---

[2] T R S Allan, 'The Constitutional Foundations of Judicial Review: Conceptual Conundrum or
Interpretative Inquiry?' *CLJ* [2002] 87.
[3] See Joseph Raz, *The Authority of Law: Essays on Law and Morality* (Oxford: Clarendon Press,
1979), 228: 'It is merely designed to minimize the harm to freedom and dignity which the law may
cause in its pursuit of its goals however laudable these may be.'
[4] Raz, *The Authority of Law*, 211.
[5] Compare Jeremy Waldron, 'The Concept and the Rule of Law' *Ga L Rev* (2008) 43: 1, 10–11.

as a constitutional value—is one better designed to bolster legal positivism than illuminate our understanding of law.[6]

In recent debate over the constitutional foundations of judicial review, Parliament and the common law courts have been juxtaposed as rival sources of authority and legitimacy. The emphasis of the ultra vires doctrine on legislative intention, as at least an implicit basis for the enforcement of judicial standards of administrative legality, has been challenged by those who locate the basis of judicial power in the common law. Either the courts are servants of a sovereign legislature, enforcing the standards of legality sanctioned by Parliament, or they are authors of principles of legality independent of any parliamentary sanction (though subject to express contrary legislative command). If not ordained by Parliament, the principles of legality are '*judicially created* standards of public behaviour'; they are 'categorically, *judicial creations*'.[7] But this competition between *sources* of administrative law is ultimately intelligible only within a legal positivist framework. The judges are conceived as devising or extending a doctrine of the rule of law as a safeguard against the abuse of law: judicial invention must match the potential for administrative tyranny, filling a void that Parliament has left unregulated.

The whole debate makes more sense, I suggest, if reconstructed as an argument over the nature of law itself and, hence, over the connections between legality, liberty and justice. Like the debate between legal and political constitutionalists, it is in essence an exploration of the roots of the constitution in moral and political principle. We cannot detach our grasp of the role of the common law from our broader inquiries into the nature of law itself. In enforcing principles of legality the common law courts seek not to usurp the powers of other branches (even if that is sometimes the effect of dubious reasoning in particular cases) but rather to identify the boundaries of legitimate state power. The various legal tests of reasonableness or rationality or proportionality are not fundamentally judicial *creations*, adopted as a political strategy to out-manoeuvre government or Parliament; they are rather the implications of a general principle of legality, understood as a moral ideal of respect for the equal dignity of independent citizens, united by loyalty to a broadly just and democratic regime.

The contests between statute and common law, as a foundation for judicial review, and between law and politics, as a foundation for constitutional democracy, reflect a similar opposition between parliamentary sovereignty and the rule of law, understood as competing constitutional principles. In each case, the familiar opposition is substantially false—largely the consequence of a misguided philosophy of legal positivism. If law is only a matter of whatever official sources have determined, regardless of the consequences for the rights of those subject to it, the identification of those sources becomes a matter of huge importance. If, instead, law is always

---

[6] Compare Nigel Simmonds, *Law as a Moral Idea* (Oxford: Oxford University Press, 2007) ch 2. Like Simmonds, I treat 'legal positivism' as the thesis (prominently endorsed by H L A Hart) that there is no necessary or conceptual connection between law and morality—a denial of law's status as an intrinsically moral idea linked to an *ideal* of legality.

[7] Sir John Laws, 'Law and Democracy' *PL* [1995] 72, 78 (emphasis added): 'They owe neither their existence nor their acceptance to the will of the legislature.'

an interpretation, in context, of the demands of *legality*—a moral value internally linked to ideals of liberty and justice—the question of sources loses its dominance. Liberty and justice are values that citizens of equal status can only seek in common as a collective endeavour: we cherish democracy as a fair means of furthering that endeavour. Judicial tests of fairness, rationality and proportionality hold officials to the standards of respect for persons that democracy itself entails. Legislative supremacy and the rule of law are interrelated doctrines, each being premised on a fundamental equality of citizenship; democracy and legality are interdependent moral ideals, aiming at the reconciliation of each person's autonomy with that of every other independent citizen.[8]

Self-styled political constitutionalists have acknowledged the links between legal and political theory; so they cannot ignore the jurisprudential questions pertinent to constitutional law. The alleged 'descriptivism' of J A G Griffith's account of the 'political constitution' has been superseded by avowedly normative accounts; but their appeal to republican values comes at a price.[9] The fundamental value prized by republicans is freedom, understood as non-domination or independence— independence from the power of another. A republican who celebrates freedom in that sense must embrace the concept of law to which it is tied, repudiating legal positivism. Law is necessarily connected to liberty in the sense that it secures the conditions of non-domination; the true republic must be an 'empire of laws', constraining all unjustified interference with people's exercise of their autonomy.[10] Liberty is not the mere absence of constraint; it is the assurance given by enjoyment of an independent sphere of decision and action, impervious to other people's demands or disapproval.[11] Providing the conditions of liberty for all, law cannot be treated as merely an instrument of governmental power for the attainment of specific ends. A genuine political constitutionalism, of a truly republican kind, marches hand-in-hand with legal constitutionalism, based on a vision of the rule of law as a moral ideal.

In affirming, in *Jackson*, that the 'rule of law enforced by the courts is the ultimate controlling factor on which our constitution is based', Lord Hope took a step towards acknowledging the interdependence of the rule of law and legislative supremacy—each doctrine embracing and qualifying the other.[12] And his observation that the 'principle of parliamentary sovereignty which . . . has been created by

---

[8] See T R S Allan, *Constitutional Justice: A Liberal Theory of the Rule of Law* (Oxford: Oxford University Press: 2001) ch 7.

[9] J A G Griffith, 'The Political Constitution' *MLR* (1979) 42: 1. See the critique in Adam Tomkins *Our Republican Constitution* (Oxford: Hart Publishing, 2005) 36–40. For an alternative normative reading of Griffith, see Graham Gee and Gregoire C N Webber, 'What Is a Political Constitution?' *OJLS* (2010) 30: 273.

[10] See Philip Pettit, *Republicanism: A Theory of Freedom and Government* (Oxford: Clarendon Press, 1997) 172–7. The phrase comes from James Harrington, *The Commonwealth of Oceana and A System of Politics* J G A Pocock (ed.) (Cambridge: Cambridge University Press 1992) 81.

[11] Compare John Locke, *Two Treatises of Government* (originally published 1690; London, 1924), II, para. 22: 'freedom of men under government is to have a standing rule to live by . . . A liberty to follow my own will in all things where that rule prescribes not, not to be subject to the inconstant, uncertain, unknown, arbitrary will of another man . . .'

[12] *R (Jackson) v Attorney General* [2005] UKHL 56, para. 107.

the common law is built upon the assumption that Parliament represents the people whom it exists to serve' can be understood as further recognition of the interdependence of legality and democracy.[13] Legislative supremacy is a common law doctrine that embodies the value of democracy as a means to equal liberty and justice; it would not apply to measures that could not reasonably be understood as advancing those ends. If, as Lord Steyn warns,[14] the courts may under certain circumstances (such as an attempt to curtail or abolish judicial review) have to 'qualify' the doctrine of legislative supremacy, the qualification would only be an elaboration of existing commitments to legality and democracy, appropriately integrated and explained. There would, however, be no divorce (as Lord Steyn asserts) between 'strict legalism' and 'constitutional legal principle'; that distinction is a relic of legal positivism with its false dichotomy between law, on one hand, and the rule of law, on the other.[15]

From the perspective of legal positivism, the rule of law is a safeguard against the abuse of powers conferred by law; the accountability of public officials and agencies consists in their answerability to independent courts for breaches of jurisdictional limits. If very broad powers are conferred by explicit legislation, legal accountability will be correspondingly weak. Even fundamental rights may be overridden (on that view) in pursuance of public policy objectives whose importance has been clearly signalled by statute. I am defending a contrasting theory of accountability, repudiating positivism. There must be respect not only for explicit statutory conditions of jurisdiction, but also for the process of law itself. The rule of law is a moral ideal that regulates all governmental interference with liberty; it cannot be extinguished without destruction of the moral foundations of British liberal democracy. It requires not only the supervision of executive officials by independent courts, but the application of principles of legality that secure due process and a reasonable balance, in particular cases, between public ends and private sacrifice. Accountability to law is ultimately a matter of conformity to the constitution, treated as the charter of a free society. In defining the limits of executive power, in doubtful instances, we interpret our constitutional tradition; we read statutory grants of power in the light of that tradition. We expose the meaning and implications of our concepts of law and legality in our deliberations over the justifiability of concrete examples of governmental action.

---

[13] *R (Jackson) v Attorney General*, para. 126.

[14] *R (Jackson) v Attorney General*, paras 101–2.

[15] The critique of these judgments in C Turpin and A Tomkins, *British Government and the Constitution: Texts and Materials*, 7th edn, (Cambridge: Cambridge University Press, 2011), 92–5, and the associated rejection of 'common law radicalism', is based on appeal to matters of 'political fact' which are conceived to be the foundations of sovereignty. But this is a mistake induced by adherence to legal positivism: the law consists not of political (or legal) facts but rather *interpretations* of legal practice, in which fact and value are deeply intertwined. See, generally, L L Fuller, *The Morality of Law* (revd edn, New Haven: Yale University Press, 1969); R Dworkin, *Law's Empire* (London: Fontana, 1986).

B. Law, freedom and justice

J A G Griffith's superficially descriptive or empirical stance, apparently resistant
to normative constitutional claims, ultimately reflected its explicit jurisprudential
basis. His opposition to a Bill of Rights, enforceable by the judiciary, and to anything
more than a minimal style of judicial review of administrative action, was rooted in
his legal positivism. He denied that the concept of law was a moral one: 'laws are
merely statements of a power relationship and nothing more'.[16] For Griffith, theories
of natural law were only sources of confusion, serving to conceal the realities of
political power; and the rule of law, beyond a basic requirement that public authorities
should not exceed their legal powers, was 'a fantasy invented by Liberals of the old
school . . . and patented by the Tories to throw a protective sanctity around certain
legal and political institutions and principles which they wish to preserve at any
cost'.[17] Griffith considered that the 'society in which government is by laws and
not by men' was an unattainable ideal; and he thought it a mistake to move power
away from elected politicians to unelected judges. It was a stark vision of political
conflict, distrustful of all reference to justice or human rights:

> I am arguing then for a highly positivist view of the constitution; of recognizing that
> Ministers and others in high positions of authority are men and women who happen to
> exercise political power but without any such right to that power which could give them a
> superior moral position; that laws made by those in authority derive validity from no other
> fact or principle, and so impose no moral obligation of obedience on others; that so-called
> individual or human rights are no more and no less than political claims made by individ-
> uals on those in authority; that a society is endemically in a state of conflict between warring
> interest groups, having no consensus or unifying principles sufficiently precise to be the
> basis of a theory of legislation.[18]

Consistently with this conception of law as the exercise of naked power, Griffith
challenged the idea of separation of powers implicit in the rule of law as a constitutional ideal. Sir Stephen Sedley's vision of a 'bi-polar sovereignty of the Crown in
Parliament and the Crown in its courts, to each of which the Crown's ministers are
answerable', was countered by an insistence on the equal sovereignty of government
(or the executive).[19] The government was not inferior in status to Parliament or the
courts. From Griffith's instrumentalist view of law, as the exercise of power to effect
particular ends, executive authority was paramount: governments have aspirations
'to which, through their majority, they require Parliament to conform'.[20]

Legal constitutionalism repudiates that striking but implausible vision of law
as political power. For a legal constitutionalist, law is a source of moral authority
deriving, in part, from the legitimate exercise of power by elected and accountable

---

[16] Griffith, 'The Political Constitution', 19.   [17] Griffith, 'The Political Constitution', 15.
[18] Griffith, 'The Political Constitution', 19.
[19] Sir Stephen Sedley, 'Human Rights: a Twenty-First Century Agenda' *PL* [1995] 386, 389; J A G
Griffith, 'The Common Law and the Political Constitution' *LQR* (2001) 117: 42.
[20] Griffith, 'The Common Law and the Political Constitution', 52.

representatives; and there is a moral obligation to obey the laws duly made by those with the requisite authority. Within this conception of law, political conflict is softened and contained by broad constitutional commitments to an ideal of human dignity and personal autonomy—sufficiently abstract to accommodate competing visions of the social order but adequate to ground a more compelling vision of a free republic.[21] From a legal constitutionalist perspective, the separation of powers is no mere arrangement of convenience or even a means of dispersing power as a defence against authoritarianism. It is an implicit requirement of the rule of law itself, as applied to government: ministers and other public authorities may exercise only the power conferred (in the usual case) by statutory grant, subject to judicial review to enforce the relevant jurisdictional limits. The overarching idea is the reconciliation of political authority and individual autonomy; the separation of powers between the principal institutions of state is critical to the citizen's independence, 'owing his existence and preservation to his own rights and powers as a member of the commonwealth, not to the choice of another among the people'.[22]

If the rule of law were only a means to promote efficiency, as Joseph Raz contends, there would be no reason for government officials to refrain from ad hoc departures from legality whenever that might prove useful to ends in view: coercion might be applied without any legal basis that a court would recognize. But since we would treat such coercion as illegitimate, it is clear that the rule of law must be understood as a basic constitutional safeguard: it is intended to protect individual liberty, limiting the scope for ad hoc or *ad hominem* (arbitrary) official action. When public officials may act against the citizen only in accordance with previously published laws, defining their powers or specifying the citizen's duties, the law secures liberty in the sense of *independence*: no one is at the mercy of any governmental choice or official whim, asserted beyond properly defined jurisdictional limits enforced by independent courts. Respect for legality is therefore a necessary element of freedom in the republican sense: the rule of law provides for the conditions of non-domination that ultimately distinguish the free man from the slave.[23]

Legal constitutionalism denies the positivist thesis that the rule of law is a principle designed to limit the dangerous potential of law itself: it is not a *negative* value, intended merely 'to minimize the harm to freedom and dignity which the law may cause in its pursuit of its goals', whatever they may be.[24] Raz is much closer to the truth in acknowledging that one of our most 'common images' of the rule of law portrays it as 'an ideal rooted in the very essence of law', so that in conforming to it 'the law does nothing more than be faithful to its own nature'.[25] The idea that

---

[21] See, generally, Allan, *Constitutional Justice*.
[22] Immanuel Kant, *The Doctrine of Right (The Metaphysics of Morals, Part I)*, in Mary J Gregor (ed.) *Practical Philosophy* (Cambridge: Cambridge University Press, 1996), 6: 314. See also Arthur Ripstein, *Force and Freedom: Kant's Legal and Political Philosophy* (Cambridge, Massachusetts: Harvard University Press, 2009), 146–7, 174–6.
[23] See Pettit, *Republicanism*, esp. 31–44.
[24] Raz, *The Authority of Law*, 228.
[25] Joseph Raz, 'Formalism and the Rule of Law', in Robert P George (ed.) *Natural Law Theory* (Oxford: Clarendon Press, 1992), 309.

force should not be used against the citizen except in response to the breach of a published and prospective rule, or only in accordance with rules that confine and control discretionary governmental powers, conferred in the public interest, must be viewed as intrinsic to the concept of law: the rule of law means, above all, compliance with law in this sense. Our concept of law is, then, the antithesis of arbitrary power, which is power exercised beyond the limits prescribed by general rules, binding on government official as much as private citizen.[26]

An acknowledgment of the moral nature of law, and its intrinsic connection with liberty as independence, provides the basis for an understanding of *democracy* as a mode of legitimate governance, reflecting fundamental assumptions about citizens' equal dignity. Liberty in the sense of non-domination is the basis of a moral conception of the self-governing community: rather than a battleground of conflicting interests, regulated by a series of temporary majorities, justice and the common good are sought within a framework that protects each person's independence. Powers may be conferred on public officials and agencies for the attainment of appropriate ends, consistent with a plausible account of the public good; but such powers must not be abused for extraneous ends, serving only private interests, nor wielded in a manner that undermines the ideal of freedom as independence. No one should be at the mercy of unfettered official discretion; and the enforcement of legal constraints on such discretion is a necessary part of the idea of government according to law.

The rule of law dictates the submission of public authorities to requirements of rationality and due process, enforceable by independent courts. Such courts must be free of any political interference or personal prejudice; and their decisions must be securely based on accurate perceptions of the relevant facts, established by duly admissible evidence. Although administrative bodies cannot, of course, exhibit a similar detachment from their own policy objectives and assessments of the public interest, they must nonetheless comply with analogous standards of rationality and fairness. An administrator must act impartially: each person's situation must be judged in the light of the proper objectives of the relevant powers, ignoring considerations of personal merit or rank or affiliation irrelevant to those objectives. There must be appropriate procedures to establish the facts in particular cases so that individuals are not subjected to unwarranted interference, unnecessary for the public purposes in view. It is a feature of government according to law, moreover, that any exercise of coercive power is consistent, not merely with the explicit terms of the grant of power, but also with the constraints implicit in the character of the legal order itself as a community of independent moral agents, claiming equal dignity or worth.

---

[26] Compare Simmonds, *Law as a Moral Idea*, 47–51. Simmonds defends a conception of law structured by an archetype, represented by Fuller's 'inner morality of law'; the archetype is an intrinsically moral ideal: Simmonds, *Law as a Moral Idea*, 51–6. Fuller's 'inner morality of law' (norms of procedural legality) largely corresponds to Raz's formal conception of the rule of law. See L L Fuller, *The Morality of Law*, ch 2.

Compliance with the rules of natural justice, by both courts and administrative agencies, is as important an aspect of the rule of law as the conformity of enacted rules with the constraints of formal or procedural legality (generality, clarity, publication, prospective effect and so forth). It is not simply that the accurate application of rules and policies to particular cases serves the goal of efficiency or effectiveness. It is primarily a question of *fairness*: discrimination between persons is unfair and arbitrary if not properly related to authorized public purposes. If, moreover, people are thought to have a moral obligation of obedience to duties or requirements imposed in the exercise of legitimate authority, they must be able to *acknowledge* such an obligation in the light of their own treatment in all the circumstances. Coercive interference with people's rights and interests must be capable of *justification*; and no one can be expected to acknowledge the justice of his treatment when it is determined by an official whose impartiality is suspect, or whose procedures are wholly unreliable. There is an implicit appeal to the citizen's duty to accommodate his interests to the wider demands of the common good; and unfairness undermines that appeal, threatening the citizen's self-respect.

Beyond the principles of natural justice or procedural fairness, however, the rule of law—in contradistinction to the rule of state officials—encompasses all the familiar requirements of rationality and legality enforced by judicial review of administrative action. If a public authority acts for improper reasons or on the basis of irrelevant considerations, or overlooks or disregards relevant matters, it exceeds its proper jurisdiction as fully as if it ignores explicit limitations on the scope of the powers conferred. Nor can we accept a formalistic distinction between having regard to relevant factors, on the one hand, and attributing to them an inappropriate *weight*, on the other. While questions of weight will often lie within the exclusive jurisdiction of the public agency, they will sometimes fall outside it. In some circumstances, perhaps involving important constitutional rights, a failure to weigh the competing considerations correctly—in accordance with considered and impartial judicial opinion—will amount to justiciable error. Unreasonable action, of the *Wednesbury* kind, is the product of just this sort of error.[27]

The concept of *Wednesbury* unreasonableness sits astride any simple dichotomy of procedure and substance. It provides for a review of administrative *process*, ensuring that the decision or action impugned can be shown to fall within a range of legitimate possibilities, respectful of both relevant statutory purposes and the gravity of the consequences for persons specially affected. In acknowledging, in *ex p Smith*, the serious damage done by government policy to the applicants' rights of privacy and personhood, the court made the rationality test properly sensitive to the constitutional context. The legality of a policy to exclude homosexuals from the armed forces depended not only on the cogency of the reasons offered in its favour, but also, in part, on the gravity of the consequences for those whose unblemished careers would be abruptly terminated. In accepting that 'the more substantial the interference with human rights, the more the court will require by way of justification

---

[27] See, further, Allan, *Constitutional Justice*, 125–48.

before it is satisfied that the decision is reasonable', Bingham LJ acknowledged the dependence of legality on legitimacy: in judging whether the decision was 'beyond the range of responses open to a reasonable decision-maker', the 'human rights context' was plainly critical.[28] Insofar as the rationality test fell short of the robust inquiry into *proportionality*, which European Convention jurisprudence required, it was surely misapplied, allowing the applicants' rights to be overridden on slender and ultimately unconvincing grounds. The court deferred to the 'primary decision-maker' to a degree that undermined the rights it purported to accept in principle.[29]

In defending the idea of a true republic as an 'empire of laws', Philip Pettit stresses that far from being a constraint on liberty, as is sometimes supposed, law is better understood as *constitutive* of liberty in securing the conditions of non-domination. The empire-of-laws condition requires, in addition to respect for the precepts of formal legality applicable to legislation, the extension of the rule of law to executive agencies: 'They should be permitted to act only under the authority of law, and only in a way that accords with the requirements of law....An empire of law requires fidelity to due process on a wide range of political fronts.'[30] There is no objection to the exercise of discretion by government officials provided that it is curtailed and confined by requirements of fair procedure and due process. And Pettit rightly distinguishes republicanism from populism. True republicans want to guard against the abuse of majoritarian power: they will endorse such counter-majoritarian measures as the bicameral division of Parliament, the recognition of constitutional limits to legislative supremacy, and the operation of a bill of rights.[31]

Richard Bellamy, by contrast, is scornful of 'legalistic conceptions of the rule of law'; for him the rule of law is simply 'the democratic rule of persons'.[32] He acknowledges the importance of ideas of impartiality and reciprocity: the ideal of equality before the law means that 'we want the law to be not only blind and free from partiality but also in the public interest'.[33] But since there is no 'privileged evaluative viewpoint' from which to decide whether government action serves the public interest, we must rely on the democratic political process, which 'allows people to speak for themselves and to contest the proposals of others'.[34] Without scope for discretion to depart from general rules, and for special laws that treat different people differently, the law itself may become arbitrary, neglecting genuine aspects of the public good. But Bellamy largely ignores the danger of arbitrariness in the sense of unfair and illegitimate discrimination, dismissing all insistence on law's proper moral form in favour of unfettered political bargaining. The rule of law, correctly conceived, is a precious safeguard against 'special laws' that victimize

---

[28] *R v Ministry of Defence, ex p Smith* [1996] QB 517, 554.
[29] Compare *Smith and Grady v United Kingdom* (1999) 29 EHRR 493 (ECtHR); Allan, *Constitutional Justice*, 177–9.
[30] Pettit, *Republicanism*, 175.   [31] Pettit, *Republicanism*, 181.
[32] Richard Bellamy, *Political Constitutionalism: A Republican Defence of the Constitutionality of Democracy* (Cambridge,: Cambridge University Press, 2007), 66, 83.
[33] Bellamy, *Political Constitutionalism*, 65.   [34] Bellamy, *Political Constitutionalism*, 66.

unpopular persons or vulnerable minorities, and against coercive action that does injury to individuals out of all proportion to any public gain.

Bellamy's depreciation of the rule of law—his failure to grasp the moral nature of the concept of law—accompanies a conception of equal democratic citizenship as implausible as it is unattractive. In his broad-brush focus on legislation, Bellamy seems entirely to overlook the problem of administrative discretion and its implications for individual liberty. If a robust republicanism is, in the political sphere, truly the antithesis of tyrannical rule, judicial review of governmental action plays a similar role in public administration. The more heavily an administrative decision bears on the rights or interests of particular persons, whose special circumstances bring them within range of an agency's pursuit of its policy agenda, the greater, in fairness, must be their opportunities to challenge its legality. Recourse to judicial review, at least in the absence of an effective statutory appeal, is the administrative counterpart to rights of opposition and challenge to legislative proposals or government policy. And here the 'privileged evaluative viewpoint' of the judge is critical, independent of both executive or administrative agency, on the one hand, and complainant, on the other.

Bellamy substitutes for Pettit's 'idealized political process' a conception of democratic politics in which everything is determined by majoritarian decision.[35] There is space neither for the exercise of delegated administrative power, nor for the general legal principles that prevent such power degenerating into arbitrary coercion of individuals. His repudiation of legal constitutionalism has striking consequences. In the absence of 'common recognizable interests', identifiable by a court of law firmly detached from the political process, everyone would be subject to domination by public officials, whose discretionary judgments in particular cases would be immune to challenge.[36]

Even when the exercise of discretionary power by public authorities is subject to inspection and challenge on the basis of its consequences for the public interest, political accountability needs to be supplemented by review for legality at the behest of those directly and specially affected. It is only in the light of the specific consequences for such persons that we can judge not merely the general effectiveness of administrative action, but its fairness and reasonableness in all the circumstances. It is as great an error to imagine that the political process can alone secure the citizen's independence as it is to suppose that the rule of law can dispense with democratic deliberation and decision.

It may be thought, nonetheless, that Bellamy's objections to judicial review of primary legislation are perfectly consistent with a vigorous regime of review of administrative action: here the judicial role, strictly subservient to Parliament, is merely to enforce the prescribed limits of the statutory powers of officials. As I shall argue more fully below, however, the limits of any administrative jurisdiction, being a matter of statutory interpretation, cannot be discerned without reflection

---

[35] Bellamy, *Political Constitutionalism*, 163–71.
[36] Compare David Dyzenhaus, 'How Hobbes Met the "Hobbes Challenge"' *MLR* (2009) 72(3): 488.

on pertinent questions of liberty and justice. We cannot determine the legality of any governmental decision or action by reading the statute in isolation: the nature and scope of a statutory power are matters of judgement, brought to bear on the circumstances in which the power has been asserted. So much depends on the consequences of administrative action for particular persons, whose interests must be accorded appropriate weight in any fair and reasonable exercise of discretion; nor can we neatly segregate questions of fairness and rationality from those of legality or jurisdictional limits. We determine the limits of a statutory power, in part, by reflection on the acceptability of particular outcomes, whether actual or hypothetical. In supervising the legality of administrative action, therefore, the court must *construct* the character of the jurisdiction under review by reference both to legitimate public purposes and independent standards of legality. The court must be as much the guardian of law as the servant of the legislature: it enforces Parliament's law in the manner appropriate to the law of a *parliament*, representative of equal and independent citizens united by an inherited tradition of justice.

If, of course, law were best understood as a heap of unrelated rules giving legislative direction on specific matters, with little or nothing by way of interconnected doctrine or principle—law as positive law in the most literal sense—the courts could only be mainly passive instruments of a superior will. Any creative judicial role would be confined to legislating, interstitially, to fill gaps in the legal order. The citizen would then be subjected to the rule of Parliament and the rule of judges and officials, rather than subject to (and protected by) the rule of law. It is part of our concept of law, indeed, that it gives the citizen a role in the rational determination of its content: he is accorded the dignity of an independent moral reasoner, encouraged to make sense of the law as a whole, and hence of its demands in particular instances. Our common law principles are ultimately the related moral ideas that enable us to find *coherence* within both legislation and judicial precedent, treated as parts of the same system of law. The law presents itself to its subjects as a 'unified enterprise of governance that one can make sense of', enabling them to understand how 'the regulation of one set of activities relates rationally to the regulation of another'.[37] The citizen is accorded the status of legal interpreter, extending deliberation and dialogue from the political into the legal domain: 'In this way, the law pays respect to those who live under it, conceiving them now as bearers of individual reason and intelligence'.[38]

It follows, however, that we cannot easily draw sharp lines between different species of judicial review, contrasting 'strong' and 'weak' varieties.[39] Even if there is no formal power to *quash* a statute for breach of fundamental rights, there is large and legitimate scope for interpretative sensitivity to such rights; an application of statute that ignored the implications for political morality (as opposed merely to political expediency or efficient administration) would result in law degenerating

---

[37] Jeremy Waldron, 'The Concept of Law and the Rule of Law' *Ga L Rev* (2008) 43:1, 35–6.
[38] Waldron, 'Concept of Law', 35–6. See also Jeremy Waldron 'The Rule of Law as a Theatre of Debate' in Justine Burley (ed.) *Dworkin and his Critics* (Oxford: Blackwell Publishing, 2004), 319.
[39] As Waldron proposes: see Jeremy Waldron, 'The Core of the Case Against Judicial Review' *Yale LJ* (2006) 115: 1346. Waldron includes within 'strong' judicial review a power to modify the statute

into official decree and administrative tyranny. While from an American or even Canadian perspective, the Human Rights Act 1998 might initially seem a weak form of review, as regards primary legislation, a focus on section 3 alters the picture.[40] Insofar as section 3 echoes the interpretative approach of the common law, making the European Convention rights critical to correct construction of relevant statutory provisions, it affirms the *collaborative* nature of parliamentary enactment and judicial application characteristic of governance according to law. The justice (and hence legitimate extent) of a penal measure intended to protect the public from dangerous criminals, for example, can be appraised in the course of its application to an individual offender, whose particular circumstances may reveal the danger of unwarranted severity—a danger averted by a nuanced interpretative approach.[41] We should not choose between unfettered parliamentary sovereignty, on one hand, and judicial supremacy, on the other; rather we should affirm a separation of powers that makes Parliament supreme within the limited, benign constraints imposed by adherence to legality as a basic political value.[42]

Our concepts of law, liberty and justice are closely intertwined; and their explication is necessary for a proper grasp of the related ideas of democracy and citizenship. Public lawyers can no more *choose* between contrasting conceptions of the rule of law, as Paul Craig suggests,[43] than political constitutionalists can choose legal positivism as a theory of law that suits their repugnance for judicial review or the judicial enforcement of fundamental rights. Their task is rather to work out the implications of the idea of legality in the specific context of governmental action. Craig warns, following Raz, that 'the adoption of a fully substantive conception of the rule of law has the consequence of robbing the concept of any function which is independent of the theory of justice which imbues such an account of law'.[44] If the rule of law were the 'rule of the good law', Raz objects, then 'to explain its nature is to propound a complete social philosophy'.[45] Craig is doubtful whether

---

'in ways that the statute itself does not envisage' (Waldron, 'The Core of the Case Against Judicial Review', 1354); but it begs the critical interpretative question to suppose that such matters of 'modification' and statutory meaning are independent of our efforts at principled, constitutional construction. Waldron presents the Human Rights Act 1998 (HRA 1998) as an example of weak review, focusing his attention on the declaration of incompatibility (having no effect on validity) under s 4.

[40] The HRA 1998, s 3 requires a court to interpret a statutory provision consistently with the European Convention rights whenever 'possible'. The Canadian Charter of Rights, while rendering invalid any statute inconsistent with it, permits express legislative override (under s 33).

[41] *R v Offen* [2001] 1 WLR 253, approved in *R v Drew* [2003] UKHL 25, para. 20; Allan, 'Parliament's Will and the Justice of the Common Law: The Human Rights Act in Constitutional Perspective' *CLP* (2006) 59: 27, 47–9.

[42] For an effective critique of Waldron's objections to judicial review along similar lines, see David Dyzenhaus, 'The Incoherence of Constitutional Positivism' in Grant Huscroft (ed.), *Expounding the Constitution: Essays in Constitutional Theory* (Cambridge: Cambridge University Press, 2008), 138, esp. 140–54. The incoherence of 'constitutional positivism' arises from its implausible combination of resistance to 'strong' judicial review and acceptance of a human rights culture informing both 'weak' review (of primary legislation) and review of administrative action (on the basis of moral principles of legality).

[43] Paul Craig, 'Formal and Substantive Conceptions of the Rule of Law: An Analytical Framework' *PL* [1997] 467, 487.

[44] Craig, 'Formal and Substantive Conceptions', 487.   [45] Raz, *The Authority of Law*, 211.

there is any 'middle ground' between purely formal and richly substantive conceptions of the rule of law, observing that the principles of judicial review are not 'self-executing': it is difficult for courts to undertake the necessary tasks of normative evaluation 'without explicitly or implicitly relying on some background theory of justice'.[46]

We should not assume, however, that a theory of justice is itself a matter of ungrounded choice, imposed by lawyers or judges as a matter of political will, independent of legal discipline and tradition. The relevant 'background theory' may be largely a matter of piecemeal construction, case by case, attempting to give a greater coherence to acknowledged legal practices and standards. While the various requirements of administrative legality are in themselves no doubt compatible with competing conceptions of justice, elaborated as abstract ideals of political morality, their consequences for the validity of official acts or decisions may depend much more on expectations and assumptions embedded in legal practice, specific to a particular jurisdiction. Just as analysis of legislative structure and purpose is required to determine whether or not an agency has acted in breach of its statutory mandate, so recourse to common law principle may be necessary to resolve any doubts about the scope of the relevant powers. In more recent work, Raz has defended a similar view of the rule of law, whose core idea is 'principled faithful application of the law'.[47] Democracy is reinforced by requiring legal institutions to be loyal to parliamentary legislation while also setting limits to majoritarianism, justification of judicial decisions being made by reference to 'the common values and shared practices of the legal culture'. It is the function of the rule of law 'to facilitate the integration of particular pieces of legislation with the underlying doctrines of the legal system'. A grant of police powers, for example, should be applied 'in a manner which is both faithful to the legislative purpose and principled in integrating it with traditional doctrines of the liberties of the citizen'.[48] Not only are those civil and political rights 'without which no democracy can prosper' presupposed by this account, but further, the rule of law 'respects those civil rights which are part of the backbone of the legal culture, part of its fundamental traditions'.[49]

What for Raz are merely contingent features of British constitutionalism, however, are better understood as necessary elements of legality, but honed and elaborated in the context of an evolving legal order. They are an attempt to understand and give expression to the requirements of freedom as independence in the specific conditions of the British legal and political order. In addition, therefore, to the procedural elements of the rule of law associated with the form of legislation and the propriety of administrative regulation and decision-making, our concept of law embraces (at least in abstract form) such basic freedoms as those of speech, conscience and association, inherent in any conception of republican liberty, as well as the prohibition of such intrinsic denials of equality as bills of attainder

---

[46] Craig, 'Formal and Substantive Conceptions', 486.
[47] Joseph Raz, *Ethics in the Public Domain: Essays in the Morality of Law and Politics* (Oxford: Clarendon Press, 1994), 357.
[48] Raz, *Ethics in the Public Domain*, 359.   [49] Raz, *Ethics in the Public Domain*, 360.

or the infliction of cruel and unusual punishments.[50] These various elements of the rule of law provide a stable framework within which people can co-operate as equals in the pursuit of justice; and British legal practice should be understood accordingly. Law is linked to justice; but the relevant conception of justice is that presupposed by legal and constitutional practice, giving local and determinate shape to the ideal of legality.[51]

C. The constitutional foundations of judicial review

Recent debate over the constitutional foundations of judicial review has been marred by an excessive concentration on competing *sources* of administrative law: the creativity of common law judges is pitted against a legislative 'intention' derived from the grant of statutory power.[52] Since the common law basis of the principal grounds of review is recognized by all, and since everyone endorses their application to any and every exercise of statutory power—in the absence, at least, of explicit provision to the contrary—it may be hard to see what really divides the different bodies of opinion. And though the ultra vires doctrine, which equates excess or abuse of power with the contravention of a legislative command (or 'intention'), has been called into question, its critics have not usually denied the orthodoxy of absolute parliamentary sovereignty. So even those scholars seeking the foundations of judicial review in the common law, as opposed to legislative intent, seem to treat the rule of law as, in the last analysis, the gift of the current parliamentary majority. And yet despite this reluctance, on all sides, to challenge Parliament's ability to curtail or even abrogate judicial review, there is also general assent to the courts' characteristic resistance to ouster clauses: no one, it seems, wants to take too literally a legislative intent that appears to threaten the rule of law.[53]

The focus on sources of law reflects assumptions characteristic of legal positivism, which treats the content of law as deriving entirely from empirical acts of law-creation. In H L A Hart's version, the law consists of the rules made in the exercise of an authority conferred by the 'rule of recognition', which is itself constituted by the facts of established official practice.[54] Such assumptions readily

---

[50] See, further, Allan, *Constitutional Justice* and also Allan, 'Constitutional Justice and the Concept of Law', in Grant Huscroft (ed.) *Expounding the Constitution: Essays in Constitutional Theory* (Cambridge: Cambridge University Press, 2008), 219. Compare Kant's *Doctrine of Right*, in which such basic freedoms are derived from the innate right of humanity, or 'independence from being constrained by another's choice', making everyone 'his own master': Kant, *The Doctrine of Right*, in Gregor (ed.) *Practical Philosophy*, 6.237–8.

[51] Compare Dworkin, *Law's Empire*, chs 6 and 7. For further discussion of the nature and value of legality, see Ronald Dworkin *Justice in Robes* (Cambridge, Massachusetts: Harvard University Press, 2006), ch 6.

[52] See the essays collected in Forsyth (ed.) *Judicial Review and the Constitution*.

[53] The 'modified' ultra vires doctrine seeks to combine common law and statutory sources; Parliament is deemed to authorize the courts to enforce the rule of law: see Mark Elliott *The Constitutional Foundations of Judicial Review* (Oxford: Hart Publishing, 2001); Christopher Forsyth and Mark Elliott, 'The Legitimacy of Judicial Review' *PL* [2003] 286.

[54] H L A Hart *The Concept of Law* (Oxford: Clarendon Press, 2nd edn, 1994), esp. 100–110.

explain the emphasis placed by the ultra vires doctrine on legislative intention, signalling the ultimate foundations of judicial doctrine in continuing statutory authority; but they also preclude effective criticism. If the alternative source of judicial doctrine is the quasi-legislative power enjoyed by common law judges, who may fashion the rules of administrative law as they see fit in the absence of any contrary parliamentary command, it is inferior to statute and so must surrender to any such overriding instructions. The ultra vires doctrine is entailed by absolute parliamentary sovereignty, which makes legislation the superior source of law acknowledged by the rule of recognition.[55] Its salience is confirmed, for all absolutists, by the threat of the statutory ouster clause. An ouster may be circumvented in any case of jurisdictional error, enabling the court to intervene by quashing the administrative decision; but since the identification of such error is a matter of statutory interpretation, it cannot (at least in positivist theory) override an explicit statutory grant of extensive, even unqualified, jurisdiction.[56]

An insistence on the *common law* basis of the grounds of review is best understood as the defence of an appropriate conception of the rule of law: the various categories of legal error are conceptual constraints, marking the boundary between legitimate and illegitimate state coercion. Law is not simply a matter of authoritative instructions, related to specific policy goals; nor is it a set of moral standards imposed by judges, unrelated to law's intrinsic form. Law is a means of attaining public ends that insulates the individual from arbitrary power, limiting coercion to what can be justified in all the circumstances. The common law grounds of review express the various dimensions of that conception of legality, subjecting coercive powers to limits whose status is wholly independent of anyone's preference or command. The corresponding duties on public authorities are no less part of the rule of law—no less implicit in the concept of law itself—than the requirements of Fuller's inner morality of law (the precepts of formal legality applicable to legislation).[57] But whereas such requirements as generality, clarity, prospective effect (and so forth) are relatively independent of a statute's substantive content, the conditions of legality applicable to administrative action necessarily concern

[55] Paul Craig denies this, observing that the courts may impose interpretative constraints on legislative power that fall short of invalidation: such constraints reflect the 'common law model' of judicial review: Craig, 'Constitutional Foundations, the Rule of Law and Supremacy' *PL* [2003] 92. Once it is acknowledged, however, that the ultra vires doctrine cannot invoke a 'legislative intention' in any literal sense (Parliament does not share a single human mind), it is *formal* only, signifying the ultimate source of the validity of any constraints on discretionary power. Moreover, Craig sometimes seems to concede the point, noting that in substance the courts resolve conflicts between statute and fundamental rights, preserving only 'the formal veneer of legal sovereignty' (Craig, 'Constitutional Foundations', 108).

[56] Ironically, Christopher Forsyth seeks to defend the ultra vires doctrine by observing that it was essential to the reasoning in *Anisminic* (see below), allowing the court to sidestep the ouster clause as being inapplicable to a decision flawed for jurisdictional error: Forsyth, 'Of Fig Leaves and Fairy Tales: The Ultra Vires Doctrine, the Sovereignty of Parliament and Judicial Review' *CLJ* [1996] 122. This convenient reconciliation between common law principle and parliamentary sovereignty works, however, only as long as it remains possible (by some suitably explicit verbal formula) to exclude judicial review even in the case of 'jurisdictional' error. If this is not in practice possible, absolute sovereignty has in substance been abandoned.

[57] Fuller, *The Morality of Law*, ch 2.

both procedure and substance. As requirements of *due process* they are sensitive to all considerations relevant to the justice or fairness of coercive state action, having regard to legitimate policy objectives and their consequences for the persons most directly concerned.

It is well understood that even the principles of natural justice or procedural fairness must be adapted to the specific context: no one thinks that every administrative hearing should be conducted in the manner of a criminal trial for a serious offence. A balance must be struck between the reasonable demands of administrative cost and efficiency, on the one hand, and the legitimate interests of those affected by proposed state action, on the other: 'what the requirements of fairness demand when any body, domestic, administrative or judicial, has to make a decision which will affect the rights of individuals depends on the character of the decision-making body, the kind of decision it has to make and the statutory or other framework in which it operates'.[58] Although the requirements of fairness are sensitive to context in this way, however, it does not follow that they are arbitrary. Consistency is maintained by recourse to well established rights and widely acknowledged human needs and interests: the greater the threat to fundamental interests in liberty or bodily security or property or reputation, the more elaborate must be the procedural constraints observed by a public authority in exercising its powers. And what is true of procedural fairness, narrowly understood, is equally the case as judicial review extends to the broader sphere of due process. Whether or not a power is abused for an extraneous purpose, or exercised in disregard of relevant considerations, is a judgement that depends on the context: the question of moral *justification* for coercive action in all the circumstances cannot be avoided.

Consistently with the focus on competing sources of administrative law, the opponents of ultra vires have tended to emphasize *doctrinal structure*, deriving from common law, at the expense of the variety and complexity of the different contexts to which common law doctrine applies. Yet the connection between general principles of legality, abstractly defined, and their concrete application to the facts of particular cases is often very complex; and matters of law and policy are inevitably intertwined. As fundamental conditions of legitimate governance, embracing all statutory functions and contexts, the various precepts of legality have a specific application which is necessarily dependent on all the circumstances. A finding of illegality, whether based on neglect of relevant considerations or the influence of irrelevant ones, or on similar grounds of irrationality or improper purposes, expresses the *conclusion* of judicial analysis—an analysis that must focus on whether the action impugned falls within a discretion delimited by constraints of purpose and context *unique to the public function in question*. The 'legislative intent', invoked by ultra vires, is best understood as a reference to the importance of the administrative context, signalling the adaptation of general doctrine to its particular needs.

There is, then, no challenge here to democratic governance: judicial review serves to bind executive agencies to their allotted tasks, making them subservient

---

[58] *Lloyd v McMahon* [1987] AC 625, 702 (Lord Bridge).

to the legislative will. At the same time the basic constraints of legality, attuned to the context in view, secure the conditions of respect for persons fundamental to a community of independent moral agents. But we cannot concede that if 'the omnipotent Parliament' chooses to override the ordinary grounds of review, in terms that are 'unequivocally clear', the courts must 'then adhere to such dictates'.[59] That would be to make legality itself vulnerable to legislative attack, echoing the claim of those defending the ultra vires doctrine that Parliament is 'competent to grant or withhold the power to contravene the principles of good administration', authorizing the exercise of arbitrary power.[60] Again the focus on a competition between rival sources of law—statute versus common law—provokes an unhelpful conflict between democracy and legality, suggesting an ultimate stand-off between competing claims of parliamentary absolutism and judicial supremacism. Instead, the demands of legality are met by bringing common law principle to bear on statutory functions in a manner that gives due weight to the demands of both individual right and public interest, according to the specific context. When, for example, personal liberty is severely curtailed on the basis of mere reasonable suspicion of links to terrorism, procedural fairness requires sufficient disclosure to enable the court to provide genuine protection (even if the literal words of the statute may suggest the opposite).[61]

The various criticisms of ultra vires can be deflected by adopting a more subtle and nuanced understanding of the 'legislative intention' it invokes. Sir John Laws is right to object to the notion that the courts' decisions, in ensuring the legality of administrative action, are 'only a function of Parliament's absolute power'; but whether or not it is objectionable that '*ultra vires* consigns everything to the intention of the legislature' depends on what we mean by the 'intention of the legislature'.[62] Since a legislative assembly composed of hundreds of members cannot literally share a conscious intention, we must understand the expression in a mainly metaphorical sense. We mean essentially that our interpretation of any particular section or clause should be consistent with what appear to be the general statutory purposes, making sense of an overall legislative scheme designed to further the public interest. When Sir William Wade observed that the judges 'have no constitutional right to interfere with action which is within the powers granted', he meant simply that the courts, being confined to matters of legality, must respect administrative decisions made within jurisdiction.[63] The judge 'must in every case be able to demonstrate that

[59] Paul Craig, 'Competing Models of Judicial Review' *PL* [1999] 428, 429.

[60] Mark Elliott, 'The Demise of Parliamentary Sovereignty? The Implications for Justifying Judicial Review' *LQR* (1999) 115: 119, 133.

[61] See *Secretary of State for the Home Dept v AF (No 3)* [2009] UKHL 28, in which the Supreme Court accepted the ruling of the European Court of Human Rights in *A v United Kingdom* (2009) 49 EHRR 29 (in respect of art 5(4) of the Convention): Lord Scott held that the Convention reflected common law standards; and Lord Hope held that the court must adhere to principle, requiring the suspect to be told what is alleged against him (*AF (No 3)*, paras 96, 84). The Prevention of Terrorism Act 2005 was thus interpreted in accordance with the rule of law, preserving the right to a fair hearing.

[62] Sir John Laws, 'Illegality: The Problem of Jurisdiction', in M Supperstone and J Goudie (eds) *Judicial Review* (London: Butterworths, 1997) 4.19.

[63] Sir William Wade and Christopher Forsyth *Administrative Law*, 9th edn (Oxford: Oxford University Press, 2004), 37.

he is carrying out the will of Parliament as expressed in the statute conferring the power' in the sense that he must point to some abuse of power, inconsistent with the statutory grant. If, however, all such grants are necessarily curtailed by implicit standards of legality, the 'will of Parliament' coincides with the requirements of the rule of law.[64]

The only question is whether the public body has exceeded a jurisdiction defined both by specific statutory purposes, inferred from the legislative scheme as a whole, and by fundamental (common law) precepts of legality. If, indeed, 'the common law is logically prior to statute', so that the court's 'obedience to Parliament's law is not an axiom on which its jurisdiction proceeds, nor a defining limitation of it', as Laws contends,[65] there is no sovereign legislative will that may override the rule of law. Parliament's will is confined by the conditions of legality, whether these relate to the proper form of legislation or the manner of exercise of any discretionary powers it confers on executive agencies. The supposed opposition between parliamentary sovereignty and the rule of law is therefore false: the former is necessarily asserted in conformity to the latter; the courts' obedience is predicated on that understanding. If, as Laws maintains, 'the developed doctrines of modern public law, including an increasing recognition of fundamental constitutional rights, are not in fact and logically cannot be a function of Parliament's law', they must instead be basic presuppositions or preconditions of that law. The common law rules of construction are themselves therefore fundamental, resistant to legislative abrogation that would violate legality. Their *form* as presumptions of 'legislative intent' should not mislead us: the relevant 'intent', properly understood, presupposes compliance with legality.

If there is no true opposition between legislative supremacy and legality, the sovereignty of Parliament reflects the sovereignty of law itself. Parliamentary sovereignty is not the narrow 'political' sovereignty, which Sir John Laws elsewhere contrasts with 'constitutional' sovereignty: it is an expression of the unity of law and democracy.[66] As primary representative of the people, Parliament enjoys supremacy in the making of new law; but as a body itself constituted by law it is subject to the principles of legality in so doing. And such principles are not confined, as some have thought, to rules that prescribe the qualifications of members of the legislature and the procedures for enactment of legislation; they prescribe also the conditions that enacted rules must meet to qualify as law, capable of altering existing rights, duties and powers. It is only a failure to perceive the fundamental character of the relevant principles of construction that would oblige a defender of the rule of law to repudiate ultra vires. Such principles, reflecting the inherent demands of legality, provide a necessary conduit between enacted provisions and

---

[64] See Wade and Forsyth, *Administrative Law*, 720–1, describing judicial review as 'a constitutional fundamental which even the sovereign Parliament cannot abolish', any attempt at abolition being 'an abuse of legislative power'.

[65] Laws, 'Illegality', 4.13.

[66] Sir John Laws, 'Law and Democracy' *PL* [1995] 72, 92: 'Ultimate sovereignty rests, in every civilized constitution, not with those who wield governmental power, but in the conditions under which they are permitted to do so. The constitution, not the Parliament, is in this sense sovereign.'

their legal consequences. Parliamentary sovereignty affirms the rule of law while giving scope for democratic change. It is for the people's elected representatives to rule through the institution of law; popular or political sovereignty is thereby transformed into the *constitutional* sovereignty that makes enforcement of the popular will legitimate.

Even though Sir John Laws acknowledges that 'the duty to obey Parliament is given by the common law', which is 'the higher premise', his acceptance of the 'conventional doctrine' of parliamentary sovereignty commits him to an unnecessary confrontation between democracy and law.[67] Rightly insisting that such values as 'justice, freedom, and order' are the '*fons et origo*' of the common law, essential to its legitimacy, his repudiation of ultra vires reflects his denial that the 'goodness of the common law' could be merely a function of the legislative power.[68] Laws is anxious that the ultra vires doctrine, by attributing everything to legislative intention, might undermine the principles of interpretation that the courts invoke to protect constitutional rights. When, however, those principles are properly recognized as *fundamental law*, the supposed danger evaporates. They cannot be swept away, even by an 'actual' intent, revealed 'on the face of the statute', because they serve to unite democracy and law, which operate in practice as interdependent values. Rather than concede that Parliament can 'abrogate the rule of law', even if only by explicit provision, we should treat the legislative will as already attuned to the implicit requirements of legality.[69] Any reasonable *interpretation* of the legislative command, respectful of legislative good faith—of the 'conscience and wisdom' of Members of Parliament[70]—would take an intention of compliance with *law* for granted.[71]

The limits of a statutory power are ascertained, then, by interpretation, which must proceed all the way from the most abstract account of the statutory scheme and purpose to the concrete consequences for the particular case. The greater the potential interference with well established or fundamental rights, in particular, the more reluctant we should be to concede the requisite statutory authority: the best interpretation is the one that offers the most persuasive reconciliation between statutory text, underlying purpose, and individual right in all the circumstances. We need for each case a general *theory* of the statute, responsive to all relevant aspects of political morality, and capable of adaptation to the constantly changing circumstances of practical administration. The ultra vires doctrine symbolizes that interdependence of legislative will and judicial reason, making the legality of an administrative decision dependent on appraisal of its statutory credentials, respectful of the legislative scheme. Its invocation, in striking down a decision, marks the combined injuries to legality and democracy: an ultra vires act is one that violates the legislative will, in the sense that it draws no support from the original grant of powers, correctly construed. Properly explained, the doctrine need not deny the

---

[67] Laws, 'Illegality', 4.12–13.   [68] Laws, 'Illegality', 4.19.
[69] Laws, 'Illegality', 4.23, 4.26.   [70] Laws, 'Illegality', 4.13.
[71] See also Allan, 'Parliament's Will and the Justice of the Common Law: The Human Rights Act in Constitutional Perspective' *CLP* (2006) 59: 27.

fundamental status of the common law grounds of review; for since Parliament could not confer any power to violate the rule of law, any such violation would be necessarily in breach of jurisdiction.[72]

As Sir John Laws recognizes, the statutory ouster clause confronts the court with a significant challenge to legality, to which it must respond: 'the vindication of the rule of law is the constitutional right of every citizen'.[73] But the principles of interpretation that preserve the common law constitution are sufficiently resilient to reconcile democracy and legality, as the specific administrative context dictates.[74] The *Anisminic* case exemplifies the fundamental status of judicial review.[75] By allowing the ouster clause to exclude review only in the case of *non-jurisdictional* error—decisions within the legitimate sphere of administrative determination—the court preserved the appropriate separation of powers. Decisions in excess of jurisdiction are made in breach of the legislative mandate, and hence in violation of democratic principle: 'What would be the point of defining by statute the limit of a tribunal's powers if, by means of a clause inserted in the instrument of definition, those limits could safely be passed?'[76] Any idea of opposition or confrontation between legislative command and judicial response is superficial and misleading: the values of democracy and legality are not in conflict. By rejecting a claim on erroneous grounds, the tribunal had exceeded its jurisdiction, rendering its 'determination' a mere nullity (or *purported* determination), obtaining no protection from the statutory barrier to any genuine determination being 'called into question in any court of law'.[77] Judicial circumvention of the ouster clause, if that be an apt description, was an evasion of its literal meaning only; and literal meanings rightly give way to more nuanced ones, reflecting the constitutional context in point.[78]

In his judicial capacity, Sir John Laws reached similar conclusions in *R (Cart & Ors) v The Upper Tribunal & Ors*: the High Court's supervisory jurisdiction could not be excluded merely by the designation of the Special Immigration Appeals Commission and the Upper Tribunal as, in each case, a 'superior court of record'.[79] Whether or not these tribunals were subject to review (and in what circumstances) was a conclusion of common law, based on analysis of their respective constitutional roles.[80] The court's 'ingrained reluctance' to permit the exclusion of judicial

---

[72] For full discussion, see Allan, 'Constitutional Dialogue and the Justification of Judicial Review' *OJLS* (2003) 23: 563. See also Allan, 'Legislative Supremacy and Legislative Intent: A Reply to Professor Craig' *OJLS* (2004) 24: 563.

[73] Laws, 'Illegality', 4.23.

[74] Compare Laws, 'Law and Democracy', 75: 'Whenever the bite of an [exclusionary] provision is challenged, the issue will always be one of statutory construction, and the construction of statutes is always and entirely within the keeping of the courts.'

[75] *Anisminic v Foreign Compensation Commission* [1969] 2 AC 147.

[76] *Anisminic*, 208 (Lord Wilberforce).　　　[77] Foreign Compensation Act 1950, s 4(4).

[78] See Allan, *Constitutional Justice*, 210–15.

[79] [2009] EWHC 3052; see Special Immigration Appeals Commission Act 1997, s 1(3) (as amended by Anti-Terrorism, Crime and Security Act 2001, s 35); Tribunals, Courts and Enforcement Act 2007, s 3(5).

[80] In affirming a broader oversight of the Upper Tribunal than the lower courts had thought appropriate, the Supreme Court assumed what Lord Phillips called 'a partnership between Parliament and the judges' in upholding the rule of law: 'It should be for the judges to decide whether the statutory

review of tribunals of limited jurisdiction reflected the pertinent principle of the rule of law: 'statute law has to be mediated by an authoritative judicial source, independent both of the legislature which made the statute, the executive government which (in the usual case) procured its making, and the public body by which the statute is administered'.[81] If the final legal interpreter were the public body responsible for administering the statute, the decision-makers 'would write their own laws'.

In affirming the requirements of the rule of law, the court also protects democracy. It permits a statutory tribunal to exercise the authority, including interpretative authority, appropriate to the constitutional function conferred by Parliament. As Laws explained, the effectiveness of statute law requires that public bodies be kept within the confines of their prescribed powers, as confirmed and clarified by judicial review:

> Accordingly, ... the need for such an authoritative judicial source cannot be dispensed with by Parliament. This is not a denial of legislative sovereignty, but an affirmation of it: as is the old rule that Parliament cannot bind itself. The old rule means that successive Parliaments are always free to make what laws they choose; that is one condition of Parliament's sovereignty. The requirement of an authoritative judicial source for the interpretation of law means that Parliament's statutes are always effective; that is another.[82]

What Laws describes here as conditions of sovereignty might be better presented as conditions of democracy: Parliament and courts co-operate to preserve the constitutional arrangements that underpin the British version of liberal democracy. An ouster clause can serve to justify a degree of interpretative freedom for the agency that would not otherwise exist: its existence is *pertinent* to the correct construction of the limits of the power conferred.[83] But it could not altogether insulate the agency against review without authorizing the exercise of arbitrary (illegal) power.

D. The principle of legality and fundamental rights

Joining the political constitutionalists, Adam Tomkins objects to the idea that government should be subject to general principles of legality, which he denounces as a dubious tenet of legal constitutionalism.[84] He has no objection to the courts enforcing specific statutory rules, such as one requiring a public authority to consider a person's representations before withdrawing a welfare benefit; but he complains that general principles of legality such as the *Wednesbury* principle are too vague, displacing executive discretion with 'untrammelled judicial discretion'.[85]

---

provisions for the administration of justice adequately protect the rule of law and, by judicial review, to supplement these should it be necessary': *R (Cart) v Upper Tribunal* [2011] UKSC 28, para. 89.

[81] [2009] EWHC 3052, para. 36.   [82] [2009] EWHC 3052, para. 38.

[83] Compare *Pushpanathan v Canada (Minister of Citizenship and Immigration)* [1998] 1 SCR 982, 1003–12.

[84] Tomkins, *Our Republican Constitution*, 10–25.   [85] Tomkins, *Our Republican Constitution*, 22.

If, however, an unreasonable action is the result of a decision-making *process* that frustrates the statutory scheme, ignoring relevant considerations or introducing irrelevant ones, or annexing the delegated powers to an improper or extraneous purpose, the courts' intervention is justified in defence of the rule of law. In identifying the specific legal errors involved, moreover, the court is engaged in a deliberative process whose integrity is open to public inspection and criticism. The legal constitutionalism Tomkins deplores is only a commitment to eradicate arbitrary power, from whatever source it derives. In the context of judicial review, it demands elaboration of the *arguments* that underlie judgments of irrationality, or illegality, exposing to public scrutiny what might otherwise remain doubtful intuitions, hidden from view.[86]

Tomkins assumes the truth of legal positivism, identifying law with whatever has been imposed by officials, regardless of content or mode of application. He supposes (like those debating the merits of ultra vires) that general principles of legality must be 'the creations of the courts', overlooking their status as conceptual limitations on administrative discretion, inherent in the idea of government according to law.[87] A court has no more *choice* over whether or not to apply a test of procedural fairness or proper purposes (or, by extension, irrationality of result) than it has over whether to countenance a claim that specific statutory provisions have been misconstrued or disregarded. A public agency that flouts the basic principles of public law necessarily exceeds its jurisdiction; and a court has no more right to ignore such principles than the agency, but instead a duty to affirm the citizen's resistance to such unlawful treatment. Even the requirement that an agency should comply with *express* legislative instructions is a general principle of legality, independent of statutory authority. Nor is it judge-made, in the sense of an assertion of political will; it is simply a common law principle, making obedience to such legitimate instructions a requirement of the rule of law.[88] (If everything really turned on the existence of specific injunctions in the statutory text, it would be necessary to find a *direction* that the courts should enforce any such specific injunctions, and perhaps a direction to enforce that one, ad infinitum.)

The common law constraints on exercise of discretionary power reflect those conditions implicit in the basic idea of a self-governing community of equal citizens. The enforcement of law means, above all, the preservation of the conditions of liberty as independence; and it is the judicial function to interpret the law, so far as possible, as a consistent scheme of regulation that meets those conditions. Courts must be guided, accordingly, in their application of enacted rules and review of administrative discretion, by a vision of the rule of law as an ideal to which English law (or

---

[86] Compare Jeffrey Jowell and Anthony Lester, 'Beyond *Wednesbury*: Substantive Principles of Administrative Law' *PL* [1987] 368. Elsewhere, Tomkins has acknowledged a role for the courts in defence both of the political constitution and of civil liberties: Adam Tomkins, 'The Role of the Courts in the Political Constitution' *UTLJ* (2010) 60: 1.

[87] Tomkins, *Our Republican Constitution*, 22.

[88] And the demands of the rule of law are a matter of *judgement*, dependent on context. Consider judicial efforts to find a more nuanced approach than the classification of procedural conditions (for all purposes) as mandatory or directory: see eg. *R v Immigration Appeal Tribunal, ex p Jeyeanthan* [2001] 1 WLR 354, 362 (Lord Woolf MR).

Scottish or European law) inherently aspires. Judges *justify* their decisions by reference
to the law, but a rule's status as law cannot be merely a matter of deriving from
a criterion of 'recognition' accepted (for whatever reason) by officials; for such
official acceptance provides no moral ground to justify coercion of the citizen. To
provide a true justification, the rule must be derivable from a system that exhib-
its certain moral properties: 'Those properties will mark the system as one that
approximates to the ideal of the rule of law; and they will be logically tied to the
notion of freedom as independence from the power of others.'[89]

It follows that the 'principle of legality' applied by English courts to statutory
powers is aptly named, acknowledging that basic constitutional principles impose
inherent limits on any grant of discretionary power. No plausible interpretation of
the Home Secretary's powers regarding the management of prisons and discipline
of prisoners, arising from the general terms of the Prison Act 1952, could ignore the
consequences of his actions for the right of access to a court and the associated right
to obtain confidential legal advice. The maintenance of a proper balance between
such rights, on the one hand, and the requirements of administrative efficiency, on
the other, is not only a feature of English legal tradition but a conceptual commitment of the rule of law. The right of recourse to legal process for the vindication
of rights is a necessary implication of recognizing legal limits to the exercise of
power. Its elimination, or unnecessary limitation, would strike at the prisoner's
status as a member of the community, making him in effect an outlaw. It is part of
the constitutional bedrock: 'Even in our unwritten constitution it must rank as a
constitutional right.'[90]

Admittedly, the court in *Leech* assumed that such a constitutional right might
be curtailed, whether by express provision or necessary implication; but the importance of the right justified a strong presumption against such curtailment: 'it can
fairly be said that the more fundamental the right interfered with, and the more
drastic the interference, the more difficult becomes the implication'.[91] Since it
makes little sense to suppose that a fundamental right, central to the rule of law,
might be swept away by ill-considered legislation, we should interpret the principle
of legality here as a requirement of rationality or proportionality: any interference
must be *justified* by recourse to legitimate public ends, compatible with respect
for basic constitutional values. The court required the Home Secretary to prove a
'demonstrable need' for the power claimed (under prison rules) to examine and,
if thought appropriate, to terminate a prisoner's legal correspondence: 'The question is whether there is a self-evident and pressing need for an unrestricted power to
read letters between a prisoner and a solicitor and a power to stop such letters on
the ground of prolixity and objectionability.'[92] Since no such need was established,
the power did not exist: it would create too grave an impediment to exercise of the
prisoner's right of access to the court. It was acknowledged that the examination of
correspondence might be necessary to detect and prevent offences or to forestall

[89] Simmonds, *Law as a Moral Idea*, 191.
[90] *R v Secretary of State for the Home Dept, ex p Leech (No 2)* [1993] 3 WLR 1125, 1134 (Steyn LJ).
[91] *R v Secretary of State for the Home Dept, ex p Leech (No 2)*, 1134.
[92] *R v Secretary of State for the Home Dept, ex p Leech (No 2)*, 1137.

plans for escapes or disturbances. There was an implied power to inspect correspondence 'in order to ascertain whether it is in truth bona fide correspondence between a prisoner and a solicitor and to stop letters which fail such scrutiny'.[93] What is *authorized* by statute, then, depends on what can be *defended* as necessary limits on the enjoyment of basic constitutional rights.

The proportionality requirement of the rule of law is also demonstrated by the House of Lords' decision in *Simms*, in which the 'principle of legality' was explicitly applied to a further question relating to the Home Secretary's powers under the Prison Act. Fundamental rights could not be curtailed by general or ambiguous words: 'In the absence of express language or necessary implication to the contrary, the courts...presume that even the most general words were intended to be subject to the basic rights of the individual.'[94] On their correct construction, notwithstanding their apparently sweeping and draconian terms, the prison rules did not permit a prison governor to prohibit interviews of a prisoner by a journalist, or prevent information obtained by the journalist being used for his professional purposes. The evidence established that such interviews were often necessary to enable a journalist to become fully informed about the case of a prisoner who claimed to be the victim of a miscarriage of justice. Where the prisoner's sole purpose was to gain access to the investigative resources of the media in order to publicize an alleged injustice, with a view to having his case referred back to the Court of Appeal, considerations of prison management and discipline should give way so far as necessary. The minister's evidence did not establish 'a case of pressing need' which could prevail over the prisoner's attempt to gain access to justice.[95]

In these circumstances, the right of access to the media can be understood as both implicit in the concept of legality—part of any effective and reliable system of law that protects freedom as independence—and intrinsic to the British instantiation of legality, as an aspect of freedom of speech, or fair trial, that finds a natural home in a liberal democracy rooted in the common law tradition. Since few such constitutional rights could be *absolute*, however, in the sense of resisting all qualification, they must be treated as rights against unwarranted interference; and the court has no choice, in defence of legality, but to determine to the best of its ability whether any interference is truly justified in all the circumstances. In stressing, in *Daly*, that the doctrine of proportionality requires the reviewing court to assess the balance struck by the decision-maker, Lord Steyn confirmed what is implicit in the recognition of fundamental rights: when such rights are threatened the 'range of rational or reasonable decisions' is necessarily curtailed.[96] A judicial appraisal of the relative weight of competing considerations is what any test of legality, applicable to an interference with established rights, would rationally require.

We must, however, resist the notion that the principle of legality is defeated by express provision or necessary implication to the contrary. Our adherence to the

---

[93] *R v Secretary of State for the Home Dept, ex p Leech (No 2)*, 1138. Compare *Campbell v UK* (1992) 15 EHRR 137, 161 (cited in *Leech* at 1141).
[94] *R v Secretary of State for the Home Dept, ex p Simms* [2000] 2 AC 115, 131 (Lord Hoffmann).
[95] *R v Secretary of State for the Home Dept, ex p Simms*, 129 (Lord Steyn).
[96] *R (Daly) v Secretary of State for the Home Dept* [2001] 2 AC 532, para. 27.

rule of law defines our allegiance to constitutionalism; we could imply an intention
to override it only by supposing an affirmation of resort to arbitrary rule, displacing law by the uncontrolled will of officials. We should therefore challenge Lord
Hoffmann's view that Parliament can 'legislate contrary to fundamental principles
of human rights' provided that it is willing 'to accept the political cost'.[97] The
political cost of interference with prisoners' basic rights may be very small indeed;
and the notion that the constraints on legislative power are 'ultimately political,
not legal', is an affront to constitutionalism.[98] A 'constitutional right' that can be
'overridden' by majority vote in the legislature is a contradiction in terms; and so is
a 'principle of legality' that surrenders to action infringing the rule of law. A wholly
disproportionate interference is a form of irrationality that cannot be attributed to
legislation without showing disrespect for its parliamentary provenance. Just as an
ouster clause is treated as inapplicable to jurisdictional error, so must sweeping executive powers be construed as subject to fundamental rights, whose proper weight in
particular contexts can no more be cancelled by express provision than the principle
of legality itself.[99]

Tomkins complains that the right of unimpeded access to the court was 'invented'
in *Leech*, as if there could be a rule of law (whether for prisoners or anyone else)
without such access.[100] And his objection to *Simms* is that, 'in the hands of the
lawyers', a 'big question' about prisoners' freedom of expression was reduced to a 'far
narrower' one concerning the legality of restrictions imposed by a prison governor
on the conduct of an interview.[101] It is, however, precisely the specific, contextual
focus of the legal issue that makes judicial resolution both necessary and legitimate.
The more wide-ranging questions of penal policy, about which people can reasonably disagree, must be reserved for political debate and decision. The narrow
question, concerning the legality of an exercise of governmental discretion, must
be settled by reflection on the true content of the rule of law. The issue of legality
was related to the basic principle that miscarriages of justice should be corrected,
and the related idea that public interest in such (alleged) miscarriages should
be fostered rather than suppressed. Since the court must tread a delicate path
between resolving issues of legality and intruding, illegitimately, into political or

---

[97] *R v Secretary of State for the Home Dept, ex p Simms*. 131.

[98] *R v Secretary of State for the Home Dept, ex p Simms*, 131. The lack of any 'political cost' is clearly
demonstrated by the hostile political reaction to the decision of the European Court of Human Rights
in *Hirst v United Kingdom (No 2)* (2004) 38 EHRR 40, holding that the automatic loss of the right
to vote accompanying a sentence of imprisonment in the UK, irrespective of the length of sentence or
nature or gravity of the offence, is an indiscriminate restriction on the right to vote (art 3 of Protocol
1) falling outside any acceptable margin of appreciation. Successive governments have so far failed to
promote reform and in February 2011 the House of Commons adopted a motion opposing it. But a
requirement that the right to vote should be removed only in accordance with a considered and proportionate scheme, reflecting relevant features of the offence concerned, is hardly (one might think)
an illegitimate assault on legislative supremacy.

[99] Compare Sir John Laws's observation on a (supposedly) effective ouster in 'Illegality', 4.24: 'The
statute would have to provide that the decision of the body in question could not be reviewed for any
failure to comply with the principles of public law; it would be tantamount to a provision to the effect
that the decision-maker was not obliged to be reasonable, or to be fair, or to act within the confines of
the Act's purpose, or according to its correct construction.'

[100] Tomkins, *Our Republican Constitution*, 23.   [101] Tomkins, *Our Republican Constitution*, 29.

administrative policy-making, it should base its decision on the narrowest grounds available.[102]

E. Conclusion

I have offered a defence of judicial review of administrative action based on the principle of legality, which is closely linked to the fundamental political values of freedom and justice. The common law constitution provides the foundations of judicial review by giving expression to the idea of legality within British legal practice and tradition; it requires executive power to be employed in a manner that conforms to the requirements of the rule of law, whereby citizens' equal independence is effectively secured. Since such independence is the very foundation of republican liberty, legality and democracy are closely connected values. In curbing arbitrary power, exercised beyond the limits of statutory authority, judicial review of governmental action simultaneously affirms both the supremacy of Parliament as law-maker and the rule of law. Properly conducted, judicial review maintains the separation of powers critical to both representative government and the rule of law.

A lengthy debate over the true foundations of judicial review has been somewhat disfigured by the failure of the common lawyers, rejecting ultra vires, clearly to repudiate the legal positivism that underlies their opponents' stance.[103] When the principles of legality and rationality are understood as rule-of-law constraints on power, akin to the precepts of formal legality applicable to statutes, we can appreciate their place as intrinsic components of our concept of law. Legislative intention or instruction cannot be the basis of judicial review because legislative action takes the idea of law for granted; in conferring powers for the attainment of public ends, Parliament *invokes* the concept of law, which judges must interpret as part of their function in enforcing the jurisdictional limits that bind executive agencies. If law is the foundation of our liberty, we must acknowledge the moral dimension of the principles of legality. Their instrumental utility is subservient to the overriding demands of liberty and justice; and our concept of law or legality is ultimately intelligible only by reference to an ideal of the rule of law that serves those fundamental values.

---

[102] Thomas Poole's objection to courts acting as 'guardian of the moral order', whereby judges reflect on what in the abstract fundamental values 'seem to require', is well founded; but his characterization of 'common law constitutionalism' is arguably very wide of the mark: see Poole, 'Questioning Common Law Constitutionalism' *LS* (2005) 25: 142, 160–2. See also Paul Craig, 'Political Constitutionalism and Judicial Review' in Christopher Forsyth et al (eds) *Effective Judicial Review: A Cornerstone of Good Governance* (Oxford: Oxford University Press, 2010), 19.

[103] In insisting on a strict division, as regards the concept of law, between factual and normative questions, Sir John Laws fails to see how law is dependent on a vision of the rule of law; he therefore treats the 'mere idea of law itself' as morally neutral: Laws, 'Judicial Review and the Meaning of Law', in Forsyth (ed.), *Judicial Review and the Constitution*, 173, 178–80, 183–4. The jurisprudential dimension of the debate was, however, clearly identified by David Dyzenhaus: see Dyzenhaus, 'Reuniting the Brain: The Democratic Basis of Judicial Review' *PLR* (1998) 9: 98, and 'Form and Substance in the Rule of Law: A Democratic Justification for Judicial Review?' in Forsyth (ed.), *Judicial Review and the Constitution*, 141.

A political constitutionalism of the sort that diminishes judicial review, rejecting the implications of a moral understanding of law and legality, undermines democracy rather than promoting it. Ignoring the consequences for the exercise of discretionary power, and rooted in a misguided philosophy of legal positivism, political constitutionalism betrays the republican values it claims to defend. In a true republic the citizen is protected from domination, whether by powerful fellow citizens, government officials or political majorities. The alternative danger of domination by courts cannot be ignored; but judicial power is tamed by adherence to legality, whose integrity depends on closely reasoned, public argument, probing the justifiability of governmental coercion in particular instances. Accountability to law means more than compliance with positive law, whether statute or precedent; it is an ideal that informs and guides the interpretation of positive law. It is ultimately respect for law and legal process, conceived as moral constraints on the nature and mode of British governance—constraints we explore and refine in making sense of our own constitutional tradition. Legality is not identical with either liberty or justice; but respect for that complex moral ideal is a prerequisite for the success of our efforts to further the other basic political values.[104]

---

[104] For an effective critique of the supposed opposition between legal and political constitutions, insisting on the legal *framework* of the political constitution, see Tom R Hickman, 'In Defence of the Legal Constitution' *UTLJ* (2005) 55: 981, esp. 1016–22. For reflection on the dialectic at the heart of constitutional democracy, see Mark D Walters, 'Common Law, Reason, and Sovereign Will' *UTLJ* (2003) 53: 65. The themes of this chapter are further explored and developed in Allan, *The Sovereignty of Law: Freedom, Constitution, and Common Law* (Oxford: Oxford University Press, 2013).

5

Adjudication as Accountability: A Deliberative Approach

*Sandra Fredman**

A. Introduction

The role of adjudication in the human rights context has always been contested. Human rights adjudication is generally accused of being anti-democratic, giving power to unelected judges to override the elected representatives of the people. This is particularly so when human rights are thought to give rise to positive duties requiring resource allocation. This chapter does not intend to re-plough the well-worked terrain which ranges justiciability against non-justiciability. Instead, it regards the real challenge as being the need to formulate a democratically justifiable role for the courts. It is by augmenting the power of the electorate to hold the executive and legislature to account that judges can enhance rather than undermine democracy in the context of human rights adjudication. This in turn requires more attention to be paid to the meaning of democracy. It is argued in this paper that the role of human rights adjudication should be to enhance the deliberative dimension of democracy by insisting that human rights decisions be taken in a deliberative manner. While the primary responsibility for interpreting and delivering human rights responsibilities should lie with Parliament, decision-makers must be in a position to persuade the court that they have fulfilled their human rights obligations, account being taken of the fact that there is room for reasonable disagreement in the interpretation and the delivery of human rights, as well as in the acceptable limits. Moreover, a Bill of Rights, properly constructed, should make judges more rather than less accountable, because they too have to justify their own decisions against a background of values reached by a process of prior consensus. In this way, a Bill of Rights acts as a mechanism for accountability for both the legislature and the judiciary.

* Rhodes Professor of the Laws of the British Commonwealth and the USA, Oxford University, and a Fellow of Pembroke College, Oxford. This paper is substantially drawn from S Fredman *Human Rights Transformed: Positive Rights and Positive Duties* (Oxford University Press: Oxford, 2008), ch 4; S Fredman, 'New horizons: incorporating socio-economic rights in a British Bill of Rights' *Public Law* (2010) 297–320 and S Fredman 'From Dialogue to Deliberation: Human Rights Adjudication and the Prisoners' Right to Vote', *Public Law* [2013] 292–311. I am grateful to the editors, Nick Bamforth and Peter Leyland, for their helpful comments on an earlier draft.

This paper begins by considering the democratic objection to human rights adjudication. The second section briefly considers a dialogical approach. The third section takes the dialogical approach further and argues for a deliberative solution. On this view, the role of the judge is to facilitate deliberative reasoning about human rights, whether in the legislature, in the court room or in civil society. It is through requiring decision-makers to account for their interpretation, delivery and balancing of human rights that courts can enhance the democratic dimension of society. This is discussed further below.

1. The democratic objection

The most cogent objection to justiciable human rights is that put forward by Jeremy Waldron. For Waldron, the most fundamental of rights is the right to participate on equal terms in social decisions. This right should not be confined to interstitial matters of social and economic policy, but should essentially concern issues of high principle such as those addressed by human rights.[1] Giving judges the power to decide issues of high principle such as the content of human rights entails a profound disrespect for people in their democratic and representative capacities. 'Disagreement about rights is not unreasonable, and people can disagree about rights while still taking rights seriously. In these circumstances, they need to adopt procedures for resolving their disagreements that respect the voices and opinions of the persons—in their millions —whose rights are at stake in these disagreements and treat them as equals in the process. At the same time, they must ensure that these procedures address, in a responsible and deliberative fashion, the tough and complex issues that rights-disagreements raise. Ordinary legislative procedures can do this, . . . and an additional layer of final review by courts adds little to the process except a rather insulting form of disenfranchisement and a legalistic obfuscation of the moral issues at stake in our disagreements about rights.'[2]

Waldron's argument against judicial review in a human rights context is premised on a society which fulfils a number of conditions. The society in question must have '(1) democratic institutions in reasonably good working order, including a representative legislature elected on the basis of universal adult suffrage; (2) a set of judicial institutions, again in reasonably good order, set up on a non-representative basis to hear individual lawsuits, settle disputes, and uphold the rule of law; (3) a commitment on the part of most members of the society and most of its officials to the idea of individual and minority rights; and (4) persisting, substantial, and good faith disagreement about rights (ie., about what the commitment to rights actually amounts to and what its implications are) among the members of the society who are committed to the idea of rights.'[3] He also focuses on what he calls 'strong judicial review' by which he means that the courts have the authority to decline

---

[1] J Waldron *Law and Disagreement* (Oxford University Press: Oxford, 1999), 213.
[2] J Waldron, 'The Core of the Case Against Judicial Review' *Yale Law Journal* (2006) 115: 1346 at 1406.
[3] Waldron, 'Judicial Review', at 1360.

to apply a statute or to modify its effect to make it conform with human rights. This he contrasts with 'weak' judicial review, where courts do not have the power to decline to apply legislation.[4] He acknowledges that his target is strong judicial review, and that there may be some role for its weaker partner.

The approach in this paper does not dissent from Waldron's fundamental premise. Indeed it reiterates the key importance of participation in decision-making about the interpretation of rights. This is particularly true for the most contested of questions: how to balance rights against other public interests. However, I argue that such participation should not be confined to what Waldron calls 'ordinary legislative procedures'. Although there may be a high level commitment to human rights, signified by the continued adherence to a Bill of Rights or human rights legislation, legislative majorities may not always evince a commitment to human rights per se. Nor can one say, in the generalized and abstract way that Waldron puts it, that contestation about rights is always about good faith disagreement amongst those who are committed to rights. While this may be generally true, it is in precisely those cases in which the commitment to human rights wavers that it may be necessary to move beyond reliance on majority decisions within Parliament. Indeed, where the issue involves marginalized or unpopular minorities, even the high level commitment might come into question. The debate about prisoners' right to vote in the UK is a good example. Opponents of prisoners' right to vote in Parliament were often shrill in their rejection, not just of prisoners' right to vote, but also of the need for the European Convention on Human Rights, or indeed of any human rights at all.[5] As Dyzenhaus has argued, opponents of strong judicial review 'are prone to romanticize their favoured institution [Parliament], one whose reputation among the people often seems rather low these days, if only because of the popular perception that legislatures act as rubber stamps for powerful governments. Far from being reason-debating forums, they often fail even to be reason-demanding forums.' He gives as an example the UK Anti-Terrorism legislation whose amendment in 2001 was driven through Parliament by ministerial order by a government uninterested in debate, discussed before an almost empty chamber.[6]

Nor should it follow from the foundational premise (namely that all important decisions should be settled by the people themselves) that Parliament should be the only forum for participation. There is little basis for asserting that the people themselves actually do make important decisions. Decision-making is in practice skewed towards those with power in society, and even where majorities do make decisions, there is a risk that they will override the rights of minorities. The prisoners' right to vote debate is again a good example. Given that prisoners do not have the right to vote, and are therefore not represented in Parliament, why should decisions about

---

[4] Waldron, 'Judicial Review', at 1354–5.
[5] See, further, Fredman 'From Dialogue to Deliberation: Prisoners' Rights to Vote'.
[6] D Dyzenhaus 'Are legislatures good at morality? Or better at it than the courts?' I•CON, Vol 7, No 1, 2009, pp 46–52 at 49.

whether they should have such an entitlement be left to Parliamentary majorities? It could be argued that if the political system is defective in the extent to which ordinary people participate, the answer is to improve the political system rather than taking away more power from the people and giving it to the courts. However, this is a false juxtaposition. Parliament's ability to function as a robust forum of accountability might well be augmented by giving courts an appropriate role in insisting on such accountability. This can go hand in hand with political reform.

Waldron's rejection of a legitimate role for judicial review of human rights also assumes that there is an inevitable conflict between judicial and legislative power. This is true for both 'strong' judicial review, which gives the courts an ultimate and non-revisable power; and 'weak' forms, which appear to require courts to defer to Parliament. However, a closer look at various models of human rights adjudication reveal a much more fluid picture, in which courts and legislatures interact in potentially fruitful ways. This is particularly true for the UK Human Rights Act 1998, which Waldron characterizes as a form of weak judicial review. Under the HRA 1998, judges do not have the power to override legislation. Instead, judges faced with a successful human rights challenge to legislation can do one of two things. They can interpret the legislation so far as possible to comply with the courts' understanding of the right at issue,[7] in which case the amended legislation may be repealed or further amended by Parliament. Alternatively, they can issue a declaration of incompatibility.[8] Such a declaration does not itself alter the law, but gives a powerful signal to the legislature that the law ought to be altered. Thus adjudication could be characterized as feeding into the political process. By making a declaration of incompatibility, the courts can reopen the political debate, as well as enriching it by the insights uniquely generated through the process of judicial deliberation. In this sense, the import of the declaration of incompatibility is political, not legal. There are those who have argued that legislatures would find it so difficult to gainsay the court that this amounts to a power of veto. However, this misunderstands the difference between legally binding decisions, and those which enter the political process as a factor, albeit weighty, which legislators consider. The HRA 1998 operates as an input into the political process, not as a point of closure. This expands rather than contracts democratic participation.

These approaches are not only relevant for situations in which the courts do not have the power to invalidate legislation, as is the case for the HRA 1998. Even where judges do in principle have the power to strike down legislation, this does not generally mean, as Waldron suggests, that the decision is permanent and non-revisable. Constitutional courts have acknowledged that constitutions contain open-textured principles whose interpretation remains open to further discussion. Bills of rights are frequently referred to as a 'living tree', where changing social norms and values infuse judicial interpretation in order to reinvigorate constitutional texts. The European Court of Human Rights expressly states that its decisions are responsive to the changing consensus in contracting states. An example concerns the extent to

---

[7] HRA 1998, s 3.   [8] HRA 1998, s 4.

which it is discriminatory for fathers to be denied the right to paternity or parental leave. In *Petrovic v Austria*[9], the Court found that a distinction on the basis of sex with respect to parental leave in the 1980s could not be regarded as a breach of the Convention, given the great disparity at that time between the legal systems of contracting states on this issue. However, in 2012, in the case of *Konstantin Markin v Russia*[10], the Court held that society had significantly advanced, and the majority of European countries now provided parental leave for both men and women. 'The Court cannot overlook the widespread and consistently developing views and associated legal changes to the domestic laws of Contracting States concerning this issue.'[11]

Similarly, it is well known that dissenting judgments from earlier cases may in time convince the majority. A salient example is the United States Supreme Court's decision in *Lawrence v Texas*[12] holding that it was unconstitutional to criminalize homosexuality by prohibiting sodomy between consenting adults. In order to come to this conclusion, the court was required to hold that its earlier contrary holding in *Bowers v Hardwick*[13] was wrong. Indeed, Kennedy J, giving judgment for the court, held that the dissenting judgment of Stevens J in the *Bowers* judgment should have been controlling. Thus, the court held, '*Bowers* was not correct when it was decided, and it is not correct today. It ought not to remain binding precedent. *Bowers* v. *Hardwick* should be and now is overruled.'[14] The Supreme Court of Canada, which similarly has an override power, is also willing to revise its decisions, as in the case of *R v Kapp*[15], where the court held that its previous use of dignity in the context of equality claims under section 15 of the Constitution had become confusing. Instead of a legal test, which had become an obstacle in the applicant's way, dignity should be regarded as an essential value underpinning the legal principles applicable under section 15.

In any event, judges, conscious of their position relative to elected decision-makers, have often been quick to carve out areas of autonomy for decision-makers. In particular, concepts such as 'reasonableness' permit ongoing interaction between judges and elected officials even in the context of a binding constitution. The South African Court, which also has the power of 'strong' judicial review, has used the textual reference to 'reasonable' measures in the socio-economic rights provisions of the Constitution to develop a strong concept of deference to elected representatives in relation to the means to deliver socio-economic rights.[16] Nor are all constitutions as difficult to amend as the US Constitution. The Indian Constitution was amended by Parliament after a series of early cases in which the Supreme Court of India struck down social legislation in the name of the right to

---

[9] *Petrovic v Austria* (2001) 33 EHRR 14 (ECtHR).
[10] *Markin v Russia* [2012] Eq. L.R. 489 (ECtHR). [11] *Markin v Russia,* para.140.
[12] *Lawrence v Texas* (2003) 123 S Ct 2472 (S Ct US).
[13] *Bowers v Hardwick* (1986) 478 S Ct 186 (S Ct US).
[14] *Lawrence v Texas,* 539 S Ct 558 at 578.
[15] *R v Kapp* (2008) SCC 41 (S Ct of Canada) paras 21 and 22.
[16] *Republic of South Africa v Grootboom (1)* (2001) (1) SA 46 (SA Cons Ct); *City of Johannesburg v L Mazibuko (489/08)* (2009) ZASCA 20.

property.[17] Although the court reasserted jurisdiction so that the 'basic structure' of the Constitution could not be amended, the possibility of legislative override nevertheless acted as a constraint on the court.[18]

2. The dialogic approach

Recent scholars have attempted a different way out of the dilemma: one which moves away from a polarization between judges and legislatures, and instead attempts to work out ways in which both can contribute to a democratic resolution of human rights disputes. An increasingly influential stream of thought characterizes the relationship between courts and legislatures as one of dialogue. The advantage of this approach is to allow courts 'to bring constitutional values... into focus in the legislative forum' but leave the final decision to the legislature[19]. Rather than courts having the final say in the matter, judicial decisions provoke a response from the legislature. Dialogic theories of adjudication, which originated in Canada, have shown how legislatures can respond appropriately to judicial decisions, ultimately achieving their legislative purpose without falling foul of their human rights commitments. The dialogic approach has also been applied to the HRA 1998 in the UK, which seems particularly apt for such a model, given that the court has power to issue a declaration of incompatibility but not to declare legislation invalid. In this paper, I build on the insights of these theories to posit a 'deliberative' model of adjudication, which likewise regards courts as complementary rather than antagonists of Parliament.

The dialogic approach originated with a highly influential article by Hogg and Bushell,[20] which argued that the record of decisions under the Canadian Charter demonstrated that judges did not in fact have the last word on the matter. Instead, the legislature was generally able to respond to judicial invalidation of legislation in ways that preserved the basic legislative objective. This was possible because of the particular structure of the Canadian Charter. Hogg and Bushell pointed to several opportunities for 'dialogue' of this kind. The first was section 33 of the Charter, which expressly allows the legislature to override judicial decisions by the inclusion of a 'notwithstanding' clause. Secondly, the qualified rights,[21] the guarantee of equality in section 15, and the justification clause in section 1 of the Charter,[22] all meant that the rights could be complied with in a number of ways. These features of the Charter ensured that 'after a law was found to be invalid by the courts, legislatures would normally be left with a range of choices as to the design of corrective legislation. . . [and] . . . while the Charter would often influence the design

---

[17] *State of Madras v Champakam Dorairajan,* AIR (1951) S Ct 226 (S Ct India).
[18] *Golaknath v State of Punjab* AIR (1967) S Ct 1643 (S Ct India); *Kesavananda Bharati v State of Kerala,* (1973) 4 SCC 225 (S Ct India).
[19] M Tushnet, 'Dialogic Judicial Review' *Ark. L. Rev* (2009) 61: 205.
[20] P Hogg and A Bushell, 'The Charter Dialogue Between Courts and Legislatures (Or Perhaps the Charter of Rights Isn't Such A Bad Thing After All)' *Osgoode Hall Law Journal* (1997), 35: 75.
[21] Ss 7–9 and 12.
[22] S 1 provides: 'The Canadian Charter of Rights and Freedoms guarantees the rights and freedoms set out in it subject only to such reasonable limits prescribed by law as can be demonstrably justified in a free and democratic society.' (See *R v Oakes* [1986] 1 SCR 103 for the tests for justification).

of legislation that encroached on a guaranteed right,' legislatures 'would usually be able to accomplish what they wanted to do while respecting the requirements of the Charter'.[23]

Their claim was primarily a descriptive rather than a normative one. Having examined the aftermath of every case in which a law had been declared contrary to the Charter by the Supreme Court of Canada, they found that most of the cases had elicited some response from the legislature. In two thirds of the total, a new law was substituted for the old one. Apart from two cases in which the legislature defied the court by re-enacting the same law (once through section 33 and once through section 1), in all the other cases, the legislature 'respected the judicial decision by adding some civil libertarian safeguards in the new version of the law, but maintained the legislative purpose'.[24] The result was that in the Canadian context, judicial review did not mean that judges had the last word.

Although Hogg and Turnbull's claims were empirical, they quickly formed the basis for normative arguments in favour of a dialogic model. Thus Iacobucci J, enthusiastically embraced the dialogic model in *Vriend v Alberta*[25] as one which enhanced the mutual accountability of legislature and judiciary:

> As I view the matter, the Charter has given rise to a more dynamic interaction among the branches of governance. This interaction has been aptly described as a "dialogue" by some.... To my mind, a great value of judicial review and this dialogue among the branches is that each of the branches is made somewhat accountable to the other. The work of the legislature is reviewed by the courts and the work of the court in its decisions can be reacted to by the legislature in the passing of new legislation (or even overarching laws under s. 33 of the Charter). This dialogue between and accountability of each of the branches have the effect of enhancing the democratic process, not denying it.[26]

The dialogic model is an attractive one. Rather than taking the side of either an unadulterated Parliamentary sovereignty or a robust judicial supremacy, it characterizes the process as collaborative. However, a closer look reveals a deep ambiguity as to the role of the judiciary. Can judges ultimately make authoritative decisions on the meaning of human rights (or other constitutional principles) or do they defer the authoritative decision to the legislature? The dialogic approach is compatible with either. Thus, Tushnet takes the view that the task of the court in constitutional adjudication should be to draw the attention of the legislature to constitutional values and then leave it to the legislature to decide how to address these.[27] Similarly, for Roach, the courts' expertise in interpreting rights justifies their drawing 'the attention of the legislature to fundamental values that are likely to be ignored or finessed in the legislative process,' but not in their attempting to 'end the conversation or conduct a monologue in which [their]... Charter rulings are the final word.'[28]

---

[23] P Hogg, A Thornton and W Wright, 'Charter Dialogue Revisited: Or Much Ado about Metaphors' *Osgoode Hall Law Journal* (2007) 45: 1 at p.3.
[24] Hogg, Thornton and Wright, 'Charter Dialogue', p.4.
[25] *Vriend v Alberta* [1998] 1 SCR 493 (S Ct Canada).   [26] *Vriend v Alberta*.
[27] Tushnet, 212.
[28] K Roach *The Supreme Court on Trial: Judicial Activism or Democratic Dialogue* (Irwin Law Books, 2001), 530–1.

By contrast, Hogg et al argue that the final authority for interpreting the Charter rests properly with the judiciary. 'In our view, societies that have a written bill of rights will require some body or institution to have the final authority to say what the bill of rights means, otherwise there would be a possibility for "interpretive anarchy." '[29] Similarly, Hickman[30] develops a model of 'strong form' dialogue to describe the workings of the HRA 1998. A strong form of dialogue reflects a belief that 'courts have a vital constitutional role in protecting fundamental principles from the sway of popular sentiment.'[31] He distinguishes his model from what he calls 'principle proposing' dialogue, according to which 'the role of the courts under the HRA is to propose to the other branches answers to substantive questions of justice' but from which the government may legitimately deviate on compet-ing principled grounds.[32] The strong form of dialogue nevertheless maintains a dialogic approach. Courts should not simply impose these principles, but work with the executive and legislature in 'evolving them and in fostering their accept-ance.' In doing so courts should have the capacity for compromise in the interests of expediency, while at the same time 'insulating fundamental principles even in the face of such compromises.'[33] In other words, a strong form of constitutional dialogue is strong in that it permits courts to establish strong principles, which are insulated from majorities, but is dialogic in that the judge 'engages on a wider dialogic enterprise with society that involves a certain degree of give and take, prudential management and persuasion in the evolution and protection of principle.'[34]

There is also ambiguity in the notion of dialogue itself. Dialogue tends to suggest an ongoing process, whereby each side has the opportunity to react to the other. Yet human rights dialogue as described by these authors for the most part consists only in the legislature's reaction to courts. For Hogg and Turnbull, any leg-islative response constitutes a dialogic response, and there is no particular need for a further judicial reaction.[35] Indeed, neither the Canadian Charter nor the HRA 1998 has any formal mechanism for a further response by the court. In later work, Hogg et al did move beyond legislative response to examine 'second look' cases, or cases in which a court has reviewed the validity of legislation aimed at replacing a law previously struck down as infringing Charter rights.[36] However, here too, the judicial response is not built in: these examples are clearly dependent on litigants returning to court. This is true too of the HRA 1998. Whereas a declaration of incompatibility may (but need not) trigger a response from the legislature, there is no in-built mechanism for the court to scrutinize the outcome. Hickman attempts to construct scenarios of different legislative reactions (no reaction, re-enactment without change, or modification). But 'dialogue' ends there. There are now some 'second look' cases, the prisoners' voting rights cases being a salient example.

---

[29] Hogg, Thornton and Wright, 'Charter Dialogue', 31.
[30] T Hickman, 'Constitutional dialogue, constitutional theories and the Human Rights Act 1998' *Public Law* [2005], 306–35.
[31] Hickman, 'Constitutional dialogue', 316.   [32] Hickman, 'Constitutional dialogue', 309.
[33] Hickman, 'Constitutional dialogue'.   [34] Hickman, 'Constitutional dialogue', 326.
[35] Hogg and Bushell, 'Charter Dialogue'; Hogg, Thornton and Wright, 'Charter Dialogue', 45.
[36] Hogg, Thornton and Wright, 'Charter Dialogue', 19ff.

But, as in the Canadian case, this depends entirely on new litigants turning to courts to evaluate the outcome.

It is of course possible to create mandatory mechanisms for continuing dialogue. For example, South African courts have tended to use a suspended declaration of invalidity, which gives the legislature the opportunity to frame its response while keeping the court cognizant of the matter.[37] The Indian Supreme Court has used the device of a continuing interim mandamus.[38] In both these cases, however, the court has the final say; an approach which is anathema to this version of dialogue.

Even if the dialogic approach could be improved to achieve a genuine to and fro discussion, it remains limited. Firstly, it is concerned only with the court and the legislature. Ideally, the process of human rights interpretation and application should be open to a much wider range of participants. Secondly, the dialogic model focuses only on the 'output' or the judicial decision itself. The deliberative model, as I will show, looks behind the decision to the process of decision-making in the course of human rights litigation. Judges are not simply expected to articulate 'principles' which, in Hickman's model, appear to be identified in some abstract way. Instead, in recognition of the fact that the interpretation of a human right need not necessarily have a single right answer, the court itself should be required to justify itself in deliberative terms. Thirdly, the dialogic model assumes that the function of the courts is to give alternative solutions to human rights questions to that offered by the legislature. The deliberative model focuses instead on the quality of deliberation. The requirement that legislative or executive decisions be justified in a deliberative manner before a court is itself an important means of protecting human rights while at the same time reinforcing democracy. Thus, the deliberative model regards the judicial output as itself part of a process of deliberation.

3. A Deliberative response

The deliberative model begins by asking the question: what unique contribution can courts make to the protection of human rights? As we have seen, one of the main sources of the difficulty in framing an appropriate role for courts in adjudicating human rights is because of the assumption of a dichotomy between majoritarian democracy and anti-majoritarian human rights. The deliberative model addresses the problem by recognizing that majoritarian democracy does not fully describe all democratic models. This in turn requires more attention to be paid to the difference between, in Habermas's terms, 'interest-governed' and 'value-oriented' co-ordination.[39] It is argued here that while both have their place in a democracy, resolution of human rights cannot by its nature take place within the interest-regarding aspect. Deliberative solutions are necessary to prevent minority interests continually being overridden by more powerful interests. By contributing to the deliberative

[37] *Minister of Home Affairs v Fourie* (2006) (3) BCLR 355 (CC)
[38] *People's Union for Civil Liberties vs. Union of India and Others* Writ Petition (Civil) 196 of 2001 (S Ct India).
[39] J Habermas *Between Facts and Norms* (Polity Press, Cambridge, 1997) pp 139–41.

dimension of democracy in the human rights context, judges can enhance rather than detract from democracy.

Habermas explains his distinction as follows. Interest–governed coordination presupposes that each party comes to the bargaining table with fixed interests, the aim being to induce the other party to accept their claim. There is no background set of values against which to measure the validity of each party's interests; instead, success depends, not on the power of reasons, but on factual power. The solution is victory, surrender, or compromise; but not a change in the parties' perceptions of their own interests. A paradigm case is that of collective bargaining. Here, bargaining takes place in the absence of a collective agreement or legislative code and arrives at a set of outcomes based on the balance of industrial power. This contrasts with value-oriented coordination. Here parties do not come to the table with fixed interests. They enter the process aiming to justify their positions by appeal to reasons that all parties can accept, while at the same time being open to persuasion.[40] Deliberation is not on the basis of fixed interests: taking the deliberative commitment seriously requires a willingness to revise one's own preferences and convictions. Thus, instead of factual power, such coordination is based on the ability to adduce reasons which participants sincerely expect to be persuasive to others. In place of defeat or victory, therefore, coordination takes place through rationally motivated consensus.[41]

Drawing on these insights, deliberative democrats characterize democratic decision-making, as a situation in which citizens 'share a commitment to the resolution of problems of collective choice through public reasoning'.[42] Deliberative democracy contests the assumption that preferences are fully formed prior to the political process. Arguing that preferences are heavily influenced by social circumstances, theorists in this school conclude that the process of decision-making can itself play a central part in shaping those premises. This in turn means that initial preferences may be revised in the course of deliberation in a way which encompasses not only one's own perspective, but also those of other members of an association. Deliberation enables participants to see the extent to which their preferences are adaptations to their own limited circumstances.[43]

Nor is the aim of the process simply to reach a compromise or to aggregate those preferences as in the case of interest-bargaining. Instead, the aim is to arrive at a decision which is capable of being justified by reasons which participants sincerely expect to be persuasive to others. Attempting to justify a position by resorting to self-interest alone is unlikely to be successful. In addition, taking the deliberative commitment seriously requires a willingness to revise one's own preferences and convictions.[44] This is particularly true for preferences which a participant discovers cannot be justified. The result is to open up the possibility of resolving disagreements by

---

[40] Habermas, *Facts and Norms,* 25–26.
[41] Habermas, *Facts and Norms,* 139–40, 165.
[42] J Cohen, 'Deliberation and Democratic Legitimacy' in A Hamlin and P Pettit (eds), *The Good Polity* (Blackwell, Oxford, 1989), 22.
[43] Cohen, 'Deliberation and Democratic Legitimacy', 27.
[44] Cohen, 'Deliberation and Democratic Legitimacy', 25–26.

reasoned persuasion. Moving from a bargaining model to a deliberative model therefore requires a substitution of interest-governed action by value-oriented action. Particularly important is the function of disciplining political representatives by requiring them to justify decisions by reference to the public interest, not to preferences (their own or voters') which could be distorted or self-seeking.[45] At the same time, deliberative democracy is postulated as being a pluralistic association whose members have diverse preferences, convictions, and ideals. Apart from sharing a commitment to deliberative democracy itself, participants need not share a conception of the good.[46] This in turn necessitates explicit discussion of what values should be the basis of community aspirations.[47]

The deliberative democracy approach is not without its difficulties, both in principle and in practice. In particular, it is difficult to see how consensus can always be achieved through deliberation, and at what point closure is declared. One way forward is to use Sunstein's notion of incompletely theorized agreements. This involves distinguishing between different levels of agreement. People might disagree at one level of abstraction, but agree on a more particular application. This allows agreement on outcomes without agreeing on the most general theory that accounts for it. There may be no need to achieve consensus on the fundamental principle if the outcome can be agreed.[48] For example, people might agree on a redistributive policy because they believe in charity for the poor, or because they believe that property is theft, or because they believe in equality. This may work in both directions: there may be general consensus on the principle but not on the particular application; in which case, the principle could be agreed and the specification left for another time. Sunstein sets out a series of benefits of incompletely theorized agreements about constitutional principles and cases. Most important is the background value of mutual respect: even if there is no detailed agreement, people agree on the need for reciprocity, harmony, and respect. Such agreements reduce the political cost of enduring disagreements, while at the same time allowing the consensus to evolve over time.

Incompletely theorized agreement modifies deliberative democracy to the extent that, in putting forward their reasons, participants are not aiming to convince others of the soundness of their reasons, but only of their plausibility, so that the background value of mutual respect permits agreement to be reached. Even in this form, however, it is clearly unrealistic to expect that all decision-making fulfils the criteria of deliberative democracy. Instead, the insights of deliberative democracy fulfil the more partial function of acting as a discipline on decision-makers. Deliberative democracy requires decision-makers to justify their decisions by reference to reasons that all can regard as sound, even if they cannot command a consensus. Thus, self-seeking or biased reasons are flushed out and regarded as unacceptable.[49]

---

[45] Sunstein 'Beyond the Republican Revival'.
[46] Cohen 'Deliberation and Democratic Legitimacy', 23.
[47] Cohen 'Deliberation and Democratic Legitimacy', 24.
[48] C R Sunstein *Designing Democracy: What Constitutions Do* (Oxford University Press: Oxford, 2001) 50–65.
[49] C R Sunstein, 'Beyond the Republican Revival', *Yale Law Journal* (1988) 97: 1539.

Similarly, reasoned persuasion might still have a role in the context of a debate in which more than one reasoned solution is possible. In such a case, majority voting may be necessary. But this does not mean that the majority votes simply to advance its own personal interests. Instead, it is a way of deciding between various reasonable alternatives on the basis of the numbers of those who find one set of reasons more persuasive than another. In such cases, even if consensus cannot be achieved, it is possible to establish a reasonable set of policies which cannot be bargained away through the use of factual power.

Deliberative procedures will always co-exist alongside interest-bargaining. Habermas concedes that in complex societies, it is often the case that interests are sufficiently diverse that consensus is not possible.[50] In such cases, resort must be had either to majority voting or to bargaining between success-oriented parties who are willing to cooperate. Similarly, Sunstein describes the legislative process as a continuum, at one pole of which interest group pressures are determinative, while at the other end, legislators engage in deliberation in which interest group pressures play little or no role. Along the continuum, outcomes depend on an amalgam of pressure, deliberation, and other factors.[51] Even for those decisions in which interest-bargaining is unavoidable, deliberative procedures are necessary to establish the background procedural requirements. This is particularly important to ensure that all interested parties are provided with equal opportunities to influence one another.[52]

Thus modern democracies are a complex amalgam of individual representation, interest-group bargaining, and deliberative procedures. However, human rights cannot be addressed on the basis of interest-bargaining. If they were, individuals and minorities may always be trumped by those with superior numerical, political or financial power. Even when blatant exclusionary practices are not in place, it is clear that, as Rawls acknowledged, social and economic inequalities in a modern democratic state are so large that those with greater wealth and position usually control political life and enact legislation and social policies that advance their interests.[53] Human rights can only be addressed within a democracy through deliberative means. The power of the principle must itself be the reason for adopting it, rather than the numbers of those who back it. It is here that the courts are in a position to make a unique contribution to democratic resolution of human rights issues.

Adjudicating human rights: bounded deliberation

To what extent, then, can courts contribute to a deliberative resolution of human rights issues? At first sight, they are an unlikely option. Adversarial litigation appears to be a paradigm interest-bargaining framework. Each side appears before the court in an entirely defensive or accusative mode, aiming to persuade the court

---

[50] Habermas, *Facts and Norms*, 166.
[51] C R Sunstein, 'Interest Groups in American Public Law' Stanford Law Review (1985) 38: 29 48–49.
[52] Habermas, *Facts and Norms*, 166.
[53] J Rawls *Justice as Fairness* (Harvard University Press: Cambridge, Massachusetts 2001), 148–50.

from a rigid position. However, on closer inspection, it is obvious that judicial decision-making is, if correctly applied, essentially deliberative. It is not the parties' political, numerical or economic strength that persuades courts, but the strength of their reasoning. The parties' input is aimed at opening up the range of different responses to judges, on the basis of which they reach their decision. Moreover, in human rights cases, rules of standing and intervention can be adapted so that a wider range of perspectives is permitted to enter into the debate. The decision as to what the 'principle' should be is itself a deliberative exercise and gains its legitimacy from its deliberative credentials. This also clarifies the role of parties to proceedings in cases of positive duties where there is no immediate benefit to the right-holder. Where a right is programmatic and future-oriented, a successful case would only yield a duty to carry out an approved plan, which may not provide an immediate tangible benefit to the winning party. Instead of a right-holder making a realizable claim to an individual benefit, the role of participants is to bring to the process a particular deliberative solution to the problem.

A more serious concern with applying a deliberative model to human rights adjudication concerns the role of human rights themselves. Deliberative models assume an open-ended approach, allowing the process to produce a solution with no preconditions. Human rights, by contrast, require a prior commitment to the observation of human rights which appears to belie the possibility of a deliberative approach. Indeed, any legal materials which are binding on the court potentially obstruct this approach. It is partly for this reason that Waldron argues that courts are unsuitable for human rights adjudication: far from being able to reason morally, judges are constrained by materials which are only tangentially relevant to the issue at hand. He cites as an example the difference between the legislative approach to abortion in the UK and the judicial approach to the same subject in the US. Whereas the UK Parliament was able to reason openly about the subject at hand, the US court was required to focus on tangential legal issues such as whether privacy was implied into the US Constitution and the role of precedent.

Human rights pose particularly complex questions because they are neither fully determined nor open to thoroughgoing deliberative solutions. If they were fully determined, then both courts and legislatures could simply apply formulaic responses. Both institutions would be bound by the same mandatory norms and neither would be superior. However, human rights are open to a range of interpretations in particular contexts. Similarly, the question of whether human rights have justifiably been limited inevitably requires a judgement. On the other hand, human rights are not simply open moral questions. They are based on a consensus which has developed over time and is universally accepted as to what the fundamentals of being human in a political society require. It is within the framework set by this prior deliberative consensus that current decision-making must take place. Thus human rights place real constraints on both judicial and legislative decision-making, while at the same time being open to interpretation.

It is in this interpretative space that the deliberative approach functions. I argue that the primary deliberative role belongs with the legislature. Human rights decisions should be taken in a deliberative, rather than an interest-based mode, and the legislature is in the best position to do so. However, courts have a supervisory role, to ensure that such decisions are indeed taken deliberatively within the constraints set by the human rights themselves. Thus the primary role of the court is to enhance the deliberative dimension to modern democracy. Judges should do more than remind legislatures of the need to consider human rights: they should insist that legislatures address interpretive disagreements on value-based rather than interest-based grounds. Decision-makers must be in a position to persuade the court that they have fulfilled their human rights obligations, account being taken of the fact that there is room for reasonable disagreement both in the interpretation and the delivery of human rights, as well as in the acceptable limits. Thus, a central function of human rights adjudication is the requirement that the state explain and justify to the court, and therefore to the litigants and the public more generally, the grounds of its decisions and the reason for the selection of particular means. A proper explanation by the state cannot be based on particular private interests, but instead requires reasons which can be publicly advocated. In other words, one of the aims of judicial intervention is to rejuvenate the deliberative process.[54] For Habermas, this need not amount to a court overstepping the grounds of legitimation by substituting for the democratic process. Instead, its aim is to insist on the 'communicative presuppositions which allow the best arguments to come into play and procedures to secure fair bargaining conditions'.[55]

Decisions taken which affect groups without the political power to affect the decision require particular attention. Moreover, participation remains crucial. Those affected must be consulted and given an opportunity to vocalize their position, especially when silenced by majoritarian politics. As Baroness Hale has emphasized in the British Supreme Court: 'It is a purpose of all human rights instruments to secure the protection of the essential rights of members of minority groups, even when they are unpopular with the majority. Democracy values everyone equally even if the majority does not'.[56] Equality also serves democracy generally. In the famous words of Justice Jackson of the US Supreme Court: 'There is no more effective practical guaranty against arbitrary and unreasonable government than to require that the principles of law which officials would impose upon a minority must be imposed generally. Conversely, nothing opens the door to arbitrary action so effectively as to allow those officials to pick and choose only a few to whom they will apply legislation and thus to escape the political retribution that might be visited upon them if larger numbers were affected. Courts can take no better measure to assure that laws will be just than to require that laws be equal in operation'.[57]

At the same time, courts are not entitled to impose their views on open-ended moral grounds. The deliberative approach is bounded in that it operates within the

---

[54] C Sunstein, 'Interest Groups in American Public Law', *Stanford Law Review* (1985) 38: 29 at 58.
[55] Habermas, *Facts and Norms,* 278.
[56] *Ghaidan v Godin-Mendoza* [2004] UKHL 30, [2004] 2 AC 557 (HL) at [132] and see also *A v Secretary of State for the Home Department* [2004] UKHL 56 at [108], [237]; and *West Virginia State Board of Education v Barnette* 319 US 624 (1943), para.3.
[57] *Railway Express Agency Inc v New York* 336 US 106 (S Ct US) at 112–13.

constraints of human rights, which are themselves a product of prior deliberative consensus. Waldron regards this as a reason why courts should be considered unsuitable for human rights adjudication: the institutional setting in which judges act and the role they adopt 'require them to address questions about rights in a particular legalistic way—indeed, in a way that, sometimes, makes it harder rather than easier for essential moral questions to be identified and addressed.' He contrasts this with 'legislative approaches, which proceed by identifying all the issues and all the opinions that might be relevant to a decision, rather than artificially limiting them in the way that courts do.'[58] However, it is paradoxical to valorize the output of legislative deliberation while at the same time regarding legal materials as irrelevant to judicial decision-making. A Bill of Rights makes judges more rather than less accountable, because they too have to justify their own decisions against a background of values reached by a process of prior consensus.

The model is illustrated well by the UK Supreme Court case of *Limbuela*,[59] in which asylum seekers, living rough in car parks and on pavements, claimed that the withdrawal of all social security support, which, together with a prohibition on paid work, left them to inevitable destitution, breached their rights under the European Convention on Human Rights art 3 (not to be subject to inhuman or degrading treatment or punishment). Asylum seekers have no voice in the political process; in the 'plural bazaar' of interest-bargaining, they would certainly lose out.[60] Deliberative accountability, however, had a very different result. Decision-makers could not resort to politically charged arguments about the need to deflect undeserving asylum seekers. Instead, they were required to produce a transparent and reasoned account, capable of convincing others, as to why it was not inhuman and degrading to exclude the most disadvantaged from basic means of survival. Such an account was not forthcoming. The asylum seekers' claims were upheld. As Lord Brown put it: 'It seems to me one thing to say, as the ECtHR did in *Chapman*, that within the contracting states there are unfortunately many homeless people and whether to provide funds for them is a political, not judicial, issue; quite another for a comparatively rich . . . country like the UK to single out a particular group to be left utterly destitute on the streets as a matter of policy.'[61] The result was not a usurpation of political power, but a deliberative solution based in the pre-existing values in article 3.

It could be argued that litigation derails rather than augments democracy, since it gives a second vote to the litigant in matters already dealt with through the ballot box. However, there is no reason why the individual's only opportunity to participate in political decision-making should be through the ballot box. Where a person is actually affected by a decision, it makes full democratic sense

---

[58] J Waldron, 'Judges as Moral Reasoners' *International Journal of Constitutional Studies* (2009) 7: 2, 2.

[59] *R (on the application of Limbuela) v Secretary of State for the Home Department* [2005] UKHL 66, [2006] 1 AC 396 (HL).

[60] B Ackerman, 'Beyond Carolene Products' *Harvard Law Review* (1985) 98: 713.

[61] *R (on the application of Limbuela) v Secretary of State for the Home Department* [2005] UKHL 66.

to allow her to participate in the process of decision-making both in respect of the particulars of her own situation and by contributing to the choice of values guiding the decision-maker.[62] More problematic is the objection that a courtroom, far from enhancing democratic participation, is an arena in which elites are able to augment their already powerful position. Litigation is sufficiently expensive, protracted, and framed in mystifying language, to make it inaccessible to most people. Thus, to the extent that litigation permits the litigants to participate in the political process, it does so in a wholly unrepresentative manner, privileging those with the resources and energy to pursue their grievance.

The current structure of many courts makes this a real criticism. However, it is not a necessary feature of justiciability. If courts are going to be taken seriously as deliberative fora, then accessibility and equality within the courtroom must be a priority. To ensure that courts properly discharge their function of holding decision-makers to account through human rights adjudication, accessibility and equality within the courtroom must be a priority. Legal aid, demystifying language, open standing rules and an accessible procedure and tone are all possible, as well as use of tribunals, human rights commissions and ombudspersons.[63] It is only by giving an opportunity to those who cannot participate fully in the democratic process that litigation supplements democracy; not by giving a further platform to those already well represented in that process. Procedural developments in Indian courts demonstrate ways in which courts can be opened up to the most disadvantaged in society.[64]

On the other hand, it should not be thought that the political process provides a more accessible or equal alternative. The ability of elites to manipulate and dominate is not confined to the courtroom. The political process, particularly where it involves interest bargaining, is highly vulnerable to such domination. In this respect, justiciable positive duties are capable of correcting rather than reinforcing inequality. A key aim of human rights is to give individuals the wherewithal to participate fully in society, including in the political process. Human rights adjudication should make it possible for even the weakest voice to be heard. At the same time, the aim is not to give any individual a veto over the broader process, but to allow all to enter into the deliberative process on an equal footing, both in terms of persuading and being persuaded.

Does the deliberative process not mean that decisions can never be made? This is problematic in a courtroom, where the parties before the court require an answer to their dispute. As Habermas argues, there is a need to reach a point of closure under pressure of time, both for the parties before the court and in creating settled expectations by which others, including state bodies, can organize their decisions and actions. How then can the paradox be resolved between the ongoing deliberative

---

[62] G Cartier, 'The Baker Effect: A New Interface between the Canadian Charter of Rights and Freedoms and Administrative Law', in D Dyzenhaus (ed.) *The Unity of Public Law* (Hart, Oxford, 2004), 83.

[63] For an analysis of the institutional changes in India see Fredman, *Human Rights Transformed: Positive Rights and Positive Duties,* ch 5.

[64] Fredman, *Human Rights Transformed: Positive Rights and Positive Duties,* ch 5.

debate, which requires revisability of judicial decisions, and the dispute before the court, which requires closure in decision-making? Clearly, judges should not have the last word on the meaning of human rights values, nor should they be fossilized by non-revisable decisions. However, courts need to be in a position to enforce the decision in the case before them, as well as creating settled expectations and consistent standards.

The way forward is to regard courts' decisions as binding for the issue before them, but revisable in the long term through the dynamic forum of deliberative democracy. This, however, does not differ from the court's role in common law disputes in general. Here too, the court's decision can be revised by Parliament, but the change in the law cannot reverse the effect on the particular parties. At the point of decision-making, the duty is fixed, and the state is required to take action or is absolved from action, as the case may be. But on the broader scale, the decision remains part of a process of continuing revisability, whether through Parliament, case law or public discourse. Similarly, the court itself can, as part of the deliberative process, revise its views. But here the principle of stability requires change to be incremental, so that state officials and private individuals can order their lives according to reasonably settled rules. The cases on parental leave from the ECtHR, cited above, are a good illustration of this process.

A particularly good example of the application of a deliberative model is the litigation in the South African *TAC* case,[65] in which the Constitutional Court struck down the government's decision to refuse to permit the use of Nevirapine to reduce mother-child transmission of the HIV-AIDS virus. The South African Constitution gives everyone the right of access to adequate housing,[66] health care services, sufficient food and water, and social security. [67] The corresponding duty of the state is to 'take reasonable legislative and other measures, within its available resources, to achieve the progressive realisation of this right.'[68] The case was brought by an NGO, Treatment Action Campaign, which argued that the government's decision could not be justified in the light of its constitutional commitments to take all reasonable measures, within its available resources, to provide access to health care. Notably, there was no difficulty in finding resources, as sufficient quantities of the drug had been offered free for three-to-five years by the manufacturer. However, the government had for many years refused to take effective measures to combat the AIDS pandemic on the grounds that it did not believe that the HIV virus caused AIDS. The result was that, despite the proven efficacy of nevirapine in diminishing the risks of mother-to-child transmission of the virus, the government refused to permit the drug to be administered in state hospitals outside of a handful of 'pilot schemes'. The court upheld the challenge.

The decision was centrally based on deliberative accountability. As the judgment notes: 'In our country the issue of HIV/AIDS has for some time been fraught with an unusual degree of political, ideological and emotional contention.'[69]

---

[65] *Minister of Health v Treatment Action Campaign (No 2)* (2002) 5 SA 721 (SA Cons Ct).
[66] South African Constitution s 26.   [67] South African Constitution s 27.
[68] South African Constitution ss 26(2); 27(2).   [69] South African Constitution, para.20.

By requiring the government to prove that its concerns over the safety of Nevirapine were based in evidence, the court introduced a strong requirement of accountability and transparency. It was not enough simply to produce reasons; they were also required to be reasonable. In this light, it was clear that the reasons put forward were lightweight relative to the enormous cost in human lives that the refusal entailed. But the judgment goes further than accountability, introducing a deliberative element into decision-making. This is because the government was required to explain its policies in a way which could convince others of their reasonableness, and on terms which were free of ideological or self-interested perspectives. Those who had previously had no voice in democratic decision-making were able to introduce their own perspectives, so that the court could create a synthesis of both. The equality parameter is also evident, in that the chief victims of the policy were the poor who could not afford to buy the drug privately.

Similarly, the South African court has developed a strong participatory dimension, through its notion of meaningful engagement. Thus in the *Olivia Rd* case, the court required the parties to 'engage with each other meaningfully … and in the light of the values of the Constitution, the constitutional and statutory duties of the municipality and the duties of citizens concerned' to resolve the dispute.[70] This is not simply an instruction to parties to settle the case: instead of interest-bargaining, meaningful engagement must follow deliberative principles, by requiring parties to reach a consensus based on the constitutional rights. Most importantly, the most disadvantaged group (here squatters in derelict inner city housing) are given a voice in a deliberative forum, when they would certainly have none outside of it. Thirdly, the duty cannot be applied in a discriminatory manner.[71]

The South African court, however, remains hesitant in the extent to which it ensures that deliberative accountability is followed through. This is reflected in its cautious approach to remedies, and particularly to structured interdicts,[72] its reluctance to specify minimum obligations,[73] and specific timetables, its use of balancing rather than proportionality, and, most recently, its preparedness to take government gestures towards 'meaningful engagement' at face value, rather than insisting on a pure deliberative forum.[74] Moreover, the deliberative standard is an exacting one, which requires constant vigilance. It is not sufficient to accept any explanation, without demanding proper evidence.[75]

---

[70] *Occupiers of 51 Olivia Road v City of Johannesburg* Case CCT 24/07 [2008] ZACC 1 (SA Cons Ct).

[71] *Khosa and Mahlaule v Minister for Social Development* 2004 (6) BCLR 569 (SA Cons Ct).

[72] G Budlender and K Roach, 'Mandatory Relief and Supervisory Jurisdiction: When is it Appropriate, Just and Equitable?' *South African Law Journal* (2005) 122: 325–51.

[73] D Bilchitz *Poverty and fundamental rights: the justification and enforcement of socio-economic rights* (Oxford University Press: Oxford, 2007).

[74] *Residents of Joe Slovo Community v Thubelisha Homes* Case CCT 22/08 [2009] ZACC 16 (SA Cons Ct); S Liebenberg 'Joe Slovo eviction: Vulnerable community feels the law from the top down' *Business Day Live*, June 22 2009, <http://www.bdlive.co.za/articles/2009/06/22/joe-slovo-eviction-vulnerable-community-feels-the-law-from-the-top-down;jsessionid=C598F61154921FE6692CD6CEA7B07EF4.present2.bdfm> accessed 17th August 2013.

[75] See, eg. *City of Johannesburg v L Mazibuko* (489/08) [2009] ZACC 28.

B. Conclusion

It has been argued in this paper that it is possible to structure adjudication of human rights in a way which strengthens rather than detracts from democracy. Judges should not substitute their opinion for that of decision-makers; but nor should they simply defer. Instead, I have proposed a model based on 'bounded deliberation': one which requires both legislatures and courts to be able to give a deliberative (rather than interest-oriented) account of their interpretation and delivery of human rights and their limits. Human rights should only be addressed within a democracy through deliberative means rather than through interest-based bargaining. The power of the principle must itself be the reason for adopting it, rather than the numbers of those who back it. It is here that the courts are in a position to make a unique contribution to democratic resolution of human rights issues.

This approach leaves open a number of questions. For example, should deliberation take place within the legislature, or is it sufficient for the government to put forward deliberative justifications for the purposes of the litigation? Is an *ex post facto* deliberative justification sufficient? Conversely, is it problematic if deliberation takes place with an eye on the 'judge over your shoulder'? That is, is it self-defeating if decisions are taken expressly with a view to conforming with judicial prescriptions? Particularly problematically, are there situations in which no explanations will meet the test of bounded deliberation? However, once we move beyond a rigid dichotomy between courts and legislatures towards more collaborative approaches, the solutions are not nearly as intractable as might be thought.

6

The Instrumental Value of
Legal Accountability

*Jeff King**

A. Introduction

Any proposal to extend the domain of adjudication can reasonably be met with the following good faith question: why? What is valuable about doing that, and about legal accountability more generally? A traditional answer suggests that it is required to protect the rule of law, or prevent the abuse of power, or protect our rights. But each of these claims is question begging, and not only because these are very ambiguous concepts. Even if we all agreed on the core content of these ideas, we would still need a deeper answer about what institutional features legal accountability possesses that makes it good for serving them.

In this essay, I set out an account of the main instrumental benefits of legal accountability, and defend that account against some common objections. It is intended to provide a general answer to the question, one that is susceptible of proof or falsification in terms that it is hoped will attain some measure of general agreement. That is, it is hoped that if a reader disagrees with any stated benefit, we will agree on what evidence would count as proof or disproof of the assertion. In Section B, I explain that my approach to evaluating the question is instrumentalist. On this view, legal accountability can be seen as a means for achieving ends, and not something to be assessed primarily in terms of its intrinsic value. There is also a list of what I consider to be the essential attributes of legal accountability, and these attributes help us to understand why it is that legal accountability has some

* Senior Lecturer in Law, University College London. The author would like to thank Paul Craig, Dimitrios Kyritsis, Richard Kirkham, Simon Halliday, Joana Mendes, Ron Levy, and the participants of a Staff Seminar held at the Faculty of Laws, University of Sheffield in November 2011, and the participants in the Workshop on Accountability in the Contemporary Constitution held at London Metropolitan in September 2010 (and especially T R S Allan and Mark Tushnet for their helpful criticisms). In particular, he would like to thank Nicholas Bamforth and Peter Leyland for penetrating and demanding editorial oversight, which improved the piece considerably. An older draft benefited from presentation to the Oxford Socio-Legal Studies Discussion Group in 2006, and from extensive and very helpful written comments from Richard Kirkham and Graham Gee.

of the benefits that it does. In Section C, I set out a list of ten prima facie benefits. I argue there that legal accountability generates ten features that have instrumental value: focus, principled reasoning, constitutional authority, independence and impartiality, rule interpretation competence, procedural fairness competence, participation, expressiveness, publicity, and inter-institutional collaboration. I defend the claim that legal accountability possesses these features, and that these features produce (or can produce) valuable ends, and I defend both types of claims against some common objections. The entire structure of the argument is in prima facie terms. I accept that the final question of the value of legal accountability is to be determined in particular contexts. It is hoped that identifying a general list of benefits will assist the task of evaluating the case for legal accountability in specific jurisdictions on particular issues.

B. Instrumentalism, legal accountability, and prima facie benefits

Prior to outlining the benefits themselves, there is a need for a rather detailed methodological detour of sorts.

1. Instrumentalism, adjudication, and institutional design

I agree with the view that the function of law generally is to serve *as a means to an end*.[1] By 'law', I mean the set of formal sources and legal standards officially recognized as constituting law,[2] and the set of institutional procedures (the legal process) used authoritatively by adjudicative institutions to identify and uphold the law. Law is used as an instrument, by its authors (and sometimes interpreters) to bring about some state of affairs. Such ends can be intrinsically valuable (eg. equality, liberty, dignity, fairness etc.), or can be ends that are themselves means for obtaining other things of intrinsic value (eg. prosperity, stability, coordination, transparency, etc.). And any instrumentalist account of law's value must acknowledge that the ends secured by law may well be negative, whether by design or accident (eg. domination, exploitation, conservation of harmful customs, etc.). Law is typically used to secure a broad range of ends.[3]

---

[1] I aim to follow the analysis in L Green, 'Law as a Means' in P Cane (ed.) *The Hart-Fuller Debate in the Twenty-First Century* (Oxford: Hart Publishing, 2010).

[2] See H L A Hart *The Concept of Law* (2nd edn, Oxford: Clarendon Press, 1997), ch VI. It is compatible with the role J Finnis sees for a rule of recognition to play in a system of positive laws, *Natural Law and Natural Rights* (Oxford: Clarendon Press, 1980), ch X, both in the 'selection of viewpoint' (ch I) and in the role for law in securing coordination for the common good (chs IX and X). It corresponds roughly to the the sources identified by legal officials as the 'pre-interpretive' material in the account of law set out in R Dworkin *Law's Empire* (Cambridge, Mass.: Harvard University Press, 1986), Chs 2–7.

[3] I follow H L A Hart in believing that it is unlikely that law serves any one end in particular, even if it is well-adapted to a variety of ends: see the Postscript in his *The Concept of Law* at 248-9. See also J Raz, 'The Functions of Law' in his *The Authority of Law* (Oxford: Oxford University Press, 1979).

We can at this point state a weak and a strong thesis about the instrumental value of law. The strong thesis is that the desirability of law is measured *exclusively* by reference to whether it produces desirable ends. On this view, there is nothing intrinsically valuable about law or legal institutions. This is a plausible view in my mind, but it is not my aim to defend it here. The weak thesis is that the worth of law and legal institutions is *predominantly* to be evaluated by reference to the ends they produce.[4] Such an account does not deny the possibility of a residual intrinsic dignity to the law or legal processes themselves, but it considers it to be marginal in any inquiry about the true value of law. This essay takes this weaker view. In the main, it is concerned to evaluate the value of some aspect of legal regulation by examining *what it does*. An important consequence of this view is that the value of legal accountability is ultimately contextual.

I consider what I have said above to be broadly consistent with the views of H L A Hart and John Finnis about the nature of (human made) law and legal institutions.[5] Ronald Dworkin's view of what constitutes the law on any given question is not straightforwardly compatible with this position, though his view of the role and desirability of different modes of adjudication plainly is instrumentalist in this manner.[6] Notably, to make such claims about law and legal institutions does not imply any strong view about the role of legal instrumentalism in adjudication.[7] That is, one can be an instrumentalist about evaluating the desirability of legal processes or doctrines, without suggesting that judges should adopt an instrumentalist attitude in their disposal of particular cases.[8] Indeed, as with rule and act consequentialism, the very best case against this type of potential opportunism may be an instrumentalist argument that such an approach undermines the proper ends of a well-functioning legal system. In my view, instrumentalist arguments are most appropriate for the level of institutional design.

2. The meaning of 'legal accountability'

In this essay, I aim to address the value of legal accountability, as defined in this sub-section, and not of *law* as a whole. Marc Bovens offers a 'narrow' sense of the

---

⁴ Note that although instrumentalists speak of law securing 'ends', and that 'ends' can be defined strictly in relation to stated, purposive objectives, instrumentalists typically mean 'ends' in a broader sense to mean 'consequences.' In this sense, legal instrumentalism is in fact best understood as a type of legal consequentialism, which employs the term 'instrumental' as emphasis upon the idea that is used by persons to achieve goals. Instrumentalists are concerned about side-effects, however. See further, A Vermeule, 'Instrumentalisms' *Harvard L Rev* (2007) 130: 2113, 2117ff.

⁵ See Hart, *The Concept of Law* n 2, ch VI; Finnis, *Natural Law and Natural Rights,* n 2, chs 2, 9, and 10 (the 'selection of viewpoint' (ch I) and in the role for law in securing coordination for the common good (chs IX and X).

⁶ Dworkin, n 2 above at 93 (setting out 'the point' of law as being to justify coercion). On adjudication, see R Dworkin, 'In Praise of Theory' *Arizona St L J* (1997) 29: 353, 364 (his theory is 'plainly consequentialist'); see also his *Freedom's Law: The Moral Reading of the American Constitution* (Cambridge, Mass: Harvard University Press, 1996), ch 1 (arguing that constitutional judicial review *may* be one effective way to give effect to the constitutional conception of democracy he sets out).

⁷ B Tamanaha *Law as a Means to an End: A Threat to the Rule of Law* (New York: Cambridge University Press, 2006), 1.

⁸ Green, 'Law as a Means', n 1 above at 3–4, is critical of Tamanaha on this point.

concept of accountability, in the effort to avoid any evaluative dimension and obfuscation sometimes found in a discourse that treats accountability as synonymous with transparency, responsiveness, controllability and so on.[9] He argues that '[a]ccountability is a relationship between an actor and a forum, in which the actor has an obligation to explain and to justify his or her conduct, the forum can pose questions and pass judgment, and the actor may face consequences.'[10] I follow Bovens in all these respects.

Bovens claims legal accountability is the most 'unambiguous' type of accountability, and he appears to equate legal accountability with resort to courts.[11] However, legal accountability cannot only be defined by pointing to the institutions that are called courts in various countries. The institutional variation in terms of training, structure of adjudication, and tenure of judges is profound. It is more useful, therefore, to offer an account of the attributes of legal accountability. This sheds light on why legal accountability offers certain prima facie benefits. And the existence of those benefits in turn explains the instrumental importance of these particular attributes of legal accountability. Accordingly, I would argue that the following are essential attributes of legal accountability:

(i)   an individual right of petition;

(ii) a functionally independent adjudicator;

(iii) adjudicators interpret and apply publically affirmed legal standards;

(iv) adjudicators give decisions that are (a) interpretations of applicable standards, which conform to reasonably demanding professional standards of rationality, consistency, and fidelity to those standards and cannons of interpretation, (b) responsive to the principal submissions, and (c) ordinarily published;

(v)   there is a remedy (which may be declaratory or coercive); and

(vi) the remedy is final (subject to appeal or reversal by due process of law).

It is not my purpose in the present essay to insist upon these attributes as being essential features or a 'central case' of legal accountability in the sense employed in general jurisprudence. I am content to stipulate, for the purposes of this essay, that the benefits claimed in Part C below are for the adjudicative institutions that manifest these attributes, subject only to the additional proviso that the output of such adjudicators is treated with respect and comity by other public institutions and by the public at large.

---

[9] M Bovens, 'Analysing and Assessing Accountability: A Conceptual Framework' *13 Eur LJ* (2007) 447.

[10] Bovens, 'Analysing and Assessing', 450.

[11] Bovens, 'Analysing and Assessing', 456. He considers ombudspersons a species of administrative accountability. J Mashaw as well appears to equate legal accountability with courts. See his 'Bureaucracy, Democracy and Judicial Review: The Uneasy Coexistence of Legal, Managerial and Political Accountability' in R F Durant (ed.) *The Oxford Handbook of American Bureaucracy* (New York: Oxford University Press, 2010), ch 24. My view, which for reasons of space cannot be pursued here, is that ombudspersons and tribunals share many of the essential attributes of legal accountability outlined in this section, and can thus reasonably be viewed as substitutes for courts of law where circumstances demand.

3. Benefits, prima facie benefits, and costs

I argue in Part C that the prima facie benefits of legal accountability are useful means for achieving valuable ends. At the most general level, I believe that they may secure respect for the following intrinsically valuable ends: individual dignity; individual well-being; equal treatment; and fairness. Furthermore, some of the prima facie benefits also, in my view, secure the following instrumentally valuable ends: the rule of law; democratic accountability (self-government); transparency; and efficiency. Each of these is valuable because it secures further, intrinsically valuable ends, such as those given in the list above.

I call the list below prima facie benefits because whether they are real benefits in the final analysis can only be determined by offsetting their positive consequences against their costs. So, 'participation' (eg. through interventions, public interest standing, etc.) may appear to be a prima facie benefit, but further study may show that wide participation rights have posed significant challenges for the political process.[12] We will only know whether a prima facie benefit is a real benefit after accounting for such costs. That exercise, furthermore, must be contextual. This therefore raises the question of whether there is any point in speaking of prima facie benefits in the first place. Why not simply defer any question of the value of legal accountability to a wholly contextual analysis that is both jurisdiction- and issue-specific? Would that not provide for a richer set of relevant variables? It certainly would, but in my view there is still a need for a general account of the prima facie benefits of legal accountability. First, it offers an index of putative general benefits, which can be subject to fruitful challenge at a general level, and not just in isolated circumstances. Much of the analysis below is concerned with those general, 'up-front' challenges to the prima facie benefits that I claim for legal accountability. If general arguments are always liable to the criticism of being non-contextual, so contextual arguments are liable to being distinguished as non-generalizable. And furthermore, a general theme emerges in my treatment there. A number of the objections to the prima facie benefits of accountability do not amount to refutations of the prima facie benefit. They amount to qualifications, ones that I believe are addressed through the deployment of interpretive doctrines or curial attitudes that manifest proper judicial restraint. (Such objections may, however, be strong reasons to avoid extending the province of legal accountability too far in particular contexts, for instance where the curative effect of the proposed solution is unrealistic).

Second, a prima facie list helps clarify the institutional component of the instrumentalist claim about law's value. In many discussions about the need for law reform, one hears about the need to respect rights, the separation of powers, the rule of law, and to provide greater accountability. Yet there is a perennial risk of obfuscation when one's case for change is entirely based on such concepts, because people disagree fundamentally on their requirements. A focus on the prima facie

---

[12] R B Stewart, 'The Reformation of American Administrative Law' *Harvard L Rev* (1975) 88: 1669; C Harlow, 'Public Law and Popular Justice' *MLR* (2002) 65: 1.

benefits listed below, which I claim are connected to desirable ends, may help better inform any such discussions by directing our attention towards a set of stipulations that are liable to proof or rebuttal in terms that will command wider approval.

C. The prima facie benefits of legal accountability

The aim of this section is to present a non-exhaustive list of the most important prima facie benefits. It is helpful analytically to think of the key claims set out below as consisting of two broad categories. First, I argue that legal accountability possesses certain *features*, which are the prima facie benefits. I outline ten of them (eg. focus, independence, principled reasoning, etc.). Second, I argue that these features can produce valuable consequences (eg. facilitating the rule of law, protecting individual dignity, etc). Some critics deny either or both of these types of claims, and I will take up and reply to some of these important objections.

1. Focus

Legal accountability prompts factual focus on the narratives of particular individuals and how some policy affects them or their rights, and legal focus on a distinct set of legal issues which is isolated in strong measure from the competing political pressures for time and attention. The right of petition, the right to reasons, and the duty to interpret and apply standards, all compel this outcome. This feature of legal accountability promotes respect for individual dignity (showing respect and concern for individuals), fairness and equality (considering legitimate grievances and claims to inconsistent treatment), and the rule of law (enabling challenges to alleged illegality). In respect of focus, legal accountability compares well with administrative, political and market-based options for redress. With administration, the problem is typically inertia. Even sympathetic managers may be unable to address a case adequately.[13] With the political process, the complaint must compete with other issues that take on grander importance on a crowded agenda. It is not a reliable working supposition that issues can be considered in isolation. And it is rare, in many countries, to resort to legal accountability to the exclusion of these avenues when they are in fact available. The market, for its part, offers little to those without bargaining power, and provides little real remedy for abuses of public power. A legal process for justiciable problems ensures that the issue is addressed formally and that there can be, depending on the strength of access to justice in

---

[13] M Lipsky *Street Level Bureaucracy: Dilemmas of the Individual in Public Services* (New York: Russell Sage, 1980); S Halliday *Judicial Review and Compliance with Administrative Law* (Oxford: Hart Publishing, 2004); J L Mashaw *Bureaucratic Justice* (New Haven: Yale University Press, 1985). Mashaw celebrates bureaucratic rationality over the moral treatment model employed by courts, but presents much data along the way showing that individualized justice is not the strength of large bureaucracies.

the community, an enforceable demand for an official response to the claimant's arguments.

Objections:

- *Appellate litigation is usually about policy or abstract principles, not discrete issues and compelling narratives.*

Jeremy Waldron argues that this purported feature is largely a myth: '[b]y the time [a case] has reached the high appellate level, almost all trace of the original flesh-and-blood right-holders has vanished, and argument such as it is revolves around the abstract issue of right in dispute.'[14] In some important cases this is true. Yet in many others it is false. There are many cases where factual narratives do provide important insight into the unjust impact of particular policies. These narratives are important, for instance, in cases concerning deportation when life-saving medical treatment is at risk,[15] or measures that condemn late-claiming asylum seekers to total destitution,[16] or national security measures that impose a Kafkaesque bureaucratic procedure upon those who have not been shown to have committed any wrong.[17] Indeed, it is precisely the poignancy of tragic choices in health care allocation, and the susceptibility of the judicial process to such 'flesh-and-blood' narratives, that in Calabresi and Bobbitt's view make adjudication improper for that purpose.[18] Lord Steyn famously said that in law, context is everything.[19] Even if that is an overstatement, it is a very long way from Waldron's caricature. At any rate, the benefit of focus is not only about personal narrative. It is about picking out one policy and considering its legality in the light of relevant facts and legal standards and, where human rights are concerned, comparing its substance with other options in the light of comparative experience. While this analysis is at times also carried out in Parliament and by government, many issues in adjudication are those not considered in the process of legislative drafting or administrative rule-making, or may be sidelined by dense timetables or aggressive party discipline.

- *Litigation is myopic*

Myopic focus on the issues before the adjudicator is the more problematic objection. Judges may have a poor understanding of the dynamic or knock-on effects of their decisions,[20] and courts are said to provide poor mechanisms for participation by those who are ultimately affected by decisions. One example of this is when a court adjudicates a heavily polycentric problem, meaning a problem that comprises an

---

[14] J Waldron, 'The Core of the Case Against Judicial Review' *Yale LJ* (2006) 115: 1379.
[15] *D v United Kingdom* (1997) 24 EHRR 423 (ECtHR); cf. *N v United Kingdom* (26565/05) [2008] ECHR 453.
[16] *R v SSHD, ex p Limbuela* [2005] UKHL 66.
[17] *A v United Kingdom* (2009) 49 EHRR 29 (ECtHR).
[18] G Calabresi and P Bobbit *Tragic Choices* (New York: W W Norton & Co. 1978).
[19] *R(Daly) v Secretary of State for the Home Department* [2001] UKHL 26 [28].
[20] A Vermuele *Judging under Uncertainty: An Institutional Theory of Legal Interpretation* (Cambridge, Mass.: Harvard University Press, 2006); Mashaw, *Bureaucratic Justice*, n 13 above.

elaborate set of interconnected relationships where changes to one relationship affect many others throughout the network.[21] Focus is needed for obvious reasons in individualized adjudications. Yet with review of broader policy questions, the costs of focus/myopia rise exponentially. This is a real problem, but there have been a host of interpretive doctrines that compensate for it. First, there are a variety of doctrines of judicial deference and restraint that apply in public law, both general and specific.[22] In addition to a constant judicial preoccupation with deference to expertise, there is also a more or less recognized distinction between adjudicative facts and legislative (or social) facts,[23] with a presumption that adjudicators exercise more restraint and caution when determining the latter. Second, there is increased specialization, both within the judiciary and among tribunals and ombudspersons. This increased expertise fosters greater awareness of the knock-on effects of particular decisions. Third, legal accountability offers a measure of remedial flexibility that can adjust to the nature of the problem. Judges can resort to declaratory relief or procedural rights, whereas ombudspersons can frame their recommendations to enable bureaucratic flexibility. Lastly, the decisions of these bodies are subject to considerable feedback, particularly those of the courts. Lessons are learned, and the side-effects of myopia are gradually cured.

2. Principled reasoning

Adjudicators are generally required to advance interpretations of the public standards that are well-reasoned. If they fail to do so, they have failed in their professional duty. The reasoning must be principled in the sense that it presents proofs and reasons in support of a particular interpretation of the relevant sources and policy considerations, and valid arguments connecting all together in the text of the decision. It is principled in the sense of not merely an appeal to preferences (unless the community's preferences are legally relevant), or to values or considerations that lie outside the sources to which it is proper to refer.

This has five important consequences that can be beneficial. First, it entails *logical rigour*. Adjudicators must consider all relevant considerations, observe consistency in their argument, and follow professional interpretive conventions. Second, it ordinarily entails *responsiveness* to the submissions and relevant arguments, and thus treatment of counter-arguments. Third, it engenders *professional scrutiny* of the product, which reinforces the first two consequences. (This third item is particularly true of

---

[21] See J W F Allison, 'The Procedural Reason for Judicial Restraint' *PL* [1994] 452–73. Cf J A King, 'The Pervasiveness of Polycentricity' *PL* [2008] 101.

[22] The literature here is vast. For more recent work, see A Kavanagh, 'Defending Deference in Public Law and Constitutional Theory' *LQR* (2010) 126: 222; T R S Allan argues against the need for any doctrine: 'Judicial Deference and Judicial Review: Legal Doctrine and Legal Theory' *LQR* (2011) 127: 96; J King *Judging Social Rights* (Cambridge: Cambridge University Press, 2012), Part II; P Daly *A Theory of Deference in Administrative Law: Basis, Application and Scope* (Cambridge: Cambridge University Press, 2012).

[23] K C Davis *Administrative Law Treatise* Vol 2 (St. Paul, Minnesota: West Publishing Co. 1958), 353, at [15.03]. See Rule 201 of the Federal Rules of Evidence (US), which sets out rules relating to judicial notice of adjudicative (not legislative) facts.

the higher decisions of the law courts; less so for lower courts and tribunal decisions). The form of professional scrutiny there includes hierarchical supervision, third-party intervention, academic commentary, comparative analysis by foreign courts, and occasionally public and political scrutiny. Common law adjudicators are in that sense extremely accountable for their decisions, even if not easily removable. Fourth, the process creates a *good faith attempt at objectivity*.[24] Even if being objective is impossible, *trying* to be objective and impartial delivers real benefits and reduces the extent to which law suffers from the vices of opportunism. Legal accountability enables the party to adduce proofs and reasons and compels the adjudicator to give a principled response, in a process largely transparent and open for scrutiny. Fifth, legal accountability enjoys a distinct advantage for *evidence assessment and fact-finding*. Courts are the exemplary institution for the establishment of adjudicative facts and can even, at times, be effective in the difficult task of determining complex questions of causation and sifting through materials relating to the establishment of legislative facts.[25] This is due to the mode of principled reasoning and adjudicator-independence inherent in legal accountability institutions. It is for this reason that judges are at times chosen to conduct important public inquiries.[26]

We have good reason for valuing these consequences. There is a range of decisions a political community may want to resolve through this type of reasoning process. Some such decisions may include jurisdictional disputes between levels of government, border disputes, criminal responsibility, certain questions of rights, deportation, and at least some aspects of the treatment of minorities and marginalized groups more generally. Furthermore, I would contend that this reasoning process is an essential precondition for the rule of law. The resort by individuals to courts would be largely pointless if there were no predictability or legitimacy to the process of reasoning used in the courts.

Objections:

- *Legal standards run out quickly, and then judging is mostly the application of judicial preferences.*

The argument above is not blind to the rise and fall of the legal process school of jurisprudence in the United States,[27] which advocated 'neutral principles' and the principle of institutional settlement.[28] Neither is it ignorant of the insights from

---

[24] See Tamanaha *Laws as a Means to an End,* n 7 above at 234–41; K Greenawalt *Law and Objectivity* (Oxford: Oxford University Press, 1992), esp. ch 10.

[25] Davis, *Administrative Law Treatise,* n 23 above at [15.03]; see also his 'Judicial Notice' Columbia L Rev (1955) 55:945. Davis pointed out judicial limitations but also felt that the adjudication of legislative facts was inescapable and necessary in litigation.

[26] J Beatson, 'Should Judges Conduct Public Inquiries?' *LQR* (2005) 121: 221.

[27] See H M Hart Jr and A M Sacks *The Legal Process: Basic Problems in the Making and Application of Law* (prepared for publication from the 1958 Tentative Edition and containing an introductory essay by W N Eskridge Jr and P P Frickey) (Westbury, New York: Foundation Press, 1994). See also N Duxbury *Patterns of American Jurisprudence* (Oxford: Oxford University Press, 1992), ch 4 for an account of the school's rise and fall.

[28] H Wechsler, 'Toward Neutral Principles of Constitutional Law' *Harvard L Rev* (1959) 73: 1 and see also the introductory essay by Eskridge and Frickey,

legal realism and critical legal studies. The claims asserted are meant to be comparative only, and furthermore subject to the important qualifications I make below.

The objection stated above would be false, if by it one means that judicial outcomes are chiefly determined by naked preferences. It amounts to a radical and outmoded form of legal realism.[29] Judges' decisions are constrained by a range of legal standards, and their conclusions within the interstices must be plausibly linked to those standards. This is reinforced by the requirements of reason giving, publication of decisions, and professional and academic scrutiny thereof.

It is true that judges will appeal to policy and moral arguments in settling legal disputes, and of course their sense of moral judgment and preferences will affect their evaluation of such arguments. However, even these arguments, to some extent unmoored from the legal standards, are subject to some important basic constraints. First, they must be *generally acceptable* forms of public reason. This does not mean that they command consensus, but it does commonly exclude certain types of arguments, such as (in many though not all liberal democracies) direct appeals to the law of God,[30] appeals to radical theories of law and the state such as those found in Communist or fascist writings, the use of theories positing racial or gender superiority, and so on. Secondly, the moral views espoused must at the very least fit with the principles recognized by the legal system. It is not typically open to judges to apply exotic moral theories, and fit (and perhaps institutional conservatism) is largely the explanation. Third, there is a presumption that policy arguments in particular will be supported by evidence, whether of a legal or factual nature. Now, obviously all of these 'requirements' are ignored from time to time in specific cases. However, when that occurs, judges are departing from their role as a judge. They become open to the criticism that they have breached professional norms of conduct. I take this much to be inherent in the nature of the reasoning process within the framework of legal accountability that I set out in Part B above. When the breach is persistent, we can consider the situation to be a crisis. But the very fact that that state of affairs would constitute a crisis confirms the appropriateness of the status quo outlined here.

No doubt, the stronger objection here is that these are very weak constraints on the application of judicial preferences. For some courts, depending on their docket, the constraints of precedent, and the nature of the legal questions submitted to them, this may well be true. However, for many others, which move incrementally, take strong account of academic views, have relatively low rates of dissent, and whose decisions are more predictable, this view is not accurate. And we must not commit the fallacy of equating apex courts with the entire system of legal accountability, or indeed, with the broader system of administrative justice. Their dockets are by their very nature made up of hard cases.

---

[29] Tamanaha, *Law as a Means to an End*, n 7 above at 237–9, also accepts that the institutional constraints of judging are real and not marginal. Attitudinal studies present a challenge to this view and are considered briefly at notes 49–50 below and accompanying text.

[30] Of course such references have occurred and continue to do so, but often in situations in which there is a high degree of consensus that such references are acceptable as evidence of a community's positive morality.

- *Legislators and administrators are better than courts at principled reasoning, so nothing is gained by subjecting their decisions to legal reversal.*

Constitutional review will often require courts to address the same principled arguments and evidence as has the legislature. Yet much of parliamentary debate is exemplary of principled reasoning. Legislatures have certain epistemic advantages as well, given the diverse range of inputs into the legislative process. The committee system in the UK Parliament, for example, has augmented this capacity to a very impressive extent. Ideally, the process works best when government appoints experts to report on an issue, solicits viewpoints at the green and white paper stages, hears further views during drafting and later the committee stages of the legislative process. This happens frequently enough.[31] However, it is common ground that legislatures are subject to pressures that distort principled reasoning in a number of ways, chief among them being party discipline. If committee votes are subject to party discipline, then independence is in fact lacking, and decisions on voting can and often are made before even hearing the evidence meant to inform the decision. Another pressure is time and priorities. Of course legislatures have more time than the courts do, but any bill comprises a massive range of matters, and parties must prioritize in ways that can marginalize even the rights-issues they sympathize with. Above all are the problems of inadequate representation of marginalized groups, and of a legislative process that fails to see the consequences of a certain enactment. All these failings and more are diagnosed and analysed by Rosalind Dixon in her insightful analysis of what she terms legislative 'blind-spots' and 'burdens of inertia.'[32]

- *Administrative agencies are better (indeed normally better) at principled reasoning, objectivity and assessment of evidence than courts.*

This statement is largely true of some very important agencies, and it ties well with the original justification for the growth of agencies in the first place. Yet the objection merely justifies an appropriate level of judicial deference, and does not eliminate the prima facie benefit contended for here. Agencies are obviously better at saying whether global warming is imminent, or whether some drug is likely to be cost-effective. This objection is especially true when the issue under determination is highly complex, and the agency applies its collective expertise to it. And such judgements are not rare either. As a managerial matter, moreover, agencies are much better than judges at evaluating costs and adjusting to the costs and benefits for most larger programmes.[33] This all justifies a strong measure of judicial restraint. However, judicial restraint is compatible with retaining general public law jurisdiction over agencies.

---

[31] It was what occurred, eg., in the lead up to the passage of the Tribunals, Courts, and Enforcement Act 2007.

[32] 'Creating Dialogue About Socio-economic Rights: Strong-form Versus Weak-form Judicial Review Revisited' *I.CON* (2007) 5: 391; see also R Dixon, 'The Supreme Court of Canada, Charter Dialogue, and Deference' *Osgoode Hall Law Journal* (2009) 47: 235, 257-60.

[33] Mashaw, *Bureaucratic Justice*, n 13 above; Vermeule, n 20 above.

In fact this is necessary, as, quite apart from review of routine matters of statutory interpretation and procedural fairness, bureaucracies have their familiar flaws in the area of principled reasoning as well. Administrative behaviour suffers from unstoppable inertia, lack of resources for careful deliberation or reconsideration, and programming and political imperatives that interfere with the reasoning process.[34] Bureaucrats adopt heuristics, which often lead to high error rates that the administration may be slow to acknowledge, and in some cases powerless to correct.[35] The less routine the decision, the more political influence is liable to exert control. All these considerations work against blanket judicial deference to administration, and qualify the familiar case for judicial restraint. Thus the objection is an important qualification, one that justifies a central principle in public law, as it should.

3. Constitutional authority

Courts have a form of constitutional authority owing to their historical constitutional role, their role in protecting the rule of law, and as a forum for asserting individual rights. They are thus accorded respect by political institutions and the public. Judges tend to have high intelligence, rigorous training, and follow transparent procedures. They play an extensive role in shaping and creating many rules governing private and public relations, most of them against a backdrop of moral considerations. Courts are regarded as having a constitutional responsibility to enforce and to some extent fashion these values. This constitutional authority is peculiar to courts, but other formal accountability mechanisms may eventually come to share this attribute.

This authority has four potentially valuable institutional consequences. The first is *political responsiveness*, namely, that government and the public ordinarily accord court rulings respect and take them seriously.[36] The power to award enforceable remedies—ranging from fairly lax to quite intrusive—can in principle ensure political responsiveness, at least in the case at bar. The second important consequence is *judicial confidence*; namely, the willingness of judges to take a controversial stand on matters with significant policy or social ramifications. There are several cases involving issues that rest significantly on this type of political confidence,[37] constituting

---

[34] See Lipsky, *Street Level Bureaucracy*, n 13 above; M Derthick *Agency Under Stress* (Washington, DC: Brookings Institution Press, 1990).

[35] K C Davis *Discretionary Justice: A Preliminary Enquiry* (Chicago: University of Illinois Press, 1971); Derthick, *Agency Under Stress*, ch 2; Mashaw, *Bureaucratic Justice*, n 13 above; King, *Judging Social Rights*, n 22 above, ch 8.

[36] P Cane, 'Understanding Judicial Review and its Impact' in M Hertogh and S Halliday (eds) *Judicial Review and Bureaucratic Impact: International and Interdisciplinary Perspectives* (Cambridge: Cambridge University Press, 2004), 15, 19: 'It is certainly arguable that the status of the Administrative Court is critical to its ability to entertain complaints against the political executive of central government in the reasonable expectation that any finding against the government will be taken seriously.'

[37] *R v Inspectorate for Pollution, ex p Greenpeace (No 2)* [1994] 4 All ER 329 (QBD); *R v Secretary of State for Foreign Affairs, ex p World Development Movement* [1995] 1 WLR 386 (QBD) (standing);

what Peter Cane describes as 'high profile judicial review.'[38] A third valuable institutional consequence is that courts (though not tribunals or ombudspersons) have *general jurisdiction.*[39] This helps to ensure that there are few holes in the regime of accountability, and that there is a general presumption of legal accountability in play that cannot be ousted easily or in piecemeal fashion. A fourth aspect is *remedial flexibility.* Judges can choose a broad range of remedial responses to problems of illegality, and the common trend in bills of rights is to give courts the power to award 'appropriate remedies' or 'just satisfaction.' This flexibility helps them adapt legal accountability to the needs of modern administration. All these features can and often do faciliate the attainment of the broad variety of ends identified in Part B.3 above.

Objections:

- *These 'benefits' are actually detriments.*

It is a fair charge that for all the above reasons, the blade of legal accountability cuts deeper into administration and politics than it ought to.[40] It is true that this 'benefit' of legal accountability is ultimately dependent on whether the costs of judicial intervention are outweighed by the benefits. It is therefore admitted that the link between the feature of legal accountability and the desirable end is less straightforward than with some of the other benefits. The benefit here is more in the realm of a potential benefit. It is akin (to borrow a familiar example) to a blade that cuts well, but which can ultimately be used for good or bad. Its potential for good makes it a prima facie benefit. If so, a sceptic may ask, why not call it a prima facie detriment? The answer here is that in my view the evidence on the whole supports the view that the practice is generally beneficial.[41] No critic of the judicial review of administrative action to my knowledge goes so far as to say that we can do without it.

- *This argument overestimates the impact of legal accountability.*

There are a range of studies about the impact of adjudication. Some focus on the impact of constitutional rights litigation in particular, and other forms of

---

Anisminic v Foreign Compensation Commission [1969] 2 AC 147 (HL) (construction of ouster clauses); *R v Secretary of State for Social Security, ex p Joint Council for the Welfare of Immigrants* [1997] 1 WLR 275 (CA) (the vires of regulations that infringe on subsistence rights); *R v North East Dev on Health Authority, ex p Coughlan* [2001] QB 213 (CA) (the enforceability of a substantive legitimate expectations); *A and others v Secretary of State for the Home Department* [2004] UKHL 56 (detention without trial); *Jones v Ministry of Interior Al-Mamlaka Al-Arabiya as Saudiya (The Kingdom of Saudi Arabia)* [2006] UKHL 26 (admissibility of torture evidence); *R v Secretary of State for the Home Department, ex p Limbuela* [2005] UKHL 66 (ministerial capacity to forbid support to certain indigent asylum seekers).

[38] Cane, 'Understanding Judicial Review', n 36 above at 18.

[39] At times courts will contract this general jurisdiction, either through doctrines of justiciability, or through procedural rulings such as the rule in *O'Reilly v Mackman* [1983] 2 AC 237 (HL) that public law rights claims could only be raised through the judicial review procedure.

[40] J A G Griffith *The Politics of the Judiciary* (5th edn, London: Fontana Press, London 1997).

[41] I consider these arguments in more depth in King, *Judging Social Rights*, n 22 above, ch 3.

cause-lawyering.[42] These studies are mostly American, and deal with a sub-set of legal accountability. In that literature, the tide has turned against (and indeed never swam with) a strong version of the 'hollow hope' argument famously offered up by Gerald Rosenberg,[43] an argument that largely overlooks (or relegates to a late chapter) the iterative relationship between law and politics that cause-lawyers have navigated with significant success over the years since the early days of the civil rights movement.[44]

The UK studies focus on the impact of conventional judicial review.[45] Halliday's study of homelessness decision-making in London local authorities provides notable insight into the limitations of judicial impact. He shows that, in the authorities he studied, there were few applications for judicial review, little absorption of legal standards into local authority behaviour, and a problem of 'creative compliance' whereby authorities use their knowledge of the legal process to evade legal control.[46] This literature is an antidote to quixotic notions of what legal accountability can deliver. It qualifies but does not refute the premise of political responsiveness, however. That responsiveness is evident in too much of judicial review, including several statutory amendments after cases taken under the Human Rights Act 1998 (HRA 1998) or won in Strasbourg, in the nearly one million tribunal cases disposed of annually, and in the near total rate of compliance with the recommendations of the Parliamentary Commissioner of Administration (Ombudsman) and local government ombudsmen.[47]

4. Independence and impartiality

The independence of the judiciary from strong political pressure is often offered as a leading argument in support of judicial review,[48] and of course recourse to

[42] Surveys of the voluminous literature are provided in the chapters by McCann and Epps in K E Whittington, R D Kelemen and G A Caldeira (eds) *The Oxford Handbook of Law and Politics* (New York: Oxford University Press 2008), chs 32 and 37. See also A Sarat and A Scheingold (eds) *Cause Lawyers and Social Movements* (Stanford: Stanford University Press, 2010).

[43] The classic is G Rosenberg *The Hollow Hope: Can Courts Bring About Social Change?* (2nd edn, Chicago: University of Chicago Press, 2008). See also D Horowitz *The Courts and Social Policy* (Washington DC: Brookings Institution, 1977), and M Klarman *From Jim Crow to Civil Rights: The Supreme Court and the Struggle for Racial Equality* (New York: Oxford University Press, 2004).

[44] See the essays cited above, n 42. I analyse the hollow hope argument and this literature in King, *Judging Social Rights,* n 22 above, ch 3.

[45] The leading current exemplar is Halliday, *Judicial Review and Compliance with Administrative Law,* n 13 above, and a survey of other current literature is available in Hertogh and Halliday, *Judicial Review and Bureaucratic Impact,* n 36 above.

[46] Halliday, *Judicial Review and Compliance with Administrative Law,* n 13 above, 61–5; see also I Loveland *Housing Homeless Persons* (Oxford: Oxford University Press, 1995), ch 11 for similar conclusions.

[47] I have answered this important objection more fully in King, *Judging Social Rights,* n 2 above, ch.3. For a snapshot of the European Convention's strong recent impact on domestic law and policy, see Ministry of Justice, *Responding to Human Rights Judgments: Report to the Joint Committee on Human Rights* (Cmnd 8432, 2012). On compliance with local government ombudsmen reports, the 2011–12 Annual Report of the Local Government Ombudsman for England and Wales states that out of 3,347 remedies issued, councils 'resisted' in two cases only (see <http://www.lgo.org.uk/publications/annual-report-2011-12-perf-measuring-success/> (accessed 5 November 2012)).

[48] *Rhodes v Chapman* (1981) 452 US 359 (Brennan, J., concurring). See also J H Ely *Democracy and Distrust: A Theory of Judicial Review* (Cambridge, Mass: Harvard University Press, 1980).

independent courts is a central feature of the rule of law. Independence here means functional (not formal) immunity from control or improper influence, and impartiality means the absence of bias in favour of one side to a dispute. Functional independence is compromised by political control of adjudicators, but also by effective control or influence by religious authorities, or private groups such as militias, nationalist or ethnic groups, threats by crime syndicates and so forth. Bias is often a byproduct of lack of independence, but it can be voluntary when adjudicators abandon professional norms of interpretation and show preference for a party. This may be done due to political or personal favouritism, or simple corruption.

Functional independence and impartiality produce clearly valuable consequences, the most notable being those associated with the rule of law. It is a precondition for any effective judicial review (of the administrative law variety). It straightforwardly reinforces many of the benefits listed elsewhere in this essay, such as principled reasoning, constitutional authority and procedural fairness competence. And there is also little doubt that independent adjudication is a precondition for reliable contracting and thus efficient commercial relationships, which can produce economic growth.

Objection:

• *Judges are political.*

When people make this objection, they may employ the term 'political' in a narrow or broad sense. The narrow sense is the claim that adjudicators and especially common law appellate judges decide some cases primarily with the objective of achieving their personal policy preferences. There has been an extensive amount of increasingly sophisticated empirical analysis exploring this premise over the last sixty years, mostly in relation to American appellate judges.[49] This literature delivers a strong blow to the conventional view that law constrains judges. However, its conclusions are not straightforward support for the claim that judges act to further political ends. The leading studies focus on the atypical US Supreme Court, and the phenomena highlighted in such studies appears more acute in America than abroad.[50]

Nonetheless, there is a broader sense of 'political' which is that adjudicators, even if they do not implement their political preferences directly, do so indirectly because of the inescapability of judicial discretion or judgement, especially when

---

[49] For a review of the different models of judicial decision-making, see L Baum, 'Motivation and Judicial Behavior: Expanding the Scope of Inquiry' in Klein and Mitchell (eds) *The Psychology of Judicial Decision-Making* (Oxford: Oxford University Press, 2010). The leading attitudinal study is J A Segal and H A Spaeth *The Supreme Court and the Attitudinal Model Revisited* (Cambridge: Cambridge University Press, 2002). I am very grateful to Cheryl Thomas for diverting me from an unduly simplistic analysis of the attitudinal studies.

[50] These points merely echo those of others and are not meant as a rebuttal of the studies: see R Posner *How Judges Think* (Cambridge, Mass: Harvard University Press, 2008), 25–9; Tamanaha, *Law as a Means to an End*, n 7 above at 240. For a detailed critique and new model, see M A Bailey and F Maltzman *The Constrained Court: Law, Politics and the Decisions Justices Make* (Princeton: Princeton University Press, 2011).

enforcing vague norms. Posner, for instance, is a critic of the narrow version of the argument that judges are political, but an advocate of this broader statement.[51] Almost no one doubts, however, that a judge's view of political morality will influence the decisions she renders.[52] But that fact does not destroy an adjudicator's independence. Indeed, in many cases of adjudication (perhaps all) we *want* judges to apply their moral sensibilities in their assessment of what the law requires in a given case. Can we imagine a morality-blind family or tort law? The claim about legal accountability made here is that the adjudicators in healthy legal systems tend to be independent and impartial as between the parties, and that they make a good faith attempt at objectivity, *not* that they are wholly objective in their application of the law.

One might argue in agreement with Marxists and structuralist philosophers that the entire institution of law is so suffused with class or ideological bias that even the noblest of adjudicators cannot help but take the wrong side by exhibiting a systematic and pernicious class bias. Yet the historian E P Thompson, himself a Marxist, refuted these claims in his *Whigs and Hunters*, a study of the use of the Black Act 1723 to criminalize the encroachment by persons onto royal forests. He did so by affirming the very benefits set out here:

It is inherent in the especial character of law, as a body of rules and procedures, that it shall apply logical criteria with reference to standards of universality and equity. [. ..] Most men have a strong sense of justice, at least with regard to their own interests. If the law is evidently partial and unjust, then it will mask nothing, legitimize nothing, contribute nothing to any class's hegemony. The essential precondition for the effectiveness of law, in its function as ideology, is that it shall display an independence from gross manipulation and shall seem to be just.[53]

Thompson showed how particular laws were tools for extending and protecting class interests, but also that a system of at least reasonably impartial legal accountability (the 'rule of law') was more or less essential for the maintenance and legitimation of that system. That system to him represented a 'cultural achievement of universal significance' and the rule of law an 'unqualified human good' .[54]

Now, to invoke Thompson in this way is not a mere appeal to leftist authority to settle the matter of the impact of class bias on the law. That would be a fallacy, and there are anyway many others who might be cited for a contrary proposition. However, as with the views of Harold Laski that I discuss in the next section, the fact that Thompson pushed back against this aspect of Marxist doctrine is telling. It was, in my view, a rare moment of clarity and honesty within an industry

---

[51] Posner, *How Judges Think*, 25–9.

[52] Certainly Dworkin does not take such a view: see his *A Matter of Principle*, (Cambridge, Mass: Harvard University Press, 1985), ch 1.

[53] E P Thompson *Whigs and Hunters: The Origin of the Black Act* (New York: Pantheon Books, 1976), 262–3.

[54] Thompson, *Whigs and Hunters*, 265. This conclusion was treated by Thompson's left-wing contemporaries as 'apostasy', as Daniel H Cole puts it in 'An Unqualified Human Good: E.P. Thompson and the Rule of Law' *Journal of Law and Society* (2001) 28: 177, esp. at 189ff. Marx himself, and his later and most influential work, owed much to the protection of the rule of law in nineteenth century England.

of obfuscation. It is important to pin down the leftist objection, furthermore, to know whether it amounts to more than an evocative and ambivalent complaint about a defect in law. When those who advance the class bias argument actually confront the spectre of unaccountable power by considering the option as a real legislative possibility,[55] or see it in comparative historical perspective (as did Thompson, by comparison with other European states in the nineteenth century, and some obvious candidates in the twentieth), one is forced to be honest about the true significance of the claim. It states the limits of the benefit, rather than a negation of it. Those who press the point too far offer solace to tyrants.

5. Rule interpretation competence

Legal adjudicators are good at rule interpretation. The type of reasoning used in legal adjudication possesses several pertinent sub-features: it employs an elaborate set of interpretive cannons of interpretation;[56] it provides a suitably forensic process and forum for considering competing interpretations of complex texts; the respect for consistency (an observable objective of all well-functioning legal systems) produces fairness between similarly situated persons, and predictability for legislators; and the publication of decisions about interpretation, coupled with intense professional and appellate scrutiny, reinforces all the above and provides transparency and thus general accountability.

The greatest advantage of all the above is that it facilitates democratic government. The rule of law is an essential feature of a proper functioning democracy, and a body with rule interpretation competence is an essential feature of the rule of law. The rule of law is required in order for Parliament to be assured that its choices will be respected. A body with rule-interpretation competence of the sort described above protects such choices. When legislation is drafted, it is done consciously in awareness of the cannons of interpretation,[57] and in the expectation that courts will pronounce upon compliance. Any new government inherits a large range of past political commitments embodied in legislation. The rule of law guarantees that the government of the day is legally accountable for such commitments, and requires that (apart from the constitutional judicial review of statutes) they only be undone through the same forum in which they were enacted.

The relevance of rule-interpretation competence extends well beyond the interpretation of statutes. The legal regime governing a modern bureaucracy is also interlaced with regulations, guidance, circulars, precedent and stated policy. These standards pervade and structure the discretion of officials throughout government, and in Kenneth Culp Davis' view, their proliferation was crucial for promoting the rule of law in bureaucracy.[58] The profusion of such written standards, coupled with

---

[55] See the discussion in the next sub-section discussing Harold J Laksi's position on special courts for interpreting statutes.

[56] F A R Bennion (K E Goodall ed.) *Statutory Interpretation* (5th rev edn, London: Butterworths, 2007).

[57] Bennion, for example, was Parliamentary Counsel (drafting UK government legislation) from 1953–65 and 1973–5.

[58] Davis, *Discretionary Justice*, n 35 above.

legal accountability, means that government must operate in a reasonably transparent and consistent manner, treating like cases alike and providing real remedies for those adversely affected by executive conduct that diverges from the stated policy. This accountability empowers persons by conferring real rights on them (whose enforcement admittedly depends on the health of access to justice), by providing recourse to a system that formally demands a consistent interpretation and application of such standards. A further byproduct of the system is the preservation of the rationality and consistency of the entire scheme, which not only furthers respect for rule of law values (eg. predictability) but is also important for the effective delivery of policy and maintenance of clear lines of political accountability.

Objection:

• *Judges have a poor track record with statutory interpretation.*

The dangers of overzealous adherence to 'extravagant' notions of the rule of law are well known.[59] There is a voluminous critical literature, particularly in the United States, on what the correct approach to the interpretation of statutes ought to be — particularly agency statutory interpretation — replete with strong criticisms of existing and past approaches.[60] Early workers' compensation and industrial legislation in Britain was often interpreted in conservative ways that impeded statutory objectives.[61] One can agree with many of the criticisms found in such literature while also maintaining that rule interpretation competence is a prima facie benefit of legal accountability. The tenor of the criticisms here again speaks to the need for judicial restraint, not in total denial of benefit. This nuance is best exemplified in the position of the political theorist and public intellectual, Harold J Laski, who sat on the Donoughmore Committee that reported in 1932 on the appropriate types of accountability that might accompany the rapidly expanding role of administrative discretion and delegated legislation in the new British welfare state. Laski set out a separate opinion in an addendum to the Report of the Committee, commenting on the issue of whether to oust the jurisdiction of the law courts from the interpretation of statutes:[62]

I wholly concur in the conclusion of the Committee that it is undesirable to transfer the interpretation of statutes which define and control the administrative process (whether

---

[59] Davis, *Discretionary Justice,* 28–42; C Harlow and R Rawlings, *Law and Administration* (3rd edn, Cambridge: Cambridge University Press, 2009), ch 1.

[60] For some of the American literature, see Vermuele, *Judging under Uncertainty*, n 20 above, ch 7; W N Eskridge Jr *Dynamic Statutory Interpretation* (Cambridge, Mass: Harvard University Press, 1994); F B Cross *The Theory and Practice of Statutory Interpretation* (Stanford: Stanford University Press, 2009). See also C R Sunstein, 'Law and Administration After *Chevron' Columbia LR* (1990) 90: 2071; C R Farina, 'Statutory Interpretation and the Balance of Power in the Administrative State' *Columbia LR* (1989) 89: 452. For an interesting contrast with the UK position, see T A O Endicott *Administrative Law* (2nd edn, Oxford: Oxford University Press, 2011) at 325–330.

[61] See the 'Note by Professor Laski on the Judicial Interpretation of Statutes', Annex V to the *Report of the Committee on Ministers' Powers* (Donoughmore Committee), Cmd 4060/1932 (1932) 135–6. See also F Frankfurter and N Greene *The Labour Injunction* (New York: Macmillan, 1930).

[62] 'Note by Professor Laski on the Judicial Interpretation of Statutes'.

local or central) to special Courts. No gain which might result therefrom in flexibility of construction seems to me to counterbalance the value of the independent assessment of statutory intention which is now afforded by the ordinary Courts. The historical principle of the rule of law cannot, I think, be better protected than by making ordinary judges the men who decide the legality of executive action.

Laski was quick to add, however, that 'this is not to say the methods of interpretation now used by the Courts are satisfactory.'[63] The bulk of his note illustrated the potential dangers of judicial interpretation, outlining a critique of legal formalism in the United States and Britain that few liberals would disagree with today.[64] His concluding remark on interpretive doctrines fits with the conclusions of this essay.

6. Procedural fairness competence

The courts' competence in respect of procedural fairness is reflected well in their history of fashioning and protecting the rules of the paradigm of procedural justice, namely, the judicial process. This is reflected in the two principles of natural justice (ie. that an adjudicator must be impartial and hear both sides). Furthermore, judges have devised and evolved procedures concerning the admissibility of evidence, and procedures for pleading, notice to opposing parties, transparent reasons etc. These practices reflect a cultivated institutional memory concerning basic procedural fairness for parties to a dispute. The role for courts in giving such protection has been recognized around the world in both administrative and constitutional law.[65] Procedural fairness secures a range of ends, including individual dignity for the affected person, equal treatment of similarly situated persons, and accuracy in administrative and judicial decision-making.

Objection:

- *The judicial conception of procedural fairness is inappropriately dominated by the model of the trial.*

One concern is that judges may seek to impose the paradigm of the judicial process upon a complex bureaucracy that can ill-afford the procedural luxuries observed in the criminal and civil courts. Bureaucracies can groan under the weight and expense created by extensive oral hearings for items such as the termination of welfare benefits. This is the crux of Mashaw's argument in *Due Process in the Administrative State* (and his particular target was constitutional due process rights in the welfare state, a particularly difficult issue). [66] Mashaw felt that judges did not understand the dynamic impact that was created by their judgments, and they

---

[63] 'Note by Professor Laski on the Judicial Interpretation of Statutes', 135.
[64] 'Note by Professor Laski on the Judicial Interpretation of Statutes' at 135–6.
[65] See, generally, D Galligan *Due Process and Fair Procedures: A Study of Administrative Procedures* (Oxford University Press, Oxford, 1996); F Michelman, 'Formal and Associational Aims in Procedural Due Process' in J Penock and J Chapman (eds) *Due Process, Nomos XVIII* (New York University Press: New York, 1977).
[66] J L Mashaw *Due Process in the Administrative State* (New Haven: Yale University Press, 1985); see also Harlow and Rawlings, *Law and Administration*, n 59 above, ch 14.

were powerless to reverse changes they promoted that turned out to be dysfunctional. This can be connected more broadly with Vermeule's concern that judges cannot see the dynamic effects of their judgments, and that they should therefore employ a type of formalism that embraces strong judicial restraint.[67]

These are potent warnings, but none of the above suggests any more than a qualification to the claim that procedural fairness is one benefit of legal account-ability. Mashaw, notwithstanding his criticism, ultimately saw an essential role for legal accountability: 'Individualized hearings, before independent decision-makers with demands for proof and judgment on the record are a major bulwark against state oppression.'[68] Furthermore, the evolution of procedural rights in public law has proceeded at a glacial pace in the United Kingdom, a special light-touch review applies to fair trial rights in the administrative process (both in the UK and in the relevant Strasbourg authority under the ECHR),[69] and the American phenomenon of regulatory ossification is largely confined to that country.

7. Participation

A number of rights advocates claim that legally enforceable rights will provide a much-needed avenue of participation for those marginalized and vulnerable groups which are effectively excluded from legislative or executive decision-making.[70] On a more pedestrian level, trials and hearings give people the right to complain about the decision affecting them, and the enforceable power to be heard. Even a lost hearing is more satisfying than no hearing at all. The take-up rate of this right to a hearing is in fact very low, an issue driving extensive studies in legal needs.[71] However, the influence of law is felt well beyond the courtroom, in settlement activity, often made possible by the ultimate recourse to judicial remedies.[72] Expanded rules on standing and intervention have facilitated greater means for participation and representation.[73]

---

[67] Vermeule, *Judging under Uncertainty*, n 20 above.

[68] Mashaw, 'Bureaucracy, Democracy and Judicial Review', n 11 above.

[69] For UK administrative law, see *R v Home Secretary, ex parte Doody* [1994] AC 531 (HL). For the interpretation of Convention rights under the HRA1998, see *Ali v Birmingham City Council* [2010] UKSC 8; and for the position of the Strasbourg Court see *Bryan v United Kingdom* (1996) 21 EHRR 342 and *Tsfayo v United Kingdom* [2006] All ER D 177; (2006) 48 EHRR 18.

[70] Ely, *Democracy and Distrust*, n 48 above; A Kavanagh, 'Participation and Judicial Review: A Reply to Jeremy Waldron' *Law and Philosophy* (2003) 22: 451; S Fredman *Human Rights Transformed: Positive Rights and Positive Duties* (Oxford University Press, 2008), 77–9, 105–7. See also *I CON* (2007) 5: 183, the entire issue being an exploration of the comparative effectiveness of courts as a forum for the participation of the marginalized.

[71] H Genn *Hard Bargaining: Out of Court Settlement in Personal Injury Actions* (Oxford: Clarendon Press, 1987); M Galanter, 'Why the Haves Come out Ahead' *Law & Society Rev* (1974) 9: 95.

[72] V Bondy and M Sunkin, 'Settlement in Judicial Review Proceedings' *PL* [2009] 237.

[73] See JUSTICE, *To Assist the Court: Third Party Interventions in the UK* (London: JUSTICE, 2009). Cf Harlow, 'Public Law and Popular Justice', n 12 above; Stewart, 'The Reformation of American Administrative Law', n 12 above, 1760ff. Despite Stewart's criticisms of the model, see 1805–13 for his more nuanced conclusions.

Objections:

- *People are alienated by the judicial process and have little say in hearings.*

This claim is no doubt partly true, but often overstated. (Access to justice is particularly jurisdiction-specific, so I have chosen the UK as my home jurisdiction in the discussion that follows). In Hazel Genn's *Paths to Justice*, broad surveys of civil justice revealed, for instance, that courts and tribunals were considered more stressful and alienating than resolution by agreement.[74] Yet while eighty-five percent of tribunals and court users said they would definitely or probably repeat the process, only sixty-seven per cent of those using mediation said the same.[75] Most interestingly, the most common response of claimants disappointed with how they resolved their justiciable problem was that they did pursue sufficiently formal means.[76] This is not an incoherent set of results. Standing up for one's rights can be both frightening and ultimately rewarding.

What about lawyers, then, who do much of the standing up? Of those court and tribunal users represented by lawyers, ninety-three per cent of represented respondents said that they would not have been better off at the hearing without representation, and ninety-two per cent thought they were represented either very well or fairly well.[77] Sixty-five per cent said they had a chance to get across everything they wanted to say at the hearing, and another ten per cent said they got most of what they wanted to say across. About ninety per cent said they understood what was going on at the hearing. While it is wise not to be romantic about civil justice in the courts, we sell legal accountability short by understating its value for most citizens.

- *Only the rich have reasonable access to courts.*

That is quite a common claim, but the true picture is far more complex. According to Genn's study, over a quarter of those respondents who incurred legal costs in Britain were legally aided.[78] Other recent studies have found that judicial review is actually higher in London boroughs that are more marginalized and poorer.[79] Indeed, the poor in Britain are actually *more likely* to consult a lawyer in a grievance against the government than are the wealthy or the middle classes.[80] This phenomenon is not only explained by the UK's relatively generous legal aid system, though that is no doubt relevant. Herbert Kritzer consolidated comparative studies on legal needs covering eight countries.[81] His findings were 'remarkably consistent' in

---

[74] H Genn (et al) *Paths to Justice: What People Do and Think About Going to Law* (Oxford: Hart Publishing, 1999) 194–5.

[75] Genn *Paths to Justice*, 218, 222.   [76] Genn *Paths to Justice,* 205.

[77] Genn *Paths to Justice*, 220.   [78] Genn *Paths to Justice,* 166.

[79] L Platt, M Sunkin and K Calvo, 'Judicial Review Litigation as an Incentive to Change in Local Authority Public Services in England and Wales' *Journal of Public Administration Research and Theory* (2010) 20: 243.

[80] H. Kritzer, 'To Lawyer or Not to Lawyer? Is that the question?' *Journal of Empirical Legal Studies* (2008) 5: 875, fig.12 (citing the data of P Pleasence, N Balmer and A Buck, *Causes of Action: Civil Law and Social Justice* (2nd edn, London: Legal Services Research Centre, 2006)).

[81] Kritzer, 'To Lawyer or Not to Lawyer?, 875.

showing that 'income has relatively little impact on decisions to seek the assistance or advice of a lawyer.'[82]

- *Judicial review in fact disrupts a more meaningful mechanism for participation; namely, voting.*

This objection is ordinarily only true of the subset of cases involving the review of legislation for its constitutionality. The objection amounts to the following argument: the remedy given to the person who comes before the court invalidates a statute adopted in a procedure that gives more meaningful participation to everyone equally. Those whose decision is represented in the statute are not represented in the hearing at which their interests are effectively decided. In that sense, the 'participation' of one person or group in court is the negation of many others' participation at the ballot box. This argument is true in a formal sense, but its significance depends on (1) the quality of a claimant's participation in the legislative process, and (2) the adequacy of the representational role played by counsel for the state in such hearings. As to the first, John Hart Ely presented the most sustained analysis of how judicial review might compensate for the representative deficiencies of the majoritarian legislative process. As for the second, we must recall that the non-participation of the aggrieved voter in the legal process does not mean that she is not represented in the process. The state and judges alike both represent that public interest. And unlike the marginalized claimant in the political process, the average voter is *well-represented* in the legal process to the point of being presumed correct until an onerous burden is met in showing otherwise. In my view, nevertheless, this objection has enough to it to merit the adoption of a theory of constitutional judicial review that gives strong prominence to the issue of representation in judicial review.[83]

- *The administrative and legislative processes are far better at facilitating inclusion.*

People can participate in the legislative and administrative process by responding to consultation exercises during the green and white paper phases of the legislative process, or submitting observations to parliamentary committees, or lobbying parliamentarians by post, in the flesh at the constituency surgery, or by e-petition. In the United States, the Administrative Procedure Act 1946 provides for a quite elaborate notice-and-comment procedure for much rule-making. Advocacy groups need no lessons on the availability and limitations of these channels. The important point is that there is no reason to think that these various avenues of participation are incompatible with using adjudicators as well. Legal accountability offers individuals the right to lodge claims about compliance with public standards (law), not merely an additional view to be added to the heap.

---

[82] Kritzer, 'To Lawyer or Not to Lawyer?, 900. This discussion has been adapted from King, *Judging Social Rights*, n 22 above at 79–81, where some relevant further studies are considered, including those expressing reservations about Kritzer's conclusion.

[83] I have done so in King, *Judging Social Rights,* n 22 above, ch 6. See also the work of Rosalind Dixon, 'The Supreme Court of Canada' n 32 above.

8. Expressiveness

Legal accountability can play an expressive function in law by applying key principles, policies or other values in the text of published decisions. These values become part of the fabric of public discourse, and can have an impact in subtle ways. In Genn's study, nearly three quarters of respondents agreed that '[c]ourts are an important way for ordinary people to enforce their rights.'[84] Scholars also recognize the expressive function of law in enshrining values and providing a normative framework for moral debate, particularly with respect to legislation.[85] This is doubtless a key part of adjudication, in both private and public law, which employs a range of normative concepts such as fairness, reasonableness, discrimination, good faith, equity and so on. There is a range of important things that society cannot do without judicial or quasi-judicial hearing: child custody and child protection, criminal conviction, deportation, eviction, and many others. Our basic understanding of courts is that they ought to provide not just dispute resolution, but *justice*. As Owen Fiss stated: 'The judicial role is limited by the existence of constitutional values, and the function of the judiciary is to give meaning to those values.'[86] Variants of this view are also advanced in the work of Ronald Dworkin, T R S Allan, and Robert Alexy.

Expressiveness is not merely empty rhetoric, but it does have an uncertain relationship to consequences; a point that threatens its value as an instrument. The expressive elements of published legal judgments do not tend to generate large and sudden changes to institutions. Yet they may have real and valuable effects. For one, they can be of immediate and profound psychological importance to petitioners, for whom a declaration alone can constitute just satisfaction even of a human rights violation. More importantly, expressiveness about basic values can reinforce systemic values (eg. the rule of law, good administration) that buttress a complex system of politics. For example, the principle of the rule of law in the United Kingdom was developed first by the courts of law, expounded by some doctrinal writers, and later recognised by both Parliament and government as being a cardinal constitutional principle.[87] If Dicey were believed, most of the civil liberties the English came to cherish (and ultimately export) also arose this way.[88]

---

[84] Genn (et al), *Paths to Justice*, n 74 above at 227.

[85] C R Sunstein 'On the Expressive Function of Law' *U of Penn L Rev* (1995–6) 144: 2021; W van der Burg, 'The Expressive and Communicative Functions of Law, Especially with Regard to Moral Issues' *Law & Philosophy* (2001) 20: 31.

[86] O Fiss, 'Foreword: The Forms of Justice' *Harvard L Rev 1* (1979) 93: 1, 11.

[87] AV Dicey *Introduction to the Law of the Constitution* (8th edn, London: MacMillan, 1915), Pt II; *R v Secretary of State for the Home Department, ex p Simms* [2000] 2 AC 115 (HL); Constitutional Reform Act 2005, s 1. There is a brief mention of the principle in *The Cabinet Manual: A Guide to Laws, Conventions and Rules on the Operation of Government* (London: Cabinet Office, 2011), 49 [6.4].

[88] Dicey, *Introduction to the Law of the Constitution*, ch.V-VII. At 124, he contrasts the law of England with foreign bills of rights by arguing that 'with us freedom of person is not a special privilege but the outcome of the ordinary law of the land enforced by the Courts.'

Objection:

- *Symbolic legality is of limited value.*[89]

This objection is true, but consistent with what has been said above. Symbolism and expressiveness are of some value on an ethical level. Suppose that midway through some human rights or sexual harassment litigation, the respondent offers to settle by giving the claimant all that he or she seeks (including an apology). Would the claimant still have a good case for taking the claim forward, or should the court dismiss the case for mootness? The answer is that the claimant has a right not just to claim compensation, but justice. Legal accountability offers authoritative resolution, publicity, and an affirmation not just of wrongdoing or mistake, but of *illegality* and *injustice*. A symbolic end still counts as a real end, as it is connected with the well-being of individuals who have legitimate interests in obtaining that type of satisfaction.

I have already noted the way in which expressiveness can have important systemic consequences. Many thought *Brown v Board of Education* had this effect, though there is much evidence to the contrary.[90] Important cases can reinforce an attitude of respect for rights and the rule of law. These influences may be weak, but they are not negligible. And as Sunstein notes, expressiveness can also have important immediate consequences.[91] The common law facilitates its own growth by grand statements of expressive principle. Today's obiter dicta become tomorrow's ratio decidendi.

9. Publicity

Legal accountability can generate publicity and political salience. Litigation can become a locus for political action and can form an instrumental part of a political campaign. This is the key observation being returned from legal mobilization studies in law and politics, which document a certain symbiosis between legal and political avenues for change used by litigators seeking policy reform.[92] Episodes of political activity are followed by legal cases, which may lead to fruitful political outcomes even when cases are lost. Even awful judgments can lead to legislative amendment.[93] Controversy surrounding judicial rulings or court activity often ignites the public

---

[89] Rosenberg, *The Hollow Hope*, n 43 above at 424 ('[S]ymbolic victories may be mistaken for substantive ones, covering a reality that is distasteful.'); Mashaw, *Bureaucratic Justice*, n 13 above at 11 ('But what are we to do when symbolic legality wears thin?').

[90] 347 US 483 (1954). Rosenberg, *The Hollow Hope*, n 43 above; Klarman, *From Jim Crow to Civil Rights*, n 43 above.

[91] Sunstein, n 86 above, at 2045–2048. This has been confirmed in some studies: P Funk, 'Is there an Expressive Function of Law? An Empirical Analysis of Voting Laws with Symbolic Fines' *American Law and Economics Rev* (2007) 9: 135.

[92] See the studies cited above, n 42. For an excellent UK/Canadian study in this vein, see L Vanhala, *Making Rights a Reality? Disability Rights Activists and Legal Mobilization* (Cambridge: Cambridge University Press, 2011).

[93] As occurred in *R v Hillingdon LBC, ex p Puhlhofer* [1986] 1 AC 485 (HL) case (reversed in Parliament, in the Housing and Planning Act 1986, s14(2), amending the Housing Act 1985, s 58),

consciousness, media and political process. The interplay between courts, parliamentary committees, advocacy groups, and Parliament itself can mean that court battles actually invigorate the overall political process by focusing its attention on rights-issues, and by providing narratives that give living colour to general social problems. In this respect, even lost cases can represent political victories, as the exposure of poignant stories can create sympathy and increase the costs of political interference or apathy.[94]

Objection:

- *Assuming legal episodes do create publicity and political salience, it can be as negative as it is positive.*

The legal mobilization studies have shown that advocates do use legal battles in iterative combination with political campaigning to achieve their objectives. However, there are other case studies as well, demonstrating the phenomenon of backlash. Anyone familiar with the tabloid press in Britain will know that the salience of the HRA 1998 on its pages is no triumph for legal accountability. The backlash phenomenon in parts of America has been much worse. It has occured when groups mobilize in reaction to litigation, but in the effort of reversing the effects of the court judgment—sometimes violently (as in the case of reactionary racist groups in southern America after *Brown*), sometimes by means of agitating for constitutional amendment (as in many American states on the issue of gay marriage), or by mobilizing to advance a political agenda (such as libertarianism) through the courts and legislature, or by politicizing the judicial appointments process to an undue extent.[95] This phenomenon is less familiar to Commonwealth countries, but the experience in Britain is that the influential tabloid press has succeeded in generating considerable political opposition to human rights legislation.[96]

This is admittedly an area in which there is evidence that cuts both ways. I have elsewhere argued that the backlash phenomenon is both disputed in the United States and at any rate is a phenomenon that may be peculiar to that country in particular.[97] The argument that anti-human rights publicity generated by legal accountability

---

and with whether private care companies ought to be regarded as public authorities under the HRA 1998 (Health and Social Care Act 2008, s 145 reversing *YL v Birmingham CC* [2007] UKHL 27).

[94] This effect is often doubted, but it was what occurred, for instance, in the famous *R v Cambridge Health Authority, ex p B* [1995] 1 FLR 1056 (QB); 2 All ER 129 (CA) case (see C Ham, 'Tragic choices in health care: lessons from the Child B case' *British Medical Journal* (1999) 319: 1258). The same occurred in the protracted dispute concerning the Chagos Islanders, as recounted in the judgment of the House of Lords in *R (Bancoult) v Secretary of State for Foreign and Commonwealth Affairs (No 2)* [2008] UKHL 61. Vanhala, *Making Rights a Reality?* n 92 above, also documents a number of such cases.

[95] On civil rights and the backlash more generally, see Klarman, above note 43, ch.7. More generally, see R Post and R Siegal, 'Roe Rage: Democratic Constitutionalism and Backlash' *Harvard Civil Rights-Civil Liberties Law Review* (2007) 42: 373.

[96] As noted with great concern in Equality and Human Rights Commission, *Human Rights Inquiry: Report of the EHRC* (London: EHRC 2009).

[97] King, *Judging Social Rights*, n 22 above, ch 3.

can be politically regressive has little support in the United Kingdom. It is true that human rights cases have generated the ire of the press, but the agitation is for a return to the status quo before the adoption of the HRA 1998. That cannot be considered regress unless the HRA 1998 is considered progress. The argument is therefore self-defeating.

10. Inter-institutional collaboration

The process of legal accountability, and its reasoned interpretive output, in my view is better understood to be in a collaborative relationship with the other branches of government, than functioning as a mere 'check' or 'veto' upon them.[98] Are procedural fairness rights best understood as an impediment or a contribution to efficient administration? Does requiring agencies and ministers to act within the powers set out in their empowering statute interfere with effective government? Should the orders of the Information Tribunal to disclose information be regarded as fundamentally punitive, or ultimately as measures that can improve administration by rendering it more transparent? We *could* in each case frame the relationships as those of warden and delinquent. However, it is more accurate to understand them as akin to that between a free press and a well-functioning government. To say they are fundamentally 'opposed' is to misunderstand the relationship. The relationship is tense at times, but good government in fact *depends* on a free press, just as it depends on a healthy respect for the rule of law. When the government does its job the press helps it get the message out to the public. When it does not do its job or is evasive, it exposes the lapse in the hopes for correction.

In my view, each of the branches essentially collaborates (at a respectful distance) with the others in the implementation of key public goals, for example respect for human rights, allocative efficiency, environmental protection, public and workplace safety, the best interests of children, and many others. Parliament scrutinizes government on the implementation of these goals, and opens it up to challenge in myriad ways. Parliamentary committees offer important guidance and criticism on a range of matters considered by both the executive and the courts. The House of Lords Constitution Committee and the Joint Committee on Human Rights, though obviously attractive to lawyers, are nonetheless exemplars in this regard. Both engage in bill scrutiny and draw upon principles expounded by courts as well as other non-legal sources of constitutional principle and policy. The executive, for its part, also engages in considerable work at promoting and giving effect to the aforementioned principles. While it takes the lead with respect to the environment, efficiency, and regulation of the workplace, it also plays a strong role in promoting respect for human rights principles. Ministers must carry out compliance research before issuing statements of compatibility under s19 of the HRA 1998.

---

[98] For a discussion of both the traditional theory and a more modern theory of the separation of powers that accords better with the view presented here, see E Carolan *The New Separation of Powers* (Oxford: Oxford University Press, 2010). For judicial review as a veto, which I consider contrary to the analysis here, see R H Fallon Jr, 'The Core of an Uneasy Case for Judicial Review' *Harvard L Rev* (2008) 121: 1693.

The government also creates and/or funds bodies that are vigilant in addressing human rights issues, such as the Equality and Human Rights Commission and Citizen's Advice. Furthermore it has issued a considerable amount of guidance to its own departments and to local authorities on the topic of human rights.[99]

This type of collaboration is a phenomenon, but it is also a prima facie benefit offered by courts because they have institutional features that can further it. In particular, general jurisdiction, an inherent law reforming power, and remedial discretion allow adjudicators, especially in public law, to complement the system of accountability by adjusting the scope of review and range of substantive remedies to shifting demand over time. For example, in the early days of the welfare state, when there was a perceived need for courts not to impede the practice of demolishing housing deemed unfit for human habitation, the House of Lords refused to extend to an aggrieved landlord a right to an oral hearing, and a right to see the report of the inspector that formed the basis for the closing order.[100] By 1964, the House of Lords decided in *Ridge v Baldwin* that there could be a duty of procedural fairness in respect of ordinary administrative decisions as well as those by judicial or quasi-judicial bodies.[101] Thirty years later, what was announced as possible in 1964 was confirmed as always applicable in *ex p Doody*, but with the caveat that the requirements of fairness were to be particularly flexible and depend entirely on the circumstances.[102] In all three cases, the courts adjusted to the needs of modernizing administration and administrative justice. The development is not always a matter of increased judicial scrutiny, either. For example, there has been an increased recent emphasis on the importance of deference to tribunal expertise,[103] which is something of a departure from the formal approach taken in cases such as *Anisminic v Foreign Compensation Commission.*[104]

When the comity between institutions is healthy, it is possible for the inherent flexibility of public law principles and remedies to be adjusted as needed to suit evolving needs for accountability in the contemporary state. The remedy of declaratory relief, in particular, offers the possibility of facilitating this type of collaboration by giving the executive latitude by way of response. A declaration of incompatibility under s 4 of the HRA 1998 offers similar latitude to Parliament in respect of primary legislation found incompatible with the European Convention. This flexibility and adaptability breeds comity and collaboration, which in turn

---

[99] On guidance, see Dept. of Health, *Human Rights in Health Care: A Framework for Local Action* (2nd edn, 2008); Dept. of Communities and Local Government, *Guidance for Local Authorities on Contracting for Services in Light of the Human Rights Act 1998* (2005); Borders and Immigration Agency, *Asylum Policy Instructions: European Convention on Human Rights* (2006, 're-branded' in 2008) and *Article 8 of the ECHR* (2009) and *Considering Human Rights Claims* (2009). Other codes of practice highlight the importance of compliance with the HRA 1998 among their general principles: see Dept. of Health, *Code of Practice: The Mental Health Act 1983* (2008) ch 1, esp.1.7. On the bureaucratic impact of the HRA 1998, see EHRC, *Human Rights Inquiry,* n 96 above.

[100] *Local Government Board v Arlidge* [1915] AC 120 (HL).

[101] *Ridge v Baldwin* [1964] AC 40 (HL).

[102] *R v Home Secretary, ex p Doody* [1994] AC 531, 560 (HL).

[103] *R (Cart) v The Upper Tribunal; MR (Pakistan) v The Upper Tribunal* [2011] UKSC 28 [48]-[49].

[104] [1969] 2 AC 147 (HL).

allows legal accountability to meet the ebb and flow of demand for it. Since accountability in modern government promotes fairness, individual dignity, the rule of law, and respect for democratic accountability, its ultimate value is or at any rate can be quite positive.

Objection:

- *Legal accountability is comparatively quite rigid.*

Adjudication initially appears to be quite rigid. It must be triggered by a petitioner. There is a limited range of remedies. The court cannot make recommendations or insist on apologies, or (generally speaking) call large meetings to thrash things out and compromise. It is also constrained doctrinally in all the ways mentioned above. And there are strong limits on what kind of further research judges can do when an issue is raised in litigation. They cannot (in the common law world) visit the site of the disturbance and knock on the neighbours' doors.

This is all true, but these limitations flow from the same features that give legal accountability its hard edge, its relative degree of autonomy, and its constitutional authority. Its working methods are not as flexible as those of a minister or inspector, but neither is the judge removable. And judges cannot change their minds from one day to the next, but nor should they when their decisions are reported and relied upon. The fact is that legal accountability is flexible enough to facilitate adaptation and collaboration over time, but its flexibility is suited to its character as a potent form of relief. Furthermore, different potential forms of legal accountability show different potential for flexible approaches. The Parliamentary Ombudsman shares many important attributes with legal accountability. Yet the ombudsman also has investigative powers, has fashioned principles of good administration, and commonly makes policy recommendations that aim to improve administration. While there are occasional areas of friction,[105] her role is essentially complementary rather than entirely antagonistic to parliamentary politics.

D. Conclusion

The ten prima facie benefits outlined above in my view constitute a core of instrumental value offered by legal accountability. In most cases, the benefit asserted is at least to some extent contingent. It is not asserted that the existence of each feature leads inexorably to the attainment of a beneficial end (net of its costs). It is rather contended that in many systems of legal accountability that possess these features, it will be common for them to function as prima facie benefits that are nonetheless rebuttable. The benefits, again, are: focus; principled reasoning; constitutional authority; independence and impartiality; rule-interpretation competence; procedural fairness competence; participation; expressiveness; publicity;

---

[105] R Kirkham, 'Challenging the Authority of the Ombudsman: The Parliamentary Ombudsman's Special report on Wartime Detainees' *MLR* (2006) 69: 792.

and inter-institutional collaboration. Whether these prima facie benefits amount to actual benefits will depend on the contexts in which they are applied. It is hoped the list will help point out fruitful areas for inquiry, and perhaps emphasize, as a form of feedback, which aspects of legal accountability stand out as particularly important for securing these prima facie benefits. For instance, the requirement of giving reasoned decisions appears to be more greatly respected in some legal systems than in others. And of course, in those systems where the judiciary is not independent, the analysis suggests that we have reason to doubt whether it is appropriately called legal accountability at all.

This leaves one difficult methodological issue that I will address by way of conclusion. It is the problem of incommensurability. A list of benefits and stated costs may imply to some that I envisage some heaven of commensuration wherein if we had all relevant information, all the variables could be compared and that an arithmetical operation would yield the answer to any question of legal institutional design. I have no such idea in mind. At the end of any fully informed analysis, some public figure will need to decide just how much individual consideration is worth a reduction of allocative efficiency, and whether some amount of judicial independence is worth a novel extension of responsibilities through, for example, a new tribunal or bill of rights. The fact that these public choices require difficult judgement and are not reducible to any calculus does not mean that an account of benefits and costs is useless to the task. Sure, someone must simply decide, but they must decide in light of the best information. And if we accept that legal accountability is a means, we must have an approach to public decision-making that is susceptible to evidence of its success and costs before any sensible choices can be made.

PART III

7

Accountability, Human Rights Adjudication and the Human Rights Act 1998

*Alison L Young**

Accountability is both an attractive and an elusive concept. Understood narrowly, it refers to the practice of 'giving account' to another, providing an explanation or justification of conduct. In its broad sense, accountability expands to incorporate a normative dimension. A body that can be held to account for its actions is more legitimate than one that is not accountable; any practice that enhances account-ability thereby enhances legitimacy.[1] Mark Bovens defines accountability in its narrow sense as 'a relationship between an actor and a forum, in which the actor has an obligation to explain and to justify his or her conduct, the forum can pose questions and pass judgement, and the actor may face consequences.'[2] Understood in this sense, human rights adjudication is but one means through which public authorities can be held to account for actual and potential human rights abuses. In its broader sense, conceptions of accountability have been used to provide a justifi-cation of human rights adjudication. This is most clearly seen in the concept of the 'culture of justification' found in the work of Etienne Mureinik, David Dyzenhaus, and Murray Hunt.[3]

The extent to which the Human Rights Act 1998 (HRA 1998) has enhanced accountability in the narrow sense has been extensively discussed in the academic literature, particularly concerning the way in which dialogue may operate to bal-ance legal and political mechanisms of control of human rights, particularly as

---

* Fellow in Law, Hertford College, Oxford. The author wishes to thank Mark Elliott and the editors for their extremely helpful comments on earlier drafts.

[1] M Bovens, 'Analysing and Assessing Accountability: a Conceptual Framework' *European LJ* (2007) 13: 447, 449-50.

[2] Bovens n 1, 450. *Cf* C Harlow and R Rawlings, who question whether sanctions are required for the narrow definition of accountability in C Harlow and R Rawlings, 'Promoting Accountability in Multilevel Governance: a Network Approach' *European LJ* (2007) 13: 542, 545.

[3] D Dyzenhaus, 'The Legitimacy of Legality' *University of Toronto L J* (1996) 46: 129; D Dyzenhaus, 'Law as Justification: Etienne Mureinik's Conception of Legal Culture' *South African Journal on Human Rights* (1998) 14:11; M Hunt, 'Sovereignty's Blight: Why Contemporary Public Law Needs the Concept of "Due Deference"' in N Bamforth and P Leyland (eds), *Public Law in a Multi-layered Constitution* (Oxford: Hart Publishing, 2003) 339; M Cohen-Eliya and I Porat, 'Proportionality and the Culture of Justification' *American Journal of Jurisprudence* (2009) 463.

regards control over legislation.[4] I have argued earlier that accountability may not be enhanced due to the way in which courts have a tendency to defer when defining Convention rights, as opposed to defining a right and using s 4 declarations of incompatibility. To use deference in this manner weakens the scrutiny of the court over human rights whilst also removing further political scrutiny following a declaration of incompatibility.[5]

This chapter will focus upon accountability in the normative sense, examining in particular the way in which 'accountability' has been used to justify judicial review and, more specifically, the extent to which the 'culture of justification' provides an account of a specific theory of human rights adjudication. It will argue that difficulties arise as to the way in which these theories of adjudication apply in practice. Far from providing the transparency required by a culture of justification, the argument is made that current case law fails to provide sufficient certainty, undermining accountability. This chapter will argue that these difficulties are not merely caused by practical problems. There are also conceptual problems arising from a mismatch between theories of proportionality and of deference. The chapter will firstly provide a brief overview of the HRA 1998 and its relationship to mechanisms of accountability. Secondly, it will explain how the culture of justification is used to legitimize human rights adjudication and how the current case law does not appear to provide sufficient clarity, before explaining these possible weaknesses and suggesting possible modifications to enhance accountability.

A. Accountability and the Human Rights Act 1998

The HRA 1998 is regarded as an example of a 'commonwealth' model of constitutionalism.[6] The HRA 1998 does not empower the judiciary to strike down legislation that contravenes human rights. Instead, it creates a series of legal and political controls over the executive and the legislature. These controls are found in ss 3, 4, 6 and 19 of the HRA 1998. Legal control is exerted over administrative acts through s 6, which makes it unlawful for a public authority to act contrary to

---

[4] See D Nicol, 'The Human Rights Act and the politicians' *Legal Studies* (2004) 24: 451; S Gardbaum, 'The New Commonwealth Model of Constitutionalism' *American Journal of Comparative Constitutional Law* (2001) 49: 707; R Clayton, 'Judicial Deference and "Democratic Dialogue": the Legitimacy of human rights intervention under the Human Rights Act 1998' *Public Law* [2004] 33; T R Hickman, 'Constitutional Dialogue, constitutional theories and the Human Rights Act 1998' *Public Law* [2005] 306; A L Young *Parliamentary Sovereignty and the Human Rights Act* (Oxford: Hart Publishing, 2009), Chs 5, 6; A S Butler, 'Interface between the Human Rights Act 1998 and other enactments: pointers from New Zealand' *European Human Rights Law Review* [2000] 249; A S Butler 'The Bill of Rights Debate: Why the New Zealand Bill of Rights Act 1990 is a bad model for Britain' *Oxford Journal of Legal Studies* (1997) 17: 323 with regard to New Zealand.
[5] A L Young, 'Is Dialogue working under the Human Rights Act?' *Public Law* [2011] 772, 778-81.
[6] S Gardbaum *The New Commonwealth Model of Constitutionalism: Theory and Practice* (Cambridge University Press: Cambridge 2012); 'The New Commonwealth Model of Constitutionalism' n 4; 'Reassessing the New Commonwealth Model of Constitutionalism' *International Journal of Constitutional Law* (2010) 8: 167.

Convention rights. This control is easily classified as a form of accountability in the narrow sense. Public authorities are held to account for their actions to another, the judiciary. There are legal consequences should their actions fail to comply with Convention rights. What is harder to ascertain is whether the legal and political controls over Acts of Parliament can be accurately described as forms of accountability.

The strongest form of legal control over Acts of Parliament is found in s 3 of the HRA 1998, which requires courts, so far as it is possible to do so, to read and give effect to Acts of Parliament in a manner compatible with Convention rights. However, there are difficulties that arise when classifying this as a form of accountability. Bovens' model of accountability has three components: (i) a forum that either investigates or passes judgment; (ii) an obligation placed upon the actor to account for or justify his actions; and (iii) possible consequences placed by the forum upon the actor held to account for his or her actions. S 3 provides a means through which actions of the legislature can be scrutinized by another body, the judiciary. However, when reading legislation so as to comply with Convention rights, the court does not focus upon the actions of the legislature, holding them to account for their inability to legislate so as to protect Convention rights. Rather, the focus of the decision of the court is upon the words of the legislation, investigating whether its provisions are capable of being read so as to protect Convention rights.[7] There is no obligation placed upon the legislature to explain or justify its conduct; its role, instead, is to argue that the legislation in question is compatible with Convention rights. A possible exception to this focus is found in the scrutiny of the actions of Parliament in *Animal Defenders International v Secretary of State for Culture Media and Sport* concerning the enactment of s 321(3) of the Communications Act 2003, where the court scrutinized the conduct of Parliament and the Joint Committee of Human Rights, reaching the conclusion that the legislative provision in question was not incompatible with Convention rights.[8] This difference may be explained as the Broadcasting Act 2003 was enacted following a s 19(1)(b) statement, where the Minister promoting the bill was not able to state that it was compatible with Convention rights but that, nevertheless, the government wished to enact the legislation in question.

Second, it is not clear that the legislature faces any consequences as a result of its legislation being interpreted so as to comply with Convention rights. It is true that Convention-compatible interpretations of legislation may mean that policy objectives of the legislation in question can no longer be achieved. However, given that most legislation is initiated by the government, this may be regarded more as a sanction for the government than for the legislature. In addition, the government called upon to argue that legislation is compatible with Convention rights may not be the government responsible for the legislation in question. It may not be their policy objectives that are called to account. In addition, obligations that arise from Convention-compatible interpretations of legislation may fall upon

---

[7] See in particular the analysis of the seminal case of *Ghaidan v Godin-Mendoza* [2004] UKHL 30, [2004] 2 AC 447.

[8] [2008] UKHL 15; [2008] 1 AC 1312, [13]-[26].

private individuals as opposed to the government or Parliament. For example, the Convention-compatible reading of legislation in *Ghaidan v Godin-Mendoza* imposed a legally enforceable obligation upon Mr Ghaidan, the landlord, to extend a protected tenancy to the same-sex partner of a deceased protected tenant. It was Mr Ghaidan and not the government that faced consequences for the legislator's failure to fulfil its human rights obligations.

Finally, it is possible for the legislature to avoid accountability by enacting legislation specifically designed to counteract a Convention-compatible re-reading of legislation by the courts. S 3 places courts under a limited obligation—to read legislation in a manner compatible with Convention rights 'so far as possible'. *Ghaidan v Godin-Mendoza* states that it is not possible for the courts to read legislation in a manner compatible with Convention rights where to do so would contradict a fundamental feature of that legislation. As such, it is possible for the legislature to undermine the legal control of the courts by enacting legislation, a fundamental feature of which is to re-instate the wording of the legislation in question. Indeed, it is possible for the legislature to go further and to overturn the HRA 1998. It is hard to conclude that the HRA 1998 provides an effective form of accountability over the legislature given this power of the legislature to effectively avoid any consequences and to undermine the very mechanism that may be used to bring it to account for its actions.

The final form of control over Acts of Parliament is found in ss 4 and 19 of the Act, which facilitate political controls. S 19 requires that the minister in charge of a bill must, before the second reading of the bill, make a statement to Parliament either that the bill in question is compatible with Convention rights,[9] or that the government wishes to enact the legislation anyway, despite the inability to assert that the bill is compatible with Convention rights.[10] These statements help to facilitate political debate which focuses upon human rights, assessing the impact of legislation upon fundamental human rights. Parliament is aided in these debates by the work of the Joint Committee on Human Rights, one of whose roles is to produce reports concerning the impact of legislation on Convention rights. S 4 of the HRA 1998 empowers courts of the level of the high court and above to issue a declaration of incompatibility when the court is unable to read and give effect to legislation in a manner compatible with Convention rights. Declarations of incompatibility do not affect the legal force, validity or effect of legislation declared incompatible with Convention rights. However, political pressure may ensure that the government responds to declarations of incompatibility, amending legislation so as to ensure its compatibility with Convention rights. In addition, individuals still retain the right to petition the European Court of Human Rights. If an individual succeeds before the Strasbourg Court, the government will be placed upon an obligation in international law to remedy the breach of Convention rights and may be required to pay damages.

These political controls are also difficult to classify as complying with the ideal of accountability. It is hard to identify a forum to which the legislature is held

---

[9] HRA 1998, s 19(1)(a).   [10] HRA 1998, s 19(1)(b).

to account for its actions. Political debate in the Houses of Parliament may be regarded as a forum in which the government is held to account for its actions by the legislature. It is, however, difficult to classify the electorate, or the media institutions who report on political events, as a specific forum. Questions may be asked in both Houses of Parliament and the Joint Committee on Human Rights is able to question ministers and frequently asks questions of ministers regarding their response, or lack of one, to declarations of incompatibility and negative judgments of the Strasbourg Court.[11] As such the government may be called to account to explain its actions. Problems arise with regard to the possible consequences for failing to protect Convention rights. The government may face consequences of losing political support either in the Houses of Parliament or with the electorate if it fails to protect Convention rights. However, as recent events concerning prisoner voting affirm, support may also be won for standing firm in the face of pressure from 'European' institutions and continuing to support legislation deemed by the Strasbourg Court to be incompatible with Convention rights.[12] In addition, as the HRA 1998 is not legally entrenched, it is possible for the government to enact legislation to overturn its provisions. Despite this, the government does respond to the majority of declarations of incompatibility, and decisions of the Strasbourg Court, by modifying legislation to ensure its compatibility with Convention rights.[13]

In conclusion, although the HRA 1998 provides for a range of political and legal controls over administrative acts and legislation, it is difficult to regard these controls as providing an effective means of holding the government to account for its legislative actions. The more traditional legal control over administrative actions of the government and public authorities provides the most effective means of accountability. These conclusions may explain the mixed reactions regarding the success of the HRA 1998. In particular, it may explain why advocates of political protections of human rights are nevertheless sceptical as to whether the enactment of the HRA 1998 has improved the protection of human rights in the UK. Although the HRA 1998 may provide for a series of political controls, the inability of these controls to match the ideals of accountability may explain why it is still regarded by some as futile.[14]

---

[11] See <http://www.parliament.uk/business/committees/committees-a-z/joint-select/human-rights-committee/> for a list of recent reports and actions regarding declarations of incompatibility and adverse judgments of the Strasbourg Court.

[12] <http://www.telegraph.co.uk/news/uknews/law-and-order/9287633/We-must-defy-Strasbourg-on-prisoner-votes.html>; <http://www.dailymail.co.uk/debate/article-2148987/Prisoner-voting-rights-David-Camerons-chance-deliver-Britain.html>; <http://www.economist.com/blogs/bagehot/2011/02/prisoners_voting_rights>

[13] See 'Enhancing Parliament's Role in Relation to Human Rights Judgments' 15th Report of the Joint Committee of Human Rights, 2009-10 Session, <http://www.publications.parliament.uk/pa/jt200910/jtselect/jtrights/85/8502.htm>.

[14] J Ewing and J-C Tham, 'The Continuing Futility of the Human Rights Act 1998' *Public Law* [2008] 668.

B. The Culture of justification

The HRA 1998 may not provide an ideal means through which to hold the government and Parliament to account for legislation which contravenes Convention rights. Nevertheless the HRA 1998 may uphold normative ideals of accountability through facilitating a culture of justification. To assess this, we need first to delineate what is meant by the culture of justification, before assessing its requirements as a normative conception of accountability and whether the HRA 1998 matches these normative ideals.

Dyzenhaus describes the culture of justification as providing a middle ground between the extremes of the culture of reflection and the culture of neutrality.[15] A 'culture' is best understood as a series of values which provide normative justification for the powers of the institutions of government, understood in its broad sense to encompass the judiciary. The culture of reflection can be illustrated by the work of Bentham, who advocated legislation as the ideal form of law-making, reflecting the majority choices of the citizens governed by this legislation. The role of courts is merely to interpret legislation, ensuring that their interpretations correspond to the wishes of the legislature, reflecting majority preferences. In contrast, the culture of neutrality regards legitimacy as stemming from liberal principles, which underpin democracy. The role of the judiciary is to uphold these liberal principles, ensuring that they are not overridden by democratic decision-makers.

From this brief outline, one can begin to see how the culture of reflection and the culture of neutrality provide competing normative accounts of the role of the court and competing models of judicial review.[16] The culture of reflection underpins the ultra vires theory of judicial review. According to this theory, judicial review is justified as a means by which the judiciary can ensure that the administration does not transgress the scope of its powers granted to it by the legislature. If the administration were to act beyond the scope of its powers, it would act contrary to the wishes of the electorate, as expressed in the legislation enacted by Parliament. Were the courts to strike down actions of the administration for any reason other than it having transgressed the scope of its powers, their actions would no longer be normatively justifiable.

The culture of neutrality is reflected in some interpretations of the common law theory of judicial review, which regards judicial review as legitimate when it upholds constitutional principles, often reflecting the values of liberalism, found in the common law. Actions of the administration are legitimate not because they are within the sphere of power granted to them by the legislature, but because they comply with legitimate principles of the common law. These principles derive their legitimacy, for the majority of common law theorists, from the value of the substantive

---

[15] D Dyzenhaus, 'The Legitimacy of Legality', n 3.
[16] The term 'model' is used here to recognize that the justifications presented here are simplifications and are meant to provide an account of general themes running through schools of thought that underpin more specific and precise theories of justification of judicial review.

principles reflected in the common law. The court is justified, therefore, in overturning actions of the administration that contravene these common law constitutional principles.

Mureinik's approach to administrative law provides the best explanation of how the culture of justification holds the middle ground between the culture of reflection and the culture of neutrality. Mureinik's approach was developed in the face of providing a normative justification for the role of the court under the Apartheid regime. Mureinik classified the prevailing culture under Apartheid in South Africa as a culture of authority. Under the culture of authority, the legislature took actions that were upheld by the judiciary, often due to the existence of ouster clauses removing judicial review, but where the legislation enacted did not reflect the view of the majority of the population governed by that legislation. As such, an application of an ultra vires theory of administrative law failed to provide a justification for judicial review. The Apartheid regime also posed problems for the culture of neutrality, particularly where this was based upon Dworkin's justification of law as integrity. Apartheid laws are hard to 'fit' with the liberal principles of morality needed to overturn it, yet without this element of fit and integrity it was in turn hard to justify the role of the judiciary to uphold these liberal principles over the will of the legislature unless these principles could be justified as universal or objective. However, Mureinik doubted the ability of the judiciary to provide a clear set of objective, non-contestable principles that could be used to justify the overriding of legislation.

Mureinik's theory aimed to respond to these pressures. The culture of justification aims, in part, to promote accountability. Mureinik argued that a focus on accountability can provide a more justifiable means of promoting substantive values when these are not reflected in the law. He does not advocate that the judiciary should strike down actions of the legislature that undermine liberal principles. Nor does he advocate that courts should correct actions of the administration that are contrary to liberal rights.[17] However, neither should courts merely ensure that the actions of the administration are within the scope of powers granted to them by the legislation. Courts are required to develop stronger procedural protections perhaps in the face of apparently contradictory legislation, particularly regarding the requirement that reasons are provided for the actions of the administration and the legislature.[18] This provision of reasons facilitates the ability of the judiciary to hold the administration and the legislature to account through a detailed scrutiny of justifications and reasons provided for their actions.

The culture of justification is not merely concerned with enforcing procedural protections and the duty to provide reasons. This can be seen in particular in the

---

[17] E Mureinik, 'A Bridge to Where? Introducing the Interim Bill of Rights' *South African Journal of Human Rights* (1994) 10: 31; D Dyzenhaus, 'Law as Justification: Etienne Mureinik's conception of legal culture', n 3.

[18] A possible example of this in English law could be *R v Secretary of State for the Home Department ex p Al Fayed* [1998] 1 WLR 763, where the court required sufficient notice of a decision to be provided to the applicants to enable them to exercise their appeal rights, despite an express statement in statutory provisions that reasons need not be provided for the decision.

work of David Dyzenhaus and Murray Hunt, both of whom use the culture of justification to justify a theory of human rights adjudication which focuses upon substantive controls, particularly relying upon proportionality and deference. There is a plethora of conceptions of proportionality. In this context, it is best understood as a legal test that is used to determine the extent to which the state can enact measures that harm human rights. When balancing rights against other legitimate aims, the state may only take a measure that places a proportionate restriction upon the human right in question. A culture of justification requires that courts examine the reasons provided by the executive or legislature to justify their actions, ensuring that any purported restriction of a right is proportionate. Deference is used to modify the intensity of the scrutiny of the court.

C. The Human Rights Act 1998 and the culture of justification

At first glance, it would appear that the HRA 1998, as interpreted by the case law, upholds the values of accountability found in the culture of justification. Ss 3 and 4 make it clear that the court cannot strike down legislation that is incompatible with Convention rights. It is also clear that courts are not merely enforcing the will of the legislature when reading and giving effect to legislation so as to ensure it complies with Convention rights. *Ghaidan v Godin-Mendoza* makes it clear that courts can read legislation in a manner compatible with Convention rights even when the wording of legislation is not ambiguous, thus providing a means whereby the courts can uphold Convention rights even though the wording of legislation may appear to contradict this.[19] Moreover, courts do use the proportionality test when applying ss 3, 4 and 6 of the HRA 1998. In addition, there is evidence that the courts are requiring that the executive and the legislature provide more detailed reasons and justifications for their actions when applying the proportionality test.[20]

However, difficulties arise when we examine the more precise requirements of a theory of human rights adjudication based upon the culture of justification. Firstly, it is clear from the work of David Dyzenhaus and Murray Hunt that judicial review for human rights requires a particular conception of deference—deference as respect as opposed to deference as submission—if it is to further the ideal of the culture of justification. Although there is evidence that English courts adopt a conception of deference as respect, there are instances when the application of deference as respect appears to collapse into deference as submission. As such, courts could fail to provide adequate scrutiny. Secondly, although there is some evidence of courts focusing on scrutinizing the reasons provided by the administration for their actions, courts still appear to focus predominantly on assessing the substance

---

[19] *Ghaidan v Godin-Mendoza* [2004] UKHL 30; [2004] 2 AC 447, [28]-[30] (Lord Nicholls); [44] (Lord Steyn); [67] (Lord Millett).
[20] *R (Quila) v Secretary of State for the Home Department; R(Bibi) Secretary of State for the Home Department* [2011] UKSC 45; [2012] AC 621.

of the legislation or the action of the administration, calling into question the extent to which courts are upholding a culture of justification and facilitating accountability, or, instead, focusing upon upholding liberal principles of human rights and overturning actions that are contrary to liberal principles of human rights. Third, Hunt and Dyzenhaus refer to a conception of deference where the courts 'give weight' to the decisions of the administration or the legislature. However, English case law does not only refer to deference as 'giving weight' but also to 'modifying the stringency' with which the test of proportionality is applied. Although this may appear a minor problem, the way in which this is applied may, in practice, mean that proportionality is no longer applied as the standard of review in human rights adjudication as required by the culture of justification. These potential deficiencies may detract from the aim of facilitating accountability and justification.

1. Respect or submission?

Deference as respect occurs when 'the court gives some weight to a decision of a primary decision-maker for an articulated reason, as part of its overall review of the justifications for the decision'.[21] It is contrasted with deference as submission, which occurs 'when the court treats a decision or an aspect of it as non-justiciable, and refuses to enter on a review of it because it considers it beyond its competence'.[22] The weight given by the court depends upon an analysis of the relative constitutional and institutional features of the legislature, the executive, and the courts. Constitutional features depend upon the relative constitutional positions of these institutions, recognizing the democratic mandate of the legislature and the constitutional function of the court to uphold the rule of law. Institutional features refer to the relative expertise of the legislature, the executive, and the courts. Both depend upon the specific context of the decision or action falling to be examined by the courts. Deference as respect occurs when the judiciary respects the opinion of the executive or legislature, but still determines for itself whether an Act of Parliament or the actions of a public authority contravene Convention rights. Deference as submission occurs when courts accept the determinations of the legislature or executive as a correct account of the definition and application of the Convention right in question.[23] However, it can be hard to delineate between the two, especially if they are viewed as a matter of degree. How much respect can be paid to the executive or legislature, or weight be given to their opinions, before the judiciary merely accepts the decision of the executive or legislature as correct?

The potential for collapse can be illustrated by Lord Hoffmann's analysis of deference in *R (Prolife Alliance) v British Broadcasting Corporation (Prolife)*.[24] Prolife

---

[21] M Hunt, 'Sovereignty's Blight: Why Contemporary Public Law needs the Concept of "Due Deference"' in N Bamforth and P Leyland (eds) *Public Law in a Multi-Layered Constitution* (2003: Hart Publishing: Oxford) 337, 347.

[22] Hunt, 'Sovereignty's Blight' n 21, 346-7.

[23] D Dyzenhaus, 'The Politics of Deference: Judicial Review and Democracy' in M Taggart (ed), *The Province of Administrative law* (Oxford: Hart Publishing, 1997) 279, 286.

[24] [2003] UKHL 23; [2004] 1 AC 185.

wished to broadcast pictures of aborted foetuses as part of its electoral broadcast. The BBC forbade Prolife from broadcasting these pictures, requiring instead that the commentary be accompanied by a blank screen with the word 'censored' in place of pictures of aborted foetuses. The Court of Appeal concluded that the broadcasting restriction contravened Prolife's right to freedom of expression found in art 10 of the European Convention on Human Rights (ECHR) and Sch.1 of the HRA 1998. The House of Lords disagreed. Lord Hoffmann in particular focused on the legislative scheme which governed the powers of the BBC. The legislation made it clear that the BBC had an obligation to restrict the material it broadcast in order to protect the moral sensitivities of the audience. He concluded that such a legislative scheme would not contravene art 10 ECHR, which would enable restrictions to be placed on the right to freedom of expression in order to protect the moral sensitivities of the audience. Once he had reached this conclusion, it was clear that the BBC was entitled to apply general standards in order to ascertain whether material would offend moral sensitivities and, therefore, should not be broadcast:

Once one accepts that the broadcasters were entitled to apply generally accepted standards, I do not see how it was possible for a court to say that they were wrong.[25]

This would appear to advocate a model of deference as submission. If it is not possible for the court to say that the BBC was wrong in its assessment of the balance to be made between freedom of expression and the protection of the moral sensitivities of others, then it would appear that the court must merely accept the opinion of the BBC. It need not make its own assessment as to the balance to be drawn between freedom of expression and the protection of moral sensitivities in order to provide its own account of whether the BBC had breached the right to freedom of expression.

However, Lord Hoffmann later argues that:

Public opinion in these matters is often diverse, sometimes unexpected and in constant flux. General accepted standards on these questions are not a matter of intuition on the part of elderly male judges... I would therefore hesitate a good deal before saying that the broadcasters must have been wrong in saying, as they did, that the images would be offensive to a very large number of viewers.[26]

To require that the judiciary 'hesitate a great deal' before deciding that the BBC had contravened a Convention right does not require the court to refrain from determining for itself whether the restriction placed by the BBC was a proportionate restriction on Prolife's right to freedom of expression. It appears instead to require that the court decides for itself whether the restriction is proportionate or not, albeit also recognizing that the court should give considerable weight to the opinion of the BBC when making this assessment.

The culture of justification aims to facilitate accountability. As such, it requires courts to scrutinize Acts of Parliament and actions of the administration. According

---

[25] [2003] UKHL 23; [2004] 1 AC 185, [79].   [26] [2003] UKHL 23; [2004] 1 AC 185, [80].

to the culture of justification, actions of public authorities are legitimate when they are reasoned, justified, and accountable. Deference as respect aims to achieve this by ensuring that actions are scrutinized by the judiciary, whilst at the same time ensuring that the judiciary does not merely determine the legality of actions of public authorities by assessing whether these actions comply with liberal principles as determined by the judiciary. Deference as submission undermines this aim. It detracts from accountability as, when applied, it effectively empowers the executive or the legislature to determine whether its actions are compatible with human rights with no scrutiny by the judiciary. Instead, the judiciary merely determines whether to defer. Not only does this reduce scrutiny, and hence undermine account-ability, but in addition it switches the focus of judicial scrutiny towards an analysis of constitutional and institutional factors influencing deference as opposed to an analysis of the actions of public authorities. This, in turn, further detracts from accountability, providing public authorities with an incentive to supply arguments as to the degree of deference owed as opposed to providing an incentive to public authorities to provide reasons for their actions.

2. Process or substance?

The culture of justification rejects theories that rely purely upon arguments from democracy to conclude that courts should not overturn legislation and that liberal principles should not form the basis of criteria of legitimacy that justify human rights adjudication. It would appear, therefore, to be ideally suited to human rights adjudication under the HRA 1998. The HRA 1998 provides for a model of human rights adjudication that combines political and legal accountability. It does not rest purely upon political accountability, with its preservation of democracy, or upon legal accountability. However, the culture of justification also prefers a more procedural as opposed to a substantive approach to human rights adjudication. It is in this sense that difficulties arise in the application of the theory of the culture of justification to the provisions of the HRA 1998 in a manner that may harm accountability.

The HRA 1998 marks a move away from a theory of adjudication that focuses upon the way in which decisions are made towards a theory of adjudication controlling the content of the decision-making process. This can be illustrated, first, from judicial discussion of the shift from *Wednesbury* unreasonableness[27] to proportionality through the application of the HRA 1998. As Lord Steyn made clear, proportionality, although perhaps leading to the same outcome in some cases as *Wednesbury* unreasonableness, is nevertheless, in theory, a more stringent form of review in three regards: it requires courts to assess the balance drawn between a right and competing interests and not merely to determine whether this is within a range of rational responses; it requires courts to examine the relative weight given to rights and competing interests; and it requires an analysis of whether there was a

---

[27] *Associated Provincial Picture Houses Ltd v Wednesbury Corporation* [1948] 1 KB 223.

pressing social need and whether the restriction placed on the right to achieve this social need really was necessary in a democratic society.[28]

Courts are required to focus much more clearly on the substance of the decision, determining whether a right has been infringed. This was made clear in *R (SB) v Governors of Denbigh High School*[29] where the House of Lords reversed the decision of the Court of Appeal, which had criticized the school for failing to apply the requisite stages of the proportionality test when determining whether its uniform policy infringed the right to religious freedom of Shabena Begum, who believed her religion required her to wear a jilbab, a garment prohibited by the school's policy. The House of Lords stressed that the role of the court was not to determine whether the school had followed the right procedure when determining whether the school uniform policy respected Shabena Begum's human rights, but whether the policy did respect those rights in substance.[30] This shift to a substantive focus was confirmed in *Miss Behavin'*.[31]

Dyzenhaus is critical of the shift away from a procedural to a substantive analysis of proportionality, particularly as this applied in the *Begum* case,[32] arguing that a shift towards a substantive analysis, especially when proportionality is coupled by deference, can undermine the culture of justification. The culture of justification requires transparency and reasoned decision-making. It places an onus on administrative bodies to provide reasons for the conclusions that they reach so that these reasons can be scrutinized by the courts through an application of proportionality and deference. Although Dyzenhaus would agree that the job of the court is not merely to ensure that proportionality has been applied in the correct way by public authorities, he is concerned that the test applied by the House of Lords inappropriately separates process from substance. Instead of human rights adjudication furthering accountability through ensuring that the administration provides a reasoned account of its decisions, and the courts check that these justifications illustrate that the public authority has limited a human right in a proportionate manner to achieve a legitimate aim, there is a danger that courts will determine for themselves whether a restriction on a right is proportionate. This may mean that courts focus too greatly on substantive principles to the detriment of democratic rights, or that courts, aiming to defer in order to protect democracy, apply a test of proportionality that is insufficiently stringent, failing adequately to protect human rights.[33]

---

[28] *R (Daly) v Home Secretary* [2001] UKHL 26; [2001] 2 WLR 1622, [27].

[29] [2006] UKHL 15; [2007] 1 AC 100.

[30] *R (SB) v Governors of Denbigh High School* [2006] UKHL 15; [2007] 1 AC 100, [29]-[31] (Lord Bingham) and [66]-[68] (Lord Hoffmann).

[31] *Belfast City Council v Miss Behavin' Ltd* [2007] UKHL 19; [2007] 1 WLR 1420, [12]-[16](Lord Hoffmann), [21]-[24] (Lord Rodger), [31](Baroness Hale), [43]-[45](Lord Mance) and [90](Lord Neuberger).

[32] D Dyzenhaus, 'Militant Democracy in the House of Lords?' <http://www.cardozo.yu.edu/uploadedFiles/Cardozo/Profiles/floersheimer-134/Dyzenhaus,%20Headscarvesrevised.pdf>

[33] For an illustration of this second danger, see D Dyzenhaus *The Constitution of Law: Legality in a Time of Emergency* (Cambridge: Cambridge University Press, 2006).

Dyzenhaus's criticisms are limited to the separation of process and substance found in the *Begum* case. His argument can be countered by referring to other examples where courts have been sensitive to the inter-relationship between process and substance. Baroness Hale in *Miss Behavin'* recognised that, had Belfast City Council addressed itself to the precise issue of whether the selling of porno-graphic literature should be restricted and how these restrictions should have been enforced in this particular area of Belfast, then the court would have given greater weight to these particular considerations. However, as the City Council had not addressed this issue, then the court was in a position where it had no choice but to decide the issue for itself. These comments demonstrate that Baroness Hale is sensitive to the way in which the proportionality test has both procedural as well as substantive aspects.[34] In a similar manner, Lady Hale and Lord Wilson in *Quila and Bibi* found the policy designed to restrict forced marriages to be dispropor-tionate because the minister had failed to provide sufficient evidence to explain why the policy was proportionate. In the words of Lord Wilson:

[o]n any view it is a sledge-hammer but [the Minister] has not attempted to identify the size of the nut. At all events she fails to establish that the interference with the rights of the respondents under article 8 is justified.[35]

The approach in *Quila and Bibi* does facilitate accountability as required by the culture of justification. The court focused upon a need for reasons for the balance struck by the legislature between the right to marry of couples who freely wished to marry and the rights of women to be able to resist forced marriages, which in turn impeded their freedom to choose not to marry. The failure to provide a justification for raising the age to 21 from 18 meant that the court concluded that the legislation was not a proportionate restriction on the right to marry. This did not require the court to substitute its assessment of the merits for that of the legislature. It did require the legislature to account for its policy, so that the court could analyse whether their reasons justified a particular policy choice. However, although a recent decision of the Supreme Court, *Quila and Bibi* does not necessar-ily reflect the general tenor of human rights decisions based upon the HRA 1998. It is difficult to conclude, therefore, whether this marks a shift towards a legitimate approach to human rights adjudication as required by the culture of justification.

3. To give weight or to modify stringency?

The culture of justification requires the application of deference as respect, where courts determine whether a public body has provided a proportionate restriction on a human right through analysing the reasons provided for the restriction, giving appropriate weight to the reasoning of the public authority in the light of its insti-tutional and constitutional features vis-à-vis those of the court. Deference as respect is referred to by Hunt as giving weight and as modifying the stringency with which

---

[34] *Belfast City Council v Miss Behavin' Ltd* [2007] UKHL 19; [2007] 1 WLR 1420, [37].
[35] [2011] UKSC 45; [2012] AC 621, [58].

the proportionality test is applied. This tension is illustrated in the academic commentary on deference as respect, with some academics referring to deference as a modification of stringency with which the test of deference is applied,[36] and others as where the court gives greater weight to the opinion of the administration when applying a particular legal test.[37] As Mark Elliott recognizes, there is a latent tension between the two.[38] This tension gives rise to two problems when assessing whether English law upholds the values of the culture of justification. First, the tension between 'giving weight' and 'modifying stringency' may detract from accountability, as confusion regarding how the court exercises deference may detract from its ability to effectively scrutinize the actions of public bodies. Public authorities may focus more on proposing arguments on deference that lower the stringency with which the court examines their actions as opposed to focusing on providing reasoned restrictions on human rights. Second, problems arise from the way in which deference relates to the test of proportionality, particularly when deference is used to modify the stringency with which proportionality is applied. It is hard to determine how far proportionality can be applied less stringently whilst still retaining the characteristics of a control of proportionality.

The case law applying the HRA 1998 does appear confused, detracting from accountability. References can be found in the case law both to the idea that deference requires giving weight to the decisions of public bodies, and that it requires a modification of stringency with which the test of proportionality is applied. Lord Steyn in *R (Daly) v Secretary of State for the Home Department* appears to adopt a conception of deference that requires a modification of the stringency with which the proportionality test is applied. Although recognizing that proportionality is a more stringent test than *Wednesbury* unreasonableness, he also relies on the statements of Laws LJ in *R (Mahmood) v Secretary of State for the Home Department*[39] recognizing that the intensity of review varies according to subject matter, even in cases applying Convention rights.[40] Similarly, Lord Hoffmann in *Belfast City Council v Miss Behavin' Ltd* equated the wide margin of appreciation with 'the broad power of judgment entrusted to local authorities by the legislature', [41] arguing that:

If the local authority exercises that power rationally and in accordance with the purposes of the statute, it would require very unusual facts for it to amount to a disproportionate restriction on Convention rights.[42]

---

[36] See M Hunt, 'Sovereignty's Blight: Why Contemporary Public Law Needs the Concept of Due Deference" ' n 3 above, 337, 340 and 352, A Kavanagh, 'Deference or Defiance?' n 17 above, J Steyn, 'Deference: A Tangled Story' [2005] *Public Law* 346.

[37] See A Kavanagh, 'Defending Deference in Public Law and Constitutional Theory' *Law Quarterly Review* (2010) 126: 222, 233; A L Young, 'In Defence of Due Deference' *Modern Law Review* (2009) 72: 554.

[38] See M Elliott, 'Proportionality and Deference: the Importance of a Structured Approach' in Forsyth, Elliott, Jhaveri, Ramsden and Scully Hill (eds) *Effective Judicial Review: A Cornerstone of Good Governance* (Oxford University Press: Oxford 2010), 264, 268-70.

[39] [2001] 1 WLR 840, 847.

[40] *R (Daly) v Secretary of State for the Home Department* [2001] UKHL 26; [2001] 2 AC 532, [28].

[41] [2007] UKHL 19; [2007] 3 All ER 1007, [16].

[42] [2007] UKHL 19; [2007] 3 All ER 1007, [16].

Although not expressed specifically in terms of modifying the stringency with which the test is applied, it is clear that this would be the result of Lord Hoffmann's approach. The broad area of discretion afforded to the local authority means that proportionality is applied less stringently—only irrational balances that ignored the purpose of the statute would amount to a disproportionate restriction of the Convention right.

The clearest support for the idea that the judiciary exercise deference by giving weight to the opinions of the executive is found in the judgment of Lord Bingham in *Huang v Secretary of State for the Home Department*, where he expressly refers to 'according appropriate weight to the judgment of a person with responsibility for a given subject matter and access to special sources of knowledge and advice.'[43] Baroness Hale in *Miss Behavin'* also expressly refers to the way in which the court may exercise deference through according the appropriate weight to the opinions of the legislature and the executive, in recognition of their greater expertise and of the better ability of the local council to be in touch with the people affected by these decisions.[44]

This duality of approaches, combined with a lack of clear statements concerning the nature of deference and the way in which it applies, detracts from the ability of English law to promote accountability as required by the culture of justification. If the standard of review to be applied to public authorities is not clear then there is the potential for this lack of clarity to detract from accountability, with legal processes focusing more on the criteria influencing deference than on analysing whether a restriction placed upon a human right is justified. In addition, as *Sinclair Collis v Secretary of State for Health* illustrates,[45] even when there is consensus determining the conception of deference and the manner in which it is applied, there can be further confusion regarding the extent to which the intensity of proportionality can and should be modified. The case concerned a ban on cigarette vending machines, the aim of the ban being to prevent harm to the health of children through smoking, particularly given the relative ease with which they may purchase cigarettes from vending machines. An issue arose as to whether this policy was contrary to EU law as a disproportionate restriction on the free movement of goods. All three judgments recognized that a greater discretionary area of judgement was left to the administration in this area, given that it concerned a matter of public health. All three agreed that this could be achieved through modifying the stringency with which the test for proportionality applied. However, disagreement arose as to the way in which this should be achieved.

Laws LJ referred to the court leaving a 'wider space for the decision-maker's own judgment as to the application of the standards', such that the 'broader the margin of appreciation, the less inclined the court will be to strike an autonomous balance of the material factors'.[46] Arden LJ recognized that courts can apply proportionality

[43] [2007] UKHL 11; [2007] 2 AC 167, [16].
[44] [2007] UKHL 19, [2007] 3 All ER 1007, [32] and [37].
[45] [2011] EWCA Civ 437; [2011] 3 WLR 1153.
[46] [2011] EWCA Civ 437; [2011] 3 WLR 1153, [50].

more flexibly by according a 'less intensive level of scrutiny than under a strict test of proportionality'[47] and Lord Neuberger MR concluded that the applicants would have to present a 'very strong case indeed' such that the court would not interfere 'unless satisfied that no reasonable Secretary of State would have concluded that it was right' to have reached that decision.[48]

Sinclair Collis also demonstrates how modifying the stringency with which proportionality applies may result in the courts applying a test for review different from proportionality—a less stringent application of proportionality can be hard to differentiate from an application of *Wednesbury* unreasonableness or a test which only deems unlawful 'manifestly inappropriate' restrictions on human rights. Laws LJ was critical of the way in which counsel for the government advocated that proportionality should be equated with a test of 'manifestly inappropriate', believing that this undercuts the standard of proportionality, particularly because this may deprive the court of the requirement to examine whether there was a less restrictive means of achieving a particular goal.[49] The test as applied by Lord Neuberger MR in the case resembled a test of *Wednesbury* unreasonableness, where decisions would be struck down if irrational.[50] Arden LJ, whilst recognising the requirement to apply a test of 'manifestly inappropriate' as devised by the Court of Justice of the European Union, disagreed with Laws LJ, regarding this as an application of the proportionality test as opposed to a different standard of review.[51]

It is hard to conclude that English law complies with the criteria of human rights adjudication advocated by the culture of justification. Confusion over whether the judiciary is to give weight or modify the stringency with which proportionality is applied may detract from its ability to provide a clear signal to public authorities regarding the standards they need to adhere to if they are to protect human rights. In addition deference as respect may collapse into a model of deference as submission and English law has a tendency to focus more on substance as opposed to process when applying a test of proportionality, meaning that the judiciary fails to concentrate fully on analysing the reasoning provided by public authorities for harming human rights. The question arises whether these difficulties are merely examples of the practical problems which arise whenever an abstract theory is applied to the real world and needs to be expressed as a legal test, or whether these tensions illustrate a deeper problem inherent to the culture of justification and to the use of accountability as a normative concept capable of justifying judicial review.

D. Practical or conceptual problems?

The previous section argued that human rights adjudication did not match the criteria advocated by the culture of justification. There are two possible reasons for

---

[47] [2011] EWCA Civ 437; [2011] 3 WLR 1153, [127].
[48] [2011] EWCA Civ 437; [2011] 3 WLR 1153, [255].
[49] [2011] EWCA Civ 437; [2011] 3 WLR 1153, [40]-[50].
[50] [2011] EWCA Civ 437; [2011] 3 WLR 1153, [240].
[51] [2011] EWCA Civ 437; [2011] 3 WLR 1153, [154]-[155].

this mismatch. First, the culture of justification is best understood as a 'constructed type'—ie. a model based on the achievement of certain normative principles which is an objectively probable account of the real world.[52] As an ideal, the requirements of the model may not be fully achievable. But constitutional arrangements should aim to match the model in order to ensure that the human rights adjudication undertaken by the judiciary is normatively defensible and that human rights are protected in as normatively justifiable a manner as possible. Difficulties arise when transforming any ideal into reality or when transcribing abstract principles into a workable legal test that accurately reflects normative ideals. Secondly, these difficulties could reflect deeper problems that arise when accountability is used normatively, particularly when accountability is seen as a justifiable end as opposed to a means of achieving a different goal. This section will argue that some of the problems faced in human rights adjudication can be explained as mere practical issues, but that there is also evidence of deeper, conceptual problems that cast doubt upon normative theories of accountability.

1. Transcription errors?

The culture of justification advocates principles of human rights adjudication based upon a test of proportionality and a principle of deference as respect, where courts give weight to the decisions of public authorities when determining whether their actions are in accordance with human rights. However, it was argued above that deference as respect was in danger of collapsing into deference as submission and that it was difficult to determine whether courts were giving weight to decisions of public authorities, or modifying the stringency with which the test of proportionality was applied, with the accompanying danger that the courts may apply a test other than that of proportionality. These problems may be explained as transcription errors, difficulties that arise when developing legal tests and principles from abstract ideals.

First, although the culture of justification refers to proportionality, there is a range of different legal tests that can be used as a means of applying a test of proportionality. The most frequently applied test in English law is the three-fold test adopted in *de Freitas v Permanent Secretary of the Ministry of Agriculture and Others* that examines:

(i) Importance—whether the aim of the measure restricting a human right is sufficiently important to merit the restriction of a human right.

(ii) Rational connection—whether there is a rational connection between the measure in question and the sufficiently important aim.

(iii) Necessity/proportionality—whether the means used to impair the right or freedom are 'no more than is necessary to accomplish the objective.'[53]

---

[52] See McKinney *Constructive Typology and Social Theory* (Appleton-Century-Crofts, New York 1964) and F Weinhart 'Weber's Ideal Types as Models in the Social Sciences', (1996) 41 *Royal Institute of Philosophy Supplement* 73.
[53] [1999] 1 AC 69, PC; (1998) 4 BHRC 563, 572.

This test, in turn, is interpreted by Paul Craig as a three-fold test of necessity, suitability, and proportionality *stricto sensu*.[54] The first stage of *de Freitas* appears to have been separated from the rest of the test, it often being dictated by Convention rights—eg. particularly arts 8-11, the 'non-absolute' rights which can be restricted only to achieve the legitimate aims set out in those articles. The third stage of *de Freitas* is expanded, with necessity and proportionality being seen as two separate elements, proportionality going beyond necessity.

Lord Bingham in *Huang* recognised a deficiency in this three-fold test of proportionality: that it failed to draw sufficient attention to the need to balance the interest of society with those of individuals and groups.[55] In *Quila and Bibi* Lord Wilson interpreted Lord Bingham as establishing the following four point test for proportionality:

   (i) 'is the legislative objective sufficiently important to justify limiting a fundamental right?'

  (ii) 'are the measures that have been designed to meet it rationally connected to it?'

 (iii) 'are they no more than are necessary to accomplish it?'

 (iv) 'do they strike a fair balance between the rights of the individual and the interests of the community?'[56]

However, this formulation of the legal test seems almost to beg further questions as opposed to supplying further answers. How do you determine whether something is 'sufficiently important' or 'no more than necessary', or that it 'strikes a fair balance'? Further difficulties arise as the interpretation of these terms depends on the context. For example, in *ANS and another v ML (Scotland)*, the Supreme Court was required to determine whether provisions of the Adoption and Children (Scotland) Act 2007, which provided for circumstances in which adoption could take place without the consent of one or more parents, was compatible with art 8 ECHR. The court concluded that this restriction on the right to family life would only be in line with Convention rights if it were necessary and proportionate, proportionality being satisfied only where there is an overwhelming need for the adoption of the child to take place and where nothing less than adoption will suffice to protect the interests of the child.[57] Proportionality is best understood here in terms of a 'least restrictive means' analysis. In *AXA v General Insurance*, the Supreme Court was required to determine whether legislation which allowed for insurance claims for those suffering from pleural plaques was a proportionate restriction on the property rights of insurers. This was particularly in the face of a potential retro-active impact of the legislation, the legislation in question having the effect of reversing a House of Lords decision excluding pleural plaques from insurance claims. Given

---

[54] P Craig *Administrative Law* (6th edn) (Sweet and Maxwell: London, 2008), 628.
[55] *Huang v Secretary of State for the Home Department* [2007] UKHL 11; [2007] 4 All ER 15, [19].
[56] *R (Quila) v Secretary of State for the Home Department; R (Bibi) v Secretary of State for the Home Department* [2011] UKSC 45; [2012] AC 621, [45].
[57] [2012] UKSC 30.

the complex social background to this legislation, and the difficulty of balancing the needs of the insured and insurance companies, the Supreme Court applied a different test of proportionality, requiring a 'reasonable relationship' of proportionality between the end and the means—it was not required that the measure in question was the least restrictive means of achieving a particular end.[58]

Problems arise because it is difficult to transform an application of proportionality into a precisely worded legal test. What is meant by a proportionate response may well depend upon the circumstances and the context in which the test is applied. Even the classic formulation of a disproportionate measure—using a sledgehammer to crack a nut—causes difficulties. Why a sledgehammer? Would it not also be disproportionate to use a strong nutcracker designed for cracking walnuts to crack a thinner shelled nut, such as a hazelnut? Could there be cases in which a sledgehammer is the least restrictive means of cracking a nut—eg. where, faced with a starving population, the only feasible food source is a supply of nuts that needs to be cracked as quickly as possible to save as many lives as possible? In this instance, maybe it is not a sledgehammer but a steamroller that is a disproportionate means of cracking a nut.

Similar transcription errors occur when assessing how to modify the stringency with which proportionality is to be applied, or to give weight to the assessments of public authorities. It is hard to see how the stringency with which proportionality is to be applied can be modified other than through the wording of the test. To return to the classic example of using a sledgehammer to crack a nut, a more stringent application of the proportionality test would not only require that sledgehammers were not used to crack nuts, but in addition would insist that walnut crackers were not used to crack hazelnuts. A less stringent application of the proportionality test may merely require that steamrollers were not used to crack nuts. To modify stringency in this way looks like a modification of the test of proportionality to a test of reasonableness. In a similar manner, it could be interpreted as an application of a necessity test that does not move on to assess proportionality *stricto sensu*.

Similar difficulties occur when we try and determine how to 'give weight' to the assessments of public authorities. Proportionality is seen in terms of 'weighing up' the rights of the individual with the interests of society. If we use the analogy of a set of weighing scales, the court places the reasons for restricting the right in one set of pans and the reasons for protecting the right in the other. Or, as in *Quila and Bibi*, where the court is balancing competing rights, the restriction on one right—the right to marry—is balanced against the restriction on the other right — the right not to be forced into marriage. 'Giving weight' to the decisions of the public authority could be seen in terms of the court accepting that the decision of the public authority is likely to be correct and so should not be interfered with. It could also be seen in terms of 'putting in extra weight' in the pans of the scales. For example, even if the court is not sure in and of itself that there are good reasons to protect the right of those who wish to marry when younger than 21 and allow their

---

[58] [2011] UKSC 46; [2012] AC 868, [37], [82], [128]-[134].

spouse to live with them in the UK, perhaps doubting the ability of those so young to have the wisdom to decide such issues, it may nevertheless see these reasons as having more weight and therefore requiring more justification to restrict, given that a public authority has determined that this is an important right. However we try and put these abstract tests into words, it is hard to see how they can be applied in reality in a clear, precise and consistent manner. Any application of these broad, abstract provisions and analogies is perhaps inevitably going to give rise to what would appear to be a plethora of legal formulations and applications. Confusion, which in turn limits the effectiveness of accountability, would appear to be inevitable.

2. A matter of degree?

In addition to transcription errors, other problems arise as both the test of proportionality and that of deference are matters of degree. Hunt argues that deference applies in a variable manner. This distinguishes deference from justiciability— where issues are removed from scrutiny by the court as beyond their jurisdiction, often on a blanket basis. Deference differs in two respects: it does not remove areas from the jurisdiction of the court and it applies on a variable basis, depending on a range of factors. The precise context and issue before the court is examined to determine the appropriate degree of scrutiny over the decisions of public authorities by the courts. To recognise the contextual nature of due deference, however, hints at further problems. Is the range of factors relevant to determining the degree of deference owed so large that it is impossible to see deference as a principle at all, its criteria essentially collapsing into a requirement that courts take all circumstances into account when determining the stringency with which they review a particular decision?[59] However, if the criteria influencing deference are applied in a rule-like manner, then the application of due deference is more likely to give rise to the clarity required to enhance accountability, but it is also in danger of being applied in a manner that produces the same results as an approach based upon justiciability. These difficulties arise because deference is a matter of degree. It does not mean that deference cannot be applied in a manner required by the culture of justification. However, it will inevitably challenge the extent to which deference can enhance accountability. It is harder for public authorities to be accountable to less clear standards. Also, public authorities may have an incentive to focus on providing reasons for greater deference as opposed to providing clear justifications for their actions.

As discussed above, deference as respect may appear to collapse into deference as submission given that greater and lesser amounts of respect are to be paid to public authorities. This can also be explained by the recognition that deference is a matter

---

[59] See T R S Allan, 'Judicial Deference and Judicial Review: Legal Doctrine and Legal Theory' *Law Quarterly Review* (2011) 127: 96; J Jowell 'Deference: Servility, Civility or Institutional Capacity?' *Public Law* [2003] 592 and J King, 'Institutional Approaches' *Oxford Journal of Legal Studies* (2008) 28: 409.

of degree. Regardless of whether deference modifies stringency, or affects the weight to be given to the reasoning of public authorities, stringency is modified to a greater or lesser degree and greater or smaller weight is given. In these circumstances, it may be hard to delineate between giving a large amount of weight and merely accepting the decisions of the public authority, or between applying proportionality less stringently and merely accepting the solution of the public authority as satisfying the test of proportionality. In a similar manner, as the wording of the test of proportionality can be modified, so it can be hard to delineate between applying a test of proportionality less stringently and applying a test other than proportionality. A requirement that a restriction 'strike a fair balance' between the rights of individuals and the interest of the community may be little different from requiring public authorities to be reasonable when weighing up these competing interests.

The difficulty of dealing with matters of degree may also explain potential confusion between the necessity and proportionality components of the four stage proportionality test post *Huang*. In *Quila and Bibi*, Lord Wilson distinguished between the necessity and the proportionality component of the test: the former concerned an assessment of whether the measures in question would have an effect on reducing forced marriages,[60] and the latter an assessment of whether the measure had a detrimental impact on unforced marriages.[61] However, it is hard to know which evidence is relied upon by Lord Wilson to explain the lack of necessity and which is used to determine the lack of a fair balance between the two interests. The two seem to merge into one another as he assesses the evidence provided by different interest groups to the Home Secretary in order to assess whether there was enough evidence to conclude that the restriction on the right to marry was proportionate. In a similar manner, Lady Hale delineates between questions appertaining to the impact of the policy on unforced marriages,[62] whether the policy really does help those in forced marriages,[63] and whether the policy does more harm than good.[64] Again, however, when assessing the evidence, the same evidence appears to provide support for finding a lack of necessity and a finding that the balance was disproportionate. If the two are matters of degree, this may explain why the same evidence is used for both aspects of the test and why it can be difficult to clearly delineate between the two stages of the test.

3. Conceptual issues

It may be that difficulties apparent in human rights adjudication are merely caused by these practical issues. As such, it is arguable that there is a tension between normative and non-normative theories of accountability. The culture of justification advocates principles of proportionality and deference in order to enhance

---

[60] *R (Quila) v Secretary of State for the Home Department; R (Bibi) v Secretary of State for the Home Department* [2011] UKSC 45; [2012] AC 621, [47]-[50].
[61] [2011] UKSC 45; [2012] AC 621, [51]-[57].   [62] [2011] UKSC 45; [2012] AC 621, [74].
[63] [2011] UKSC 45; [2012] AC 621, [75].   [64] [2011] UKSC 45; [2012] AC 621, [76]-[77].

accountability. However, due to issues arising when transcribing these theoretical ideals into practical legal tests, and due to problems arising from both proportionality and deference being understood as a matter of degree, it may well be that accountability is not enhanced. The lack of clarity may make it difficult to hold public authorities to account for their actions. In addition, public authorities may find it hard to ensure that their actions comply with human rights standards. The varying standards of proportionality and deference may provide public authorities with an incentive to focus on legal arguments that apply a weaker standard of review to their actions as opposed to arguments that explain how their actions are not contrary to human rights. However, this section will argue that there is a deeper conceptual issue that arises from an analysis of criticisms of proportionality and deference. The most challenging criticisms of these principles stems from academics who adopt alternative theories of human rights adjudication, particularly concerning whether the judiciary is the primary or the secondary decision-maker of human rights issues. This question is not fully answered by advocates of the theory of the culture of justification. This not only calls into question the validity of this theory of human rights adjudication, but also questions normative theories of adjudication. Can a decision of a public authority be justified merely because it is held to account for its actions, or does the justification depend upon the principles applied by the body holding the public authority to account? In other words, can 'accountability' be an end in itself, or is it merely a means through which to ensure other ends are achieved?

The strongest academic criticism of the principle of deference is found in the work of Trevor Allan. It was argued above that the difference between deference as respect and deference as submission is a matter of degree and, therefore, this may explain the danger of applications of deference as respect sliding into applications of deference as submission. Allan takes this argument further, arguing that deference as respect inevitably collapses into deference as submission.[65] Any exercise of deference, even deference as respect, involves the courts reneging on their constitutional duty. He also argues that any application of deference amounts to double counting. The role of the court is to define human rights and to correct decisions of public authorities that fail to comply with human rights as defined by the courts. Any relevant 'margin of appreciation' to be granted to public authorities depends upon the definition of the right in question and will be accorded when properly defining the right. To then defer to public authorities after defining the right amounts to double counting. The same criteria used to define the right are then used again to defer to the public authority.[66]

Allan's criticism is based upon his understanding of the court as the primary decision-maker for human rights issues. If Allan were analysing the facts in *Sinclair Collis*, for example, he would argue that there is no need for the court to 'defer'

---

[65] T R S Allan, 'Human Rights and Judicial Review: a Critique of "Due Deference"' *Cambridge Law Journal* (2006) 65: 671 and 'Judicial Deference and Judicial Review: Legal Doctrine and Legal Theory', n 59.

[66] T R S Allan, 'Judicial Deference and Judicial Review: Legal Doctrine and Legal Theory' n 59, 110-6.

because the right to the free movement of goods would recognize the need to accommodate a range of possible proportionate restrictions when applied to issues of public health and public policy, recognizing that the right could be restricted to a greater extent in the face of public health issues. To defer further would be to accord too much deference to the executive; effectively deferring twice over as the court would have already taken factors influencing deference into account when determining the content of the right to the free movement of goods. Deference does not give rise to double counting, nor does deference as respect collapse into deference as submission, if we regard the courts as the secondary decision-maker. The job of the court is not to define human rights. Rather, it is to set the boundaries of lawful restrictions that can be placed by public authorities on human rights. When ascertaining these boundaries, the courts first define rights broadly, using proportionality and deference to determine the range of lawful decisions that can be taken by public authorities. In *Sinclair Collis*, the courts would first recognize that the restriction on tobacco vending machines would restrict the free movement of goods, when broadly defined. In order to analyse whether this restriction is justified, the court will apply proportionality, using deference to determine the stringency with which proportionality is analysed. There is no double counting because the role of the court is different and, in turn, the precision with which the right is first defined is different.[67]

An understanding of the different roles of the judiciary, as either a primary or a secondary decision-maker, may also explain distinctions between conceptions of proportionality and the relationship between proportionality and deference. Julian Rivers distinguishes two conceptions of proportionality—optimizing and state-limiting. Optimising conceptions of proportionality are more relevant to theories of human rights adjudication that regard the court as the primary decision-maker. Here, proportionality is used as a means of defining a human right. State-limiting conceptions of proportionality are more relevant to theories of human rights adjudication that regard the court as the secondary decision-maker. Here, proportionality is used to define the limits of legitimate actions of public authorities when restricting a human right.[68] Deference appears inappropriate when courts are regarded as primary decision-makers. However, this does not mean that courts do not defer. Courts can grant a margin of appreciation to public authorities when defining human rights. Such a test regards the principle of proportionality as a means of determining the definition of a Convention right. When adopting a theory that focuses on the role of the court as a secondary decision-maker, then deference can apply in this model without contradiction of the constitutional role of the court.

Problems arise as the culture of justification could be interpreted in a manner compatible both with the ideology of the judiciary as the primary and as the secondary decision-maker in human rights decisions. When the judiciary acts as the primary decision-maker, it may appear as if the role of the judiciary is more compatible with

---

[67] A Kavanagh, 'Defending Deference in Public Law and Constitutional Theory' n 37, 228-40.
[68] J Rivers, 'Proportionality and Variable Intensity of Review' *Cambridge L J* (2006) 65: 174.

the ideology of a culture of neutrality. The judiciary holds governmental institutions to account by defining rights according to liberal principles and ensuring that public bodies comply with these rights. However, it may be compatible with a culture of justification if courts define rights in such a manner as to include a broad discretionary area of judgement, essentially deferring to public authorities, but through modifying an optimizing conception of proportionality and applying a weaker standard of accountability. The culture of justification may also be exemplified in a system where the courts act as secondary decision-makers. Here, the judiciary is not applying a culture of neutrality as it acts to check the actions of public authorities. Its check also ensures that the judiciary is not merely upholding a culture of reflection. However, applying a test of state-limiting proportionality and using deference to modify the stringency with which proportionality is applied causes difficulties for the culture of justification. The test of proportionality may be transformed into a weaker test of reasonableness and the multiplicity of factors determining the degree of deference may provide an incentive for both the judiciary and public authorities to focus on deference as opposed to human rights. To resolve these problems, the theory of accountability required by the culture of justification needs to be bolstered by an account of whether the judiciary should be the primary or secondary decision-maker.

Another way of resolving these difficulties would be to require the culture of justification to include a theory of the nature of human rights. A theory of human rights that regards rights as being clearly delineated is more suited to an optimizing conception of proportionality, where the judiciary plays the primary role in determining human rights issues. A theory of human rights that regards rights as essentially contestable, capable of more definite definitions only in specific situations where there is a need to determine how far a right can be restricted by another right or interest, is more suited to a state-limiting conception of proportionality where the judiciary is recognized as a secondary decision-maker. These difficulties hint at a deeper problem with normative theories of accountability that view accountability as an end as opposed to a means to an end. To equate a decision or action of a public authority as normatively justifiable merely because a public authority can be held to account for its actions provides only a weak justification, especially when notions of accountability are fluid and can be applied to a greater or lesser degree.[69]

E. Conclusion

The HRA 1998 establishes both legal and political mechanisms for checking the actions of public authorities with regard to human rights, providing a means of control over executive and legislative actions. However, this chapter has argued that neither form of check is ideal. Ss 3 and 4 may enable courts to check legislation, but

---

[69] Dyzenhaus *The Constitution of Law: Legality in a Time of Emergency*, n 33 above.

the use of deference and the need to determine the extent to which the court can read and give effect to legislation so as to render it compatible with Convention rights may weaken accountability. Judicial decisions may focus more on the relative institutional and constitutional features of the legislature, the executive and the scope of interpretation than upon an assessment of human rights. This detracts from accountability both in terms of the primary control by the courts and in terms of the extent to which legal accountability mechanisms will provide an incentive to public authorities to ensure their actions are compatible with Convention rights. Political checks may also fall short of the requirements of ensuring effective accountability. There may be no clear forum in which the public authority is held to account. In addition, there are often no clear sanctions for human rights breaches. Accountability may often be more a matter of political preference than a focus on human rights.

This chapter has also examined the extent to which the HRA 1998 upholds a normative theory of accountability through investigating the culture of justification. The culture of justification advocates a theory of human rights protection through an application of proportionality and deference. As well as pointing out ways in which English law does not fully adhere to this theory, the chapter has argued further that a clearer understanding is required of the precise conceptions of proportionality and deference that should be deployed by the courts. A lack of clarity about these legal doctrines, and their relationship to one another, detracts from accountability in two ways. Firstly, a lack of clarity detracts from the transparency needed to enhance accountability. If the principles to which a public body is to be held to account are unclear, then it is harder to ensure that public authorities are adhering to these principles. Second, this lack of clarity may mean that more time is focused on determining the standard to which the public authority should be held to account than on determining whether the public authority has met this standard, detracting from the ability to ensure human rights are adequately adhered to.

Moreover, the chapter has questioned normative theories of accountability. Our analysis of human rights adjudication under the HRA 1998 argues that the culture of justification needs to be supplemented by a theory as to whether the judiciary should be the primary or the secondary decision-maker for human rights issues, as well as a theory as to the nature of human rights. Without these additions, it may be difficult for the theory of adjudication advocated by the culture of justification to achieve its aim of facilitating accountability. In a similar manner, normative theories of accountability may provide only a weak justification. The analysis suggests that accountability works better as a means to achieving a particular end as opposed to an end in and of itself.

8

Accountability and Judicial Review in the UK and EU: Central Precepts

*Paul Craig**

A. Introduction

Judicial review is one method of securing accountability in the modern state. It is not the only one, but then accountability is not in this respect a zero sum game. This is so notwithstanding the fact that commentators might legitimately disagree on the ambit of judicial review, or on its relative importance as a mechanism to secure accountability when compared to other methods. The very fact that all developed legal systems have some regime of judicial review is indicative of its perceived importance in securing the values of the liberal state, using that phrase in broad terms for these purposes. This does not mean complacency in this regard. To the contrary, discussion of accountability entails not merely estimation of the relative efficacy of different mechanisms to secure this end, but also evaluation of the credentials underlying any particular accountability mechanism itself, the latter being the objective of this chapter.

This chapter is concerned with judicial review as developed in the United Kingdom and in the European Union. It does not directly address the impact of the latter on the former. There is literature dealing with the effect of EU law on judicial review, more especially the way in which EU general principles of law have affected domestic judicial review. This chapter does not replicate this discourse. The focus is rather on the cardinal features that define and shape judicial review in a legal system in order to see how the UK and the EU compare in this regard. To this end the subsequent analysis considers the two systems in terms of conceptual foundations, legitimacy, hierarchy of norms and rights. This exercise has not to my knowledge been undertaken in relation to UK and EU models of review. It sheds interesting light on domestic debates in the UK and on the foundations of judicial review in the EU. The discussion will be addressed principally in relation to judicial review of executive action rather than primary legislation, although there will also be consideration of the latter, more especially because the divide between the two has not in the past been either clear

* Professor of English Law, St John's College and the University of Oxford.

or central to the application of judicial review in the EU. For the sake of clarity it should be noted at the outset that the EU principles of judicial review bind not only the EU institutions, but also the Member States when they act in the scope of EU law.

B. Conceptual foundations

It is fitting to begin with the conceptual foundations of judicial review. The ultra vires debate is well known. It was concerned with whether the principles of judicial review had to be legitimated via some connection with legislative intent, whether conceptualized as a specific legislative intent in relation to the particular principle of judicial review, or some more general legislative intent that there should be principles of judicial review of the kind developed by the courts. Some argued that such intent was a necessary conceptual foundation for review, while others contended that the courts could develop the principles of judicial review pursuant to the rule of law. I have no wish to re-open this discourse.[1] The objective is rather to consider the foundations of judicial review in EU law in the light of this debate. It will be seen that, although the EU courts had express authorization for judicial review in the original Rome Treaty, the principles of such review were fashioned by the Union courts pursuant to the rule of law in a manner analogous to that in the UK.

Thus, viewed from one perspective the EU courts have been more secure in relation to the foundations of judicial review. The European Court of Justice (ECJ) had, from the very inception of the EEC, an express authorization to undertake judicial review derived from art 173 EEC, now art 263 TFEU, thereby obviating concerns about the legitimacy of engaging in judicial review of the kind that plagued UK scholarship. Yet the matter is more interesting and less straightforward than a mere glance at art 173 EEC would suggest. The reason resides in the general principles of law that fashioned EU judicial review. These were, as is well known, read into the Treaty by the ECJ, in particular during the 1970s. The conceptual foundation for this development has rarely been examined in detail, and the ECJ itself was not unduly forthcoming about the justificatory arguments for the flesh that it read on to the bare bones of art 173.

Article 19 TEU, the old art 220 EC, under which the ECJ is charged with the duty of ensuring that the 'law' is observed, is a possible foundation for this case law. This might have been interpreted in a limited manner to connote the idea that, for example, Commission decisions should be made within the limits of the primary Treaty articles and secondary legislation. The word 'law' within this article was, however, open to a broader interpretation that was used by the ECJ to fashion a system of general principles through which the legality of Union and Member State action could be determined. The generality of art 19 reveals nonetheless the

---

[1] Many of the articles are collected in C Forsyth (ed.), *Judicial Review and the Constitution* (Oxford: Hart, 2000).

ECJ's creativity in interpreting it as the foundation for the elaborate tapestry of general principles of law that constitutes EU judicial review.

The injunction in art 263(2) TFEU, which specifies the grounds of judicial review, is more promising in this respect. It states that the ECJ shall, inter alia, review for infringement of the Treaties 'or any rule of law relating to their application'. The *travaux préparatoires* for the original Rome Treaty were not available for over thirty years. This is a blessing, since it means that we have not been beset with debates about original intent of the kind that have plagued US constitutional scholarship. The very absence of the *travaux préparatoires* meant, however, that the ECJ developed its own interpretation of the scope of art 263(2).

The intent might simply have been to ensure that Commission decision-making complied not only with the primary Treaty articles, but also Regulations, Directives, etc. passed pursuant thereto. If this had been the intent it could, however, have been expressed more directly. The intent might alternatively have been to capture not only compliance with secondary legislation, but also with other rules of law relating to the application of the Treaty that might be developed by the courts. This interpretation might be enhanced by the fact that French juristic thought is clearly imprinted on the grounds of review in art 263 and French doctrine includes *principes généraux du droit*.[2] In any event, the very ambiguity in the phrase provided the ECJ with a window through which to justify the imposition of administrative law principles as grounds of review.

The judicial task of elaborating principles of judicial review was further facilitated by more specific Treaty articles, which made reference to, for example, non-discrimination. It was then open to the ECJ to read these particular Treaty references as indicative of a more general principle of equal treatment and non-discrimination that underpinned the legal order.[3]

The very fact that some foundation for the judicial exercise of power might be located in art 19 TEU and art 263 TFEU should not, however, mask the creativity involved. The ECJ created the principles of EU judicial review in order to enhance the rule of law, and did so in a manner directly analogous to the UK courts when fashioning the principles of judicial review.

This substantive creativity was matched by interpretive creativity. It was the ECJ that decided which systems of administrative law to draw on in shaping Community principles of judicial review. To be sure the structure of what is now art 263(2) bore a French imprint, in terms of the four generic categories of review. This nonetheless left the ECJ with considerable interpretive discretion when developing general principles of law. It certainly did not regard itself as bound to French doctrine, nor did it systematically trawl through the legal systems of each Member State in order to find common principles. The approach was, rather, to consider principles in the major legal systems of the Member States, to use those that were

---

[2] The French version of art 263(2) TFEU is, however, worded as follows: 'violation des traités ou de toute règle de droit relative à leur application'.

[3] Cases 117/76 and 16/77 *Ruckdeschel v Hauptzollamt Hamburg-St. Annen* [1977] ECR 1753, [7]; Case 8/78 *Milac GmbH v Hauptzollamt Freiburg* [1978] ECR 1721, [18].

felt to be best developed and to fashion them to the Community's own needs. Thus, while French juristic thought might have been the principal force behind the Treaty provisions, it was German law that became most influential. It was German jurisprudence on, for example, proportionality and legitimate expectations that was of principal significance for the development of Community law in these areas.

The substantive and interpretive creativity can be evidenced by the way in which the EU courts decide whether to add to existing general principles of law. Thus, for example, the precautionary principle[4] was promoted into the 'premier league' of general principles via the creative jurisprudence of the Court of First Instance (CFI) in *Artegodan*[5] and *Pfizer*.[6] The cases are an object lesson in the similarities in legal reasoning by judges from a common law and civil law background. The judgments are classic examples of generating, or perhaps more importantly being willing to generate, a general principle from diverse and hitherto limited references to the precautionary principle in the jurisprudence of the ECJ and the Treaty.[7] In *Audiolux*,[8] by way of contrast, the ECJ was unwilling to recognize a general principle of EU law requiring the dominant shareholder of a company to protect minority shareholders in certain respects during a takeover, and this was reflected in the way in which the ECJ distinguished instances in which minority shareholders were afforded protection in existing EU legislation.

Judicial review is regarded as one mechanism for securing accountability in the modern state. The focus of this chapter is, as stated at the outset, on the credentials underlying this particular accountability mechanism. It is interesting and noteworthy that the conceptual foundation for judicial review in EU law has been fashioned pursuant to the rule of law in a manner analogous to that in the UK.

C. Legitimacy

The literature contesting the legitimacy of constitutional review could fill an office block or mansion, whichever architectural metaphor you prefer.[9] The legitimacy of non-constitutional review has not been as contentious as its more famous sibling.

---

[4] V Heyvaert, 'Facing the Consequences of the Precautionary Principle in European Community Law' *E L Rev* (2006) 31: 185; J Corkin, 'Science, Legitimacy and the Law: Regulating Risk Regulation Judiciously in the European Community' *E L Rev* (2008) 33: 359.

[5] Cases T-74, 76, 83–5, 132, 137 and 141/00 *Artegodan GmbH v Commission* [2002] ECR II-4945.

[6] Case T-13/99 *Pfizer Animal Health SA v Council* [2002] ECR II-3305.

[7] P Craig, *EU Administrative Law* (Oxford: Oxford University Press, 2nd edn, 2012), ch 21.

[8] Case C-101/08 *Audiolux SA e.a v Groupe Bruxelles Lambert SA (GBL)* [2009] ECR I-9823.

[9] See, eg. R Dworkin, *Freedom's Law: The Moral Reading of the American Constitution* (Oxford: Oxford University Press, 1996); P Pettit, *Republicanism, A Theory of Freedom and Government* (Oxford: Clarendon Press, 1997); C Eisgruber, *Constitutional Self-Government* (Cambridge, Mass: Harvard University Press, 2001); L Sager, *Justice in Plainclothes: A Theory of American Constitutional Practice* (New Haven: Yale University Press, 2004); J Waldron, *Law and Disagreement* (Oxford: Oxford University Press, 1999); T R S Allan, *Constitutional Justice: A Liberal Theory of the Rule of Law* (Oxford: Oxford University Press, 2003); J Waldron, 'The Core of the Case against Judicial Review' *Yale LJ* (2006) 115: 1346; R Bellamy, *Political Constitutionalism, A Republican Defence of the Constitutionality of Democracy* (Cambridge: Cambridge University Press, 2007); M Tushnet, *Taking the*

The academic discourse on the latter occupies a more modest dwelling, but has nonetheless been prominent in the common law world.[10] This is not the place to engage generally with the complex arguments entailed in the debates about the legitimacy of non-constitutional review, some of which are not pertinent to this chapter. There is nonetheless an aspect of the common law debate about the legitimacy of judicial review, which is apposite for comparative analysis of the foundational precepts of judicial review in the UK and the EU.

It is common for criticism to be voiced against the legitimacy of legal constitutionalism and judicial review in the UK on the ground that the doctrine is not justified, except through recourse to abstract concepts such as natural law, fundamental values or the rule of law. This critique is predicated on mistaken assumptions about the development of any body of legal doctrine, whether in public or private law. The common law develops at three interconnected levels.

There will, firstly, be some imperative for judicial involvement in the area, such as the need for legal rules to deal with delictual harm, the regulation of consensual relations and the like. The objectives served by these rules may be eclectic, and may alter over time. These will be reflected in principles, which shape the applicable legal doctrine.

The second level is the fashioning of particular categories of legal doctrine applicable within the salient area, such as mistake, misrepresentation and illegality in contract, or negligence, nuisance and defamation in tort. These legal doctrines will be developed because they serve the background imperatives and principles that underlie that area of the law. The doctrine is perforce based on certain assumptions about the important values within that legal sphere, whatsoever those might be. In that sense the values embodied within legal doctrine will be regarded as fundamental, when viewed in the light of the principles and objectives served by that body of law. The doctrine may also be influenced by values that transcend the particular legal area.

The third level concerns the more detailed meaning of the doctrinal areas established. Thus, there will be further questions as to the nature of liability for nuisance, the type of defences that should be available, and the like. Resolution of these issues will necessarily involve an admixture of normative and practical considerations, with assumptions being made concerning the type of conduct that should give rise to legal responsibility, and the moral considerations that provide the foundation for an excuse or defence.

Constitution away from the Courts (Princeton: Princeton University Press, 1999); L Kramer, *The People Themselves: Popular Constitutionalism and Judicial Review* (Oxford: Oxford University Press, 2004).

[10]   See, eg. A Tomkins, *Our Republican Constitution* (Oxford: Hart, 2005); T Poole, 'Back to the Future? Unearthing the Theory of Common Law Constitutionalism' *OJLS* (2003) 23: 453; T Poole, 'Questioning Common Law Constitutionalism' *LS* (2005) 25 142; T Hickman, 'In Defence of the Legal Constitution' *UTLJ* (2005) 55: 98; P Craig, 'Political Constitutionalism and Judicial Review', in C Forsyth, M Elliott, S Jhaveri, A Scully-Hill, M Ramsden (eds), *Effective Judicial Review: A Cornerstone of Good Governance* (Oxford: Oxford University Press, 2010); A Tomkins, 'The Role of the Courts in the Political Constitution' *UTLJ* (2010) 60: 1; P Craig, 'Political Constitutionalism and the Judicial Role: A Response' *I-CON* (2011) 9: 112; T R S Allan in this volume ch 4.

There are certain noteworthy features of this pattern of development. Thus it is incremental and analogical. This is true not only for case law, but also for the concepts that inform the levels adumbrated above. These concepts do not emerge 'perfect' and 'fully-formed'. They are fashioned, re-fashioned, developed, altered, and changed over time. The courts may well proceed relatively cautiously in this respect.[11]

The relationship between the three levels is symbiotic, with developments at one level impacting on the others. Thus, articulation of categories of legal doctrine at the second level may well prompt reconsideration of the overarching values to be served by that body of law as a whole. Or more detailed consideration of particular legal doctrine at the third level may be the catalyst for rethinking the very division between the categories that comprise the subject.

The content of the three levels will, moreover, evolve over time; it is not static. The very values that underpin a body of the law change over time. So too will the categories of legal doctrine that comprise the second level, or their more detailed meaning, the third level. The changes may come from within the common law itself, or they may result from legislative intervention.

The preceding framework facilitates understanding of the legitimacy of judicial review. When viewed from an historical perspective, the most basic rationale for judicial review was the need to render public power accountable, which connoted the twin ideas that an institution complied with conditions laid down in the enabling grant of power, and with certain precepts of good governance, thereby enhancing legitimacy.[12] This was the imperative for judicial involvement. It constituted the background objective and value at the first level identified above. Subsequent development of judicial review refined this basic precept.

It might be argued by those opposed to judicial review that the preceding rationale for judicial intervention is unconvincing. This requires argumentation, and has not to my knowledge been undertaken. It would be a daunting task, given that a very similar rationale is found in pretty much all developed legal systems. While 'is' does not make 'ought', it reinforces the conclusion that the basic normative premise for judicial review in the UK is plausibly grounded. Thus, if political constitutionalists wish to challenge the legal status quo, then it must be at the second and third levels, concerning the doctrinal implications drawn from the basic premise.

It is common, as we have seen, for criticism to be voiced against legal constitutionalism and judicial review on the ground that the doctrine is only justified through recourse to abstract concepts such as natural law, public reason or fundamental values. The historical development of doctrine rests, however, on more secure, specific and discrete foundations. This does not mean that the doctrinal categories

---

[11] C Sunstein *One Case at a Time, Judicial Minimalism on the Supreme Court* (Cambridge, Mass: Harvard University Press, 1999); C Sunstein, 'Incompletely Theorized Agreements in Constitutional Law', Chicago, Public Law and Legal Theory Working Paper No 147.

[12] S A de Smith, 'The Prerogative Writs' *CLJ* (1951) 40; S A de Smith, 'Wrongs and Remedies in Administrative Law' *MLR* (1952) 189; L Jaffe and E Henderson, 'Judicial Review and the Rule of Law: Historical Origins' *LQR* (1956) 72: 345; E G Henderson, *Foundations of English Administrative Law* (Cambridge, Mass: Harvard University Press, 1963); A Rubinstein, *Jurisdiction and Illegality* (Oxford: Oxford University Press, 1975); P Craig, 'Ultra Vires and the Foundations of Judicial Review' *CLJ* (1998) 63.

are value-free, nor does it mean that they are premised on some universal theory of value. What it does mean is that the existence of these categories, and their more specific meaning, levels two and three, are the result of reasoned analysis that draws on, and gives more concrete expression to, the foundational ideas that underlie judicial review explicated above. Such doctrinal development is incremental and symbiotic in the manner described above and thus may well lead to refinement or modification of the foundational precepts that underlie this body of law. The nature of the connection between the three levels can be briefly exemplified.

Consider in this respect certain core doctrines of judicial review that constitute what was termed the second level. It is axiomatic that if the courts are to render public power accountable, then there must be legal doctrine that serves to keep the relevant body within its assigned sphere of power. It is equally axiomatic that there must be controls to determine whether the power has been used for an improper purpose. Such legal doctrine is fundamental in the sense that if we are to have any body of law to check public power, then there must be doctrinal categories of this kind. This is equally true for the law dealing with the consequences of invalidity, which is grounded on the fundamental precept that where a public body makes an invalid decision, it should, in principle, be retrospectively void. It is therefore unsurprising that these doctrinal categories have existed from the seventeenth century, and have been refined since then. This still leaves a plethora of issues at the third level, concerning the more detailed content of these doctrinal categories, as exemplified by the debates concerning the criterion for jurisdictional review, the test for misuse of power where the public body pursues multiple purposes or the qualifications that should be made to retrospective nullity. Resolution of these issues will perforce entail normative assumptions, and commentators may disagree about the 'best solution'. Analogous debates occur in all areas to which the common law applies.

Consider also in this respect the fact that the courts developed from the outset principles of legality that took account of moral precepts and were designed to enhance good governance. A prime instance is natural justice. It was central to the objective of rendering public power accountable: in instrumental terms, decisions were more likely to be correct if people were heard before the decision was taken; in non-instrumental terms, it was part of what it means to be a person to be heard before the state took action against the individual.[13] Natural justice was therefore reflective of the twin precepts underlying judicial review identified above. It helped to ensure that public bodies remained within their assigned area, since a correct decision was more likely if a person was heard before it was taken, and it also functioned as a principle of legitimate good governance, as reflected in the non-instrumental rationale for natural justice. Another less well known principle of legality is that public or quasi-public bodies with monopoly power could charge

---

[13]   J L Mashaw, *Due Process in the Administrative State* (New Haven: Yale University Press, 1985); D J Galligan, *Due Process and Fair Procedures: A Study of Administrative Procedures* (Oxford: Oxford University Press, 1996).

no more than a reasonable price.[14] The principled reasoning in the seminal cases was posited on grounds that were part economic, and part concerned with precepts of good governance that should be demanded from bodies 'imbued with a public interest', given their de facto or de jure monopoly power. The fact that such doctrinal categories were shaped by normative and moral considerations is neither surprising nor illegitimate, and the same occurs when categories are forged in private law. It does not mean that we should simply accept any such judicial evaluation. The justification for the relevant category must rest on the strength of the normative argument, viewed against the objectives and values of the overall area.

Consider in this respect a third example concerning discretionary power. The courts recognized that the primary decision-maker had been given discretionary power by Parliament and therefore that they should not substitute judgment on the merits. They recognized also that certain public authorities, such as ministers and local authorities, had some democratic mandate. Legal intervention was nonetheless deemed warranted because of the twin precepts that underpin judicial review identified above: the imperative of checking that discretionary power was exercised in accordance with the enabling legislation, plus the belief that good governance demanded judicial oversight over choices made by the administration. The result was limited rationality review. There is no doubt that rationality review accords the judiciary a measure of interpretive choice, that the meaning ascribed to rationality has altered over time, and that there is debate as to the meaning that the term ought to bear.[15] These debates, which include the choice between rationality and proportionality, exemplify the discourse that commonly occurs about any body of law at the third level, viz, the more particular meaning to be accorded to a doctrinal category. The reality is nonetheless that if some control over discretionary power is warranted for the preceding reasons, then it will perforce be undertaken through criteria such as rationality or proportionality, which allow for differences of interpretation.

It is interesting and instructive to reflect on the legitimacy of EU administrative law in the light of the preceding analysis. This is more especially so, given that the EU courts did not have the luxury of having three centuries in which to fashion the tools of judicial review. The judicial creativity evident in the crafting of general principles of law was noted in the previous section. The EU courts were helped in this respect because this creative enterprise, the central pillars of which were fashioned in the 1970s and 1980s, was held to be legitimate for reasons analogous to those embraced three hundred years earlier in the UK.

Thus, judicial review was felt to be warranted at what was termed the first level, because of the twin imperatives of the need to ensure that EU institutions remained within the remit of their allotted power, and that their decision-making complied with certain precepts of good governance. It was readily apparent by the 1970s

[14] *Allnutt v Inglis* [1810] 12 East 527; *Bolt v Stennett* [1800] 8 TR 606; *Gard v Callard* [1817] 6 M & S 69; *Wright v Bruister* [1832] 4 B & Ald 116; P Craig, 'Constitutions, Property and Regulation' *PL* [1991] 538.
[15] *R v Chief Constable of Sussex, ex p International Trader's Ferry Ltd* [1999] 2 AC 418, 452; *R v Secretary of State for the Home Department, ex p Daly* [2001] 2 AC 532, 549.

and 1980s that the EEC had considerable power and that a schema of judicial review was required in order to ensure that norms of Community law were subject to proper oversight. The ECJ's jurisprudence could therefore be depicted as legitimate in enhancing the rule of law by ensuring that Community decision-making was subject to controls by way of judicial review that were analogous to those in the Member States. The imperfections in the Community legislative process enhanced the legitimacy of judicial review in furtherance of the rule of law. The period from the inception of the Community until the Single European Act 1986 was marked by the dominance of the Commission and Council in the decision-making process. This was aptly captured in the aphorism that 'the Commission proposes, the Council disposes'. The Assembly, rechristened the European Parliament, had little formal input into Community decision-making, being largely limited to consultation rights, and then only where a particular Treaty article so provided. This was reflected in its substantive exclusion from most Community decision-making. Change came slowly, but can be dated from the creation of the cooperation procedure in the Single European Act 1986 and its application to important areas such as art 95 EC, which was the legal foundation for measures to complete the single market. The cooperation procedure modified the dynamics of Community decision-making and laid the foundations for the more powerful co-decision procedure introduced in the Maastricht Treaty, renamed the ordinary legislative procedure by the Lisbon Treaty. It is therefore unsurprising in the light of the decision-making process that the ECJ should feel the need to put flesh on the bare bones of art 263 through the development of general principles, and it is equally unsurprising that its jurisprudence was seen as pushing at an open door, being welcomed as a method of rendering technocratic Community decision-making more accountable.

The doctrinal categories in EU law, and their more specific meaning—levels two and three as explicated earlier—are the result of reasoned analysis that draws on, and gives more concrete expression to, the foundational ideas that underlie EU judicial review, just as they do in the UK. There are doctrinal similarities and differences between the two systems. The latter are reflective of different conclusions concerning the specific implications that should be drawn from the background values that underpin EU judicial review. The relationship between levels one to three, and the similarities and differences between UK and EU law, can be revealed through examples that mirror those discussed in relation to UK law.

Consider in this respect the way in which the ECJ rapidly developed doctrinal controls dealing with error of law, error of fact, use of power for improper purposes, and invalidity. Legal doctrine of this kind is necessary in order to fulfil the background purpose of EU administrative law, which is in part to ensure that decision-makers remain within the remit of the powers assigned to them. Given this background objective, controls of the kind elaborated here are a necessary part of the doctrinal architecture at level two. They receive less attention than some of the better known precepts of EU administrative law, such as proportionality or legitimate expectations, but they have nonetheless formed an integral part of the doctrinal terrain since its inception. Many cases continue to be decided on grounds of error of law, error of fact and misuse of power.[16] The more particular meaning accorded to these concepts differs in some respects from analogous doctrine in UK law, thereby reflecting different value assumptions that play out at what was termed level three. Thus, to take but one example, the EU courts have from the outset undertaken judicial review of all questions of fact, with intervention grounded on the applicant being able to show a manifest error.[17] This stands in contrast to the difficulties that have plagued UK law in this area. Although the UK courts have clarified the scope of intervention for mistake of fact, uncertainties still remain.[18] The particular differences in legal doctrine can also result from legislation, or in the case of the EU, from Treaty provisions. Thus, UK law on invalidity struggled to balance the principled imperative that an ultra vires act should be retrospectively void, with the factual difficulties that unmitigated application of this precept can generate, the result being for many years covert manipulation of the terms void and voidable rather than open discussion of the circumstances in which the invalidity should be prospective rather than retrospective. EU law, by way of contrast, benefited from the fact that the Treaty at its outset stipulated in art 174 EEC[19] that, while the prima facie consequence of invalidity was that the act was void, it was nonetheless open to the ECJ to consider which effects of the challenged norm should be held to be definitive. The ECJ used this power to deal with cases where retrospective nullity would lead to very real difficulties for institutions and/or individuals.[20]

Consider as a second example the way in which EU courts rapidly developed within the doctrinal armoury, at what was termed level two, general principles of law that embodied moral precepts designed to enhance good governance. This is most readily apparent in the recognition of fundamental rights within general principles of law. It is true that the ECJ was pressed to take this step by the German and Italian courts, which threatened to test EU Regulations for compliance with national constitutional rights in the absence of EU fundamental rights' protection.[21] It is nonetheless very likely that the ECJ would have taken this step, even if it had not been pushed to do so by national courts. It was creating general principles of law at this time, and inclusion of fundamental rights was a natural step. The ECJ was fully aware of the increasing power wielded by the EEC even in the 1970s, and the fact that the power transcended the purely economic sphere. It was cognizant of the fact that the quid pro quo for increased governmental

---

[16] Craig, *EU Administrative Law*, ch 15.   [17] Craig, *EU Administrative Law*, ch 15.

[18] P Craig, *Administrative Law* (London: Sweet & Maxwell, 7th edn, 2012), ch 17.

[19] Now art 264 TFEU.

[20] Case 81/72 *Commission v Council* [1973] ECR 575; Case 51/87 *Commission v Council (Generalized Tariff Preferences)* [1988] ECR 5459, [21]-[22]; Case C-41/95 *European Parliament v Council* [1995] ECR I-4411; Case C-392/95 *European Parliament v Council* [1997] ECR I-3213, [25]-[27]; Case C-1159/96 *Portugal v Commission* [1998] ECR I-7379, [52]-[53]; Case C-445/00 *Austria v Council* [2003] ECR I-8549, [103]-[106]; Case C-93/00 *European Parliament v Council* [2001] ECR I-10119, [47]-[48]; Case C-378/00 *Commission and European Parliament v Council* [2003] ECR I-937, [73]-[77]; Cases C-402 and 415/05 P *Kadi and Al Barakaat International Foundation v Council and Commission* [2008] ECR I-6351, [373]-[376].

[21] M Dauses, 'The Protection of Fundamental Rights in the Community Legal Order' *ELRev* (1985) 10: 398; A Cassese, A Clapham, and J Weiler (eds), *European Union: The Human Rights Challenge*

power within liberal polities was recognition of some form of rights-based limit on its exercise, in order thereby to enhance the legitimacy of the political order.[22] The judicial development of fundamental rights within EU law bore many of the hallmarks of 'common law' reasoning, being incremental and analogical. Indeed the ECJ's very recognition of fundamental rights as an integral part of Community law prior to the EU Charter of Rights bears analogy with the process whereby the UK courts 'discovered', prior to the Human Rights Act 1998 (HRA 1998), that such rights were embedded in the common law. The principal difference was that the ECJ, unencumbered by Diceyan impediments to the recognition of rights, reached this solution a whole lot quicker than its UK counterparts. Due process is integral to any administrative law regime, and it was conceptualized as part of fundamental rights by the ECJ.[23] The principle had to be respected both where there was no specific legislation and where legislation existed, but did not give sufficient protection to the principle.[24] While the catalyst for the ECJ's recognition of process rights was in part the common law precepts of natural justice, it was also shaped by civilian conceptions of the rights of the defence. The moral precept of equality of arms that is integrally related to civilian conceptions of rights of the defence helps to explain some of the significant differences of detail between EU and UK law at what was termed level three, which is concerned with the detailed working out of legal doctrine. This is exemplified by recognition of access to the file as an important aspect of EU process rights,[25] and its absence from common law concepts of natural justice.

Consider finally a third example concerning discretionary power. The EU courts recognized, analogously to their UK counterparts, that the primary decision-maker had been given discretionary power pursuant to EU legislation and therefore that they should not substitute judgment on the merits. The ECJ also concluded, in common with courts in the UK, that there should be constraints on the exercise of discretionary power over and beyond those already considered. It considered that

(Berlin: Nomos, 1991); A Clapham, 'A Human Rights Policy for the European Community' *YEL* (1990) 10: 309; K Lenaerts, 'Fundamental Rights to be Included in a Community Catalogue' *ELRev* (1991) 16: 367.

[22] The relationship between review for fundamental rights and the EU legislative process will be explicated more fully below. Suffice it to say at this stage that the initial recognition of fundamental rights' review was less controversial than in common law jurisdictions for two related reasons. Firstly, civilian legal systems which predominate in the EU legal order are less troubled by constitutional review than their common law counterparts. Secondly, when such review was developed by the ECJ the EEC legislative process was imperfect, with scant involvement of the Assembly.

[23] Case C-49/88 *Al-Jubail Fertilizer v Council* [1991] ECR I-3187, [15]; Cases T-33-34/98 *Petrotub and Republica SA v Council* [1999] ECR II-3837; Case C-458/98 P *Industrie des Poudres Spheriques v Council and Commission* [2000] ECR I-8147, [99]; Case C-141/08 P *Foshan Shunde Yongjian Housewares & Hardware Co Ltd v Council* [2009] ECR I-9147, [83].

[24] Case T-260/94 *Air Inter SA v Commission* [1997] ECR II-997, [60].

[25] Case T-7/89 *SA Hercules Chemicals NV v Commission* [1991] ECR II-1711, [53]-[54]; Cases T-30-32/91 *Solvay SA v Commission* [1995] ECR II-1775; Cases C-204-205, 211, 213, 217, 219/00 P *Aalborg Portland v Commission* [2004] ECR I-123; M Levitt, 'Access to the File: the Commission's Administrative Procedures in Cases under Articles 85 and 86' *CMLRev* (1997) 34: 1413; C D Ehlermann and B Drijber, 'Legal Protection of Enterprises: Administrative Procedure, in particular

even if the primary decision-maker, normally but not always the Commission, acted for a proper purpose there should still be some constraint on the way in which the discretionary power was exercised. The particular EU legal solution differed from that chosen by UK courts, thereby reflecting a difference in doctrinal choice at levels two and three. Whereas the UK courts opted for limited rationality review, the EU courts chose to proceed via a general test of proportionality that was applied with varying degrees of intensity.[26] This is not the place to rehearse the arguments for and against proportionality being a general head of review in the UK.[27] Nor is that the purpose of this contribution, which is rather to stress the way in which legal doctrine develops through the instrumentality of the three levels adumbrated above. The doctrinal differences between the two systems are reflective of different conclusions concerning the specific implications that should be drawn from the background values that underpin EU judicial review. It should, moreover, be noted that the existence of such doctrinal variations does not preclude the existence of similar values informing the application of the legal doctrine, and this is so irrespective of whether it is accorded the same linguistic tag or not. Thus, EU courts do not articulate the varying intensity of proportionality review through language cast in terms of deference or respect for the primary decision-maker. It is clear, nonetheless, that the predominant test for proportionality review of social, political or economic discretionary power, whereby it is for the claimant to show manifest disproportionality,[28] is informed by similar considerations. The very fact that the exercise of such discretionary power entails complex social, political or economic assessment, and that the primary decision-maker has been given this responsibility either by the Treaty or a norm made pursuant to the Treaty, is the reason why intervention is pitched in terms of manifest disproportionality. The very test for review therefore embodies respect accorded to the primary decision-maker in the making of such complex assessments.

The credentials underlying any particular accountability mechanism must necessarily include analysis of the legitimacy of the detailed precepts used when holding others to account. Opponents of judicial review have been critical in this respect, particularly in the UK, arguing that it is only ever legitimated by recourse

Access to Files and Confidentiality' *ECLRev* (1996)375; H Nehl, *Principles of Administrative Procedure in EC Law* (Oxford: Hart, 1999) ch 5.

[26] G de Búrca, 'The Principle of Proportionality and its Application in EC Law' *YBEL* (1993) 13: 105; N Emiliou, *The Principle of Proportionality in European Law* (London: Kluwer, 1996); G Gerapetritis, *Proportionality in Administrative Law* (Athens: Sakkoulas, 1997); D U Galetta, *Principio di Proporzionalità e Sindacato Giurisdizionale nel Diritto Amministrativo* (Milan: Giuffrè, 1998); Craig, *EU Administrative Law*, ch 19.

[27] M Taggart, 'Proportionality, Deference, Wednesbury' *NZLR* [2008] 423; M Hunt, 'Against Bifurcation', in D Dyzenhaus, M Hunt and G Huscroft (eds), *A Simple Common Lawyer—Essays in Honour of Michael Taggart* (Oxford: Hart, 2009) ch 6; T Hickman *Public Law after the Human Rights Act* (Hart, Oxford, 2010) ch 9; P Craig, 'Proportionality, Rationality and Review' *NZLR* [2010] 265; T Hickman, 'Problems for Proportionality' *NZLR* (2010) 303; J King, 'Proportionality: a Halfway House' *NZLR* [2010] 327; Craig, *Administrative Law*, ch 21.

[28] Case C-491/01 *R v Secretary of State for Health, ex p British American Tobacco (Investments) Ltd and Imperial Tobacco Ltd* [2002] ECR I-11453, [123]; Case C-210/03 *The Queen, on the application of Swedish Match AB and Swedish Match UK Ltd v Secretary of State for Health* [2004] ECR I-11893, [48].

to general precepts of the rule of law. This view is misconceived. It is predicated on mistaken views about the way in which any body of law develops, whether public or private. The principles of judicial review are not value-free, but nor are any of the foundational or doctrinal precepts in other parts of the law, public or private. The detailed rules of judicial review in the UK and the EU have developed in a manner analogous to other types of legal doctrine, and can be explicated in accordance with the tripartite analysis set out above.

D. Hierarchy of norms

The discussion thus far has focused on the conceptual foundations and legitimacy of judicial review in the UK and EU. We now turn to the status of the principles of judicial review within their respective legal regimes, and their place within the hierarchy of norms. There is a marked contrast in this respect between the UK and EU, and the difference is significant in terms of the balance between judicial and legislative power.

In UK law, the principles of judicial review can be used to invalidate secondary norms and to interpret primary legislation, but they cannot be used to invalidate the latter. This is true even in relation to rights-based review pursuant to the HRA 1998, since legislation that is incompatible with Convention rights is not invalidated, but is subject to a declaration of incompatibility that does not affect its legal status. The government has, it is true, complied with such declarations of incompatibility, thereby reducing the difference between classic constitutional review of the US or German variety and the softer form that exists in the UK.[29] This does not alter the fact that the courts under the HRA 1998 do not formally invalidate legislation, nor does it alter the fact that the other grounds of judicial review can only be used to invalidate secondary norms and interpret primary legislation.

In EU law the position is different. The general principles of law sit below the Treaties, but above all else. They can therefore be used to interpret and invalidate EU legislative acts, delegated acts and implementing acts.[30] They can also be used to challenge primary legislation in Member States where the subject matter falls within the scope of EU law. It is important to emphasize that this status attaches to all general principles of law, not merely to that part dealing with fundamental rights. Thus, if a claimant can show that an EU legislative act is contrary to, for example, the principle of legitimate expectations or the precautionary principle and that it cannot be interpreted to be in conformity with such precepts, then it will be declared void. This conclusion will also follow if, for example, the claimant is able to show that an EU legislative act infringes proportionality even if the case

---

[29] S Gardbaum, 'The New Commonwealth Model of Constitutionalism' *AJCL* (2001) 49: 707; J L Hiebert, 'Parliamentary Bills of Rights: An Alternative Model' *MLR* (2006) 69: 7; J L Hiebert, 'New Constitutional Ideas: Can New Parliamentary Models Resist Judicial Dominance when Interpreting Rights?' *Texas LR* (2004) 82: 1963.
[30] Arts 288–91 TFEU.

has nothing to do with fundamental rights. Where the clash is between a general principle of law and national law, the ECJ does not declare the offending national norm void, but finds it inconsistent with EU law, with the result that national institutions including courts have an obligation to remove the inconsistency pursuant to the EU supremacy principle.

It is tempting to seek easy rationalizations for the difference. Consider the following explanation. It might be argued that the principles of UK judicial review could not be superior to primary legislation, albeit below constitutional norms, because there is no written constitution. It might be argued further that the contrasting status of general principles of EU law is to be explained simply by way of domestic analogy with French law, in which the *principes généraux du droit* sit above legislation but below the Constitution. The temptation to rationalize the law in this manner should nonetheless be resisted, because both parts of the preceding formulation are wrong, or at the very least incomplete.

The error is most obvious in relation to UK law. The mere fact that we have an unwritten constitution does not per se preclude principles of judicial review from being above primary legislation. It would be perfectly possible to imagine an unwritten constitution in which this was so. The rationale for the position in the UK is not because we have an unwritten constitution, but because its dominant principle is the sovereignty of Parliament, the corollary being that UK principles of judicial review may serve as interpretive guides concerning primary legislation, but cannot lead to its invalidation.

The error is less obvious in relation to EU law. The explanation for the status accorded to general principles in EU law cannot, however, rest per se on the analogy with *principes généraux du droit* in France. At the inception of the EEC the *principes généraux du droit* were not fully developed in French law. More importantly the Conseil d'Etat could not invalidate primary legislation, and the Conseil Constitutionnel had not yet undergone its (re-)birth. The renaissance of the Conseil Constitutionnel in the 1970s facilitated challenge to primary legislation, but only ex ante and there was no possibility for challenge ex post prior to the recent constitutional reforms in France.[31]

Thus any idea that the status accorded to general principles in EU law was somehow pre-ordained by domestic analogy is flawed. The reality was, rather, that the status accorded to such principles was a choice made by the ECJ, which was facilitated by the wording of what is now art 263 TFEU. Thus, once the ECJ interpreted the magic phrase 'any rule of law relating to their application' as the grounding for general principles of law, it was an easy step to place them above legislative acts in the hierarchy or norms, since art 263(1) TFEU was predicated on such acts being susceptible to judicial review.

This very wording of art 263(1) in rendering EU legislative acts susceptible to judicial review should, moreover, be viewed in the historical context sketched

---

[31] M Rogoff, 'Fifty Years of Constitutional Evolution in France: The 2008 Amendments and Beyond' (2011) 6 *Jus Politicum*. See also the debate in (2012) 7 *Jus Politicum* as to whether the Conseil Constitutionnel is the guardian of fundamental rights.

above. At the inception of the EEC the legislative process was dominated by the Commission and Council. It was imperfectly democratic to say the least; hence the idea that judicial review in accordance with general principles of law should sit 'above' norms made in this manner could be accepted with relative equanimity. The structural relationship between arts 263(1) and (2) has however remained unchanged in the subsequent years, notwithstanding the significant development and democratization of the EU legislative process.

The status accorded to general principles of law gives the EU courts a very powerful tool to shape the emerging EU legal and political order, since they are the ultimate deciders as to whether EU legislation is consonant with the ever-expanding list of general principles of EU law. The EU legislature may respond to invalidation of a legislative act for non-compliance with a general principle of law by re-drafting it to remove the legal infirmity. This does not alter the fact that the judicial view as to what is demanded by general principles of law will trump any such estimation made by the EU legislature, irrespective of whether the case is concerned with fundamental rights. There are various possible responses to the preceding analysis, three of which can be sketched here.

It might be argued, as intimated above, that the status of general principles of law in the hierarchy of norms is legitimate because the wording of art 263(1) is expressly predicated on legislative acts being reviewable in accordance with the criteria in art 263(2). It could be argued further that the framers of the Lisbon Treaty were fully mindful of review for compliance with general principles of law, which had existed for over forty years, and were content that the new Lisbon category of legislative act should be subject to this same regime. There is force in this view. There is nonetheless scant, if any, evidence from the deliberations that led to the Constitutional Treaty[32] to suggest that thought was given to this issue. There was discussion of the hierarchy of norms, which led to the Lisbon distinctions between legislative, delegated and implementing acts. There is, however, no indication of considered reflection on the status of general principles of law within the hierarchy of norms in a regime where the passage of legislative acts has some real democratic legitimacy.[33]

It might alternatively be contended that the status of general principles of law is justified in normative terms. A proponent of this view would maintain that the placing of general principles of law below the Treaties, but above other EU norms, is correct in normative terms. This argument must, however, be sustained, not merely stated as if self-evidently correct. Asseveration is not argumentation. Such an argument could be constructed. It would, however, necessarily be premised on contestable arguments concerning legal and political theory. The normative premise might be positivist in orientation, drawing on the wording of art 263 as the

---

[32] The Constitutional Treaty was never ratified, but much of the content was taken over into the Lisbon Treaty.

[33] This point could indeed be made pre-Lisbon, and post-Maastricht, given that the co-decision procedure, the precursor to the ordinary legislative procedure, had democratic legitimacy in the areas to which it applied.

source-based legitimation for judicial articulation of general principles of law. The normative premise might alternatively be a non-positivist theory of law, in which it was accepted as legitimate for courts to create general principles of law that bind the legislature, irrespective of the precise wording of art 263 in this regard.

It might be maintained as a third type of response that the distinction between the UK and EU in terms of the status accorded to the principles of judicial review is less dramatic than might be thought, because the line between invalidation and interpretation is not clear cut. There is, so it might be argued, ample evidence that courts which cannot invalidate primary legislation can nonetheless achieve much the same ends through strong principles of interpretation. The principle of legality used by UK courts, whereby they refuse to read primary legislation as invasive of fundamental rights in the absence of clear and unequivocal words showing that the legislature had understood the implications of its action, exemplifies what can be achieved through principles of interpretation.[34] The preceding argument might be further reinforced by reference to intensity of review. A legal system such as the EU that allows legislation to be invalidated for non-compliance with general principles can moderate the effect of this through intensity of review. Thus, for example, legislative acts may be invalidated for infringement of proportionality, but the claimant will have to show manifest disproportionality for this to occur where the legislative act encapsulates complex discretionary assessments involving social, political or economic choice. There is force in the previous arguments. Courts can achieve much by way of interpretation, and claimants may have to surmount high hurdles to show breach of the general principle that is the condition precedent for invalidation. These arguments should nonetheless be kept in perspective. The fact that the line between interpretation and invalidation may be less stark than initially thought does not mean that it is irrelevant in terms of practical outcome, or in terms of what it signifies symbolically about the relationship between courts and legislatures. The fact that courts can condition invalidity on high hurdles must also be kept in perspective. The status accorded to general principles in EU law applies to all such principles, and not simply proportionality in relation to which the courts have developed variable intensity of review.

The credentials underlying any particular accountability mechanism must necessarily include analysis not only of the legitimacy of the detailed precepts used when holding others to account, but also of their status within the legal order as a whole. The placing of such precepts within the hierarchy of norms reflects a choice as to their status as compared to other legal norms. That choice has been made differently in the UK and the EU and while one might seek to diminish the difference in the manner considered above, it remains of significance, in both practical and normative terms.

---

[34] *R v Secretary of State for the Home Department, ex p Simms & O' Brien* [2000] 2 AC 115; *R (Morgan Grenfell & Co Ltd) v Special Commissioner of Income Tax* [2003] 1 AC 563; *R (Anufrijeva) v Secretary of State for the Home Department* [2004] 1 AC 604; *A v HM Treasury* [2010] 2 AC 534.

E. Rights

The protection of rights of the kind commonly found in a Bill of Rights is certainly not the only focus of judicial review. There are many cases that come before the courts in all legal systems that do not entail any such right. The way in which rights-based cases are treated is nonetheless instructive when thinking more generally about accountability secured through judicial means, and when considering the central precepts of any system of judicial review. We have already touched on this issue in the preceding discussion when considering the role of fundamental rights within the regime of EU judicial review, and when analysing general principles in relation to the hierarchy of norms. It is nonetheless important to address the issue directly. There are, as will be seen, similarities and differences between UK and EU law in this respect.

We can begin with the similarities. Prior to 1998, the UK courts made it clear that fundamental rights were embedded in the common law and would be protected by the UK courts in judicial review actions.[35] The advent of the HRA 1998 nonetheless transformed judicial review in the UK. There was a significant expansion in the number of cases that raise rights-based arguments in the context of judicial review actions. The lesson from this is that enshrining fundamental rights in statutory form had a marked impact on the extent to which they would be relied on in legal actions. This is not surprising. Claimants are likely to feel on more secure foundations when relying on a statute that clearly lists rights and has received Parliament's imprimatur.

The pattern was similar in the EU. The ECJ engaged in fundamental rights review since the 1970s. The number of such cases was nonetheless limited. Claimants, Advocates-General, the CFI and more recently the ECJ relied on the EU Charter of Fundamental Rights[36] for interpretive guidance even prior to the Lisbon Treaty. The fact that the Charter is now rendered legally binding by the Lisbon Treaty[37] is likely to increase the profile of rights-based claims within judicial review actions. Claimants can point to a clear set of rights, which are legally binding on EU institutions and Member States when they act within the sphere of EU law. The profile of judicial review cases is therefore likely to change in the EU in a manner that bears analogy to the development that occurred in the UK. The change may indeed be greater because of the very breadth of the Charter. The HRA 1998 incorporated rights from the European Convention on Human Rights. The list of rights in the ECHR is considerably narrower than that in the Charter, and that is so notwithstanding the fact that some Charter provisions are deemed to be principles rather than rights.[38] The very breadth of the Charter provisions will therefore fuel claims testing their meaning, scope and interpretation. The number of complex rights-based claims is likely to increase because of other changes made

---

[35] *A-G v Guardian Newspapers (No 2)* [1990] 1 AC 109, 283–4; *Derbyshire County Council v Times Newspapers Ltd* [1993] AC 534.
[36] Charter of Fundamental Rights of the European Union [2010] OJ C83/389.
[37] art 6(1) TEU.   [38] art 52(5) Charter.

by the Lisbon Treaty. It brought the Area of Freedom, Security and Justice (AFSJ) within the general framework of EU law, including judicial control. Many AFSJ measures involve conflicts with classic civil and political rights, and claimants will increasingly seek recourse to EU courts to resolve these complex issues. The possibility of bringing such actions has been rendered somewhat easier by changes made in the Lisbon Treaty to the rules for locus standi for direct actions.[39]

There are two related differences in relation to the treatment of rights within the schema of review in the UK and EU. The first was touched on in the previous discussion, which is the placing of rights-based protections within the hierarchy of norms. The difference between UK and EU law was considered above. Review for compliance with fundamental rights can be used to interpret primary law in the UK, whereas it can be employed to interpret and invalidate EU legislative acts, although this should be read subject to the earlier discussion as to how this distinction might be qualified. The difference has become more marked after the Lisbon Treaty. This is because the EU Charter now has a status distinct even from other general principles of law, having the same legal value as the constituent Treaties themselves.[40] Detailed discussion of the implications that this might have is beyond the scope of this chapter. Suffice it to say that even prior to the Lisbon Treaty the ECJ's fundamental rights jurisprudence could be used in relation to Treaty articles, in order to interpret them in the manner that was most compatible with protected rights, and Member States could only formally alter the content/application of a general principle of law through Treaty amendment. The elevation of the Charter to the same status as the constituent Treaties is nonetheless at the very least symbolically significant.

The second difference between the UK and EU in relation to rights concerns the way in which this exercise of judicial power is viewed within the respective systems. We have already noted the common law preoccupation with the legitimacy of constitutional and non-constitutional review. The exercise of rights-based review in the EU has, by way of contrast, been viewed with relative equanimity.[41] This was in part because the counter-majoritarian difficulty that lies at the heart of rights-based constitutional review was not initially relevant in the EU, given the nature of the initial decision-making process in which power was divided between Commission and Council to the exclusion of the Assembly. It was in part because civilian legal systems dominate within the EU and those trained in such systems are generally less troubled by judicial invalidation of primary legislation pursuant to constitutional rights-based guarantees than their common law counterparts. This point should be kept in perspective. It would be wrong to imagine that civilian systems make no accommodation for legislative choice when undertaking rights-based constitutional review. They have done so through variable proportionality review,

---

[39] art 263(4) TFEU.   [40] art 6(1) TEU.

[41] There has of course been much literature dealing with various aspects of fundamental rights, such as the derivation of the rights, whether the courts were taking such rights seriously, and the extent to which such rights could and should bind the Member States. This does not alter the point made in the text, which is that commentators were not troubled by the legitimacy of rights-based review on the grounds that have given rise to concern in the common law world.

the intensity of which can alter depending on the nature of the right,[42] and this same technique is evident in ECJ case law.[43]

It is nonetheless still true that concern about the legitimacy of constitutional review predicated on the anti-majoritarian argument, combined with the fact of disagreement about the meaning and application of constitutional rights, does not have the same academic or judicial prominence in civilian regimes. The complex rationale for this difference between common law and civilian systems cannot be explored here. Suffice it to say that the rationale is eclectic, drawing on diverse factors including the background positivist legal theory that informs much civilian adjudication and the relative trust placed in courts and legislatures.

It remains to be seen whether amendments made by the Lisbon Treaty herald any change on this issue in the EU. The legislative acts challenged before the Union courts will normally be made via the ordinary legislative procedure, with input from the Commission, Council and European Parliament. The extension of the ordinary legislative procedure, and the symbolic change in name from that of co-decision, has strengthened the European Parliament's role in the EU political order and further enhanced the democratic legitimacy of EU legislation. The interpretation of Charter rights will be contestable. There will inevitably be cases in which the EU courts substitute their view for that of the legislature on the meaning and interpretation of such a right. The counter-majoritarian aspect of constitutional review and the prevalence of disagreement about the meaning of constitutional rights will be more apparent than hitherto.

It may be that the quiet equanimity that has attended EU constitutional review hitherto will continue in the future. The Council and European Parliament may accept such judicial decisions, on the assumption that courts are 'naturally' entitled to the last word on such matters. Concern about the legitimacy of constitutional review may continue to be regarded as primarily a common law preoccupation. This may be so; time will tell. It is, however, also possible that the perennial issue about the balance between the rule of law and democracy, which has been long debated in common law regimes, will become a live issue in the EU in a way that it has not done hitherto. We should at the very least be aware of the changed circumstances in which fundamental rights review will take place under the Lisbon Treaty.

The credentials underlying any particular accountability mechanism include analysis of the status accorded to the detailed precepts used when holding others to account. This issue has been especially contentious in common law regimes in discussion of rights-based constitutional review, where the courts use fundamental rights as the reason for invalidating primary legislation. It has also featured in the

---

[42] V Goesel Le-Bihan, 'Réflexion iconoclaste sur le contrôle de proportionnalité exercé par le Conseil constitutionnel' [1997] RFDA 227; 'Le contrôle de proportionnalité dans la jurisprudence du Conseil constitutionnel: figures récentes' [2007] RFDA 269; 'Le contrôle exercé par le Conseil constitutionnel: défense et illustration d'une théorie générale' [2001] RFDA 67; BVerfG 53, 135 (145); BVerfG 115, 276 (308); BVerfG 103, 293 (307).
[43] Case C-491/01 *British American Tobacco* (n 28) [149]-[152]; Cases C-20 and 64/00 *Booker Aquacultur Ltd and Hydro Seafood GSP Ltd v Scottish Ministers* [2003] ECR I-7411; Craig, *EU Administrative Law,* ch 19.

discourse about review of primary legislation under the HRA 1998, even though the UK courts cannot formally invalidate primary legislation that is inconsistent with the rights protected by that Act. The EU has for the reasons adumbrated above largely escaped such controversy, but whether it continues to do so remains to be seen.

F. Conclusion

This chapter has sought to enhance our understanding of judicial accountability through consideration of certain features that are central to the systems of judicial review in the UK and the EU. To this end the chapter has examined the conceptual foundation for judicial review, its legitimacy, its place within the hierarchy of norms and the treatment accorded to rights. There are not surprisingly similarities and differences between the respective systems. There are doubtless other features that might have been included within such an analysis, but limits of space place constraints in this respect. It is in any event difficult to think of additional features that would displace those discussed. The most significant additional factor that shapes the respective systems is the way in which they respond to the challenges posed by other legal regimes with which they inter-relate, such as the ECHR and the international legal order. The integration of this complex material with that discussed in the present chapter is a task for another day.

9

Parliamentary Accountability and the Judicial System

Andrew Le Sueur*

A. Introduction

Tensions between political and legal accountability are a backdrop to many debates about the character and future direction of the British constitution.[1] This essay explores a juncture of these two modes of accountability by examining how the UK Parliament exercises accountability in relation to the judicial system of England and Wales.

Part A defines 'the judicial system' and what may be meant by parliamentary accountability and judicial independence in this context. Part B takes an institutional and procedural approach to examining the opportunities Parliament has for engaging in accountability activities in relation to the judicial system, focusing in particular on the evolving role of Select Committees. Part C uses an inductive approach to map current accountability practices in Parliament in relation to particular aspects of the judicial system by drawing on examples from the parliamentary record to develop an explanation of what is and ought to be the reach of MPs' and peers' accountability functions relating to judges and courts.

1. The judicial system

The term 'judicial system' is used in this study to define an area of state activity that is narrower than the whole legal system (so, for example, legal aid and the legal professions are left out) but broader than 'the judiciary' or 'the judicial power of the state'. Deciding cases and, for the higher courts, judgment writing to create precedents are the core activities of the judicial system. Closely connected to these are the practices and procedures of courts. Around this core is a penumbra

* Professor of Constitutional Justice, University of Essex. I am grateful to Nicholas Bamforth, Graham Gee, and Peter Leyland for comments on a draft; and to Christopher Luff for research assistance; but of course any errors and omissions are mine alone.

[1] An overview of the debates can be found in A Le Sueur, M Sunkin and J Murkens *Public Law: Text, Cases, and Materials* (Oxford: Oxford University Press, 2013), ch 2.

of other activities and features that support and facilitate the judicial role. This includes the foundational texts (legislation and 'soft law') creating new courts and shaping the governance of the judiciary; decision-making about judicial careers (appointments, terms and conditions of service, salaries and pensions, discipline and dismissals); deployment; training; and the management of the physical estate and infrastructures of the courts and tribunals.

Viewed as a set of institutions and decision-making processes, the judicial system comprises judges, ministers (in particular the Lord Chancellor/Secretary of State for Justice), officials, and holders of public office (such as the commissioners of the Judicial Appointments Commission for England and Wales)—all of them potential targets of accountability according to their responsibilities.

2. Parliamentary accountability

Parliamentary accountability centres on formal questioning, comment, and critical evaluation of past decisions or changes to existing or proposed practices or policy by MPs and peers, as reported in *Hansard* and other parliamentary publications. The occasional criticism of judges by ministers and other parliamentarians in interviews, conference speeches,[2] and extra-parliamentary writing[3] are important in setting the tone of relations with the judiciary but they fall outside the scope of this essay, as they are not part of the formal parliamentary record.

The constitutional imperative for *some* kind of accountability in relation to *some* aspects of the judicial system cannot now be seriously doubted.[4] As a relevant principle, parliamentarians have accepted it,[5] as have the judiciary of England and Wales,[6] and ministers.[7] This reflects the general importance now attached to clear lines of accountability across all public services; the legitimacy of most kinds of public power now depends on satisfactory accountability mechanisms. The challenge that remains is to define more closely the circumstances in which

---

[2] See eg. Home Secretary Theresa May's remarks at the 2011 Conservative Party conference disparaging a tribunal judge whom, she claimed, had ruled that an illegal immigrant could not be removed from the UK because of a pet cat: Adam Wagner, 'Cat had nothing to do with failure to deport man' (*UK Human Rights Blog*, 4 October 2011) <http://ukhumanrightsblog.com/2011/10/04/cat-had-nothing-to-do-with-failure-to-deport-man/> accessed 10 March 2012.

[3] For example, in 2012 steps were taken by the Northern Ireland Attorney General to prosecute Peter Hain MP (a former Secretary of State for Northern Ireland) for the ancient form of contempt known as 'scandalizing a judge' over remarks he made about a judicial review judgment of Lord Justice Girvan in his memoirs *Outside In* (London: Biteback 2012). The charges were dropped in May 2012 after Hain wrote to the Attorney General to explain and clarify his remarks.

[4] See Andrew Le Sueur, 'Developing mechanisms for judicial accountability in the UK' 24 *LS* (2004) 73.

[5] See eg. House of Lords Constitution Committee, *Relations between the executive, the judiciary and Parliament* (HL 2006-7, 151), para. 121; House of Lords Constitution Committee, *Relations between the executive, the judiciary and Parliament: Follow-up Report* (HL 2007-8, 177).

[6] 'The Accountability of the Judiciary' (2007) <http://www.judiciary.gov.uk> (accessed 22 April 2013). The essay focuses on England and Wales and addresses issues relating to the UK Supreme Court only in passing.

[7] Department for Constitutional Affairs, *Constitutional Reform: a new way of appointing judges* (CP 10/03, 2003).

parliamentarians may legitimately operate in relation to the judicial system, which accountability tools are best for the job, and what aspects of the judicial system should remain off-limits, or subject only to light-touch accountability oversight, by reason of the need to respect the constitutional principles of independence of the judiciary and separation of powers. This essay is a contribution to that debate.

a. *The orthodox approach*

The conventional account of the limits of parliamentary accountability for the judicial system rests on two main ideas. The first is that the constitutional principle of judicial independence prohibits parliamentary scrutiny of the core aspect of the judicial system (deciding cases and setting precedents). In 2004 Chris Leslie MP, a junior minister, explained the point as follows :

> Judicial decisions are taken and explained in public (save where the circumstances of a case demand confidentiality) and any decision which a judge makes is liable to be scrutinised, and if necessary overturned, on appeal, which is also a public process. Judges are therefore fully accountable for their judicial decisions through the appeal system. Judges are not, however, accountable through a political process for the decisions they take, as this would not be consistent with judicial independence. The Lord Chancellor and Secretary of State therefore does not monitor appeals against decisions made by individual judges, and it is not his role to intervene in judicial decisions or consider complaints about judicial decisions.[8]

The constitutional principle of judicial independence is a multifaceted concept.[9] It relates to individual judges (who should not be placed under such personal pressure through inquiries or criticism by politicians as to influence or risk influencing their decision making) and to the judiciary as a whole (which as an institution of the state should enjoy a relatively high degree of autonomy vis-à-vis government and parliament). Orthodox thinking priorities judicial independence over accountability: the latter must yield to the former in day-to-day practices and in constitutional design. It will be argued later that the broad *cordon sanitaire* around the judicial system that is often called for in the name of orthodox approaches to judicial independence is out of step with actual developments in the UK Parliament. Parliamentarians believe they can, and they do, question aspects of the judicial system more than orthodox thinking suggests is proper.

The other main idea in the orthodox approach is the assumption that accountability practices associated with ministerial responsibility are adequate to scrutinize other aspects of the judicial system beyond the prohibited zone. In other words, ministers are and should be answerable through parliamentary questions, in debates, in Select Committee inquiries; and this delivers a satisfactory level of accountability. Before 2005, the Lord Chancellor was the member of government

---

[8] HC Deb 22 January 2004, vol 416, col 1448W (answering a question from Vera Baird QC MP).
[9] For a detailed statement of the particular norms contained under its umbrella, see *The Mount Scopus Approved Revised International Standards of Judicial Independence* (March 2008) <http://www.jwp.org> (accessed 30 July 2013).

responsible for judicial appointments, for allocation of resources to the courts, and so on—and he was answerable to Parliament for these matters. Whether in practice, ministerial responsibility was an effective form of accountability is open to question, not least because the Lord Chancellor's Department was the last of the major government departments to become shadowed by a House of Commons Select Committee.[10]

b. Recent innovations

This approach to accountability of the judicial system (that is, a prohibited zone plus ministerial accountability for the penumbra) is no longer satisfactory. First, remarkable changes to the scope of the 'judicial power of the state'[11] have taken place, through the development of common law powers of judicial review, the impact of the Human Rights Act 1998, and of European Union law. Judicial decision-making now impacts on government policy-making and parliamentary legislation in ways unthinkable two generations ago. It is unrealistic, against the background of these developments, to imagine that Parliament and parliamentarians will or should want to maintain a *cordon sanitaire* around judicial decision-making. Insofar as court decisions impact on the national interest and the lives of constituents, parliamentarians will want to debate and criticise them.

Second, since 2005 there have been equally remarkable changes to the governance arrangements for the judicial system. The radical reforms to the office of Lord Chancellor mean that traditional notions of ministerial responsibility are no longer adequate to secure accountability for leadership roles, budgets, and decision-making powers that have been transferred or shared beyond the government department responsible for the judicial system—which was the Lord Chancellor's Department ('LCD') up to 2003, the relatively short-lived Department for Constitutional Affairs 2003-7 (nicknamed 'DeCaf' by some wags but more respectfully 'the DCA') and the Ministry of Justice ('MoJ') since May 2007.

The Lord Chancellor/Secretary of State provides political leadership in the Ministry of Justice, with four junior ministers. The Lord Chancellor and Secretary of State are two distinct ministerial offices to which the Prime Minister appoints the same person. Legislation dealing with judiciary-related matters normally specifies the Lord Chancellor to be the responsible minister, though on occasion there has been debate as to which is the appropriate minister.[12] The distinction is of constitutional importance as the Constitutional Reform Act 2005 places broad duties on the Lord Chancellor to 'have regard' to 'the need to defend' the independence of the judiciary and 'the need for the public interest in regard to matters relating to the judiciary or otherwise to the administration of justice to be properly

---

[10] See generally Dawn Oliver and Gavin Drewry *The Law and Parliament* (London: Butterworths 1998).

[11] The turn of phrase used in the Contempt of Court Act 1981, s 19.

[12] The bill that became the Legal Services Act 2007 initially had the Secretary of State as the responsible minister; it was amended to Lord Chancellor: see HL Deb, 9 January 2007, vol 688, col 136.

represented in decisions affecting those matters'.[13] Other ministers have the lesser duty to 'uphold the continued independence of the judiciary'.[14] The Ministry is a major department of state (no longer the sleepy backwater that the LCD once was), with an annual budget of £8.58 billion in 2011-12, of which £1.21 billion is allocated to HM Courts and Tribunals Service. The Ministry employed over 78,000 FTE staff in 2009-10.

In the new governance arrangements, several important functions are now carried out by public bodies that have an arm's length relationship to the Ministry, some with executive powers, some dispute resolution and inspection roles, and some advisory. This judicial comitology is set out in Appendix 1 below. Several have been or shortly will be abolished under the Public Bodies Act 2011 as part of government policy to reduce the number and cost of quangos.

Other roles have been transferred directly to the judiciary, under the ultimate leadership of the LCJ; a network of boards and committees carry out executive decisions and advisory work (see Appendix 2). The Judicial Office consists of approximately 190 FTE civil servants who report directly to the Lord Chief Justice rather than to ministers.[15] It has five groups of staff: strategy, communications, and governance; human resources; senior judicial support through private offices and jurisdictional teams; the Judicial College; and corporate services. There are plans to transfer decision-making power to accept, reject, or ask for reconsideration of selections by the Judicial Appointments Commission for some judicial posts from the Lord Chancellor (in the Ministry of Justice) to the Lord Chief Justice (in effect, to the Judicial Office); presumably a transfer of staff from the Ministry of Justice will accompany this.[16] The Judicial Executive Board (JEB), 'which appears to be envisaged as a sort of judicial Cabinet',[17] is chaired by the Lord Chief Justice and comprises nine senior judges with management responsibilities and the chief executive of the Judicial Office.

A more varied range of accountability mechanisms is needed to respond to these redistributions and fragmentations of responsibility. This essay focuses on what happens (or does not happen) in Parliament, but it is instructive to note developments in accountability elsewhere. One is that as head of the judiciary of England and Wales, the LCJ holds an annual press conference, the transcript of which is published online. In December 2011, Joshua Rozenberg, Frances Gibb (*The Times*) and other journalists from the *Daily Telegraph*, the *Guardian, Daily Mail, Evening Standard,* BBC, ITV News, and the Press Association questioned Lord Judge for 45 minutes.[18] The LCJ expressed diffidence in answering several

---

[13] CRA 2005, s 3(6).   [14] CRA 2005, s 3(1).

[15] <http://www.judiciary.gov.uk/training-support/jo-index> (accessed 22 April 2013).

[16] Ministry of Justice, *Appointments and Diversity: 'A Judiciary for the 21st Century'* (London: Ministry of Justice 2011); Crime and Courts Act 2013.

[17] HLConstitution Committee, *Relations between the executive, the judiciary and Parliament* (6th report of 2006-7) para. 100.

[18] 'Press conference held by the Lord Chief Justice of England and Wales' (London, 6 December 2011) <http://www.judiciary.gov.uk/Resources/JCO/Documents/News%20Release/lcj-press-conference-06122011.pdf> (accessed 22 April 2013).

questions on matters of current political controversy (legal aid reform, mandatory life sentences for murder) or because they dealt with particular cases (contempt of court). Other questions related to parliamentary privilege, sentencing after the summer 2011 riots, and the prison population. Asked about a controversial public lecture given by Jonathan Sumption QC shortly before his swearing in as a Justice of the Supreme Court,[19] Lord Judge said he was 'very sympathetic with Mr Sumption and the views he has expressed', telling Steve Doughty of the *Daily Mail* that 'I would love to give you something to write down'. Lord Judge said 'Judges have to be careful to remember that we are enforcing the law. As to that, we have no choice. We enforce the law as we find it to be. I think we have to be careful to remember that we cannot administer the responsibilities which others have'.

Since the 2010 coalition government came to power, new political priorities for accountability across the whole of government have been articulated. In a speech to civil servants, David Cameron MP outlined the Conservatives' approach:

We want to replace the old system of bureaucratic accountability with a new system of democratic accountability—accountability to the people, not the government machine. We want to turn government on its head, taking power away from Whitehall and putting it into the hands of people and communities. We want to give people the power to improve our country and public services, through transparency, local democratic control, competition and choice.[20]

Courts boards provide an illustration of the new approach in relation to the judicial system. The Courts Act 2003, s 4 provided that 'England and Wales is to be divided into areas for each of which there is to be a courts board'. Boards had the duty 'to scrutinise, review and make recommendations about the way in which the Lord Chancellor is discharging his general duty in relation to the courts with which the board is concerned'.[21] Boards consisted of at least one judge, two lay magistrates, and at least four others, two of whom were 'representative of the people living in the area'.[22] Over time, their number was reduced from 42 to 19. They are abolished under the Public Bodies Act 2011; during the passage of that bill, the minister explained 'there are now other structures in place such as the Justice Issues Group and area judicial forums to ensure that magistrates' views are heard. There are also strong local relationships with magistrates' bench chairs' and 'there are other ways to ensure that the needs of the community are met, such as customer surveys, open days and more effective use of court user meetings'.[23]

---

[19] Jonathan Sumption, 'Judicial and political decision-making: the uncertain boundary' (The FA Mann Lecture, London, 9 November 2011) <http://www.guardian.co.uk/law/interactive/2011/nov/09/jonathan-sumption-speech-politicisation-judges> (accessed 22 April 2013). For a response, see Stephen Sedley, 'Judicial Politics' *London Review of Books* Vol.34, No.4, (2012) 15.
[20] David Cameron, 'We will make government accountable to the people' (8 July 2010) <http://www.conservatives.com/News/Speeches/2010/07/David_Cameron_We_will_make_government_accountable_to_the_people.aspx> (accessed 22 April 2013).
[21] Courts Act 2003, s 5.   [22] Courts Act 2003, sch 1, para. 2.
[23] Minister of State, Ministry of Justice (Lord McNally), HL Deb 11 January 2011, vol 747, col 1305-6.

Transparency has swept through the judicial system in recent years. The Ministry of Justice's business plan makes a commitment 'to ensure that the Department can be held to account as it moves this work forward and we will do this through our information strategy. Along with the rest of government, the Department will publish an unprecedented amount of data so the public can hold us to account. This will cover who we are, what we spend and what we achieve'.[24] The Ministry now publishes, by court: what sentences are given for each type of offence; conviction rates; how long it takes for cases to be decided; the number of sitting days; and financial allocation and spend.[25] A similar commitment to transparency can be seen in the arm's length bodies, down to trivial expense claims.[26] More significantly, the whole judicial selection process is described in great detail on the Judicial Appointment Commission's website and in its publications.

B. Opportunities for parliamentary accountability

Against this background of dramatic increases in the judicial power of the state, changes in governance and new approaches to accountability, what role does Parliament have in oversight of the judicial system? What role should it have? Finding answers to these questions is not straightforward, not least because of the need to protect judicial independence from inappropriately targeted accountability claims.

1. The accountability toolkit

Parliament has at its disposal a variety of accountability mechanisms that can be deployed for oversight of the judicial system. Examples of how these are used are provided below:

i. There are opportunities to scrutinize legislative proposals. In relation to bills, this now includes the possibility of pre-legislative scrutiny (if the government publishes a bill in draft), the legislative process in each House (with the parallel scrutiny of committees including the Joint Committee on Human Rights and the House of Lords Constitution Committee), and relatively new practices of post-legislative scrutiny (where the responsible government department reviews legislation five years or so after enactment and reports to a Select Committee).

---

[24] Ministry of Justice, *Business Plan 2011-15* (London, 2011) <http://www.number10.gov.uk/wp-content/uploads/MOJ-Business-Plan1.pdf> (accessed 22 April 2013).
[25] See <http://www.justice.gov.uk/statistics/previous-stats/criminal-annual> (accessed 22 April 2013).
[26] Anybody interested can, for example, find on the JAC's website detailed information on expenses such as that Dame Lorna Kelly claimed £4.25 for meals on 28 July 2011 in relation to a selection and character committee and diversity forum: JAC, 'Senior Management Team and Commissioner Expenses Q2' <http://jac.judiciary.gov.uk/about-jac/1112.htm> (accessed 8 March 2012).

ii. A variety of different kinds of debate may be held on the floor of the House, including government motions, topical debates, substantive motions for the adjournment, and daily adjournment debates.

iii. Ministers are obliged to answer oral and written questions. 'The purpose of a question is to obtain information or press for action; it should not be framed primarily so as to convey information, or so as to suggest its own answer or to convey a particular point of view, and it should not be in effect a short speech'.[27]

iv. Early Day Motions proposed by backbench MPs drawing attention to an event or cause, which MPs sign to register their support. Hardly any are actually debated.[28]

v. Select Committee inquires enable MPs and peers (usually working in a non-partisan, cross-party manner) to carry out detailed evidence-based investigations, receiving oral and written evidence. Reports may be debated on the floor of the House or in Westminster Hall. The relevant government department is expected to make a formal response to the committee's findings and recommendations.

vi. Pre-appointment Select Committee hearings for appointments to various senior public offices.[29] In relation to the judicial system, the House of Commons Justice Committee is responsible for scrutinizing the government's preferred candidate for the chair of the Judicial Appointments Commission and the Chair of the Office of Legal Complaints. Some commentators have argued in favour of extending pre-appointment scrutiny to senior judicial posts but so far Parliament has viewed this as anathema.[30]

These may form a network of interconnected activities: for example, what a judge says in oral evidence to a Select Committee may be quoted in the committee's report, which in turn will prompt a debate in the House and a response from ministers; another illustration of the connectedness of the mechanisms is that information obtained by an MP from a written parliamentary question may be used to lobby a minister or in a speech on the floor of the House.

2. Select Committees

Select committees have acquired a central role in accountability practices relating to the judicial system. They provide the most rigorous sort of parliamentary scrutiny, conducting thematic inquiries based on oral and written evidence.

---

[27] M Jack (ed), *Erskine May's Treaties on The Law, Privileges, Proceedings and Usage of Parliament* (24th edn, London: LexisNexis, 2011), 357.
[28] See <http://www.parliament.uk/edm> (accessed 22 April 2013).
[29] House of Commons Liaison Committee, *Pre-appointment hearings by Select Committees* (2007-8, 384); Paul Waller and Mark Chalmers, *An evaluation of pre-appointment scrutiny hearings* (London: UCL Constitution Unit 2010).
[30] See section C3 below.

On occasion, the launch of an inquiry makes front-page news.[31] Sometimes a Select Committee oral evidence session ends with the publication of a transcript on the relevant committee's web page. Normally, however, the Select Committee produces a report containing findings and recommendations, often accompanied by a press release. The government is expected to make a formal written response within two months, which in turn is published by the Select Committee (with or without further comment). Subject to the pressures on the parliamentary time-table, a Select Committee will attempt to secure a debate on the floor of the House for a significant inquiry. Thus, on 18 November 2008 the Constitution Committee's two reports on relations between the executive, judiciary and Parliament were the subject of a 'take note' debate in the 'dinner hour' during which ten speeches were made.[32] They are able to engage in follow-up inquiries if it is thought desirable to return to an issue. The practice of the Constitution Committee and the Justice Committee of having periodic meetings with the LCJ and the Lord Chancellor also enables some 'triangulation' to take place, whereby one is able to comment on the evidence previously given by the other.

One of the most notable developments in recent years is the phenomenon of judges appearing to give oral evidence to Select Committees and submitting written evidence.[33] Appendix 3 summarises the inquiries at which judges have appeared to give oral evidence on 38 separate occasions between 2006 and August 2012. Eight different Select Committees received evidence, though appearances were concentrated in the House of Commons Justice Committee and the House of Lords Constitution Committee. During the passage of the Constitutional Reform Bill there was discussion about the pros and cons of establishing a Select Committee on the judiciary. This might be a joint committee of both Houses and have a statutory basis.[34] So far, this has not been thought necessary or desirable.[35]

The 35 individual judges contributing to the work of Select Committees come from all levels of the court hierarchy, from the magistrates' courts to the Supreme Court. Unsurprisingly, it is those judges with leadership responsibilities who appear most frequently (in particular the LCJ and Heads of Division); there is now an expectation, firming up into a constitutional convention, that the LCJ will meet the House of Commons Justice Committee and the House of Lords Constitution Committee on an annual basis. Clearly, Select Committees are also keen to hear from judges with experience of the coalface in the lower courts and tribunals. From time to time, judges have expressed or implied concerns about the amount of time it takes to prepare and appear before committees—time away from other

---

[31] eg. *The Times* led with the launch of the House of Lords Constitution Committee's 2011 inquiry into the judicial appointments process: Frances Gibb and David Brown, 'Too male, white and elitist? Too right, admit top lawyers' *The Times* (London, 6 July 2011) 12-13.

[32] HL Deb 18 November 2009, vol 705, col 1102.

[33] Judges may also appear before House of Commons public bill committees: Dame Janet Smith (Smith LJ) gave oral evidence to the Health and Social Care public bill committee drawing on her experiences as the chair of the Shipman inquiry (2007-8, 8 January 2008).

[34] Select Committee on the Constitutional Reform Bill, *Report* (2003-4,125-I), para. 420.

[35] HL Constitution Committee, *Relations* (2006-7, 151) para. 129.

administrative responsibilities or sitting in court. In *The Lord Chief Justice's Report 2010–12*, Lord Judge notes that 'Since the General Election, there has been an increase in the number of judges invited to assist Parliament with their enquiries' and continued:

Judges are able to provide valuable technical advice to Parliament, which is particularly useful in an era of increasingly complex legislation. However, for appearances to be mutually beneficial both the judiciary and Parliament need to be mindful of their respective roles—as Parliamentarians are aware, there are some areas of enquiry in which it is not appropriate for judges to become involved, for example in relation to political matters or issues relating to a particular case. Being drawn into such matters would be damaging for both future involvement in the work of committees and for the impartiality and reputation of the judiciary. For this reason, care is exercised by those involved when responding and in considering invitations to judges to appear before Parliament.[36]

There appears, however, to be a feeling on the part of the judiciary and parliamentarians that meetings with Select Committees are generally valuable experiences for both sides.

Over time, the judiciary has taken a more coordinated approach to requests to appear before committees. The Judicial Office explains:

Should a Select Committee feel they require a judge to appear before them, the normal process is for the relevant Committee to contact the Lord Chief Justice's Office seeking for an appropriate judge to be identified, or to approach the judge directly. On some occasions judges are unable to attend Committee hearings due to sitting and other prior commitments. On other occasions it may be suggested to the Committee that judicial attendance would not be appropriate, as the issues to be discussed are 'political' in nature or might require adjudication at a later date. This has never caused difficulties in the past; either the Committee accepts an alternative judge, or it would be inappropriate for a judge to give evidence. Neither the Lord Chief Justice, nor the Judicial Office acting on his behalf, has ever prohibited attendance of a judge before a Select Committee.[37]

In July 2008, the Judicial Executive Board issued 'Guidance for Judges appearing before or providing written evidence to parliamentary committees'.[38] The document provides a list of types of questions which judges may not be willing to answer or in respect of which they will need to exercise caution: 'the merits of individual cases'; 'cases over which they have presided'; 'the merits or personalities of particular serving judges and politicians'; 'the merits of Government policy'; and bills or proposed legislation, 'save where the policy in question affects the administration of justice within his or her area of judicial responsibility'; the administration of justice which falls outside the judge's area of responsibility or previous responsibility; and matters on which the government is consulting to which the judiciary will but has not yet responded. In fact, it is rare for a judge to be asked a

[36] Lord Chief Justice of England and Wales, *The Lord Chief Justice's Report 2010-12* (Judicial Office 2012) paras 23-4.
[37] Letter to the author, 13 December 2011.
[38] <http://www.judiciary.gov.uk/Resources/JCO/Documents/Guidance/select_committee_ guidance0708.pdf> (accessed 22 April 2013).

question during a Select Committee hearing that the judge feels it inappropriate to answer. The committee clerk drafts lines of questioning, often with the assistance of a part-time specialist adviser.[39] The practice in the House of Lords is for witnesses to be sent the proposed lines of questioning several days in advance of the hearing, though this does not happen routinely in the Commons. The extent to which members of a committee depart from the suggested lines of question varies, but for the most part the interview proceeds along the pre-prepared lines.

Judicial appearances before Select Committees have different kinds of function. In some inquiries the judiciary is the focus of scrutiny. As the Constitution Committee states, Select Committees 'can play an important role in holding the judiciary to account by questioning the judges in public'.[40] Into this type fall the annual appearances of the LCJ. Where necessary, committees may be critical of the judiciary: thus, in 2007 the Constitution Committee gently suggested that the LCJ needed to re-appraise his media and public communications strategy and that the judges needed to make the Judicial Communications Office 'more active and assertive in its dealing with the media in order to represent the judiciary effectively'.[41] Later in the essay, two further examples of inquiries which included a focus on the judiciary are considered in which judges *did not* give evidence: the Joint Committee on Human Rights' inquiry into how the judiciary were interpreting s 6 of the Human Rights Act 1998 (wrongly, the committee found);[42] and an inquiry by the House of Commons Culture, Media and Sport Committee which considered the judgments of Mr Justice Eady in relation to privacy (finding that the judge had not, contrary to the assertions of a newspaper editor, departed from precedent in cases on privacy rights).[43] One possible reason for not hearing from judges in these inquiries is that any lines of questioning would have quickly taken the committees into forbidden territory—the merits of cases and the merits of particular serving judges.

A further function of judicial evidence is to comment on or criticize government policy or action in relation to the administration of justice or areas of public policy in which judges have particular experience or expertise. Thus, Sir Nicholas Wall (President of the Family Division of the High Court) was quoted in a committee's report on the government's proposed reform of legal aid as saying that the government 'is very ill-advised to concentrate on violence' rather than use the term 'domestic abuse'; and he said that the proposals created 'a perverse incentive' to take out injunctive proceedings against a former spouse.[44] His predecessor, Sir Mark Potter, described earlier proposals as 'a series of extremely crudely averaged

---

[39] To declare an interest: the author has served as specialist adviser to the House of Commons Constitutional Affairs Committee, the House of Lords Select Committee on the Constitutional Reform Bill, the House of Lords Constitution Committee, and the House of Commons Justice Committee in relation to judiciary-related matters.

[40] HL Constitution Committee, *Relations* (2006-7, 151) para. 124.

[41] HL Constitution Committee, *Relations* (2006-7, 151) paras 160, 171.

[42] See Example 1.1. below.   [43] See Example 1.4 below.

[44] House of Commons Justice Committee, *Government's proposed reform of legal aid* (HC 2010-11, 681) paras 83-4.

fixed fees', concluding that 'the whole thing has to be radically revised'.[45] In relation to inquiries of this sort, Select Committee evidence is one way in which judges may make known to Parliament their misgivings about government proposals.

A third function of judicial evidence is educative: to explain to parliamentarians what the judges' role involves and what the limits of that role are. Examples include Baroness Hale's evidence to the JCHR on a British bill of rights (about adjudication on social and economic rights)[46] and Ryder J's evidence to the Justice Committee on the operation of family courts (on the difference that hearing the voice of the child could make).[47] The Constitution Committee has suggested that there might be more of this kind of interaction, with judges 'encouraged to discuss their views on key legal issues in the cause of transparency and better understanding of such issues amongst both parliamentarians and the public'.[48] As the committee noted, judges discuss issues such as the interpretation of the Human Rights Act 1998[49] or the use of *Pepper v Hart*[50] in public lectures and in academic writing.

Measuring the concrete influence of the work of Select Committees is far from straightforward.[51] This is as true of inquiries in relation to the judicial system as it is in other contexts. It may be that the importance lies in the activity of engagement by parliamentarians with judges and others about the judicial system (rather than any specific 'wins' in influencing policy or practice). Select committee hearings now provide the only official forum in which parliamentarians and judges may have a public conversation. Before the CRA 2005, the senior judiciary who were peers (the Law Lords and the Lord Chief Justice) were able to make contributions to debates on the floor of the House and, the conscientious objectors apart,[52] did so until disqualified in the new constitutional arrangements.[53] A sense of proportion is, however, needed: concern for judiciary-related matters is something of a niche interest among parliamentarians. Except perhaps where an MP's constituency is affected by court closures or reorganisation, the judicial system barely registers on

---

[45] HC Justice Committee, *Implementation of the Carter review on legal aid* (HC 2006–7, 223) para. 107.

[46] Joint Committee on Human Rights, *A bill of rights for the UK?* (2007-8, 165) paras 170, 189–90.

[47] HC Justice Committee, *Operation of the family courts* (2010–12, 518) para. 146.

[48] HL Constitution Committee, *Relations* (2006–7, 151) para. 126 (but noting that 'under no circumstances must committees ask judges to comment on the pros and cons of individual judgments'.

[49] Examples of lectures by serving judges on the HRA include: Lord Justice Elias, 'The rise of the Strasbourgeoisie: judicial activism and the ECHR' (Annual Lord Renton Lecture, Statute Law Society, 24 November 2009); Lord Bingham, 'The way we live now: human rights in the new millennium' (Earl Grey Memorial Lecture, University of Newcastle-upon-Tyne, 29 January 1998), and Baroness Hale, 'Salford Human Rights Conference' (4 June 2010) <http://www.supremecourt.gov.uk/docs/speech_100604.pdf> (accessed 22 April 2013).

[50] *Pepper (Inspector of Taxes) v Hart* [1993] AC 593 (holding that ministerial statements reported in *Hansard* made during the passage of a bill could be used as an aid to interpreting ambiguous statutory provisions); the judgment was criticized by eg. Lord Steyn 'Pepper v Hart: a re-examination' (2001) 21 OJLS 59.

[51] See Meg Russell and Meghan Benton, *Selective Influence: the policy impacts of House of Commons Select Committees* (UCL Constitution Unit 2011).

[52] Some, such as Lord Bingham in his role as Senior Law Lord, Lord Steyn and Baroness Hale took no part in legislative proceedings in the House of Lords while serving Law Lords.

[53] CRA 2005, s 137.

the political agenda of most parliamentarians. Some Select Committee hearings with judges have been poorly attended by MPs.

C. Mapping accountability practices in Parliament

The previous section focused on the institutional mechanisms through which Parliament exercises accountability functions in relation to the judicial system. To develop a more nuanced and contextual understanding, attention now shifts to particular aspects of the judicial system. Five areas have been selected: (i) court judgments on points of law; (ii) the legislative and other texts that form the foundations of the judicial system; (iii) judicial appointments; (iv) judicial discipline; and (v) judicial leadership. An inductive approach is adopted to map out current accountability practices based on observation of the parliamentary record and to sketch out some basic principles that emerge from the realities of work in the Palace of Westminster. In several different ways there is tension between what happens, what the 'rule book' indicates ought to happen (or not happen), and understandings of how basic constitutional principles such as the independence of the judiciary ought to operate.

1. Scrutiny of court judgments on points of law

The parliamentary rulebook discourages parliamentary scrutiny of the core judicial function of deciding cases and setting precedents. *Erskine May* states that questions to ministers 'seeking an expression of opinion on a question of law, such as the interpretation of a statute, or of an international document, a Minister's own powers, etc, are not in order since the courts rather than Ministers are competent in such matters'.[54] *Sub judice* rules adopted by each House seek generally to prevent references being made to active court proceedings in any motion, debate or question (subject to the discretion of the Speaker or committee chair).[55] Moreover, questions 'which reflect on the decision of a court of law' are not in order.[56] As already noted, the Judicial Executive Board guidance to members of the judiciary appearing before Select Committees urges judges to avoid answering questions which deal with the 'merits of individual cases'. In between these obstacles, there is, however, scope for parliamentary scrutiny of judgments.[57] Parliamentarians, from time to time, have reason to consider rulings of the courts and have the ultimate power to change the law if a majority of both Houses agree, in legislation, that the law as enunciated by the courts is not in the public interest. Consider the following examples.

Example 1.1. The Joint Committee on Human Rights (JCHR) issued two reports critical of the way in which courts had interpreted the meaning of 'public function'

---

[54] M Jack (ed.), *Erskine May's Treaties on The Law, Privileges, Proceedings and Usage of Parliament* (24th edn, LexisNexis, 2011).

[55] *Erskine May*, pp 364, 441-2.   [56] *Erskine May*, p 365.   [57] See section B2 above.

in s 6 of the Human Rights Act 1998. The first report criticized the case law as 'in human rights terms, highly problematic', finding that the 'development of the case law has significant and immediate practical implications'. It called for the government to intervene in a future case to argue for a change in the courts' approach to interpretation.[58] The second report was made while an appeal on the relevant point of law was pending before the House of Lords, preventing the committee from commenting on the particular case.[59] Both reports drew on written evidence from a variety of public bodies and interest groups. The reports led to an unsuccessful private member's bill seeking to reverse the precedent set by a series of judgments, including House of Lords authority; a change of law was brought about by s 145 of the Health and Social Care Act 2008, resulting in care homes being subject to the Convention rights.

The methodical work of the JCHR in reviewing case law and bringing together a body of evidence about the impact of the approach taken by the courts to interpreting the HRA 1998 should not be regarded as undermining judicial independence, so long as parliamentarians are clear that their views expressed in reports and debates are opinions expressed in a political arena. In the UK, it is safe to assume that the courts will exclude politicians' views as generally irrelevant to their adjudicatory task. This can be seen in the leading case of *YL v Birmingham City Council* in which the Law Lords had to consider the same issue canvassed by the JCHR. Lord Mance, noting the existence of the two reports, said 'such statements must be left to one side' and 'So far as these reports proceed on the basis that Parliament had any particular intention, that is the issue which the [Appellate Committee of the] House has to determine according to the relevant principles of statutory construction'.[60] Reference was also made to the written evidence to the JCHR from Age Concern England.[61] A majority of their Lordships gave an interpretation of the HRA at odds with the desired approach advocated by the JCHR.

Example 1.2. The Compensation Act 2006, s 1 sought to ensure that 'desirable activities' were not discouraged because of fear of liability under the common law of negligence or breach of statutory duty if it resulted in harm by clarifying the approach of courts to assessing what constitutes reasonable care in individual cases. During its passage as a bill, a Select Committee took evidence and reported on the 'compensation culture'.[62] In carrying out post-legislative scrutiny[63] of the Act in 2012, the Ministry of Justice told the Justice Select Committee it had not carried out any detailed examination to assess the impact of s 1. To do so would, the Ministry said, be 'impractical in resource terms' but also would not be appropriate

---

[58] Joint Committee on Human Rights, *The Meaning of Public Authority under the Human Rights Act* (HL 2003-4, 39; HC 2003-4, 382).
[59] Human Rights, *Public Authority* (HL 2006-7, 77; HC 2006-7, 410).
[60] [2007] UKHL 27, [2008] 1 AC 95, [90].   [61] [2007] UKHL 27, [2008] 1 AC 95, [117].
[62] HC Constitutional Affairs Committee, *Compensation Culture* (HC 2005-6, 754-I).
[63] See Office of the Leader of the House of Commons, *Post-legislative Scrutiny: The Government's Approach* (Cm 7320, 2008).

'as it could be seen as undermining the independence of the judiciary and casting doubt on the way in which they have interpreted the law'.[64]

Clearly there is a difference between the Ministry's and the JCHR's understanding of the constitutional propriety of a body other than the courts discussing the case law flowing from relatively recent legislation. The judiciary did not seem to share the Ministry's concerns when the idea of post-legislative scrutiny was first being worked out in recommendations of the House of Lords Constitution Committee and the Law Commission.[65] The Law Commission heard from the Association of District Judges that the 'most important considerations for review were likely to be "difficulties in interpretation and unintended legal consequences" '.[66] The Judges' Council envisaged that 'individual judges might send any comments they have made about legislation in judgments to the body undertaking the scrutiny work and that judges should be made aware of this possibility but not obliged to follow this route'.[67] So long as Parliament does not trespass into retrospective interference with individual cases (which must remain exclusively for the courts), the sort of corrective instigated by the JCHR in relation to s 6 of the HRA ought to be viewed as a welcome tool of accountability for Parliament, which does not undermine judicial independence.

Example 1.3. In May 2011, the High Court interpreted provisions of the Police and Criminal Evidence Act 1984 on police bail in an unexpected way, a judgment that was reported as leaving the position of 85,000 suspects in doubt.[68] In June, the Minister for Policing and Criminal Justice (Nick Herbert MP) made a statement saying 'There seems to be general agreement that this was an unusual judgment, which overturned 25 years of legal understanding. We cannot wait for a Supreme Court decision, and emergency legislation is therefore sensible and appropriate'. Responding to a question ('Does my right hon. Friend agree that judgments such as this, which fly in the face of common sense, run the risk of bringing our justice system into disrepute?'), the minister said: 'I think that the best way that I could respond would be by quoting the legal expert Professor Michael Zander QC, whom my hon. Friend may have heard on the "Today" programme this morning. He said: "The only justification for the ruling is a literal interpretation of the Act which makes no sense" '.[69] The House of Lords Constitution Committee criticized the Government's decision to introduce a bill while an appeal to the Supreme Court was pending; this gave rise to 'difficult issues of constitutional principle as regards both the separation of powers and the rule of law' (a point that government appeared not to accept).[70] The minister responsible for the bill in the Lords

---

[64] Ministry of Justice, *Memorandum to the Justice Select Committee: Post-Legislative Assessment of the Compensation Act 2006* (Cm 8267, 2012) paras 62-3.

[65] The Law Commission, *Post-legislative Scrutiny* (Law Com No 302, Cm 6945, 2006).

[66] Law Comm, *Post-legislative Scrutiny* para. 2.4.

[67] Law Comm, *Post-Legislative Scrutiny* para. 3.67.

[68] *R (Manchester Police) v Hookway* [2011] EWHC 1578 (Admin), [2011] 3 All ER 521.

[69] HC Deb 30 June 2011, vol 530, cols 1133-42.

[70] HL Constitution Committee, *Police (Detention and Bail) Bill* (HL 2009-11, 143); and subsequent correspondence with the minister <http://www.parliament.uk/business/committees-a-z/lords-select/constitution-committee/correspondence-with-ministers1/parliament-2010/bill-scrutiny> (accessed 22 April 2013).

responded that the government 'really do not believe that we are undermining the constitutional separation of powers by asking Parliament to legislate to reverse the effect of a High Court decision in advance of the issue having been decided by the Supreme Court'.[71] The fast-tracked bill, which had retrospective effect, became the Police (Detention and Bail) Act 2011 and the Greater Manchester Police withdrew their appeal.

The parliamentary response to the PACE ruling highlights the question of timing: the general rules of *sub judice* discourage Parliament from scrutinizing judgments or commenting on cases which are actually pending before the courts while retaining the ultimate right to legislate on any matter.[72] Comity and practical coordination between the judicial, legislative and executive limbs of the state require a principled approach to be taken in relation to cases that are awaiting decision on appeal to the Supreme Court; it is far from clear that this happened.

Example 1.4. The House of Commons Culture, Media and Sport Committee, carrying out an inquiry into press freedom and privacy, reported under the heading 'Mr Justice Eady and Privacy Law' that they had 'received no evidence in this inquiry that the judgments of Mr Justice Eady in the area of privacy have departed from following the principles set out by the House of Lords and the European Court of Human Rights', adding that 'If he, or indeed any other High Court judge, departed from these principles, we would expect the matter to be successfully appealed to a higher court'.[73] In reaching that conclusion, the committee heard from journalists, judges and lawyers. The review into the jurisprudence and ideology of Mr Justice Eady is probably best seen as turning on the specific circumstances of a particular Select Committee inquiry: the committee was faced with allegations made by an editor of a national newspaper and they felt could not, in the context, be ignored. The committee's report was carefully worded and favourable in outcome to the judge. There is, however, a significant threat that *individual* judicial independence is compromised if a Select Committee embarks on a line of inquiry into a body of case law by a named judge.

2. Foundations

In the absence of a written constitution, the constitutional framework of the judicial system has to rest on ordinary legislation (primary and secondary), 'soft law' and constitutional conventions. Under the new architecture, the principal statutes are the Constitutional Reform Act 2005 and the Tribunals, Courts and Enforcement Act 2007. (Provisions intended by the government to be included in the Constitutional Reform and Governance Act 2010 were dropped to enable the bill to receive royal assent before the 2010 general election). Examples of 'soft law' include: the 2004 concordat between the Lord Chancellor and the

---

[71] HL Deb 12 July 2011, vol 000, col 603 (Baroness Browning).   [72] *Erskine May* 441-2.
[73] House of Commons Culture, Media and Sport Committee, *Press Standards, Privacy and Libel* (2009-10, 326-I) para. 76. Paul Dacre, editor of the *Daily Mail*, was a consistent and vitriolic critic of Eady J, labelling his judgments 'arrogant' and 'amoral'.

LCJ;[74] the 'Memorandum of Understanding between the Office for Judicial Complaints, the Ministry of Justice and the Directorate of Judicial Offices for England and Wales';[75] Her Majesty's Courts and Tribunals Service Framework Document;[76] and the list of 'qualities and attributes' required for judicial office—in other words, how 'merit' is defined—published by the JAC.[77]

The following two examples provide contrasting approaches to policy formation and legislative scrutiny:

Example 2.1. In 2003, the government made a surprise announcement of plans to abolish the office of Lord Chancellor, create a Supreme Court in place of the Law Lords, and establish a new system for judicial appointments in England and Wales. There had been no consultation with the senior judiciary. The proposals were subject to protracted parliamentary debate and scrutiny before the bill was published: in an unusual move, the Conservative Opposition in the House of Lords successfully moved an amendment to the Loyal Address after the Queen's Speech (calling on the government 'to withdraw their current proposals and to undertake meaningful consultation with Parliament and the senior judiciary before proceeding with legislation'); a major inquiry and report by the House of Commons Constitutional Affairs Committee; and a 'take note' debate in the Lords.[78] The House of Commons Constitutional Affairs Committee criticized the Government for not publishing a draft bill.[79] At second reading of the Constitutional Reform Bill in March 2004, the Lords voted to refer the bill to a special committee with powers to take evidence and amend the bill before recommitting it to a Committee of the Whole House (a procedure that had lain dormant for several decades). Several members of the judiciary took part in Lords debates and one voted in a division (Lord Hoffmann, against the government). 'Carried over' to the 2004-5 session, the bill was modified in significant ways in both Houses before receiving Royal Assent five days before Parliament was prorogued for the 2005 general election.

Example 2.2. In 2000, the government appointed an independent panel, chaired by retired judge Sir Andrew Leggatt, with broad terms of reference to undertake a review of 'the delivery of justice through tribunals other than ordinary courts of law' leading to a report in 2001.[80] The Department for Constitutional

---

[74] *Constitutional Reform: The Lord Chancellor's judiciary-related functions: Proposals* (2004). <http://webarchive.nationalarchives.gov.uk/+/http://www.dca.gov.uk/consult/lcoffice/judiciary.htm> accessed 9 March 2012.

[75] <http://judicialcomplaints.judiciary.gov.uk/docs/Memorandum_of_Understanding.pdf> (accessed 22 April 2013).

[76] HM Courts & Tribunals Service, *Framework Document* (Cm 8043, 2011).

[77] JAC, 'Qualities and abilities' <http://jac.judiciary.gov.uk/application-process/112.htm> accessed 7 March 2012.

[78] See Andrew Le Sueur, 'From Appellate Committee to Supreme Court: A Narrative' in Louis Blom-Cooper, Brice Dickson and Gavin Drewry (eds), *The Judicial House of Lords 1876-2009* (Oxford: Oxford University Press, 2009), ch 5.

[79] HC Constitutional Affairs Committee, *Judicial appointments and a Supreme Court (court of final appeal)* (HC 2003-4, 48) para. 118 ('The Constitutional Reform Bill is a clear candidate for examination in draft').

[80] Andrew Leggatt, *Tribunals for Users One System, One Service* (2001) <http://webarchive.nationalarchives.gov.uk/+/http://www.tribunals-review.org.uk/leggatthtm/leg-00.htm> (accessed 22 April 2013).

Affairs responded in 2004 with an equally wide-ranging White Paper, accepting the thrust of the Leggatt recommendations and proposing a new principle of 'proportionate dispute resolution' to avoid disputes arising and to encourage Alternative Dispute Resolution (ADR).[81] In 2006, the Government published a draft Tribunals, Courts and Enforcement Bill.[82] Neither the House of Commons Justice Committee nor the House of Lords Constitution Committee felt able to find time to carry out pre-legislative scrutiny of the draft bill. As well as completely re-designing the tribunal system (or 'maze' as critics dubbed it), the bill would amend the eligibility criteria for all judicial appointments. The House of Lords Constitution Committee successfully called for a provision on ADR included in the draft bill but removed from the bill 'proper' to be reinstated.[83]

The legislation in these two examples was of great practical and constitutional importance. In the first, 'back of the envelope' policy-making and a government decision not to publish a draft bill was countered by careful (albeit often partisan) parliamentary scrutiny that left few clauses unturned. In the second, careful policy making with judicial involvement, a White Paper and a draft bill were met with relative indifference by parliamentary Select Committees.

Example 2.3. In January 2004, the Lord Chancellor (Lord Falconer) and the LCJ (Lord Woolf) announced that agreement had been reached on the principles and practices governing the transfer of functions from the former to the latter under the government's proposals. This came to be known as 'the concordat'. In their 2007 report, the House of Lords Constitution Committee stated that, although many aspects of the concordat had been put on a statutory footing by the CRA 2005, 'it is clear to us that the concordat continues to be of great constitutional importance'.[84] In a debate on the Constitution Committee's report, Baroness Royall of Blaisdon (President of the Council, speaking for the government) said 'The Government will consult and work with the judiciary to ensure that the concordat remains live and relevant, and that changes to both the framework document and the concordat are properly put before this House'.[85] In February 2011, Lord Judge told the House of Lords Constitution Committee that in the event of the LCJ failing to negotiate a satisfactory annual settlement for funding the judicial system:

I think we would have to renegotiate a new concordat, and I would expect that this Committee would be following very closely how we were reaching the concordat that we were trying to reach. I do not regard the concordat agreement between the Lord Chief Justice and the Lord Chancellor of the day as private between them. It is a public document, and anybody can look at it at any time. If the situation were to reach such a parlous state that it broke down completely, I suspect the Lord Chief Justice of the day—because this will not happen in my time—would be very anxious to exercise such power as is left

[81] Department for Constitutional Affairs, *Transforming Public Services: Complaints, Redress and Tribunals* (White Paper, Cm 6243, 2004).
[82] *The draft Tribunals, Courts and Enforcement Bill* (Cm 6885, 2006).
[83] HL Constitution Committee, *Tribunals, Courts and Enforcement Bill* (2006-7, 13).
[84] HL Constitution Committee, *Relations* (2006-7, 151) para. 13.
[85] HL Deb 18 November 2008, vol 704, col 1124.

to him in the context of the parliamentary process: (a) this Committee, (b) the Justice Committee and (c) the exercise under Section 5 of the Constitutional Reform Act of, in effect, writing to Parliament and setting out his or her concerns.[86]

Example 2.4. In January 2007, the Home Secretary (John Reid MP) wrote an article in the *Sunday Telegraph* hinting strongly that the government was minded to create a Ministry of Justice (merging some policy areas of the Home Office and the Department for Constitutional Affairs).[87] The senior judiciary had not been consulted at that point. The Prime Minister announced the creation of the Ministry of Justice by a written statement to Parliament on the day it rose for the Easter recess.[88] The House of Commons Constitutional Affairs Committee carried out an inquiry into the decision, taking evidence from Lord Phillips CJ, Lord Justice Thomas, then twice from the Lord Chancellor (Lord Falconer) and permanent secretary (Alex Allan). The committee's July 2007 report criticised the government for having failed to learn lessons from the way changes to the Lord Chancellor's office had been announced in 2003 and for causing 'a highly undesirable public conflict between the senior judiciary' and the government.[89] The House of Lords Constitution Committee, which was midway through an inquiry on relations between government, judges and Parliament, also considered the handling of the creation of the new ministry.[90]

These two examples demonstrate the importance of non-statutory foundations for the judicial system. In relation to the concordat, there are several statements about its perceived importance, but parliamentarians have not been specific about what exactly their continuing role might appropriately be in scrutiny of the future developments of the concordat. This uncertainty is a reflection of doubts about the constitutional status of the concordat. On one view, its importance has faded since most of its provisions have been put on a statutory footing by the CRA 2005 and the conventions and institutional arrangements that have subsequently developed. Example 2.4 shows the mediating role Parliament is able to play when fundamental disagreements arise between government and the judiciary. A carefully planned campaign by senior judges allowed them to use Select Committee hearings to vent their concerns about the manner in which the government had acted in setting up the MoJ as well as the substance of the government's plans.

3. Judicial appointments

The 2005 constitutional settlement gave responsibility for selecting candidates for judicial office to an arm's length body, the Judicial Appointments Commission

---

[86] HL Constitution Committee, *Meetings with the Lord Chief Justice and Lord Chancellor* (2010-11, 89) Q11.
[87] Patrick Hennessy, 'Reid wants to split the Home Office in two', *Sunday Telegraph*, (London, 21 January 2007) 1.
[88] HC Deb 39 March 2007, vol 458, col 133WS.
[89] HC Constitutional Affairs Committee, *The Creation of the Ministry of Justice* (2006-7, 466).
[90] HL Constitution Committee, *Relations* (2006-7, 151) para. 3.

(JAC) while reserving powers to the Lord Chancellor to have the final say on accepting, rejecting or asking the JAC to reconsider a recommendation.[91] Parliament has no role in individual appointments; its function (unstated on the face of the CRA) is to exercise overarching accountability functions in relation to the process as a whole. As the following examples show, a range of methods is used to achieve this.

Example 3.1. Lord Marks of Henley-on-Thames (a QC) asked an oral question 'To ask Her Majesty's Government what progress is being made in improving gender and ethnic diversity in judicial appointments'. After the minister's reply, five other peers asked supplementary questions.[92]

Example 3.2. During 2011-12, the House of Lords Constitution Committee carried out a major inquiry into the judicial appointments processes in England and Wales and for the Supreme Court.[93]

Example 3.3. In the calendar years 2010 and 2011, 37 written questions in the Commons dealt with aspects of the appointments process and judicial careers.

Example 3.4. The House of Commons Justice Committee has held evidence sessions on the work of the JAC: two sessions in 2007;[94] and in 2010, hearing from Baroness Prashar (the chair), Jonathan Sumption QC (as he then was), and Edward Nally (legal practitioner members).[95]

The picture that emerges is of some parliamentarians in both Houses keen to have oversight of the judicial appointments system as a whole, and to exercise scrutiny on a regular and rigorous basis. So far, however, parliamentarians have consistently rejected suggestions that they should have any role in individual senior appointments, as House of Commons Select Committees now have in relation to several public offices for which they carry out pre-appointment hearings with the preferred candidate.[96] One of the main reasons for eschewing this direct form of accountability is that parliamentary involvement would risk undermining judicial independence, in fact or perception, if appointment hearings were to be conducted along partisan lines. This is a concern that needs to be taken seriously, though in an era when the LCJ subjects himself to an annual press conference and judges are content to give public lectures openly critical of government, the concern may be overstated.[97]

---

[91] CRA 2005, Pt 4.   [92] HL Deb 17 March 2011, vol 725, col 347.

[93] HL Constitution Committee, *Judicial Appointments*, 25th Report of 2010-12 (HL Paper 272).

[94] <http://www.publications.parliament.uk/pa/cm200607/cmselect/cmconst/cmconst. htm>(accessed 22 April 2013).

[95] HC Justice Committee, *Minutes of Evidence: The work of the Judicial Appointments Commission* (HC 2009-10) <http://www.publications.parliament.uk/pa/cm201011/cmselect/cmjust/449-i/10090701. htm> (accessed 22 April 2013).

[96] See eg. Select Committee on the Constitutional Reform Bill, *Report* (2003-4,125-I), paras 412-14; HL Constitution Committee, *Relations* (2006-7, 151) para. 131.

[97] See eg. Lord Phillips, 'Judicial independence and accountability: a view from the Supreme Court' (UCL Constitution Unit launch of research project on the politics of judicial independence, London, 8 February 2011).

4. Judicial discipline

The British constitution allocates to Parliament alone the power to dismiss judges of the High Court, Court of Appeal and Supreme Court: judges hold office 'during good behaviour, subject to a power of removal by Her Majesty on an address presented to Her by both Houses of Parliament'.[98] No judge has been subject to this procedure in modern times, but it is important to recognise that Parliament has this ultimate 'sacrificial' tool of accountability. Dismissal of judges below the level of the High Court on grounds of misbehaviour is by the Lord Chancellor with the concordance of the LCJ. *Erskine May* is clear that 'Unless the discussion is based upon a substantive motion, reflections must not be cast upon the conduct of... judges of the superior courts of the United Kingdom, including persons holding the position of a judge, such as circuit judges and their deputies, as well as recorders'.[99] The parliamentary record reveals MPs do, from time to time, want to criticize the conduct of individual judges.

Example 4.1. An Early Day Motion by Mildred Gordon MP called for the dismissal of Judge Sir Harold Cassel QC over sentencing remarks in a child abuse case.[100] It seems that the judge had, in fact, already tendered his resignation.

Example 4.2. Mark Todd MP led a debate on 'Judicial Error (Compensation)' in Westminster Hall. He dealt in detail with the case of a constituent who had been convicted of indecent assault, which was subsequently held to be unsafe by the Court of Appeal. The MP was critical of the trial judge (whom he did not name) and went on to say:

> The straight answer is that I do not know what happened to the judge after his decision was corrected. Although I can appreciate that the objectivity and independence of the judiciary might be harmed by, say, the ability of a complainant to sue the judge for damages where their error causes harm, I would expect some accountability to be exercised for judicial error. On my observation, we instead enter into a polite and largely private world. Some of the texts that I have read, which were written by learned lawyers, point out that it can be argued that the appellate process offers some accountability, in that it demonstrates where a correction is required of a judge.[101]

For the government, Harriett Harman MP accepted that this individual case 'raises a number of important and difficult points of principle' and went on to explain the compensation schemes available for wrongful convictions (which did not apply) and the new Office of Judicial Conduct.

Example 4.3. An MP used the daily adjournment debate to raise the 'somewhat esoteric subject of ex parte applications in the family courts' and a specific case involving constituents. He said that 'I understand that in 2006-7...two

---

[98] Senior Courts Act 1981, s 11; Constitutional Reform Act 2005, s 33.   [99] *Eskine May*, 443-4.
[100] EDM 83, 1988-9 (29 November 1988); Anon, 'His Honour Sir Harold Cassel, Bt (obituary)', *Daily Telegraph,* (London, 21 September 2001) <http://www.telegraph.co.uk/news/obituaries/1341145/His-Honour-Sir-Harold-Cassel-Bt.html> (accessed 22 April 2013).
[101] HC Deb 8 March 2006, vol 443, col 312WH.

complaints were upheld out of the 938 complaints made against judges. That tells us how much accountability m'learned friends in that high office have. It seems that judges have power without responsibility to anybody but themselves and one another'.[102]

Example 4.4. The annual report of the Office for Judicial Complaints is published by the Lord Chancellor, with the concurrence of the LCJ. This event is put on the parliamentary record by a written statement.[103] It appears that there has never been Select Committee scrutiny of the report or any debate of it in Parliament.

It is difficult to see how individualized censure can ever be appropriate in the light of (a) the principle of independence of the judiciary and (b) the existence of the Office for Judicial Complaints, established as part of the new CRA arrangements. Parliament's attention would be better directed at ensuring effective systematic scrutiny of the general work of the OJC, but this it has failed to do despite the availability of a detailed annual report.

5. Judicial governance

The final aspects of the judicial system that will be examined are the new institutions of self-governance, with the LCJ at its apex. As noted above, there has been a transfer of management and leadership power to the judiciary under the CRA 2005.[104] The making of annual reports is an accountability tool in its own right but is also capable of being the basis of further parliamentary scrutiny.

Example 5.1. The LCJ has no statutory duty to make an annual report. In May 2006, Lord Phillips CJ told the House of Lords Constitution Committee that this 'is something we are considering'. In July 2007, he announced that the Judicial Executive Board would publish an annual report.[105] The House of Lords Constitution Committee welcomed this, as 'the report will provide a useful opportunity for both Houses of Parliament to debate these matters on an annual basis, and for the Lord Chief Justice to engage effectively with parliamentarians and the public'.[106] The Lord Chancellor told Parliament that 'The Lord Chief Justice views this as a way to demonstrate the judiciary's accountability to the public and parliamentarians without compromising judicial independence'.[107] There then followed uncertainty about the procedural mechanism whereby such a report could be made to Parliament. CRA 2005, s 5 provides that the LCJ 'may lay before Parliament written representations on matters that appear to him to be matters of importance relating to the judiciary, or otherwise to the administration of justice'. Initially, this had been seen as a 'nuclear option', to be used only in circumstances approaching

---

[102] HC Deb 20 January 2010, vol 504, col 408 (Peter Kilfoyle MP).
[103] See eg. HC Deb 25 February 2010, vol 506, col 78-9WS.   [104] See section A2b above.
[105] HL Constitution Committee, *Relations* (2006-7, 151) para. 136.
[106] HL Constitution Committee, *Relations* (2006-7, 151) para. 139.
[107] HC Justice Committee, 'Jack Straw MP: Memorandum submitted by the Ministry of Justice', *Minutes of Evidence* (2007-8) <http://www.publications.parliament.uk/pa/cm200708/cmselect/cmjust/913/8070201.htm> (accessed 22 April 2013).

a constitutional crisis.[108] The first report was published in March 2008, covering the period April 2006 to September 2007. It was neither published in Hansard nor debated. In 2008, Lord Phillips appeared to have 'resiled from the commitment to publish such a report on a strictly annual basis', though that seemed to be to avoid binding his successor, Lord Judge (who was to assume the office of LCJ in October 2008).[109] Lord Judge told the Constitution Committee that he felt 'it may not be sensible to produce [a report] every year'.[110] Two further reports have been published: one in February 2010 for the legal year 2008-9; and the other in August 2012 for the period January 2010 to June 2012.[111] These have not been debated in Parliament. The judiciary website states: 'Future reviews will be produced to provide information about the preceding Legal Year'.[112]

Example 5.2. In February 2010, the Senior President of Tribunals presented his first annual report. The foreword explained that it was 'not intended as a formal report under section 43 of the Tribunals, Courts and Enforcement Act 2007' under which the Senior President 'is required to report annually to the Lord Chancellor, specifically about "cases" rather than the function of the new system of tribunals in general'.[113] The report is succinct but informative. It deals with organisational matters and with tribunal law and jurisprudence. It includes contributions from different tribunal judges. A second annual report appeared in February 2011. There was no discussion of either report on the parliamentary record.

These two examples reveal uncertainty about the scope and purpose of the reporting duties contained in legislation. The examples also show varying degrees of eagerness by Select Committees to follow-up annual reports with evidence sessions.

D. Conclusions

It has been argued that the orthodox approach to parliamentary accountability practices in relation to the judicial system—a prohibited zone plus ministerial responsibility—is no longer viable given the dramatic changes that have taken place in the judicial power of the state, the governance of the judiciary, and rising expectations about the degrees to which all public bodies are held to account. Additional tools of accountability are needed. This study has sought to examine the ways in which MPs and peers have and use opportunities to exercise an accountability role: all the accountability procedures at their disposal are used to some

---

[108] Joshua Rozenberg, 'Lord Phillips prepares to gain more power', *Daily Telegraph,* (London, 19 July 2007); HL Constitution Committee, *Relations* (2006-7, 151) para. 113.

[109] HL Constitution Committee, *Relations: Follow-up Report* (HL 2007-8, 177) para. 22; Lord Goodlad, HL Deb 18 November 2008, vol 705, col 1105.

[110] HL Constitution Committee, *Relations: Follow-up Report.*

[111] Judiciary of England and Wales, *The Lord Chief Justice's Review of Administration of Justice in the Courts* (London, 2010) and *The Lord Chief Justice's Report 2010-12* (London, 2012).

[112] <http://www.judiciary.gov.uk/media/media-releases/2010/0510> (accessed 22 April 2013).

[113] Senior President of Tribunals, *Annual Report: Tribunals Transformed* (Ministry of Justice, 2010) 12.

extent. Select committees appear to be regarded as especially important, both for parliamentarians and the judiciary.

Although constitutional principle and standing orders discourage parliamentary scrutiny of the core activities of the judicial system (deciding individual cases and setting precedents), parliamentarians can and do inquire into case law and approaches to statutory interpretation, though there are unresolved questions about the constitutional propriety of doing so, for example in carrying out post-legislative scrutiny. Parliament's record in examining legislative change is mixed: the CRA 2005 shows Parliament responding in a thorough if rather partisan way to poorly prepared government policy; the failure of any Select Committee to undertake pre-legislative scrutiny of the draft Tribunals, Courts and Enforcement Bill demonstrates the difficulties parliamentarians have in finding time and enthusiasm for effective legislative scrutiny. There seems no appetite among MPs or peers for involvement in individual judicial appointments. From time to time, MPs seek to criticize individual judges for their conduct but there has been little or no interest in scrutinizing the work of the complaints system that now exists. In relation to judicial leadership and governance, there is a lack of clarity about when and why statutory duties to make annual reports should exist and variations in practice in making and scrutinizing reports.

Effective parliamentary accountability mechanisms, respecting the independence of the judiciary, are important for the legitimacy of the judicial system. They may also help to dissuade ministers and their speechwriters from taking cheap shots at judges and judgments.[114]

---

[114] See n 2 above.

Appendix 1
Arm's length bodies relating to the English judicial system

Body	Function	Status	Governance	Reporting duties/activities
HM Courts and Tribunals Service	'responsible for the administration of the criminal, civil and family courts and tribunals in England and Wales and non-devolved tribunals in Scotland and Northern Ireland'	Executive agency of the MoJ	Board, including 3 judicial members and senior MoJ official 'It uniquely operates as a partnership between the Lord Chancellor, the Lord Chief Justice and the Senior President of Tribunals as set out in our Framework Document'	Annual report presented to Parliament: Courts Act 2003, s 1(4) Pages on MoJ website
Judicial Appointments Commission for England and Wales	'We select candidates for judicial office on merit, through fair and open competition, from the widest range of eligible candidates'	NDPB sponsored by the MoJ	15 Commissioners; 'leadership team' of a chief executive and two directors	Annual report presented to Parliament: CRA 2005, sch 12 para 32 Own website
Judicial Appointments and Conduct Ombudsman	Deals with complaints about the judicial appointments and discipline process.	Appointed by the Queen on the recommendation of the Lord Chancellor	Corporation sole 'completely independent of Government and the judiciary'	Annual report presented to Parliament: CRA 2005, sch 13 para 15 Pages on MoJ website
Office for Judicial Complaints	Deals with complaints from members of the public about judge's conduct	Up to 2011: an 'associated office' of the MoJ, set up to support Lord Chancellor and LCJ in their joint responsibilities for judicial discipline. From 2011: part of the Judicial Office	Civil servants work 'jointly and equally to the Lord Chancellor and LCJ'. Head is senior civil servant appointed by open competition	Annual report published by Lord Chancellor and LCJ; announced by Lord Chancellor in written statement to Parliament Own website

Body	Function	Status	Governance	Reporting duties/activities
Civil Justice Council	'We promote the needs of civil justice in England and Wales and monitor the system to ensure that progress to modernise it continues'	Advisory NDPB funded by MoJ: Civil Procedure Act 1997	Since October 2010, sponsored by Judicial Office	Business plan, news and reports regularly appear on pages on judiciary website
Civil Procedure Rules Committee	Makes rules of court for the Civil Division of the Court of Appeal, the High Court and the county courts	NDPB created by Civil Procedure Act 1997	Chaired by Master of the Rolls; 15 other members, mostly legal practitioners	Annual report published by MoJ; Page on MoJ website
Family Justice Council	'We promote better and quicker outcomes for the families and children who use the family justice system'	Advisory NDPB funded by MoJ; since October 2010 sponsored by Judicial Office	The national Council of 30 members meets quarterly; 39 local FJCs	Page on judicial website
Family Procedure Rules Committee	Makes rules of court governing the practice and procedure to be followed in family proceedings in the High Court, county courts and magistrates' courts	NDPB created by Courts Act 2003 s 77	Chaired by President of Family Division; 16 other members	Page on MoJ website
Criminal Procedure Rule Committee	'Responsible for modernising court procedure and practice and making the Criminal Procedure Rules'	NDPB created by Courts Act 2003 s 70	Chaired by LCJ with membership of judges, lawyers and police officers	'What's new?' page on MoJ website but no annual report
Sentencing Council	'To promote greater transparency and consistency in sentencing, whilst maintaining the independence of the judiciary'	NDPB sponsored by the MoJ created by Pt 4 of the Coroners and Justice Act 2009	LCJ is president; chaired by a CA judge with 13 other members appointed by LCJ or LC	Annual report: Coroners and Justice Act 2009 s 119(2)Own website

Key: CA = Court of Appeal of England and Wales; LC = Lord Chancellor; LCJ = Lord Chief Justice; MoJ = Ministry of Justice; NDPB = non-departmental public body; quotations taken from organisations' web pages. 'MoJ website' is < http://www.justice.gov.uk>; 'Judiciary website' is <http://www.judiciary.gov.uk>. Several bodies have been or are planned to be abolished under the Public Bodies Act 2011: Court boards; Crown Court Rule Committee; Her Majesty's Inspectorate for Court Administration; Magistrates' Courts Rule Committee.

Appendix 2
Judicial self-governance

Body	Role	Governance	Reporting duties/activities
Lord Chief Justice of England and Wales	Head of the judiciary and president of the courts of England and Wales; representing the views of the judiciary to Parliament and ministers; welfare training and guidance of the judiciary; deployment and allocation of work within the courts Decision-making about judicial appointments: see Crime and Courts Bill 2012	New functions conferred on office of LCJ by CRA 2005 s 7	Periodic formal reports (latest one covers period January 2010 to June 2012); annual 45 minute press conference, transcript published; information on judiciary website Power to lay written representations before Parliament on 'matters of importance relating to the judiciary, or otherwise to the administration of justice': CRA 2005, s 5
Senior President of Tribunals*	'the independent and statutory leader of the tribunal judiciary' Decision-making about deployment and appointments to the tribunal judiciary: see Crime and Courts Bill 2012	Office created by Tribunals, Courts and Enforcement Act 2007, s 2. 'The office…is independent of both the Executive and the Chief Justices'	Formal annual report to LC: Tribunals, Courts and Enforcement Act 2007, s 43 Other annual report (see above); page on judiciary website

Other judicial leadership posts, not set out in detail here, include: the Master of the Roles, Heads of Division, Head and deputy head of criminal justice; head and deputy head of family justice, senior presiding judge.

Body	Role	Governance	Reporting duties/activities
Judicial Executive Board (JEB)	To support LCJ in executive and leadership responsibilities	LCJ, 8 other senior judges and chief executive	Page on judiciary website
Judicial Office	To support LCJ by civil servants including 'professional trainers, legal advisers, HR and communication experts, policy makers and administrators'	Led by a chief executive 'who reports to the LJC rather than to ministers, and its work is directed by the judiciary rather than the administration of the day'	Annual business plan published on judiciary website

Body	Role	Governance	Reporting duties/activities
Judicial College (part of Judicial Office)	'to ensure that high quality training is delivered to enable those who discharge judicial functions to carry out their duties effectively, in a way which preserves judicial independence and supports public confidence in the justice system'	'an independent judicial body and part of the Judicial Office' it 'draws its funds, staff and much of its corporate support directly from the MoJ'	Prospectus published on judiciary website
Judges' Council	• 'to be a body broadly representative of the judiciary as a whole which will inform and advise the Lord Chief Justice on matters as requested from time to time' • Selects judicial members of JAC • Judicial input on resourcing of courts	Meets 4 times a year; Standing Committees and working groups meet as required. Membership: JEB members plus 17 other judges from all levels	Annual report published in 2009 (but none in 2010 or 2011).
Association of HM District Judges	'gives pastoral advice and assistance to its members. It also represents the district bench in varied discussions and meetings with the senior judiciary, HMCS and many other organisations'	National committee, with six officers	Web page judiciary website

(Continued)

Appendix 2 Continued

Body	Role	Governance	Reporting duties/activities
Association of High Court Masters	'The association will represent the views, interests, opinions and resolutions of the Masters to the Lord Chief Justice and other judicial office-holders'	No information	Brief statement on judiciary website
Council of HM Circuit Judges	'collects the views of circuit judges, and acts on their behalf by negotiating with the government on matters such as salaries and other terms of service'	National committee	Web page judiciary website
UK Association of Women Judges	'The UKAWJ is the only organisation for the judiciary that is primarily concerned with issues that affect women'	Unofficial membership organisation. President: Baroness Hale	Own website

* The LC and judiciary have agreed that there should be a single head of the judiciary in England and Wales; functions of the Senior President of Tribunals will be transferred to the LCJ in forthcoming primary legislation.

Judicial evidence to Select Committees 2006 to August 2012

Accountability purpose	Oral evidence	Committee and date of hearing	Written evidence
Scrutiny of the office of Lord Chief Justice	Lord Phillips, Lord Judge CJ, Goldring LJ	HLCC Dec 2010, HCJC Oct 2010, JCJC Jul 2008, HLCC May 2006,	Lord Phillips CJ (HCJC 2007)
Scrutiny of constitutional relationships, inc. creation of Ministry of Justice	Lord Phillips, Lord Judge, Thomas LJ, Judge LJ, Lord Mackay of Clashfern,* Lord Lloyd of Berwick*	HLCC Jul 2008, HLCC Dec 2007, HLCC May 2007, HCJC May 2007, HLCC Feb 2007, HLCC Jan 2007	
Scrutiny of government proposals for human rights	Baroness Hale, Maurice Kay LJ	JCHR March 2008, HCJC Oct 2006	
Scrutiny of operation of family courts	Sir Nicholas Wall P, Pauffley J, Ryder J, Sir Mark Potter P, John Thomas LJ, Munby J, District Judge (Magistrates' Courts) Nicholas Crighton	HCJC May 2011, PAC Oct 2010, HCJC May 2006	HH Judge Clifford Bellamy (HCJC 2011)
Scrutiny of legal aid reforms	Sir Nicholas Wall P, Sir Anthony May P, Judge Robert Martin, Lady Butler-Sloss,* Sir Mark Potter	HCJC Feb 2011, HCJC June 2009, HCJC Jan 2007	Sir Anthony May (HCJC Dec 2010), Sir Mark Potter P (JCJC Jul 2009)
Scrutiny of sentencing	Leveson LJ,*** Sir Igor Judge P, HH Judge Julian Hall, Lord Phillips CJ, Lord Woolf*	HCJC Jun 2011, HCJC Dec 2010, HCJC Jan 2008, HCJC Jul 2007, HCJC Jun 2007, HCHA Apr 2007	Leveson LJ (HCJC Jul 2011, JCJC Jan 2011)
Scrutiny of reform of coroner's system	Smith LJ	HCJC Feb 2006	

(Continued)

Appendix 3 Continued

Accountability purpose	Oral evidence	Committee and date of hearing	Written evidence
Scrutiny of judicial appointments process	Lord Mackay LC,* Lord Phillips PSC, Lord Judge CJ, Baroness Hale JSC, Lord Neuberger MR, Hallett LJ, Lord Woolf,* Lord Carswell,* Toulson LJ,**** Auld JL	HLCC Dec 2011, HLCC Nov 2011 (three meetings); HLCC Oct 2011 (two meetings); HCJC Jul 2006	Baron J, Sir Konrad Schiemann,** Baroness Hale, Judge Hugo Storey, Judge Robert Martin, Arden JL, Lord Mance, Carnwath LJ; Judicial Executive Board—all to the HLCC 2010.Lord Judge CJ and Lord Phillips, jointly (JCDCRB 2008)
Ombudsman and the Equitable Life affair			Lord Judge, PASC 2009
Tribunals	Hodge J, Andrew Collins J, HH Judge Robert Martin	HCJC Mar 2006, HCWPC Nov 2010	
Domestic violence	District Judge Marilyn Morgan, Wall LJ	HCHA Jan 2008	
Privacy and injunctions	Sir Nicolas Wall P, Baker J, Lord Neuberger MR, Tugendhat (recently retired Sir Stephen Sedley also gave evidence)	Joint Committee on Privacy and Injunctions, 2012	
Extradition	Judge Riddle (Senior District Judge, Westminster Magistrates' Court)	HCHA, February 2012	

Key: HLCC = House of Lords Constitution Committee; HCJC = House of Commons Justice Committee; JCHR = Joint Committee on Human Rights; PAC = Public Accounts Committee; PASC = Public Administration Select Committee; HCHA = House of Commons Home Affairs Committee; JCDCRB = Joint Committee on the Draft Constitutional Renewal Bill; HCWPC = House of Commons Work and Pensions Committee.

* Retired judge.

** Justice of the Court of Justice of the European Union.

*** Chair of the Sentencing Council.

**** Member of the JAC.

PART IV

10

Ombudsmen, Tribunals, Inquiries: Re-fashioning Accountability Beyond the Courts

*Mark Elliott**

A. Introduction

In the United Kingdom today, courts play a part in securing accountable government that goes far beyond the role they fulfilled just a few decades ago. This paper does not dissent from the (admittedly contestable) view that this has, on the whole, been a beneficial development. It does, however, contend that the contemporary prominence of judicial review should not be permitted to obscure the value of non-court-based accountability institutions. It will be suggested that there is a tendency in the UK to regard the court-based model as a paradigm in relation to securing government accountability, but that this view should be resisted. Instead, it will be argued, an effective accountability system requires a degree of diversity, and accountability to courts should therefore be regarded neither as a panacea, nor as a necessarily adequate substitute for other forms of accountability. This raises questions about the proper balance between legal and political control of government, and it will be argued that the perceived shortcomings of the latter should not lead ineluctably to greater reliance upon the former. These points will be developed by reference to tribunals, ombudsmen and inquiries as instruments by which the UK government may be held to account.

* Reader in Public Law, University of Cambridge; Fellow, St Catharine's College, Cambridge. I am grateful to Carol Harlow, Martin Matthews, Robert Thomas, Nick Wikeley and the editors for their comments on, or for discussion of the issues addressed by, this chapter. The usual disclaimer applies.

B. Accountability and accountability institutions

1. Accountability

Accountability is a protean concept: it is pressed into service in a wide array of circumstances; and, depending on the context, it may carry radically different meanings. The compass of the present inquiry is necessarily limited, in that it is concerned with the nature of accountability in the public arena. Even confined thus, the notion of accountability remains a broad one. However, it can be calibrated, and its different senses identified, by considering three sets of related issues: the *subjects* that may form the focus of an accountability inquiry; the *criteria* or *standards* by reference to which such an inquiry may proceed; and the *purposes* that might be served by such an inquiry.

First, then, what do, and should, accountability institutions examine? There is a wide range of possibilities here. The subject-matter of the inquiry might be an administrative measure—which could be a specific decision affecting one individual, or a broad policy potentially affecting large swathes of the population. Or the inquiry might be concerned with the competence, credentials, effectiveness or good faith of a given administrative actor or institution. Or the inquiry might be broader still: it might, for instance, be concerned with systemic issues such as how different institutions relate to one another.

Second, it stands to reason that if there is a broad range of matters capable of forming the subject-matter of accountability inquiries, there is also likely to be an array of criteria, or standards, by reference to which the object of the inquiry may be evaluated. It is also likely that there will be a relationship between these factors: that the appropriate evaluative criteria will depend, in part, upon the type of matter that is under investigation. The applicable criteria might, then, be legal ones, such as statutory restrictions upon the powers of the body being held to account, principles of good administration developed by the courts in exercise of their judicial review jurisdiction, or fundamental rights such as those protected by the Human Rights Act 1998 (HRA 1998). Alternatively (or as well) the criteria might be political: the question might, for instance, be whether it was wise, or prudent, or in the national interest, to pursue a given course of action. Or the applicable standards might be financial, bureaucratic or managerial. Does the matter under scrutiny fulfil value-for-money criteria? Is the system an administratively effective one that is fit for purpose? Have relevant benchmarks and targets been met—and, if not, why not?

Third, accountability inquiries can be, and are, undertaken for a number of purposes. The notion of accountability is often equated with the attribution of responsibility or blame. But just as ministerial accountability is about far more than the circumstances in which ministers should resign, so may accountability inquiries be conducted for ends other than the delivery of a scalp. The objective of an accountability inquiry might, then, be to secure the reversal or cancellation of administrative measures if they fail to meet the benchmark against which they fall to be assessed; the improvement of the quality of future administrative conduct; reform on the policy level; the learning of lessons; catharsis by authoritatively establishing what actually happened; or simply the promotion of transparency—that is, putting information into the public domain in order, inter alia, that the democratic process might be augmented by equipping the electorate to make informed judgments about an elected public body. And of course several of these purposes may be served by a single accountability process. Judicial review of a ministerial decision might, for instance, result in judicial annulment of an unlawful administrative measure, but might also bring to light wider failings within a bureaucracy that may in turn result in operational or policy changes,[1] or affect public perceptions (and so the electoral prospects) of the government of the day.

2. Accountability institutions

Any effective accountability institution must possess two general characteristics. The first is that there must be (and must appear to be) a form of tension, or distance, between it and the body being held to account. The accountability institution must, then, posses a measure of independence. Second, the accountability institution's outputs—its findings—must be imbued with a sufficient degree of impact. An accountability institution whose findings or recommendations can be ignored with impunity is not an effective accountability institution: to hold a public body to account must entail something more than the expression of a view that can readily evaporate into the ether.[2]

These two characteristics are found most readily in the courts. Of all public institutions, courts can most plausibly claim that they are independent of government, judicial independence being, in the UK, the most ample manifestation of an otherwise ambivalent commitment to separation of powers. Meanwhile, doubts about the integrity and effectiveness of the wider political system mean that accountability institutions such as ombudsmen and inquiries, whose outputs sound ultimately in the political rather than the legal realm, may be perceived as the poor relations of judicial bodies with the capacity to issue binding remedies.

The possibility therefore arises of the judicial model of accountability being regarded as a form of paradigm, in the sense that it most obviously and abundantly possesses the basic prerequisites of an effective accountability mechanism. But, for two reasons (among others), the judicial model should not be placed on a pedestal. Firstly, it creates a risk that judicial review will be perceived as a sort of panacea that can substitute for other accountability models that less amply possess the two characteristics mentioned above. That risk must be avoided because, important

---

[1] Equally, however, the wider bureaucratic impact of a court's decision might be slight or non-existent: see generally Halliday, *Judicial Review and Compliance with Administrative Law* (Oxford: Hart, 2003).

[2] Beyond these two general characteristics, what effectiveness requires turns, in part, on the specific goals of the relevant accountability institution. The concern for the time being, however, is with general prerequisites.

though the courts' role is, judicial review is self-evidently capable of supplying only a subset of the forms of accountability sketched in the previous section.

Secondly, treating judicial review as a paradigm may be symptomatic of an underlying misapprehension: namely, that the judicial model furnishes the only, or the best, way of securing the general characteristics required of an effective account-ability institution. In fact, it will be argued, investing such an institution with judicial-style independence is not the only way of creating the sort of distance, or tension, that is necessary. Similarly, impact may be created otherwise than through a power to issue legally binding remedies.[3] The outputs of an accountability process may have seismic consequences simply by virtue of precipitating public pressure (most likely channelled through the media, whether traditional or, now, social)— although this, in the first place, requires that the institution is well-placed to attract publicity to its findings.

Against this background, it will be argued that non-court accountability mechanisms have a valuable and distinctive role to play in the contemporary accountability system. In developing this argument, particular attention will be paid to each mechanism's relationship with court-based accountability, in which regard it will be contended that certain discernible tendencies to view that model as a paradigm should be resisted. Throughout the chapter, the focus will be on holding the UK government to account and, therefore, on those accountability institutions that are particularly relevant to that endeavour.

C. Tribunals

In 1957, the Franks Committee found the predominant view to be that tribunals 'should properly be regarded as part of the machinery of administration, for which Government must retain a close and continuing responsibility'.[4] The Committee, of course, did not share that view, and the Tribunals and Inquiries Act 1958 more clearly established tribunals as part of the adjudicative, as opposed to admin-istrative, apparatus of the state. If Franks, together with the 1958 Act, was the beginning (in earnest) of the judicialization of tribunals, then the Leggatt Report[5] and the Tribunals, Courts and Enforcement Act 2007 (TCEA 2007) arguably marked the logical conclusion of that process. One of the primary effects of those reforms has been to make tribunals more court-like: as Sir Robert Carnwath, the inaugural Senior President of Tribunals, put it, the reforms represent 'a profound constitu-tional change, completing the process of embedding the tribunals' judiciary in the judicial system'.[6] Yet while tribunals are now uncontroversially regarded as judicial

---

[3] As Harlow and Rawlings, *Law and Administration* (Cambridge: Cambridge University Press 3rd edn, 2009), 39, put it, 'control' need not be limited to *judicial* control.
[4] Cm 218, *Report of the Franks Committee on Administrative Tribunals and Enquiries* (London, 1957), para. 40.
[5] *Tribunals for Users: One Service, One System* (London, 2001).
[6] *Second Implementation Review* (London, 2008), para.11.

bodies, this does not, and should not, mean that they are indistinguishable from (regular) courts.[7]

1. Institutional position of tribunals and the separation of powers

The Franks Committee's insistence on the adjudicative nature of tribunals notwithstanding, they could certainly not, prior to the recent reforms, straightforwardly be characterized as part of the judicial branch. For instance, tribunals were commonly 'sponsored' (meaning, among other things, funded) by the very government departments against whose decisions they heard appeals. Such arrangements reflected the fact that tribunals constituted a custom-designed form of accountability, originally tailored for each policy area, rather than functioning as a continental-style administrative court. However, departmental sponsorship was regarded—by the Council on Tribunals[8] and Leggatt, among others—as highly problematic in separation of powers terms. The latter argued that such arrangements gave rise, at best, to a perceived lack of independence and, at worst, to a culture in which tribunal members might actually be influenced in their decision-making by the tribunal's relationship with the sponsoring department.[9] This issue was addressed by shifting administrative responsibility for tribunals from individual sponsoring departments to the Tribunals Service, an executive agency of the Ministry of Justice—a department that does not itself make the sort of decisions that are subject to appeals in tribunals, and which (as the white paper that presaged the reforms put it) has 'a particular mission to protect judicial independence'.[10] (The Tribunals Service has now been superseded by a new executive agency of the Ministry of Justice: HM Courts and Tribunals Service.) Of course, judicial independence is secured not only through institutional independence, but also by judicial seclusion: that is, the insulation of individual judges from pressures that might improperly influence their decision-making. It is noteworthy, therefore, that tribunal judges now enjoy considerable security of tenure.[11]

The judicial status and independence of tribunals and tribunal judges is emphasized under the new arrangements in a number of further ways. Legally qualified tribunal members are known as 'tribunal judges'[12]—to whom the guarantee of 'continued judicial independence' provided for by the Constitutional Reform Act 2005 extends[13]—and all High Court and Court of Appeal (and equivalent) judges are *ex officio* tribunal judges.[14] The Upper Tribunal,[15] meanwhile, is statutorily

---

[7] See, eg. Leggatt Report, paras 1.11-1.13, n 5 above,; *Gillies v Secretary of State for Work and Pensions* [2006] UKHL 2; [2006] 1 WLR 781, paras 36-43, *per* Baroness Hale.

[8] Cm 3744, *Tribunals: Their Organisation and Independence* (London, 1997).

[9] *Tribunals for Users,* para.2.20, n 5 above.

[10] Cm 6243, *Transforming Public Services: Complaints, Redress and Tribunals* (London 2004), para.6.14.

[11] TCEA 2007, sch.2, paras 3-4; sch.3, paras 3-4.

[12] TCEA 2007, ss 4-5; sch.2, para.1; sch.3, para.1.

[13] Constitutional Reform Act 2005, s 3(7A) and sch.14.

[14] TCEA 2007, ss 4(1)(c) and 5(1)(g) read with s 6(1).

[15] The role of the Upper Tribunal is considered in more detail below.

designated as a 'superior court of record'[16] and is invested with powers of judicial review.[17] And the new tribunals system is judicially led by the 'Senior President',[18] who is currently—and who will normally be[19]—a Court of Appeal judge (or equivalent). Moreover, the Ministry of Justice has proposed the abolition of the office of Senior President in order to make way for a single head of the courts and tribunals judiciary. The inaugural Senior President saw this as 'a logical step in the evolution of the tribunal system in accordance with the Leggatt vision', conceding that the need for the office was diminished 'now that tribunal judges and members are accepted as full members of the judicial family'.[20]

The upshot of all of this is that tribunals are now situated firmly within the judicial branch. In this sense, then, the distinction between courts and tribunals has largely been eroded—and rightly so. Both courts[21] and tribunals supply a form of accountability that is adjudicative in nature: their prime focus is upon assessing administrative decisions by reference to objective legal criteria, overturning or righting such decisions if they are found to be unlawful or incorrect, and so equivalent cases for judicial-style independence can be made in relation to each.

2. Courts and tribunals: functional differentiation

However, this does not mean that the two sets of institutions should resemble one another in every respect. Certain points of similarity notwithstanding, there have traditionally been—and still are—very substantial differences between what courts and tribunals do, and how they do those things. For instance, tribunals operate in a more informal manner than courts, with the intention that individuals should be able to participate in their proceedings without need for representation.[22] At the same time, the tribunal system is divided into a number of different jurisdictions, whereas the Administrative Court is generalist in nature.[23]

These differences exist—and continue to exist—as a matter of empirical *fact*. But they can be *explained*, to some extent at least, by reference to two broader differences between courts and tribunals. First, the tribunal system is, and the Administrative Court is manifestly not, a mechanism for supplying mass administrative justice. For instance, in 2011, there were 11,200 applications to the Administrative Court for permission to apply for judicial review, permission being granted in only 1,220 cases.[24] In contrast, in the 12-month period beginning on 1 April 2011, tribunals received 553,300 appeals and disposed of 621,800.[25]

---

[16] TCEA 2007, s 3(5).   [17] TCEA 2007, s 15.   [18] TCEA 2007, s 2.
[19] This is implicit in the appointment arrangements set out in the TCEA 2007, sch.1.
[20] *Senior President of Tribunals' Annual Report* (London, 2011) 7.
[21] That is, those courts, such as the Administrative Court, that entertain challenges to executive action.
[22] Leggatt Report, ch 4, n 5 above.
[23] This remains the case under the TCEA 2007: although many separate tribunals have been swept away in favour of the new First-tier and Upper Tribunals, jurisdictional divisions remain within the new system. This is discussed in more detail below.
[24] Ministry of Justice, *Judicial and Court Statistics 2011* (London, 2012), table 7.12.
[25] Ministry of Justice, *Annual Tribunals Statistics 2011-12* (London, 2012) at 3-5. These figures pertain only to tribunals that were administered by HM Courts and Tribunals Service in the relevant

Secondly, first-instance tribunals are generally concerned with both the merits and legality of impugned administrative action, whereas the Administrative Court is concerned only with the latter.[26]

Taken together, these overarching distinctions between the respective roles of courts and tribunals help to explain many of the more specific differences between them. For instance, the fact that tribunals are dispensers of mass administrative justice inevitably requires them to be more accessible than the Administrative Court: while procedures have never been uniform across the tribunals spectrum, tribunals generally adopt a more enabling approach, which, at least in theory, facilitates direct participation and obviates the need for representation (for which most complainants would be unable, and the state unwilling, to pay).[27] Of course, it is well established that the position of unrepresented parties is often not fully ameliorated by the procedural approach adopted by the tribunal—and that such parties are often surprised by an approach that is more formal and legalistic than they anticipated.[28] And even if, as some research suggests,[29] lack of representation at hearings is not inevitably of decisive importance, it appears that legal advice prior to a hearing does (unsurprisingly) make a difference to the appellant's prospects of success.[30] The harsh reality, however, is that public funds are not available to provide legal representation or advice to tribunal appellants as a matter of course— and so, as Leggatt acknowledged in 2001,[31] and as the Justice Select Committee has recognized more recently,[32] the emphasis must be upon facilitating effective direct participation in tribunal proceedings. The fact that the tribunals system does not (and probably never will) do this perfectly does not alter the fact that it does so (and, as a dispenser of mass administrative justice, must of necessity do so) to a far greater extent than the Administrative Court.

Against this background, the following *dictum* of Lady Hale is instructive:

[Tribunals] were set up by statute to administer complex and rapidly changing areas of the law. Their judges were expected to know this law without having to have lawyers for

---

period, and (because the present concern is with individual-versus-government tribunals as an instrument of executive accountability) exclude Employment Tribunals.

[26] Admittedly, the Administrative Court, exercising judicial review powers, is more concerned than it once was with questions pertaining to merits (thanks, for instance, to the development of more substantive grounds of judicial review). However, the Administrative Court is not unambiguously and explicitly concerned with merits in the same way as a first-instance tribunal might be.

[27] The scope for direct participation was identified by Leggatt as a key characteristic of tribunal adjudication: para.1.11 n 5 above.

[28] See, inter alios, Baldwin, Wikeley and Young *Judging Social Security* (Oxford, 1992); Genn 'Tribunals and informal justice' *MLR* (1993) 56: 393; Adler and Gulland, *Tribunal Users' Experiences, Perceptions and Expectations: A Literature Review* (London, 2003),11.

[29] It appears that unrepresented appellants who receive 'pre-hearing advice' do not fare significantly worse than represented appellants: Adler, 'Tribunals Ain't What They used to Be' (ADJUST Newsletter, March 2009). However, public funding (where it presently exists) for such advice is now under threat. See, generally, Justice Committee, *Government's proposed reform of legal aid* (HC681-I, 2010-11).

[30] Adler, 'Tribunals Ain't What They used to Be', n 29 above; Justice Committee, para.130, n 29 above.

[31] *Tribunals for Users*, paras 7.2-7.6, n 5 above.

[32] Justice Committee, para.132, n 29 above.

the parties to explain it to them. Their members were expected to have relevant expertise or experience in the subject matter of the dispute, not only so that they would be able to adjudicate upon factual issues without the help of lawyers for the parties, but also so that the parties could feel confident that the overall balance of the panel (for example between employers and employees) would produce impartial results. Their procedures were also tailored to the subject matter of the dispute and they were not bound by the technical rules of evidence.[33]

These remarks echo Leggatt's view that the relative expertise of tribunals—a function of their differentiated nature—may go some way towards facilitating the more effective participation of unrepresented appellants that is essential if tribunals are to function as dispensers of mass administrative justice.[34] Yet the extent to which such differentiation and expertise will persist within the reformed system is currently uncertain. One of the most eye-catching structural changes ushered in by Leggatt was the consolidation of disparate tribunals into a unified two-tier structure. Most appeals are now heard by the First-tier Tribunal—which is divided into several chambers, many of which are further subdivided into jurisdictions—with a right of appeal on points of law to the Upper Tribunal, which is itself divided into chambers. There are many reasons to welcome these changes: the new structure is more rational, less haphazard, potentially more efficient, and has clearer and more consistent pathways through it in terms of rights of appeal. It is, however, unclear to what extent it will result in the preservation of the expertise of the old, separate tribunals (which was arguably already on the wane, given decreasing reliance upon non-legally qualified chairs and wing members).[35] Under the new system, judges can be 'ticketed' to hear cases falling within more than one jurisdiction within a given chamber, and can also be 'assigned' to hear cases in other chambers.[36] There is therefore at least the possibility[37] that specialization will diminish under these arrangements.[38] As Lady Hale has observed, 'There must be some risk that the amalgamation of very different jurisdictions in the new chambers will dilute rather than enhance the specialist expertise of their judges and members.'[39]

It is too early to assess the extent to which cross-ticketing and assignment may have effects of this nature, but it is already clear that the availability of these techniques is being capitalized upon. For instance, the President of the Social Entitlement Chamber of the First-tier Tribunal reports that 'the flexibility of deployment offered by the [new regime] has been seized upon by the Chamber', with 'substantial

---

[33] *R (Cart) v Upper Tribunal* [2011] UKSC 28; [2011] 3 WLR 107 at [13].

[34] *Tribunals for Users*, para.1.12, n 5 above.

[35] See, eg. Wikeley, 'Burying Bell: Managing the Judicialisation of Social Security Tribunals' *MLR* (2000) 63: 475.

[36] TCEA 2007, sch.4.

[37] Mullen, 'A Holistic Approach to Administrative Justice?' in Adler (ed.), *Administrative Justice in Context* (Oxford, 2010), 407.

[38] Albeit that the Senior President has indicated that judges' 'suitability' will be considered before final decisions on assignment are made and that 'a training system [will be introduced] for assigned judges prior to their sitting in a new jurisdiction': *Assignment: Senior President's Policy Statement* (London, 2009), para.21.

[39] *R (Cart) v Upper Tribunal* (UKSC), at [54], n 33 above.

cross-ticketing of judges between [the Asylum Support and Social Security & Child Support jurisdictions within the Chamber] and of medically qualified members between [the Social Security & Child Support and Criminal Injuries Compensation jurisdictions]'.[40] Meanwhile, there have been 'assignment exercises between the Social Entitlement Chamber and [three] other Chambers [of the First-tier Tribunal]',[41] and 26 judges have (by means of assignment) been transferred into the Administrative Appeals Chamber of the Upper Tribunal.[42]

In his recent study of tribunals adjudication, Cane suggests that tribunals are now best regarded as a species of court, not merely as a court-substitute.[43] This argument is undoubtedly persuasive, in that tribunals, as well as performing a role that is functionally similar to that of courts (in the sense of adjudicating upon individual disputes according to settled and objective legal principles), also possess many institutional characteristics that are classically associated with regular courts. It is even the case that the Upper Tribunal is statutorily authorized to exercise High Court-style powers of judicial review in limited circumstances.[44] Nevertheless, the point remains that even if tribunals can, or should, be regarded as a type of court, they continue to supply legal accountability in a manner that makes them readily distinguishable from those regular courts (principally the Administrative Court) that hold government to account.

The raw, pragmatic reason for this consists, of course, in the need for tribunals, unlike the Administrative Court, to act as dispensers of mass administrative justice in a way that is financially sustainable and which therefore (among other things) facilitates direct participation. And although the byzantine nature of the old system was rightly criticized, it reflected, at root, what Lady Hale has called one of the fundamental 'facts of tribunal life':[45] namely, that the role, and so the *modus operandi*, of the tribunal system demands a somewhat differentiated, specialized set of institutions that are able to bring a measure of expertise to bear upon challenges to administrative decisions. Whereas differentiation (being a function of fragmentation) was hard-wired into the old system, this is not true (at least to the same extent) of the new structure. In this sense, a tension lies at the heart of the new system—between, on the one hand, its malleability (and the efficiency interests that will militate in favour of that characteristic's exploitation) and, on the other hand, the need for differentiation and specialization. The new system creates opportunities to trade these interests off against one another in a way that its predecessor did not. This is not to doubt the wisdom of adopting a rationalized structure; but it will be important, as the new system beds down, to ensure that its capacity to dispense high-quality mass administrative justice is not undercut by diluting the expertise of the former individual tribunals through undue invocation of the new structure's greater jurisdictional flexibility.

---

[40] *Senior President of Tribunals' Annual Report,* 42, n 20 above.
[41] *Senior President of Tribunals' Annual Report,* 42.
[42] *Senior President of Tribunals' Annual Report,* 21.
[43] Cane, *Administrative Tribunals and Adjudication* (Oxford, 2009), 72.
[44] TCEA 2007, ss 15-21.   [45] *Gillies,* [41], n 7 above.

3. Relationship between the courts and tribunals systems

So far we have considered where tribunals stand today within the accountability system—and, in particular, with reference to ordinary courts—in terms of their institutional status (and independence) and their functional differentiation from regular courts. We now turn to a third, and final, issue. What is the relationship between the new tribunal *system* and the court *system*—and what does this tell us about tribunals' role today?

One of the hallmarks of the pre-2008 tribunals regime was that tribunals' relationships with ordinary courts were somewhat haphazard, with inconsistencies in terms of the existence, nature and destination of rights of appeal. The position has now been rationalized, the norm being that there is a right of appeal against an administrative decision to the First-tier Tribunal; an onward right of appeal, on a point of law only, to the Upper Tribunal;[46] and a further right of appeal, again on a point of law only, to the Court of Appeal.[47] For four interlocking reasons, the effect of this new regime is that it is now relatively rare for ordinary courts to intervene in relation to matters that fall within the purview of the tribunal system.

First, there is little prospect of the Administrative Court judicially reviewing decisions of the First-tier Tribunal, given that in respect of most such decisions there is a right of appeal to the Upper Tribunal. Judicial review, being generally regarded as a remedy of final resort, is normally available only if any alternative remedies (by way of appeal) have been exhausted.[48]

Second, the latter inhibition upon judicial review does not apply to the small category of First-tier Tribunal decisions against which no right of appeal exists. However, any judicial review of such decisions would most likely be carried out not by the Administrative Court but by the Upper Tribunal. This is because the Upper Tribunal has been invested with statutory powers of judicial review,[49] and has exclusive judicial review jurisdiction in relation to, inter alia, First-tier Tribunal decisions against which there is no right of appeal.[50]

Third, the right of appeal to the Court of Appeal against decisions of the Upper Tribunal is highly constricted. It lies (as noted above) only on points of law;[51] only with the permission of the Upper Tribunal or the Court of Appeal;[52] only if the appeal would raise 'some important point of principle or practice' or if there is 'some other compelling reason' for the appeal to be heard;[53] and does not lie at all in respect of certain matters.[54]

Fourth, while the statutory scheme does not purport to exclude the possibility of judicial review of the Upper Tribunal, such review will be rare in practice. In *Cart*[55] and

---

[46] TCEA 2007, s 11.   [47] TCEA 2007, s 13.
[48] *R v Inland Revenue Commissioners, ex p Preston* [1985] AC 835 at 852, *per* Lord Scarman.
[49] TCEA 2007, ss 15-21.
[50] TCEA 2007, s 18(6) and the Lord Chief Justice's Direction made thereunder.
[51] TCEA 2007, s 13(1).   [52] TCEA 2007, s 13(4).
[53] Appeals from the Upper Tribunal to the Court of Appeal Order 2008. This restriction applies to appeals against decisions made by the Upper Tribunal in appeals to that Tribunal against decisions of the First-tier Tribunal.
[54] TCEA 2007, s 13(1) and orders made thereunder.
[55] *R (Cart) v Upper Tribunal (UKSC)*, n 33 above.

Eba,[56] the Supreme Court had to decide on the circumstances, if any, in which an Upper Tribunal decision against which (unusually) there was no right of appeal[57] could instead be challenged by way of judicial review. Endorsing the view of Laws LJ in the Divisional Court,[58] the Supreme Court held in *Cart* that the statutory designation[59] of the Upper Tribunal as a 'superior court of record' does not formally exempt it from judicial review. However, the Supreme Court also considered that (for reasons addressed below) the Upper Tribunal's decisions should not generally be vulnerable to review. The court therefore held that judicial review of the Upper Tribunal should occur only in cases raising an important point of principle or practice or disclosing some other compelling reason for judicial review. These are, quite deliberately, the same criteria as those which apply to second appeals to the Court of Appeal (both from the Upper Tribunal[60] and generally).[61] Those criteria, as they apply generally, have been interpreted quite narrowly,[62] and in *PR (Sri Lanka) v Home Secretary*[63] a powerfully-constituted Court of Appeal[64] adopted a notably restrictive interpretation of the criteria as they apply to the Upper Tribunal. This is consistent with Lady Hale's observation in *Cart* that while the 'adoption of the second-tier appeal criteria' as the means by which to determine the availability of judicial review creates the possibility of a 'further check, outside the tribunal system', it is 'not one which could be expected to succeed in the great majority of cases'.[65]

The upshot is that the new tribunal system is, to a significant degree, self-contained, in that it is subject only to limited oversight by regular courts. In restricting the scope for judicial review (and aligning the applicable criteria with those pertaining to second-tier appeals), the Supreme Court was evidently influenced by pragmatic concerns about the efficient use of scarce judicial resources—a point that emerges from frequent references to the need to avoid extending to complainants 'disproportionate' opportunities for challenge. As Lady Hale put it, while judicial fallibility means that 'there should always be the possibility that another judge can look at the case and check for error', 'it is not obvious that there should be a right to any particular number of further checks after that'.[66] On this view, then, it may be perfectly proper for denial of permission by the Upper Tribunal to mark the end

---

[56] *Eba v Advocate General for Scotland* [2011] UKSC 29; [2011] 3 WLR 149.
[57] As explained in the previous paragraph, there is generally a limited right of appeal to the Court of Appeal against decisions of the Upper Tribunal. However, *Cart* and *Eba* were concerned with decisions by the Upper Tribunal to deny permission to appeal to that Tribunal against decisions of the First-tier Tribunal. There is no right of appeal to the Court of Appeal (or, in Scotland, to the Court of Session) against such permission decisions by the Upper Tribunal.
[58] *R (Cart) v Upper Tribunal* [2009] EWHC 3052 (Admin); [2010] 2 WLR 1012.
[59] TCEA 2007, s 3(5).
[60] Appeals from the Upper Tribunal to the Court of Appeal Order 2008.
[61] Civil Procedure Rules 1998, r 52.13.
[62] See, generally, Jenns, 'Is it all downhill for second appeals?' *CJQ* (2006) 25: 439.
[63] [2011] EWCA Civ 988.
[64] Lord Neuberger MR, Sir Anthony May P and Carnwath LJ.
[65] *R (Cart) v Upper Tribunal (UKSC)*, [56], n 33 above.
[66] *R (Cart) v Upper Tribunal (UKSC)*, [56], n 33 above .

of the road in a given case. It is significant, however, that, in the tribunals context, neither the first instance judge nor the judge carrying out the 'check for error' will be a judge of the ordinary courts acting in that capacity.[67] The question then becomes to what extent, if any, it is necessary for the ordinary courts to exercise oversight. In addressing this matter, the Supreme Court took account of considerations of both institutional capacity and constitutional propriety. It sought to balance avoidance of unnecessary 'duplication of judicial process' (as Lord Phillips put it)[68] against the need to ensure 'that errors on important points of principle or practice do not become fossilized within the [tribunals] system' (as Lord Dyson put it),[69] while acknowledging that it would be inconsistent with the rule of law for ordinary courts to foreclose on the possibility of overseeing tribunals. In concluding that this balance was best struck by limiting review (as well as appeal) by reference to the second-tier appeal criteria, the court acknowledged the institutional competence of the tribunal system. In doing so, it echoed, but crystallized, earlier *dicta* to the effect that ordinary courts should be slow to conclude that specialist tribunals have committed errors of law, given the relative expertise of the latter.[70]

One of those dicta[71] led Sir Robert Carnwath, when Senior President of Tribunals, to postulate (extrajudicially) an 'antihierarchical approach to the relationship between courts and tribunals', according to which the Upper Tribunal would enjoy substantial freedom to develop a distinctive approach to its supervision of the tribunals system.[72] That freedom would have been more substantial still had the Supreme Court adopted the Divisional Court and the Court of Appeal's view that the Upper Tribunal should be vulnerable to review only in the event of a 'denial...of fundamental justice'[73] or an excess of jurisdiction in the narrow (pre-*Anisminic*) sense.[74] The Supreme Court's rejection of that view was somewhat elliptical, in that it approached the matter from a perspective different from that adopted by the lower courts. Whereas those courts were centrally concerned with the extent of the Upper Tribunal's legal powers per se, the Supreme Court's concern was with the circumstances in which an allegation that the Tribunal has exceeded its jurisdiction should be capable of being pursued by means of judicial review proceedings.

It is not entirely clear what the Supreme Court would, in the first place, count as an excess of jurisdiction on the part of the Upper Tribunal. In *Cart*, the Justices certainly rejected (implicitly or explicitly) the lower courts' minimalistic assessment

---

[67] Although it might (or might not) be a judge of one of those courts acting in his or her *ex officio* capacity as a judge of the Upper Tribunal.

[68] *R (Cart) v Upper Tribunal (UKSC)*, [89], n 33 above.

[69] *R (Cart) v Upper Tribuna (UKSC)*, [130], n 33 above.

[70] *Cooke v Secretary of State for Social Security* [2001] EWCA Civ 734; [2002] 3 All ER 279 at [15]-[17]; *R (Wiles) v Social Security Commissioner* [2010] EWCA Civ 258 at [53]-[54]; *AH (Sudan) v Secretary of State for the Home Department* [2007] UKHL 49; [2008] 1 AC 678 (HL) at [30].

[71] *Per* Lady Hale in *Cooke*, [15]-[17], n 70 above.

[72] 'Tribunal Justice - A New Start' *PL* [2009] 48: 57. For instance, he suggested that although appeals to the Upper Tribunal normally lie only on points of law, it might fashion for itself an appellate jurisdiction more ample than that criterion would normally imply, by adopting a view of the fact/law distinction at odds with that which prevails in the ordinary courts.

[73] *R (Cart) v Upper Tribunal* [2010] EWCA Civ 859; [2011] QB 120 at [36] (*per* Sedley LJ).

[74] *R (Cart) v Upper Tribunal* (CA) [36] (*per* Sedley LJ).

of the limits applying to the Tribunal's jurisdiction, but it would be surprising if the pre-TCEA 2007 approach favouring restrained review of specialist tribunals did not persist. Lord Dyson, for instance, assumed that it would, and accepted that this, in itself, represented a significant restriction upon the extent of judicial oversight of the tribunal system.[75] The Supreme Court returned to this matter in *R (Jones) v First-tier Tribunal*. Lords Hope and Carnwath suggested—with disarming frankness—that the distinction between issues of fact and law could legitimately be manipulated, so as to avoid characterizing as (jurisdictional) questions of law matters that ought properly to be left to the expert judgement of a tribunal.[76] The upshot, then, is that oversight of the Upper Tribunal by ordinary courts is likely to be relatively rare, given the restrictiveness of the second-tier appeal criteria which now constrain both appeal and review; and, even if such oversight takes place, it is likely to be relatively light-touch in nature at least in circumstances where the matter in question engages the expertise of the Upper Tribunal.

It is too early to say with certainty what the practical ramifications will be of the decisions in *Cart* and *Eba*, and, in particular, the extent to which they leave intact the potential, identified by Carnwath, for a distinctive tribunals jurisprudence. The likelihood, however, is that much of that potential remains, albeit that whereas the lower courts' approach carved out a sharply-defined area of autonomy, the Supreme Court's approach is more subtle. It relies upon limiting the circumstances in which permission will be granted, as well as upon the somewhat elastic concept of deference in the face of relative institutional competence and the (apparently almost infinitely) flexible nature of the law/fact distinction. On this view, then, while tribunals are now a firmly entrenched part of the judicial system, they are a distinctive component of it. In particular, the courts' willingness—revealed in *Cart* and *Eba*—to engage in only very limited oversight of the new tribunals system means that the judicialization of tribunals does not amount to the assimilation of courts and tribunals.

D. Ombudsmen, inquiries and political accountability

A degree of diversity *within* the judicial system is one thing; but a more radical form of diversity is also necessary. Legal-judicial control of government must be complemented by other techniques if the full spectrum of forms of accountability sketched at the beginning of this chapter is to be supplied. Our focus therefore shifts to ombudsmen and inquiries, both of which provide non-legal forms of accountability. In relation to each, it is argued that failings in the wider political system within which those accountability mechanisms sit can be, and sometimes are, perceived as arguments in favour of their augmentation by means of borrowing from the judicial model. It will be argued that while it does not follow that the

---

[75] *R (Cart) v Upper Tribunal* (UKSC) [113], n 33 above.
[76] [2013] UKSC 19; [2013] 2 WLR 1012.

'pull' of the judicial model should invariably be resisted, the appropriateness of yielding to it must be carefully weighed if the diversity of the overall accountability system is to be maintained.

1. Ombudsmen

The form of accountability supplied by public sector ombudsmen[77] is clearly different from, and complementary to, that which is provided by courts and tribunals. For instance, ombudsmen are generally more accessible than courts; they can evaluate administrative action against standards of good administration that are in some senses broader, and more demanding, than those applicable in judicial review proceedings;[78] and they are (sometimes) able—for instance by drawing general conclusions after examining a multiplicity of individual complaints—to identify problems, and secure change, at a systemic level.[79]

Like most ombudsmen systems, the office of Parliamentary Ombudsman[80]— which forms the focus of this part of the chapter—is, by design, part of the political as opposed to legal arrangements for holding government to account. This is not to suggest that the Parliamentary Ombudsman is not constituted on a legal basis, or lacks legal powers for such purposes as holding investigations and obtaining evidence. However, the outputs of the Ombudsman's investigations sound in the political, not the legal, realm. So, for instance, the Ombudsman's finding of maladministration does not per se undermine the legal validity of the executive act in question. Equally, the Ombudsman's recommendation that a decision-maker guilty of maladministration occasioning injustice should take certain remedial steps does not impose any legal obligation to do so.

It was argued earlier in this chapter that effective accountability institutions must be imbued with two key characteristics. Firstly, there must be a degree of tension between the accountability institution and the body being held to account. Here, the Ombudsman serves a valuable purpose as an independent outsider capable of conducting a thorough inquiry and uncovering vices ranging from individual ineptitude to systemic failure. Secondly, however, accountability institutions must also have clout, effective accountability being impossible if the output of the process is so readily dismissible as to have no meaningful impact. The fact that most of the Ombudsman's recommendations are accepted by public bodies is testament to the fact that an accountability institution can have considerable impact without possessing legal powers of enforcement. Administrative resistance is unlikely in run-of-the-mill cases, given their relatively self-contained nature and the modest scale of the remedial

---

[77] On which see, generally, M Seneviratne, *Ombudsmen: Public Services and Administrative Justice* (Cambridge: Cambridge University Press, 2002); Buck, Kirkham and Thompson, *The Ombudsman Enterprise and Administrative Justice* (Farnham: Ashgate, 2011).

[78] See, eg., Parliamentary Ombudsman, *Principles of Good Administration* (London, 2009).

[79] See, eg., Parliamentary Ombudsman, *Six Lives: The Provision of Public Services to People with Learning Disabilities* (HC203 2008-9).

[80] Or Parliamentary Commissioner for Administration, as the office is formally, but today rarely, called.

action generally recommended by the Ombudsman. Wide-ranging, high-profile cases are, though, a different matter. Here, resistance is more likely: indeed, recent years have witnessed an unprecedented number of instances of rejection by central government of the Parliamentary Ombudsman's findings and recommendations.[81] Even in controversial cases in which resistance is more likely, it does not follow that the Ombudsman's inability to issue court-like binding decisions is fatal to effectiveness—but much depends upon the vagaries of the political and media climate. Even controversial findings of maladministration and hard-to-swallow remedial recommendations may be accepted by a government faced with public or media opprobrium against the background of an Ombudsman's report capable of serving as an objective stick with which to beat the administration.[82]

However, the Ombudsman's relatively low public profile means that such 'soft' forms of enforcement will not necessarily succeed: much will depend upon the extent of public, political and media sympathy for the plight of the relevant victims of maladministration. The Ombudsman's relationship with the Public Administration Select Committee (PASC)—which both scrutinizes the Ombudsman's work and acts, in certain instances, as the Ombudsman's champion in Parliament—is therefore crucial. In this way, the Ombudsman is plugged into the wider parliamentary system for securing accountable government, and there is certainly evidence that the Committee's involvement can add real political bite to a critical report by the Ombudsman.[83] Yet in the face of the Ombudsman's apparent legal impotence and (occasional) government intransigence facilitated by the executive's dominance of Parliament, the pull of the judicial model may be keenly felt. It is against this background that the courts have in recent years been invited to consider the extent, if any, to which the government's freedom to reject the Ombudsman's findings and recommendations is legally constrained.

2. The *Bradley* and *Equitable Life* cases

Perhaps tellingly, Ann Abraham, when she was the Ombudsman, argued in favour of legal constraint. She advanced this position in *R (Bradley) v Secretary of State for Work and Pensions*, in which the claimants argued that ministerial decisions rejecting certain of the Ombudsman's findings of maladministration should be quashed.[84] The Ombudsman, making submissions as an interested party, argued that 'the Secretary of State must proceed on the basis that the ombudsman's findings of

---

[81] Only six special reports under the Parliamentary Commissioner Act 1967, s 10(3) alerting Parliament to a government failure to remedy injustice caused by maladministration, have ever been issued; four of those six have been issued since 2005.

[82] eg. in the *Equitable Life* case, discussed below, the Ombudsman's reports formed a focal point for criticism and campaigning activity, albeit that full compliance with the Ombudsman's recommendations is still awaited and may not be forthcoming.

[83] See, eg., PASC, *A Debt of Honour* (HC735 2005-6).

[84] *R (Bradley) v Secretary of State for Work and Pensions* [2008] EWCA Civ 36; [2009] QB 114.

injustice caused by maladministration are correct unless they are quashed in judicial review proceedings'.[85] Refusing to accede to this argument, Sir John Chadwick, giving the leading judgment in the Court of Appeal, endorsed the view that '[i]f he is prepared to take the consequences, and defend his position in Parliament, ... a minister who believes that he and his department have been unfairly criticized by the [Ombudsman] clearly has the right to say so'.[86] This suggests a particular underlying view according to which the Ombudsman's findings sound only in the political realm, such that a government with sufficient political muscle is free to reject them.

However, the position adopted by the Court of Appeal is more subtle than its dismissal of the Ombudsman's view may seem to imply. The Court reached the prima facie unsurprising view that the government is legally free to reject the Ombudsman's findings provided that it is not *Wednesbury* unreasonable to do so. Yet the court adopted a somewhat unconventional conception of unreasonableness, equating it with an absence of 'cogent reasons'.[87] That this involves stricter scrutiny than normal *Wednesbury* review is evident from the fact that the government's reasons were held not to pass muster—the Minister's 'preference for his own view' was not an adequate reason for rejection[88]—and from the gloss subsequently placed upon the 'cogent reasons' test in *R (Equitable Members Action Group) v HM Treasury*, in which it was said to require the court to engage in a 'careful examination of the facts of the individual case'.[89] However, the court signalled in *Equitable Members* that ministerial rejections of the Ombudsman's *recommendations*, as distinct from *findings*, would attract review only on 'conventional irrationality', not cogent reasons, grounds.[90]

Does this represent an acceptable level of 'judicialization', in the sense of imbuing the fruits of the Ombudsman's inquiries with a degree of legal force? On one view, it might be argued that the courts have gone too far. Criticizing the Court of Appeal's approach in *Bradley*, Varuhas argues that 'an orthodox *Wednesbury* standard ... should be applied when reviewing a governmental rejection of a finding of the [Ombudsman]'.[91] More searching scrutiny 'could displace Parliament as the central institution for ensuring accountability' and would 'run against the grain' of the Ombudsman system.[92] Varuhas is certainly right to warn that over-zealous judicial intervention would risk upsetting the balance between legal and political control of government; but how much judicial intervention, in this context, is too much?

---

[85] *R (Bradley) v Secretary of State*,[135]. The Law Commission (Law Com No 329, *Public Services Ombudsmen* (London 2011)) has also recommended that Ombudsmen's findings (as opposed to their recommendations) should be binding unless successfully challenged on judicial review.

[86] *R (Bradley) v Secretary of State*,[41], quoting Royal Institute of Public Administration, *The Parliamentary Ombudsman: A Study in the Control of Administrative Action* (1975), 503.

[87] *R (Bradley) v Secretary of State*, [72], n 84 above.

[88] *R (Bradley) v Secretary of State*, [91].

[89] *R (Equitable Members Action Group) v HM Treasury* [2009] EWHC 2495 (Admin) at [66].

[90] *R (Equitable Members Action Group)*, [132].

[91] 'Governmental Rejections of Ombudsman Findings: What Role for the Courts?' *MLR* (2009) 72 91 at 110.

[92] 'Governmental Rejections of Ombudsman Findings', 111.

It would be hard to argue plausibly that courts should readily be able to force ministers to implement the Ombudsman's recommendations by means of (say) strict judicial scrutiny of rejections of such recommendations. Ann Abraham, the former Ombudsman, has acknowledged this. Referring to the government's refusal in the *Equitable Members* case to provide compensation on the basis that she had recommended, she accepted that ministers were entitled 'to bring into play legitimate considerations of public policy and purse'.[93] This is surely correct: it is not for the Ombudsman to force the government to commit large sums of public money in any particular way, and it is not for the courts, by means of intensive judicial review, to enable the Ombudsman to do so.

But should review of ministerial rejections of *findings* be similarly restrained? Judicial quashing of such rejections is likely to have relatively modest effects. If a court rules that it was unlawful for a minister to have rejected a given finding of maladministration (or of injustice occasioned thereby), the finding is, on a political level, placed back on the table. This will, inter alia, strengthen the hand of those pressing the government for a remedy: to the extent that the prior justification for not granting a remedy[94] consisted in the dismissal of a given finding of maladministration or injustice, that justification will be weakened. But this does not necessarily compel the government to do anything: whether, in these circumstances, it finds itself under irresistible pressure to provide a remedy will depend upon the political weather, including the extent of public and media criticism of government intransigence and the administration's political capacity to withstand it. Meanwhile, the legal implications of quashing a ministerial rejection of a finding are likely to be somewhere between slight and non-existent. The 'reinstatement' of a finding by means of quashing its rejection does not, in itself, generate a legal obligation to do anything. An Ombudsman's report could only create such an obligation if it contained a *recommendation* that could not lawfully be rejected—but, as noted above, the court's view in *Equitable Members* was that such circumstances will arise only if rejection is unreasonable in the conventional, highly limited, sense.[95]

It follows that the principal—and, most likely, only real—consequence of quashing a ministerial rejection of a *finding* is political in nature. This, in turn, suggests that judicial intervention (including by means of relatively strict scrutiny) in this sphere is acceptable in that it is not inconsistent with the principally political form of the accountability supplied by the Parliamentary Ombudsman system. Indeed, it is possible to go further, and to argue that such judicial intervention is desirable in that it augments the political impact of the Ombudsman's findings, while preserving the government's freedom to respond as it wishes, subject only to any

---

[93] Public Administration Select Committee, *Sixth Report* (HC219, 2008-9) at Ev1.
[94] Or for granting a remedy less generous than that recommended by the Ombudsman.
[95] It might be harder to demonstrate the reasonableness of a decision to reject a *recommendation* if a *finding* whose administrative dismissal helped to justify departure from the recommendation is judicially reinstated, but the practical significance of this point is likely to be limited, given that the level of reasonableness that falls to be demonstrated when rejections of *recommendations* are reviewed is the standard, undemanding one.

constraints that flow from the political process. Of course, in an ideal world, it might be unnecessary to resort to the courts in order to enhance the impact of the Ombudsman's reports: the political process would, in itself, be sufficient to secure administrative respect for the Ombudsman process and its outputs. The reality, however, is that the British constitution is a decidedly lop-sided one in which the executive branch is unusually powerful and the legislature relatively weak. It is important, in such circumstances, to resist the counsel of despair which holds that politics is so broken that our only hope lies in ever-greater resort to judicial control. This means, inter alia, that it is necessary to consider how the parliamentary system might better support the Ombudsman[96] by ensuring that the government's ultimate freedom to reject her findings and recommendations with impunity is subject to robust scrutiny.[97] At the same time, however, it is unobjectionable that courts should augment the political process by constraining ministers' freedom to dismiss the Parliamentary Ombudsman's findings. For this reason, the position arrived at in *Bradley* and *Equitable Members*, whereby the effect of judicial review in this area is rendered principally political in nature, is one that strikes a sensible balance between legal and political forms of control.[98]

3. Inquiries into matters of public concern

Inquiries come in many different shapes and sizes—from routinely-held planning inquiries to inquiries into the making of highly controversial decisions about such matters as the waging of war. The focus here is upon inquiries of the latter type. The former sort of inquiry is best regarded as part of the decision-making process itself, whereas inquiries into matters of public concern supply ex post scrutiny of that process (and its outputs), and can therefore properly be regarded as a form of accountability institution. In the light of the argument, advanced above, that an effective accountability system requires diversity, what are the distinctive features of inquiries and the accountability that they supply?

There are several senses in which inquiries occupy a different niche from courts and tribunals.[99] The standards against which an inquiry can judge administrative action are far wider than those applicable in legal proceedings; for instance, inquiries can ask questions about such matters as the wisdom of making particular policy choices that would fall well outside the remit of a court engaged in judicial review. Moreover, whereas courts necessarily deal with individual, isolated challenges to

---

[96] As already noted, the PASC already plays an important role in this regard.

[97] For instance, the PASC (*Parliament and the Ombudsman* (HC107, 2009-10)) has suggested that a special report by the Ombudsman should automatically trigger a Commons debate. In the absence of such arrangements, the possibility of forcing a debate in such circumstances is enhanced by the creation of the Backbench Business Committee.

[98] The position outlined here bears some resemblance to that which obtains in relation to declarations of incompatibility under the HRA 1998. The effect of that legal remedy is principally political: while it imposes no legal obligation upon the executive or legislature to amend inconsistent legislation, it affects, potentially profoundly, the political environment within which the political decision whether to do so is taken.

[99] See also Steele, 'Judging Judicial Inquiries' *PL* [2004] 738.

executive decisions, inquiries can consider the wider picture by looking at a whole series of administrative actions. Meanwhile, whereas litigation is (normally) initiated by individuals, and therefore serves (at least in part) to secure litigants' private interests,[100] inquiries are initiated and owned by the government, the inquiry's intended role being to examine matters for the benefit of the public. Finally, inquiries can be, and often are, explicitly concerned with lesson-learning in a way that litigation is not, and cannot, be.[101]

Inquiries' role can also be readily distinguished from that of the Parliamentary Ombudsman (and, for that matter, ombudsmen more generally). While the Ombudsman can and does look at the bigger picture with a view to facilitating lesson-learning, this is generally done through the prism of individual complaints. In contrast, inquiries are generally concerned first and foremost with the bigger picture (albeit that the macro-level investigation might be into an administrative failure that caused myriad individual hardships). Furthermore, although the Ombudsman's assessments of administrative action can (as noted above) take account of certain benchmarks not available to courts or tribunals, examining the merits of administrative decisions is off limits.[102] So, while both inquiries and the Ombudsman operate in the political realm—whether a government acts upon or ignores their reports is ultimately a matter of *realpolitik*, not legal obligation—inquiries are capable of supplying a more explicitly political (albeit non-partisan) form of accountability. Whereas the Parliamentary Ombudsman's remit is statutorily restricted to questions of administrative effectiveness and implementation, inquiries (subject to their terms of reference) are able to examine matters in a way that potentially contributes to political discourse, and to the evaluation of government, at a deeper policy level.

From all of this, it follows that inquiries do not simply replicate other accountability institutions. Rather, inquiries complement the judicial and ombudsman systems, allowing issues to be explored in notably wide terms and from a perspective that differs from those necessarily adopted by the other accountability institutions. In this sense, inquiries contribute to the diversity of, and so enrich, the accountability system. However, this begs further questions. Why is it considered necessary to establish ad hoc public inquiries rather than leaving it to Parliament—and, in particular, Select Committees—to inquire into matters of public concern? And why are judges so often called upon to lead public inquiries? These questions fall to be addressed here because they engage the issues that are of central concern in this chapter—namely, the relationships between different accountability institutions (and so the diversity of the accountability system taken as a whole) and, in particular, the 'pull' of the judicial model.

---

[100] This is not to deny that judicial scrutiny of administrative action also serves an important public function.

[101] eg. part of the Iraq Inquiry's remit is to 'identify the lessons that can be learned' (statement by Sir John Chilcot, 30 July 2009).

[102] Parliamentary Commissioner Act 1967, s 12(3).

4. Judges and inquiries

The answers to these questions consist partly in concerns about institutional capacity. While parliamentary committees can and do conduct inquiries into matters of public concern, they are ill-equipped to undertake the sort of large-scale evidence-gathering that is often necessary in order for an inquiry to be conducted in meaningful depth. Public inquiries, on the other hand, can be imbued with the institutional resources necessary to perform this task. Meanwhile, the assumption is that *judge-led* public inquiries are equipped not merely to gather large amounts of evidence, but to bring to bear upon such material forensic techniques that will enable the inquiry to get to the bottom of things.

There is, however, a further, crucial, strand to the narrative which holds that the judicial inquiry is the Rolls Royce of the accountability system: judicial independence. It is unremarkable that independence per se is regarded as a desirable characteristic of a public inquiry; and it is clear that other potential conductors of inquiries, such as Select Committees, are not obviously imbued with it.[103] But why *judicial* independence in particular? An important part of the answer is that, as noted towards the beginning of this chapter, judicial independence is an unusually clear manifestation of the separation of powers in the UK. That is why the risk arises of the judicial model of accountability being regarded as a paradigm—a possibility that has arguably been realized in the present context, judicial inquiries being treated as a gold standard. Indeed, the need for independence is arguably especially great in this sphere. Since it is the executive that has 'ownership' of public inquiries—in that they are established and funded, and their terms of reference set, by the administrative branch[104]—the need to demonstrate the independence of an inquiry, executive ownership notwithstanding, is most obviously and completely met by appointing as its chair a judicial figure. This point arguably acquires even greater force under the Inquiries Act 2005, which explicitly authorises ministers to suspend or terminate inquiries.[105]

As others have noted, there are many potential drawbacks to relying upon judges in this way: appointing a judge 'will not depoliticise an inherently controversial matter', such that judicial involvement in inquiries risks compromising perceptions of judicial independence;[106] judges' capacity to handle legal and evidential issues in the courtroom may not be readily transferrable to the inquiries context[107] and may result in an unduly legalistic approach that renders the inquiry process almost impossibly unwieldy and expensive;[108] and judicial involvement in inquiries represents a drain on judicial resources.[109]

---

[103] Although Select Committees' credentials in this regard are arguably now stronger, in that the whips no longer play an explicit role in the determination of their membership.

[104] Following the enactment of the Inquiries Act 2005 and the repeal of the Tribunals of Inquiry Act 1921, there is now no established mechanism whereby Parliament can cause an inquiry to be held.

[105] Ss 13 and 14.

[106] Beatson, 'Should Judges Chair Public Inquiries?' *LQR* (2005) 121: 221 at 235.

[107] Jowell, 'The wrong man for the job', *The Guardian*, 3 February 2004.

[108] Blom-Cooper, 'What went wrong on Bloody Sunday: a critique of the Saville inquiry' *PL* [2010] 61.

[109] eg. the Bloody Sunday Inquiry took Lord Saville out of active judicial service for more than a decade.

Alongside these specific objections to judicial involvement in inquiries is a set of wider considerations which call into question the place of judicial inquiries within the broader accountability landscape. Beatson notes that the 'skills argument' in favour of judicial leadership of inquiries 'is strongest where the task of the inquiry is solely to find facts'.[110] Establishing the facts is certainly important, and some inquiries—including some with non-judicial chairs—regard this as their only, or main, function. For instance, Lord Butler said of his inquiry into the handling of intelligence in the run-up to the Iraq war that 'having given a full account of the facts, we left it to Parliament and the public to draw their own conclusions'[111] (although Butler's report in fact did rather more than that). Indeed, transparency—in the sense of uncovering the truth, and placing hitherto unavailable information in the public domain—is arguably one of the most important functions performed by any inquiry. For example, although the Hutton Inquiry's conclusions were trenchantly criticized by some, there was general recognition that it had served a valuable role by shining an unusually bright light upon the darker recesses of the government machine. Inquiries that do this make a major contribution to accountability by equipping members of the public—as well as the commentariat—to reach informed opinions about the matter concerned and the conduct of those involved. Viewed in this way, one of the principal virtues of inquiries is that they augment the democratic process by making available the raw informational material upon which individuals are able to base judgements about those in positions of power. And although such information is still channelled to a significant extent through traditional media—with the attendant possibility of distortion—widespread use of the internet now means that individuals are able, to an unprecedented extent, to access directly the material brought into the public domain by inquiries.[112] But, having said all of this, most inquiries are called upon to do more than establish the facts, important though that is. This begs two obvious questions. What are the broader functions of inquiries? And are they functions that it is constitutionally and practically appropriate for judges to discharge?

The potential reasons for holding, and so the purposes of, inquiries are myriad;[113] but, along with fact-finding, two are particularly significant. In the first place, an inquiry may be established with a view to ascribing responsibility by means of evaluating the conduct of relevant actors (whether institutional or individual). It may be thought that judges are ideally suited to performing this function, given their experience of the ostensibly comparable exercise of determining legal liability. However, this argument in fact holds relatively little water. For one thing, conduct can be evaluated, and so responsibility ascribed, only with reference to particular standards or criteria: and the criteria relevant to a public inquiry will inevitably be more

[110] Beatson, 'Should Judges Chair Public Inquiries?' 230, n 106 above.

[111] Public Administration Select Committee, *Government by Inquiry: Minutes of Evidence* (HC606-vi, 2003-4).

[112] The use of a website by the Hutton Inquiry—in a way that was, at the time, pioneering—was widely praised in this regard.

[113] For a useful summary, see Howe, 'The Management of Public Inquiries' *Political Quarterly* (1999) 70: 294.

diffuse, less objective and more contestable than those applicable to the determination of legal liability. The tasks, which necessarily fall to the inquiry, of both determining and applying those criteria are potentially controversial ones (creating the risk of judicial 'politicization') and ones, as Jowell has pointed out, to which judges are arguably not uniquely or even particularly well suited.[114] For instance, whereas the Hutton Inquiry was widely praised for bringing to light a wide range of relevant facts that might otherwise have remained behind a veil of secrecy, it arguably came unstuck because of the way in which Lord Hutton went on to evaluate the conduct of the principal protagonists. It has been suggested that Hutton's report reflected his 'qualities as a judge, meticulous and superb in the analysis of details and evidence, but more evidently questionable on matters of wider judgment'.[115] There is also a risk that determination of 'liability' may be accorded an unduly prominent place within a judicial inquiry: as Blom-Cooper puts it, 'Blameworthiness on the part of individual actors in the public disaster or scandal under inquiry is often unnecessary and frequently distractive from the main thrust of any inquiry ... Public inquiries are essentially creatures of public administration ...'[116]

On this analysis, reliance upon judge-led inquiries both presupposes and invites an unduly narrow conception of accountability which borrows too heavily from the model adopted by the judicial system. The ascription of 'liability' in judicial proceedings is explicitly purposeful, in that it results in concrete remedial consequences. Yet this phenomenon (rightly) has no precise analogue in the political realm that inquiries inhabit. Notions of fault, blame and responsibility are necessarily subtler in this sphere. Indeed, the inquiry panel's views on such matters are simply that: *views*. As a result, the ascription-of-responsibility function potentially served by inquiries, while not unimportant, shades into—in some senses, exists in the shadow of—the broader transparency function addressed in the previous paragraph, which serves to equip the public, politicians, and the media to form their *own* views.

A similar point can be made in relation to the other main task that inquiries habitually perform—namely, the facilitation of lesson-learning by means of analysing the relevant issues and formulating proposals for reform in areas ranging from substantive policy and administrative practice to institutional design and interaction. Of course, situations arise in which judges are ideally suited to this task; but such situations are rare, and are inevitably confined to technical areas concerning such matters as the administration of justice.[117] Outside of such circumstances, it is unclear in what sense judges are equipped to perform this function, save to the extent that they (like many others) are able to consider evidence and competing arguments and to arrive at a (most likely highly contestable) view. Take, for instance, the Leveson Inquiry, which was required, inter alia, to make recommendations about media regulation and the future conduct of relations between the press,

---

[114] Jowell, 'The wrong man for the job', n 107 above.
[115] Blom-Cooper and Munro, 'The Hutton Inquiry' *PL* [2004] 476 at 476.
[116] Blom-Cooper, 'What went wrong on Bloody Sunday', 78, n 108 above.
[117] eg. Lord Woolf's inquiry into reform of the civil justice system: *Access to Justice: Final Report* (1996).

on the one hand, and politicians and the police, on the other.[118] This remit took the inquiry deep into the policy arena, and it is far from clear why a judge—whatever his capacity to inquire into and establish the causes of the phone hacking scandal that precipitated the inquiry—was an appropriate person to undertake such a task. Indeed, it is regarded as wholly improper for judges to undertake such assessment and formulation of policy when (for example) they decide judicial review cases, not least because they are institutionally ill-equipped to do so.

The foregoing does not, however, reduce to the argument that judges should have no involvement in public inquiries. Rather, judges' involvement in inquiries should be confined to performing those functions that they are uniquely well placed to perform.[119] One version of this argument consists in the view that judges should be involved only in inquiries that specifically call for their particular skill-set.[120] The difficulty, however, is that this putative condition *for* legitimate judicial involvement may be fulfilled in circumstances that also disclose strong arguments *against* such involvement. A forensic approach (and one that is conducted in a transparently independent manner) to matters factual and evidential may be necessary, but as a precursor to very different tasks such as evaluating relevant actors' conduct by reference to soft, contestable criteria, and making detailed recommendations in specialized and esoteric areas.

Inquiries can—and should—supply a form of accountability that differs fundamentally from that which the legal system provides by means, inter alia, of judicial review. Accountability in the present sense calls for evaluation (of past events) and prescription (for the future) by reference not to legal standards, but with regard to a range of more diffuse bureaucratic, financial, institutional, moral and political criteria. It would be unduly dogmatic to oppose judges' involvement in the fact-finding phase of inquiries, but their involvement should be confined to that phase. This is, as the foregoing discussion suggests, an argument based partly upon technical considerations about the extent of judges' skills. But it also forms part of a wider argument about where constitutional responsibility ought to lie for providing the type of accountability that inquiries are capable of furnishing—an argument which, if accepted, would necessarily constrain, but not eviscerate, the role of judges in this sphere.

The present situation is that the executive branch, on occasions, chooses (whether freely or under irresistible political pressure) to establish inquiries into controversies caused by the conduct of one of its constituent parts, and drafts in the judiciary to run such inquiries even though they involve tasks well beyond that branch's practical competence and constitutional remit. Such arrangements illustrate,

---

[118] *An Inquiry into the Culture, Practices and Ethics of the Press* (HC 780, 2012–13).

[119] Although even here, the obvious question is begged whether judges are *uniquely* equipped to perform tasks such as the questioning of witnesses and the analysis of large volumes of evidence. Consider, for instance, the widely-praised role played by Robert Jay QC, counsel to the Leveson Inquiry, and the chairing by Robert Francis QC of the Stafford Hospital Inquiry. On the latter, see *Report of the Mid Staffordshire NHS Foundation Trust Public Inquiry* (HC 898, 2012-13).

[120] Bingham, 'Judicial Ethics' in Cranston (ed.), *Legal Ethics and Professional Responsibility* (Oxford: Clarendon Press, 1995), 43.

in microcosm, many regrettable truths about the British constitution, including executive hegemony, the marginalization of Parliament, and undue veneration of the judicial model of accountability as a result, in part, of the judiciary's unique status, under the UK's quasi-separation of powers, as an independent counterweight to the legislative-executive apparatus.

One solution, as the PASC has recognised, would be for Parliament to assume a greater role in this area.[121] At present, an inquiry under the Inquiries Act 2005 can be triggered only by the administrative branch (albeit that Parliament can, of course, bring pressure to bear), which means, inter alia, that the executive determines whether an inquiry takes place at all,[122] and, if so, what its terms of reference are[123] and who chairs it.[124] The implications of such executive control are arguably apparent from the way in which the terms of reference of the initial Iraq-related inquiries[125] were constrained, with the 'full' inquiry—the Chilcot Inquiry—conceded only once the main protagonists had left, or were destined shortly to leave, the political limelight. Of course, the fact that the government has established an inquiry on terms of its choosing does not prevent Select Committees from conducting their own investigations on their own terms. The difficulty, however, as noted above, is that such committees generally lack the institutional capacity to conduct detailed investigations of the type typically undertaken by government-established public inquiries.

Against this background, the PASC proposed the creation of 'parliamentary commissions of inquiry', using the relationship between the National Audit Office and the Public Accounts Committee as a model. Under the PASC's proposal, Select Committees would be able to establish 'commissions of inquiry' 'in order to establish factual information on complex subjects which would otherwise occupy too much committee time'.[126] It would then be for the Select Committee to examine the commission's findings and report to the House. Presumably, that examination process would involve the evaluation of the evidence as found by the commission and, where appropriate, the determination of responsibility and the making of proposals in the interests of lesson-learning.

Although the PASC did not discuss the possibility, there is no good reason why external commissions should not consist of or be led by a judge in circumstances where judicial expertise is relevant. Such a model would inherently limit judges' roles within the wider inquiry process, harnessing their skills where relevant while acknowledging that inquiries supply (or ought to supply) a form of accountability that is fundamentally different from that which the judicial model is capable of providing. It would also better reflect underlying separation of powers concerns, according to which ultimate constitutional responsibility for holding the executive

---

[121] *Government by Inquiry* (HC606, 2003-4), ch 7; *Parliamentary Commissions of Inquiry* (HC473, 2007-8).

[122] Inquiries Act 2005, s 1.   [123] Inquiries Act 2005, s 5.   [124] Inquiries Act 2005, s 4.

[125] That is, the Hutton Inquiry (*Report of the Inquiry into the Circumstances Surrounding the Death of Dr David Kelly CMG* (HC247, 2003-4)) and the Butler Inquiry (*Review of Intelligence on Weapons of Mass Destruction* (HC898, 2004-5)). (The establishment of these inquiries preceded the enactment of the Inquiries Act 2005.)

[126] *Government by Inquiry*, para.208, n 121 above.

to account by reference to non-legal accountability criteria should rest not with judges running government-initiated inquiries, but with Parliament.

There is no immediate prospect of the PASC's proposals being adopted. But something of the PASC model is discernible in the Parliamentary Commission on Banking Standards, which was established in July 2012 in the wake of the scandal concerning the fixing of Libor (the rate at which leading banks can obtain unsecured funding in the London interbank market). The Commission is technically just an ad hoc joint committee of the House of Commons and the House of Lords. Unusually, however, it has 'the power to invite specialist advisers appointed by the Commission (including counsel appointed as specialist advisers) to examine witnesses'.[127] It has also established several 'panels' to examine particular issues.[128] However, the Leader of the House of Commons said that he did not anticipate that this would 'become the modus operandi of other Select Committees'—something that other MPs lamented. John Mann MP, for instance, argued that if these powers were 'good enough for this new Commission, they should be made available to any Select Committee looking at any issue'.[129] This point notwithstanding, the Commission on Banking Standards is a rare (in this sphere) example of institutional innovation. If, in due course, it is deemed to have been a success, it may come to be regarded as the basis for an alternative inquiry model, thereby diminishing the kneejerk tendency to insist upon a judge-led inquiry whenever a crisis erupts.[130]

E. Conclusions

The British constitution is not short of the type of striking features that, at least at first glance, make outsiders wonder how on earth the system manages to function. One of those features is the closeness of the relationship between the legislative and executive branches. Few facets of the UK's constitutional architecture have more profound or far-reaching effects on the system of government and the arrangements for holding it to account. One such effect is that as the scale and impact of government has grown in recent decades, the relative weakness of Parliament within the legislative-administrative machine has become increasingly apparent, and so greater store has been set by the judiciary as a counterweight. As Lord Mustill put it, the courts stepped in to 'to occupy the dead ground' arising from the perceived inadequacies of Parliament, in order to avoid 'a vacuum in which the citizen would be left without protection against a misuse of executive powers'.[131]

---

[127] HC Deb, 16 July 2012, col 810.

[128] For detailed information on the Commission, see http://www.parliament.uk/bankingstandards.

[129] HC Deb, 16 July 2012, col 801.

[130] This is not, however, to suggest that the model adopted in relation to the Commission on Banking Standards is perfect. In particular, there are serious questions about the government's involvement in choosing who sits on such ad hoc committees, and about their relationship with departmental Select Committees.

[131] *R v Secretary of State for the Home Department, ex p Fire Brigades Union* [1995] 2 AC 513 at 567.

Yet while this account may be historically accurate, it is normatively questionable, in that it appears to presuppose that judicial and political modes of accountability are interchangeable such that one can substitute for the other.

It has been argued in this chapter that accountability can, and should, take several forms. This, in turn, demands that accountability be supplied by a range of functionally-complementary institutions applying a diversity of criteria and approaches. Against this background, the judicialization of accountability should be regarded with a degree of suspicion, as should the assumption that judicial accountability can fill the gap where other modes of accountability are found wanting. This suspicion will not, of course, always turn out to be well-founded. The judicialization of the tribunal system is, for reasons examined above, to be welcomed in that it aligns the institutional characteristics of that system with the (legal) form of accountability that it is intended to provide. It does not, however, follow that tribunals should unthinkingly be cast in the precise image of regular courts; for all that tribunals can now be regarded as a species of court, they remain a distinct species which provides a form of legal accountability that differs sharply from that supplied by the Administrative Court. This much was recognized in *Cart*, in which the Supreme Court acknowledged the fundamental constitutional shift effected by the creation of an integrated tribunals system by conceding that there should only be minimal supervision of it by regular courts. The Supreme Court thus accepted and underlined the independence—in the sense of the separateness and distinctiveness—of the new tribunals system. In doing so, it acknowledged—at the risk of making Dicey turn in his grave—that the rule of law is not, after all, threatened by what approximates to a system of administrative courts largely free from oversight by their regular counterparts.

The phenomenon of judicialization is less pronounced, and more subtle, in the ombudsmen and inquiries contexts—but is nevertheless discernible in the recently demonstrated (albeit limited) willingness of courts to afford a degree of protection to the Parliamentary Ombudsman's findings (by substantially limiting executive discretion to dismiss them) and the well-established practice of relying upon judges to chair inquiries into issues of public concern. In both spheres, it is arguable that part of the impetus for such judicialization lies in the dysfunctional (in accountability terms) relationship between Parliament and the executive. If Parliament cannot be trusted to make sure that the government takes the Ombudsman seriously, then perhaps the courts should do so? And if Parliament, thanks to executive domination, has failed to adopt a framework within which it can take the lead on public inquiries, perhaps the least-worst alternative is for the executive to meet the public clamour for an inquiry by appointing a palpably independent figure, in the form of a judge, to conduct one? It would be going too far to argue—and it has not been argued in this chapter—that such forms of judicialization must be comprehensively resisted and reversed. But it must be recognized that, if the British constitution is to embody an adequately rich set of arrangements for holding the government to account, it must also exhibit the sort of institutional diversity that is jeopardized by an undue degree of judicialization.

11

Accountability of and to the Legislature

*Nicholas Bamforth**

Carol Harlow has suggested that Parliamentary accountability is 'the form of democratic accountability to which greatest weight is attached by the public as well as theorists'.[1] Using a 'conventional' or 'classical' approach, it is thus the first item for discussion when accountability is considered in a constitutional setting.[2] Considered in a broad sense, the term 'Parliamentary accountability' encompasses the accountability of the legislature for its (and its members') actions and decisions, as well as the accountability of actors to the legislature. The centrality of this notion may well be demonstrated by the public concern surrounding the 'expenses' scandal which affected the Westminster Parliament in the run-up to the United Kingdom general election in 2010. In the UK, which forms the primary focus of this essay, accountability to Parliament encompasses such notions as ministerial responsibility and/or accountability, Parliamentary questions and debates, and the role of Parliamentary committees. Accountability of Parliament is encompassed in legal form via judicial review of executive action allegedly authorized by legislation and scrutiny of the meaning and limits of legislation more generally, and through political channels via debate and questioning as well as public and media scrutiny. The priority one accords to different forms of accountability will, it will be suggested in this essay, depend upon the underlying account of legal or political constitutionalism to which one is committed. On this basis, and by reference to practical examples, it might be said that a mixture of techniques deriving from the political and legal constitutionalist positions underpin accountability of and to the legislature.

Argument about accountability and the legislature is conventionally discussed with reference to procedures within Parliament, parliamentary select and Standing Committees and parliamentary questions. These classic political accountability mechanisms have been subjected to much high-quality analysis,[3] which need not

---

* Fellow in Law, The Queen's College, Oxford. The author would like to thank Peter Leyland for his comments.
[1] C Harlow, *Accountability in the European Union* (Oxford: Oxford University Press, 2002), p 84.
[2] Harlow, 2002, p 109; see also pp 109-10 and p 190.
[3] See eg. D Oliver, *Constitutional Reform in the United Kingdom* (Oxford: Oxford University Press, 2003), chs 9 and 10; D Oliver and G Drewry (eds), *The Law and Parliament* (London: Butterworths, 1998); V Bogdanor, *The New British Constitution* (Oxford: Hart, 2009), chs 5 and 6; M Russell,

be repeated here. The focus of the argument in the present essay will instead be rather different, and will proceed in three stages. It will first be necessary to evaluate how we go about defining political and legal accountability. Such an exercise in methodology, to be conducted in the first section of the essay, provides a foundation for substantive analysis of accountability to and of the legislature. In the second section, substantive aspects of relevant accountability arrangements will be examined: in particular, and perhaps unusually, the role of parliamentary privilege will be emphasized given that political and legal accountability mechanisms cannot fully be understood without reference to it. The third section will contain an analysis of political and legal accountability conducted via a case study of the roles played by legislative and judicial actors in the field of national security. Given the centrality and sensitivity of this field in the politics of northern and western countries since 2001, national security provides a key example for such evaluation, and in turn for consideration of political and legal accountability.

A. Explaining and justifying political and legal accountability

Elizabeth Fisher has argued that accountability is 'closely related to issues of democracy'[4] and 'has a profoundly normative aspect'.[5] It is 'not an autonomous principle' or a neutral concept,[6] and an 'argument for *more* accountability is really an argument about wanting to align governance regimes to a particular normative vision. The process of holding a decision-maker to account is a process of debating what the standards should be'.[7] To quite some extent, this position must be correct: the term 'accountability' assumes a situation or process which is normatively desirable, a point underscored by Carol Harlow's and Richard Rawlings' suggestion that accountability is one of a trilogy of 'administrative law values' (the others being transparency and participation) around which a 'growing consensus' of support has 'crystallized' as something which it is thought appropriate for the law to promote.[8] Debate concerning the exact meaning of accountability and the content of the best or least bad accountability regime tends to be normative in character, even if only because the theorists concerned are assuming at a very general level that some value attaches to the idea of accountability: for otherwise, there would be little or no point in debating the best or least bad interpretation. This point can be made even before consideration is given to the well known assertion of Harlow and Rawlings that 'Behind every theory of administrative law there lies a theory of

---

' "Never Allow a Crisis Go To Waste": The Wright Committee Reforms to Strength the House of Commons' (2011) 64 *Parliamentary Affairs* 612.

⁴ E Fisher, 'The European Union in the Age of Accountability' (2004) 24 *Oxford Journal of Legal Studies* 495, 508.

⁵ Fisher, 2004, 509.

⁶ Fisher, 2004, 508 (compare with 496).

⁷ Fisher, 2004, 513.

⁸ C Harlow and R Rawlings, *Law and Administration* (Cambridge: Cambridge University Press, 3rd edn, 2009), 46.

the state'[9]—'theory' meaning *normative theory*—although the two clearly reinforce one another.

It is thus unsurprising that leading normative accounts of the proper roles of courts, legislatures and executive bodies—more specifically, the accounts known as legal and political constitutionalism[10] —entail their own assumptions about or views concerning accountability. As is well known, Harlow and Rawlings talk of 'red light' and 'green light' theorists: loosely-defined camps, some of the distinctions between which broadly echo the divisions between legal and political constitutionalism.[11] Adam Tomkins characterizes 'red light' theorists as believing:

(1) that law is autonomous to and superior over politics; (2) that the administrative state is something which needs to be kept in check by the law; (3) that the preferred way of doing this is through rule-based adjudication in courts.[12]

By contrast, 'green light' theorists believe:

that law is nothing more than a sophisticated (or elitist) discourse of politics...[and] that the objective of administrative law and regulation is not merely to stop bad administrative practices, but to encourage and facilitate good administrative practices...and...that the best institutions to achieve these aims will not necessarily be courts.[13]

Harlow and Rawlings, while acknowledging that 'accountability' is nowadays championed as a value by both red and green light theorists,[14] are nonetheless clear that on an historical and conceptual basis, 'Red light theory prioritizes courts; green light theory prefers democratic or political forms of accountability'.[15] An analogous point is made by Tomkins, using the broader language of political and legal constitutionalism: 'A political constitution is one in which those who exercise political power (let us say the government) are held to constitutional account through political means, and through political institutions (for example, Parliament). Thus, government ministers and senior civil servants might be subjected to regular scrutiny in Parliament...A legal constitution, on the other hand, is one which imagines that the principal means, and the principal institution, through which the government is held to account is the law and the court-room'.[16]

---

[9] Harlow and Rawlings, 2009, 1. As is made clear at 48 and in subsequent chapters, the authors do not assume that any one theory can be associated on an empirical basis with the content of the current body of administrative law, considered in the round.

[10] For a well known legal constitutionalist account, see R Dworkin, *Taking Rights Seriously* (London: Duckworth, 1977), chs 4, 5 and 7, *A Matter of Principle* (Oxford: Oxford University Press, 1985), chs 1 and 2, and *Law's Empire* (London: Fontana, 1986). For a well known political constitutionalist account, see J Waldron, *Law and Disagreement* (Oxford: Oxford University Press, 1999), esp. chs 1, 4, 5, 10, 11-13, *The Dignity of Legislation* (Cambridge: Cambridge University Press, 1999), ch 1, and 'The Core of the Case Against Judicial Review' (2006) 115 *Yale Law Journal* 1346.

[11] Harlow and Rawlings, 2009, ch1.

[12] A Tomkins, 'In Defence of the Political Constitution' (2002) 22 *Oxford Journal of Legal Studies* 157, 158; M Loughlin, *Public Law and Political Theory* (Oxford: Oxford University Press, 1992), 60-1.

[13] Tomkins, 2002, 158-9; see also Loughlin, 1992, 60-1.

[14] Harlow and Rawlings, 2009, 46.

[15] Harlow and Rawlings, 2009, 38.

[16] A Tomkins *Public Law* (Oxford: Oxford University Press, 2003), 18-9.

As Harlow makes clear, 'important choices' therefore have to be made about 'the proper balance between different forms of accountability and the extent to which, in any given situation, legal, political, or regulatory accountability is preferable'.[17] Such choices are to a significant extent normative, focusing on the values promoted by the form of accountability in issue—and, in turn, on one's general view concerning the proper role of the institutions in play (including, but not only, the legislature). For example, Tomkins suggests that the weight one places on values such as openness, transparency, participation, representativeness, deliberation, and the safeguarding of minorities—all normative concerns, and sometimes in competition—may affect one's general support for political or legal constitutionalism and associated account-ability mechanisms.[18] A not-dissimilar point can be made about the accountability of legislators to the electorate (an issue to which considerable attention has recently been paid in the UK): the extent to which one believes that a member of the leg-islature should explain decisions to the electorate, and/or take account of the electors' will but exercise independent judgment, and/or be mandated, will have very direct implications for the accountability relationships which should exist— for example, whether there should be some form of direct popular accountability in addition to the political checks and balances which exist within the legislative process—as well as resting on a normative view of the proper role of legislators and the legislature in a democracy.

Nonetheless, to fully understand the distinction between political and legal accountability, it remains necessary to pay attention to *certain* descriptive or definitional issues (hence the slightly qualified endorsement given to Fisher's argument above[19]). For it is plainly the case that, whatever the normative *aspects* of argu-ments concerning accountability, such arguments can also have linguistic or purely analytical *components*. This point is captured in Dawn Oliver's understanding of accountability arrangements as things which, while promoting the public interest (conceived of in normative terms as an ideal which legitimates government), can also be divided analytically into four categories. First, political accountability is owed to politicians, encompassing ministerial accountability to Parliament (in the UK) or local authority accountability to central government and Parliament. Within this category, accountable actors and bodies are exposed to possible political censure and electoral risk, with political costs sometimes being exacted at a personal level (for example, via the forced resignation of a minister) if performance falls

[17] Harlow, 2002, 165. Harlow herself articulates some of the central doubts about legal accountability: given that it tends to be left in the hands of the judiciary, it expands and contracts as judges think appropriate; and heightened accountability to un-elected judges (at the suit of individuals) tends, in turn, to inhibit the forms of collective political and democratic accountability which modern society values most highly (Harlow, 2002, 165-7; see also 182-6).
[18] Tomkins, 2003, 18-9.
[19] In fairness, it is important also to note Fisher's own comments at Fisher, 2004, 495 at 497, 499-500 and 511. See also C Scott, 'Accountability in the Regulatory State' (2000) *Journal of Law and Society* 27 and R Mulgan, '"Accountability": An Ever Expanding Concept?' (2000) 78 *Public Administration* 555, 557-8.

below the expected standard.[20] Secondly, public accountability is owed to the general public or interested sections of it. Most obviously, elected national and local politicians are politically obliged to explain and justify their actions to electors, with political penalties to be paid at the ballot box if an adequate account is not offered..[21] Thirdly, legal accountability is owed to the courts, most obviously in the UK via judicial review of executive action, something which hopefully encourages transparency in decision-making.[22] Fourthly, administrative accountability entails the duty to account to non-political regulatory bodies such as the Parliamentary Commissioner for Administration.[23] Analytical components can also be found in Carol Harlow's treatment of accountability in the European Union. Thus, Harlow associates legal accountability as a category with proportionality review, in the sense that administrative measures need to be appropriate as well as necessary to achieve their desired objectives, and with the requirements of due process.[24] She also argues that: '[T]here is always an adversarial element in accountability, the purpose of which is to encourage admissions of responsibility and to hold people to account for their actions'.[25] In addition, she suggests that effective accountability may, as a mechanism, entail a measure of externality and autonomy given that it becomes hard for those who have taken part in a decision or in policy-making to censure or blame the decision-maker.[26]

The arguments just discussed go to the structure of accountability viewed, analytically, as a distinct concept: this is why they can be described as descriptive or definitional. A further approach operating beyond the purely normative level is set out by Tomkins. He has suggested that appropriate roles for political and legal constitutionalism can be evaluated not only by reference to the values promoted by each—a clearly normative criterion—but *also* by assessing their efficacy as *tools* for promoting the values concerned.[27] This additional criterion is clearly normatively-tinged, it being hard to detach one's assessment of the effectiveness of a constitutional tool from *any analysis at all* of the desirability of its underlying values. Nonetheless, Tomkins' explicit separation of the two evaluative methods would, in logic, be difficult to explain without accepting to some extent that it is possible to assess a constitutional tool by reference to its success 'by its own lights': that is, by reference to how effective it is (including by comparison with other possible tools) in promoting its own demonstrable goals. Since many such goals are normative, it would plainly be artificial to claim that an efficacy-focused assessment of this type could plausibly be seen as *purely* empirical (at least where

---

[20] D Oliver, *Government in the United Kingdom: The Search for Accountability, Effectiveness and Citizenship* (Milton Keynes: Open University Press, 1991) pp 23-5, *Constitutional Reform in the UK* (Oxford: Oxford University Press, 2003), pp 49-50.
[21] Oliver, 1991, pp 25-6, Oliver, 2003, pp 50-1.   [22] Oliver, 1991, pp 26-7.
[23] Oliver, 1991, pp 27-8.   [24] Harlow, 2002, pp 164-5.   [25] Harlow, 2002, p 101.
[26] Harlow, 2002, p 106.
[27] Tomkins, 2003, pp 19-30. (Note also the 'mixed' evaluation of legal accountability at pp 206-11). For Tomkins' analysis of the proper ordering of the various functions of the legislature, see 'What is Parliament For?', ch 3 in N Bamforth and P Leyland (eds), *Public Law in a Multi-Layered Constitution* (Oxford: Hart, 2003).

normative goals are in play). Nonetheless, it *is* clearly different from an evaluation which asks only whether the tool concerned promotes *normatively desirable* goals, and judges the tool on that basis. For an assessment of efficacy 'by its own lights' does not entail a prior evaluation of the (un)desirability of the goals in play. The goals are instead presupposed and the focus of assessment is on how well the tool serves in assisting with their delivery. It should thus be possible to assess constitutional rules from the standpoint of their efficacy in promoting a given type of accountability, and for this exercise—while quite possibly normatively-tinged—not to be an out-and-out argument 'for a particular normative vision' in the sense envisaged by Fisher.

For the sake of completeness, two further points need to be stressed. First, while it seems obvious that judges' interpretations of the workings of individual constitutional mechanisms, including those with implications for accountability, will be affected by the properties of the broader constitutional setting (or judicial understandings of such properties) within which the mechanisms concerned operate,[28] constitutional theorists' analyses—of the general idea of accountability and the distinction between political and legal accountability as well as of individual mechanisms—may well be similarly affected, albeit at varying levels. For example, a theorist whose primary focus is the constitutional law of the UK may well be content to equate legal accountability (that is, to courts) with statutory interpretation and (so far as it is distinct) judicial review of executive action[29]; a United States constitutional theorist, by contrast, is more likely to see the main tool of legal accountability as judicial review of legislation, with statutory interpretation and review of executive action being placed slightly lower down the list of significant accountability devices. In consequence, it may be a matter of degree how far these two theorists can share a workable understanding of legal accountability. Despite this, however, it is also clear that some general ideas can be and are shared. An obvious example is the notion that certain privileges and immunities attach to those engaged in the business of the legislature, a protection that seems to apply—albeit with different boundaries from case to case—in jurisdictions where legislation is open to judicial review by courts as well as in the small number where it is not.[30] Furthermore, the two efficacy criteria for evaluating accountability arguments (normative desirability and 'by its own lights') would seem, in logic, to be applicable regardless of localized constitutional characteristics.

---

[28] Within English law, a good example is provided by the House of Lords' analysis in *British Railways Board v Pickin* [1974] AC 765, of the implications of the bedrock constitutional rule of parliamentary sovereignty for the operation of parliamentary privilege in precluding questions from being raised about conduct within Parliament (see particularly Lord Simon of Glaisdale's analysis at 798-9).

[29] It is interesting that Aileen Kavanagh's analysis of statutory interpretation under ss 3 and 4 of the Human Rights Act 1998 (HRA 1998) goes so far as to suggest that this is in substance akin to judicial review, despite the absence of a set-aside power in the courts. See A Kavanagh, *Constitutional Review under the UK Human Rights Act* (Cambridge: Cambridge University Press, 2009), 280.

[30] Despite noting the implications of the underpinning concept of sovereignty for privilege in *British Railways Board v Pickin*, therefore, it may be that Lord Simon slightly overstated the matter in declaring that it was a 'concomitant of the sovereignty of Parliament . . . that the Houses of Parliament enjoy certain privileges' (*Pickin*, at 798).

Secondly, normative theories about desirable accountability arrangements some-times rest on 'best case' assumptions about the performance or characteristics of the institutions under scrutiny. Sandra Fredman, for example, suggests by reference to UK and South African legislative debates about voting rights for prisoners that key political constitutionalist Jeremy Waldron 'idealizes legislative decision-making', from which 'much relevant evidence and opinion is frequently omitted' in practice.[31] By analogy, leading legal constitutionalist Ronald Dworkin conceded that the US Supreme Court had come in the late 2000s to be dominated, in implicit contrast to his ideal of integrity-driven decision making, by a 'right-wing phalanx' which seemed 'guided by no judicial or political principle at all, but only by partisan, cultural, and perhaps religious allegiance'.[32] These examples may help reinforce the suggestion that in practice, constitutional accountability is likely to be most effectively promoted not through 'best case' idealizations of the role to be played by a single institution, but instead through a *combination* of political and legal mechanisms.

A more principled version of this suggestion has been articulated, originally by reference to the Canadian Charter of Rights and Freedoms, by Janet Hiebert. Hiebert puts forward a 'relational approach' whereby Parliament and the courts can both offer valid insights into the best interpretation of legislative objectives. From this perspective:

The normative goal is not that Parliament aspire to ensure that legislation addresses all judi-cial concerns or, alternatively, that the judiciary defer to Parliament's judgment. Rather, it is that each body satisfy itself that its judgment reflects [constitutional] values, particularly when faced with the other's contrary judgment. Thus, a relational approach is informed by the assumption that parliamentary and judicial judgments be guided by a degree of modesty about the superiority of their conclusions and by respect for the other's contrary interpretation. Respect is measured by a sincere effort to understand the reasons and motivations that led to a contrary assessment, even if each ultimately disagrees with the other.[33]

On this view, the legislature and judiciary should each satisfy themselves that their assessment is justified. When differences arise, the two institutions should 'reflect on the opinion of those situated differently, relative to the.... conflict' and '[i]n Parliament's case, a court's contrary judgment should be considered and its different concerns addressed, even if ultimately disagreed with'.[34] This forms part of a 'call for shared responsibility', whereby the legislature is encouraged to

---

[31] S Fredman, 'From Dialogue to Deliberation: Human Rights Adjudication and Prisoners' Right to Vote' [2013] *Public Law* 292, 298. By contrast, it has been argued that legal constitutionalists some-times demonize legislatures: LD Kramer, *The People Themselves: Popular Constitutionalism and Judicial Review* (New York: Oxford University Press, 2004), pp 239, 242, 247.

[32] R Dworkin, *The Supreme Court Phalanx: The Court's New Right Wing Bloc* (New York: New York Review of Books, 2008), pp 47-8. For a sustained critique of judicial decision making, see R Hirschl, *Towards Juristocracy: The Origins and Consequences of the New Constitutionalism* (Cambridge, MA: Harvard University Press, 2004).

[33] JL Hiebert, *Charter Conflicts: What is Parliament's Role?* (Montreal: McGill-Queen's University Press, 2002), p 52.

[34] Hiebert, 2002, p 220.

'exercise principled judgment about the merits of legislative decisions' involving careful and deliberate evaluation of the goals of legislative proposals relative to individual rights, even if its judgment ultimately differs from that of a court.[35]

In turn, Tom Hickman categorizes approaches of this type as involving a 'constitutional dialogue between courts, legislatures and executives'.[36] In the UK, such approaches are often associated with the Human Rights Act 1998, although there have been important disagreements between 'dialogue' theorists about their exact operation: for example, about whether the idea of 'dialogue' entails the adoption of divergent judgments by courts and the legislature, whether courts are essentially engaged as political actors in the process of persuading Parliament to reach a final judgment, or whether the nature of the interaction between the two institutions depends upon the contestability of the issue in play.[37] Questions have also been raised about the point at which the process of 'dialogue' can be seen as beginning and ending, and about the quality of the deliberation required on each side.[38] It is perhaps unsurprising that Alison Young, a supporter of 'dialogue' theory, acknowledges its 'malleability'.[39]

Debate about the best approach to 'dialogue' theory lies beyond the scope of this essay. Instead, the aim of the next two sections is to tie discussion of the respective roles of the legislature and courts to an analysis of accountability issues, ultimately through the lens of 'dialogue' arguments. It will be suggested that an effective analysis of the accountability arrangements prevailing in relation to the Westminster Parliament—that is, arrangements surrounding ministerial responsibility and/or accountability, Parliamentary questions and Parliamentary debate, as well as judicial scrutiny of executive power—must be understood in terms of legal *and* political components viewed in combination. More particularly, the combination of judicial and political scrutiny in the anti-terrorism context provides a key—and centrally focused—illustration of the correlation between the promotion of accountability and the existence of judicial and political methods working in tandem.

B. Accountability and Parliament

In the previous section, it was argued that there can be both normative and analytical/ empirical dimensions to what we define as political and legal accountability, and to how we seek to draw the boundary between the two mechanisms. The task in this

---

[35] Hiebert, 2002, p 226.

[36] TR Hickman, 'Constitutional Dialogue, Constitutional Theories and the Human Rights Act 1998' [2005] *Public Law* 306, 306.

[37] Compare TR Hickman, 2005, D Nicol, 'Law and Politics after the Human Rights Act' [2006] *Public Law* 722, 744-751, T Hickman, 'The Courts and Politics after the Human Rights Act: A Comment' [2008] *Public Law* 84, AL Young, 'Is Dialogue Working Under the Human Rights Act 1998?' [2011] *Public Law* 773.

[38] See S Fredman, *Human Rights Transformed: Positive Rights and Positive Duties* (Oxford: Oxford University Press, 2008), pp 103-113, and Fredman, 2013, 293-8.

[39] Young, 2011, 774.

section is to engage in a more specific analysis of certain key aspects of accountability in relation to the Westminster Parliament.

This requires us, as a first step, to demarcate the accountability mechanisms to be considered. Harlow has noted that, 'parliaments everywhere have found increasing difficulty in holding governments accountable as governments have grown steadily more presidential in their ambitions and more global in reach'.[40] While this may be true, a variety of devices or techniques are open to legislatures when seeking to hold the executive to account. Terence Daintith has categorized some techniques available to *government* when implementing its policies as examples of *imperium*, and others as examples of *dominium*: respectively 'the government's use of the command of law in aid of its policy objectives, and...the employment of the wealth of government for this purpose'.[41] *Imperium* measures, which are typically but not necessarily legally enforceable, set a standard or rule for the behaviour of particular individuals or bodies and provide sanctions for non-compliance. Measures concerned with *dominium*, by contrast, tend to lay down the substantive criteria to be met before expenditure can be allowed.[42] As Anne Davies has suggested, a similar distinction can be applied to 'the accountability mechanisms which apply to the traditional mode of governmental activity, [namely] legislation or "*imperium*", and those which apply to contract or "*dominium*"'.[43] In reality, some mechanisms—especially when they are encapsulated in legislation—more closely resemble *imperium*, and others *dominium*. Harlow suggests that the accountability mechanisms open (or potentially open) to the legislature include the power to appoint the government, to support it in power and to withdraw political backing;[44] the power to exercise control over budgetary and financial powers;[45] and the operation of the committee structure, 'without which no parliament can hold government to account'.[46] The right to establish an independent investigatory inquiry may constitute an additional mechanism: for as Harlow notes, 'In recent years, quasi-judicial inquiries have emerged as an important technique for securing accountability, and have often been preferred to parliamentary investigative committees'.[47] Finally, is the power to make law. For Harlow, this concerns accountability since 'In all modern systems of government, law-making is largely a function and a monopoly of government' so that 'The contribution to accountability made by the law-making process is that government is put to the trouble of an explanation and may on occasion be forced to re-think'.[48]

It should be stressed that while many or most of these mechanisms are associated with political accountability and operate entirely in the political realm, some of

---

[40] Harlow, 2002, pp 79-80. See also pp 34-5.
[41] T Daintith, 'The Techniques of Government', ch 8 in J Jowell and D Oliver (eds), *The Changing Constitution* (Oxford: Oxford University Press, 3rd edn, 1994), 213.
[42] Daintith, 213-9.
[43] ACL Davies *Accountability: A Public Law Analysis of Government by Contract* (Oxford: Oxford University Press, 2001), ix.
[44] Harlow, 2002, pp 92, 94-6. See also Tomkins, 2003, pp 90-7.
[45] Harlow, 2002, pp 92, 96-9. See also Tomkins, 2003, pp 90-7.   [46] Harlow, 2002 p.92.
[47] Harlow, 2002, p 99.   [48] Harlow, 2002, p 95; see also p 93.

them—most obviously, the ability to question or seek information—depend upon legal underpinnings (in the case of the UK, the idea of parliamentary privilege) for their unhindered operation. Of course, their efficacy in practice will be heavily influenced by political factors (for example, the role of party loyalty as a bar or encouragement to robust questioning), but the prior existence of an absence of legal restrictions on questioning is clearly crucial. The Westminster Parliament therefore illustrates the importance of understanding the close connections between the 'purely' political and legal dimensions when considering the construction and operation of relevant accountability relationships. In the rest of this section, the two dimensions will be considered in turn.

Turning first to the 'purely' political, Adam Tomkins has suggested that 'Parliament has three main ways of holding the executive to account: debate, parliamentary questions, and Select Committees'.[49] More specifically, Colin Scott argues that Parliament has 'enhanced its capacity for holding ministers and officials to account through the development of Select Committee structures, in some cases linked to new oversight bodies such as the Parliamentary ombudsman and the National Audit Office'.[50] However, when considering the abstract question of the *roles* of political and legal accountability, two more general points deserve emphasis. The first is that, as clearly political accountability mechanisms, the success of Parliamentary debates, questions and Select Committees must depend both upon the political will of the politicians involved and on how widely the issues under scrutiny are publicized and analysed via the news media and in public debate more broadly.[51] The second issue, to be highlighted here, is that while debate about the efficacy and desirability of political accountability mechanisms visibly involves the deployment of views about what was earlier described as the effectiveness of those mechanisms measured 'by their own lights', it also engages (even if only implicitly) arguments concerning the appropriate boundary between political and legal accountability.

Against this background, an obvious starting point is the constitutional convention of ministerial responsibility, which demarcates the relationship between the executive and the legislature—a relationship of fundamental constitutional importance—and was traditionally seen as a primary vehicle for promoting accountability of members of the executive to Parliament. Adam Tomkins, for example, has argued that it is a 'political form' of accountability which despite certain 'fault lines' remains central to our system of public law.[52] However, the growth in size and complexity of government departments in the post-Second World War period, coupled with the operation of a strong system of party discipline within the House of Commons, has long been thought to make it difficult for MPs to establish who was responsible

---

[49] Tomkins, 2003, p 160. See also M Loughlin, *The British Constitution: A Very Short Introduction* (Oxford: Oxford University Press, 2013), pp 63-64.

[50] Scott, 41. Note, however, Harlow's more general concerns about the role of committees in relation to government accountability: Harlow, 2002, p 33.

[51] A Select Committee Report which might be thought to illustrate this is the Health Committee's *Commissioning: Third Report of Session*, 2010-11 H.C. 513-1, 18th January 2011.

[52] Tomkins, 2003, pp vii, 49 and 135ff.

for a decision and for Parliament collectively to hold that person to account.[53] In addition, the widespread contracting out of functions once performed by central government, frequently using legal arrangements with strong confidentiality provisions, has more recently generated intense debate about the limits and effectiveness of ministerial responsibility as an accountability mechanism.[54] In consequence, Colin Scott suggests that while ministerial responsibility may have been 'central' to the 'concern' of holding public actors accountable to the democratic will, '[t]he problem arises from an acknowledgement that traditional mechanisms of accountability within the British state are weak instruments for achieving these objectives'.[55] Meanwhile, Harlow and Rawlings concede that nowadays, '[f]ew would wish to set sail in a barque as frail as that of ministerial responsibility',[56] and Elizabeth Fisher has suggested that it is old-fashioned to place this convention utterly centre-stage in relation to Parliament.[57]

The formal position in relation to individual ministerial responsibility is now stated in printed form in the Ministerial Code, most recently reissued in 2010.[58] The Code has its origins in (and incorporates the text of) Resolutions passed by both Houses of Parliament in 1997 following controversy initially triggered by the publication of the Scott Report.[59] The Code asserts that 'Ministers have a duty to Parliament to account, and be held to account, for the policies, decisions and actions of their departments and agencies',[60] and that it is 'of paramount importance that Ministers give accurate and truthful information to Parliament'[61] and be 'as open as possible' with it,[62] with those who knowingly mislead Parliament being required to offer their resignation. While the Code sets out the political accountability requirements of ministers to Parliament in a fashion which is clearer and more accessible than was previously the case, it is nevertheless still a constitutional convention which is enforceable only at the political level (ultimately via the political penalty of forced resignation).

However, law enters the picture, alongside prevailing political mechanisms, in relation to civil servants and ministerial special advisers. The Constitutional Reform

---

[53] See, generally, Q Hogg, 'Elective Dictatorship', the Richard Dimbleby Lecture 14th October 1976, *The Listener*, Vol 21, 496-500; N Lewis & D Longley, 'Ministerial Responsibility: The Next Steps' [1996] *Public Law* 490; N Bamforth, 'Political Accountability in Play: the Budd Inquiry and David Blunkett's Resignation' [2005] *Public Law* 229, 230-1.

[54] For discussion, see D Woodhouse, 'Ministerial Responsibility', ch 8 in V Bogdanor (ed), *The British Constitution in the Twentieth Century* (Oxford: Oxford University Press, 2003); Tomkins, 2003, pp 148-159.

[55] C Scott, 'Accountability in the Regulatory State', 39.

[56] Harlow and Rawlings, 2009, p 38.

[57] Fisher, 2004, 397 (fn 14). She thus dismisses (at 497) as 'traditional constitutional scholarship' Tomkins's account (Tomkins, 2003, chs 5 and 6) for holding accountability to be 'synonymous with a set of particular processes such as ministerial responsibility and judicial review'.

[58] Ministerial Code, Cabinet Office, May 2010.

[59] For the Resolutions, see H. C. Deb., vol. 292, cols. 1046-7 (19th March 1997) and H. L. Deb., vol. 579, col. 1057 (20th March 1997). Ministerial Code, 2010, section 1.6. For discussion of the Scott Report, see Tomkins, 2003, pp 152-4.

[60] Ministerial Code, 2010, section 1.2.b   [61] Ministerial Code, 2010, section 1.2.c.

[62] Ministerial Code, 2010, section 1.2.d.

and Governance Act 2010 required the minister for the civil service to publish and lay before Parliament an official code governing civil servants and which was to form part of their (legally enforceable) terms and conditions of employment.[63] An equivalent but more detailed set of requirements was required to be attached to special ministerial advisers.[64] The resulting codes embody both political and legal dimensions. On the political side, the Civil Service Code specifies that 'Civil servants are accountable to Ministers, who in turn are accountable to Parliament'[65] and that civil servants must not 'deceive or knowingly mislead Ministers, Parliament or others'.[66] On the legal side, the Code reiterates the Act's statement that it forms part of the contractual relationship between the civil servant and their employer[67] and notes that the statutory basis for the management of the civil service is contained within the Act.[68] The Code of Conduct for Special Advisers in turn makes clear that such advisers are generally subject to the provisions of the Civil Service Code[69] and that they must not 'deceive or knowingly mislead Parliament'.[70] Politically, responsibility for the management, conduct and discipline of advisers rests with the appointing minister and ultimately the Prime Minister,[71] but the incorporation of relevant aspects of the Civil Service Code would appear to inject a (legally enforceable) contractual dimension.

What is clearly interesting here is the incorporation of a legal dimension, both generally via the 2010 Act and more specifically via the references to terms and conditions of employment, to the arrangements governing civil servants and special advisers, when the arrangements for ministerial responsibility to Parliament remain enforceable only in the political realm.[72] The question clearly arises whether it is appropriate in constitutional terms for the accountability mechanism relating to ministers to be solely political, whereas the arrangements governing civil servants and advisers possess a legal dimension. In practice, of course, this question is intimately associated with one's understanding of the separation of powers and the priority one affords to political as opposed to legal accountability mechanisms. In short, the answer one gives will depend on one's underlying constitutional theory. It is very likely that most constitutional theorists would *not* want the courts to become involved in enforcing ministerial accountability to Parliament (as it is currently explained in the Ministerial Code). Nonetheless, that viewpoint clearly requires the adoption of a position concerning the appropriate boundary between the legal and the political: in other words, about the relationship between them.

A similar point becomes obvious in relation to the role played by the legal concept of parliamentary privilege as a basis for the promotion of effective political

---

[63] Constitutional Reform and Governance Act 2010, s 5; see also ss 6 and 7.
[64] Constitutional Reform and Governance Act 2010, s 8.
[65] Civil Service Code, Cabinet Office 2010, section 2.   [66] Civil Service Code, 2010, section 9.
[67] Civil Service Code, 2010, section 20.   [68] Civil Service Code, 2010, section 1.
[69] Code of Conduct for Special Advisers, Cabinet Office June 2010, section 4
[70] Code of Conduct for Special Advisers, 2010, section 5
[71] Code of Conduct for Special Advisers, section 4.
[72] On the accountability-related role of ministerial responsibility/accountability, see Harlow, 2002, p 32.

accountability to Parliament, as well as the more debatable question of how far parliamentary privilege hampers the political accountability of elected legislators. As the European Court of Human Rights noted in *A v United Kingdom*, the Council of Europe and the European Union, alongside many individual European nations, extend certain privileges and immunities to members of their legislatures so as to enable the relevant representatives to fulfil their functions.[73] Within the UK, parliamentary privilege plays an important, if double-edged, role in relation to accountability and the legislature. It is classically associated with the stipulation, found in Art. 9 of the Bill of Rights 1689, that 'the freedom of speech and debates or proceedings in Parliament ought not to be impeached or questioned in a court or place out of Parliament'. By safeguarding freedom of expression *within* Parliament, privilege plays a legally crucial role (against the backdrop of English law's traditionally strong regime of defamation liability) in underpinning political accountability to the legislature. However, it also serves to uphold the status of the institution and/or its members, and as was highlighted by the 2010 parliamentary expenses scandal, is sometimes assumed to have questionable implications for the accountability *of* the legislature and/or its members. Since the Supreme Court emphasized in *R v Chaytor* (a case resulting from the 2010 scandal) that the roots of parliamentary privilege lay in *both* Art. 9 *and* Parliament's exclusive cognizance or jurisdiction in particular areas,[74] it is perhaps not surprising—however the exact relationship between the two components is understood[75]—that the concept plays the double-edged role it does in relation to accountability.[76] The creation of independent regulatory bodies—most obviously, the Parliamentary Commissioner for Standards and the Independent Parliamentary Standards Authority—are also crucial to the operation of accountability in this context. In the remainder of the present section, these issues will be considered in turn.

The role of parliamentary privilege in promoting free expression within Parliament, and in turn the open questioning and criticism of decision-makers by the legislature, has been emphasized by both parliamentarians and the courts. On the parliamentary side, the Joint Committee on Parliamentary Privilege noted in its 1999 Report that 'Freedom of speech is central to Parliament's role. Members must be able to speak and criticize without fear of penalty. This is fundamental to the effective working of Parliament, and is achieved by the primary parliamentary privilege...guaranteed by [A]rticle 9'.[77] The Committee was clear that 'The public interest in the freedom of speech' in parliamentary proceedings was 'of a

---

[73] *A v United Kingdom* Application (35373/97), (2003) 36 EHRR 51, paras [33]-[58]. A notion of privilege has, historically, also extended to members of the US Congress: for an early example, see *Kilbourn v Thompson* (1880) 103 US 168.

[74] [2010] UKSC 52, [2011] 1 AC 684.

[75] The judgments contain slightly variable (if overlapping) formulations of the relationship between the two elements: see paras [25] to [78] (Lord Phillips PSC), [101]-[104] (Lord Rodger), and [130]-[133] (Lord Clarke).

[76] Needless to say, debate has long existed about the exact jurisdictional basis, ambit and workings of privilege. Compare *Stockdale v Hansard* [1839] 9 Ad & E 1; *Case of the Sheriff of Middlesex* [1840] 11 Ad & E 273.

[77] *Parliamentary Privilege—First Report* (30 March 1999), HL Paper 43-I, HC 214-I, para.12.

high order',[78] and—in a clear tilt towards accountability—that it was 'of utmost importance that there should be a national public forum where all manner of persons, irrespective of their power or wealth, can be criticized. Members should not be exposed to the risk of being brought before the courts to defend what they said in Parliament. Abuse of parliamentary freedom of speech is a matter for internal self-regulation by Parliament'.[79]

On the judicial side, Lord Browne-Wilkinson stressed in *Pepper v Hart* that Art. 9 'ensures the ability of democratically elected Members of Parliament to discuss what they will (freedom of debate) and to say what they will (freedom of speech)'.[80] His Lordship elaborated on this in *Prebble v Television New Zealand*, where it was noted that 'the basic concept underlying [A]rticle 9' is 'the need to ensure so far as possible that a member of the legislature and witnesses before committees of the House can speak freely without fear that what they say will later be held against them in the courts. The important public interest protected by such privilege is to ensure that the member or witness *at the time he speaks* is not inhibited from stating fully and freely what he has to say'.[81] In *Chaytor*, Lord Phillips PSC asserted that 'the principal matter to which [A]rticle 9 is directed is freedom of speech and debate in the Houses of Parliament and in parliamentary committees. This is where the core or essential business of Parliament takes place',[82] and entailed 'freedom for Parliament to conduct its legislative and deliberative business without interference from the Crown or the Crown's judges'.[83]. This is seemingly consistent with Lord Denman CJ's historic association of parliamentary privilege, in *Stockdale v Hansard*, with Parliament's role 'as the grand inquest of the nation'.[84]

A not dissimilar view appears to have been taken by the European Court of Human Rights in *A v United Kingdom*, where it was accepted that parliamentary privilege pursued legitimate aims, including the protection of freedom of expression,[85] while not constituting a disproportionate restriction on the claimant's right of access to a court (the claimant, a private individual, had been the subject of disparaging remarks made by a Member of Parliament during a House of Commons debate).[86] Drawing

---

[78] *Parliamentary Privilege—First Report*, para 39.

[79] *Parliamentary Privilege—First Report*, para 40.

[80] [1993] AC 593 at 638. While Lord Browne-Wilkinson emphasized that Art. 9 'should not be narrowly construed' (at 638), Lord Phillips PSC suggested in *R v Chaytor* (at paras [32]–[48], [61]) that the same need not be true in relation to matters which were incidental to proceedings on the floor or in committee.

[81] [1995] 1 AC 321 at 334. See also Lord Bingham's statement for the Privy Council in *Buchanan v Jennings* [2005] 1 AC 115, para [17].

[82] [2010] UKSC 52; [2011] 1 AC 684, para [47]. His Lordship thus tied the application of privilege to a particular activity to whether a failure to do so was likely to impact adversely on Parliament's core or essential business.

[83] *Chaytor* at para [61]. See also para [62]. Note also Lord Simon's observation in *Pickin v British Railways Board* [1974] AC 763 at 798.

[84] *Stockdale v Hansard* (1839) 9 Ad & El 1 at 115.

[85] *A v United Kingdom* [2002] All ER (D) 264, para [77]. The claimant accepted these aims at para [76].

[86] *A v United Kingdom*, para [83]; see also para [89]. This conclusion was notwithstanding the court's observation at para [88] that the comments which the claimant sought to challenge, made by an MP in the course of a House of Commons debate, were 'extremely serious and clearly unnecessary'.

attention to the findings of the 1999 Joint Committee Report,[87] the Court was clear that freedom of expression was especially important for an elected representative: 'He or she represents the electorate, draws attention to their preoccupations and defends their interests. In a democracy, Parliament or such comparable bodies are the essential fora for political debate. Very weighty reasons must be advanced to justify interfering with the freedom of expression exercised therein'.[88] The court also pointed out that MPs' absolute immunity from being sued for defamation for things stated during a House of Commons debate was designed to protect the interests of Parliament *as a whole*.[89]

The importance for the promotion of political accountability of these expression-based accounts of parliamentary privilege becomes clear if we recall English law's somewhat chequered history when it comes to safeguarding free expression about public bodies and political actors.[90] It was only in 1993 that the House of Lords accepted[91]—after earlier lower-level decisions to the contrary[92]—that elected public authorities did not have the right to sue for defamation, by contrast with private parties (a principle accepted rather earlier, in 1964, by the US Supreme Court in *New York Times v Sullivan*[93]). Later, in *Reynolds v Times Newspapers*, it was established that attempts by political figures to sue could in certain circumstances be defeated by a qualified privilege defence, the rationale again lying in the need to protect freedom of expression[94]: but even then it took courts further time to fully accept that the relevant defence needed to be interpreted in an expression-friendly, rather than unduly claimant-friendly, fashion.[95]

The argument that free expression about political figures and institutions (and within those institutions) helps promote accountability and, in turn, democracy is well established. John Gardner, for example, points out that freedom of expression 'is justified in part by the contribution it makes, when it is respected, to maintaining a free flow of information'.[96] Freedom of expression is not just a right to engage in political analysis and debate: it also includes art, culture, work, recreation, education, and matters ranging from the avant-garde to the humdrum. Nonetheless, 'the importance of democracy does lend extra weight to the right to freedom of expression in some contexts', and democracy 'can function adequately only if a good deal

---

[87] *Parliamentary Privilege—First Report*, paras 32 and 82.

[88] *Parliamentary Privilege—First Report*, para 79.

[89] *Parliamentary Privilege—First Report*, para 85.

[90] See generally E Barendt, *Freedom of Speech* (Oxford: Oxford University Press, 2nd edn, 2005), 40, 160; H Fenwick and G Phillipson, *Media Freedom under the Human Rights Act* (Oxford: Oxford University Press, 2006), 4-6.

[91] *Derbyshire County Council v Times Newspapers* [1993] AC 534.

[92] *Dutton* v. *Bognor Regis D.C.* [1972] 1 QB 373. See JA Weir's powerful expression-based attack on the decision: 'Local Authority v Critical Ratepayer—A Suit in Defamation' (1972A) 30 *Cambridge Law Journal* 238.

[93] *New York Times v Sullivan* [1964] 376 US 254.

[94] *Reynolds v Times Newspapers* [2001] 2 AC 127.

[95] See *Jameel v Wall Street Journal* [2006] UKHL 44.

[96] 'Freedom of Expression', ch 7 in C McCrudden and G Chambers (eds), *Individual Rights and the Law in Britain* (Oxford: Oxford University Press, 1994), at p 210.

of information is freely available'.[97] More broadly, Eric Barendt highlights the role played by the promotion of democracy as one of a number of justifications—albeit the 'most easily understandable'[98] and 'most influential'[99] of them—for protecting expression. As Barendt acknowledges, this justification is not uncontentious,[100] but it seems clear that—in so far as the full accountability of decision-makers to an elected legislature is thought to play a central role in a properly-functioning democracy—freedom of expression within the legislature, as a crucial mechanism for facilitating the questioning of ministers and officials, plays an extremely important part in facilitating such accountability. The absence of potential legal liability in defamation allows—assuming the political will is present—for questioning and analysis at whatever intensity the unfettered demands of political accountability dictate.[101] By removing the potential 'chilling effect' of defamation liability, parliamentary privilege acts—as the findings of the European Court of Human Rights in *A v United Kingdom* imply—as a crucial guarantor of the accountability to Parliament of institutions (and powerful individuals) in a way which is central to facilitating the effective working of a constitutional democracy. As Lord Bingham noted in *Buchanan v Jennings*, 'in...liberal democracies, a very high value is attached to freedom of speech and expression as the necessary condition of good government'.[102] In Carol Harlow's words, 'Accountability and representative government go together'.[103]

The second and seemingly broader basis for determining the ambit of parliamentary privilege is the idea of Parliament's 'exclusive cognizance'. This was an area in which, according to Lord Phillips in *Chaytor*, the courts have accepted that 'any issues should be left to be resolved by Parliament rather than determined judicially'.[104] Perhaps more broadly, Lord Rodger suggested that it concerned matters within Parliament which are 'core activities of members of the House which the privilege of exclusive cognizance exists to protect—their right, for example, to speak, to vote, to give notice of a motion, to present a petition, to serve on a committee, and to present a report to the House', something he summarized as 'legislative or deliberative processes'.[105] The Supreme Court was clear that, historically, inroads had been made into areas that had previously fallen within Parliament's exclusive competence, that the courts had jurisdiction to try crimes committed within Parliament, and that the prosecution of parliamentarians for allegedly dishonest

---

[97] Gardner, p 210. [98] Barendt, 2005, p 18. [99] Barendt, 2005, p 20.

[100] Barendt, 2005, pp 18-23. Other, clearly distinct, justifications are considered at pp 6-18.

[101] Something which may also apply to powerful private actors, an example being the Select Committee on Culture, Media and Sport's questioning of Rupert Murdoch in the course of its analysis of phone-hacking: see *11th Report –News International and Phone Hacking*, HC 903, 1 May 2012.

[102] *Buchanan v Jennings* [2005] 1 AC 115, para.[6].

[103] Harlow, 2002, p 190.

[104] *Chaytor*, para [63].

[105] *Chaytor*, para [122]. Lord Rodger's arguable difference of approach from Lord Phillips is also evident at paras [102]-[104], where he explains that he regards art 9 as only legitimately applying to matters for which Parliament can (also) claim exclusive cognizance, the latter category being the broader of the two.

expenses claims related to an area of administrative activity and did not touch on the essential business of Parliament.[106]

In earlier cases, factors associated with this second basis have been evident, sometimes associated with Parliament's specific status as an institution or with more general separation of powers concerns. For example, in *Bradlaugh v Gossett*, Lord Coleridge CJ invoked the 'great dignity' of the House of Commons[107]—seemingly, concern for its collective status *as opposed to* concerns for the promotion of accountability—to stipulate that 'What is said or done within the walls of Parliament cannot be inquired into in a court of law',[108] and in justifying this conclusion, Stephen J drew attention to the 'disrespectful' nature of any potential judicial declaration that a resolution of the House of Commons was beyond the powers of the House.[109] Meanwhile, both judges referred to the seemingly status-associated problem that, were the courts to become involved in determining the legality of the internal proceedings of the House of Commons, the Judicial Committee of the House of Lords—then the highest court in the land—might ultimately be drawn into the matter, leading to one Chamber determining the privileges of the other.[110] Respect for the separation of powers was in turn emphasized in *British Railways Board v Pickin*, with Lord Simon stating that 'Parliament and the courts have each been astute to respect the sphere of action and the privileges of the other'[111] and Lord Wilberforce stressing the constitutional undesirability of the courts inquiring into the procedures followed within Parliament when it was legislating.[112] In *Buchanan v Jennings*, Lord Bingham asserted that 'It is . . . an important principle that the legislature and the courts should not intrude into the spheres reserved to another',[113] and in *A v United Kingdom*, the European Court of Human Rights identified as a legitimate aim of parliamentary privilege the maintenance of the separation of powers between Parliament and the judiciary.[114]

Nonetheless—and admittedly less visibly than is the case with freedom of expression—the second basis for parliamentary privilege can clearly be associated with a concern to promote accountability. At first sight, the 1999 Joint Committee on Parliamentary Privilege Report was concerned only with the status of the legislature when stating that: 'The legislature and the judiciary are, in their respective spheres, estates of the realm of equal status . . . Parliamentary privilege is founded on the principle that the proper conduct of parliamentary business without fear or favour, let or hindrance, requires that Parliament shall be answerable for the conduct of its affairs to the public as a whole . . . It must be free from, and protected from,

---

[106] See *Chaytor*, esp. paras [78]-[90] (Lord Phillips), [105]-[24] (Lord Rodger).
[107] *Bradlaugh v Gossett* (1884) 12 QBD 271 at 273.
[108] *Bradlaugh v Gossett*, 275; see also Stephen J at 278–82.
[109] *Bradlaugh v Gossett*, 282.
[110] *Bradlaugh v Gossett*, 275 (Lord Coleridge CJ), 286–7 (Stephen J). Note, though, the apparent limitations to the proposition, in the reassertion of the point that a mere resolution of the House of Commons cannot change the law of the land.
[111] *British Railways Board v Pickin*, 799. See also 787–8 (Lord Reid), 790 (Lord Morris of Borth-y-Gest).
[112] *British Railways Board v Pickin*, 796.   [113] *Buchanan v Jennings*, para [18].
[114] *A v United Kingdom*, paras [76], [77].

outside intervention'.[115] However, the Report's reference to answerability to the public clearly suggests a direct association between legislators' political freedom and accountability. This also seems evident in the Report's concern that the *sole* justification for parliamentary privilege lay in enabling 'the two Houses of Parliament and their members and officers... to carry out their parliamentary functions effectively',[116] and in its assertion that without parliamentary privilege 'members would be handicapped in performing their parliamentary duties, and the authority of Parliament itself in confronting the executive and as a forum for expressing the anxieties of citizens would be correspondingly diminished'.[117]

The implications of the second basis for parliamentary privilege for the promotion of effective political accountability can be categorized in two more specific ways. The first concerns accountability to the legislature. While the reasoning in *Bradlaugh* seems to have been entirely associated with status-related factors,[118] the decision nonetheless had important *implications* for the ability of the legislature to hold ministers and other decision-makers to account, given the Lord Chief Justice's ruling that nothing said within Parliament could be questioned in a court—thereby spelling out in absolute terms Members' immunity in relation to defamation liability for questions asked or points raised within the chamber. It is also interesting that the European Court of Human Rights stressed in *A v United Kingdom* that most, if not all, Convention signatory states had some form of immunity for members of their national legislatures.[119] It can surely be no coincidence that legislative privilege is widely safeguarded—even in jurisdictions like the US with far stronger traditions of constitutionally-protected speech than that found in the UK. As Tomkins notes, 'Parliamentary privileges enable the Houses of Parliament to undertake their constitutional functions without interference from the Crown or from the courts'.[120] In the UK, such privileges include (apart from freedom of expression) freedom from civil arrest, the right of Parliament to regulate its own composition and procedures, and Parliament's right to enforce its privileges: but the implications of Tomkins' assertion—that the privilege for legislatures and/or their members enables such institutions effectively to carry out their business—are surely clear in relation to accountability, at least provided that we have faith in legislators to use their legally unique position to hold government to account.

---

[115] *Parliamentary Privilege—First Report*, para 23. Indeed, the Committee associated these points with the separation of powers (para.24) and mutual respect between the two institutions (para.25).

[116] *Parliamentary Privilege—First Report*, para 3; see also para 4.

[117] *Parliamentary Privilege—First Report*, para 3. How far this is compatible with the reasoning in *Chaytor* is perhaps an interesting issue.

[118] An assessment arguably reinforced by the point that, while the subject of the case could be said to have been the accessibility to judicial scrutiny of the internal proceedings of the House of Commons, the dispute on its facts concerned an expressive act in the form of the repeated refusal of an elected MP to swear the oath in the required doctrinal form prior to taking up his seat (in other words, a protest against the discrimination then practiced by the House of Commons against elected Members from certain religious affiliations).

[119] *A v United Kingdom*, para [80]; see also paras [81] and [84].

[120] Tomkins, 2003, 125. See also 125–7.

Secondly, though, factors associated with the second basis may have implications for the accountability *of* the legislature. The expenses scandal which lay behind the litigation in *Chaytor* was but one of a series of episodes which have raised questions in the public mind about the dedication and good faith of legislators. [121] Ian Loveland has thus drawn attention to what he categorizes as Parliament's unwillingness to accept full public scrutiny of the finances and ethical standards of its members, its inadequate political mechanisms for self-regulation, and some of its members' attacks on those who have shown 'contempt' by asking unduly serious questions in the public realm.[122] From this standpoint, it might be suggested that ethically improper behaviour by parliamentarians results from an environment in which status-related factors are assumed to entitle them to special consideration. Furthermore, Loveland appears to imply that if, as a conceptual matter, accountability demands an element which is independent of the subject under scrutiny, a mechanism genuinely independent of Parliament—perhaps involving the courts—might be the best way to secure the accountability of individual legislators, at least where accusations of malfeasance are levelled.[123] The expenses scandal might thus be thought to highlight the need for more robust political scrutiny of individual legislators, and/or the dilution of Parliamentary privilege so as to allow for legal regulation. It should be noted, however, that such developments might also involve a *cost* in accountability terms if the ability of parliamentarians to question decision-makers was in any way undermined by granting courts a greater role in assessing the legality of Parliamentary proceedings.

It is against this background that the emergence of independent regulators of legislators' conduct is relevant. As Patricia Leopold notes, until 2009 'enforcement procedures were internal to the House', implemented by the Parliamentary Commissioner for Standards, the House of Commons Committee on Standards and Privileges, and potentially the full House of Commons.[124] The relevant procedures, contained in a Code of Conduct, applied generally to the public conduct of MPs, but with particular reference to financial matters.[125] This form of accountability was thus political. However, the Parliamentary Standards Act 2009, as amended by the Constitutional Reform and Governance Act 2010, created the Independent Parliamentary Standards Authority to determine and pay MPs' allowances and salaries. While the 2009 Act contemplated the possibility of legal intervention in some cases given that it created the criminal offence of providing false or misleading information as part of a claim for allowances, [126] in practice the determination of official payments to MPs remains with the Authority and the statutory Compliance Officer. As a practical matter, though, accountability for the financial matters concerned may be thought to have shifted (or begun to shift)

---

[121] See, generally, P Leopold, 'Standards of Conduct in Public Life', ch.15 in J Jowell and D Oliver (eds), *The Changing Constitution* (Oxford: Oxford University Press, 7th edn, 2011).
[122] I Loveland, *Constitutional Law, Administrative Law, and Human Rights: A Critical Introduction* (Oxford: Oxford University Press, 6th edn, 2012), pp 248–59.
[123] Loveland, pp 248-59.   [124] Leopold, at 403.   [125] See H.C. 735 (2009-10).
[126] Parliamentary Standards Act 2009, section 10.

from the political to the independent regulatory arena. Nonetheless, it is perhaps also significant that section 1 of the 2009 Act stipulates that none of its contents (as amended in 2010) 'shall be construed by any court...as affecting' Art.9 of the Bill of Rights. As such, the legal interpretation given to the ambit of privilege in *Chaytor* would now appear to serve as the key guide to the width of application of the regulatory accountability regime administered by the Authority.

It might be asked what this analysis of parliamentary privilege can tell us about our more general understanding of and approach to political and legal accountability. Two points are of particular importance. First, the material seemingly underscores the argument that the context in which we deem it appropriate to use one form of accountability rather than another—most obviously, here, legal rather than political—rests in part on our normative stance (red-light, green-light, etc.) but also partly on some of the more neutral criteria discussed in section A: for example, on our definition of accountability as a device. Secondly, while legal issues underpin the efficacy of political accountability—hence the need to examine parliamentary privilege at length—political factors also directly affect the practical willingness of actors to make such accountability effective, as Loveland's critical scrutiny (whether or not one accepts his conclusions) perhaps suggests. The direct connections between the legal and political components of the accountability regime which operates in relation to the Westminster Parliament thus become visible. In narrow legal terms, legislators are free to question, debate and scrutinize as they choose only because of the immunity from being sued provided by parliamentary privilege. However, the practical importance of that freedom very much depends upon their good faith and the strength of their political will.

An obvious consequence flows from the material considered in this section: however strong one's normative convictions about the priority of legal over political accountability mechanisms (or vice versa), in practice it seems difficult to contemplate— at least in relation to the Westminster Parliament—the complete detachment of the political mechanisms for promoting government accountability from relevant legal underpinnings. It becomes easier, this being so, to analyse situations in which legal and political accountability mechanisms are more visibly connected in terms of the 'dialogue' approach highlighted earlier. This issue will be considered, in relation to national security measures, in the next section.

C. Human rights, national security and accountability

National security has long been identified as a sensitive policy issue,[127] but it has assumed particular contemporary prominence in western Europe and north America

---

[127] The UK has a long history of relevant legislation: for discussion, see C Gearty, *Terror* (London: Faber and Faber, 1991), esp. chs 2 and 8; L Lustgarten and I Leigh *In From The Cold: National Security and Parliamentary Democracy* (Oxford: Oxford University Press, 1996); D Feldman, 'Human Rights, Terrorism and Risk: The Roles of Politicians and Judges' [2006] *Public Law* 364, 364-72; D Bonner, *Executive Measures, Terrorism and National Security: Have the Rules of the Game Changed?* (Aldershot: Ashgate,

following the 11th September 2001 attacks in the US. This being so, the roles played by courts and legislatures in holding governments to account for their proposals, decisions and actions in this area could be thought to provide a particularly vivid illustration of the constitutional parts played by legal and political accountability, particularly given that, as Lucia Zedner has noted, 'we should not underestimate the extent to which security measures... erode the freedom of ordinary citizens'.[128] It will be argued in this section that good illustrations of 'dialogue' between the courts and Parliament (and its limits) are visible in relation to the Anti-terrorism, Crime and Security Act 2001 and Prevention of Terrorism Act 2005. In addition, national security measures illustrate that 'dialogue' cannot necessarily be reduced to a binary process involving just two distinct types of institution engaging in different types of scrutiny. As the roles played by independent national security-related scrutiny bodies illustrate in the UK, 'dialogue' concerning national security has in fact involved a *variety* of institutional actors. As such, the connections between political and legal accountability mechanisms within any 'dialogue' can be variable and subtle.

Adam Tomkins suggested, writing in 2003, that national security was 'an area of government from which the courts generally prefer to keep away',[129] helping to highlight the law's 'significant limitations' when it came to holding the government to account[130] and contributing to the conclusion that it was 'unsafe to assume that greater judicial power, even greater judicial power that is ostensibly confined to the enforcement of human rights',[131] was necessarily appropriate or democratic, especially considering the 'significant role that political accountability, notwithstanding its imperfections, can and should continue to play'.[132] However, during the period in which both Parliament and the courts have had to consider the Convention-compatibility of anti-terrorism legislation, it is perhaps significant that for many theorists, the balance appears to have altered somewhat, not least with the House of Lords' decision in *A (FC) v Secretary of State for the Home Department* (the '*Belmarsh*' decision).[133] Here, it was accepted that section 23 of the Anti-terrorism, Crime and Security Act 2001, which provided for the indefinite detention without trial of foreign nationals reasonably suspected of involvement in international terrorism by the Home Secretary, contravened Arts. 5 and 14 of the European Convention on Human Rights (the rights to liberty and non-discrimination respectively), and should be subject to a declaration of incompatibility under section 4 of the Human Rights Act 1998. Furthermore, the Human Rights Act 1998 (Designated Derogation) Order 2001, giving voice

2007); C Walker, *Blackstone's Guide to The Anti-Terrorism Legislation* (Oxford: Oxford University Press, 2nd edn, 2009), pp 1-22.

[128] L Zedner 'Securing Liberty in the Face of Terror: Reflections from Criminal Justice' (2005) 32 *Journal of Law and Society* 231, 242. For discussion of political pressures encouraging government action (and, by implication, heightening the need for accountability) in the national security field, see Walker, 2009, pp 15-17.

[129] Tomkins, 2003, p 207.   [130] Tomkins, 2003, p 208.   [131] Tomkins, 2003, p 210.
[132] Tomkins, 2003, p 210.
[133] *A (FC) v Secretary of State for the Home Department* [2004] UKHL 56.

to Parliament's attempt to invoke Art. 15 of the Convention to justify the derogation, was quashed.

The *Belmarsh* case offers an important illustration of the roles of judicial and
political accountability for at least four reasons. The first two are as follows: at
the heart of the case lay the question of the compatibility of Parliament's initial,
post-11th September 2001 response to the perceived terrorist threat—namely,
provisions of the 2001 Act—with the Convention, which had been brought into
national law by the Human Rights Act 1998 when it came into force just a year
earlier; and secondly, and on a connected basis given that the courts were still seeking to clarify and categorize their constitutional roles as accountability agents in
Human Rights Act litigation, the decision contains important observations about
the judicial role (which, while not openly couched in the language of accountability,
can easily be adapted to it.)[134]

In his majority judgment, for example, Lord Bingham emphasized that it was
preferable to approach the deference owed by courts to political authorities as going
to 'demarcation of functions or... "relative institutional competence"'. The more
purely political (in a broad or narrow sense) a question is, the more appropriate it
will be for political resolution and the less likely it is to be an appropriate matter
for judicial decision. The smaller, therefore, will be the potential role of the court.
It is the function of political and not judicial bodies to resolve political questions.
Conversely, the greater the legal content of any issue, the greater the potential role
of the court, because under our constitution and subject to the sovereign power
of Parliament it is the function of the courts and not of political bodies to resolve
legal questions'.[135] In particular, Lord Bingham stressed, it was 'wrong to stigma-
tize judicial decision-making as in some way undemocratic': while judges were
not elected, have different functions from and 'are not answerable to Parliament',
the 'function of independent judges charged to interpret and apply the law is
universally recognized as a cardinal feature of the modern democratic state'.[136]
Lord Rodger in turn stressed that 'deference to the views of the Government and
Parliament...cannot be taken too far. Due deference does not mean abasement
before those views, even in matters relating to national security'.[137] Of perhaps
particular importance to accountability was Lord Rodger's observation that '[o]n a
broader view... scrutiny by the courts is appropriate. There is always a danger that,
by its very nature, a concern for national security may bring forth measures that
are not objectively justified.... good faith does not eliminate the risk that, because
of an understandable concern for national security, a measure may be taken which,
on examination, can be seen to go too far'.[138]

---

[134] On the general constitutional role of the decision, see TR Hickman, 'Between Human Rights
and the Rule of Law: Indefinite Detention and the Derogation Model of Constitutionalism' (2005)
68 *Modern Law Review* 655, 666-8.

[135] *Belmarsh*, para [29].

[136] *Belmarsh*, para [42]. See also Lord Hope at paras [99],[107], [108]; Lord Walker (dissenting),
para [192].

[137] *Belmarsh*, para [176].   [138] *Belmarsh*, para [177].

Returning to Tomkins' scepticism about the appropriateness of legal rather than political accountability, it is interesting to note that Helen Fenwick has described *Belmarsh* as a 'dramatic rejection of deference in relation to national security matters',[139] while Aileen Kavanagh suggests that the national security case law of recent years embraces a '"constitutional shift" from a completely hands-off approach (as embodied in the doctrine of non-justiciability) to a more hands-on approach (as embodied in the idea of a variable intensity of review combined with a degree of deference)'.[140] Kavanagh thus describes *Belmarsh* as 'remarkable and significant' not because it involved a total sweeping aside of judicial deference in national security matters—it did not—but rather because the House of Lords insisted on keeping its legitimate reviewing role while acknowledging that 'the primary decision on what national security was, first and foremost, a decision of the elected branches of government'.[141] Viewed in these terms, *Belmarsh* appears to represent a recognition by the House of Lords of both the power of and the limits to the judicial role in relation to the accountability of the executive.

The third basis for the significance of the *Belmarsh* decision is that among factors repeatedly mentioned by Lord Bingham in his majority judgment were the views expressed on the 2001 measure by Parliament's Joint Committee on Human Rights[142] and a Committee of Privy Counsellors chaired by Lord Newton with a mandate to investigate the in/compatibility of legislation and legislative proposals with Convention rights. This seemingly suggested that the results of certain types of non-judicial and ultimately political scrutiny could play an important evidential role in a context in which the focus was on assessing the legal legitimacy of legislative and executive action.[143] The fourth, connected, basis is that the House of Lords' decision can arguably be classified as having encouraged a lengthy 'dialogue' between the legislature and the highest court about what might be included in

---

[139] H Fenwick, 'Recalibrating ECHR Rights, and the Role of the Human Rights Act Post 9/11: reasserting International Human Rights Norms in the "War on Terror"?' (2011) 64 *Current Legal Problems* 153, 156; see also 231-3.

[140] 'Constitutionalism, Counter-Terrorism and the Courts: Changes in the British Constitutional Landscape' (2011) 9 *International Journal of Constitutional Law* (2011) 9(1): 172, 173-4: the phrase 'constitutional shift' is taken from Sedley LJ's judgment in *Redmond-Bate v Director of Public Prosecutions* [2000] HRLR 249.

[141] Kavanagh, 2011, 183.

[142] The Committee's terms of reference are set out at H.C. Vol. 361, cols. 482-490 (January 17th 2001) and H.L. Vol. 621, cols. 11-12 (January 22nd 2001). For analysis, see JL Hiebert, 'Parliament and the Human Rights Act: Can the JCHR help facilitate a culture of rights?' (2006) 4 *International Journal of Constitutional Law* 1.

[143] Lord Bingham, paras [23], [32], [34], [43], [64], [65] (discussing the Report of the Committee of Privy Counsellors chaired by Lord Newton of Braintree, *Anti-Terrorism, Crime and Security Act 2001 Review*, H.C. 100, 18th December 2003), and paras [24] and [65] (discussing Reports of the Joint Committee on Human Rights, H.L. Paper 37/H.C. 372, H.L. Paper 59/H.C. 462, H.L. Paper 38/H.C. 381, H.L. Paper 158/H.C. 713). A more direct focus on Parliament's role in any 'dialogue' might be associated with Lord Nicholls' statement in his concurring judgment that he could 'see no escape from the conclusion that Parliament must be regarded as having attached insufficient weight to the human rights of non-nationals' (para [81]) and Lord Hope's focus (para [119]) on ministerial statements to Parliament about the security threat and the government's response to the report of the *House of Commons Select Committee on Defence on the Threat from Terrorism* (H.C. 348).

terrorism legislation on a Convention-compatible basis, involving an active exchange between political and legal institutions and the promotion of accountability through both routes.[144]

Some of these points can be highlighted by considering subsequent developments. Following *Belmarsh*, Parliament replaced Part 4 of the 2001 Act, including the disputed section 23, with the Prevention of Terrorism Act 2005, which allowed the Home Secretary to impose restrictions on a person (for example, relating to their association or communications, their place of residence, or their movement within the UK) for purposes connected with protecting the public from a risk of terrorism.[145] Robert Wintemute has pointed out that Parliament would have needed to consider new legislation anyway given that s 29 of the 2001 Act was a 'sunset' provision which would have caused Part 4 automatically to expire in early 2005.[146] Nevertheless, Peter Hain MP, Leader of the House of Commons, drew attention to the implications of the Law Lords' *Belmarsh* decision as a reason for the short timetable for Parliamentary debate concerning what became the 2005 Act,[147] and the decision itself as a reason for introducing the legislation.[148] Furthermore, Charles Clarke MP, the Home Secretary, emphasised that he 'accept[ed]'[149] the *Belmarsh* decision and described the legislation as 'designed to meet the Law Lords' criticism that the previous legislation was both disproportionate and discriminatory'.[150] Indeed, '[i]f the Law Lords say that we have discriminatory and disproportionate legislation...then there is an obligation on the whole House, not simply on the Government, to address that'.[151] From this perspective, the contents of the 2005 Act—including its distinction between 'non-derogating' and 'derogating' control orders and its general application in place of a focus on foreign nationals—could be seen as a *Belmarsh*-driven move beyond the 2001 Act.[152] Notwithstanding this, concerns have however been expressed that the government would have preferred a rather harsher measure to the one eventually passed, and that the final content of the 2005 Act was due in

---

[144] Note, however, Alison Young's concerns about the consequences of judicial deference for a meaningful 'dialogue': Young, 2011.

[145] Prevention of Terrorism Act 2005, ss 1 and 15.

[146] R Wintemute, 'The Human Rights Act's First Five Years: Too Strong, Too weak, Or Just Right?' (2006) 17 *King's College Law Journal* 209, 217-8.

[147] H.C. Deb., 21st February 2005, Cols. 21-22; see also Cols. 23-4, 26 (The Leader of the House also referred to the forthcoming lapse of the powers in Pt 4 of the 2001 Act as a consequence of the Law Lords' judgment. This is incorrect when the powers were due to lapse anyway because of the 'sunset' provision, but the surrounding language suggests that the minister was perhaps just failing to distinguish with sufficient clarity between the consequences of that provision and the judicial decision).

[148] H.C. Deb., 21st February 2005, Col. 22.

[149] H.C. Deb., 22nd February 2005, Col.152; see also H.C. Deb., 26th January 2005, Col.306.

[150] H.C. Deb., 22nd February 2005, Col.151; see also Col.155.

[151] H.C. Deb., 22nd February 2005, Col.158 (interestingly, the Home Secretary went on to make the inaccurate statement that the Law Lords has 'struck down' the 2001 provisions); see also Col.168.

[152] See, eg. the Home Secretary's explanation: H.C. Deb., 26th January 2005, Cols. 305-6; Walker, 2009, pp 28-9, 213-4. Tom Hickman also argues that 'It was...only the Law Lords' decision that provoked a full – albeit rushed – Parliamentary re-consideration and which led to...the Prevention of Terrorism Act 2005' (Hickman, 2005, 667);.

no small part to the work of independent minded back-benchers and the Joint Committee on Human Rights.[153]

In any event, a spirit of 'dialogue' seemed to be evident when the House of Lords later assessed the compatibility of various control orders made under the 2005 Act with Arts. 5 and (occasionally) 6 of the Convention in the *JJ*, *MB* and *E* cases. The general Convention-compatibility of the 2005 legislation was assumed by the Judicial Committee,[154] while Lord Carswell noted the 'tension between the opposing imperatives of protecting the safety of the public and protecting individual human rights' and the difficulty of 'finding an acceptable resolution', and stressed that the government had sought to discharge its duty to protect the public but was subject to regular challenges from those affected by the resulting measures, that Parliament needed to legislate in accordance with Convention rights, and that the courts were required to adjudicate upon the Convention-compatibility of the legislation.[155]

Furthermore, as in *Belmarsh*, Lord Bingham sought to draw attention to the views of the Joint Committee on Human Rights and—on this occasion—to those of the Independent Reviewer of Terrorism Legislation.[156] Such remarks draw attention to the point that, viewed by reference to a 'dialogue', the post-September 2001 national security statutes seem to go beyond initiating a simple exchange between Parliament and the courts in that their provisions may also be subject to periodic review by non-judicial actors. First, sections 122 and 123 of the 2001 Act required the Home Secretary to appoint a Committee of Privy Counsellors to review and report on that Act within two years of its passage.[157] It has been suggested that the Report of the Committee—chaired by former Cabinet minister Lord Newton and referred to above[158]—in reality received what was at best an 'unenthusiastic' response from the executive,[159] but as was also noted above the Report was clearly influential in *Belmarsh*.[160] Furthermore, while its contribution was merely acknowledged by the Home Secretary when outlining proposals for what became the 2005 Act,[161] Parliament's Joint Committee on Human Rights (the views of which were also cited in *Belmarsh*) described the Report's criticisms of Part 4 of the 2001 Act as 'valuable' and as contributing to the Committee's own 'conclusion [that] there are serious weaknesses in the protection for human rights under Part 4'.[162]

---

[153] JL Hiebert, 'Parliamentary Review of Terrorism Measures' (2005) 56 *Modern Law Review* 676.

[154] *Secretary of State for the Home Department v JJ* [2007] UKHL 45; *Secretary of State for the Home Department v MB* [2007] UKHL 46; *Secretary of State for the Home Department v E* [2007] UKHL 47.

[155] *JJ*, para[65].

[156] *JJ*, paras [20] and [22]; *MB*, paras [16] and [22].

[157] These sections were added following debate during the passage of the Bill: see H.L. Deb., 10th December 2001, Cols. 1203-4; H.C. Deb., 12th December 2001, Cols. 952-3; H.C. Deb., 13th December 2001, Col. 1110.

[158] *Anti-terrorism, Crime and Security Act 2001 Review: Report*, 2003.

[159] Walker, 2009, p 28; see also p 213 and C Walker, 'Keeping Control of Terrorists Without Losing Control of Constitutionalism' (2007) 59 *Stanford Law Review* 1395, 1406.

[160] Note, however, Tom Hickman's more nuanced assessment: Hickman, 2005, 666-8.

[161] H.C. Deb., 26th January 2005, Col. 305.

[162] *Anti-terrorism, Crime and Security Act 2001: Statutory Review and Continuance of Part 4*, Sixth Report of Session findings being invoked in judicial decisions or 2003-04, H.L. Paper 38/H.C. 381, para. 33. Other recommendations in the Report were variously 'welcomed', 'endorsed' or 'accepted'.

The Newton Committee's evaluation was confined to the 2001 Act, but the Independent Reviewer of Terrorism Legislation serves as a second, more long-standing non-judicial scrutineer. Under Parliamentary pressure, the government agreed to the creation of an independent reviewer during the passage of the 2001 Act, and the position—the holder of which was appointed by the Home Secretary and confined under section 28 only to reviewing certain aspects of Part 4—was filled by Lord Carlile QC until 2011.[163] Section 14 of the Prevention of Terrorism Act 2005 in turn (and under Parliamentary pressure) mandated annual independent review of that Act, and under the Terrorism Act 2006—which replaced the 2005 Act—section 36 mandated the appointment of an independent person to conduct an annual review of the Terrorism Act 2000 and Part I of the 2006 Act. Lord Carlile was also appointed to these latter roles, arguably giving the impression that he had become a general scrutineer. His reports have often been cited in Parliament and by the Joint Committee on Human Rights,[164] and as noted above Lord Bingham referred to his conclusions in *JJ* and *MB*.[165] Lord Carlile's successor, David Anderson QC, thus argued that while '[s]ome of Lord Carlile's recommendations were rejected or ignored... through his public reports and private interventions, he repeatedly demonstrated the Reviewer's capacity both to affect the public and political debate on the shape of counter-terrorism laws and to bring about changes to their operation'.[166] Nonetheless, Clive Walker criticises the independent review scheme as 'muddled' given how far its application varies from statute to statute,[167] and suggests that to some extent an appearance of coherence may simply have been the result of the same person being appointed to act as reviewer for all the relevant statutes. In addition, the Joint Committee on Human Rights has suggested that the Independent Reviewer may be seen as insufficiently independent from the government and that the post should be reformed 'so as to be Parliament's Reviewer rather than the Government's: appointed by Parliament and reporting directly to Parliament'.[168] It is thus interesting that while declining to comment on the merits of this suggestion, David Anderson accepted that future Reviewers must be 'strong and independent'.[169]

The first two non-judicial reviewers clearly comprise or are members of the social/political 'great-and-good': in other words, 'above criticism' and usually former political

---

[163] Lord Carlile of Berriew Q.C., *Anti-terrorism, Crime and Security Act 2001, Part IV Sections 28 Review of Operation in 2004*, Paras I.1. and I.2.

[164] See Walker, 2007, 1444-6.

[165] Lord Bingham, *JJ*, paras [20] and [22]; *MB*, paras [16] and [22]..

[166] D Anderson, 'The Independent Review of Terrorism Legislation' [2011] *European Human Rights Law Review* 544, 546.

[167] Walker, 2009, p 301.

[168] *Counter-Terrorism Policy and Human Rights: Bringing Human Rights Back In*, H.L. Paper 86/H.C. 111, para 116. The Joint Committee also drew attention to the issues raised by the location of the Reviewer's supporting secretariat in the Home Office. See also Walker, 2009, pp 301-2 (and JCHR criticizes him in 2005-6 (see also Kent Roach, 'Must We Trade Rights for Security? The Choice Between Smart, Harsh, or Proportionate Security Strategies in Canada and Britain' (2006) 27 *Cardozo Law Review* 2151, fn 137; Roach himself criticizes Carlile at 2181-3 and 2193 (torture issues), 2199 (on detention time limits)).

[169] Anderson, 548.

actors rather than currently elected politicians. However, a third non-judicial scrutiny mechanism—the Parliamentary Joint Committee on Human Rights—comprises members of both Chambers with a special interest in human rights, and (as noted above) evaluates proposed and enacted anti-terrorism measures for their compatibility with Convention rights: something which may offer practical help to legislators in identifying the human rights implications of Bills.[170] While some of the Committee's evaluations have been heeded by the government, Murray Hunt observes that the executive also 'frequently rejects' the Committee's recommendations, not least in the area of national security.[171] However, Hiebert notes that '[i]ncreasingly, parliamentarians refer to JCHR reports in their deliberations, although this occurs more often in the House of Lords than the Commons and is more likely to happen among opposition members or cross-benchers than government party members'.[172] Meanwhile, Hunt is clear that 'there has been more independent scrutiny within Parliament of the Government's record on human rights'.[173] The judiciary seems also to have been keen to note the Committee's concerns.[174] At a conceptual level, and very much in line with the notion of 'dialogue', Hiebert therefore suggests that the Committee assumes a 'central role' in the 'dialectical relationship' between government, Parliament and the judiciary contained within the Human Rights Act.[175]

The three non-judicial reviewers mentioned here have all, to varying extents, played a role in political and/or (through judicial citation) legal evaluation of national security measures, hopefully on balance reflecting Kent Roach's suggestion that '[i]ndependent reviews of both legislation and police actions have the potential to provide increased accountability for national security activities'.[176] Sometimes this has involved their findings being invoked in judicial decisions or Parliamentary debates as supporting justifications for the decision-maker's own conclusion; sometimes it has involved mutual citation for the same purpose by two or more of the non-judicial reviewers—almost emphasizing such reviewers' collective and individual expertise in national security matters, going above and beyond that generally

---

[170] C Evans and S Evans, 'Legislative Scrutiny Committees and Parliamentary Conceptions of Human Rights' [2006] *Public Law* 785, 786. One widely noted report of the Joint Committee was its *Anti-terrorism, Crime and Security Act 2001: Statutory Review and Continuance of Part IV*, 6th Report of Session 2003-4, HL Paper 38/HC 381

[171] 'The Impact of the Human Rights Act on the Legislature: A Diminution of Democracy or a New Voice for Parliament?' [2010] *European Human Rights Law Review* 601, 607.

[172] Hiebert, 2006, 31 (a point she particularly associates with legislative deliberations following the *Belmarsh* decision: Hiebert, 2005). For discussion of how the Committee's effectiveness might be measured, see Hiebert, 2006, 14-17, 23-7, 35-8; D Feldman, 'Parliamentary Scrutiny of Legislation and Human Rights' [2002] *Public Law* 323, 333-48; Hunt, 603-6.

[173] Hunt, 607. See also the empirical survey conducted by Francesca Klug and Helen Wildbore, attached to the Joint Committee on Human Rights's *The Committee's Future Working Practices*, H.L. Paper 239, H.C. 1575 (Twenty-third Report of session, 2005-6).

[174] See, for example, Lord Bingham, *Belmarsh*, paras [23], [32], [34], [43], [64], [65], *JJ*, paras [20] and [22], and *MB*, paras [16] and [22]..

[175] Hiebert, 2006, 27. See also Evans and Evans, 787; Hunt, 602-3, 606-8.

[176] Roach, 2171. It should be noted that this comment was not made in relation to the Parliamentary Joint Committee on Human Rights.

possessed within Parliament or by the judiciary.[177] Nonetheless, given that all three reviewers have their roots in the legislature, they must ultimately—and as is implied by the label 'non-judicial'—be seen as political, even if they or their members are no longer involved in or at least focusing on the day-to-day business of party politics. These reviewers' role in the 'dialogue' concerning national security measures therefore implies that courts and contemporary politicians are perhaps involved in a somewhat three-sided process, when seeking to hold government to account, rather than engaging only in 'dialogue' with one another.[178]

Given this background, it is interesting to see that the Joint Committee—as a part of the *legislature*—has seemingly recognized the important role played by legal accountability, while also suggesting that scrutiny within Parliament has been inadequate. In its 2010 Report, revealingly entitled *Counter-Terrorism Policy and Human Rights: Bringing Human Rights Back In*, the Committee emphasized 'the serious democratic deficit in the making of counter-terrorism policy' since 2001.[179] In particular, 'Much of what we now know' about anti-terrorism measures effected using executive action 'has only seen the light of day *because of litigation* or the release of previously classified documents by foreign governments'.[180] The Committee thus felt it important to critically assess whether Parliament's accountability mechanisms had been operating effectively enough, causing it to conclude that 'the mechanisms of democratic accountability for counter-terrorism policy have largely been found wanting'.[181] For example, the Court of Appeal's judgment in *R. (Binyam Mohamed) v Secretary of State for Foreign and Commonwealth Affairs*[182] raised serious doubts about the Intelligence and Security Committee's effectiveness as a mechanism for scrutinizing the security services, causing the Joint Committee to recommend that it be converted into a 'proper' Parliamentary committee with an independent secretariat, legal advice and investigatory mechanisms.[183] While the focus of these comments was on executive action, it is clearly significant from the standpoint of accountability that a body which might be described as a non-judicial part of the 'dialogue' relationship was nonetheless emphasizing the crucial nature of the judicial contribution.

It should thus be clear that the 2001 and 2005 Acts provide an important case study of the roles played by political and legal accountability.[184] While courts have traditionally been reluctant to become involved in national security matters,

---

[177] Also note Roach's observation: 'The normal checks and balances of legislative and judicial review...often may not be available' in the national security context, and that '[i]n some cases, only independent reviewers with appropriate security clearances will be in a position to evaluate the propriety or effectiveness of anti-terrorism policies' (Roach, 2167).

[178] For critical discussion in the U.K. context, see Walker, 2009, p 20.

[179] Sixteenth Report of Session 2009-10, H.L. Paper 86/H.C. 111, Para [107]. On the Terrorism Act 2000, see Walker, 2009, p 25.

[180] Para.[107], emphasis added. See also Feldman, 2006, 380-4.

[181] Para.[107]. In relation specifically to the Counter-Terrorism Act 2008, however, see Walker, 2009, pp 31-2.

[182] [2010] EWCA Civ. 65.   [183] Paras [108]-[112].

[184] As (*Gentle*) v. *Prime Minister* [2008] UKHL 20 arguably demonstrates, there may also be fact situations in which no meaningful political or legal accountability mechanism is open to the claimant.

Belmarsh may suggest that this reticence has slightly declined, while still remaining powerful. Legal challenges, as a basis for holding government to account, may seem a more promising option than was once the case, albeit one to which there are limits. Within the political sphere, an active role has been played by the Joint Committee on Human Rights (acknowledged by Lord Bingham in two of his judgments). The Committee does not seem itself to feel that its Reports have been accorded sufficient weight elsewhere in the political process, and has doubts about the efficacy of other ingredients of that process as mechanisms for securing proper accountability for national security measures, but some commentators are more optimistic.[185] From the standpoint of accountability of the legislature, the key lesson seems thus to be that the debate and litigation concerning the 2001 and 2005 Acts may plausibly suggest that some sort of 'dialogue' concerning national security legislation has taken place between Parliament and the courts, albeit an exchange in which other institutional actors associated with the political process have been involved.[186] It might also be ventured, given the central and difficult place occupied by national security issues in contemporary politics, that the material considered here makes it hard to imagine a workable approach to security measures which did not involve inter-institutional 'dialogue' and include some combination of legal and political accountability mechanisms

D. Conclusion

Three central arguments have been made in this essay. First, while the definition of accountability and our understanding of the appropriate point of division between its legal and political forms depends to quite some extent upon our underlying normative perspective, it is nonetheless possible to engage in definitional/analytical rather than normative arguments about the concept, as is demonstrated by certain of the arguments concerning what constitutes political accountability. This conclusion may also be underlined by the acceptance of theorists such as Tomkins that political accountability (and the location of its boundary with legal accountability) can be assessed not only in normative terms but also from the standpoint of efficacy in promoting the goals of the concept. Analysis of political accountability at this theoretical level thus offers important lessons for our understanding of accountability as a whole. Secondly, many of the constitutional principles and practices associated with the legislature—ministerial responsibility being an obvious example—can be associated with political accountability, depending upon how that concept is defined, but require an acknowledgement of the role played by legal mechanisms in order to understand their operation, demonstrating the connection

---

[185] See, for example, Walker, 2009, pp 71, 310.
[186] A further debate relevant to the efficacy of political accountability as exercised on the floors of both Houses of Parliament may concern the use of 'sunset' provisions, which on one view have the effect – where they are used – of subjecting relevant national security measures to useful annual debate, but on another view sometimes or often result in cursory scrutiny.

between those mechanisms. These points hopefully help underline the importance of debate about political accountability for our understanding of accountability as a whole, and of debate about accountability for practical analysis of the constitutional architecture. Thirdly, the case study of national security, human rights and accountability provides an illustration of the extent to which—in an area of absolutely central importance to contemporary government and to political and constitutional debate—a combination of legal and political accountability mechanisms has been maintained, seemingly involving a 'dialogue' between relevant institutions.[187].

---

[187] As may be indicated by the hostile reaction to the invitation extended to the Westminster Parliament by the European Court of Human Rights to reconsider national rules concerning prisoners' voting rights (see *Hirst (No 2) v United Kingdom* [2005] EHRR 68, paras [83]-[84]), the prospects for 'dialogue' between that Court and the legislature may be more remote, at least in relation to 'sensitive' policy questions.

12

Accountability and the Foundations of British Democracy—the Public Interest and Public Service Principles

*Dawn Oliver**

A. Introduction: the purposes of accountability in the UK constitution

In this chapter[1] I wish to develop a hypothesis about the purposes—or one of the purposes—of public accountability mechanisms as they operate in the United Kingdom. Discussion of accountability commonly revolves around ways in which public office-holders (including Members of the two Houses of Parliament and of the government, and other elected people—for instance in the devolved bodies and in local authorities, civil servants, local authority officers, police officers and others exercising public functions) are answerable to public bodies of various kinds or to the electorate: officials to the courts; ministers to Parliament and the electorate; civil servants to ministers; public authorities to ombudsmen; local authorities to their electorates. I take accountability to entail, in this context, a legal, political, social or moral duty on the part of an accountor to explain and justify his or her action or inaction to particular bodies demanding explanations—accountees —according to standards set by or associated with the role of the accountee. If the courts are involved, the standards will be legal; if the ombudsman, the standard will be whether there has been maladministration resulting in injustice, and so on. If the accountee considers that mistakes or errors have been made, the accountor may be required—whether by law or other social norms—to put matters right by meeting the requirements of the accountee, for instance by apologizing, making amends, ensuring that similar errors are not made in future, resigning or submitting to punishment.

We do not often ask exactly why a web of accountability mechanisms exists in a democracy such as the UK; what good the mechanisms are supposed to achieve;

* Emeritus Professor of Constitutional Law, University College London. Some of the ideas and material in this chapter were first developed in my article D Oliver, 'Psychological Constitutionalism' in *Cambridge Law Journal* (2010): 639–75.

what evils they are supposed to avoid; or whether the wide range of established and approved accountability mechanisms have anything in common.

We know that election of members of the legislature and the executive is not enough to produce and maintain a well-functioning democratic system in which the rule of law is observed, human rights and civil and political liberties are respected, and it is accepted that no party or government has a monopoly of wisdom; ie. that authority is not enough and justifications for action may be expected[1]—these being the essential elements of a liberal democracy, in my view. Without appropriate (and appropriateness is crucial) accountability mechanisms, election alone could produce imprudent, partisan, sectarian, discriminatory, illegitimate, corrupt government that would be inconsistent with the very concepts of democracy and the rule of law. And access to the courts alone cannot protect us from bad government. Further mechanisms of accountability are required. I shall suggest that what most accountability arrangements in the UK have in common is recognition of the need to uphold two important constitutional principles: public bodies should seek to promote the general or public interest and not sectional or partisan interests (the public interest principle); thus, they should serve, altruistically, the public and not their own interests (the public service principle). These principles are elaborated in the next part of this chapter. While I am focusing on the UK system in this chapter, in fact these principles are commonly included in the constitutional texts of western democracies.[2]

Some concepts need to be clarified before we can proceed. First: accountability. I have sketched the meaning of accountability in the first paragraph of this chapter. In exploring the workings of accountability mechanisms in the context of the British constitution and the public service and public interests principles, we need to be aware that 'accountees' vary widely: many of them are expected, and consider their role to be, to promote public interests rather than sectional or sectoral interests. Ministers are 'responsible'—nowadays 'accountable' is a better term—to the two Houses of Parliament: they are supposed to be concerned about public interest in, among other things, the competence and integrity of ministers. Ministers are required to explain and justify their own or their officials' actions to Parliament in terms of public interest standards and not, for instance, in terms of partisan standards that they know conflict with public interests.

Of course, politicians are liable to focus on short-term rather than long-term problems and their solutions, or on winning or retaining votes in the next election. They may lack expertise where it is needed and they may panic in emergencies or when faced by heavy public pressure. The system in the UK therefore involves many non-party political or expert bodies—executive agencies and quasi-autonomous non-governmental organisations (Quangos)—which work under mandates (framework documents in

---

[1] The idea of a shift from a culture of authority to a culture of justification was first discussed by E Mureinik in 'A bridge to where? Introducing the interim Bill of Rights' in *SA Jnl of Human Rights* (1994) 10: 31, at 32, in relation to South Africa.

[2] For examples in the Constitutions of France, Germany, Greece, the Netherlands, and Spain: see Oliver, 'Psychological Constitutionalism', pp 644-5 and 649-50; see also L Duguit *Law and the Modern State* (New York, B W Huebsch, 1919), p.44.

the case of executive agencies, statutory or other legal mandates in the case of many Quangos) which spell out the public interests and how they should be weighed against one another, or against sectional interests. Given the inevitability of differences of opinion as to how conflicting public interests are to be weighed in particular instances, safeguards are to be found in the public servant's duties under the Nolan Committee's Seven Principles of Public Life —selflessness, integrity, objectivity, accountability, openness, honesty, and leadership[3]—and their 'enforcement' via, for instance, rights of access to information under the Freedom of Information Act 2000, the possibility of judicial review (as is illustrated by some of the cases discussed below), and a whole range of other accountability mechanisms.

Thus, ministers are accountable to the Prime Minister, and the Prime Minister is responsible/accountable to the House of Commons in relation to his ministers' performance (since he alone can dismiss them). The Parliamentary Ombudsman and other ombudsmen in the system are entitled to investigate complaints of maladministration by public bodies leading to injustice, which is assumed to be contrary to the public interest[4] and are accountable to the Public Administration Select Committee of the House of Commons and to Parliament generally. The Comptroller and Auditor General and the National Audit Office are charged with securing that the limits of expenditure authorized by Parliament are not exceeded, and with value-for-money and efficiency auditing.[5] The Comptroller and Auditor General is accountable to the House of Commons Committee for Public Accounts for his work and that of the National Audit Office.

The votes of the electorate at election time respond to the record of the incumbent government: elections are accountability moments. Individuals may exercise their votes in accordance with their own interests, but the assumption is that the aggregate of individuals' votes will reflect or promote the general interest and the public service principle. And—very importantly—sections of the public to whom information about the work of officials is disclosed, whether by the press or on freedom of information requests or in other ways—will articulate the standards they expect of public bodies: criticisms may well result in resignations—as when a number of MPs resigned or did not stand for re-election in the wake of the 'sleaze' scandals of 1995 and the MPs' expenses scandals of 2009.[6]

It should not be assumed that the principal role of accountees is to criticize their accountors. They may need to support them. The National Audit Office is supported

---

[3] *First Report of the Committee on Standards in Public Life* (Cm 2858, 1995).

[4] Parliamentary Commissioner Act 1967.

[5] National Audit Act 1983; see John McEldowney, 'Public expenditure and the control of public finance' in J Jowell and D Oliver, (eds) *The Changing Constitution*, (7th edn, Oxford, Oxford University Press, 2011).

[6] See P Leopold, 'Standards of conduct in public life' in J Jowell and D Oliver *The Changing Constitution* (7th edn 2011); P Leyland *Public Law* (2009) 675; G Rayner 'The Complete Expenses File', *Daily Telegraph,*, 20 June 2009; *Committee on Standards in Public Life Report* (Cm 7274, November 2009). Further examples of the influence of negative public reactions to revelations of conduct considered to be inappropriate include the resignation of Damian McBride as Head of Communications at the Treasury on 11 April 2009 when it was disclosed that he had exchanged emails with another Labour government supporter about disseminating fabricated rumours about the private lives of Conservative politicians; the resignation of Liam Fox MP, Secretary of State for Defence, in October

generally by the House of Commons Public Accounts Committee, though it may be criticized by government departments. The Parliamentary Ombudsman is supported by the House of Commons Public Administration Select Committee and criticized by ministers. Thus, if accountors are to do their jobs well, they may need the support of their principal accountees when faced with, for instance, public or political criticism.[7] Thus, accountability is commonly owed to a number of accountees—in these examples to the Prime Minister, to Parliamentary Committees, to ministers, to individual complainants, and to the general public. The existence of a range of possibly conflicting accountability mechanisms—an accountability web—can have both positive and negative effects on officials' performance of their duties of service in the public interest. It is crucial that the balance between different accountabilities is in favour of public interest and public service, and not skewed in favour of sectional interests, or the selfish interests of accountors, or so intense as to make it difficult for the accountable body to perform its functions effectively.

In the next two parts of this chapter I shall expand upon the elements of the public service and public interest principles and how they are 'enforced' and implemented, legally, politically, and socially in the UK. In Section D I shall discuss wrong kinds of accountability. My argument will be that if accountability mechanisms undermine rather than uphold these principles, the legitimacy of state bodies in the UK will be weakened and problems of corruption are likely to arise; and that such developments undermine or destroy the workability of the UK's constitutional system. The history of Northern Ireland during much of the twentieth century provides an illustration of this point.

In Section E I reflect on some of the implications of this line of argument and develop my hypothesis that the principles of public service and public interest are foundational in the UK, and in fact in other liberal democracies; more so even than what are often called 'fundamental' principles such as—depending on the country—a Bill of Rights, direct or representative democracy, parliamentary sovereignty; even legality. These principles, I suggest, have been developed in large part to promote the public service and public interest principles and not, as may be supposed, the other way round.

B. The public service principle

Let us first consider the principle that public officials should act in the service and interests of the public and not, for instance, in the interests of their kin, family, friends, religious bodies, parties and others with whom they have connections; nor

---

2011 over the activities of his unofficial adviser Adam Werrity including his attendance at many of the Secretary of State's official engagements without security clearance; and the resignation on 21 January 2011 of Andy Coulson, the Prime Minister's Director of Communications, over suspicions that he had been involved in phone hacking when he was editor of the *News of the World* newspaper.

[7] Section D of this chapter, 'Wrong kinds of accountability' discusses this issue.

should they act against the interests of, for example, women, children, or racial, religious, or ethnic minorities, or dissidents, on the basis of irrational stereotypes or personal animosity.[8]

1. Public service and soft law

The public service principle has come to be broadly recognized in the hard and soft law of the UK since at least the nineteenth century. It was given institutional expression in the Northcote–Trevelyan Reforms to the civil service in 1854[9] which provided for a permanent, professional civil service, appointed on merit and not as a matter of patronage. The principle is nowadays expressed in many soft law sources: I have already noted the Seven Principles of Public Life which were elaborated by the Committee on Standards in Public Life in its first Report in 1995[10]; these are now incorporated in the Ministerial Code[11], Ministers' and Special Advisers' Codes of Conduct[12], the Civil Service Code[13], the Codes of Conduct for Members of Parliament[14] and for Peers[15], Local Government Codes of Conduct[16], and many other codes which regulate the conduct of public bodies, including special advisers, so as to articulate and promote the public service principle.

Though not 'hard law' in the sense of being judicially enforceable, these requirements are 'enforced' in a range of ways. They are commonly obeyed. The Prime Minister is responsible to Parliament for his operation of the Ministerial Code: it is for him or her to respond to claims that the Code has not been obeyed, and to require a minister who has breached the provisions to resign. The two Houses of Parliament each have their own enforcement mechanisms, operating through the House of Commons Standards and Privileges Committee[17] and the Parliamentary Commissioner for Standards[18], and the House of Lords Privileges Committee. The *Parliamentary Ombudsman's Principles of Good Administration*[19] set out six standards for public bodies: getting it right; being customer-focused; being open and accountable; acting fairly and proportionately; putting things right; and seeking continuous improvement. These are informally

---

[8] See, for instance, the report of the Public Administration Select Committee *The Public Service Ethos*, HJC 263 (2001/2).

[9] The Report is reprinted as an Appendix to the Fulton Report, 1968, *The Civil Service* (Cmnd 3639).

[10] (Cm 2850–I, 1995).

[11] 2010. See https://www.gov.uk/government/uploads/attachment_data/file/61402/ministerial-code-may-2010 (accessed 25 April 2013) at Annex A.

[12] See *Code of Conduct for Special Advisers,* June 2010,:https://www.gove.uk/) and the Ministerial Code (above) which places responsibility for their special advisers on their ministers

[13] Available via the Cabinet Office website. Civil Service values set out in the Code include: 'integrity…putting the obligations of public service above your own personal interests'.

[14] HC 1885, 2010-12.

[15] See O Gay, *Regulation of Standards of Conduct in the House of Lords*, HC Library Standard Note SN/PC/04950, 7 April 2010.

[16] The Localism Act 2011 requires local authorities to adopt codes of conduct. Breach of certain standards of conduct is criminalized under the Act.

[17] See Erskine May *Parliamentary Practice* (24th edn.) (London, Butterworths, 2011), ch 5, p.76 and ch 37, pp 846-7.

[18] Erskine May, *Parliamentary Practice*, p.76.

[19] February 2009, available on the Parliamentary Ombudsman website.

enforced by the ombudsman and the Public Administration Select Committee to which he or she is accountable, and which exercises political pressure on departments to comply with the ombudsman's reports and findings.

The public service principle is also expressed in some of the decisions of the Committee of Standards and Privileges of the House of Commons and the Committee of Privileges of the House of Lords, and parliamentary resolutions[20], in particular the principle that MPs should not be harassed[21] or mandated by outside bodies such as trade unions or sponsors[22], and that the offering or taking of bribes to or by a member of either House is a serious contempt of Parliament.[23]

2. Statutory provisions on public service

Many hard law responses—both in Acts of Parliament and in case law—to breaches of the public service principle are targeted at ensuring that the public service values prevail against incompatible pressures. This is done by a combination of statements of the principle and provisions for institutionalized responses to its breach. The following illustrate the point.

- The Constitutional Reform and Governance Act 2010 provides by section 7 that the civil service code that is to be published under section 5 'must require civil servants to carry out their duties (a) with integrity and honesty, and (b) with objectivity and impartiality'; section 9 establishes complaints procedures when a civil servant may have been required to act in breach of the code or has acted in breach; section 10 provides that appointments to the civil service shall be on merit. These provisions were included in part in response to concerns that ministers may seek to use the services of civil servants for party political purpose, and that there were insufficient channels for civil servants to complain of ministers' misuse of their services.

- The Bribery Act 2010 criminalises the performance of a function of a public nature if it is done in breach of an expectation that it will be exercised in good faith, impartially or if the person is in a position of trust.[24] This Act was passed in response to concerns, in particular, about private companies offering bribes for contracts.

---

[20] See Erskine May, *Parliamentary Practice*, chs 12,13,15.
[21] HC 22 (1975-6) (Gary Allighan's case); HC 27 (1956-7) (The *Daily Graphic* case); Erskine May, *Parliamentary Practice*, ch 15.
[22] See Reports of the Committee of Privileges: 118 HC Deb., (1946-7) and 440 HC Deb., col. 284 (the Case of W J Brown); 512 HC (1976-7) (the NUPE Case); 634 HC (1974-5) (the NUM Case); Erskine May, *Parliamentary Practice*, ch 15.
[23] Resolution of the House of Commons that 'the offer of money or other advantage to any Member of Parliament for the promoting of any matter whatsoever, depending or to be transacted in Parliament, is a high crime and misdemeanour' (CJ (1693-97) 331). It is not clear whether MPs are subject to prosecution under the Bribery Act 2010 if they solicit or accept a bribe; they may be protected by parliamentary privilege: see *Parliamentary Privilege*, (Cm 8318, 2012), chs 3, esp. paras 93, 100, 106-11, 5, esp. para. 216, and 6; *Bribery Bill,* House of Commons Research Paper 10/19, March 2010, para.3.2; *R v Chaytor and others* [2010] UKSC 52.
[24] Ss 1-4. As noted above, it is not clear whether this applies to MPs.

- The Parliamentary Standards Act 2009 as amended by the Parliamentary Voting System and Constituencies Act 2011 section 30 removes the regulation and administration of MPs' expenses arrangements from the House of Commons and puts them on a formal legal basis with provision by section 10 for the prosecution of Members who make false claims for expenses. This Act was passed in response to the MPs expenses scandal in 2008–09.

3. The courts on public service

A number of cases illustrate how the public service principle is treated by the courts.

In *Amalgamated Society of Railway Servants v Osborne*[25] one of the issues was the effects of assertions by unions or political parties within or outside Parliament of a right to mandate Labour MPs, to limit their freedom to vote as they thought right and to punish them for failing to comply with the demands of their 'mandators'. Lord Shaw of Dunfermline stated that such assertions were unconstitutional, and that any contract that purported to bind an MP was in law unenforceable and void as being contrary to 'sound public policy'.[26] On the issue of a contractual relationship between the MP and his party, Lord Shaw noted that: 'Unless a member becomes bound to the society and to the Labour party by these conditions, and shapes his parliamentary action in conformity therewith, and with the decision of the parliamentary party, he has broken his bargain'; and held: 'I do not think that such a subjection is compatible either with the spirit of our parliamentary constitution or with that independence and freedom which have hitherto been held to lie at the basis of representative government in the United Kingdom'.[27]

In *R (on the application of Corner House Research and others) v Director of the Serious Fraud Office*[28] the question was whether it had been unlawful for the Director of the Serious Fraud Office to discontinue a criminal investigation into alleged bribery involving Saudi Arabia. Baroness Hale indicated how accountability to the courts operates in such a case:

It is common ground that *it would not have been lawful for [the Director of the Serious Fraud Office] to take account of threats of harm to himself,* threats of the 'we know where you live' variety. That sort of threat would have been an irrelevant consideration. So what makes this sort of threat different? *Why should the Director be obliged to ignore threats to his own personal safety (and presumably that of his family) but [be]entitled to take into account threats to the safety of others? The answer must lie in a distinction between the personal and the public interest.* The 'public interest' is often invoked but not susceptible of precise definition. But it must mean something of importance to the public as a whole rather than just to a private individual.[29]

---

[25] *Amalgamated Society of Railway Servants v Osborne* [1910] AC 87.

[26] *Amalgamated Society of Railway Servants v Osborne* p.111.

[27] *Amalgamated Society of Railway Servants v Osborne.* These comments were made *obiter*, as the main issue in that case was that trade unions were not permitted by the Trade Union Acts of that time to administer political funds or to levy contributions from their members for political purposes. The Trade Union Act 1913 reversed the position and legitimated contributions and political funds.

[28] *R (on the application of Corner House Research and others) v Director of the Serious Fraud Office* [2008] UKHL 60.

[29] *R (on the application of Corner House Research)*, para.53. My italics.

There have been a number of cases about the public service duties of local authorities and the legality of decisions in which members have felt themselves bound by decisions of their local party organizations, or have felt entitled to give effect to their own moral or ideological views without pinning them to their understanding of where the public interest lies. The issue arose at about the time of the Campaign for Labour Party Democracy which gained currency after the defeat of the Labour party in the 1979 general election. The campaigners claimed that Labour party MPs should be bound by the policy of the party in its election manifesto, and that the manifesto should be drafted by the National Executive Committee of the Labour party. This raised sharp issues about the meaning of democracy and whether the mandate of elected representatives by non- or extra-parliamentary bodies could be consistent with the liberal democratic nature of the British constitution.[30]

The case best known for dealing with this issue is *Bromley London Borough Council v Greater London Council.* [31] The decision was strongly criticized[32] for the failure of the House of Lords to appreciate the realities of transport policy, and for holding that the council owed fiduciary duties to its ratepayers. But a major issue was whether and to what extent the elected Labour party members of the council were bound by the policy of the London Labour Party. Lord Diplock maintained that the elected members of the council had 'a collective legal duty to make choices of policy and of action that they believe to be in the best interests (weighing, where necessary, one against the other) of all those categories of persons to whom their collective duty is owed'; and that 'A council member once elected is not the delegate of those who voted in his favour only; he is representative of all the electors'.[33]

Issues as to the treatment of party policies arose in a number of cases, most of them in the 1980s when local authorities were more politicized than they are nowadays. In *R v Amber Valley District Council, ex p Jackson*[34] the council had contracted with a company to manage a proposed development and was obliged by the contract to use its best endeavours to obtain the necessary planning permissions, failure to do so resulting in liability in damages. The local group of the party having political control of the council resolved to support the company's planning application. An objector sought judicial review on the basis that in light of the contractual terms the council's decision was likely to be biased and unfair, contrary to the statutory duty of the council; in effect, that the accountability of the council to the contractors would prevent them from deciding fairly and impartially. It was held by Woolf J

---

[30] The CLPD claims were reminiscent of those of communist countries whose constitutions referred to 'the leading role' of the Communist party and entrenched that institution and, of course, with it, its ideology in the political system: see Constitution of the USSR 1977, art 6 'The leading and guiding force of Soviet society and the nucleus of its political system, of all state organizations and public organizations, is the Communist Party of the Soviet Union'.

[31] *Bromley London Borough Council v Greater London Council* [1983] 1 AC 768.

[32] See, for instance, M Loughlin, *Local Government in the Modern State* (London, Sweet and Maxwell, 1986); P. McAuslan 'Administrative Law, Collective Consumption and Judicial Policy', *Modern Law Review* (1983) 46: 1, at 14-15.

[33] *Bromley* para.107.

[34] *R v Amber Valley District Council, ex p Jackson* [1985] 1 WLR 298.

(as he then was) that the council had a general duty to act fairly and a statutory duty to consider the applicant's representations, and that the mere fact that the majority group was predisposed in favour of the applicant did not disqualify it from participating in the decision. In the absence of other evidence that the council would fail to consider the planning application and representations on their merits, there were no grounds for the court to intervene. The point for our purposes is that it would have been unlawful for members of the council not to act fairly and not to consider the representations, but to consider themselves bound in their decision-making by the contractual liability of the council: in effect, they were given the benefit of any doubt; a presumption of compliance with the public service principle in the absence of evidence to the contrary.

In *R v Waltham Forest London Borough Council, ex p Baxter and others*[35] the members of the majority group on the council had met before the meeting to determine the rate. The standing orders of the group required members to refrain from voting in opposition to the decisions of the group on pain of withdrawal of the party whip. A number of ratepayers applied for judicial review of the council's rate decision on the basis that members of the majority group had voted in favour of the new rate, despite the fact that at the time of the earlier meeting they had opposed it. It was held that these matters were not evidence that the councillors' discretion had been fettered; party loyalty or party policy were relevant considerations for the councillors as long as they did not dominate; that the evidence showed that the councillors who had initially opposed the decision had voted after making their own minds up; and that their freedom to vote as they thought fit had not been fettered. The case illustrates the fine balance that politicians are expected to make between party loyalty—accountability to the party group—and their own inclinations. The point for us again is that the decision upholds the principle against mandate or interference with the freedom to exercise individual judgement in line with the public service principle.

In *R v Somerset County Council, ex p Fewings*[36] the council owned land to which the local hunt wished to have access. The council resolved to ban hunting on its land as an exercise of its ownership rights on the basis that these were not different from the ownership rights of private bodies. Members of the hunt applied for judicial review on the basis that the ban had been made on purely moral grounds and without reference to the statutory duty of the council to act for the benefit of the area—a local version of the public service and public interest principles. By a majority, Sir Thomas Bingham MR and Swinton Thomas LJ, the Court of Appeal held that the council ought to have considered expressly its duties to promote the benefit of the area and that, having failed to do so, its decision was unlawful. One judge, Simon Brown LJ, was prepared to give the council the benefit of the doubt and to assume that it had indeed taken its duty to the public interest into account, although it had not said so. An important point in the decision is that

---

[35] *R v Waltham Forest London Borough Council, ex p Baxter and others* [1988] 2 WLR 257 at 259-60.
[36] *R v Somerset County Council, ex p Fewings* [1995] 1 All ER 513 (QB); [1995] 3 All ER 20 (CA).

public bodies do not have the same freedoms of action as private bodies; they are not entitled to impose their moral principles on others without consideration of their public service duty.[37]

In the fourth of this series of cases, *Porter v Magill*[38], it was held that the selling of council-owned flats to Conservative supporters in the City of Westminster in order to increase the Conservative vote there—on the assumption that owner-occupiers were more likely than tenants to vote Conservative—was unlawful. In effect, pursuit of party interests was contrary to the public service principle.

In *Padfield v Minister of Agriculture*[39] it was held that for a minister to seek to avoid personal political embarrassment by refusing to exercise a statutory power to refer an issue to a committee would be unlawful: protection of personal interests at the expense of the public interest is not permitted.

4. Social controls

Of course, the fact that the public service principle has been articulated in soft law, in Acts of Parliament, and in judicial decisions in these ways illustrates the fact that public bodies and politicians, like all humans, are capable of the opposite: partisan, selfish, nepotistic, or untrustworthy action.[40] So, the public service principle is also underpinned by—in fact I suggest that it reflects general awareness of the existence of—non-legal, social controls. Breach of the Seven Principles of Public Life, even before they were elaborated, resulted in ostracism, anger and shaming of the miscreant who had accepted payment for tabling parliamentary questions[41] by the public, the press and opposition parties. This also demonstrates the existence among the general population of senses that they share interests which public bodies should be promoting, a topic discussed in the next section of this chapter on the public interest principle. The public as accountees can be an effective check on breaches of these principles. Breaches of the public service principle may lead to disciplinary action. A minister may be dismissed or demoted by the Prime Minister for breach of the Ministerial Code; civil servants may be disciplined by their line

---

[37] See also *Wheeler v Leicester City Council* [1985] AC 1054 (HL) in which it was held that a local authority should not impose its view as to how to counter apartheid by refusing to allow a football club continued access to the council's practice ground when a member had agreed to take part in a football tour to South Africa.

[38] *Porter v Magill* [2001] UKHL 67.

[39] *Padfield v Minister of Agriculture* [1968] AC 997.

[40] Examples include: the sales of honours by Lloyd George which led to the passage of the Honours (Prevention of Abuses) Act 1925, which criminalizes the sale of honours; the Poulson scandals in local government in 1972 when John Poulson was convicted of fraud in connection with the award of building contracts by a local authority, a scandal in which a number of MPs were implicated; and the 'sleaze' scandals of the 1990s involving MPs taking payments for the asking of parliamentary questions, which led to the setting up of the Committee on Standards in Public Life and implementation of the recommendations in many of its reports; MPs' abuses of their expenses which were disclosed in 2008-09 resulted in the passing of the Parliamentary Standards Act 2009: see for instance P Leopold, 'Standards of conduct in public life' in J Jowell and D Oliver *The Changing Constitution* (7th edn, 2011); O Gay and P Leopold, (eds) *Conduct Unbecoming: The Regulation of Parliamentary Behaviour* (London, Politico's, 2004).

[41] G Locke, 'The Hamilton Affair' in Gay and Leopold, *Conduct Unbecoming*.

managers or ministers for breach of the Civil Service Code. Thus breaches of the public service principle are dealt with by a web of accountability mechanisms, not by any means all of them of a formal nature.

Many of the legal provisions for dealing with breaches of the public service principle came into effect as a result of prior social concerns about their importance and demands for them to be formally upheld, as with the establishment of the Independent Parliamentary Standards Authority after the MPs' expenses scandal.[42] In summary, the public service principle as embodied in soft law, in formal legal requirements, and in social norms entails that public bodies and officials should not act selfishly or in the interests of their own careers or families or political parties to the exclusion of public interests; nor should they indulge their own whims, moral or other, or otherwise act arbitrarily or irrationally. The articulation of these principles has the effect of creating or strengthening accountability mechanisms of various kinds in order to ensure that the principles are adhered to, for example by publishing standards which had previously lacked authoritative texts, by making provision for supervisory mechanisms in local government[43], for the investigation of complaints about conduct in the House of Commons by the Parliamentary Commissioner for Standards[44], and for civil servants to raise concerns about ministerial misuse of civil service resources with their line managers and ultimately the Civil Service Commission.[45] These will be considered in due course below.

Many of the articulations of this principle that are summarized in the following paragraphs illustrate the point: they have arisen because of instances of breaches of the previously unarticulated or unsure principles—for instance, the exercise of patronage in the appointment of civil servants leading to incompetence in public administration resulted in the Northcote-Trevelyan reforms of 1854; attempts by sponsoring trade unions to punish MPs for failing to vote as instructed by them resulted in resolutions setting out the limits of relationships between MPs and outside bodies;[46] cases of 'sleaze' among MPs who accepted payments for asking parliamentary questions resulted in appointment of the Commissioner for Parliamentary Standards and the tightening of rules relating to interests;[47] abuses of MPs' expenses resulted in the appointment of the Independent Parliamentary Standards Authority and the transfer of responsibility for the administration of the expenses system from the House of Commons to the Authority.[48] Thus each of these 'breaches' gave rise to public concern. That fact is itself interesting in that it illustrates the connections between the public's expectations of government and the need for governmental responses when public concern is manifest.

---

[42] See note 6 above.
[43] The Localism Act 2011 requires local authorities to adopt codes of practice and to supervise them. Some breaches of standards are criminalized by the Act.
[44] See Leopold, 'Standards of conduct in public life' and Gay and Leopold, *Conduct Unbecoming*.
[45] Civil Service Code paras 16-9.
[46] *Report of the Committee on Privileges* 118 HC Deb., (1946-7) and 440 HC Deb., col. 284 (the Case of W J Brown).
[47] See G Locke, n 42.   [48] See discussion in Section D of this chapter.

The public service principle is underpinned, not only by formal and informal punishments for its breach, but also by socially valuable rewards for its observance. Many rewards and punishments operate informally, not in justiciable ways.

If a person has given public service, and if those with honours to bestow believe that the service to the public has not yet been sufficiently rewarded, then an honour may be awarded: Knighthoods, CBEs, OBEs and MBEs, some peerages (eg. for independents), are rewards for public service.[49] The honoured person is thus rewarded, in a politically neutral, merit-based (not patronage based) process[50] with visible and titular tokens. According to researchers in the fields of social and evolutionary biology and psychology, these rewards may give rise to heightened social status, which in turn generates trust on the part of the others with whom s/he deals, and their cooperation. This brings benefits to the individual—who may continue to provide public service—as well as to society at large.[51] These examples illustrate the significance of the attitudes of the general public and of politicians and others who are expected to serve the public interest, in the operation of the public service principle. In fact, many countries have public honours systems. In the UK, an effort has been made in recent years to involve the public in making nominations (perhaps reflecting the idea that honours are for *public* service) and scrutiny machinery has been created to help ensure that nominations for honours are appropriate.[52]

C. The public interest principle[53]

1. Origins of the public interest principle

The public service principle is closely linked to the public interest principle. It rests on an assumption on the part of rulers and the ruled that there exist among the population substantial shared common—and in that sense 'public'—interests. This is not the case in all populations, and where it is absent it may not be possible for a liberal democracy in the sense noted above to function. The short case study of Northern Ireland in Section D of this chapter illustrates the point.

The origins of the concept of public interest and of its development as a constitutional principle in democracies, or at least in the UK, are ancient. John Locke in *Two Treatises of Government* wrote:[54]

[49] For information on the honours system see: <http://www.direct.gov.uk/en/Government citizensandrights/UKgovernment/Honoursawardsandmedals/DG_176328> (accessed 22 April 2012).

[50] See P Leopold 'Standards of conduct in public life', p.412-3; *Report of the Public Administration Select Committee* HC 212 (2003-4); Government response (Cm 6479, 2005).

[51] For a brief summary see Oliver, 'Psychological Constitutionalism' pp 662-5 and the sources referred to there.

[52] The system has been made more transparent in recent years: see <https://www.gov.uk/honours/overview> (accessed 25 April 2013) <http:// www.direct.gov.uk/Governmentcitizensandrights/UKgovernment/Honoursawardsandmedals/TheUKHonourssystem.index.htm> (accessed 22 April 2013).

[53] Some of the material in this Section is taken from Oliver, 'Psychological Constitutionalism' p.654ff.

[54] P Laslett (ed.) *Second Treatise* (Cambridge, Cambridge University Press, 1988), chapter XI, para. 136. My italics.

Whatever form the commonwealth is under, the Ruling Power ought to govern by declared and received laws and not by extemporary dictates and undetermined resolutions...For all the power the Government has, being only for *the good of society*, as it ought not to be: arbitrary and at pleasure, so it ought to be exercised by establish[ed] and promulgated law: that both the people may know their duty, and be safe and secure within the limits of the law, and rulers too kept within their due bounds, and not to be tempted, by the power they have in their hands, to imploy it to such purposes, and by such measures, as they would not have known, and own not willingly.

The assumption that the people who form the whole population are a group—and one whose welfare and interests the government and Parliament are responsible for—was reflected very strongly in the statement of the theory of representation put by Edmund Burke in his famous speech to the Electors of Bristol:

Parliament is not a congress of ambassadors from different and hostile interests which interests each must maintain, as an agent and advocate, against other agents and advocates; but parliament is a deliberative assembly of *one nation, with one interest, that of the whole*; where not local purposes, not local prejudices ought to guide, but the *general good*, resulting from the general reason of the whole. You choose a member indeed but when you have chosen him, he is not member of Bristol, but he is a member of parliament.[55]

Dworkin stated in *Taking Rights Seriously*:

Arguments of policy justify a political decision by showing that the decision advances or protects some collective goal of *the community as a whole*...Arguments of principle justify a political decision by showing that the decision respects or secures some individual or group right.[56]

Of course the concept of 'the community as a whole' or 'the public as a whole' is problematic, as is the balancing of community, individual and sub-group rights and the resolution of conflicts between them. The identification of common or public interests may be done differently by different sections of society and it may be highly subjective. But the public interest principle at least requires that rulers operate on the basis of the public interest as expressed in law, and that where there is no law they form their own honest, altruistic and considered concept of the public interest, in line with their duties of public service, and promote it.

Lord Diplock acknowledged the difficulties of weighing up interests in the passage from *Bromley LBC* case noted above. Nowadays the populations of the UK and of many democracies are diverse, due to many generations of immigration[57], free movement of workers in the EU, and other developments. But the general proposition that it is the duty of rulers to govern selflessly in the interests of the

---

[55] E Burke, 'Speech to the Electors of Bristol', 3 November 1774. My italics.
[56] London, Duckworth,1977, pp 82–3. My italics.
[57] For discussion of the psychology of acculturation of immigrants into their 'host' community and acceptance of immigrants by host communities see J P Van Oudenhoven and others, 'Patterns of relations between immigrants and host societies' *International Journal of Intercultural Relations* (2006) 30: pp 637–51; Van Oudenhoven, 'Attitudes of minority and majority members towards adaptation of immigrants' *European Journal of Social Psychology* (1998) 28, pp 995–1013; D L Sam and J W Berry (eds)

community as a whole is, in my view, 'foundational' in liberal democratic systems. Duguit suggests that:

There exists then an intimate relation between the possession of power and the obligation to perform certain services. It is a relation so clearly understood and desired as in itself to provide a sufficient basis for the legal duties of government. *All over the world to-day every ruler, emperor, king, president, minister, parliament, holds power not for his own but for his subject's advantage,* and the idea is so widespread that every statesman repeats it to nauseation even while in fact he tries to obtain the greatest advantage from his position.[58]

2. The courts and the public interest principle

The public interest principle finds expression in both hard and soft law in the UK. Many Acts of Parliament refer to 'the public interest' or 'the interests of the area', implying, among other things, that the general public in an area shares common interests. I have already noted that in the *Fewings* case[59] local authority action banning stag hunting on council-owned land was required to be justified by the authority as being for the benefit of the area and not as a simple exercise of the ownership rights of the council or the indulgence of councillors' personal morality.

In *Chandler v DPP*[60] the House of Lords found that the interests of the state are not the interests of the government of the day. (This is another example of the operation of the public service principle.) However, given that the courts do not consider that they are the constitutionally competent institution to determine what the substantive interests of the state are in any given situation, the House of Lords held in that case that the interests of the state were to be determined (presumably honestly and in good faith) by the government of the day rather than by the courts. In *R (on the application of Corner House Research)* noted above, Baroness Hale stated that 'the public interest' must mean something of importance to the public as a whole rather than just to a private individual'. [61] In that case, the government of Saudi Arabia had threatened to withdraw from the existing bilateral counter-terrorism cooperation arrangements with the UK and cooperation in relation to UK strategic objectives in the Middle East unless a bribery investigation was discontinued. That withdrawal would have had detrimental implications for national security and British foreign policy objectives in the Middle East. The House of Lords held that it had not been unlawful for the Director of the Serious Fraud Office to discontinue the investigation in the light of the threats from Saudi Arabia. He had been entitled to form his own view of the predominant public interest and to act to safeguard it.[62] This decision upheld the statutory personal responsibility

---

The Cambridge Handbook of Acculturatation Psychology, (Cambridge, Cambridge University Press, 2006), chs 11 (Van Oudenhoven) and 23 (L Robinson).

[58] L Duguit *Law and the Modern State*, p.44.
[59] *Rv Somerset County Council, ex p Fewings* [1995] 3 All ER 20.
[60] *Chandler v DPP* [1964] AC 763.
[61] *R (on the application of Corner House Research)* [2008] UKHL 60, at para.53. This case is also discussed in Section B, part 3 above.
[62] *R (on the application of Corner House Research)*.

of the Director to exercise his judgement independently and in good faith, thus preventing him from delegating it to ministers or others who had not been granted statutory powers to decide.

3. Politicians and the public interest principle

The principle that the substance of some 'public interests' is to be determined by the government of the day (or by Parliament, or the official with legal responsibility for the decision) rather than by the courts must, it is suggested, be right, but only if—as is supposed to be the case in the UK—the government or Parliament are operating in a system of checks, balances and *accountability* that is weighted in favour of the public interest and not the interests of politicians. Weighting in favour of the public interest is promoted, if not guaranteed, by the conventions of ministerial responsibility to Parliament, openness via the Freedom of Information Act 2000, appointments of civil servants and other officials on merit, and the availability of judicial review—among other checks and balances. These combine to put pressure on officials determining where the public interest lies to do so without regard to their own interests. This is why the appropriateness of accountability mechanisms is crucial: some accountability mechanisms, eg. accountability to religious bodies, might not promote the interests of the whole community, only those of adherents to the religion. Parallel points can be made about accountability to financial and commercial interests and to extra-parliamentary political party organizations.

Much of the discussion of the public interest in this section of the chapter so far has been of the notion that the whole of the public has shared or joint interests, and of the question by whom the general interest is to be determined. The focus has not, then, been on arguments about the *content* of 'the public interest'.[63] In many constitutional arrangements in the UK, it is assumed that the accountability mechanisms in place, including the public service principle, should ensure that the public interest principle prevails in governmental decisions.[64] The Human Rights Act 1998 (HRA 1998), with its incorporation into UK law of most of the articles of the European Convention on Human Rights, assumes broad, nationwide public interests in, for instance (depending upon the right at stake) national security, territorial integrity, public safety, the economic well being of the country, the prevention of disorder or crime, the protection of health or morals, public order, and the protection of the rights and freedoms of others. These public interests can form elements of legitimate justifications for overriding an individual's Convention rights. The courts are guided in the weighing exercise by s 3 of the HRA 1998, which imposes a duty of

---

[63] For discussion of what is *in* the public interest (what its content is) and how it is to be determined (eg. by deliberation), see for instance B M Barry, 'The Use and Abuse of the Public Interest' in C J Friedrich (ed.) *Nomos V: The Public Interest* (New York, 1962); V Held *The Public Interest and Individual Interests* (New York 1970); C Sunstein *After the Rights Revolution: Reconceiving the Regulatory State* (Cambridge Mass, Harvard University Press,1990); M Feintuck *The Public Interest in Regulation* (Oxford, Oxford University Press, 2004).

[64] I shall note in the next section, however, that some accountability mechanisms can be inappropriate.

compatible interpretation of UK law with Convention rights, and by s 4 which, by granting the courts powers to make declarations of incompatibility, returns responsibility for the weighing of interests to the government by way of remedial orders to remove incompatibility. These provisions thus demarcate the political responsibility of the executive and Parliament from the legal responsibility of the court for, and their duties in relation to, weighing up public and private interests.

4. Social conventions and the public interest

The public interest principle has parallels in social conventions governing the many sub-groups in the population. It is not just a matter of the national interest. Within any collection of people who consider themselves to constitute a group—Scots, Welsh, Londoners, Brummies, members of churches, football clubs and so on—there will be expectations that members will sometimes subordinate their own interests to the general good of the group. Those who do so will be rewarded by other members with respect, cooperation, trust, social status. And those who always put their own interests first or 'defect' will be ostracized; perhaps punished as free-riders or cheats. This is a matter of innate human predispositions.[65] But in the UK—and no doubt in other liberal democracies—the general assumption is that, given shared interests among the population, it is legitimate and expected of rulers that they will observe the public service and public interest principles.

D. Wrong kinds of accountability

We need to bear in mind that not all accountability mechanisms in the UK promote the public interest and public service principles: not all of the 'accountees' who seek to hold officials to account by criticizing them, demanding explanations or redress, and calling for their resignation if they consider that they are wrong, will be concerned to promote the public interest and public service; they may rather be preoccupied with their own personal interests, ideologies, or preferences. Political parties and other unelected bodies may seek to impose their views of where the public interest lies on elected ministers and MPs or on local authorities. The cases on the public service principle discussed earlier illustrate this point: *Osborne* and *Bromley* were litigated because of concerns that MPs and elected councillors allowed themselves to be mandated by outside bodies; *Padfield* was litigated because of concern that a minister had been influenced by his personal interest in avoiding embarrassment if he were to refer the question of milk pricing to a committee; *Fewings* was litigated because of concerns that councillors considered themselves to enjoy the same freedom of action as private property owners, entitled therefore to impose their own moral opinions about stag hunting on others. Thus it is obvious that the principles of public service and public interest can conflict with the interests of

---

[65] See Oliver, 'Psychological Constitutionalism', pp 654–8.

MPs and councillors, and of government, or the wishes of many electors. That is inevitable. But if public bodies were so sensitive to pressures that conflict with their own honest judgements of where the public interest lies that they gained reputations for weakness, their very legitimacy would be undermined.

There follow some further illustrations of what are currently widely regarded as inappropriate elements in accountability webs. Public officials may feel impelled to respond positively to criticisms from partisan or sectional representative bodies so as to mollify them; they may even feel pressed to abandon policies they believe to be in the public interest because of partisan pressures. For instance, if MPs act as consultants to bodies which are concerned with their own interests or those of their members, they are likely to be lobbied by them to promote their interests or to support their views. It is in order to prevent such relationships from undermining the ability of MPs to act in a spirit of public service and to pursue public interests that parliamentary rules require MPs not to accept mandates from their sponsors, and sponsors not to mandate MPs.[66] But these rules alone will not prevent MPs from being influenced by their relationships with their sponsors in what they do. It is in recognition of these problems that MPs are required to register their interests, to declare them, and not to act as paid advocates or to lobby for reward or consideration.[67]

Some—for instance, excessive—impositions of accountability on public officials can interfere with their proper exercise of public functions in the public interest. Derek Lewis, the Director of Prisons who resigned after a prison breakout in 1995, complained that the Home Secretary, Michael Howard MP, involved himself so much in the work of the service that it damaged his ability to do the job.[68] The Independent Parliamentary Standards Authority, set up by Act of Parliament in 2009 (as amended by the Constitutional Reform and Governance Act 2010, ch 3) in the wake of the 2009 scandals over MPs' expenses, has been greatly resented and criticized by individual MPs and others, including some members of the Speaker's Committee for the Independent Parliamentary Standards Authority [69] in ways that may have made it difficult for it to cope with its remit. There are no doubt differences of interpretation of the facts of each of these examples, but they serve at least to show that accountabilities can operate counter-productively so as to frustrate the mandate of the accountor.

The history of Northern Ireland during the period from 1923 to 1972 is the strongest example close to home of the damage that can be done by the wrong kinds of accountability.[70] Direct rule was imposed in 1972 because of the Troubles there

---

[66] The Code of Conduct together with The Guide to the Rules Relating to the Conduct of Members, HC 735, June 2009, updated May 2010; and see Erskine May, *Parliamentary Practice* ch 15.

[67] HC 735, June 2009.

[68] See The Learmont Report, *Review of Prison Service Security in England and Wales and the Escape from Parkhurst Prison on Tuesday 3 January 1995*, (Cm 3020, 1995); Derek Lewis *Hidden Agendas. Politics, Law, and Disorder*, 1997.

[69] See, for instance, the corrected transcript of oral evidence from members of IPSA taken before the Speaker's Committee for IPSA on the IPSA Draft Estimate 2012–13 on 22 May 2012.

[70] On this period in the history of Northern Ireland see, for instance, P Dixon *Northern Ireland: The Politics of War and Peace*, 2nd edn. (Basingstoke: Palgrave Macmillan, 2008); B O'Leary and J McGarry

that were caused by permanent unionist majoritarian government at Stormont which promoted the interests of the unionists/protestants/loyalists over those of the nationalist/Catholic/republican populations—which in other words did not operate on the basis that there were shared interests in the province which it was the duty of the government at Stormont and the public service there to promote. The Northern Ireland government and the majority parties in the Assembly were effectively accountable only to the majority population, not to the minority or to the population as a whole. This situation resulted in violent conflict between members of the two communities, and this in turn led to direct rule from Whitehall and Westminster; to the abandonment of jury trial; to judges being threatened and having to be placed under tight security protection; to lawyers and journalists being murdered—in other words not only were state institutions which failed to observe these two principles suspended, but the rule of law itself was under threat. The conflict could only be brought to an end through the laborious negotiation of an agreement to share power between the two communities, the Belfast Agreement 1998 and its endorsement in referendums held in the Province and in the Republic of Ireland, followed by the Northern Ireland Act 1998.

In sum, although accountability mechanisms in the UK will commonly operate positively to promote the public service and public interest principles, they may operate negatively. It is likely that the same is true of other liberal democracies.

E. Reflections and concluding remarks on public service, the public interest, accountability and liberal democracy in the UK

There remain many areas of concern about whether accountability mechanisms in the UK need to be tightened up to protect and promote the public interest and public service principles: currently, for instance, the regulation of lobbying of ministers by powerful interest groups is under consideration.[71] No doubt new areas of concern will open up from time to time: the sleaze and expenses scandals of the 1990s and 2000s were surprises, but they will not have been the last ones.

The present web of accountability in the UK system, then, is not perfect. But let us reflect on what the position would be if inappropriate accountability mechanisms were to develop or not be constrained in the UK system. Reminding ourselves of some of the scandals and cases discussed above, MPs would not be acting unlawfully, and nor would their sponsors be doing so, if they were bound to vote and act in Parliament in compliance with instructions from outside. The same is

---

The Politics of Antagonism: Understanding Northern Ireland (Atlantic Highlands:NJ, Athlone Press 1992); J Whyte *Interpreting Northern Ireland* (Oxford: Clarendon Press,1990); D Birrell and A Murie *Policy and Government in Northern Ireland: Lessons of Devolution* (Dublin: Gill and Macmillan,1980); D Oliver 'Psychological Constitutionalism' *CLJ* (2010) 69: 669–74.

[71] See Second Report of the House of Commons Political and Constitutional Reform Committee, *Introducing a Statutory Register of Lobbyists*, HC 153, 2012–13, 11 July 2012/Government Response,/ HC 593, 13 July 2013; Lobbyists (Registration of Code of Conduct) Bill, 2013.

true of relationships between MPs and elected councillors on the one hand and extra-parliamentary party organizations and caucuses on the other hand. But for the rules of parliamentary privilege and contempt, it may well not be a crime for MPs to take bribes in return for favours.[72] Nor would it be unlawful for ministers or civil servants or other public bodies to do so. It would not be unlawful for local authorities to manage public property and exercise their powers to as to maximize support in their areas for their party—or to maximize opposition to their political rivals. Ministers and councillors would be free to impose their moral or religious views on private bodies or individuals with whom they have contractual or property-based relationships. Each of these 'not unlawful' activities would be contrary to the public service or public interest principles. And this is the point: the standards that current accountability mechanisms are designed to uphold have not always been observed in public life—and of course, despite current arrangements, such standards are still breached from time to time—and if they were repealed or regularly disregarded it is obvious that the public service and public interest principles themselves would be at risk.[73]

I suggest therefore that it is essential to the public interest and public service principles not only that officials are committed to them, but that the general population too is committed to them and confident that they are generally observed. If the population or the majority were not so committed it would not be contrary to generally accepted norms, standards or codes for Parliament, ministers and local authorities to discriminate against sections of the population and to give preferential treatment to those they consider to be members of their own groups, or to grant special access to representatives of sectional interests so as to put themselves in a position which calls their commitment to the general interest into question; it would not be considered inappropriate for ministers or civil servants to go straight from their elected positions into employment by bodies with whom their departments were connected on leaving the service, though this would put a question mark over their commitment to the public service and public interest during their period of office. The particular importance of these examples is that such conduct would undermine the general public respect for and confidence in officials, on which the public interest and public service principles are based; and if it did not do so we would know that in fact there is little sense of shared interests in the population.

This may appear self-evident. But the reason I am highlighting the importance of these obvious principles and the lessons of past experience is that it supports my argument that the two public interest and public service principles are in fact foundational to the operation of the UK system—and no doubt of other liberal democratic states.

---

[72] As noted above, it is not clear whether MPs could be prosecuted under the Bribery Act 2010 for soliciting or accepting bribes.

[73] An area in which such problems could arise is the introduction of 'Community Rights' under the Localism Act 2011: these rights could be factional or partisan in character and thus could potentially trump the wider public interest at local government level.

F. Conclusion

I draw from experience in Northern Ireland that the workability and survival of liberal democratic systems in the sense outlined above (systems in which the executive and legislature are elected and in which the rule of law is observed, human rights and civil and political liberties are respected, and it is accepted that no party or government has a monopoly of wisdom) depends upon there existing among the general population a sufficiently strong sense of shared interests so that the efforts of public bodies to promote those interests, and to do so altruistically and in a spirit of public service, command the broad if not universal support, or at least the acquiescence, of the people. Whether a sufficiently strong sense of shared interests exists in a population is an empirical question; a matter of the culture and psychology of the groups within the population. It is part of the role of governments to promote senses of shared interests and identities. If they do not exist, then the government and the system will lack legitimacy. Here is my hypothesis. A country in which conformity with the public service and public interest principles is not generally demanded of those in power by the population; which expects or reluctantly accepts or even demands instead that those in power favour particular sections of society; or where those not in official positions are allowed to control public officials; and where the principles are not broadly adhered to by public bodies — for instance, where there is corruption or partisanship or sectarianism — cannot be a liberal democracy. We can no doubt all of us think of countries which are not liberal democracies: my bet is that all of them suffer from an absence from the culture of the population and from officials of commitment to these two principles—whether from corruption which undermines the public service principle, or tribalism, racism, classism, or religious sectarianism, all of which deny the very existence of public or shared interests or the principle that the pursuit of those interests, if they exist, should be the goal of government. And the webs of accountability in all countries will reveal the extent of commitment to these principles.

13

Multi-Layered Constitutional Accountability and the Re-financing of Territorial Governance in the UK

Peter Leyland*

A. Introduction

The introduction of devolution transformed the constitutional landscape of the United Kingdom by establishing a layer of sub-national government which was tailored to fit the prevailing conditions in each of the home nations, but since it was established in 1999 the economic and political circumstances have fundamentally changed with the onset of a deep economic recession and with a referendum for an independent Scotland in prospect for 2014. In a number of ways we will see that devolution, notwithstanding its asymmetrical shape, has been designed to deliver enhanced levels of democratic and legal accountability, at least for the devolved parts of the UK. However, the absence until recently of any major dispute over funding allocation has been one of the most remarkable features of devolution. In part this feature can be attributed to the arrangements for its introduction at an administrative level as the responsibility for functions shifted from central government at Westminster to the newly-formed executives in Edinburgh and Cardiff, with a strong emphasis on achieving seamless continuity in the delivery of policy. From the standpoint of ordinary citizens dependent on the state, there was little perception of any change. Perhaps an even more compelling reason for the acceptance of the existing system was that the so-called 'Barnett Formula' already provided a financial settlement which took account of local circumstances in Scotland, Wales and Northern Ireland. This formula had already been applied for more than 30 years and delivered relatively generous levels of funding to the devolved parts of the UK. With the exception of the variable tax rate included in the Scotland Act 1998, the approach of the then government was to accept this block-grant settlement as the baseline.

* Professor of Public Law, London Metropolitan University. I would like to thank Professor George Jones, Mark Elliott, Professor Gordon Anthony, Professor Andrew Harding and Nicholas Bamforth for their helpful comments on an ealier draft of this chapter.

As the political situation changed, particularly with the electoral success of the SNP in Scotland and the implications of the economic recession, the sleeping dog has well and truly woken up and begun to bark. After considering the main features of accountability as part of the multi-layered constitution, this chapter argues there is a wider meta-narrative framing the discussion which encapsulates the policy of successive governments—a conflict between the accepted approach to devolution where funding is largely handed over without strings attached and the approach to local government which has been faced with precisely the opposite trend in the form of severe legal constraints and more recently funding cuts at the hands of central government.[1] But first it will be argued from a general constitutional standpoint that certain accountability mechanisms have been radically modified and that accountability has been compounded by multi-layered considerations through the introduction of devolution. Nevertheless, there has been only limited attention to establishing direct financial accountability at the devolved level. Second, it will be argued that in regard to the allocation of funding, although there may be negotiation between central and devolved government over funding levels, no special parliamentary procedures were introduced to scrutinize the proposed allocation of resources under the Barnett Formula to the devolved administrations. The next concern is to consider in the light of the recommendations of the Calman Commission and Holtham Commission whether there is a convincing argument from the standpoint of constitutional accountability for the replacement of the Barnett Formula with a needs-based alternative supported by an independent grants commission. While the politicians have yet to agree on an answer to the problem of block-grant funding, the Scotland Act 2012 has to some extent addressed the correlation between taxation and spending by changing the capacity of the Scottish Parliament to impose taxes at the level of devolved government. In identifying the meta-narrative it becomes clear that devolution was designed to bring government closer to the electorate in the devolved nations by allowing scope for policy preferences to be expressed. The relatively generous financial settlement produced a flexibility that can be starkly contrasted with the suffocating controls imposed on local government.[2] Against a background of economic contraction rather than expansion, it is argued that the rules of the game are having to change as assumptions about the nature of the modern welfare state are in danger of being undermined by the disparities caused by geographical variations in policy delivery. In turn, these trends exert further pressure on the integrity of the UK as a nation state.

---

[1] Since the coalition government took office in 2010, the Localism Act 2011 proposes to make further changes at local government level set against a background of a 27 per cent cut to their formula grant from Whitehall over 4 years. See eg. 'Council cuts: UK local authorities respond to budget cuts' *Financial Times*, 22 March 2011.

[2] It will be explained below that the Localism Act 2011 changes the ground rules of local government by seeking to employ referendums as means of controlling excessive expenditure.

B. Accountability in a 'multi-layered' constitution

This section considers the general issue of constitutional accountability from the standpoint of sub-national governance. As we survey the manner in which devolution was set up it will become apparent that, despite establishing improved accountability mechanisms at devolved level, certain features of devolution have undermined particular aspects of constitutional accountability. There is an assumption that, to provide accountability, most codified constitutions adopt a template that also sets out different types of checks and balances including a definition of the respective positions of national and sub-national government, but notions of accountability under the uncodified UK constitution have evolved with the constitution itself. Since the introduction of universal suffrage there has been political accountability in that governments are elected at regular intervals of at least every 5 years. The so-called Westminster model version of the constitution was roughly based on the assumption that all public administration is ultimately handled by ministers who are, in turn, answerable to Parliament under the doctrine of individual ministerial responsibility.[3] While there has been a debate over the degree of effectiveness of ministerial responsibility[4], for many commentators the ability of the party machine at Westminster managed by the party whips to dominate Parliament meant that the Whitehall model of executive dominance, or what Lord Hailsham termed 'elective dictatorship', transcended the Westminster model.[5] In effect, this approach suggested that the roles of Parliament as a site for debate and for calling government to account have been marginalized because the government is able to use its support to get its way, not only over legislation, but whenever Parliament divides and votes on controversial policy matters.

As part of this analysis we can see that the mechanisms for accountability must under current constitutional arrangements (post 1999) be considered as a feature of an increasingly multi-layered constitution where the exercise of power has been redistributed both upwards and downwards.[6] But the change has not been under a formal written constitution or a more traditional federal system. This multi-layering means that there are not only additional levels of government, but as part of the contracting state an increasing number of inter-related strands responsible for the exercise of power. These additional layers of government have impacted on the way accountability mechanisms operate in the sense that the strands have become more complex and the layers are uneven or frequently overlap in ways that may not have been fully anticipated.[7] For instance, the 'West Lothian Question' provides

---

[3] J Mackintosh *The Government and Politics of Britain* (London: Hutchinson, 1977), 16.

[4] A Tomkins *Public Law* (Oxford: Oxford University Press, 2003), 134.

[5] A King *The British Constitution* (Oxford: Oxford University Press, 2007), 82.

[6] See N Bamforth and P Leyland 'Introduction: Public Law in a Multi-Layered Constitution' in N Bamforth and P Leyland (eds) *Public Law in a Multi-layered Constitution* (Oxford: Hart Publishing, 2003), 4ff.

[7] Mount convincingly argues that any straightforward dichotomy between a unitary system where power radiates from a single source and a federal system where power is divided symmetrically is

an obvious manifestation of the accountability gap precipitated by the asymmetry of devolution. Scotland, Wales and Northern Ireland each have a distinctive form of devolution based on a new form of elected government, but England lacks an equivalent level of government which might have been provided under a symmetrical federal system. One of the incidental effects of the devolution legislation is that English MPs no longer have the right to vote on the policy areas that have been devolved, but Westminster MPs returned from constituencies in Scotland, Wales and Northern Ireland have retained the right to vote on legislation coming before the Westminster Parliament about England.[8] It will be immediately apparent that the role of the Westminster Parliament as a representative body for Scotland, Wales and Northern Ireland has been modified since the introduction of devolution.[9]

In the absence of a codified constitution, the original devolution statutes established revised terms of reference under which accountability issues might be considered by redefining the formal boundaries of power.[10] Indeed, the form of democratic accountability under a devolved system can be justified for obvious practical reasons. Hopkins maintains that this outcome is because 'the issues of concern in specific localities, particularly in the peripheral and less populous territories, will be less prominent. This leads to a government that is responsive only to certain issues and specific territorial concerns. Although national issues are important, specific regional concerns and those of the periphery must be addressed if the government is to represent the whole electorate.'[11]

A constitutional framework for each of the home nations apart from England is established to confer powers on a new set of institutions. In each case the core concept of sovereignty is preserved.[12] The Scottish Parliament and the Assemblies in Cardiff and Belfast are based on creating variants of a democratic model of accountability with a different electoral cycle from the Westminster Parliament. After an election in Scotland and Wales the new legislature[13] votes for a first minister who appoints a cabinet forming the devolved government which is formally answerable to the elected legislature.[14] Northern Ireland differs in that there must be a multi-party executive chosen on the basis of the 'd'Hondt Formula' to ensure power-sharing between the communities, with the first minister and deputy first

incorrect and points to other asymmetries that have been accepted including the unequal distribution of parliamentary seats. See F Mount *The British Constitution Now* (London: Mandarin, 1993), 199.

[8] V Bogdanor, 'The West Lothian Question' *Parliamentary Affairs*, Vol 63, No 1, 2010, 156–72.

[9] The Conservative-Liberal Democrat agreement reached after the 2010 general election included a commitment to establish a commission to consider how the West Lothian question might be addressed. See V Bogdanor *The Coalition and the Constitution* (Oxford: Hart Publishing 2011).

[10] See Scotland Act 1998, Government of Wales Act 1998 and Northern Ireland Act 1998.

[11] J Hopkins *Devolution in Context: Regional, Federal and Devolved Government in the European Union* (London: Cavendish, 2002), 32.

[12] Scotland Act 1998, ss 29, 31 and 32.

[13] Wales was at first granted a form of only executive devolution under the Government of Wales Act 1998. However, following a referendum held in March 2011 under the Government Wales Act 2006, the Assembly gained law-making powers roughly equivalent to those enjoyed by the Scottish Parliament and the Northern Ireland Assembly. See P Leyland *The Constitution of the United Kingdom: A Contextual Analysis* (2nd edn, Oxford: Hart Publishing, 2012), 254ff.

[14] N Burrows *Devolution* (London: Sweet and Maxwell, 2000), 82ff.

minister and the other ministerial portfolios allocated accordingly.[15] The basic UK constitutional convention making the government accountable to Parliament is not exactly replicated under devolution.[16] This change is because all three elected bodies serve for a fixed term of office, but in each case there are statutory limits to these law-making powers.[17] If the executive lose a no-confidence motion, although the First Minister and other ministerial office-holders might be expected to resign, an executive of some kind is still expected to emerge and gain the confidence of the elected body.[18] At Westminster, the spectre of a no-confidence motion puts the party whips in a powerful position in securing electoral support for government measures. The fact that the executive will not necessarily fall potentially allows more scope for individual members who are dissatisfied with any proposal to vote against the ruling devolved government with relative impunity. Notwithstanding this emphasis on establishing democratically-accountable institutions, devolution was distinctive for not fundamentally modifying the formal position on the funding allocated to devolved government from central government. The block-grant provision under the Barnett Formula was retained, but the Scottish Parliament was granted additional revenue-raising powers as essentially a top-up provision.[19]

In shaping the Parliaments and Assemblies, access and participation have been encouraged and they have been assisted by active citizen engagement in policy-making[20] through more systematic consultation and involvement with the routine publication of draft bills and in the current information age by websites which also help facilitate more effective consultation. While the Westminster system has been criticized because individuals and organizations found it difficult to inform and influence the policy-making process before the introduction of legislation,[21] in Scotland, more attention has been placed on the pre-parliamentary stage of introducing a bill to encourage increased accessibility and participation in the law-making process: 'The emphasis on public engagement has resulted in much more detailed scrutiny of proposals at the pre-legislative stage and stage one of the legislative process... This has allowed much greater public involvement than exists at Westminster.'[22] Before

---

[15] Devolution in Northern Ireland was suspended three times between 1999 and 2002 with powers reverting to the Northern Ireland Office before being finally relaunched in May 2007. See C McCrudden, 'Northern Ireland and the British Constitution since the Belfast Agreement' in J Jowell and D Oliver (eds) *The Changing Constitution* (6th edn, Oxford: Oxford University Press, 2007).

[16] In an annual statement to the Parliament, the Executive (now government) should be required to outline its main aims, objectives and policy priorities, and the various means— administrative, executive, legislative— by which it intends to achieve them. If possible, this outline might look beyond one year, but could be updated annually. The statement might take the form of an annual report, reporting on progress made in the previous year. The statement might include an element of performance review, for which appropriate performance indicators would need to be set.

[17] See eg. pre-legislative and post-legislative scrutiny under Scotland Act 1998, ss 31 and 32.

[18] Burrows, *Devolution*, 108.

[19] No equivalent provision was present in the Government of Wales Act 1998 or the Northern Ireland Act 1998.

[20] See eg. Your Scotland, Your Voice.

[21] See Report of the Consultative Steering Group on the Scottish Parliament *Shaping Scotland's Parliament*, December 1998, section 2 para.18.

[22] J Johnston, 'The Legislative Process: the Parliament in Practice' in C Jeffrey and J Mitchell (eds) *The Scottish Parliament 1999–2009: The First Decade*, (Edinburgh: Luath Press, 2009), 29.

the introduction of a measure a minister may be required to advise the relevant committee of his/her proposals and the committee monitors the consultation exercise. It may also take its own evidence at this preliminary stage. At the same time as the devolution legislation was being introduced, the Westminster government reacted by moving towards a two-year legislative programme in Parliament with the publication of several draft bills.[23]

Devolution provides a new approach to executive oversight at the devolved level. A good illustration is the transformation of the role of the committees undertaking the routine work of the Scottish Parliament and the Assemblies in Wales and Northern Ireland. The so-called 'subject committees' corresponding to the main policy areas perform the function of executive oversight, as well as having responsibility for scrutinizing legislation.[24] Some commentators maintain that these relatively expert committees, exercising this dual function, represent an improvement on the approach adopted at Westminster where the task is divided between ad hoc public-bill committees and more specialized Departmental Select Committees.[25] In Wales 'Subject committees should have a significant role in reviewing the effectiveness of policies and in developing new policies. They should scrutinise the performance of non-departmental public bodies and other bodies funded by the Assembly, reporting to the full Assembly on that performance from time to time.'[26] Rawlings notes that through '...inclusiveness and partnership working, these committees offered an alternative and more transparent conduit for external inputs—evidence-taking, public consultation etc'.[27] Oversight of the executive is further assisted by an enhanced culture of openness through freedom of information laws with a lower threshold for insisting on disclosure in Scotland than is included for England and Wales under the Freedom of Information Act of 2000 (FOI).[28]

Devolution operates at a formal level but also relies on less formal soft law to coordinate the process of inter-governmental relations post-devolution which are dealt with by series of mainly bilateral, but also multilateral, concordats.[29] These are agreements between Westminster and the governments in Edinburgh, Cardiff and Belfast. The respective statutes merely provide an outline which has been

---

[23] M Ryle, 'House of Commons Procedures' in R Blackburn and R Plant *Constitutional Reform: The Labour Government's Constitutional Reform Agenda* (London: Longman, 1999) p.130: See also the Hansard Society Commission proposals.

[24] Following pre-parliamentary consideration, the first parliamentary stage in Scotland is to discuss general principles by referring the bill to the relevant subject committee which takes evidence as the 'lead' committee. Also, other committees relevant to the proposals (eg. subordinate legislation, equal opportunities and finance) are involved at this point. This procedure helps tackle the boundary disputes which arise when dealing with issues that cross conventional departmental boundaries.

[25] C Himsworth, 'Parliamentary Accountability: Aspiration or Reality' in C Jeffrey and J Mitchell (eds) *The Scottish Parliament 1999–2009: The First Decade*, (Edinburgh: Luath Press, 2009), 60.

[26] National Assembly Advisory Group, *National Assembly for Wales: A Consultation Paper* (1998) paras 5.7 and 5.12.

[27] R Rawlings *Delineating Wales: Constitutional, Legal and Administrative Aspects of National Devolution* (Cardiff: University of Wales Press, 2003), 109.

[28] P Birkinshaw, 'Regulating Information' in J Jowell and D Oliver (eds) *The Changing Constitution* (7th edn, Oxford: Oxford University Press, 2011), 377.

[29] See R Rawlings, 'Concordats of the Constitution' *LQR* (2000) 116: 257.

sketched out in varying degrees of detail to describe each of the respective systems of devolved government, featuring the main institutions and the disparate powers conferred on each administration[30]. The concordats amount to a form of codification of the processes of government which have been drawn up as the principal mechanism for policy coordination between central and devolved government and as such they arguably go beyond other similar systems.[31] In particular, these agreements seek to determine how issues of policy overlap between the tiers of government are to be approached and how any disputes which arise are to be resolved without resort to litigation. There is provision for a Joint Ministerial Committee (JMC) to act as the final arbiter for disputes. In regard to this discussion it is important to mention that disputed issues of financial allocation between central and devolved tiers of government can be resolved through these mechanisms. The task of coordination under the concordats is acted out by officials from central government, from the devolved administrations and occasionally politicians (in the case of the JMC on an irregular basis with representatives from the Westminster government and devolved governments) behind closed doors, often in Whitehall. This feature is viewed as a design flaw which undermines accountability. Professor Rawlings stresses that 'Characterized by a lack of transparency, machinery like the JMC constitutes a "black hole" at the heart of the emergent artchitecture of the Union state'. Moreover, these inter-governmental concordats are not subject to regular scrutiny by the Departmental Select Committees of the Westminster Parliament or by the subject committees at devolved level.[32]

In what is yet another example of multi-layering, the responsibility for auditing the spending of the Scottish Government and the executives in Wales and Northern Ireland has been placed in the hands of devolved auditing bodies. The Scotland Act 1998 requires the Scottish Parliament to establish effective scrutiny and audit arrangements with an Auditor General for Scotland and the requirement that Scottish Ministers prepare proper accounts with the standing orders providing for the consideration by the Parliament of accounts and reports.[33] There is explicit provision for audit, but at the same time reference to cross-border authorities with the intention of avoiding dual accounting. Assistant Auditor General, Russell Frith, said: 'The NFI (National Fraud Initiative) is a prime example of how the audit process can make a measurable difference for public bodies and the citizens they serve. While there are significant financial results from this exercise, it can also have a major impact in reducing fraud and error, and providing assurance to the public.... [These results suggest] previous NFIs have identified the most significant frauds and errors; the NFI is acting as a deterrent; and public bodies are improving

---

[30] See Scotland Act 1998, Government of Wales Act 1998, Northern Ireland Act 1998. Each statute might be regarded as equivalent to a constitution for the respective parts of the UK.

[31] See J Poirier, 'The Functions of Intergovernmental Agreements: Post-Devolution Concordats in a Comparative Perspective' *Public Law* [2001] 134–57, 135. This comparative study refers to the various roles of informal agreements in eg., Canada, Australia, Germany and Belgium, as well as describing the part played by concordats in the UK devolution arrangements: Rawlings, *Delineating Wales*, 392.

[32] Rawlings, *Delineating Wales*, 403.   [33] Scotland Act 1998, ss 69 and 70.

their systems.'[34] The NFI in Scotland is similar to exercises undertaken elsewhere in the UK. Accounting and auditing standards are not required where already imposed by other legislation. There are equivalent provisions for Wales[35] and Northern Ireland.[36] In Wales '[t]he work of the Audit Committee is especially noteworthy since it illustrates the official purpose in Welsh devolution of securing greater accountability. The model effectively involves patrialization of Westminster-type arrangements, which in turn allows for a sharper and more regular form of financial scrutiny in the conditions of small-country governance.'[37] It seeks to ensure the highest standards of management in financial affairs through checks on probity and value-for-money audits. Rawlings argues that 'the Audit Committee is another fine example of the interplay of the twin elements of continuity and change in the devolutionary development'.[38]

Finally, the courts have been granted a role in policing the boundaries of devolution, but to date the judicial contribution dealing with 'devolution issues' has been of limited significance for intergovernmental disputes.[39] Nevertheless, in the recent *Axa Case*[40] the UK Supreme Court considered the status of legislation at the devolved level. The case amounted to a challenge to the legislative competence of the Scottish Parliament. Some insurance companies sought to test the validity of the Damages (Asbestos-related Conditions) (Scotland) Act 2009 which allowed victims of asbestos-related conditions to pursue actions for personal injury in the Scottish courts. The lawfulness and legitimate aim of this statute was challenged. On final appeal the Supreme Court acknowledged that insurance companies were victims and that the possessions of the insurance companies were interfered with by the Act, but the attempt to challenge the lawfulness and legitimate aim of the statute was rejected. In Lord Hope's view, the function of a modern legislature in eliminating what it perceived as an injustice had a reasonable foundation. It had been argued that it was simply disproportionate to expect the insurance industry to bear what it believed to be an excessive and unfair burden of compensation, but it was recognized by the court that there were limiting factors implicit in the legislation which mitigated the effect: namely, that exposure to compensation arose only if the employer's negligence were established and defences were available.

The challenge on common law grounds also failed. The Supreme Court had to consider whether in principle irrationality was available as a ground for reviewing legislation at the devolved level. The assumption was that an Act of the Scottish Parliament was so unreasonable that no reasonable Parliament would enact it. It was held that legislative decisions that were made on political grounds could not be challenged on grounds of rationality, but at the same time it was recognized that some sort of final judicial safeguard should be available. While judges should not be able to substitute their views on such issues, the Scottish Parliament should not be regarded as totally immune from challenge. The courts should be able to intervene in exceptional

---

[34] Audit Scotland, News Release, 31 May 2012.   [35] Government of Wales Act 1998, ss 90–103.
[36] Northern Ireland Act 1998, ss 64 and 65.   [37] Rawlings, *Delinneating Wales*, 227–8.
[38] Rawlings, *Delinneating Wales,* 229.
[39] See G Gee, 'Devolution and the Courts' in R Hazell and R Rawlings (eds) *Devolution, Law Making and the Constitution* (Exeter: Imprint Academic, 2005), 266.
[40] *AXA General Insurance Ltd, Petitioners* [2011] UKSC 46, paras 32, 42, 52.

circumstances. If a Scottish government were to use its legislative power to abolish the right to judicial review or to diminish the role of the courts in protecting the interests of the individual, in principle the courts would be capable of intervening.

In this section we have seen that devolution creates an institutional framework of democratically elected government at sub-national level with its own account-ability mechanisms, while also establishing a modified interface between central government and the devolved administrations. Although the respective devolution statutes place legal limits on devolved powers with ultimate resort to the courts, in practice, there has been a strong preference for the use of soft law methods such as concordats to achieve policy coordination and to resolve disputes between central and devolved government.

C. The oversight of devolution finance by the Westminster Parliament

When devolution was launched, Professor Bogdanor wrote that: 'Finance is the spinal cord of devolution, for it is the financial arrangements which will largely determine the degree of autonomy enjoyed by the devolved administrations; the financial settlement, therefore, will exert a dominant influence on whether the aims of devolution are sustained or frustrated.'[41] However, when viewed from the perspec-tive of the financial arrangements which underpin devolution, the procedures for distribution and oversight have been only partially modified to take account of the changes that devolution brought in its wake. Formally, Scotland has been different from the outset.[42] After the devolution referendum in 1997[43] had delivered a decisive affirmative vote to both Scotland having a devolved Parliament (74.3 per cent) and a Parliament with tax-varying powers (63.5 per cent), the Scotland Act 1998 included the power to vary the rate of Scottish income by up to 3p in the pound.[44] This tax-varying power has never been used, which has meant that the base level of devolution-funding was established by Westminster under the block grant referred to as the Barnett Formula. Since the inception of devolution in 1999, this Formula has provided a stable financial basis for devolution. Lord Barnett has acknowl-edged that his Formula was originally set up under the Labour government in the mid-1970s to allow diverse spending levels between the various parts of the UK to reflect a range of variables. They included: population scarcity; transport needs; relative levels of ill health; rural needs for education; and industrial needs.[45] As a block-grant formula, Barnett is not, however, technically a needs-based formula. Rather, it is calculated according to the change in planned spending in departments in England.

---

[41] V Bogdanor *Devolution in the United Kingdom* (Oxford: Oxford University Press, 1999), 235.
[42] No equivalent provision was present in the Government of Wales Act 1998 or the Northern Ireland Act 1998.
[43] See the Referendums (Scotland and Wales) Act 1997.
[44] See Scotland Act 1998, Pt IV.
[45] R Twigger, 'The Barnett Formula', Research Paper 98/8, House of Commons Library, 12 January 1998.

Under Barnett, the devolved administrations receive the amount allocated in the previous year, plus or minus a population-based share of changes to similar UK government spending for England. The Formula is based on calculating the changed spending level in England which is then calculated according to a given fraction for Scotland, Wales and Northern Ireland. If there are changes to the spending plans for the English programmes in the same policy domain, then a fixed proportion is added to or subtracted from the amount allocated. These proportions are population-based.[46] Since the 1998 Comprehensive Spending Review, for the purposes of this calculation the spending of all UK spending departments (Whitehall departments and the devolved administrations) is divided between the Departmental Expenditure Limit (DEL) and Annually Managed Expenditure (AME) budgets. DEL public expenditure is that which can be planned and controlled on a three-yearly basis through spending reviews. This calculation applies to the cost of providing services which can be reasonably predicted: typically education, health and transport. On the other hand, AME expenditure is public expenditure which varies according to external circumstances and cannot reasonably be subject to firm multi-year limits. The main categories of domestic AME spending comprise social security benefits and Ministry of Defence spending. The Barnett Formula applies only to spending that is territorially identifiable and forms part of a DEL. While the stability guaranteed by a secure financial underpinning should be regarded as a key positive feature, the lack of any built-in correlation between taxation and spending (or financial accountability to voters) has often been presented as the fundamental weakness of devolution.[47]

Given that issues of funding for regional, devolved or federal government in other jurisdictions are frequently matters of political controversy, often requiring final settlement in the courts, it is next worth viewing the issue of accountability for the Barnett Formula from the standpoint of existing scrutiny procedures at Westminster. Each year there is a spending review by central government and the amounts set aside for devolution form part of the review. After it has been calculated by the Treasury as part of the annual parliamentary financial procedure by which Parliament votes to make monies available for general disbursement by government, the amount allocated for devolution under the Barnett Formula makes up part of the consolidated fund. The consolidated fund bill is presented to Parliament annually and its approval provides Parliamentary authority for funds requested by the government.[48] The proceedings on this bill are formal and governed by a parliamentary convention which dictates

---

[46] For the 2007 Comprehensive Spending Review, the Welsh population as a proportion of England's was 5.84 per cent. Since the comparability percentage for transport was 68.3 per cent, if £1 billion were to be added to transport across England, then £39.9 million (£1bn x 0.0584 x 0.683) would be added to the Welsh assigned budget. See E Roy, 'The Barnett Formula: funding the devolved administrations', National Assembly of Wales, Paper number: 09/012/ER.

[47] See eg. *Serving Scotland Better: Scotland and the United Kingdom in the 21st Century, Final Report-June 2009*, 3.86; *First Report: Funding devolved government in Wales: Barnett and beyond, July 2009*, paras 1.4–1.6.

[48] The Consolidated Fund Bill authorizes provision sought in the Winter Supplementary Estimates and New Estimates and in the Vote on Account.

that there is never any debate on the consolidated fund.[49] Once passed, the bill authorizes the release of money from the consolidated fund which is, in effect, the government's bank account.[50]

While there is a virtual absence of parliamentary scrutiny at this point in the financial cycle, there is provision for resolution of disputes about funding allocations from Westminster. First, there is consultation between the Chief Secretary to the Treasury and the devolved executives before his statement of funding policy is issued. The dispute resolution procedure comes into play for resolving disputes on all financial matters if there is disagreement between Treasury ministers and devolved administrations about changes to the statement, or about any aspect of its application to determining funding. This procedure for resolving disputes on all financial issues at devolved level mirrors the arrangements between the Treasury and UK departments. The relevant devolved administration or secretary of state can first pursue the issue with Treasury ministers. As a last resort, any such matters can be raised for resolution at the Joint Ministerial Committee (as explained above) which will include the relevant ministers and officials from the UK government and ministers and officials from the devolved administrations.[51]

From the perspective of the Westminster Parliament, it is widely recognized that Departmental Select Committees of the House of Commons which shadow the main departments of state perform an important role in delivering oversight of the executive.[52] The Scottish Affairs Committee, Welsh Affairs Committee and Northern Ireland Affairs Committee have undertaken this role over the Scottish, Welsh and NI Offices since 1999 rather than for devolved responsibilities which now fall under the remit of the Scottish Parliament or the Assemblies in Cardiff or Belfast.[53] However, no attempt has been made to raise the issue of the supply estimates or detailed budgeting questions about the devolved executives. The official position is that these committees do not have a formal remit over other UK departments, including the Treasury. In practice, this limitation does not prevent Departmental Select Committees from initiating wide-ranging inquiries on matters affecting Scotland, Wales and Northern Ireland. The Scottish Affairs Committee in the course of reviewing the general effectiveness of devolution has asked questions on the annual spending review conducted by the Treasury which forms the basis for

---

[49] In any event, the House of Lords is expressly prevented from intervening in money bills since the passage of the Parliament Act 1911.

[50] P McEldowney, 'The Control of Public Expenditure' in J Jowell and D Oliver (eds) *The Changing Constitution* (7th edn, Oxford: Oxford University Press, 2011), 342.

[51] HM Treasury, 'Funding the Scottish Parliament, National Assembly for Wales and Northern Ireland Assembly: Statement of Funding Policy', October 2007, 29. This summarizes the process drawn up in concordats between HM Treasury and the devolved administrations.

[52] See A Tomkins, 'What is Parliament for?' in N Bamforth and P Leyland (eds) *Public Law in a Multi-Layered Constitution* (Oxford: Hart Publishing, 2003); M Russell ' "Never Allow a Crisis Go to Waste": The Wright Committee Reforms to Strengthen the House of Commons' *Parliamentary Affairs*, Vol 64, No 4, 2011, 612–33.

[53] The Public Accounts Committee assisted by the National Audit Office looks retrospectively to see if money has been wisely spent by central government, including the residual departments for Scotland, Wales and Northern Ireland, but it no longer has jurisdiction over funding allocated to the devolved executives.

the computation of the Barnett Formula. The reply of the Scottish Officer Minister confirmed that: 'In the course of the Spending Review one of the outcomes is that decisions are taken on spending programmes of United Kingdom departments. These are the key components of the consequentials from which will be calculated the Scottish budget. We, and indeed the Scottish Executive, have access to those figures to make sure that a fair share is coming to Scotland.'[54] Furthermore, the Scottish Office provided supplementary data from the spending review to the committee, which allowed the calculation of the Barnett Formula to be replicated.[55] The investigation by the Northern Ireland Affairs Committee into the possible effects of reducing corporation tax on the economy in Northern Ireland provides a more recent example of a Departmental Select Committee addressing financial questions about devolution.[56]

D. Financial autonomy and the Barnett Formula

The main task in this section is to evaluate the strategies for addressing the relative absence of financial autonomy in the allocation of devolution funding and the consequent accountability implications for subnational forms of government. The Scottish variable rate has never been used because of political reasons. A party promising to tax more heavily, even if it were to increase the services on offer, was likely to lose popularity and support at the ballot box, and besides, there was no need to pursue this course as long as the Barnett Formula ensured Scotland received relatively generous funding. The same basic reasoning applies to Wales and Northern Ireland. Indeed, the continuation of the same financial arrangements for more than a decade masked the impact of devolution both in England and in Scotland, Wales and Northern Ireland. Until recently the effects of devolution were barely noticed south of the border with a lack of public controversy over financial matters[57], but since 2009 there have been important official reviews of the financing of devolution, mainly triggered by growing dissatisfaction with the Barnett Formula. The original devolution settlement limited the action the Scottish Parliament could take in a number of significant areas, and the Welsh and NI Assemblies operated under similar constraints.[58] The Calman Commission was set up by the opposition parties in the Scottish Parliament (Labour, Lib Dem, Conservative) to recommend changes to existing constitutional arrangements and to improve the financial accountability of the Scottish Parliament (within the UK), but all the main political parties in Scotland, including the SNP, favoured some

---

[54] See Scottish Affairs Select Committee, Session 2001–02, 7 November 2001, question 68.

[55] See David Heald and Alasdair McLeod (2002), 'Public Expenditure', in *Constitutional Law, 2002, The Laws of Scotland: Stair Memorial Encyclopaedia*, Edinburgh, Butterworths, 'The origins and role of the Barnett Formula', para.530.

[56] *Corporation Tax in Northern Ireland: First Report of Session 2010–12, Volume 1,* HC 558–1.

[57] D McCrone, 'Conundrums and Contradictions: What Scotland wants' in C Jeffery and J Mitchell *The Scottish Parliament 1999–2009: The First Decade*, Hansard Society, 2010, p.111.

[58] B Crawford, 'Ten Years of Devolution' *Parliamentary Affairs* Vol 63, No 1, 2010, 89–97 at 95.

change to devolution financing.[59] In similar fashion, the Holtham Commission was established by the Welsh Assembly Government to provide an independent assessment of the merits of current funding arrangements for Wales. It reported in the summer of 2010, finding that Barnett was now the 'random outcome of formula driven increments, unforeseen population movements and ad hoc adjustments'.[60] More transparency in this process was required to allow for direct comparison annually on similar expenditure. In sum, the debate was no longer about whether change is needed, but what form that change should take. Although a consensus is lacking on the precise mechanism to adopt, there appears to be agreement that Barnett is flawed and should be replaced.

In principle, there is general recognition across these studies that to improve accountability the Barnett Formula should eventually be replaced by a needs-based formula of some kind.[61] The incremental approach adopted under Calman and Holtham[62] acknowledges that the Barnett Formula must remain in place until a mechanism is conceived to provide for the equitable assessment of need. Moreover, there are further parallels when considering the institutional shape of a new body charged with responsibility for assessing the relative wealth of the devolved parts of the UK, which would take account of, for instance, local geography, transport, health requirements and social security. The objective is to find a solution which seeks to avoid routine haggling over the allocation of such financial provision. While far from being an exact parallel, the example of the Australian Commonwealth Grants Commission is often cited as an independent expert body performing this kind of role.[63] It advises the federal government in Australia with terms of reference framed by the Commonwealth Treasurer after consultation with the states and the territories. Crucial to that operation is that its impartiality is accepted by the states and the territories and the fact that the Commission's advice has always been accepted by the federal government without hesitation. The Commission could serve as a model for a new UK funding commission operating as an independent body at arm's length from the Treasury and from the devolved administrations.[64] Holtham goes so far as to suggest the English local government funding criteria should be applied to Wales based on: (i) relative needs; (ii) relative resources; (iii) central allocations; (iv) 'damping'.[65] A UK funding commission designed as an independent quango has the potential to make an important contribution to the complex task of needs assessment, but giving such a non-directly accountable

---

[59] para.68.
[60] *Funding devolved government in Wales: Barnett and Beyond, Independent Commission on Funding and Finance for Wales*, July 2009 at 6.3.
[61] B Hadfield, 'Devolution: A National Conversation' in J Jowell and D Oliver (eds) *The Changing Constitution* (Oxford: Oxford University Press, 2011), 221.
[62] Holtham argued there should be no further convergence in relative funding per head until a new funding system is in place.
[63] *First Evidence from the Independent Expert Group to the Commission on Scottish Devolution*, Pt 3: *Some experiences from around the World*, November 2008, 31ff.
[64] Serving Scotland Better: Scotland and the United Kingdom in the 21st Century, Final Report, June 2009, para.3.31.
[65] Funding devolved government in Wales: Barnett and Beyond, Independents Commission on Funding and Finance for Wales, July 2009.

body the final say in determining devolution funding priorities would be a much more controversial step. Holtham also envisages that concordats would remain the principal mechanism for coordinating financial policy between Westminster and the devolved administrations. It recommends that the UK government and the Assembly Government should jointly agree a new ministerial concordat on the detailed funding arrangements for Wales.[66]

In its overall assessment of the Barnett Formula, the House of Lords Select Committee commended its 'simplicity, stability and the absence of ring-fencing' as crucial characteristics which should be maintained whatever the future method of allocating funds to the devolved administrations.[67] The process associated with Barnett may give rise to opaque decision-making and warrant clearer application, but notwithstanding drawbacks the Formula has been the accepted basis for the foundation and continuation of devolution by both the Westminster government and the devolved governments.[68] This package was the deal on the table as devolution was launched. Given the recent trend in favour of referendums, it could be argued that a change to one of the accepted fundamentals of devolution by a needs-based replacement package should first receive popular approval from the local electorate. A radical change of the financial parameters has the potential to open up endless disputation and perhaps contribute to the eventual break of the UK. The introduction of a fiscal federalism in Italy, as a form of devolved taxation, has been perceived as being fundamentally divisive.[69] Despite its shortcomings, the Barnett Formula has acted as a crucial unifying ingredient of devolution precisely because it has tended to minimize conflict between Westminster and the devolved administrations.

E. The Scotland Act 2012: linking taxation and spending

The central recommendations of the Calman Commission about the introduction of a significant element of linkage between taxation and spending in Scotland have been enacted by the Scotland Act 2012.[70] For the adoption of new forms of locally raised funding, Calman discussed not only the respective strengths and weaknesses of several forms of taxation, but also whether the options were viable in the scale of revenue raised and whether they would be perceived as fair. Devolving corporation tax was advocated by some presenting evidence to the Commission on the grounds it might be used to promote a more competitive business environment in Scotland

---

[66] *Funding devolved government in Wales*, July 2009.

[67] 'The Barnett Formula', The House of Lords Select Committee on the Barnett Formula, 1st Report of Session 2008–09, HL Paper 139 at para.51.

[68] I McLean *What's Wrong with the British Constitution* (Oxford: Oxford University Press, 2009), 171.

[69] P Leyland, ' "Fiscal Federalism" and Reforming the Financial Parameters of Devolution: Italy and the UK compared' *Percorsi costituzionali*, Rubbetino, Anno II, 2009, 239–49.

[70] Scotland Act 2012, Pt 3, s 80A, to set a rate of income tax to be paid by Scottish Taxpayers, and under s 80B the power to add new devolved taxes.

but on the other hand such a change might have detrimental consequences for the remainder of the UK.[71] In addition, there was evidence that it would raise only limited revenue, and in any case corporation tax is not paid by individual voters so this change would not help address the core issues: namely, the relationship between taxation and spending, and accountability. Another proposal would have been to allow different rates of excise duty, but this change was rejected as it was likely to create incentives for tax avoidance.[72] The scope for changing the level of VAT at devolved level is further constrained by EU law.[73]

A new Scottish rate of income tax which will be charged on the non-savings income of Scottish taxpayers from 2016 is the most important change under the Scotland Act 2012.[74] The rate paid will be calculated by reducing the basic, higher and additional rates of income tax levied by the UK government on Scottish tax-payers by 10 pence in the pound.[75] The block-grant allocation under the Barnett Formula, or any needs-based formula which eventually replaces it, will be adjusted downwards to allow for the revenue raised under the Scottish income tax. Under these arrangements, if spending levels remain as they are, the financial allocation will remain more or less at a parity with existing levels. However, the Scottish Parliament, by adjusting the Scottish rate, will be able to raise as much or as little in income tax as it wishes. This new power places in the hands of the Scottish Parliament a progressive tax which is earnings-related and thus fair in the sense that the amount paid is related to the capacity of individual taxpayers to pay it.

In addition, it was envisaged by Calman that the Scottish Parliament would have the power to introduce new taxes applying in Scotland, but only with the consent of the Westminster Parliament.[76] Calman recognized that the taxes most suitable for devolving would be those with a fixed tax base.[77] In line with this recommendation, stamp duty, landfill tax and the aggregates levy have now been devolved to the Scottish Parliament under the Scotland Act 2012.[78] However, the yield of such taxes is likely to be modest, with a contribution of around 2 per cent of the total of tax receipts in Scotland.[79] Finally, the recommendation that Scottish ministers should be granted additional borrowing powers has been included in the Scotland Act 2012. It is estimated that, following the introduction of these changes, 35 per cent of revenue in Scotland will be raised locally. If spending levels

---

[71] *Evidence from the Independent Expert Group to the Commission on Scottish Devolution*, 2009, para 6.15.

[72] Ibid, para.5.3.

[73] Ibid, para.7.5.

[74] See Scotland Act 2012. A new Scottish rate of income tax which will be charged on the non-savings income of Scottish taxpayers.

[75] 'Clarifying the Scope of the Scottish Rate of Income Tax', HM Revenue and Customs, Technical Note, May 2012.

[76] *Serving Scotland Better: Scotland and the United Kingdom in the 21st Century, Final Report,* June 2009, Recommendation 3.1–3.7.

[77] *Serving Scotland Better*, Recommendation 3.2.

[78] Air passenger duty falls into this category of taxation and could be added at a later date.

[79] *Evidence from the Independent Expert Group to the Commission on Scottish Devolution*, 2009 para. 7.6.

were to be increased in Scotland, there is now an assumption that any funding shortfall would be met by increased revenue raised at the local level.

The challenges of multi-layered governance necessarily give rise to the technical questions of tax collection and distribution.[80] This related issue has arisen because the Scotland Act 2012 provides for the levying of a proportion of income tax at the devolved level.[81] Since the variable tax rate was never implemented post 1999, no distinct mechanism was introduced to perform this task. During the passage of the 2012 Act through Parliament, the government set up a High Level Implementation Group (HLIG), jointly chaired by the Exchequer Secretary and the Secretary of State for Scotland, but with input from the relevant representative devolved bodies, to implement the introduction of the Scottish rate.[82] The 2012 Act empowers the Scottish Parliament to raise stamp duty on the purchase and leasing of land and a landfill tax from April 2015.[83] The Scottish government has announced that these taxes will be collected locally by a new Scottish tax body. When there are severe cuts in public expenditure in England and questions over the viability of fiscal autonomy for Scotland, the introduction of a new customized Scottish quango to collect relatively modest amounts of taxation might be regarded as an unnecessary duplication of resources.[84]

There is a sense in which this otherwise significant development, which goes a considerable way towards incorporating financial accountability and thereby correcting one of the perceived deficiencies of Scottish devolution, runs the risk of being swamped by wider political events. A referendum on the issue of independence is scheduled for September 2014. The SNP is seeking full control of the economic levers of an independent country.[85] The Scotland Act 2012 has been attacked by the SNP because it fails to transfer adequate fiscal powers to the Scottish Parliament. It maintains that the Scottish government is unable to create a competitive tax structure, boost growth, provide the necessary fiscal stimulus, and tackle Scotland's 'economic underperformance' in the long term.[86] Although other constitutional models of devolved governance can be cited by expert commentators to support or refute demands for greater fiscal autonomy[87], the extent to which the Scottish

---

[80] 'HMRC could veto any new Holyrood tax plans' *The Herald*, 31 May 2012.

[81] It is assumed the Scottish rate of income will be administered by the HMRC for Scottish taxpayers.

[82] 'Clarifying the Scope of the Scottish Rate of Income Tax' HM Revenue and Customs, Technical Note, May 2012, paras 17–19.

[83] Scotland Act 2012, section 25 which amends section 80 of the SA 1998.

[84] A Midwinter 'Fiscal Autonomy in Scotland: an assessment and critique' *Public Money and Management* (2012) 32:1, 49–52.

[85] In a multi-levelled system, this objective may be problematic. Currently, the SNP is committed to retaining the pound in the event of support in the referendum for Scottish independence. Not having control over key aspects of financial policy would appear to conflict with the demand for 'full control' of fiscal policy.

[86] This view is strongly contested in some quarters: 'Scotland's economic performance is better than the SNP suggests, and their analysis is superficial. It rests wholly on a single, partial economic indicator, Gross Domestic Product...' See A Midwinter, 'Fiscal autonomy in Scotland: an assessment and critique' *Public Money and Management* (2012), 49–52, 51.

[87] I Docherty and R MacDonald, 'Debate: Scotland's fiscal options–a response to Midwinter' *Public Money and Management* (2012) 32: 3, 161–163, 163. Eg. the regeneration in the Basque region can be related to the devolved corporation tax impacting on economic growth.

Parliament acquires such fiscal powers comes down to a political choice which will ultimately depend on whether there is popular support in a referendum for the status quo ante under the Scotland Act 2012 or for an independent Scotland. While side-stepping the politics of independence, the grant of full fiscal autonomy for Scotland under what has been termed 'devolution-max' would presumably mean the Scottish Parliament would set, and the Scottish government collect, all taxes in Scotland, remitting to London an amount to cover the cost of common UK public services.[88] There is an equally good case for modifying the arrangements for devolution in Wales and Northern Ireland to include a similar element of taxation and spending to the one due to be introduced under the Scotland Act 2012.[89]

F. Financial accountability of sub-national government and the welfare state

This final section argues that the overall financial policy which has been applied to devolution and to local government by central government can be viewed as two contradictory trends which comprise part of a meta-narrative of the contemporary multi-layered constitution.[90] To put it at its most basic, on the one hand, devolved government has been given latitude to determine how budgets are spent, while on the other, local government has faced increasing financial restraint at the hands of central government. If this dichotomy is viewed from a wider focus which also takes account of the effect of the radical cuts in public expenditure, it becomes clear that not only are both these trends called into question, but so are certain assumptions about the nature of a nationwide welfare state and the form of local and devolved governance as part of the state.

The first policy that has applied to all three devolved systems since they were established has permitted a high degree of autonomy in the manner in which funding is allocated by the devolved administration. Once the amount has been calculated under the Barnett Formula, the sum made available can be distributed according to preferences decided at the devolved level. As Keating explains: 'Scotland's financial settlement is unusual in international comparison, since it combines a transfer of accounting of the whole of the Executive's spending with complete freedom of

---

[88] See eg. Swinney, 'Opportunities for Scotland's economy' <http://www.snp.org/blog/post/2012/jun/swinney-opportunities-scotlands-economy> (accessed April 2013).

[89] The Silk Commission on Devolution in Wales was established in October 2011 by the Secretary of State for Wales to review the case for the devolution of fiscal powers to the National Assembly of Wales and to review the powers of National Assembly for Wales. See the report: *Empowerment and Resonsibility: Financial Powers to Strengthen Wales*, Commission on Devolution in Wales, November 2012.

[90] Bailey and Elliott also point to this distintion between, on the one hand, local government which is treated as an object of central government policy where intervention is frequent, substantial and acceptable and, on the other, devolution which is not regarded as manipulable by the centre. See S Bailey and M Elliott, 'Taking local government seriously: democracy, autonomy and the constitution' *CLJ* (2009) 455.

allocation.'[91] The same principle applies to Wales and Northern Ireland. Where a devolved administration decides to pursue a policy different from that followed or approved of by Westminster, it cannot be financially constrained from doing so. This flexibility has permitted significant policy divergence as compared with England. For instance, with residential care for the elderly, the Scottish Parliament has decided to provide a general entitlement to such care considerably beyond that available in the remainder of the UK.[92] As a result of devolution, the non-English parts of the Kingdom have been able to develop their own distinctive priorities in public policy.

In contrast, the second policy-trend has been a concern to limit strictly the financial autonomy afforded to local government, particularly in England and Wales.[93] The objective of successive governments, at least since 1979 and continuing right up to the present with the Localism Act 2011, has been to impose increasing control over local government expenditure by a variety of means. Moreover, the character of local democracy has been modified by the straitjacket imposed on it. Professor King claims there is a reluctance: 'to admit that local government has all but ceased to exist... The effect, inevitably, has been to diminish the role that political parties and democratic elections play in the government, or the governance of localities'.[94] Viewed from a historical standpoint, the consequences of what Loughlin describes as 'the Benthamite principle of utility dressed in the modern garb of value-for-money'[95] has to be confronted. The centre has become wedded to the single-minded pursuit of austerity and efficiency, and has constructed a rule-based regime to ensure particular types of policy delivery. This central priority has impacted on local government in the sense that it comes to be viewed purely as an instrumental agency to deliver central government's objectives. The overall effects of the programmes of rate-capping, compulsory competitive tendering and best-value dating back to 1979 have been cumulative. They add up to the progressive emasculation of local democracy through the imposition of centralization by a range of legislative initiatives with central-local relations reconstructed in much more explicitly hierarchical terms.[96]

The need for increased financial accountability has been *the* pretext employed by successive governments for these initiatives. Professor Leigh observes that: 'A recurrent plea from bodies recommending reform is to decrease local government dependence on central grant'.[97] The corollary for any such aspirations is to deliver reforms of local government finance which shift the balance away from a

---

[91] M Keating, 'Policy Convergence and Policy Divergence in Scotland under Devolution' *Regional Studies*, Vol 39.4 pp 453–63, June 2005, p.459.

[92] See, eg. A Bowes and D Bell, 'Free Personal Care for Older People in Scotland: Issues and Implications' *Social Policy and Society* (2007), 6:3: 435–45.

[93] The same trend was discernible in Scotland.

[94] A King *The British Constitution* (Oxford: Oxford University Press, 2007), 175.

[95] M Loughlin *Legality and Locality: The Role of Law in Central-Local Government Relations* (Oxford: Clarendon Press, 1996), 75.

[96] M Loughlin *Legality and Locality*, 417.

[97] I Leigh *Law, Politics and Democracy* (Oxford: Oxford University Press, 2000), 113.

dependence on central government and at the same time embed a fundamental linkage between taxation and spending at local government level. Professor Jones argued during the parliamentary stages of the Localism Bill in 2011 that: 'There is a huge gap in the Bill; a Localism Bill that lived up to its name would have dealt with the financing of local government. Centralism will prevail as long as local authorities are massively dependent for their resources on central government. They become supplicants for funding from central government rather than engaging in a dialogue with their citizens about local priorities'.[98] The trend towards centralism under the coalition will not be confined to this measure. The distribution of funding by central government under the Local Government Finance Act 2012 has been defended by the Westminster government on the basis that the department is better placed to redistribute the revenue in order to support the less economically buoyant parts of the country. Nevertheless, this bill which seeks, among other things, to allow local retention of business rates has been criticized for giving the Secretary of State for Communities and Local Government the power to decide the share of these rates which will be channelled back to local authorities.[99]

While the Localism Act 2011 steps back from a policy based crudely upon rate-capping, the Act in other ways reinforces the powers of central government to control expenditure and taxation at the local government level. The capacity for municipal governance to express itself as a purveyor of the 'big-society' vision rings hollow when faced with the prospect of central government intervention to keep local authorities within centrally determined expenditure and taxation limits. The 2011 Act provides that referendums may be used as a means of controlling expenditure by the Secretary of State for Communities and Local Government.[100] Local authorities are placed under a statutory duty to determine whether the council tax they propose to levy is 'excessive' according to principles set by central government. The referendum requirement arises where an authority proposes to sets council tax at a level higher than that permitted under the principles formulated by the Secretary of State. Under the new procedure, before the referendum is held the authority is required to calculate an alternative budget which complies with the criteria set by the secretary of state. If the result of the referendum favours the council, the original 'excessive' budget will be introduced. On the other hand, if the council's favoured budget is not approved by the local electorate in the referendum, the substitute budget will take effect in its place.[101] If a rise that is regarded as excessive according to the government's criteria is proposed, the council must make arrangements to hold a referendum. The crucial point is that the secretary of state is empowered to set the parameters for determining whether a proposed increase in council tax is deemed to be 'excessive'. In effect, the referendum requirement is triggered, albeit indirectly, by the judgment of the secretary of state.[102] By this mechanism the Localism Act 2011 keeps the purse strings

---

[98] Professor George Jones: <http://blogs.lse.ac.uk/politicsandpolicy/2011/03/11/localism-bill-and-centralism>.

[99] Local Government Finance Act 2012, cl.1; See Local Government Finance Bill 2012–13 Bill No 4, 2012–13, Research Paper 12/24, 16 May 2012, 2–4.

[100] Localism Act 2011, Sch.5, 52ZB.   [101] Localism Act 2011, Sch.5, 52 ZH.

[102] Localism Act 2011, s 72 and Sch., 52ZC.

in the hands of the minister and it grants local authorities very limited financial autonomy in setting their own annual budget.

These potentially conflicting trends have not been reconciled with another fundamental assumption which has underpinned the welfare state from its inception: the recognition of a relatively uniform base level of consistency in service provision applying to policy areas such as health, pensions and other welfare benefits. The welfare state was founded on the principle that the needs of the citizen should be determined, not on a geographical basis, but by central government, which is uniquely placed to balance the requirements of different parts of the kingdom. Professor Bogdanor claims: 'What cannot be denied is that devolution threatens the power of the government of the UK to secure equal social rights for all of its citizens. It is difficult to see how the state can secure these equal rights if has been fragmented and cut into pieces by devolution'.[103] The calculation of the devolution block grant relies on funding levels in England. The use of the Barnett Formula as the method for allocating funding to the devolved parts of the UK has survived to date because it has guaranteed relatively generous rates of funding for Scotland, Wales and Northern Ireland. The prospect of replacing the Barnett Formula by needs-based arrangements is called into question by the regime of cuts which is currently being introduced. Against this background it would be difficult to justify a relatively generous baseline level of funding allocation for a needs-based system. This problem would be fundamental for any funding body to confront. It raises the prospect of regular conflict on the annual determination of block-grant funding by the Treasury. Alternatively, if the Westminster government were to legislate to ring-fence categories of funding on a national basis, such provisions might restrict the scope of devolved government to pursue distinctive policies in accordance with preferences in the devolved parts of the nation.

This tendency towards fragmentation is accentuated by the Localism Act 2011. The 'big-society' initiative which lies behind the legislation is an attempt by the coalition government to square the circle of further reducing the role of the state. This diminution is to be achieved partly by new initiatives conferring a general power of competence on local authorities and stripping away their regulatory infrastructure, while at the same time requiring new forms of citizen participation involving what is termed civil society.[104] The problem is that the government is at the same time making substantial cutbacks in public expenditure, disproportionately so with local government, while stating a commitment in principle to health and social welfare.[105] The result will be that local government as an agency for policy delivery is undermined as it is faced with massive shortfalls in funding that occur because of Treasury-driven policies.[106]

---

[103] V Bogdanor, 'West Lothian Question' *Parliamentary Affairs* Vol 63, No 1, 2010, 156–72,171.

[104] See V Lowndes and L Pratchett, 'Local Governance under the Coalition Government: Austerity, Localism and the "Big Society"' *Local Government Studies*, Vol 38, No 1, 21–40, February 2012. 26.

[105] M J Smith, 'From Big Government to Big Society: Changing the State-Society Balance' *Parliamentary Affairs*, Vol 63, No 4, 2010, 818–33, 832.

[106] See also A Davies in this collection, who recognizes this point.

G. Conclusion

The evolving design of devolved institutions continues to be generated by political debate in Scotland, Wales and Northern Ireland and by the asymmetry of the original design with the conspicuous omission of any serious attempt to tackle the so-called 'English question'.[107] This chapter has argued that, although devolution introduces effective constitutional oversight at devolved level, together with mainly soft law approaches to coordinating policy between the layers of government, the relative lack of attention to the detailed financial arrangements has led to a number of problems which have been exacerbated by the current economic downturn. Having the Barnett Formula in place was a significant advantage when devolution was launched, because it not only provided a relatively generous distribution of funding to Scotland, Wales and Northern Ireland, but also prevented squabbling between Westminster and the devolved administrations over the size of the block grant. For the first time, the Scotland Act 2012 addresses the issue of relating tax raising and levels of spending in Scotland. It introduces a devolved tax regime by making provision for over a third of taxation to be raised locally. The piecemeal approach to devolution is illustrated here too, as there have been no similar proposals for Wales and Northern Ireland despite the parallels in powers and responsibilities, and accountability issues.

In response to increasing dissatisfaction with the Barnett Formula, other options have been investigated and in general terms recommendations to replace it with a needs-based system calculated by a new independent body have found support from the expert commissions looking into its replacement.[108] However, any fundamental departure from Barnett will inevitably provoke disputes over resource allocation which in turn will involve the contentious interpretation of complex economic and social indicators. The potential difficulty in achieving a new consensus as a starting point for a revised settlement accounts for the reluctance of politicians at Westminster to grasp this particular nettle. Finally, worsening economic conditions will also affect the conflicting meta-narrative which both restricted the spending of local authorities and allowed the devolved parts of the UK scope to pursue their own brands of policy. The fundamentals of the nationwide welfare state are under threat and the consequences will be confronted at the points closest to policy delivery: that is, by devolved government and by local government.

---

[107] See eg. R Hazell, 'Conclusion: What are the answers to the English Question' and M Russell and G Lodge 'The government of England by Westminster' in R Hazell (ed.) *The English Question* (Manchester: Manchester University Press, 2006).
[108] 'The Barnett Formula' The House of Lords Select Committee on the Barnett Formula, 1st Report of Session 2008–09, HL Paper 139 at para.72/73; *Serving Scotland Better: Scotland and the United Kingdom in the 21st Century,* Final Report—June 2009, para.3.31. *Funding devolved government in Wales: Barnett and Beyond,* Independents Commission on Funding and Finance for Wales, July 2009 at 6.3

PART V

14

Beyond New Public Management: Problems of Accountability in the Modern Administrative State

*A C L Davies**

A. Introduction

New Public Management (NPM) came to the fore under the Conservative governments of the 1980s and 1990s as a radical set of policy prescriptions for curing the perceived ills of the public sector. Its proponents argued that wasteful and unfriendly public services could be transformed by introducing traditionally private sector ideas such as contracts and competition. Instead of providing services, the government's role would be to purchase them from specialist providers, some in the public sector and some in the private sector. Contracts (or pseudo-contracts where both parties were in the public sector[1]) would be used to set targets for the cost and quality of the services to be delivered, and competition for government business would motivate providers, whether public or private, to meet their targets.

The relationship between NPM and the government's accountability for the delivery of public services was a complex and contested one. Its advocates argued that NPM would improve accountability in two main respects. First, government departments would have a clearer sense of what services they were providing and how much they cost. Better information would enhance politicians' accountability to the electorate. Second, NPM emphasized the direct accountability of public services to citizens and service users, who were often referred to (in private sector terminology) as 'consumers'. For example, a contract might require the provider to

* Garrick Fellow and Tutor in Law, Brasenose College, Oxford; Professor of Law and Public Policy, Oxford University. I am grateful to participants in the Accountability in the Contemporary Constitution conference and a workshop at Tilburg University, Netherlands, for their comments on an earlier draft of this paper. Responsibility for errors remains my own. This paper considers developments up to early January 2012.

[1] A term coined by C Harlow and R Rawlings, *Law and Administration* (2nd edn, London: Butterworths 1997), 210, to describe agreements used within government as if they were contracts but which were not legally enforceable as such, either because of specific statutory provisions to that effect or because the 'parties' did not have separate legal personality.

reduce the level of user complaints or, more radically, users themselves might be given the right to choose among possible providers of a particular public service. By contrast, the critics of NPM argued that the division of responsibility between government and contractors would create obstacles to accountability. Most obviously, if something went wrong, the government and the contractor might blame each other for the problem, making it difficult for Parliament or the electorate to determine where responsibility lay.

While the concept of NPM and the debate surrounding the accountability of public services delivered through NPM mechanisms are relatively familiar to public lawyers, there is much less awareness of how NPM has developed under the Labour governments from 1997–2010, and under the Conservative and Liberal Democrat coalition since 2010. Although NPM is particularly associated with Thatcherism, it has not been abandoned. Rather, it has continued to evolve in significant ways. In this chapter, it will be argued that while NPM in its original form did present some problems for accountability, it was broadly compatible with traditional understandings of the role of the state and the accountability of politicians to the electorate for the delivery of public services. The more recent evolutions of NPM—which have been the subject of much less public attention and scholarly analysis—are much more worrying from an accountability perspective because they call into question the very role of the government.

The chapter will proceed as follows. In Part B, we will examine the relationship between NPM and accountability by way of background. Part C will outline the evolution of NPM since 1997, focusing on the emergence of what will be termed 'deep' NPM—in which the government contracts out the purchasing of services as well as the provision of services—and 'post' NPM, where specialization in service provision is rejected in favour of grouping services together, both within and across public bodies. Part D offers the use of commissioning support in the National Health Service (NHS) as an example of deep NPM, and Part E considers recent reforms in local government as a case study of post NPM. Each illustration focuses in particular on the implications of these developments for accountability. Part F concludes.

B. NPM and accountability

Accountability expresses the simple idea that where one person acts on behalf of another, he or she should be prepared to 'account for' his or her activities.[2] For the purposes of analysis, it is usually best to think in terms of 'mechanisms' of accountability—the practical manifestation of accountability—rather than accountability as a desirable but vague goal.

---

[2] For a full discussion of accountability, see A C L Davies, *Accountability: A Public Law Analysis of Government by Contract* (Oxford: Oxford University Press, 2001), ch 4.

An accountability mechanism should generally involve four components: setting standards against which performance can be judged; collecting information about performance; judging the performance against the agreed standards; and applying any consequences such as incentives for good performance or sanctions for poor performance.[3] There are many factors involved in creating a successful account-ability mechanism. Firstly, and most obviously, the respective roles of the caller to account and the body being called to account must be clearly defined. Otherwise, the parties may become distracted by disputes about the operation of the account-ability mechanism itself. Secondly, the standards set must be realistic: otherwise the person discharging the responsibility may ignore them or seek strategies for 'creative compliance'.[4] Thirdly, it is important that the person calling to account is more powerful than the person being called to account. If the sanctions for a poor performance are weak, the accountability mechanism will not work effectively.[5]

Accountability mechanisms can be grouped in various ways. A popular classifica-tion focuses on the nature of the standards being applied.[6] This divides accountability mechanisms into categories such as legal, financial or political. So, for example, audit is a financial accountability mechanism, concerned with the efficient use of the public body's resources, whereas judicial review is a legal accountability mechanism con-cerned with the lawfulness of the public body's actions.

This chapter is particularly concerned with the accountability of those at the 'front line' of public service delivery, so for our purposes a more helpful approach is to divide accountability mechanisms into those which are 'internal' and 'external' to the public body.[7] 'Internal' mechanisms are those that enable people at the top of the public body in question (senior managers, councillors, ministers and so on) to call to account those who are directly involved in service delivery at the 'front-line'. 'External' mechanisms are those that enable interested parties outside the public body (MPs, citizens, service users) to call it to account.

External mechanisms can be sub-divided into two groups according to whether or not they are dependent on internal mechanisms for their effectiveness. So, for example, a complaints procedure for aggrieved service users allows members of the public to call the service provider to account for its performance directly, whereas when an MP asks the minister a question in Parliament, the answer will be fed to the minister through internal accountability mechanisms. It is sometimes tempting to suggest that failures in internal accountability mechanisms can be offset by direct external accountability from the service provider to service users: through com-plaints procedures, consultation exercises and citizens' panels, for example. Indeed, the idea of accountability up through the organizational hierarchy to ministers or councillors can sound rather old-fashioned. Nevertheless, it is an important aspect

---

[3] D Oliver, 'Law, Politics and Public Accountability: the Search for a New Equilibrium' *PL* [1994] 238, 246.

[4] D McBarnet, 'Law, Policy and Legal Avoidance: Can Law Effectively Implement Egalitarian Policies?' *Journal of Law and Society* (1988) 15: 113.

[5] Davies, *Accountability: A Public Law Analysis*, 84–5, n 2 above.

[6] See, eg., P Day and R Klein, *Accountabilities: Five Public Services* (London: Tavistock, 1987).

[7] Davies, *Accountability: A Public Law Analysis*, 77, n 2 above.

of the democratic governance of public services and should enable a broader perspective than just that of service users to be brought to bear on the evaluation of those services.

The difficulties surrounding NPM and direct *external* accountability mechanisms have been well-documented. A key feature of NPM was the more-or-less enthusiastic contracting out of public services. But once a service has been contracted out, it can often be unclear whether the contractor is subject to judicial review or Human Rights Act review at the suit of an aggrieved service user.[8] Where a service is provided in-house by a public body (in the traditional hierarchical way that prevailed prior to the emergence of NPM) public law scrutiny is, of course, always available. After contracting out, the availability of review turns on whether the contractor can be said to be performing a 'public function'.[9] The courts have concluded that where a contractor determines entitlement to use a particular service, it is performing a 'public function',[10] but if it is simply providing a service such as accommodation and meals, it is not.[11] Similarly, it is often argued that NPM limits access to the information needed for accountability mechanisms of various kinds to work effectively. For example, a Freedom of Information Act request for details about a particular contract is likely to be rejected on the grounds of the commercially sensitive nature of the information.[12]

However, from the perspective of *internal* accountability, NPM could be regarded— up to a point at least—as a positive development.[13] The shift from hierarchical management structures to contractual or pseudo-contractual relationships arguably introduced a more effective mechanism of accountability. The contract offered the potential to state in a clear way what standards were expected of the provider (an important starting-point for any accountability mechanism) both in terms of the contract price or budget for the services, and the quality of performance. Mechanisms for obtaining information from the contractor about performance could be specified in the contract. The prospect of deductions from the contract price offered new leverage for the public body in terms of ensuring compliance. And, in extreme circumstances, the possibility of losing the contract altogether to a competitor could act as a motivating force, although the extent to which competitive markets have emerged in practice for public services has varied considerably between sectors. In conceptual terms, the contractual or pseudo-contractual relationship slotted into the place vacated by the managerial hierarchy, but with potential advantages in terms of clarity and enforceability. This improved internal

---

[8] For critique, see P P Craig, 'Contracting Out, the Human Rights Act and the Scope of Judicial Review' *LQR* (2002) 118: 551; S Palmer, 'Public, Private and the Human Rights Act 1998: an Ideological Divide' *CLJ* (2007) 66: 559.

[9] Human Rights Act 1998, s. 6.

[10] *Poplar Housing & Regeneration Community Association Ltd v Donoghue* [2001] EWCA Civ 595; [2002] QB 48.

[11] *YL v Birmingham City Council* [2007] UKHL 27; [2008] 1 AC 95.

[12] Freedom of Information Act 2000, s. 43.

[13] Davies, *Accountability: A Public Law Analysis*, n 2 above.

accountability mechanism could then feed into the external accountability of ministers, councillors and others for the performance of public services.

Of course, there were problems. Any division of roles creates opportunities for blurred boundaries and the shifting of blame from one party to the other. In the central government context, one of the best known examples of this was the well-documented dispute between the Home Secretary and the head of the Prison Service Agency as to who was responsible for a series of prison escapes.[14] The Home Secretary blamed the agency head as the person with operational responsibility; the agency head blamed the government for failing to provide sufficient resources. This was exacerbated by the government's initial promotion of a very market-orientated version of NPM without recognizing that public service delivery contracts might not share all the characteristics of a contract for the supply of paper-clips.[15] Public bodies were encouraged to keep their suppliers at arm's length, and to assume that competition for contracts would offer the main mechanism for ensuring good performance. In practice, contracts for public service delivery are highly complex and are likely to be awarded for relatively long periods of time. They are 'relational', not 'discrete'.[16] Over time, it was recognized that public bodies needed to invest in contract management and in building good relationships with their contractors as part of the ongoing contractual accountability process.[17] Where problems arose, it was seen as more important to work together to find solutions, instead of trying to blame each other for what had happened.

With these modifications, it is possible to give a cautiously optimistic assessment of the effect of NPM on internal accountability and, indirectly, on some aspects of external accountability. The obvious culture clash between the public sector and the market was mitigated, but some of the advantages of contract over managerial hierarchy were retained. Although purchaser/provider splits inevitably involve some blurred boundaries, it was reasonably clear who was responsible for what. And public bodies were in charge of public services: they could specify what they wanted and they could get rid of poorly-performing contractors. Against this backdrop, we are now in a position to examine some of the latest trends in public service delivery.

C. The evolution of NPM since 1997

In many respects, the story of NPM since 1997 has been one of continuity. Successive governments of different political complexions have maintained purchaser/provider splits where they already existed, and have extended the policy to previously

---

[14] See C D Foster and F J Plowden, *The State Under Stress: Can the Hollow State be Good Government?* (Buckingham: Open University Press, 1996), 166–7, and A Tomkins, *The Constitution After Scott* (Oxford: Clarendon Press, 1998), ch 1, esp. 45–9.

[15] A C L Davies, *The Public Law of Government Contracts* (Oxford University Press, 2008), ch 7.

[16] The terminology is associated with I R Macneil, 'The Many Futures of Contracts' *S Cal LR* (1974) 691.

[17] HM Treasury, *Managing Risks with Delivery Partners* (2005), 3.

untouched areas of service provision. However, NPM has also developed in new directions that pose significant challenges for accountability.

1. Continuity

It might have been expected that a Labour government would oppose NPM on ideological grounds, but an important part of Labour's 'reinvention' as New Labour involved abandoning the party's traditional preference for public over private service provision, and adopting instead the 'third way' approach to politics as described by Giddens.[18] The 'third way' sought to draw on the strengths of both the public and the private sectors and was neatly captured in Tony Blair's mantra 'what counts is what works'.[19] Thus, the government continued to advocate the use of contracts and pseudo-contracts in the delivery of public services, and extended the approach into new sectors such as London Underground (through the ultimately unsuccessful Public Private Partnership for infrastructure maintenance).[20] Nevertheless, there were some subtle differences in the presentation and operation of NPM after 1997. In terms of rhetoric, the use of 'private sector' terminology was reduced significantly. For example, in the National Health Service, the term 'purchasing' was replaced with 'commissioning' in official documents. More importantly, there was much greater recognition that contracts or pseudo-contracts for public services should be regarded as long-term, relational arrangements with complex quality standards rather than short-term, discrete contracts for standard goods or services. The most obvious manifestation of this was the replacement of compulsory competitive tendering in local government with the 'Best Value' policy.[21] Local authorities were still encouraged to contract services out but they were allowed to make decisions based on quality and service design instead of being required to award the contract to the lowest bidder.

Since 2010, the Conservatives have returned to power in coalition with the Liberal Democrats. Although it is too early to form a settled view, the evidence so far suggests that—as might be expected—NPM techniques are likely to remain at the heart of the government's approach to public service delivery. A number of features of current government policy render NPM a particularly attractive model. Both coalition partners are committed, perhaps with slightly different ideological emphases, to the delegation of power to the local level and to public participation in decision-making.[22] The NPM approach of encouraging entrepreneurship and responsiveness to 'consumers' among those delivering public services fits well with these ideas. But perhaps most importantly, the substantial budget cuts required to address the deficit in public spending are generating an unprecedented need to do

---

[18] A Giddens, *The Third Way* (Cambridge: Polity, 1998).   [19] Labour Party manifesto, 1997.
[20] See Davies, *The Public Law of Government Contracts*, 23–4, n 15 above.
[21] Local Government Act 1999, and for discussion see P Vincent-Jones, 'Central-Local Relations under the Local Government Act 1999: a New Consensus?' *MLR* (2000) 63: 84.
[22] HM Government, *The Coalition: Our Programme For Government* (London: Cabinet Office, 2010), 8.

more with less. The proponents of NPM often present contracting out as a way of achieving this, because the government can set out its objectives and leave to potential bidders the task of developing innovative ways of meeting those objectives at a lower cost. Of course, critics argue that contractors will make savings by cutting corners, not least because private firms will want to extract a profit from the contract price.

2. New developments

NPM, then, is here to stay. But as governments and public bodies have made use of NPM techniques, they have also changed and developed those techniques in new directions. Here, we will introduce two of these new versions of NPM, labelling them deep NPM and post NPM.

Under NPM as originally conceived, the role of the state was to be the 'purchaser' of public services. Public bodies would be able to focus more clearly on determining what services were needed and on monitoring the quality of those services if they were freed from the distractions of provision. In the well-known boating metaphor coined by Osborne and Gaebler, the founding fathers of NPM, the state should 'steer' not 'row'.[23] In recent times, there has been a growing trend—which we will label 'deep' NPM—of contracting out some or all of the government's *purchasing* tasks in a particular sector. At its simplest, this involves using management consultants to assist with the procurement process. At its most complex, it might involve contracting out the procurement function altogether, an option currently under consideration by the Ministry of Defence.[24] Under deep NPM, the purchaser side of the purchaser/provider split is also split (to varying degrees depending on the arrangements) between the public body and a contractor.

Another central tenet of NPM as originally conceived was that service providers should be encouraged to specialize. It was argued that large public bodies providing a variety of different services were 'jacks of all trades; masters of none'. The quality of provision would improve if providers (whether firms or smaller units within public bodies) focused on a particular service. More recently, there has been something of a backlash against this idea. Critics have expressed concern that small specialist units can become what are pejoratively referred to as 'silos': they are closed off from the rest of the world and are unable or unwilling to communicate with each other.[25] From an efficiency perspective, these small specialist bodies may either be duplicating each other's efforts, or achieving their own targets by shifting costs onto other bodies. And from the perspective of service users, it can be difficult to know where to turn for help or how to deal with the situation in which several different

[23] D Osborne and T Gaebler, *Reinventing Government: How the Entrepreneurial Spirit is Transforming the Public Sector* (New York: Plume, 1993), ch 1.
[24] HC Deb, 17 July 2012, cols 844–52.
[25] See, eg. Organisation for Economic Co-operation and Development, *Breaking out of Policy Silos: Doing More with Less* (2010).

public bodies blame each other for problems. This has led to the emergence of what we might term 'post' NPM arrangements in which public bodies have been encouraged to pool their budgets—particularly in a local area—to tackle a shared set of problems, or have opted to contract out several services to the same provider under a single contract. In both cases, the aim is to create opportunities to redesign services. Most obviously, this might be a way to save money in a time of budget cuts, but there may also be opportunities to make the services more user-friendly.

3. Implications for accountability

Both deep and post NPM are much more challenging from the perspective of accountability than NPM itself. As we saw above, NPM gave the government a clear role as the purchaser of public services and an opportunity to set and enforce budgets and targets for the provision of particular public services. Although there were many failures, the lines of accountability—from providers to purchasers to ministers or councillors—remained reasonably obvious. By contrast, under deep NPM, the government's role as purchaser is shared with private contractors. As we shall see, it is sometimes claimed that contractors can be used simply to support the government's decision-making, while the decisions themselves remain in public hands. However, the boundary between these two activities is hard to draw, opening up the prospect of private firms taking on the traditionally public role of deciding what services should be provided. Although the public body should, in theory, be able to call the contractor to account for these decisions, this is problematic in practice because the public body is dependent on the contractor for information and expertise. Under post NPM, similar problems appear. Sharing budgets between public bodies is worrying since it may no longer be clear what role each particular public body played in decision-making for the purposes of calling that body to account. Where a contractor is invited to provide multiple services and permitted to redesign them, the government's role in deciding what should be provided is, again, much reduced. And, in order to facilitate the adoption of post NPM, the government may remove some mechanisms of accountability previously applicable to public bodies so that they have greater discretion to reorganize or to participate in shared arrangements.

To illustrate these claims, the next two sections will present two case studies. The first, an example of deep NPM, is the use of management consultants and others to provide 'commissioning support' to purchasers in the NHS, a policy which began under Labour and has continued under the coalition government, forming an important plank of the reforms under the Health and Social Care Act 2012. The second case study is an example of post NPM and involves an examination of the Labour government's Total Place policy for local government and the coalition's development of that policy, particularly through community budgeting and the new powers for local authorities introduced by the Localism Act 2011. In both cases, our focus will be on the issues they raise for accountability.

D. Deep NPM—commissioning support in the NHS

The NHS has been the subject of NPM techniques since the creation of the 'internal market' in the 1990s.[26] This involved the introduction of a purchaser/provider split and a system of pseudo-contracts. Since then, the fundamentals of the internal market have remained roughly the same, though the identity of the bodies with responsibility for purchasing has changed. We will begin by considering the use of management consultants by Primary Care Trusts (PCTs) to assist with their purchasing tasks. Under the Health and Social Care Act 2012, PCTs will be abolished in 2013 and the purchasing role will be assumed by Clinical Commissioning Groups (CCGs). The government has made significant efforts to create a market for commissioning support to assist CCGs, so we will consider this development too.

It is important to be clear that there is no bright line distinction between deep NPM and the purchaser/provider split under NPM. The precise division between the roles of the purchaser and the provider in a public service contract has always been a matter of debate. For example, in a Private Finance Initiative contract for a hospital, the main contractor—not the public purchaser—will usually be responsible for re-tendering contracts for catering and other services at regular intervals. Thus, even under NPM, private firms could get involved in purchasing. Nevertheless, the deep NPM trend is not just an example of blurred boundaries: as we shall see, it involves a different way of thinking about the public sector's role altogether.

1. The use of external consultants by PCTs

PCTs were formed from the old system of Health Authorities to purchase health services for patients in their local area, primarily from NHS providers but with some use of the private and voluntary sectors.

A study in 2009 found that just over three-quarters of the PCTs surveyed had made use of management consultants to help with their purchasing activities.[27] Interestingly, there were examples of consultants being involved at all stages of the purchasing process, including assessing the needs of the local population, awarding contracts, and evaluating providers' performance.

The government sought to institutionalize this use of external assistance by procuring it at national level, through the Framework for External Support for Commissioning (FESC).[28] Fourteen firms were hired by the Department of Health through a framework agreement to provide consultancy services for PCTs on an 'as required' basis. The advertisement in the Official Journal of the European Union (OJEU) invited bids from interested parties with expertise in 'identifying population health needs; data collection, analysis and distribution to managers and clinicians;

---

[26] Davies, *Accountability: A Public Law Analysis*, 28–35, n 2 above.
[27] C Naylor and N Goodwin, *Building High-Quality Commissioning: What Role Can External Organisations Play?* (London: The King's Fund, 2010), ch 4.
[28] Department of Health, *Commissioning a Patient-Led NHS* (2005), 7.

designing care pathways; implementing and managing contractual arrangements in accordance with those needs'.[29] After an outcry in the media, the government was forced to withdraw the Official Journal notice and redraft it in order to make clear that the commissioning role itself was not being contracted out.[30] The revised version contained the following important passage: 'Primary Care Trusts are and will remain public, statutory bodies that are accountable locally and nationally for how they discharge their responsibilities. They cannot outsource this accountability'.[31] Nevertheless, most PCTs preferred to hire management consultants outside the FESC framework because they found it 'cumbersome'.[32]

The 'next step' from the use of management consultants to help with commissioning functions was to hire a firm to perform all aspects of commissioning. In 2005, Thames Valley Strategic Health Authority suggested that it might invite private firms to bid for the commissioning functions of the Oxfordshire PCT.[33] These proposals were criticised by the Health Select Committee of the House of Commons and were subsequently withdrawn.

2. Commissioning support for CCGs

CCGs will replace PCTs in 2013 as the purchasers in the NHS. They have been created as part of a drive to shift decision-making away from 'bureaucrats' and into the hands of General Practitioners (GPs).[34] This change has been presented as a way of drawing on GPs' knowledge of their patients' needs, though it seems likely that the government is also keen to give them financial responsibility for their clinical decision-making as a way of achieving greater control over the NHS budget.

An obvious difficulty with the reforms is that CCGs lack expertise in the purchasing role: although GPs have close contact with patients, they do not necessarily have the capacity to assess population needs or negotiate and monitor contracts. The government expects the gap to be filled in one of two ways. First, some CCGs might continue to draw on private sector expertise from management consultancies, as PCTs did.[35] Second, the government is seeking to create commissioning support services (CSSs) run by the staff who used to work for PCTs.[36] This is designed to avoid the problem of staff with relevant expertise being lost to the NHS when PCTs are abolished. Although these bodies will initially be in the public sector, the government expects them to be privatized by 2016.[37] If CCGs make widespread

[29] *OJEU* S135 (19 July 2006), Contract Notice 2006/S 135-145353, S II, para.1.5.
[30] Department of Health press release, 30 June 2006.
[31] *OJEU*, n 29 above.
[32] C Naylor and N Goodwin, *Building 'World Class Commissioning': What Role Can External Organisations Play? Results from a Survey of PCTs* (London: The King's Fund, 2009).
[33] House of Commons Select Committee on Health, *Changes to PCTs* (Second Report, Session 2005–6; HC 646; 2006), paras 182–7.
[34] Department of Health, *Equity and Excellence: Liberating the NHS* (Cm 7881, 2010).
[35] Naylor and Goodwin, *Building High-Quality Commissioning*, ch 9, n 27 above.
[36] For detail, see NHS Commissioning Board, *Developing Commissioning Support: Towards Service Excellence* (2012).
[37] NHS Commissioning Board, *Developing Commissioning Support*, 29, n 36 above. This process has been criticized by some private firms for failing to create a level playing field, and for possibly

use of either of these options, the deep NPM trend looks set to continue, though of course it is possible that some CCGs will prefer to recruit their own purchasing teams.[38]

Although it is difficult to know what role might be played by management consultants, since it is up to CCGs to contract with them, more information is available about the potential roles of CSSs. It is clear that the NHS Commissioning Board expects CCGs to use commissioning support for all aspects of their activities:

> ...CCGs...will require support in undertaking both the transactional (eg. contracting and procurement) and the transformational functions (clinicians leading change and improvement through service redesign, and engaging with local stakeholders to set agreed priorities) associated with good commissioning.[39]

Moreover, although this support may be provided on a short-term basis for a specific issue (perhaps a consultation exercise with the local population, for example) it is clear that many CCGs are expected to use 'one stop' or 'end-to-end' services.[40] This jargon denotes the use of a single CSS or firm to support all the CCG's commissioning activities.

Not surprisingly, the NHS Commissioning Board is at pains to stress that commissioning support does not involve carrying out CCGs' statutory commissioning functions.[41] However, some provisions of the Health and Social Care Act 2012 cast doubt on whether this distinction can be maintained in practice. Schedule 2 of the Act inserts a new Sch.1A into the National Health Service Act 2006 to regulate the practical operation of CCGs. Each CCG must have a constitution which must 'specify the arrangements made by the clinical commissioning group for the discharge of its functions'.[42] These arrangements may include provision for the functions of a CCG to be exercised by a committee on its behalf.[43] Importantly, a committee may 'consist of or include persons other than members or employees of the clinical commissioning group'.[44] Of course, the CCG would itself retain statutory responsibility for the discharge of its functions, but it seems clear from these provisions that there is no statutory obstacle to empowering a committee of people providing commissioning support to perform those functions on a day-to-day basis.

3. Accountability issues

We are now in a position to elaborate the claim, made above, that the contracting out of purchasing under deep NPM poses a serious problem from the perspective

---

breaching state aid or procurement rules: S Gainsbury and G Plimmer, 'NHS "host" role raises legal concerns', *Financial Times*, 18 March 2012.

[38] A decision to do this would be subject to NHS Commissioning Board approval: *Developing Commissioning Support,* 29, n 36.

[39] NHS Commissioning Board, *Developing Commissioning Support,* 8, n 36 above.

[40] NHS Commissioning Board, *Developing Commissioning Support,* 8, n 36 above.

[41] NHS Commissioning Board, *Developing Commissioning Support,* 9, n 36 above.

[42] NHS Act 2006, Sch.1A, para.3(1).   [43] NHS Act 2006, Sch.1A, para.3(3).

[44] NHS Act 2006, Sch.1A, para.3(2).

of accountability. The key concern here is that the body with statutory responsibility for purchasing should be in control of and accountable for purchasing decisions, and well-placed to call service providers to account.

The first and most obvious difficulty is that—despite the government's assertions—it may prove impossible to maintain the boundary between the statutory function of commissioning (which should remain in public hands) and the (potentially private) task of providing commissioning support. Imagine the situation in which a healthcare commissioner has put a service out to tender and is about to choose the successful bidder. Its commissioning support firm would, presumably, prepare a report setting out the legal constraints on the commissioner's decision and comparing the advantages and disadvantages of the eligible bids. The ultimate decision might remain with the commissioner, but it is very easy to see how the commissioning support firm could steer that decision in a particular direction. Of course, the distinction between purchasing and provision has always been open to a degree of blurring, but the distinction between purchasing and purchasing support seems even more elusive.

This gives rise to a related problem of conflicts of interest. In the NHS at least, it seems likely that some of the private firms that might become involved in commissioning support are the same firms that provide health care services to the NHS. This brings with it the risk that the commissioning 'arm' of a firm might persuade a public body to purchase services from its service provision 'arm'. This might be dealt with in a relatively straightforward way through rules on conflicts of interest.[45] However, the problem is more complex where these firms are operating on a national level. It is much more difficult to stop a firm which purchases services in one locality from using knowledge gained there (about its competitors' prices, for example) for its own benefit in other localities in which it is a provider.

Of course, one response to these concerns might be to say that if the public body uses its contract with the commissioning support firm to ensure that the firm is accountable for its activities, it will still be able to fulfil its statutory responsibilities and prevent bad behaviour. But the problem here is that the public body may find it difficult to obtain independent advice about the contractor's performance. For example, if the contractor is responsible for assessing the population's health needs, the only information the public authority will have about the population's health needs will be from the contractor. How will the authority be able to check the accuracy of the data or the methodology the contractor has used in preparing the data? The only way to do so would be to duplicate the contractor's efforts, either using the public body's own staff or by hiring in yet more external advice. This seems wasteful and is likely to increase costs.

---

[45] Some rules on this are beginning to emerge: see NHS Commissioning Board, *Towards Establishment: Creating Responsive and Accountable Clinical Commissioning Groups* (2012), ch 4, but the focus is on GPs' interests rather than those of commissioning support providers.

Finally, in some situations there is a worry that public bodies might exploit the contracting out of purchasing as a means of avoiding their own accountability. Even ministers have admitted that this might be the case:

[Managers] get in, they have to make a difficult decision, and rather than make it, as they are paid to do, some of them are getting in some management consultants to look at it, paying these management consultants a lot of money, in order to protect the chief executive's back. That should not be happening.[46]

For example, if (due to budget cuts) there is a need to close one out of several possible services, a way of evading responsibility for this decision might be to employ consultants to investigate the matter and produce a report. The public body can then claim simply to be implementing the external, objective report when deciding which services should be closed. This is extremely problematic from the perspective of public accountability. It is the role of public bodies to take these difficult decisions and to face the consequences, either in terms of media criticism or electoral impact. It is not appropriate to use contracting out as a means of shifting the blame.

As we saw above, critics feared that NPM would inhibit public bodies' accountability. Deep NPM poses much greater risks in this regard because it involves private firms in commissioning support activities which are hard to distinguish from—or at least highly influential over—commissioning decisions, which are public bodies' statutory responsibility. We will consider some alternatives in the conclusion, below, after examining the second case-study.

E. Post NPM: from 'Total Place' to community budgets

In this section, we will illustrate post NPM policies—in which the NPM emphasis on specialization among service providers is abandoned in favour of 'generalist' service provision—by examining developments in local government. Under the Labour government, the relevant policy was known as Total Place and involved a series of pilot projects designed to get different bodies in the local area (the council, police, fire service and hospitals, for example) to work together across institutional boundaries. The coalition government has instituted even greater delegation of responsibility to local areas through the financial tool of 'community budgets'. This has been accompanied by a significant reduction in the accountability mechanisms applicable to local authorities, for example, through the relaxation of legal constraints on their powers under the Localism Act 2011, and the abolition of performance indicators. These changes have been presented as a means of giving local authorities greater discretion to change the way they work and to participate in shared service delivery arrangements.

---

[46] House of Commons Health Committee, *Commissioning* (4th Report, Session 2009–10, HC 268-I), para. 175, quoting Mike O'Brien MP, then Minister of State for Health.

1. Total Place

Total Place was launched in 2009.[47] It involved a set of thirteen pilot projects covering some 11 million people. These pilots brought together 63 local authorities, 34 PCTs, 12 fire authorities and 13 police authorities. The government defined Total Place in the following terms:

Total Place involves local public services working together to deliver better value services to citizens by focusing on joint working and reducing waste and duplication.[48]

The pilot areas adopted two main strategies. First, the various public bodies analysed what resources they were spending in the local area and how they were spending those resources. This was intended to highlight examples of duplication and waste. One result of this has been increased sharing of 'back office' functions between public bodies. Thus, it is now the case that some district councils share a chief executive and senior officers with local NHS bodies.[49] Second, the bodies engaged in 'mapping' exercises designed to examine a citizen's 'journey' through the system. These exercises were intended to highlight problems faced by citizens in getting help from public bodies and dealing with many different agencies. For example, in Leicester and Leicestershire, a project was set up to provide a single point of contact for local public services, so that citizens would be able to get the help they needed by calling a single number.[50] This also cut costs because the councils were able to reduce the number of different call centres they operated.

Central government's role in promoting Total Place focused primarily on the obstacles facing different local bodies where they wanted to work together. For example, a major part of local council spending was 'ring-fenced': in other words, councils were legally obliged to keep it separate from their general funds and to use it for specific purposes. Of course, this provides a way of protecting particular services, but it also limits the flexibility councils have to use their resources in novel ways. In the 2010 budget, the then Labour government announced that £1.3 billion of local authority funding would cease to be ring-fenced. The government also took the view that some of its own performance monitoring of local government, through the Comprehensive Area Assessment (CAA) run by the Audit Commission, got in the way of joint working between local authorities and other bodies. It therefore proposed to reduce the number of performance targets that would be monitored in areas with successful Total Place projects.[51]

---

[47] HM Treasury and Department for Communities and Local Government, *Total Place: A Whole Area Approach to Public Services* (2010).
[48] HM Treasury, *Total Place*, para. 1.8.
[49] HM Treasury, *Total Place*, para. 6.5, citing Hammersmith and Fulham, and Herefordshire.
[50] HM Treasury, *Total Place*, paras 2.8 and 3.2.
[51] HM Treasury, *Total Place*, paras 2.20–2.22.

2. New 'freedoms' for local authorities

The coalition government has continued the Total Place idea, but under new policy labels and in more radical ways. To quote the Secretary of State for Communities and Local Government, Eric Pickles:

Credit where it's due, Total Place . . . was a step in the right direction . . . But . . . in the end it was far more talk than action. As I've said before, it was a bit like your Dad letting you go down the disco. And then hanging around outside all night cramping your style.[52]

A key characteristic of the government's approach is the removal of various kinds of regulatory constraints on local authorities' activities, with a view to freeing them up to reorganize the services they provide either internally or in collaboration with other councils or public bodies. The changes have three main elements: the extension of local authorities' legal powers under the Localism Act 2011; the grant of greater financial freedoms; and substantial reductions in audit and assessment requirements. We will consider the place of private contractors in these developments towards the end of the section.

The coalition has used financial tools as its main mechanism for pursuing and developing the Total Place agenda. In 2011, the government piloted 'community budgets' in 16 areas of England.[53] These are place-based budgets which pool public funding for a local area drawn from a range of different sources. The pilot projects have focused on services for so-called 'problem families' and involved bringing together money from local government budgets, Department for Education money for 'early intervention' projects for children, and European Social Fund money for job creation via the Department of Work and Pensions. The aim is to increase the number of areas with community budgets for problem families in future years.[54] The government is also planning to pilot community budgets for other specific policy issues and, more radically, community budgets that put all public resources for a local area together into a single 'pot'.[55]

This has been accompanied by a significant move to reduce the financial constraints on local authorities. One of the coalition government's major criticisms of Total Place was that it did not go far enough in giving local authorities flexibility in how to spend their resources because of the ongoing use of ring-fencing in budgets. The government therefore abolished ring-fencing in local authority budgets in 2010 with the exception of funding for schools and for public health responsibilities.[56]

---

[52] Speech by the Secretary of State for Communities and Local Government, the Rt Hon Eric Pickles MP, 29 March 2011.

[53] <http://www.communities.gov.uk/localgovernment/decentralisation/communitybudgets/>, (accessed 22 April 2013).

[54] Department for Communities and Local Government, 'Community Budgets to be Rolled Out Countrywide', press release, 29 June 2011.

[55] Department for Communities and Local Government, '14 Areas Get 2012 Starter Gun to "Pool and Save" Billions', press release, 21 December 2011.

[56] Department for Communities and Local Government, *Business Plan 2011–15* (2010).

The removal of constraints did not stop there. The government has also made significant changes to local authorities' legal powers. It is a long-established principle that local authorities, as creatures of statute, must be able to identify specific statutory authority for their actions.[57] This has not, on the whole, proved difficult, since local authorities in fact have wide-ranging statutory powers. However, there have been some successful challenges to the vires of certain local authority actions, particularly during the 1980s when authorities engaged in some risky financial transactions in an attempt to combat the effects of budget cuts.[58] The coalition government has taken the view that local authorities might be inhibited from adopting innovative ways of working because of the constraints on their legal powers. Section 1 of the Localism Act 2011 therefore contains a 'general power of competence' which is worth quoting at length:

(1) A local authority has power to do anything that individuals generally may do.

(2) Subsection (1) applies to things that an individual may do even though they are in nature, extent or otherwise—

   (a) unlike anything the authority may do apart from subsection (1), or

   (b) unlike anything that other public bodies may do.

(3) In this section 'individual' means an individual with full capacity.

(4) Where subsection (1) confers power on the authority to do something, it confers power (subject to sections 2 to 4) to do it in any way whatever, including—

   (a) power to do it anywhere in the United Kingdom or elsewhere,

   (b) power to do it for a commercial purpose or otherwise for a charge, or without charge, and

   (c) power to do it for, or otherwise than for, the benefit of the authority, its area or persons resident or present in its area.

In one sense, this provision is less radical than it seems. Central government has extensive powers because of the Crown's inherent common law capacity to act.[59] However, in a modern democracy founded on the rule of law, any move away from the principle that a public body must have a statutory source for its powers should be seen as a backward step.

There are some constraints on the new power under the Localism Act 2011. Where the general power overlaps with a pre-existing statutory power conferred on local authorities, and that pre-existing power is subject to limits, those limits also apply to the general power under the Localism Act 2011.[60] Thus, the new power cannot be used to get round pre-existing constraints on local authorities' activities. However, s 5(1) of the Act contains a broad Henry VIII power for the Secretary of State:

---

[57] *R v Somerset CC, ex p Fewings* [1995] 1 WLR 1037, 1042 (per Sir Thomas Bingham MR).
[58] See Davies, *The Public Law of Government Contracts*, 104–6, n 15 above.
[59] Davies, *The Public Law of Government Contracts*, 86–7, n 15 above.
[60] Localism Act 2011, s 2.

If the Secretary of State thinks that a statutory provision (whenever passed or made) prevents or restricts local authorities from exercising the general power, the Secretary of State may by order amend, repeal, revoke or disapply that provision.

This means that pre-existing restraints or, for that matter, subsequent restraints can be removed by ministerial order.

Sections 3 and 4 of the Act place limits on the extent to which local authorities can charge for their services and on their use of the general power for commercial purposes. Nevertheless, the new power is striking in its breadth. A particularly surprising feature is the grant of power to local authorities to do things 'otherwise than for ... the benefit of ... [their] area',[61] which seems to go against the very purpose of local government.

Finally, the coalition government has been highly critical of the detailed performance management regime put in place by the Labour government. As we saw above, the Labour government was itself proposing to reduce the number of targets applicable in areas pursuing Total Place policies. But the coalition government has gone several steps further: it has abolished the CAA altogether, along with the Audit Commission, the public body responsible for its monitoring and management.[62] It claims that the CAA inhibited innovations in service delivery because the need to meet its targets dictated to local authorities what to do. And, of course, there are savings to be made at both local and national level if CAA data no longer need to be collected and processed.

It seems highly likely that private firms will play a role, in some councils at least, in redesigning services in response to these new flexibilities. Indeed, this process had already begun in some areas before the new regime came into force. According to press reports, the most radical such proposal was Essex County Council's planned £5.4 billion eight-year contract to design and run a wide range of council services.[63] The council initially awarded two smaller contracts to IBM to run its 'back office' and procurement functions, with the prospect of further contract awards over time.[64] A similar plan to outsource multiple services to a single private provider, including both 'back office' functions and the provision of some services to the public, seems to be ongoing in the London Borough of Barnet, though it has met with an angry response from unions representing council workers.[65] In both cases, it is possible to discern a combination of deep and post NPM strategies at work. The post NPM element is the award of a contract for multiple services, with the requirement that the contractor achieve savings by redesigning the services to make them more efficient. Once this has been done, a deep NPM element emerges in which the

---

[61] Localism Act 2011, s 1(4)(c).

[62] Department for Communities and Local Government, *Business Plan 2011–15* (2010), and see Department for Communities and Local Government, 'Grant Shapps: Next Phase of Local Public Audit', press release, 4 January 2012.

[63] Jane Dudman, 'IBM has Landed a Far-Reaching Deal with Essex Council', *The Guardian*, 22 December 2009. It is difficult to obtain detailed information about the contract itself.

[64] IBM, 'IBM Signs Eight-Year Strategic Transformation Services Agreement With Essex County Council', press release, 21 December 2009.

[65] BBC News online, 'Barnet Council Staff in Fourth Strike over Outsourcing', 9 February 2012.

contractor either supports the council in procuring different aspects of the redesigned services, or simply subcontracts for those services itself.

3. Accountability issues

The implications of post NPM policies for accountability are, if anything, more troubling than those of deep NPM. This has become particularly apparent as the coalition government's radical approach to post NPM has emerged. Traditional mechanisms of accountability are being abandoned in favour of much less obvious or certain replacements.

The post NPM agenda focuses on giving local authorities greater freedom to decide how to deliver services. This is no bad thing in itself, and indeed is likely to be regarded by many as a beneficial reversal of many years of excessive meddling from central government in local authorities' affairs. However, it is important not to over-estimate the extent of the change in central-local relations that is likely to be brought about by these reforms, for two reasons. First, the trend of stripping local authorities of key responsibilities continues in many policy areas, so although they are being given more freedom to make decisions, the scope of their policy responsibilities may still be in decline. Developments in education, such as academies and free schools, are a good illustration of this.[66] Second, central government retains its most significant lever over local authorities' behaviour: its control of the purse-strings. And in a time of austerity, local authorities' new-found freedom will be limited by substantial budget cuts. It is a freedom to spend as they see fit, but only to spend what little money they are given.

The reforms discussed above to local authorities' legal, financial and administrative accountability have been presented in terms of removing opportunities for central government control, in other words, as reforms to internal accountability from local to central government. However, the changes will also limit local authorities' *external* accountability to the public in significant ways. After the Localism Act 2011, it is almost impossible to envisage how an aggrieved council tax payer might frame a successful application for judicial review on the ground that a local authority has acted ultra vires. Of course, we should not expect the courts to act as the primary accountability mechanism for local government, but they have acted as an important 'emergency brake' in the past.[67] Similarly, the abolition of the CAA will reduce the amount of information available to the public to help them assess their local authority's performance.

The government would probably respond to these criticisms by pointing to other ways in which local authorities can be held to account. The 'redesigning services' agenda is driven by the traditional NPM desire to improve the responsiveness of public services to their consumers, for example, by making services easier

---

[66] Though the traffic is not all one-way: the Health and Social Care Act 2012 will transfer public health responsibilities from the NHS to councils.

[67] Davies, *The Public Law of Government Contracts*, n 58 above.

for users to navigate. And, of course, local authorities remain accountable to local people through the electoral process. Nevertheless, it is not obvious how voters will find out whether or not the local authority is delivering better services, particularly if they have no direct personal experience of those services.

Where a local authority chooses to provide services jointly with other bodies, or to contract out on a large scale, the problems are compounded by the difficulty of discerning who is responsible for particular decisions. For example, if the pooled community budget for 'problem families' in a particular area is overspent, a dispute may arise between the various public bodies involved as to who is responsible for the deficit. One response to this might be to say that it is up to the project partners to reach a clear agreement at the outset that addresses some of these concerns: who is responsible for auditing the accounts, who sets the quality standards, and so on. The drafting of such agreements will require careful thought, but—in the rush to embrace new techniques—there is no clear government guidance on the matter.[68]

Finally, and perhaps most worryingly, joint provision and contracting out in this area seem to limit the role of elected councillors in significant ways. Imagine the scenario in which there is widespread public dissatisfaction with local service provision and the political control of the council changes at an election. It is not clear whether the council's new leaders will be able to renegotiate agreements with other public bodies in pooled budgeting arrangements. Their ability to renegotiate or terminate contracts with private firms will depend on the drafting of those contracts and any break clauses they contain, and their ability to place new contracts will be constrained by the public procurement rules.[69] Of course, elected officials have always operated in a constrained environment in which a variety of factors may limit their ability immediately to reverse the previous administration's policies, but under post NPM they may find themselves unable to take any action until a particular agreement is due for renegotiation. Again, therefore, the role of the state is compromised by these developments.

F. Conclusion

NPM was by no means perfect. But at least it produced a system that gave public bodies a reasonably clear role as the purchasers of public services from specialist providers (whether public, private or voluntary). Public bodies had contractual tools for calling providers to account, and public bodies could themselves be held to account for their performance as purchasers. The deep and post NPM trends identified in this chapter threaten this framework. Deep NPM involves splitting

---

[68] See HM Government, *Community Budgets Prospectus* (2011), 27, leaving it to the parties to decide.
[69] See, generally, Davies, *The Public Law of Government Contracts*, chs 5 and 6, n 15 above. A 'fettering' argument may be possible in these circumstances but probably at some cost to the authority's reputation.

the public task of purchasing from the potentially private activity of purchasing support, but since the distinction between the two is elusive, it may in practice give private firms control over public bodies' performance of their statutory functions. Post NPM blurs responsibility between different public bodies (and, possibly, private firms too) as they pool budgets and group services together. Local authorities' participation in post NPM arrangements has been facilitated by the abolition of some important mechanisms for calling them to account.

One possible reason for the emergence of deep NPM seems to be a perception on the part of public bodies that they lack procurement expertise.[70] Although there are many examples of failed government projects in areas such as defence or information technology to support this view it is, nevertheless, a surprising proposition. Under NPM, one of the state's core functions was to buy services from public or private providers. In the early years, this did involve acquiring new skills that were not previously found in the public sector, such as drawing up invitations to tender and conducting competitive bidding exercises.[71] What is genuinely puzzling is why, years after the introduction of NPM, it is not regarded as essential for every public body to have a core of employees with highly developed purchasing skills.[72] Of course, CCGs are new bodies to which this criticism does not apply, but in their case it is not clear why they are being encouraged to contract for commissioning support services instead of simply employing people with the necessary skills. At the very least, public bodies should be required to compare the costs and benefits of contracting out their purchasing activities against the alternative: training existing staff or hiring new staff so that the relevant expertise exists in-house.

The post NPM agenda has some laudable aims, as we have seen. However, from the perspective of accountability, there are two important points to consider. First, it is essential to strike a balance between giving local authorities freedom to participate in these arrangements and subjecting them to an appropriate package of accountability mechanisms. Accountability always involves some tension between those who are calling to account and those who are being called to account, since greater control for the former generally means less discretion for the latter. But local authorities, as public bodies, should be accountable not just at election time but routinely, through a variety of different internal and external mechanisms. The abolition of the CAA and the removal of important elements of local authorities' legal and financial accountability seem to have proceeded without regard to this important consideration. Second, if there is a problem about getting bodies to work together at the local level, perhaps we need to ask why we have so many separate public bodies, not just separate budgets. One way to bring local services together would be to give local authorities more power, not in the sense of making them less

---

[70] In the NHS see, eg. Naylor and Goodwin, *Building High-Quality Commissioning*, 13–14, n 27 above.

[71] See, eg. Foster and Plowden, *The State Under Stress*, 116, n 14 above.

[72] Interestingly, one component of the Essex County Council contract with IBM, discussed above, is the provision of training to staff dealing with procurement: IBM, 'Essex County Council Transforms its Procurement Function', available at <http://www-935.ibm.com/services/uk/bcs/pdf/EssexCCProcurement_111027.pdf> (accessed 22 April 2013).

accountable, but rather by giving them more policy responsibilities, for example, in areas such as education and policing. This would provide a way of breaking down bureaucratic boundaries between public services, whilst at the same time maintaining formal mechanisms of accountability from the 'front line' to elected councillors, and thus to local people. But for now at least, radical institutional reform of this kind does not seem to be on the political agenda.

Writing about NPM back in 1997, Harlow and Rawlings noted that it was 'hard to exaggerate the scale and significance of the contractual revolution in government'.[73] The impact of NPM on the traditional, hierarchically-managed public sector was indeed considerable. As a result, it may seem rather difficult to imagine reforms with the potential to have an even greater impact than NPM did but, as this chapter has sought to demonstrate, such reforms are already being implemented in large parts of the UK public sector. Perhaps the most important lesson to emerge from the discussion is that, in a public sector driven by big policy ideas and limited resources, the continued existence of effective accountability mechanisms should never be taken for granted. To quote Harlow and Rawlings again, 'in the brave new world of government by contract administrative lawyers must do more to make themselves heard'.[74]

---

[73] Harlow and Rawlings, *Law and Administration*, 250, n 1 above.   [74] Ibid 294.

15

Calling Regulators to Account: Challenges, Capacities and Prospects

Julia Black[*]

A. Introduction

Since their inception, the accountability of independent regulatory agencies has been of concern to scholars of public law and political science. Writing in the 1930s in the context of the United States, Landis observed that the literature 'abounds with fulmination' at the 'inappropriate' combination of legislative, judicial and executive functions within regulatory agencies and their lack of accountability.[1] Some eighty years later, a House of Lords committee commented, 'The question of who regulates the regulators has not been answered and will not go away.'[2] In the interim, considerable energy has been spent by scholars on analysing what accountability is,[3] and in developing frameworks of analysis, typologies of mechanisms, and categorizations of goals.[4] Accountability, it has been said, is an 'ever expanding concept'.[5] It is also a Goldilocks one: for accountability can be argued to be too little, too great, but rarely just right.[6] So whilst there are observations that

[*] Professor of Law, London School of Economics and Political Science. I am grateful to Steve Brooker, Carol Harlow, Rick Rawlings and the editors for their helpful comments on a previous draft. The usual responsibilities remain my own. Note that all URLs cited were accessed and confirmed on 10 April 2012.

[1] J M Landis *The Administrative Process* (New Haven: Yale University Press, 1938), p.4.

[2] House of Lords Select Committee on Regulators, *UK Economic Regulators* 1st Report of Session 2006–7, HL 189-I (London: TSO, 2007), para.1.29.

[3] Eg. M Bovens, 'Analysing and Assessing Public Accountability: A Conceptual Model' *European Governance Papers (EUROGOV)* 2006 C-06-01 (EUI, 2006); R Mulgan *Holding Power to Account: Accountability in Modern Democracies* (Basingstoke: Palgrave, 2003).

[4] Eg. J Mashaw, 'Accountability and Institutional Design: Some Thoughts on the Grammar of Governance' in M Dowdle (ed.), *Public Accountability: Designs, Dilemmas and Experiences* (Cambridge: Cambridge University Press, 2006),115–56; C Scott, 'Accountability in the Regulatory State' *Journal of Law and Society* (2000) 23: 38; M Lodge and L Stirton, 'Accountability in the Regulatory State' in R Baldwin, M Cave and M Lodge (eds) *Handbook of Regulation* (Oxford, 2010); C Pollitt *The Essential Public Manager* (London: Open University Press, 2003).

[5] R Mulgan, 'Accountability—An Ever-Expanding Concept' *Public Administration* (2000) 78(3): 555–73.

[6] M Bovens, T Schilleman and P t'Hart, 'Does Public Accountability Work? An Assessment Tool' *Public Administration* (2008) 86(1): 225–42.

accountability demands are counter-productive or subverted, prevent the agency from performing its role effectively[7], or create cultures of blame,[8] others (usually the majority) argue that accountability of independent regulatory agencies is deeply inadequate.[9]

This chapter does not attempt to evaluate the accountability of UK regulatory agencies across all the different dimensions of accountability, not least because it is not clear what success would look like.[10] Instead, it explores the current operation of the political mechanisms for calling independent regulatory agencies to account in the UK (or more specifically in England and Wales, where regulatory functions are devolved). It argues that, whilst it would be an exaggeration to say that there is a 'crisis' of regulatory accountability,[11] nor can we be complacent. This is not, however, because regulatory agencies on the whole try to be unaccountable—on the whole they do not, and indeed there are many examples where regulators 'go beyond compliance' with the accountability requirements placed on them, even if they conflict.[12] Rather, it is often because the tension between independence, political control and political accountability creates an ambiguity in the responsibilities of the core executive and regulatory agencies which both, but particularly the executive, can seek to exploit. As a result, lines of responsibility and thus of accountability can be unclear, to say the least.

Problems of accountability are exacerbated by the fact that all UK regulators sit within the multi-level governance structure of the European Union. Significant elements of the regulatory requirements that they have to implement are written at EU level. EU Regulations and Directives can also contain quite prescriptive requirements on regulatory processes, for example the number of inspections that have to be performed in areas such as food safety, medical devices and environmental regulation; they also in some areas stipulate the governance and funding structures of regulatory agencies themselves, notably in the areas of telecommunications and energy regulation. In turn, those requirements can emanate from international regulatory bodies, which can themselves impose requirements as to the content of

---

[7] Eg. J Meyer and K Shaugnessy, 'Organizational Design and the Performance Paradox', in R Swedberg (ed.), *Explorations in Economic Sociology* (New York: Russell Sage, 1993); C Pollitt, X Girre, J Lonsdale *Performance or Compliance?: Performance Audit and Public Management in Five Countries* (Oxford: Oxford University Press, 1999); P t'Hart and A Wille, 'Living Together, Growing Apart? Politicians and Bureaucrats in The Netherlands' *Public Administration* (2006) 84(1): 121–46.

[8] C Hood, *The Blame Game: Spin, Bureaucracy, and Self-Preservation in Government* (Princeton, 2011).

[9] Eg. R Behn, *Rethinking Democratic Accountability* (Washington DC: Brookings Institution Press, 2001); M Dowdle, 'Public Accountability: Conceptual, Historical, and Epistemic Mappings', in Dowdle, *Public Accountability: Designs, Dilemmas and Experiences*, 1–26.

[10] For a detailed discussion of the legal powers and accountability arrangements of ten UK regulatory agencies see T Prosser *The Regulatory Enterprise: Government Regulation and Legitimacy* (Oxford, 2010).

[11] C Graham, *Is there a Crisis of Regulatory Accountability?* (Bath: Centre for Regulated Industries, 1995).

[12] Eg. Dowdle, *Public Accountability: Designs, Dilemmas and Experiences*; J Black, 'Constructing and Contesting Legitimacy and Accountability in Polycentric Regulatory Regimes' *Regulation and Governance* (2008) 2: 1–28.

regulatory provisions and the nature of regulatory structures.[13] As a result, there can often be a mismatch between the national-level accountability structures and the EU or international-level locus of decision-making. And with neither national government nor regulators accepting responsibility for critical aspects of regulatory decisions (on the basis that those decisions are for the other to make, or for neither to make because they have been made elsewhere), trying to pin down responsibility can be akin to trying to catch a will o' the wisp: an image of apparent solidity which recedes and dissipates as it is approached.

There are numerous ways in which discussions of accountability can be organized — by goals, mechanisms, institutions — and each mode of organization serves a different purpose. The aim of this chapter is to explore accountability by looking at the significance of capacity and institutional position in an organization's ability to call a regulatory agency to account, ie. to act as 'accountor'. These concepts are explained in the first section. The second section builds on this analysis to explore some of the key challenges facing the accountors in performing their role. It also looks at some of the strategies regulators have adopted to manage their legitimacy, often 'going beyond compliance' with their formal accountability requirements. The third section then focuses on recent developments in the roles of the four main accountors in the political domain in turn (the core executive, Parliament, the National Audit Office (NAO) and consumer panels), exploring their relationships both with the accountees (the regulators) and with other bodies which are calling those regulators to account, noting throughout how accountability relationships can turn to blame games in times of crisis. The fifth section concludes.

B. Analysing accountability dynamics—an institutional perspective

The term accountability is usually used to mean a relationship between an actor (accountee) and another (accountor) in which the accountee is called to explain and justify its actions against one or more sets of different criteria after the fact. In some definitions, there is an added element, which is that the accountor may impose consequences.[14] However, given the highly variable nature of the consequences that can be imposed, in identifying a body as an 'accountor' this chapter focuses on their capacity to perform at least the first, core element of accountability: calling to account.

---

[13] Eg. Basle Committee on Banking Supervision, *Core Principles for Banking Supervision* (Basle: Department for Business, Innovation and Skills, 2006); Council Directive (EC) 2009/72 concerning common rules for the internal market in electricity, Arts 35-7; Council Directive (EC) 2009/140 amending Council Directives (EC) 2002/21 on a common regulatory framework for electronic communications networks and services, 2002/19 on access to, and interconnection of, electronic communications networks and associated facilities, and 2002/20 on the authorization of electronic communications networks and services.

[14] Bovens, 'Analysing and Assessing Public Accountability', n 4 above.

The cast of accountors for regulatory agencies in the UK is a familiar one. There is the core constitutional triumvirate of judiciary, legislature and executive. Accountability also extends upwards, outwards and/or downwards (depending on your perspective), to consumer panels, advisory groups and other 'stakeholder' bodies,[15] to the media, to the EU institutions, and even to transnational regulatory organizations and/or international institutions.[16] Regulators[17] thus have accountability relationships with a number of different bodies or 'accountors', in the sense that they are asked, and often agree, to give an account of their operations and performance against a range of criteria. Those criteria may relate to one or more sets of issues, such as whether they have acted in accordance with their legal mandate; whether they have used their financial resources appropriately; whether they have operated in accordance with fair procedures; whether they have engaged in adequate consultation and participation in decision-making; and/or whether the goals that they are seeking to achieve are normatively acceptable.

In orthodox legal descriptions of accountability, it is normal to map the legal powers: who is required to give account to whom, when, how and in respect to what. However, if we view accountability arrangements through a more sociological and/or political lens, then it becomes clear that the ability of those accountors to call to account and to impose consequences can be highly variable, notwithstanding their legal powers. A highly critical media campaign can be more effective in causing the resignation of a chief executive of a regulatory body than any legal power to sack him, for example.

Moreover, accountability relationships are just that: relationships. Again, standard legal accounts tend to focus on the accountor: what powers it has; what criteria it is using. However, the accountee is also a part of the process. An effective accountability relationship requires the full engagement of both accountor and accountee. For just as those who are regulated can appear to be complying with the rules to which they are subject, whilst in fact subverting them, those who are being held to account can conform with the formal requirements (producing annual reports and accounts, for example), whilst in practice operating in quite a different way. Furthermore, roles can be fluid: an organization may act as an accountor with respect to a regulator, but also at different times as a participant in regulatory decision-making, as discussed below. The boundaries between accountability and control can also become blurred, again as discussed below.

If we are to really understand how accountability relationships are operating, we therefore need to look beyond formal legal structures. Moreover, we need to bear in

---

[15] The term 'stakeholder' is often used by regulators, government and others to refer to interested groups, such as trade associations and business groups, trade unions, consumer groups, non-governmental organizations, and others with particular interests in a policy area.

[16] Scott, 'Accountability in the Regulatory State', n 5 above.

[17] The terms 'regulators' and 'regulatory agencies' will be used interchangeably throughout to refer to independent regulatory agencies, ie. organizations which have a separate legal status and mandate, which are not chaired or staffed by elected politicians or subject to their operational control, which are charged with a specific set of objectives and/or functions, and are given a set of powers to achieve those objectives/carry out those functions.

mind that those formal structures may not have been created in order to achieve any functional purpose, but rather for reasons of history or constitutional convention, or for symbolic purposes. Thus in the international regulatory context in which most national regulators sit, those accountability arrangements may have been put in place simply because they are required by EU regulation, or by international organizations.[18] Alternatively, or in addition, they may exist to legitimize the regulator and the goals which it is pursuing in the eyes of different legitimacy communities.[19] In such cases, we should not be surprised if there is a decoupling of formal processes of accountability from the organization's de facto operations, or if accountability arrangements 'look good' but turn out to be functionally weak: they were introduced primarily for symbolic, not functional, purposes.

Analysing accountability relationships thus requires us to go well beyond formal legal powers and constitutional conventions. It is argued here that the ability of an accountor effectively to call a regulator to account, and the consequences that it can impose, is largely dependent not on its legal powers per se, but on the accountor's 'accountability capacity' and the institutional position that it has vis à vis both the accountee and other accountors. By 'institutional position' is meant not only the legal powers the accountor possesses to call an agency to account, but also the normative or cognitive acceptance by others (including the accountee) of its 'right' or appropriateness to act as accountor, and the strategic position that it has, political or otherwise, to do so. The institutional position of the accountor within the broader political and constitutional arrangements (widely defined), including, but not limited to, their legal powers, will affect the relationship that it has with the accountee. To given an obvious example, judges engaged in judicial review can impose legally binding decisions on agencies, but face institutional constraints in determining how interventionist to be (whether it is more appropriate for them to be 'red lights' or 'green lights');[20] parliamentary Select Committees will have no such qualms as to the appropriateness of criticizing the decisions of ministers, but they have little practical ability to impose legal consequences directly. Nonetheless, they can inflict significant reputational damage, which itself may be a catalyst for legislative or operational changes.

Moreover, accountors also have different capacities to make use of the accountability potential that their institutional position gives them. By accountability capacity, I mean (by analogy with regulatory capacity)[21] that the accountor has certain resources which it can use to call a regulator to account. In particular, it has (or has access to) information, technical expertise, financial resources, appropriate organizational

---

[18] Eg. Basle Committee on Banking Supervision, *Core Principles for the Supervision of Banks,* n15 above; Organisation for Economic Co-operation and Development (OECD), *Recommendation of the Council on Regulatory Policy and Governance* (Paris, 2012); OECD, *Guiding Principles for Regulatory Quality and Performance* (Paris 2005).

[19] Black, 'Constructing and Contesting Legitimacy and Accountability', n13 above.

[20] C Harlow and R Rawlings, *Law and Administration* (3rd edn, Cambridge: Cambridge University Press, 2009).

[21] J Black, 'Enrolling Actors in Regulatory Processes: Examples from UK Financial Services Regulation' *Public Law* [2003] 62–90; K Abbot and D Snidal, 'Strengthening International Regulation Through Transnational New Governance: Overcoming the Orchestration Deficit' *Vanderbilt Journal Transnational Law* (2009) 42: 501.

processes and practices to manage information and respond dynamically, and legitimacy and authority (its 'right' to call that person to account has to be recognized both by the accountee and by those on whose behalf, if any, the accountor is purporting to act). The capacity needed is relative to the nature of the task: greater capacity is needed to call to account regulatory agencies whose activities are opaque, technically complex, dynamic, difficult to assess, significant in scale and scope and who interact with a number of other organizations in performing their tasks and achieving outcomes. Unfortunately for accountors of regulatory bodies, that is exactly the scale of the task they face, and it is to this set of challenges that we now turn.

1. Challenges facing accountors

The challenges of calling regulators to account are many, but can be distilled for these purposes into five: the scale and scope of the regulatory landscape; the number and relationship between the different bodies involved (and their propensity to blame-shift); the technical complexity and contestability of the regulatory task; the opacity of regulatory processes; and the willingness of the accountor to be called to account.

a. The scale and shifting topography of the regulatory landscape

The scale and scope of the regulatory landscape is significant, and mapping it has been hindered by a number of definitional challenges, notably: what is 'regulation', what is an 'independent agency' and therefore what is an 'independent regulatory agency'. Unfortunately, the legislation which creates an organization does not always specify whether the organization is a 'regulatory agency' or not, not all are constituted in the same way (for example whilst most are non-departmental public bodies, some such as the Food Standards Agency, are non-ministerial departments, and a few, such as the Financial Services Authority (now the Financial Conduct Authority) are companies) and regulatory functions can also be performed by government departments or units within them. Successive attempts have been made by organizations such as the Better Regulation Taskforce, or indeed by parliamentary Select Committees, to 'map' the organizational landscape of regulation but the task can exhaust even the most dedicated cartographers. As one report by the Better Regulation Task Force commented in 2003, 'we question whether even Ministers could be certain that they know of all the independent regulators that surround their Departments'.[22] The review of public bodies in 2010 identified over 900 organizations, which at least addressed the question of knowing what bodies existed, but the categorization problem remained.[23] The Public Accounts Committee (PAC) recommended that the government introduce a taxonomy and common nomenclature and status for different types of bodies but the government

---

[22] Better Regulation Task Force, *Independent Regulators* (London, 2003).
[23] Cabinet Office, *Public Bodies Reform—Proposals For Change* (London, 2010).

responded that its aim was to reduce their number rather than to classify them, and so no attempt was even made to identify which organization was regulatory and which was not.[24]

Accountors have therefore tended to focus their accountability efforts on the main peaks: the economic regulators (the Rail Regulator, Ofcom, Ofwat and Ofgem), with the Financial Services Authority, Civil Aviation Authority and Office of Fair Trading sometimes being included in that group and sometimes not, and to a lesser extent on the 'social' regulators (notably food safety, environment and health and safety). The remaining swathes of the regulatory landscape are often left indistinctly drawn, with only a vague warning sign indicating 'there be dragons' marking their existence, until of course, a crisis strikes—for example the recent inquiries into the Care Quality Commission[25] or the Commission for Equality and Human Rights.[26]

b. The problems of 'multiple hands' and shifting roles

The second challenge is that frequently more than one regulator is engaged in regulating a particular sector and/or in achieving particular goals (often under the remit of different government departments), and, moreover that these tasks are shared with different parts of government. In most areas of regulation, there are multiple organizations involved, even where the regulators are 'mega-regulators', or the amalgamation of several pre-existing regulators. There are over twenty different bodies involved in the regulation of farming, for example, including Defra,[27] the Environment Agency,, the Rural Payments Agency, the Food Standards Agency, Natural England, and trading standards officers employed by local government.[28] Responsibilities in food safety, health and safety, and environmental regulation are split between local authorities and national regulators, calling into question who is responsible for setting and attaining overall outcomes.[29]

There are other examples. In the regulation of water, Ofwat is responsible for setting price controls on the water companies, and has to take account of the representations of Consumer Council for Water, as well as the strategic objectives set both by the Westminster government and by the Welsh Assembly. Those companies are also under obligations as to water quality, which is the responsibility of the

---

[24] Cabinet Office, *Government Response to the Public Administration Select Committee Report, 'Smaller Government: Shrinking the Quango State'* (Cm 8044, London, 2011).
[25] Public Accounts Committee, *The Care Quality Commission: Regulating the quality and safety of health and adult social care*, 78th Report of Session 2010–12, HC 1779 (CQC report).
[26] Public Accounts Committee, *Equality and Human Rights Commission*, 15th Report of Session 2009–10 HC 124 (EHRC report).
[27] Department for the Environment, Farming and Rural Affairs.
[28] Independent Farming Regulation Task Force *Striking a Balance: Reducing Burdens; Increasing Responsibilities; Earning Recognition-A Report on Better Regulation in Farming and Food Business* (London, 2011) (Farming Task Force report).
[29] It is notable that the Lofstedt review recommended that the HSE should take over responsibility and authority for all health and safety inspections, removing the role of local authorities: R Lofstedt *Reclaiming Health and Safety for All: An Independent Review of Health and Safety Legislation* (Cm 8219, London, 2011) (Lofstedt review).

Drinking Water Inspectorate (DWI) and the Environment Agency (EA). However, the level of financial resources that firms have available to invest in meeting their water quality obligations is significantly dependent on Ofwat's decisions in the price review process. It can thus be difficult to work out who is responsible if those quality objectives are not met: is it the companies (for not complying), the EA or the DWI (for not regulating properly to ensure compliance), the Consumer Council for Water (for not making adequate representations), Ofwat (for not allowing companies to make sufficient profits to invest to meet quality requirements), the Westminster government or the Welsh Assembly (for setting inappropriate and/ or conflicting objectives)?[30] Financial regulation provides another good example. Despite a memorandum of understanding (MOU) between the Treasury, the Bank of England and the Financial Services Authority (FSA), there were significant failures in coordination and considerable misunderstandings as to whose responsibility it was to do what with respect to the rescue of Northern Rock in 2007.[31]

Moreover, the roles of organizations which are acting as accountors can also be fluid. As discussed below, a consumer panel may play the role both of engaged participant in the regulatory process, as well as an ex post accountor of that regulator's activities; parliamentary involvement can demonstrate similar fluidity of roles. The question of 'who guards the guardians' is thus even further compounded, if the 'guardian' is an active participant in the very processes it is seeking to guard.

c. The nature of the regulatory tasks

The nature of the regulatory tasks and the ways in which regulators perform them can also pose challenges for accountors. First, the overall outcomes that regulators are meant to achieve are usually specified in highly general terms: for example, to protect consumers or the environment, to ensure competition, to maintain financial stability or to uphold the rule of law. Moreover, their legal mandates often specify a range of objectives which they have to achieve, which may in some instances compete with one another. However, those mandates rarely give any indication of how trade-offs between objectives are to be made. There are also considerable difficulties in measuring performance against generally framed outcomes, in distinguishing which elements of that performance are due to the regulator and which to other causes, and determining the time period over which performance will be measured.[32] Furthermore, assessing performance can require judgements to be made on counter-factuals: if there is no environmental degradation, is that because the environmental regulator has done a good job in preventing it and thus

---

[30] D Gray, *Review of Ofwat and Consumer Representation in the Water Sector* (London, 2011) (Gray Review), p.17.

[31] Treasury Select Committee *The Run on the Rock,* 5th Report of Session 2007–8 HC 56-1 (London 2007); J Black, 'The Credit Crisis and the Constitution' in D Oliver, T Prosser and R Rawlings (eds), *The Regulatory State* (Oxford: Oxford University Press, 2010).

[32] For good discussions of the issues see C Coglianese *Evaluating the Impact of Regulation and Regulatory Policy*, (Paris: OECD, 2012); C Radaelli and O Fritsch, *Evaluating Regulatory Management Tools and Programmes*, (Paris: OECD, 2012).

is a success, or does that show that it has not been sufficiently active, as environmental indicators, though remaining stable, have not improved? Or is it because there has been an economic downturn and so industries are producing less pollution? If the financial system has remained stable, is that because of the regulators' actions or in spite of them?

Regulators are also often tasked with roles which require a high degree of technical and specialized knowledge, but which are often highly contestable. Regulators in the area of telecommunications, water and energy, for example, have increasingly been required to consider a wide range of social objectives in addition to their economic objectives, and which in some cases may conflict with them. For example, there is an economic case for charging those in rural areas more for receiving some services than those in urban areas, but the social objectives require universal service at uniform prices, and cross-subsidy of one set of consumers by the other.

Regulators' tasks also often involve managing risk: resolving such questions as how much money should be spent on installing safety equipment on trains, for example, requires difficult questions to be addressed of how much should be spent to save a person's life, and whether that sum should differ between rail, road or air transport.[33]

Regulators' decisions can also be contestable because technical rules can have significant economic or redistributive consequences: how a 'market' is defined for the purposes of competition law is central to an assessment of whether a company has a dominant position within it, for example. In order to call regulators to account for the effectiveness of their decisions, accountors therefore need to have the technical knowledge necessary to understand what areas to probe, what questions to ask, and what answers to believe: should leverage ratios rather than risk models be used to set capital requirements for banks; how should a market be defined for the purposes of defining market abuse under competition law; what levels of nitrates should be allowed to be disposed in watercourses? However, by their very nature, specialist regulators have far greater technical knowledge of the substantive area they are regulating than do those calling them to account.

In the face of ill-specified and contested outcomes, and substantive decisions which require highly specialized knowledge to evaluate, accountors often resort to calling regulators to account not for their decisions but for their procedures instead: was appropriate consultation undertaken; was a regulatory impact analysis conducted; were sanctions imposed after following fair procedures?[34] Whilst these issues are important, it can mean that accountors are unable to engage with substantive aspects of complex decisions in any depth.

d. *The opacity of regulatory processes*

Accountors face a further problem, which is that the nature of regulatory activities can also present them with difficulties. Some aspects of these activities are highly

---

[33] See, eg. the Lofstedt review; E Fisher *Risk, Regulation and Administrative Constitutionalism* (Oxford: Hart Publishing, 2007).

[34] M Power *Managing Uncertainty* (Oxford, 2010); M Power *The Audit Society* (Oxford, 1997).

visible, such as public consultation processes. Enforcement decisions are also published, though details of informal settlements reached are usually not. There is little surprise, therefore, that most attention of those calling regulators to account focuses on the 'input' processes of consultation or numbers of officials assigned to particular functions, and that 'outputs' are measured in terms of highly visible indicators such as numbers of inspections undertaken, successful enforcement actions or levels of fines imposed.

However, most of regulation occurs in practice between those two visible poles of 'inputs' and 'outputs'. Regulation is a continuous process of negotiation, compromise and challenge—on both sides of the regulator-regulatee[35] relationship. It is very hard for outsiders to penetrate or have clear sight of that process. Moreover, it has been argued by some that the move away from 'command and control' regulation (reliance on detailed rules backed by legal sanctions) to 'new governance' strategies which rely more on the professional judgement of regulators, such as regulation based on principles, or regulatory strategies which require firms to develop their own systems and processes which are then approved by the regulator (which is the norm in health and safety regulation) render the regulatory process more opaque, as there are no clear standards with which regulatees have to comply, and to which regulators can be held to account. There are fears that they can thus open the regulator up to 'capture' by the regulated industry unless appropriate safeguards are put in place.[36] Whether or not such strategies are more porous and thus open to capture than a traditional 'command and control' approach is a moot point.[37] However, such 'new governance' strategies make far stronger demands on the professional judgement of a regulator, who is charged with ensuring that outcomes have been achieved rather than simply assuring that there has been technical compliance with a set of rules. Correspondingly, they also require greater professional judgement on the part of accountors.[38] Whilst it is neither possible nor desirable for accountors to have access to the day-to-day activities of regulators, they need a greater understanding of regulatory strategies and the trade-off and choices that they involve, particularly where regulators have conflicting objectives and/or limited resources. The statutory requirement for Ofcom (regulator of telecommunications and postal services) to explain how it reconciles the interests of the citizen and the consumer in its decision-making is an interesting example of how some transparency can be brought in to this complex area. But often trade-offs require difficult decisions over the application of resources; understanding that there may simply not be sufficient resources

---

[35] 'Regulatee' is a term of art common in the regulatory literature to refer to those who are being regulated.

[36] J Black, 'Forms and Paradoxes of Principles Based Regulation' *Capital Markets Law Journal* (2008) 3(4): 425–58; C Ford, 'New Governance in the Teeth of Human Frailty: Lessons from Financial Regulation' *Wisconsin LR* (2010) 441–487.

[37] Writers such as Pearce and Tombs, for example, argue that a 'compliance' approach to the enforcement of CAC rules is an indication of capture, eg. F Pearce and S Tombs, 'Ideology, Hegemony and Empiricism' *British Journal of Criminology* (1990) 30: 424.

[38] See P May, 'Regulatory Regimes and Accountability' *Regulation & Governance* (2007) 1: 8–26.

to allow for regulators to monitor or enforce regulations with the intensity that politicians or the public may want can be hard to accept, as the controversy over border controls in 2012 illustrated.

Moreover, if they are holding a regulator to account in terms of how effective it has been in achieving its statutory objectives, then accountors need a reliable way to assess the effectiveness of a regulator's activities. However, both regulators and accountors have been struggling for some time to find appropriate ways to assess performance in terms of outcomes, rather than simply inputs or outputs.[39] There are nonetheless welcome attempts by regulators to assess their own outcomes such as the FSA's Outcome Performance Reports, for example. Some accountors do the same, such as the Consumer Impact Report of the Legal Services Board's Consumer Panel.[40]

e. The role of accountees in the accountability relationship

Finally, accountability is a two-sided relationship: the accountee has to accept the 'right' of the accountor to hold them to account. The agencies discussed here have all been given legal mandates and powers, and are expected to operate independently from political control (and from 'capture' by the regulated industry). The balance between independence and accountability is inevitably one which is being continually negotiated between accountees and accountors. As a result, even organizations which are apparently in a strong institutional position, due perhaps to their legal powers, can find their 'right' to act as accountor called into question. So the constitutional supremacy of the Westminster Parliament is strongly embedded in the UK's constitutional settlement (broadly defined), but there are practical limits to its ability to call regulators to account. Moreover, Parliament's 'right' to call to account is not necessarily recognized by those it is trying to call to account, who may be less impressed with the niceties of constitutional law than orthodox accounts of Parliament's powers may suggest. Refusals by public bodies to provide parliamentary Select Committees with the information they require are not frequent, but they do happen. A striking example is the recent refusal by the Court of Directors of the Bank of England to disclose details of discussions held during the financial crisis to the Treasury Select Committee (TSC) on the basis that they were not required to by the Freedom of Information Act 2000.[41] Another example, though this time from a department, is the refusal by the government to disclose financial details relating to Network Rail to a recent PAC inquiry, which was justified on the basis that the Office of National Statistics had classified it as a private company, notwithstanding that its debt is underwritten

---

[39] See eg. NAO *Ofcom: The Effectiveness of Converged Regulation* HC 490 Session 2010–11 (London, 2010); Coglianese, *Evaluating the Impact;* and Radaelli and Fritsch, *Evaluating Regulatory Management Tools and Programmes.*

[40] See FSA, Outcomes Performance Reports at <http://www.fsa.gov.uk/about/aims/performance/opr>; Legal Services Board Consumer Panel, *Consumer Impact Report 2012* (London, 2012).

[41] Treasury Select Committee *Accountability of the Bank of England* 21st Report of Session 2010–12 HC 874 (London, 2011).

by the government.[42] (As an aside, in giving evidence to the PAC, the Permanent Secretary to the Department of Transport thought the debt was so guaranteed, but the Alternate Treasury Officer of Accounts did not, though both agreed it was a private company).[43]

However, for the most part, regulators are used to being held to account, and whilst they may not enjoy the process, they do engage with it, not least to maintain their own legitimacy and reputation.[44] For example, although it initially refused to publish its report on the supervision of the Royal Bank of Scotland (RBS) in the period prior to its rescue, citing the need for confidentiality, the FSA did capitulate in the face of strong political and media pressure, stemming initially from the TSC.[45] It also allowed the TSC to appoint two special advisors to review the report prior to publication and make amendments.[46]

Indeed, regulatory agencies are often active participants in their own accountability processes, doing much which goes beyond what is required by formal accountability arrangements. Regulators frequently engage in consultation and reporting practices which go beyond those required by statute, such as roadshows, focus groups, seminars, stakeholder meetings, annual public meetings, publication of minutes of board meetings (prior to the Freedom of Information Act 2000),[47] the appointment of expert reviewers,[48] or the creation of consumer panels (for example, Ofcom).[49]

---

[42] Public Accounts Committee, *Office of Rail Regulation: Regulating Network Rail's Efficiency*, 41st Report of Session 2010–11 (London, 2011), Minutes of Evidence, Q 183–225. The ONS plays an interesting role—when Northern Rock's debt became underwritten by the government in October 2007, the ONS classified it as a public company four months before legislation was passed to nationalize it: Black, n 31 above. Note that the NAO also assumed that Network Rail's debt is underwritten by the government: NAO *Office of Rail Regulation: Regulating Network Rail's Efficiency* HC 828 Session 2010–2011 (London, 2011).

[43] Public Accounts Committee, *Office of Rail Regulation: Regulating Network Rail's Efficiency*, 41st Report of Session 2010–11 (London, 2011).

[44] Eg. D Carpenter, *Reputation and Power: Organizational Image and Pharmaceutical Regulation at the FDA* (Princeton, 2010).

[45] Letter from Andrew Tyrie, Chair of the Treasury Select Committee, to Lord Turner, Chair of the FSA, 13 December 2010, available on the TSC website. The report was published in December 2011: FSA, *The Failure of Royal Bank of Scotland—FSA Board Report* (London, 2011).

[46] Letter from Lord Turner to Andrew Tyrie, 28 March 2011.

[47] Eg. M Thatcher, 'Regulation after Delegation: Independent Regulatory Agencies in Europe' *Journal of European Public Policy* (2002) 9: (6), 954; H Rothstein, 'Precautionary Bans or Sacrificial Lambs? Participative Regulation and the Reform of the UK Food Safety Regime' *Public Administration* (2004) 82: (4) 857.

[48] Eg. the Office of the Rail Regulator appointed regulatory experts to review its methodology for its periodic review process of Network Rail and publishes its processes including consultants' reports on its website: NAO *Office of Rail Regulation-Regulating Network Rail's Efficiency* HC 828 Session 2010–11 (London: HMSO 2011).

[49] See, eg. Ofgem's response to DECC's Ofgem Review detailing its transparency arrangements: DECC, *Ofgem Review-Final Report* (London, 2011), Annex A. For an account of similar actions by US agencies see D Rubinstein Reiss: 'Account Me In: Agencies in Quest of Accountability' *Journal of Law and Policy* (2011) 19 (2) 611–81; for accounts of how an agency can manipulate the accountability processes by the personnel that represent it see D Carpenter, *Reputation and Power* (Princeton: Princeton University Press, 2010).

Regulators also seek to manage their legitimacy by publicizing their activities, though as Hood and colleagues have noted, some are more publicity-seeking than others.[50] As Yeung has argued, regulators' presentational activities reveal the criteria by which they consider their legitimacy to be judged by others.[51] This is usually achieved by publicizing enforcement actions, but regulators use also publicity to try to change the public image of the regulator and the regime it is implementing. For example, the Health and Safety Executive has for several years published a 'myth of the month' on its website to dispel notions of 'health and safety regulation gone mad', though to little obvious effect either on behaviour or on the public's views.[52]

However, agencies can misread what is required to maintain their legitimacy, or find themselves caught between conflicting accountability regimes. As noted above, the FSA's initial refusal to publish its report on RBS was driven in significant part by concern that RBS would take legal action for breach of confidentiality, but it was a considerable political miscalculation, and it was rapidly forced to reverse its position.[53]

Thus, whilst it is conventional to bemoan the lack of accountability of regulatory agencies, the counter-argument is that they are often active participants in their accountability relationships, and even if they do not go beyond their statutory remits, at least they have a (relatively) clear mandate which a clearly defined set of individuals and governance structure (chairman, chief executive and governing board) is accountable for delivering. If regulatory functions are simply swallowed up into large departmental behemoths, there is no clear organizational structure for their performance; tasks are fungible, as are the departmental units performing them; opportunities for meaningful stakeholder participation are limited in the absence of dedicated advisory committees; and the scale of departments combined with the weaknesses of ministerial responsibility is such that accountability is lessened, not enhanced. For example, in commenting on the coalition government's Public Bodies Bill, the PAC argued that 'bringing functions back into sponsor departments is likely to undermine other channels of accountability, particularly with relevant stakeholder groups, and risk leaving policies fighting numerous other priorities for ministerial attention. This will mean less effective accountability and challenge on a day-to-day basis.'[54] Whilst the government, predictably, disagreed with this comment, as indeed it stridently disagreed with most

[50] C Hood, C Scott, O James, et al, *Regulation Inside Government: Waste-watchers, Quality Police, and Sleaze-Busters* (Oxford: Oxford University Press, 1999).

[51] K Yeung, 'Presentational Management and the Pursuit of Regulatory Legitimacy: A Comparative Study of Competition and Consumer Agencies in the United Kingdom and Australia' *Public Administration* (2009) 87: (2) 274–294.

[52] The Lofstedt review also noted the role of occupational health and safety consultants, insurance companies and fears of litigation in significantly ratcheting up the health and safety obligations of firms and local authorities.

[53] FSA, *The failure of the Royal Bank of Scotland: Financial Services Authority Board Report* (London: FSA, 2011).

[54] Public Administration Committee, *Smaller Government: Shrinking the Quango State* 5th Report Session 2010–11 (London, 2010), para.96.

of the report (whilst of course, 'welcoming' it), it is argued that there is considerable force in the PAC's view.

C. Accountability in the political domain

Those seeking to call regulators to account thus face a significant set of challenges, which they have differing capacities to address. However, it has to be remembered that agencies are not passive actors in the accountability process: they are active participants who can act to manage their accountability relationships through communicative and other strategies in order to enhance their political and social legitimacy.

This section explores these dynamics by examining the role of four key regulatory accountors in the political domain. It looks first at accountability within the executive, focusing on the ways in which the 'better regulation' agenda is used both to control regulatory bodies and to call them to account. Although the core executive's 'better regulation' processes may not always engage the independent regulatory agencies, they provide an important context in which the activities of such regulators are often assessed by other accountors, notably parliamentary Select Committees and the NAO. The second part focuses on the role of parliamentary Select Committees, highlighting the constraints that Parliament has in practice to meet the challenges outlined above in calling regulators to account, the ways in which it is meeting those challenges, and the blurring of the boundaries between its role as accountor and other roles that it may play with respect to a regulatory body. The discussion then turns to the NAO, and explores how its institutional position limits its ability to act as accountor, notwithstanding its considerable capacity. Finally, the fourth part looks at a group of accountors, consumer panels which have legal mandates to represent the views of consumers to specified regulatory agencies, and draws on current debates on their reforms to highlight both the significance of accountability capacity, and the fluidity of roles that an accountor can play in regulatory processes, constantly moving from participant to accountor.

1. Intra-executive accountability—from the periphery to the core

Although we may speak of 'the executive' as a single entity, in practice it is internally fragmented. We can distinguish broadly between the 'core' executive, which in essence is the Cabinet Office and the Treasury; the 'extended' executive, by which is meant government departments and their various units; and the 'periphery', which includes the regulatory agencies which have separate legal status, mandates and powers. In practice, different parts of the executive can have a significant role in calling other parts to account.[55] There is a strong functional and political

---

[55] Hood et al, *Regulation Inside Government*, n 51 above.

reason for this. Politicians who are in power pass legislation to create regulatory agencies to which they delegate important public functions and around which they put in place legal structures to ensure the independence of those agencies from political control. One of the challenges that the executive in particular faces is how to exercise some control over those agencies without violating (or being seen to violate) that act of delegation. There is thus a significant tension between the centrifugal forces which push functions out to the periphery, and the centre's need for control.[56] As a result, whilst we might have witnessed an internal fragmentation of the executive into a vast array of regulatory bodies, public-private contracting, outsourcing and so forth, we have seen a corresponding rise (though it may be with some considerable time-lag) in mechanisms being put in place by the core executive to enhance its capacity to control and coordinate the many-headed Hydra it has created.[57]

One way to address the problem of control over regulatory or other 'arm's length' bodies is to reduce their number. 'Quango-burning' is nothing new; the allocation of functions has oscillated between agencies and departments since the establishment of inspectorates in the Victorian 'revolution in government' in the nineteenth century.[58] In 2010, the coalition government engaged in its own review exercise and announced that four hundred and eighty one out of over nine hundred public bodies were to be reformed, reconstituted or abolished.[59] Nonetheless, despite some rationalization, significant functions remain in the hands of independent or quasi-independent public bodies which may or may not have a separate legal mandate. It is important to note that there is a considerable spectrum of operational autonomy between organizations carrying out regulatory functions, with (broadly speaking) executive agencies which have no independent legal status enjoying the least independence, and those further out on the periphery with separate legal mandates having far more autonomy. Moreover, even within the latter group, there can be a far closer operational relationship in practice between some, formally independent, regulatory agencies and their departments than there is between others. Formal powers do not necessarily give a true picture of what the relationships are in practice.

The main instrument that the core executive (ie. the Cabinet Office and the Treasury) have to control regulators and call them to account is through their

---

[56] J Black, 'Tensions in the Regulatory State' *Public Law* [2007] 58–73.

[57] See, in particular, Hood et al, *Regulation Inside Government*, n 51 above.

[58] H R Greaves *The Civil Service in the Changing State* (1949); FMG Wilson, 'Ministers and Boards: Some Aspects of Administrative Development since 1832' *Public Administration* (1954) 32: 43; Fulton Committee, *The Report on the Committee on the Civil Service* (Cmnd 3638, HMSO, 1967); P Holland, *The Governance of Quangos* (London: Adam Smith Institute, 1981); C Hood, 'The Politics of Quangocide' *Policy and Politics* (1980) 8: 247; *Report on Non-Departmental Bodies* (Cmnd 7797, London: HMSO, 1980).

[59] Cabinet Office, *Public Bodies Reform—Proposals For Change* (London, 2010). The Public Bodies Act 2011 confers on Ministers power to abolish or merge bodies, modify a body's constitutional or funding arrangements, or transfer its functions elsewhere, subject to approval by parliamentary resolution. In addition, triennial reviews of non-departmental public bodies have been introduced.

budgets, for the majority (though not all) are at least part-funded by the state, with budgets set by the Treasury.[60] There is no doubt that the Treasury can have a significant impact on a regulator's capacity through its funding decisions, and has recently imposed significant budget cuts (Ofcom's budget, for example, was cut by 28 per cent in 2011). Whilst the House of Lords review of economic regulators found that, on the whole, the independence of those regulators had not been compromised by the funding arrangements in place,[61] the issue of funding does considerably complicate Parliament's attempts to determine whether responsibility for regulators' performance should in specific instances lie with the executive or with the regulatory agency.

With respect to regulatory functions, it is through the 'better regulation' agenda that we have seen the marked 're-centring' of control by the core executive over regulatory processes, if not directly over regulatory decisions, particularly with respect to those regulators with considerable inspection and enforcement functions. Indeed, the development of better regulation processes, at least in the UK, can be largely explained as attempts to develop intra-executive mechanisms of control by the core over the periphery.[62] Despite its highly technical and often mundane nature, regulation has been a key political priority for successive administrations since the 1980s. The common mantra, through both Conservative and Labour governments, is that regulation is bad for business, and so bad for economic growth. Since the mid-1980s successive administrations, of whatever political hue, have tried to re-engineer regulatory processes under the banner of 'better regulation': trying to get independent regulators and the rest of government to 'do regulation better', and indeed to 'do "better regulation" better'.

Three strategies in particular have been used in the last fifteen years.[63] These are, firstly, the use of organizations within either the Cabinet Office or the department for business (the name changes frequently) to monitor regulatory proposals issuing from within government departments and some of their associated bodies, though not the independent regulatory agencies. Secondly, to establish specialist advisory bodies to advise the executive on what both departments and independent regulators are doing, and to appoint ad hoc independent reviews to investigate either particular independent regulators or particular functions of a number of agencies, and to report and advise. Thirdly, to impose cross-cutting duties on regulatory agencies through legal requirements and codes of practice. Each of these has the potential to make significant inroads into the exercise of discretion by independent regulators, blurring the boundaries between independence, accountability and control, though their impact in practice is mixed.

---

[60] For details on funding, see Prosser, *The Regulatory Enterprise*.

[61] House of Lords, *Review of Economic Regulators*. The exception was the funding of Postcomm, now absorbed into Ofcom.

[62] C Radaelli, 'Regulating Rule-Making via Impact Assessment' *Governance* (2010) 23: (1) 89–108.

[63] For a brief history see R Baldwin, M Cave and M Lodge *Understanding Regulation* (2nd edition Oxford: Oxford University Press, 2011).

a. Getting government to 'do "better regulation" better'—structuring decision-making

The move by central government to attempt to push the 'de-regulation' and subsequently the 'better regulation' agenda through government began in 1985 with the creation of individual departmental deregulation units, responsible for identifying areas where regulation could be simplified or removed. Responsibilities were moved to the very top of government with the creation of a central deregulation unit as part of the Cabinet Office in 1995. The incoming Labour government kept the unit, though reconstituted, and renamed it the Regulatory Impact Unit in 1997. All new regulatory proposals were to be accompanied by a 'regulatory impact assessment' setting out predicted costs and benefits. On the recommendation of the Hampton Review, to which we return below, this was replaced in 2005 with the Better Regulation Executive (BRE), initially attached to the Cabinet Office but which moved in 2007 to the Department of Business, Enterprise and Regulatory Reform (BERR). Its emphasis broadened to comprise not only regulatory impact assessments, but as discussed below, a wider focus on burden reduction and regulatory processes, again following Hampton's recommendations. It performed twice-yearly reviews of departments, which were not published but were submitted to the Prime Minister for review.[64]

Both the previous Labour administration and the current coalition government introduced further organizational and procedural reforms. The BRE's role in reviewing departmental performance and further driving the 'better regulation' agenda across government continues. It is now advised now by the Better Regulation Strategy Group, which is an advisory group comprised of business and consumer representatives, and the two bodies share the same non-executive chairman.[65] The cabinet has also replaced the Regulatory Accountability Panel with two new bodies. These are the Regulatory Policy Group, which scrutinizes all new regulatory proposals and the impact assessments accompanying them. It then passes all proposals with satisfactory impact statements to the Reducing Regulation Committee, a body comprised of external members which considers the impact assessments and the associated rules which are proposed to be removed to 'make way' for the new requirements, including those implementing EU legislation.[66]

As a mechanism of simultaneous control and accountability, the better regulation agenda is felt more strongly the closer the regulator is in its operations to government departments, at whom these efforts are principally directed. However it is not clear what impacts they have really had. Successive NAO reviews of regulatory impact assessments performed by departments have shown them to be inadequate

---

[64] Baldwin et al, *Understanding Regulation*. In addition, the Regulatory Accountability Panel, a cabinet sub-committee chaired by the Chief Secretary to the Treasury, scrutinized departmental simplification plans and major policy proposals which were likely to impose a cost of over £20 million per annum or disproportionately impact a particular sector.

[65] HM Government *Reducing Regulation Made Simple—Less Regulation, Better Regulation and Regulation as a Last Resort*, (London, 2010).

[66] NAO *Department for Business, Innovation and Skills—Delivering Regulatory Reform*, HC 758 (London, 2011).

in a number of respects—often with significant operational consequences.[67] The NAO recently concluded, in effect, that government could do better in trying to do 'better regulation'.[68] Nonetheless, whilst the outcomes remain unclear, the drive for internal control over regulatory processes from the very top of the political executive is indisputable.

b. Using specialist advisors and reviewers

Executive control over regulatory policy-making within departments has been accompanied by the use of specialist advisory bodies and independent reviews to advise on regulatory reform across the whole of the regulatory landscape. The Better Regulation Taskforce was created in 1997 and devised five principles of 'good regulation' which are now enshrined in legislation and widely referred to as the 'PACTT' principles: proportionality, accountability, consistency, transparency and targeting.[69] It conducted a considerable number of reviews into specific areas of regulation and into the conduct of regulation overall.[70] It was reconstituted as the Better Regulation Commission in 2006, but still reported to the cabinet. Arguably two of its two most influential reports were *Less is More*, which set the current policy agenda on administrative burden reduction, and *Public Risk—the Next Frontier for Better Regulation*, which was produced at the request of the Prime Minister and in fact advocated its own demise.[71] On the basis of the latter it was abolished and replaced by the Risk Regulation Advisory Council in 2008, which produced a series of reports, guides and tools to help policy-makers and the public tackle public risk. Its work programme ended in 2009, and it has not been replaced. Political attention has moved elsewhere.

The appointment of specialist advisors to investigate particular areas of regulation, either particular sectors or particular processes across sectors, has also been increasingly used. Most influential of these has been the Hampton Review of Inspection and Enforcement in 2005, which reviewed the inspection and enforcement activities of the non-economic regulators including the Environment Agency, the Food Standards Agency, the Health and Safety Executive, the Financial Services Authority and the Civil Aviation Authority.[72] The Hampton Review marked a shift to scrutinizing more closely not just the consultation practices of regulators or the decisions they make, but their operational systems and processes. Amongst other things, it recommended that regulators should adopt a risk-based approach to

---

[67] A review by the NAO found that proposals to restructure organizations in particular often had no or inadequate assessments of costs and benefits: NAO, *Reorganizing Central Government,* HC 452 (London, 2010).

[68] NAO, *Delivering Regulatory Reform.*

[69] See Baldwin et al, *Understanding Regulation,* n 64 above.

[70] Reports included *Alternatives to State Regulation* (London, 2000); *Economic Regulators* (London, 2000); *Independent Regulators* (London, 2003); *Imaginative Thinking for Better Regulation* (London, 2003); *Avoiding Regulatory Creep* (London, 2004); *Less is More—Reducing Burdens, Improving Outcomes* (London, 2005); *Risk, Responsibility, Regulation* (London, 2005).

[71] The report, and request, followed its report, *Risk, Responsibility, Regulation* (London, 2007).

[72] Hampton Review of Inspection and Enforcement (London, 2005).

inspection and enforcement, focusing resources on areas of greatest risk, and that regulators should be accountable for the efficiency and effectiveness of their processes, whilst remaining independent in the decisions they take.[73] Sector-specific reviews have also been instrumental in prompting regulatory reform. Most recent are the reviews of Ofwat[74] and Ofgem,[75] of the regulation of the railways,[76] of the inspection and enforcement of the regulation of farming (which spans several agencies)[77] and of the enforcement policies and practices of the Health and Safety Executive,[78] each of which is likely to be the basis of legislation going forward, and which are discussed further below.

Whilst they may not form part of any formal 'map' of accountability relationships, such reviews do require regulators to give an account of their activities, and can provide a valuable resource for others seeking to hold them to account. Moreover, it is striking the extent to which such reviews set the agenda for other accountors. The Hampton review has been particularly influential in defining the 'better regulation' agenda for inspection and enforcement activities, and in particular for driving the development risk-based regulation as a further element of the better regulation agenda. In the wake of the report, the government codified the 'Hampton Principles' in the Legislation and Regulatory Reform Act 2006, and set up the Macrory Review of regulatory sanctions, which also led to the Regulatory Enforcement and Sanctions Act 2008, both discussed below. The Treasury and BERR[79] also appointed the NAO to evaluate how well five regulatory agencies were operating in accordance with Hampton principles, and reviewed a further thirty-six.[80] Parliamentary Select Committees have picked up on the agenda without questioning it, and have urged regulators to adopt more principles-based approaches to regulation, and also to be more 'risk-based'.[81] It is worth pointing out how quickly accountability criteria shifted in the wake of the financial crisis, however, when all of a sudden not only did principles-based regulation lose its allure, but accountors conveniently forgot that it had ever had one.[82]

c. Using principles and codes—the juridification of better regulation

In the last few years, we have also seen the increasing 'juridification' of principles of better regulation as they have morphed from general exhortations to statutory

---

[73] Hampton Review of Inspection and Enforcement (London, 2005).   [74] Gray review.

[75] DECC *Ofgem Review—Final Report* (London, 2011).

[76] R McNulty *Realising the Potential of GB Rail-Report of a Value for Money Study* (London, 2011) (McNulty report).

[77] Farming Task Force report.

[78] Lord Young *Common Sense, Common Safety* (London, 2010); Lofstedt review.

[79] Department for Business, Enterprise and Regulatory Reform, since renamed Department of Business, Innovation and Skills.

[80] For summary of reports on the initial five regulators see NAO, *Regulatory quality: How regulators are implementing the Hampton vision* (NAO, 2008).

[81] House of Lords Regulatory Committee, *Economic Regulators*.

[82] J Black, 'The Rise, Fall and Fate of Principles Based Regulation', in K Alexander and N Moloney (eds) *Law Reform and Financial Markets* (Cheltenham: Edward Elgar, 2011).

obligations. Thus, what started off as instruments of political accountability evolved into ones of legal accountability. The extent to which they are embedded in the legal mandates of individual regulators varies: the FSA, Ofcom and Ofgem are under statutory obligations to conduct regulatory impact assessments, for example, but Ofwat and the Office of the Rail Regulator (ORR) are not. However, there has been an increased move to introduce legal responsibilities to adhere to different parts of the better regulation agenda on a cross-regulator basis. The PACTT principles, for example, began as self-imposed guidance for one regulator (the Health and Safety Executive), were then adopted and promoted by the Better Regulation Taskforce as cross-cutting principles for all regulators, as noted above, then enshrined in a non-legal enforcement concordat in 1998, incorporated in the legislative mandates of some regulators (for example, Ofcom and the Legal Services Board), and are now enshrined in the Legislative and Regulatory Reform Act 2006 (LRR Act) as statutory principles of good regulation.[83] In addition, those regulators who wish to receive enhanced enforcement powers under the Regulatory Enforcement and Sanctions Act 2008 have to demonstrate their compliance with the principles before the government will introduce an order conferring the powers on them. Thus far, only the Environment Agency and Natural England have been granted additional powers.[84]

The LRR Act also introduced the statutory Regulators' Compliance Code, which enacts the principles recommended by the Hampton review, to which regulators are now required to have regard in the exercise of their general functions.[85] It is not clear that the code has had a significant impact on the way that regulators operate, however. In its recent review of regulatory enforcement practices, the coalition government has expressed concern that the compliance code has not received the attention from regulators that it should have, though its greatest concern is that business feels that regulators are too onerous in their enforcement practices (it is notable that the review did not seek the views of other stakeholders, including consumers).[86]

So for the core executive at least, the better regulation agenda defines the criteria against which regulatory processes should be assessed, and it is through better regulation processes that the centre tries to exercise both control and accountability simultaneously. These processes have greater purchase with respect to government departments than they do on independent regulators on the far periphery. Nonetheless, even those regulators at the periphery have felt the pressure of the better regulation agenda through the injection of some of its core components into their legal mandates, as political accountability morphs into a source of legal accountability.

---

[83] Regulatory Reform Act 2006, s 21(2).
[84] Others, eg. the Health and Safety Executive, have decided not to apply on the basis that they do not need them.
[85] BERR, Regulators Compliance Code, Statutory Code of Practice for Regulators (2007), para.9.
[86] Department for Business, Innovation and Skills, *Transforming Regulatory Enforcement* (London, 2011).

2. Parliamentary Select Committees

a. *Parliament—organizing itself to be an accountor*

Whilst parliamentary Select Committees may appear to be in a strong position to hold regulators to account, given the constitutional supremacy of Parliament, as noted above the complexity of the regulatory landscape and the number, range and scope of regulatory agencies that exists pose a significant challenge to their capacity to do so.

As a result, Parliament has struggled with the question of how best to organize itself to call independent regulators to account.[87] In a recent report, the House of Lords Liaison Committee admitted as much: despite successive Select Committee reports from both Houses recommending the creation of a joint committee to scrutinize regulatory bodies, it argued that the scope was too broad for the remit of such a body to be successfully defined: ' "Regulation" in the sense of the establishment and enforcement of legal and other standards encompasses a huge sweep of public policy. The ad hoc committee [on economic regulators] found that the breadth of its remit was problematic, even in its more focussed form.'[88] It concluded that the scale of the task, together with the current upheaval in the regulatory landscape, meant that Departmental Select Committees were better placed to perform such a role on a regular basis.[89]

There have been cross-sector investigations by ad hoc committees in both Houses. Nevertheless, Parliament's accountability activities remain principally the preserve of Departmental Select Committees, certainly in the House of Commons. The House of Commons Select Committee structure deliberately follows the structure and responsibilities of government departments. However, whilst there is a clear rationale for it, this mirroring of the executive's organizational structure has limitations, at least with respect to the accountability of regulatory agencies. As noted above, often the regulation of a particular sector is distributed between two or more regulators, which can in turn have different lead departments. This can create organizational silos within the executive, and indeed gaps in regulatory regimes, which are reinforced, rather than addressed, by the Departmental Select Committee structure.[90]

Moreover, in practice Parliament is an accountor that speaks with many voices. There is little apparent coordination between House of Commons Select

---

[87] HL Constitution Committee, *The Regulatory State: Ensuring its Accountability*, 6th Report 2003–04, HL Paper 68 (London, 2004); House of Lords, *Report from the Select Committee on Regulators, UK Economic Regulators*, 2006–07, HL Paper 189 (London, 2006).

[88] HL Liaison Committee, *New Proposals for Committee Activity* 2nd Report of Session 2010–12 (London, 2010), para.10.

[89] HL Liaison Committee, *New Proposals for Committee Activity*, paras 8–12.

[90] Eg., responsibility for defined contribution pensions is split between the Pensions Regulator (Department for Work and Pensions) and the FSA, now FCA (Treasury), which can result in gaps being created in regulatory regimes which are not picked up either by the lead departments or the relevant Select Committees, and thus which reinforce the gaps rather than correcting them: see eg. NAO, *The Pensions Regulator—Regulating Defined Contribution Schemes* HC 466 (London, 2012).

Committees on their agendas, and certainly no clear systematization in the timing, scope and incidence of review of regulators by each individual committee. Indeed, it was this lack of systematic attention to regulatory agencies which the proponents of a single committee hoped such a body could address.[91] Moreover, Select Committee reports show inconsistencies in the approach taken to reviewing the regulatory bodies, either by the same committee over time or between committees, with little cross-referencing. This is not surprising given that the membership of committees changes regularly, but it does not facilitate systematic review. There can also be disputes as to which committee is responsible for what (for example, differences between the Lords and the Commons as to who should call the UK Statistics Office to account)[92], and diverging responses to the same event (for example, the different responses of the PAC and TSC to the non-disclosure of the government indemnity to the Bank of England during the financial crisis).[93]

It could be argued that there are merits in having unpredictable reviews—it keeps regulators on their toes.[94] That is true, but it is suggested that such randomized strategies are best when part of a broader systematic process which ensures that the same bodies are not reviewed over and over again whilst others are in effect ignored. One way to systematize Parliament's review function could be for the committees of each House to agree a rolling timetable of review for the most important regulatory agencies, for example a convention to review every five years unless events make a review necessary within that period, and to agree a common set of core issues to investigate, adjusted as appropriate to the agency's mandate and functions.[95]

Even if Select Committees in both Houses were to adopt such a process, however, two issues remain. The first is that the parliamentary timetable may simply preclude it from paying an active accountability role in a crisis. The financial crisis exploded in the summer of 2008, during parliamentary recess. Decisions had to be taken with such speed that the affirmative resolution procedures put in place to ensure parliamentary accountability, though followed, were simply a matter of form.[96] Crises do not follow parliamentary session dates.

The second issue is that of motivating either the rest of Parliament or the government to take note of committee reports of either House. Select Committees can sometimes be quite despondent about their ability either to call to account or to impose consequences. For example, in reviewing the proposals to merge Postcomm's functions into Ofcom, the House of Commons Select Committee for Business and Enterprise commented that the model of accountability proposed (which was in fact the standard constitutional one of an annual report to

---

[91] HL Constitution Committee, *The Regulatory State: Ensuring its Accountability*, 6th Report 2003–04, paras 199–204.
[92] HL Liaison Committee, 1st Report of Session 2007–8, HL 33 (London, 2008), App.3.
[93] Black, 'The Credit Crisis and the Constitution', n. 32 above.
[94] Hood et al, *Regulation Inside Government*, n 51 above.
[95] It may be that the government's newly introduced triennial review process for non-departmental public bodies may help Parliament to organize its attention in this regard.
[96] Black, 'The Credit Crisis and the Constitution', n. 31 above.

Parliament, followed by scrutiny by the relevant Select Committee) was 'fundamentally misconceived. . . . Select Committees have no power to direct; we can only make recommendations in reports to the House. It is for the Government to take action.'[97] It argued in effect that its previous reports had been in vain, as it had had no power to make either the government or the regulator think again. It concluded, perhaps rather fatalistically, 'only the Government has the resources and powers to monitor a regulator.'[98]

However, we should not underestimate the significance that the reports can have. Despite the difficulties Parliament faces in calling regulators and the executive to account, it has nonetheless had some considerable impacts. The reviews of both Ofwat and Ofgem noted below stemmed in part from Select Committee recommendations. It was on the basis of the PAC report and witness evidence on the Care Quality Commission (CQC) that the government postponed the proposed abolition of the Human Fertilisation and Embryology Authority and the Human Tissue Authority and the transfer of their functions to the CQC.[99] Moreover, the detailed engagement of the TSC in calling both the regulator and the executive to account in the financial crisis, which has continued with the change in government, suggests that if they so wish, parliamentary Select Committees can be formidable accountors. Indeed it may be that reforms within Parliament to the procedures for appointing members to Select Committees could serve to give those committees a greater sense of independence, which could enhance their willingness to call regulators to account.[100]

b. Determining responsibility and apportioning blame—from 'many hands' to 'no hands'

Although capacity is important, it is recognized that some accountability challenges cannot be resolved by throwing more resources at them. One of the most intractable difficulties in calling regulators to account is trying to determine who is responsible in any particular instance — regulators or the government — and therefore who to blame when things go wrong. As noted above, the regulatory landscape is highly complex with responsibilities frequently shared between regulators and the government, and with an inherent tension in their relationship between independence, control and accountability. In operational terms, coordination is at a premium, issues can fall between gaps, and responsibilities can be unclear, to say the least. There is a risk that both the government and the regulator use the organizational complexity and ambiguity as to their respective roles to avoid responsibility.

---

[97] House of Commons Business and Enterprise Committee, *The Postal Services Bill* 5th Report of Session 2008–09 HC 172-I, para.96.

[98] HC Business and Enterprise Committee, *The Postal Services Bill*, para.97.

[99] The government has since begun consultation on the issue: Dept.of Health *Consultation on proposals to transfer functions from the Human Fertilisation and Embryology Authority and the Human Tissue Authority* (London, 2012).

[100] See HC Liaison Committee *Rebuilding the House-Select Committee Issues* 1st Report Session 2009–10 (London, 2010).

If we recall Christopher Hood's argument that institutional structures are often designed largely to ensure that blame can be shifted away from their designer,[101] then we should not be surprised at this outcome, though it does not make it any easier to address. When things go wrong, blame can pass quite quickly and easily to whoever seems to be the most proximate cause. However, as Hood argues, the challenge of calling to account 'many hands' can also turn into the challenge of finding there are 'no hands' when crises erupt, as each actor seeks to blame the other.[102] Moreover, lack of clarity as to the responsibilities of each organization can lead to paralysis, or at least severe bungling. As noted above, it was clear in the case of Northern Rock's collapse, for example, that each of the Treasury, Bank of England and FSA felt that the responsibility to act lay with the other, leading not only to difficulties in ascribing responsibilities after the event in the accountability process, but to significant failings in operations leading up to its failure and in its immediate management.[103]

Successive parliamentary Select Committee reports have criticized the government for blurring the boundaries between its roles and responsibilities and those of the regulators in almost every area. For example, in a recent report reviewing the management of the risk of floods, the PAC commented that there were no clear lines of responsibility between local authorities, the Environment Agency and the department. The Agency relied on the department for funding flood protection initiatives, but that budget had just been cut and the department had told the agency to find funding elsewhere and had told local authorities to increase their contributions, whilst again cutting their budgets. In short, the committee argued that the department was failing to accept ultimate responsibility.[104]

Responsibilities can also be particularly unclear in the period when the agency is being established. For example, in a highly critical report on the CQC, the PAC argued that although the Commission's governance and operations were poor, the Department of Health had considerably underestimated the task facing the CQC in merging three pre-existing regulators into one, requiring it to take on an expanded role with a reduced budget and without a defined set of objectives. In short, even though it was responsible for the Commission, it had not 'had a grip' on what the Commission was doing.[105] Similarly, although the PAC criticized the leadership of the Equality and Human Rights Commission, it found that the lead department (which changed three times in the period leading up to its creation) did not have a clear project plan for the creation of the Commission, that there was no budget in place, and that the Commission's executive had had no say in which staff were to be transferred to it, leaving it without staff who had the necessary

---

[101] Hood, *The Blame Game*, n 9 above.   [102] Hood, *The Blame Game*, n 9 above.
[103] Treasury Select Committee *Run on the Rock*; NAO *Maintaining Financial Stability Across the UK Banking System*, HC 91 Session 2009–10 (London, 2009).
[104] HC Committee of Public Accounts *Flood Risk Management in England* HC 1659 (London, 2012).
[105] HC Committee of Public Accounts *Care Quality Commission: Regulating the Quality and Safety of Health and Adult Social Care* 78th Report of Session 2010–12 HC 1779 (London, 2012), para.1.

skills.[106] In this case, rather than try to apportion responsibility, the PAC simply (and probably rightly) blamed both for bringing the Commission into operation before it was properly prepared.

Another recurrent problem has been to identify who is responsible for defining the political, social or public interest goals that regulators should be pursuing, particularly with respect to the economic regulators. The McNulty report into the regulation of the railways, for example, argued that the ways in which responsibilities for the regulation of Network Rail (the infrastructure provider) and the train operators was shared between the ORR, the Department of Transport and the industry was unclear.[107] In addition, the report argued that the 'high level objectives' that the department set every five years for the regulator and the industry were often contradicted by political decisions made in the interim to meet short-term needs. It proposed that the ORR's remit and capacity should be considerably enhanced and that it should take over complete responsibility for regulation of the train operating companies as well as Network Rail, removing the department's regulatory role, but leaving it the task of setting long-term strategic goals.[108]

Finding the balance between the operational independence of the regulator and the exercise of strategic direction by elected politicians is not an easy matter, however.[109] The recent review of Ofwat by David Gray, for example, emphasized the need for greater clarity in the respective roles of Ofwat and the government.[110] The Gray report found a widespread demand among stakeholders for greater clarity on the government's objectives for the sector and on the respective roles of government, Ofwat and the other regulators. The regulation of water services is further complicated by the fact that Ofwat is also accountable to the Welsh Assembly, and the report found there was a need for greater coordination between the Westminster government and the Welsh Assembly on what their policy goals are. It recommended that they agree a MOU setting out their respective goals, and that their policy statements should be combined with clearer guidance to Ofwat as to how it should seek to balance its various duties in arriving at regulatory decisions. Moreover, in view of the number of regulatory bodies involved, government objectives for the water sector should be specified in a way that minimized the scope for conflict between the regulators.[111]

A similar finding was made in the review of Ofgem conducted by the Department of Energy and Climate Change (DECC).[112] The review found that as Ofgem's role had become more complex, there had been a 'blurring of responsibilities between the Government and Ofgem causing some erosion of the regulatory certainty that independent regulation was designed to provide'. It concluded that there was a need for 'an enduring solution that sees Government clearly taking responsibility

---

[106] HC Committee of Public Accounts *Equality and Human Rights Commission* 15th Report of Session 2009–10, HC 124 (London, 2010).
[107] McNulty report.   [108] McNulty report, para.4.3.
[109] See eg. the evidence of Stephen Carter on his Report *Digital Britain*: HC 331-i Q 18, and the report of the HC Business and Enterprise Committee *The Postal Services Bill* 5th Report of Session (2008–09) HC 172-I, para.99.
[110] Gray review.   [111] Gray review, Recommendation 1.   [112] DECC review.

for setting and communicating strategic direction, Ofgem's independent regulatory decisions forming a logical and coherent part of this broader strategic policy framework, and ad hoc interventions avoided where possible.'[113]

The DECC review recommended that the government should introduce a new, five-yearly statutory 'Strategy and Policy Statement'.[114] The statement would set out the government's policy goals for the sector; describe the roles and responsibilities of government, Ofgem, and other relevant bodies; and define policy outcomes that government considers the regulator to have a particularly important role in delivering. The regulator would then be expected to set out annually how it will deliver its contribution and monitor progress, and where progress is not on track, explain why and what action may need to be taken to mitigate the problems.

Such statements could bring a welcome degree of transparency to the relationship between government and the independent regulators, though as we saw in the case of Northern Rock, statements (or in that case a MOU) can prove to be less clear in ascribing responsibilities in any particular case. They can also become out of date, and/or departed from by governments, who instead intervene on an ad hoc basis to address short-term political goals, as both the McNulty and Gray reports respectively found with respect to rail and water. However, if the government could commit to such statements for a five-year period, it could go some way to providing both the strategic direction that a regulator needs, and some clarity as to the respective responsibilities of each.

c. Shifting roles

The recommendations of the Ofgem review also raised the question of how closely Parliament should become involved in policing the boundaries between control, independence and accountability. In the case of Ofgem, the DECC review proposed that the statement and any subsequent revisions would also be subject to Parliamentary approval through the affirmative resolution procedure, which would require Parliament to debate and approve the statement before it could come into force.[115] This was presented as an opportunity to involve Parliament in holding the regulator to account, but a cynic could argue that it is also a way of ensuring Parliament signs off on the statement, thus restricting its ability to criticize later on—allowing responsibilities between the accountor (Parliament) and the accountees (Ofgem and the government) to become unclear.

There is already a blurring of the boundaries of Parliament's role as accountor of Ofgem, because under the EU Third Package for Energy, it is national legislatures which have to approve the budgets of their energy regulators, not the executive.[116] At present, the annual process for setting the budget is linked to Ofgem's consultation on its annual corporate plan, which provides an opportunity for interested parties, including DECC and the Treasury to raise any concerns. Following the consultation, Ofgem sets out its main estimates for Parliament, which then votes

[113] DECC review, para.6.   [114] DECC review, para.6.   [115] DECC review, para.88.
[116] Council Directive (EC) 2009/72 concerning common rules for the internal market in electricity.

on whether to approve the budget.[117] This process may be seen as giving Parliament a welcome voice, and of empowering it to 'impose consequences', but it may complicate Parliament's role as an accountor.

This raises a broader question: whether, and to what extent, does ex ante engagement preclude the organization concerned from being an impartial ex post accountor? Does their ex ante involvement implicate them too greatly in the decisions and actions for which they then seek to hold the regulator to account? For example, Parliament (acting as accountor) may criticise Ofgem ex post for failures to achieve certain outcomes, but Ofgem may reply that it needs more funding in order to perform effectively, so that the reason it has failed is due to Parliament (acting as ex ante approver of its budget) and its refusal to allow it greater resources, thus implicating Parliament in the blame game. Moreover, who (realistically) calls Parliament to account for the budget Parliament provides to Ofgem is less than clear. The NAO, perhaps?

3. The National Audit Office

The role of the NAO in calling regulators to account has been steadily increasing over the last ten to fifteen years, and there is no doubt that the NAO has now become a significant actor in the political accountability of regulators in the UK. This is not necessarily because it can impose any direct consequences on those regulators that it criticizes: it has no power to do anything other than report. It is rather because it has become a well respected and valuable 'accountability resource' for other political actors, notably the executive and Parliament. In other words, by providing both the core executive and Parliament with detailed information and evaluation of regulators' activities, it enhances their capacity to call those regulators to account. Indeed, Parliament's accountability capacity would be severely reduced in the absence of the NAO. The NAO has developed considerable accountability capacity in terms of access to information, technical expertise in performance evaluation, and in regulatory techniques, drawing on external advisors for sectoral expertise, and its reports are generally of a high quality.

However, as it cannot comment on policy, strictly speaking the reviews that it undertakes are meant to be focused on the 'value for money' that a regulator provides. Thus, it cannot criticize policy per se, only its implementation (though the line in practice may be blurred). Furthermore, it can only examine the accounts and performance of those regulators which it is given the legal powers to examine: it was never granted the power to audit the FSA, for example, on the basis that the FSA did not receive public funds (although the Treasury did commission a review by the NAO on specific aspects of the FSA's work).[118]

---

[117] NAO *Performance of Ofgem—Briefing for the House of Commons Energy and Climate Change Select Committee* (London, 2010).
[118] This situation was criticized by the HL Constitution Committee, *The Regulatory State*, paras 204–12. Under the Financial Services Bill 2011 the FSA's replacement, the Financial Conduct Authority is now included in the NAO's remit.

Moreover, its institutional position as government auditor has arguably limited the role that it could potentially play in providing a wider evaluation of a regulatory regime, as opposed to an evaluation of the performance of individual organizations. That said, there are signs that the NAO is taking a more expansive view of its role, and it has engaged in cross-government evaluations recently, notably a highly critical review of reforms of the structure of government, and, less scathingly, of competition regulation.[119] In particular, it found that successive governments were both very keen on reorganization (there were over 90 reorganizations of government between May 2005 and June 2009), and very bad at it. In a conclusion which is relevant for the current exercise in reorganization, it stated: 'The value for money of central government reorganisations cannot be demonstrated given the vague objectives of most such reorganisations, the lack of business cases, the failure to track costs and the absence of mechanisms to identify benefits and make sure they materialise.'[120] In order for any change to occur, however, the NAO relies on the executive to take notice, and on Parliament, the media and others to ensure that it does.

The NAO can nonetheless play a significant role in helping Parliament call regulators and the government to account. In particular, its capacity to undertake detailed investigations is extremely important. For example, it played a critical role in the accountability processes relating to the 2007–9 financial crisis, providing Parliament and the public with two detailed reports on the handling of the crisis and assessing whether the billions of pounds of taxpayers' money that was used to prop up the system was in fact well spent.[121] It concluded that it was,[122] but its inquiries did reveal some failings. Notable among these was that the Treasury had failed to inform the chairs of the PAC and TSC of an indemnity of up to £18 billion provided to the Bank of England at the height of the crisis to enable the Bank to provide emergency loans to RBS, Lloyds and HBOS of up to £60 billion in October 2008. The government's response was that it had been concerned that the information would leak, exacerbating the crisis, but it is notable that no ex post disclosure was made once this danger was over.[123] Without the NAO's investigations, it is difficult to see how this information would have emerged.

The NAO is also becoming the 'accountability resource of choice' for both the core executive and for Parliament. The NAO has been used by the core executive (Cabinet Office and Treasury) to perform specific reviews to monitor the regulators' implementation of policies and recommendations, and to perform successive reviews of departmental regulatory impact assessments. As noted above, the NAO conducted reviews jointly with the Treasury of the implementation of the

---

[119] NAO *Reorganising Central Government* HC 452, Session 2009–10 (London, 2010); NAO *Review of the UK's Competition Landscape* (London, 2010).

[120] NAO *Reorganising Central Government*, para.10.

[121] The government provided $690 billion in direct support to RBS, Lloyds and HBOS, and provided $2.06 trillion in guarantees to these and other banks: Bank of England, *Financial Stability Report* June 2009.

[122] NAO, NNR and Maintaining Financial Stability.

[123] NAO *Maintaining Financial Stability;* Black, 'The Credit Crisis and the Constitution', n 31 above.

Hampton recommendations by the five largest regulatory agencies.[124] Committees of both Houses of Parliament have also asked the NAO to perform specific reviews on their behalf, for example of regulators' regulatory impact assessments, and to provide it with briefing papers on regulators or regulatory issues.[125] Indeed, a number of Select Committees have recommended that the NAO play a greater role in scrutinizing regulators. For example, the House of Lords report on economic regulators recommended that the NAO be charged with reviewing the regulators' own post-implementation evaluations for their quality and objectivity, or conducting such evaluations itself.[126]

However, there are indications of some confusion, at least on the part of the government, over the questions of for whom the NAO acts, and to whom the NAO itself is accountable. In formal terms, the NAO acts on behalf of the PAC, to whom it presents its reports. However, as the government also uses the NAO to perform reviews on its behalf, the issue of for which it is acting can become unclear in the minds of some, at least. For example in giving evidence to the recent PAC review of the ORR, the Permanent Secretary for the Department of Transport argued that the government determined the NAO's activities, only to have to be corrected by the committee, which pointed out that the NAO was funded directly by Parliament, not by the executive, and acted on Parliament's behalf, not the government's.[127] However, NAO reports on regulators, or in this case Network Rail, are approved by the lead department before they are presented to the PAC,[128] which leaves the question unclear of who, in reality, the NAO is reporting to. Its institutional position is thus blurred: is it acting on behalf of Parliament, the government, or both (but at different times)? Blurring boundaries, shifting positions and the endless question over the accountability of the accountors (or who guards the guardians)—each of these issues continues to pose challenges for regulatory accountability.

4. Consumer advocacy bodies

The final group of accountors to be considered here are consumer panels or advisory bodies. Engagement by 'civil society' in regulatory issues is usually far weaker than that of business, but to the extent that it exists at all, it is usually stronger at the 'input' stages of policy processes (through consultation) than at other stages. For reasons that cannot be explored here, the last fifteen to twenty years have seen an increase in the creation of specialist consumer representative committees or panels which are attached to individual regulators, or given a legal mandate to make representations to and to review the activities of a group of regulators. Such

---

[124] NAO *Regulatory Quality.*
[125] Eg. NAO *Performance of Ofgem; NAO, A Review of Economic Regulators' Regulatory Impact Statements for the House of Lords Select Committee on Regulators* (London: NAO, 2007).
[126] HL *UK Economic Regulators* para.1.10.
[127] HC Committee of Public Accounts *Office of Rail Regulation: Regulating Network Rail's efficiency* 41st Report of Session 2010–12 HC 1036 (2011), qq 205 & 206.
[128] HC Committee of Public Accounts *Office of Rail Regulation*, Q 218.

bodies are often created by statute, charged with representing consumer views, and performing reviews and issuing reports; and in many instances the regulator is under a statutory duty to respond publicly to their comments. Specialist consumer representative organizations exist in a number of key sectors, notably financial services (FSA (now FCA) Consumer Panel), water (CC Water), transport (Passenger Focus), aviation (Aviation Consumer Advocacy Panel), legal services (Legal Services Consumer Panel), telecommunications and broadcasting (Communications Consumer Panel), and Healthwatch (CQC). In addition, Consumer Focus was created in 2008 to take over the consumer advocacy functions of the National Consumer Council, Energywatch, and Postwatch. Some of these organizations have an official link with the regulator as dedicated advisory panels; others, such as CC Water, Passenger Focus, and Consumer Focus, are separate external sectoral bodies. The development of consumer panels which are embedded within regulatory structures is a good example of a form of accountability which is ongoing and 'interstitial', sitting between the formal processes of consultation prior to decisions and ex post reviews of performance. There has been no systematic study of their effectiveness, but whilst some consumer panels have been criticized as ineffective, lacking sufficient information, expertise and influence,[129] others have been praised for their engagement and expertise, as discussed below. The engagement of consumers or other individuals in the regulatory process and in calling the regulator to account has the potential to be considerably enhanced through the operation of both panels and external sectoral bodies, but only if certain conditions are in place. Notably, their accountability capacity has to be adequate (including possessing appropriate personnel, technical expertise, financial resources, and access to information and research), they have to be able to respond quickly to changing events, their members need to have adequate negotiating and advocacy skills, and their personal authority and institutional position has to be such that they are respected by consumers, regulators and industry alike.[130] In other words, irrespective of any legal requirement that regulators take their views into account, consumer panels have to be afforded sufficient recognition by the regulator such that the regulator really does take note of what they say, and does not just 'go through the motions' of appearing to listen but in practice disregarding them.

In this regard, there can be advantages gained in having specialist consumer panels which are able to develop the highly technical knowledge and expertise required to engage properly with issues arising in each sector. However, the coalition government is currently proposing to abolish the majority of these specialist panels (with the exception of those in financial and legal services, as they are not

---

[129] Eg. Henry Rothstein's study of the Food Standards Agency's Consumer Committee, which was in place from 2002–5: 'Talking Shops or Talking Turkey? Institutionalizing Consumer Representation in Risk Regulation' (2007) 32(5) *Science Technology Human Values* 582–607.

[130] An interesting perspective is provided by Consumer Focus, *Through Consumers' Eyes* (London, 2011).

publicly funded) and instead to merge them all into a single 'regulated industries' unit within an expanded Citizens' Advice Service.[131]

There are strong arguments against such a proposal, but at least the consultation paper has has prompted a fascinating debate on the relative capacities of different types of consumer organizations, both to represent consumers and to call regulators to account. The government argued that an integrated consumer body would be able to create greater capacity by developing stronger cross-sectoral expertise and capability; to consider the cumulative impact on consumers of changes across sectors; to develop an integrated ombudsman system to deal with complaints and redress; to raise public awareness and understanding of who is representing their interests; and to reduce overall costs and improve efficiency[132] (though it should be noted that the proposals have not been costed).[133] However the proposals have met significant opposition from regulators, consumer advocates and industry. Opponents of the proposals fall into two main camps: those who think that specialist consumer panels should be merged into a single 'regulated industries panel' but do not think that the function should be given to the Citizens' Advice Service, and those that think that specialist panels should be retained.

The generalist consumer advocacy bodies, such as Which?, Age UK, the National Consumers Federation and Consumer Focus sit in the first camp (and indeed the proposal for a single cross-sector advocacy body originated with Consumer Focus).[134] However these bodies expressed strong doubts as to whether the Citizens' Advice Service, which is a charity, would have sufficient skills, funding, powers and status to perform this role.[135] It would require a significant re-focusing of the Citizens' Advice Service, as well as a radical expansion and shift in the technical skills of its personnel. As the consultation paper itself recognizes, ensuring that consumer interests are fully represented in these highly complex areas requires significant technical knowledge and expertise, an understanding of the trade-offs involved, and (though the paper does not note this), considerable political, advocacy and negotiation skills.[136] New powers would also have to be given. For example, Consumer Focus at present has strong powers with respect to energy and postal services to force companies or regulators to disclose information which it requires to fulfil its remit, powers which would be lost with the transfer of its functions to the Citizens' Advice Service. Moreover, accountability to Parliament and

---

[131] BIS *Empowering and Protecting Consumers: Consultation on Institutional Changes for Provision of Consumer Information, Advice, Education, Advocacy and Enforcement* (London, 2011), though CC Water, which was praised for its effectiveness in the Gray review, will remain until after the 2014 price review. The proposals only cover BIS sponsored regulators; the eventual decisions on the transfer of sectoral consumer bodies into the proposed arrangements are a matter for the relevant departments and devolved administrations.

[132] BIS *Empowering and Protecting Consumers.*

[133] See also NAO *Reorganizing Central Government.*

[134] Regulated industries and the consumer, Consumer Focus (March 2011), <http://www.consumerfocus.org.uk/publications/regulated-industries-and-the-consumer>.

[135] Response of Age Concern, available at <http://www.ageuk.org.uk/Documents/EN-GB/For-professionals/Policy/BIS%20Empowering%20and%20protecting%20consumers%20(Sept%202011).pdf?dtrk=true>.

[136] BIS *Empowering and Protecting Consumers.*

the NAO risks being lost. Under the current proposals, the Citizens' Advice Service would remain a charity and as such would not be accountable to Parliament for its role, nor to the Welsh Assembly.[137] Its accountability to government would also be unclear—a familiar problem, as discussed above. Instead, proponents of a generalist consumer advocacy body argue that the remit of Consumer Focus should be expanded. This would have the advantage of having a specialist body with a specific legal mandate, with an established position and expertise and a dedicated budget.

However, as a number of other responses argued, there are also considerable arguments against the creation of a generalist advocacy body, even if it had greater powers and accountability. There is a real risk that specialist knowledge will be lost, that the skills, financial resources and attention of any such organization, and particularly a multi-function body such as the Citizens' Advice Service, would be too widely spread. Moreover, as a significant part of the regulatory agenda is set at EU level, consumer advocacy has to have an international as well as a national dimension. It is doubtful, to say the least, that a single organization could respond adequately at both national and EU levels to issues which cover most of the economy unless it was as equally well-resourced as all the existing consumer bodies.

Further, as it would lose the privileged access to information that many currently enjoy, a generalist consumer representative body which was external to the regulators would have to engage in more formal procedures to get the information that it needed from industry and the regulatory body. As a result, a non-specialist organization is likely to become too detached from the regulators and from the issues involved, able only to observe and comment rather than engage and negotiate. As the Consumer Council for Water argued in its response: 'In our experience, most benefits for consumers are delivered by negotiating in detail on key issues at senior level in the sector, backed by real expertise and respect by the parties in that sector. In the water sector there are 22 companies and four main regulators with whom we negotiate. The complex nature and extent of the negotiations in water on behalf of consumers should not be underestimated.'[138] The result is likely to be a diminution in the accountability of regulators to consumer interests, rather than an enhancement.

It is striking that many of the regulators who have specialist panels responded that they would be reluctant to lose them.[139] Those regulators argued that consumer panels which are embedded within regulatory structures, in other words which may share premises, some staff, and have good access to internal meetings or meetings with other interested parties, perform quite differently to generalist advocacy bodies—they are advisory bodies, not lobbyists, campaigners or consumer

---

[137] Response of Consumer Focus, available at <http://www.consumerfocus.org.uk/files/2009/06/Paper-5-Draft-consumer-landscape-response-27-September.pdf>.

[138] Response of the CC Water, available at <www.ccwater.org.uk/.../Final_response_BIS_Landscape_Review_-_2011>.

[139] See, eg. responses from Ofcom, Financial Services Consumer Panel, OFT, National Consumer Federation, Legal Services Consumer Panel (endorsed by the Legal Services Board), Which?, Consumer Focus, and the findings of the Gray review *Review of Ofwat and consumer representation in the water sector* (Defra, 2011).

advisors.[140] As the National Consumers' Federation observed, there is a distinction between 'campaigning advocacy' and 'participatory advocacy'.[141] Panels which are embedded to operate within the regulatory framework can have privileged access to policy processes and can provide targeted interventions at an early stage before policies are fully formed.[142] Moreover, they provide regulators with the ability to 'test out' proposals at an early stage of their development, prior to public consultation.[143] Such panels can be a valuable source of information for regulators as to what consumer interests are on significant but highly technical issues which can have both national and international dimensions. There is a real risk that their abolition would lead to the loss of a valuable counterbalance to the views of industry representatives, which are far more vocally expressed. Further, the panels were seen as inexpensive and offering good value for money (a key government criterion). As Ofcom summarized: 'An expert panel can foster a close and constructive relationship with a regulator, respond quickly and flexibly across a wide range of issues, and operate with a small team of advisors and very low overheads.'[144] Moreover, regulators themselves recognized the importance of specialist consumer panels in providing legitimacy to the regulatory process and reassurance to consumers that their interests were being effectively represented and taken into account.

The debate over the reform of the structure and role of consumer advocacy bodies provides a valuable insight into the complexity of the accountability relationships that can exist between accountor and accountee and highlights the fluidity of the roles that any one organization can play within that relationship; in this case as the role of a consumer representative organization shifts between representative, participant and accountor. Moreover, it illustrates that the capacity of an accountor to hold a regulator to account is determined by factors well beyond legal powers, but based in the possession of resources and of an institutional position which is such that both the regulator and others recognize the 'right' of that organization, in this case both to participate and to hold to account.

Again, however, the balance between independence and engagement is inevitably a difficult one to strike, in this case between the role of the consumer body as a participant and its role as an accountor. The key challenge is to ensure that consumer representative bodies have sufficient information, access and status to make a real impact on the regulators' decision-making process, whilst remaining sufficiently

[140] Eg. response of Legal Services Consumer Panel, available at <http://www.legalservicesconsumer panel.org.uk/publications/consultation_responses/documents/2011-09-27_BIS_Empoweringand ProtecingConsumers.pdf>.

[141] Response of National Consumers Federation, available at <http://www.ncf.info/sites/default/files/ NCF%20response%20to%20BIS%20consultation%20Empowering%20and%20Protecting%20 Consumers_0.pdf>; Welsh Affairs Select Committee *Representation of consumer interests in Wales* 7th Report 2011–12 Session (2011).

[142] D Tambini *Reforming Consumer Representation in UK Communications*, LSE Media Policy Brief 4 (LSE, 2011) available at <http://eprints.lse.ac.uk/38616/1/LSEMPPBrief4.pdf>; responses of Ofcom (available at <http://stakeholders.ofcom.org.uk/binaries/consultations/ofcomresponses/ consumer-landscape-ofcom.pdf>) and the Legal Services Consumer Panel.

[143] Response of Ofcom and Legal Services Consumer Panel.   [144] Response of Ofcom.

independent from it.[145] Consumer representative bodies also need to be sufficiently accountable to those whose interests they are meant to be representing, and to ensure that they are representing the interests of all consumers, not just one particular sub-set. To this end, ensuring that consumer bodies have adequate funding to pursue independent research into consumers' needs and opinions, and into the impacts of policies on them, is vital. Without such research, consumer bodies are inevitably prey to the risk (and accusation) that they represent only themselves, or at best a small sub-set of what is in reality a highly heterogenous group. Conducting such research also enables them to build their own legitimacy in the absence of clear accountability arrangements. For at present, it is not clear to whom, if anyone, consumer panels are accountable, even if they are subject to requirements to issue and publish reports to the world at large. That makes them accountable to everyone, but as we know, tasks that are assigned to everyone tend to be performed by no one. Again, the question of to whom the accountors are accountable remains unanswered.

D. Summary and prospects

Although there is a far wider array of accountability actors than those considered here, calling regulators to account is a challenging exercise. As we have seen, the key challenges are five-fold: notably the scale and scope of the regulatory landscape; the number and relationship between the different bodies involved (and their propensity to blame-shift); the technical complexity and contestability of the regulatory task; the opacity of regulatory processes; and the willingness of the accountee to be called to account. In addition, as we have seen, not only are the lines between independence, accountability and control often blurred, the roles of organizations which are acting as accountors can also be fluid. A consumer panel may play the role of engaged participant in the regulatory process as well as that of ex post accountor of that regulator's activities; parliamentary involvement can demonstrate similar fluidity of roles, particularly if Parliament is determining the budget of the regulatory body. As noted at the outset, the difficulties in answering the question of 'who guards the guardians' are further compounded, if the 'guardian' is an active participant in the very processes it is seeking to guard.

Moreover, the capacity of different actors to call regulators to account is highly variable. There has been no 'grand design' of the current political structures of accountability; rather, each has evolved and continues to evolve. Parliament, for example, has a strong institutional position as accountor, but its capacity is limited and it has struggled to organize itself in such a way as to perform a systematic and ongoing accountability function with respect to the 'regulatory state'. In contrast, the institutional position of the NAO can at times seem confused, with

---

[145] Tambini, *Reforming Consumer Representation in UK Communications*, n 142 above; Rothstein, n 129 above; J Black *Report on consumer involvement in regulatory decision making* (IDA Taskforce to Modernize Securities Regulation in Canada, 2006).

both Parliament and the government arguing that the NAO is acting for it, but its capacity to engage in the forensic investigations and technical analysis which are the necessary bedrock of any accountability process is significant. In an ideal world, the weaknesses in the institutional position and accountability capacity of one accountor would be compensated for in the strengths of another. But whilst there are some areas where this is so (such as the role of the NAO in supporting Parliament's capacity to call regulators to account), gaps still exist.

Other issues also remain: although there are signs that accountors are recognizing the significance of the EU in setting the agenda, and in some cases the structures and processes, of regulatory agencies, this recognition has been too slow in coming, and accountors risk calling regulators to account for decisions over which they have little control, or in finding that their role has been displaced by EU organizations.[146] The lack of clarity over responsibilities for setting strategic objectives or for handling crises remains. The accountability problems raised both by 'many hands' and by 'no hands' can be acute. Concerns remain as to the ongoing effectiveness and impact of parliamentary mechanisms of accountability, despite some successes in Parliament's reforms of its internal operations. As for accountability on behalf of consumers, there are real risks that the current proposals to reform consumer advocacy will prove to be yet another reform which is ill-thought through, ill-costed, will bring no real benefits, and indeed could severely weaken regulatory accountability to citizens and consumers.

However, regardless of how well-designed a system could be, or how capacities could be enhanced, the political accountability of regulatory agencies will always be complex and contested. Regulators operate in a broader context of multi-level and polycentric regimes in which responsibilities are widely dispersed, even at the national level. Furthermore, the core executive will continue to try to play a double game of delegation and control with respect to regulatory agencies, and to blur responsibilities whenever convenient to do so. It will always be the role of accountors to police the boundaries between the independence of regulatory agencies and their control by either the executive or industry, for that is not something that can be left either to the government or the agency themselves, but in so doing the role of accountors can sometimes blur into one of engaged participant. However, it should not be surprising that accountability relationships that regulators have with their accountors are complex, that accountability can be challenging or difficult for both accountors and accountees; or that roles are shifting, that lines are blurred, and that values are contested and contestable. It is the nature both of the relationship and the task of accountability that these tensions will exist, and it is right that they do, at least up to a point. Unless those tensions start to have pathological effects on the agency itself, they need not be a bad thing. For without those tensions, both regulators and their accountors will become complacent, which will be to their detriment as well as ours.

---

[146] For examples with respect to the financial crisis see Black, 'The Credit Crisis and the Constitution', n 31 above.

16

Legal Accountability and Social Justice

Colm O'Cinneide*

A. Introduction

In the UK, questions of social or 'distributive' justice are usually treated as exercising a type of repulsion effect on the reach of legal accountability. Public authorities enjoy a wide margin of discretion when deciding how to allocate resources to different social groups, while courts play a very limited role in reviewing whether such decisions are rational, compatible with individual rights, or otherwise comply with principles of justice.

However, strong arguments can be made that excessive restrictions have been imposed on the scope of judicial review in this context. A good case can be made that courts should play a greater role in holding public authorities to account for how the substance of their resource allocation decisions impacts upon the lives of individuals, especially when such decisions expose individuals to a risk of destitution, deprive them of support essential to maintain a dignified existence, or otherwise have a grave impact on their well-being. In general, it is time to reconsider the relationship that currently exists between legal modes of accountability, resource allocation decision-making, and the concept of social justice.

B. The expanded role of legal accountability in regulating public administration

As the modern administrative state came into being in the first half of the twentieth century, it was widely assumed that the legal process should play a peripheral role in regulating its functioning. In the United Kingdom, Robson and Laski preached the virtues of judicial self-restraint and deference to administrative

* Reader in Law, UCL.

decision-making,[1] while Frankfurter and Brandeis sounded a similar chord on the other side of the Atlantic.[2]

Much has changed. Legal accountability mechanisms now play an important role in regulating the activities of public authorities.[3] Legislation has been a key driver of this transformation: statutes such as the Human Rights Act 1998 (the HRA 1998) and the Equality Act 2010 have imposed new legal controls on public authorities, while tribunal jurisdiction has been expanded by legislation such as the Special Education Needs and Disability Act 2001. The willingness of courts to expand and deepen the scope of judicial review has also contributed significantly to the enhanced role now played by legal accountability in public governance. The tribunal system has also become a key element of the regulatory landscape, handling over half a million cases a year.[4] In general, the 'judge over the shoulder' has come to cast a long shadow over the functioning of public administration. Few areas of state activity are now exempt from the supervisory jurisdiction of the senior courts and public authorities have become subject to an expanded range of administrative law controls.[5]

The expanded reach and substance of legal accountability controls reflects how public law has moved away from the positivism that dominated early twentieth century legal theory towards a greater embrace of principle- and value-based reasoning and the discourse of human rights.[6] This has generated new expectations that laws regulating the relationship between the citizen and the state should be based upon a more substantive concept of the rule of law and protect important human interests such as autonomy, equality and dignity which risk being marginalized by the utilitarian focus of most public authority decision-making and the majoritarian orientation of party political democracy.[7] As a result, legal accountability mechanisms are now expected to play an active role in protecting individual rights and promoting adherence to values such as transparency, participation, fairness and respect for the rule of law.[8]

---

[1] W A Robson *Justice and Administrative Law* (1st edn., London: Macmillan & Co., 1928); H Laski *Studies in Law and Politics* (New Haven, Connecticut: Yale University Press, 1932).

[2] For analysis of Louis Brandeis's complex views on the appropriate role of courts, see S J Konefsky *The Legacy of Holmes & Brandeis: A Study in the Influence of Ideas* (New York: Macmillan, 1995). For a taste of Felix Frankfurter's views on judicial deference, see his concurring opinion in *Dennis v United States* (1951) 341 US 494.

[3] Bovens has defined accountability as a 'relationship between an actor and a forum, in which the actor has an obligation to explain and to justify his or her conduct, the forum can pose questions and pass judgement, and the actor may face consequences': see M Bovens, 'Analysing and Assessing Accountability: A Conceptual Framework' *ELJ* (2007) 13: 447–68, 450. Both courts and tribunals play a role in holding public authorities to account for how they have complied with their legal obligations.

[4] R Carnwath, 'Tribunal Justice-A New Start?' *Public Law* [2009] 48–69.

[5] For an example of the current reach of the supervisory jurisdiction of the courts, see *R (Abbasi) v Secretary of State for Foreign and Commonwealth Affairs* [2002] EWCA Civ 1598.

[6] See Harlow and Rawlings *Law and Administration* (3rd edn., Cambridge: Cambridge University Press, 2009), ch 1.

[7] See eg. J Jowell, 'The Rule of Law and Its Underlying Values', in J Jowell and D Oliver (eds.) *The Changing Constitution* (6th edn., Oxford: Oxford University Press, 2007), 5–24.

[8] For discussion of the limits that exist on the capacity of public law controls to play this role, see C Harlow and R Rawlings *Law and Administration*, 711–48.

C. The detached relationship between legal accountability and social justice

However, while its reach has expanded in recent decades, legal accountability controls in the UK to remain focused on ensuring that public authorities conform to a quite specific range of normative standards. They require public authorities to treat those affected by their actions in a manner that adheres to a conventionally 'corrective' view of justice, ie. which reflects their formal status as notionally equal subjects of concern to the law.[9] They do not aim to provide 'social' or 'distributive' justice, ie. to allocate resources and opportunities in a just manner so as to ensure that all individuals have a meaningful opportunity of participating in social, economic and cultural life.[10]

Public authorities can thus be held legally accountable for failing to respect the civil and political rights of individuals, or for subjecting them to irrational, unlawful or procedurally unsound decision-making, or for otherwise interfering unjustly with their day-to-day autonomous existence as equal subjects before the law. However, it is usually not possible to hold public authorities legally accountable for failing to provide individuals with adequate levels of social support, or for neglecting their socio-economic rights, or for otherwise failing to act in a manner that is compatible with the requirements of social justice. The state in general is expected to distribute resources in a manner that is broadly fair and just: however, administrative law, human rights law and other court- and tribunal-centred legal accountability mechanisms confine themselves to a much narrower normative remit.

This is not to say that the various forms of legal accountability do not exert any influence on how the state engages with issues of social justice. Law plays an important role in regulating the *manner* in which public authorities allocate public resources. Complex legal frameworks, comprised of a mixture of statutory provision and case law, regulate the provision of social welfare, public housing and education. As Jeff King notes, the Department of Work and Pensions' guide book *The Law of Social Security* (the 'Blue Volumes') lists fifty-seven pieces of relevant primary legislation alone, along with over one thousand statutory instruments.[11] The tribunal system decides thousands of cases every year on matters relating, inter alia, to social security, housing and the provision of special educational needs. The higher courts are also regularly asked to adjudicate intricate

---

[9] Weinrib drawing on Aristotle defines corrective justice as focused on the maintenance and restoration of the 'notional equality with which the parties enter the transaction' in question: see E Weinrib, 'Corrective Justice in a Nutshell' *University of Toronto Law Journal* (2002) 52(4): 349–56, 349.

[10] This definition of social justice is deliberately couched in broad terms, to capture the range of meanings associated with this term. For further analysis, See P Boucher and D Kelly (eds) *Social Justice: From Hume to Walzer* (London: Routledge, 1998); D Miller *Social Justice* (Oxford: Oxford University Press, 1979); by the same author, *Principles of Social Justice* (Harvard, MA: Harvard University Press, 1999); B Barry *Why Social Justice Matters* (Polity, 2005).

[11] J King *Judging Social Rights* (Oxford: Oxford University Press, 2012), 423.

legal disputes concerning the interpretation of the web of primary and secondary legislation that regulates how public authorities should go about allocating resources to individuals and groups in need.[12]

Furthermore, resource allocation decisions by public authorities which fail to respect legitimate expectations, do not take into account relevant considerations, fail to follow appropriate procedure, or otherwise breach the formal requirements of the rule of law, can be subject to judicial review. Thus, for example, in *R v North and East Devon Health Authority ex p Coughlan*,[13] the Court of Appeal held that a health authority had failed to follow its own guidance and to respect the applicant's substantive legitimate expectation that she would continue to receive NHS funded long-term health care. In *R (W) v Birmingham City Council*,[14] a decision by the respondent local authority that it could only afford to fund social care which met critical needs was held to be unlawful because of deficiencies in the process by which this decision was reached: Birmingham had failed to comply with its obligations under the disability equality duty set out in s 49A of the Disability Discrimination Act 1996.[15]

However, comparatively little control is exercised over the *substance* of resource allocation decisions taken by public authorities. When it comes to this type of issue, the 'green light' approach to legal accountability outlined by Harlow and Rawlings still prevails.[16] Public authorities enjoy a wide margin of discretion when determining what resources should be allocated to particular individuals and groups, and courts and tribunals play a very limited role in reviewing whether such decisions are rational, compatible with individual rights, or otherwise in accordance with principles of justice.

This distinction between how legal accountability mechanisms regulate the manner and the substance of resource allocation decisions is a matter of degree rather than a hard and fast rule. The line between procedure and substance is often blurred, and close scrutiny of how a public authority reaches a decision may at times cross over into an analysis of its substance. For example, in both the *Coughlan* and *R (W)* cases referred to above, the courts assessed the extent to which the procedural defects in question had 'tainted' the substance of the resource allocation decisions at issue. However, the manner/substance distinction is still important, as illustrated by two recent decisions of the UK Supreme Court.

In *R (McDonald) v Royal Borough of Kensington and Chelsea*,[17] the appellant suffered from severe mobility problems and could only access the toilet at night with the help of a carer provided by the respondent local authority. The respondent

---

[12] King, *Judging Social Rights*.

[13] *R v North and East Devon Health Authority ex p Coughlan* [2000] 2 WLR 622.

[14] *R (W) v Birmingham City Council* [2011] EWHC 1147 (Admin).

[15] This duty has now been replaced by the general equality duty set out in the Equality Act 2010, s 149.

[16] C Harlow and R Rawlings *Law and Administration*, 2nd edn. (Oxford: Oxford University Press, 1997), 67–90.

[17] *R (McDonald) v Royal Borough of Kensington and Chelsea* [2011] UKSC 33.

reassessed the care needs of the appellant and concluded that they could be satisfied by a reduced package of services which required her to use incontinence pads and/or absorbent sheets at night instead of being assisted by the night carer. The appellant alleged that the local authority had not adhered to the proper procedure as set out by primary and secondary legislation in reaching this decision: she also claimed, inter alia, that the decision violated her right to a private life under art 8 of the European Convention on Human Rights (ECHR).

The Supreme Court subjected the manner in which the local authority had arrived at this decision to close scrutiny. It concluded that it had followed the correct procedure, consulted with the appellant and generally adhered to the relevant statutory duties which regulated how it should arrive at such a decision. It then held that art 8 ECHR was not engaged, on the basis that the state enjoyed considerable discretion in allocating public resources and that an interference with Convention rights would usually only be established to exist in such circumstances if the appellant had been subject to treatment sufficiently inhuman and degrading so to engage art 3 ECHR (see below for further discussion of this point.) Baroness Hale dissented, on the basis that the local authority had acted irrationally in how they had classified the appellant's needs: in Baroness Hale's view, the authority had failed to recognize that she had a need to access toilet facilities in a dignified and humane manner. However, the majority strongly disagreed with her analysis: in their view, a conclusion of irrationality could not be sustained on the evidence.[18]

In *McDonald*, the Supreme Court thus closely scrutinized the manner in which the local authority had adhered to the relevant statutory guidelines in reaching its decision.[19] However, it then applied a very light standard of review to the substance of the decision, ie. the determination that the appellant's needs could legitimately be met by the provision of incontinence pads. It concluded that no interference had taken place with her art 8 right to a private life: furthermore, it chose not to subject the local authority's definition of the appellant's needs to close scrutiny (with the exception of Baroness Hale), or to assess in detail whether it had given sufficient weight to Ms McDonald's interests in reaching its decision.

A similar approach was adopted by the Supreme Court in *R (KM) v Cambridgeshire County Council*.[20] Here, a severely disabled man challenged the amount of a personal care budget that had been provided to him by the respondent local authority. Once again, the Supreme Court engaged in close analysis of the manner in which the local authority had arrived at its decision. In delivering the judgment of the Court, Lord Wilson emphasized that local authorities had to respect legitimate expectations and give clear reasons in support of their determination. He also made it clear that the intensity of review of how a public authority had reached a decision in such a community care case would depend upon the seriousness of its impact on the individual affected, and that in this case 'the necessary

[18] *McDonald*, see, in particular, Lord Walker's comments at 28–32.
[19] *McDonald*, see eg. Lord Kerr's very close reading of the relevant statutory guidelines at 34–40.
[20] *R (KM) v Cambridgeshire CC* [2012] UKSC 23.

intensity of review' was high.[21] The appellant lost his claim, but the judgment of the court confirmed that the courts would closely scrutinize the manner in which local authorities decided such cases. However, the actual substance of the decision, ie. whether the amount allocated to the appellant was sufficient to enable him to live in a dignified manner, was not reviewed in any detail: a challenge to its rationality was quickly rejected on the basis that the local authority had followed the relevant procedure and arrived at a 'rational computation' of the appellant's needs.[22]

Both *McDonald* and *KM* thus demonstrate that the courts are prepared to closely scrutinize how public authorities comply with procedural requirements in situations where their resource allocation decisions have a grave impact on an individual's wellbeing. However, the situation is different when it comes to the substance of such decisions, in respect of which public authorities enjoy wide discretion, Convention rights have little, if any, purchase, and courts will only strike down a decision if it meets the *Wednesbury* standard of irrationality. In general, legal accountability mechanisms play a very limited role when it comes to resource allocation decisions that raise substantive issues of social justice. By and large, their role is confined to ensuring conformity with procedural requirements, in line with the overall 'corrective' orientation of the legal process in the UK.

D. Maintaining the detachment between legal accountability and social justice

This limitation on the scope of legal accountability is partially the product of political reluctance to extend the powers of courts and tribunals in this area. Parliament has not made socio-economic rights enforceable through law: there is no socio-economic equivalent of the HRA 1998, and the rights set out in international human rights instruments such as the United Nations Covenant on Economic, Social and Cultural Rights or the European Social Charter have not been incorporated into domestic law. Section 1 of the Equality Act 2010 made provision for a duty to promote socio-economic equality to be imposed upon public authorities. However, this duty has not been given effect by ministerial order, as the legislation requires, and in any case its provisions are solely focused on regulating the process through which public authorities went about the process of 'making decisions of a strategic nature'.[23]

Furthermore, legislation is often deliberately drafted so as to limit the extent to which it could give rise to legally enforceable rights or obligations. In particular, statutes governing welfare provision, housing allocation, or other aspects of social policy are often carefully worded so as to establish target duties as distinct from clearly defined individual entitlements. As Palmer has argued, such duties are often

---

[21] *KM* para.36: see also *R(L) v Leeds City Council* [2010] EWHC 3324 (Admin).
[22] *KM* para.38.
[23] S Fredman, 'Positive Duties and Socio-economic Disadvantage: Bringing Disadvantage onto the Equality Agenda' *European Human Rights Law Review* [2010] 290.

'qualified by reference to factors such as the "reasonable practicability" of implementing the strategies, or "by the impact of proposed measures on the economy"', while 'duties to achieve designated targets or implement strategies are moderated by reference to differently formulated considerations of resources'.[24]

This is illustrated by the example of the positive equality duties which were imposed upon public authorities by several different pieces of legislation between 2000 and 2006, and then merged into a single cross-ground duty by s 149 of the Equality Act 2010. These equality duties require public authorities to pay 'due regard' in performing their functions to the need to promote equality and eliminate discrimination.[25] If an authority fails to adhere to these requirements, this may result in the relevant decision being quashed if the procedural error is deemed to be sufficiently serious.[26] The courts have even shown a willingness to require evidence that the equality duties have been given due weight in the process of setting a local authority budget or cutting financial support for social services, as illustrated by the *R(W)* case referred to above.[27] However, the impact of such duties remains confined to controlling process rather than dictating substantive outcomes.[28] For example, the courts have been clear that the equality duties impose no obligation on public authorities to take proportionate steps to achieve greater equality of opportunity for disadvantaged groups in how they allocate resources, or to demonstrate that their decision-making *as a matter of substance* engages adequately with equality concerns.[29]

The higher courts have also been very reluctant to subject the substance of resource allocation decisions to close scrutiny, in contrast to their readiness to review the exercise of state power in other contexts.[30] This reluctance has been manifested in a number of ways which, taken together, have limited the extent to which the courts play an active role in holding public authorities to account for

---

[24] See E Palmer, 'The Child Poverty Act 2010: Holding government to account for promises in a recessionary climate?' *European Human Rights Law Review* [2010] 305–16, 311. See also *R (on the application of Friends of the Earth) v Secretary of State for Energy & Climate Change* [2010] EWHC 49 (Admin).

[25] For analysis of the general nature of the positive equality duties, see S Fredman, 'Breaking the Mold: Equality as a Proactive Duty' (*American Journal of Comparative Law* (2011) 60(1): 263–88; S Fredman, 'Changing the Norm: Positive Duties in Equal Treatment Legislation' *Maastricht Journal of European and Comparative Law* (2005) 12: 369–98; C O'Cinneide, 'Positive Duties and Gender Equality' *International Journal of Discrimination and the Law* (2005) 91–119; J Halford, 'Statutory Duties and the Public Law Courts' *JR* [2007] 89.

[26] See eg. *R (Equality & Human Rights Commission) v Secretary of State for Justice Secretary of State for the Home Department* [2010] EWHC 147 (Admin); *R (C) v Secretary of State for Justice* [2008] EWCA Civ 882; *Secretary of State for Defence v Elias* [2006] EWCA Civ 1293.

[27] [2011] EWHC 1147 (Admin). See also *R (Rahman) v Birmingham City Council* [2011] EWHC 944 (Admin); *R (Hajrula and Hamza) v London Councils* [2011] EWHC 448 (Admin).

[28] S Fredman, 'The Public Sector Equality Duty' *Industrial Law Journal* (2011) 40 (4): 405–27.

[29] See eg. *R (Domb) v London Borough of Hammersmith and Fulham* [2009] EWCA Civ 810; *Child Poverty Action Group v Secretary of State for Work & Pensions* [2011] EWHC 2616 (Admin); *R (JG and MB) v Lancashire CC* [2011] EWHC 2295 (Admin); *R (Fawcett Society) v Chancellor of the Exchequer* [2010] EWHC 3522.

[30] For a comprehensive analysis of the case law, see E Palmer *Judicial Review, Socio-economic Rights and the Human Rights Act* (Oxford: Hart Publishing, 2007).

how the substance of their resource allocation decisions impact upon individual wellbeing.

First of all, the courts have taken the view that 'polycentric' decisions involving the balancing of competing social and economic interests, or which turn on complex questions of economic efficiency and resource maximization, should attract a very 'light touch' standard of rationality review. Thus, in *R v Cambridge Health Authority, ex p B*, the Court of Appeal took the view that the courts should not be prepared to subject resource allocation decisions in the provision of health care to close scrutiny.[31]

Secondly, a similar set of assumptions have been applied in the context of statutory interpretation, even where the wording of statutes has left it open to the courts to adopt a different approach. The courts have indicated that legislation governing the provision of social services should generally be interpreted in a manner that grants public authorities a considerable margin of administrative discretion.[32] In line with this approach, the courts have been reluctant to read statutes as imposing a requirement on public authorities to meet the care needs of individuals, as illustrated by the controversial decision of the House of Lords in *R v Gloucestershire County Council, ex p Barry*.[33] A similar reluctance to intervene can be seen in the context of breach of statutory duty cases in tort, where the courts have applied a presumption that statutes governing the allocation of public resources should not be interpreted as giving rise to a duty of care in respect of particular individuals.[34]

Thirdly, the rights set out in the ECHR have been interpreted in a manner that limits the extent to which they establish an individual entitlement to receive social support from the state. There are times when giving effect to Convention rights will require public authorities to provide resources to disadvantaged groups. For example, human rights law requires legal aid to be provided where necessary to avoid a breach of the right to a fair trial protected by art 6 ECHR.[35] Furthermore, public authorities cannot discriminate in a manner that violates the requirements of art 14 ECHR when it comes to distributing resources.[36] Indeed, the Strasbourg Court concluded as far back as 1979 in *Airey v Ireland* that 'the mere fact that an interpretation of the Convention may extend into the sphere of social and economic rights should not be a decisive factor against such an interpretation; there is no water-tight division separating that sphere from the field covered by the Convention.'[37] However, both the English courts and the European Court of

---

[31] *R v Cambridge Health Authority, ex p B* [1995] 1 WLR 898. See also *R v North West Lancashire Health Authority ex p A* [2000] 1 WLR 977; *R (AC) v Berkshire West Primary Care Trust* [2011] EWCA Civ 247.

[32] Note the comments of Lord Scarman in *R v Secretary of State for the Environment ex p Nottinghamshire CC* [1986] AC 240, 247, and of Lord Bridge in *R v Secretary of State for the Environment ex p Hammersmith and Fulham LBC* [1991] 1 AC 521, 594–7.

[33] *R v Gloucestershire County Council, ex p Barry* [1997] AC 584. Baroness Hale in her dissenting judgment in *McDonald* was very critical of specific elements of the *Barry* decision, and Lord Wilson in *KM* also expressed doubts about its correctness: however, for now, it remains a key precedent.

[34] See eg. *O'Rourke v Camden LBC* [1997] 3 All ER 23.

[35] *Airey v Ireland* (1979–80) 2 EHRR 305.

[36] See eg. *Burnip v Birmingham City Council* [2012] EWCA Civ 629.   [37] *Airey* para.26.

Human Rights have been very reluctant to interpret Convention rights as establishing an entitlement to receive state support in ordinary circumstances, taking the view that the ECHR is an instrument designed to protect core civil and political rights rather than a wider range of human interests.[38] Furthermore, in applying proportionality analysis to determine whether a qualified Convention right has been violated, the courts have again tended to give considerable leeway to government decision-making in the socio-economic field, with the latitude given to public authorities in this context resembling at times a doctrine of non-justiciability.[39]

In certain limited circumstances, a failure to provide a bare minimum of social support to individuals and families in need may violate the Convention.[40] In the UK, cases such as *R (Bernard) v London Borough of Enfield*[41] and *R (on the application of Adam) v Secretary of State for the Home Department*[42] have established that a failure by public authorities to provide welfare and/or housing support for impoverished individuals in circumstances where state responsibility for their plight is directly engaged may constitute a violation of art 3 (or art 8 if the right to family life is affected), if the 'treatment' they endure crosses the art 3 threshold of being 'inhuman and degrading' or comes close to meeting that exacting standard. In *MK and AH v Secretary of State for the Home Department*, Foskett J took the view that 'street homelessness, or imminent street homelessness, caused by the positive action of the State would ordinarily amount to a breach of Article 3'.[43] Similarly, in the 2011 case of *MSS v Belgium and Greece*,[44] the Strasbourg Court held that the Greek authorities had violated the art 3 rights of the claimant by failing to have due regard for the applicant's vulnerability as an asylum seeker, with the result that the state was responsible for the state of extreme poverty to which he was reduced, namely 'living in the street, with no resources or access to sanitary facilities, and without any means of providing for his essential needs'.[45]

However, both the Court of Appeal in *Anufrijeva v Southwark*[46] and subsequently the Supreme Court in *McDonald* have made it clear that a failure by a public authority to provide an individual with social support will only constitute a violation of Convention rights in exceptional circumstances.[47] In *McDonald*, as

---

[38] See *O'Rourke v UK* Application No 39022/97, Decision of 26 June 2001; *Pentiacova v Moldova* (2005) EHRR 23; *Anufrijeva v Southwark* [2003] EWCA Civ 1406; *R (Condliff) v North Staffordshire Primary Care Trust* [2011] EWCA Civ 910; *R (AC) v Berkshire West Primary Care Trust* [2011] EWCA Civ 247.

[39] *Hatton v UK* (2003) 37 EHRR 611. See also M Cousins, 'Human Rights, Anti-discrimination and Social Security Benefits: Recent UK Case Law' *Journal of Social Welfare and Family Law* (2011) 32(4): 391–400.

[40] C O'Cinneide, 'A Modest Proposal: Destitution, State Responsibility and the European Convention on Human Rights' *European Human Rights Law Review* [2008] 5: 583–605.

[41] *R (Bernard) v London Borough of Enfield* [2002] EWHC 2282 (Admin).

[42] *R (on the application of Adam) v Secretary of State for the Home Department* [2005] UKHL 66.

[43] *MK and AH v Secretary of State for the Home Department* [2012] EWHC 1896 (Admin), para.100.

[44] *MSS v Belgium and Greece* Application No 30696/09, Decision of 21 January 2011 (Grand Chamber).

[45] *MSS* para.254.   [46] *Anufrijeva v Southwark* [2003] EWCA Civ 1406.

[47] See also *R (Condliff) v North Staffordshire Primary Care Trust* [2011] EWCA Civ 910; *R (AC) v Berkshire West Primary Care Trust* [2011] EWCA Civ 247.

already discussed above, the Supreme Court considered that the local authority's decision to only fund the provision of incontinence pads had not subjected Ms McDonald to 'inhuman and degrading treatment' or come sufficiently close to crossing that threshold to warrant a finding that art 8 had been violated in her case. Furthermore, Lord Brown indicated that, even if this threshold had been crossed, the interference with the claimant's rights would have been justified on the basis that that the local authority had taken her needs into account and enjoyed wide discretion when it came to resource allocation decisions.[48]

The substance of resource allocation decisions may also be vulnerable to challenge under administrative law if they endanger an individual's life or risk exposing them to intolerable living conditions. For example, in the 'Herceptin' case of *R (Rodgers) v Swindon Primary Care Trust*, the Court of Appeal indicated that state action which endangered the right to life would be subject to 'rigorous scrutiny', even where art 2 ECHR was not in itself directly engaged.[49]

If followed to its logical conclusion, this approach could conceivably act as a 'tin-opener' to expose resource allocation decisions which could have grave effects on individual wellbeing to heightened reasonableness review.[50] However, the case law in this area is far from settled. The decision in *Rogers* ultimately turned on a very specific procedural issue, namely that Swindon Primary Care Trust had no rational basis for distinguishing between the circumstances where they would or would not fund breast cancer treatment using the new 'wonder drug' Herceptin. The court was also careful to emphasize that 'this is not a case about the allocation of scarce resources', where it would be 'very difficult, if not impossible' to conclude that a public authority had acted arbitrarily or irrationally.[51] Therefore, for now, *Rogers* only offers a tantalizing hint that the courts may be willing to subject the substance of resource allocation decisions to heightened scrutiny when they affect fundamental individual interests such as the right to life.

Subsequent cases have tended to confirm the reluctance of courts to probe too deeply into the substance of resource allocation decisions, even when they may have grave consequences for specific individuals. For example, in *R (FL) v Lambeth LBC* the High Court was not prepared to depart from the *Wednesbury* standard of review in a case involving a challenge to a decision not to re-house a young woman who was facing threats of serious violence from a group of young men living near to where she was currently residing. The claimant had been raped, and the rapist and members of his gang subsequently made threats against her life when they met her in the street near where they all lived. She asked to be provided with alternative accommodation elsewhere in London, but the

---

[48] *McDonald* paras 15–19. For criticism of the court's reasoning in this case, see L Clements, 'Disability, Dignity and the Cri de Coeur' *European Human Rights Law Review* [2011] 675–685.

[49] *R (Rodgers) v Swindon Primary Care Trust* [2006] EWCA Civ 392 para.56.

[50] The metaphor of a 'tin-opener' is borrowed from Harlow and Rawlings, *Law and Administration*, 126.

[51] As Harlow and Rawlings suggest, the decision in *Rogers* 'might have gone very differently'. See Harlow and Rawlings, *Law and Administration*, 125; see also Palmer, *Judicial Review, Socio-Economic Rights and the Human Rights Act*, 214–7.

defendant local authority refused her application on the grounds that her existing accommodation had not been shown to be unsafe. Counsel for the claimant suggested that the reasonableness of the local authority's decision should be subject to heightened scrutiny, given the circumstances of the case and the threats that had been made against the claimant's life. However, the court ruled that the standard *Wednesbury* approach should be applied: '[i]f in making their value judgments they act reasonably, take into account those matters that are relevant and put on one side those matters that are irrelevant then it seems to me this Court should not interfere'.[52] This judgment is very difficult to reconcile with the willingness of the Court of Appeal in *Rogers* to apply 'rigorous scrutiny' when the right to life was potentially affected by a resource allocation decision.[53] However, it illustrates the extent to which the courts are reluctant to probe too deeply into resource allocation decisions and the uncertainty of the current case law position.

Other tantalizing hints exist in the case law that the courts may be prepared to adopt a more robust approach in reviewing the substance of resource allocation decisions which appear to be contrary to notions of human dignity. In the remarkable *JCWI* decision, the Court of Appeal recognized the existence of a common law entitlement not to be driven into a state of destitution by a failure to provide state support. In his leading judgment, Simon Brown LJ (as he was then) commented as follows:

...the Regulations necessarily contemplate for some a life so destitute that to my mind no civilised nation can tolerate it. So basic are the human rights here at issue that it cannot be necessary to resort to the European Convention on Human Rights to take note of their violation...Parliament cannot have intended a significant number of genuine asylum seekers to be impaled on the horns of so intolerable a dilemma: the need either to abandon their claims to refugee status or alternatively to maintain them as best they can but in a state of utter destitution. Primary legislation alone could in my judgment achieve that sorry state of affairs.[54]

However, *JCWI* has rarely been cited as relevant precedent in subsequent cases.[55] Furthermore, there are few signs that the judiciary is eager to extend common law rights into socio-economic terrain. For example, the House of Lords in *Bancoult*

---

[52] [2010] EWHC 49 (Admin), para. 145.

[53] This decision was appealed, partially on the basis that the first instance judge had erred in not applying a more intensive standard of review in respect of the housing decision in question: the case was settled before the appeal hearing commenced.

[54] *R v Secretary of State for Social Security, ex p Joint Council for the Welfare of Immigrants* [1997] 1 WLR 275, 292–3. As discussed further below, Parliament subsequently introduced primary legislation expressly designed to subject certain categories of asylum-seekers to the regime of enforced destitution which had been condemned by the Court of Appeal: see A Sweeney, 'The Human Rights of Failed Asylum Seekers in the United Kingdom' *Public Law* [2008] 277.

[55] *JCWI* was singled out by Jonathan Sumption QC (as he then was) in his F A Mann lecture in November 2011 as representing a problematic intrusion into the political realm. See J Sumption, 'Judicial and Political Decision-making: The Uncertain Boundary', F A Mann lecture, 8th November 2011, text available at <http://www.legalweek.com/digital_assets/3704/MANNLECTURE_final.pdf> (accessed 20 January 2012).

(No 2) was notably unsympathetic to the idea that the population of a territory enjoyed a positive right to obtain state support.[56]

In general, questions of social justice are usually treated as exercising a type of repulsion effect on the reach of legal accountability. Both the legislature and the courts have taken the view that the substance of resource allocation decisions should be largely insulated from the reach of legal accountability. Public authorities enjoy comparatively unfettered discretion when it comes to allocating resources between different social groups, and the role of courts and tribunals is mainly confined to ensuring that resources are distributed in a manner that accords with proper procedure.

E. The case for keeping legal accountability detached from social justice

Various justifications can be offered in support of this detached relationship between legal accountability and social justice, and in particular of the limited role that courts play in English law in reviewing the substance of resource allocation decisions.[57] To start with, general agreement exists that politicians should play the leading role in deciding how to allocate resources. The political control exercised over public administration by elected politicians is the most direct means by which a relationship of democratic accountability is established between public authorities and the electorate at large. Furthermore, the distribution of communal resources is an area where democratic input should be maximized, on account of how it affects every person in society and directly impacts upon the common interest. As Michael Walzer puts it, social rights 'have their origin in a shared social life, and they partake of the rough and ready character of that life'.[58] Therefore, any self-respecting democracy must place substantial limits on the power of courts and other non-elected bodies to determine contested issues of social justice, and leave key decisions in this field to be resolved by the political process.

Resource allocation decisions also often involve a complex balancing of various policy considerations which affect a wide diversity of parties. Doubts have been expressed about the ability of the legal process to handle such polycentric disputes in a just and effective manner.[59] Furthermore, very different views exist as to what social justice entails. If courts and tribunals are dragged too deeply into these debates it may, as Carol Harlow has argued, undermine the 'very qualities of certainty, finality and especially independence for which the legal

---

[56] *R (on the application of Bancoult) v Secretary of State for Foreign and Commonwealth Affairs (No 2)* [2008] UKHL 61.

[57] For an overview, see C Gearty and V Mantouvalou, *Debating Social Rights* (Oxford: Hart Publishing, 2010).

[58] M Walzer, 'Justice Here and Now', in M Walzer, *Thinking Politically: Essays in Political Theory* (Yale, Connecticut: Yale University Press, 2007), 68–80.

[59] See L Fuller, 'The Forms and Limits of Adjudication' *Harvard Law Review* (1978) 92(2): 353–409.

process is esteemed'.[60] It might also disrupt how public authorities currently deal with the complex issues of resource allocation in areas such as social security, health care, and public housing. In particular, it could encourage public authorities to adopt an excessively cautious and defensive approach.[61] It could also skew their priorities towards appeasing potential litigants at the expense of other groups.[62]

Taken together, all of these arguments support the idea that it would be foolish to rely on legal controls to give effect to a 'total' vision of social justice, ie. a comprehensive system of resource distribution that satisfies a particular philosophical ideal of group justice. They also suggest that caution is warranted before free rein is given to courts or other legal adjudicative bodies to interpret, apply and enforce compliance with a wide-ranging set of social policy principles. The reach and scope of legal accountability may have expanded greatly over the last few decades, but this does not mean that it can or should serve as a vehicle for remedying multiple forms of social injustice.

All this is relatively uncontroversial. Few jurisdictions expect their courts to play a leading role in reviewing resource allocation decisions. Many state constitutions now make socio-economic rights legally enforceable, including South Africa, Mexico, and Kenya. However, it is only perhaps in Brazil, Colombia, and India that the courts have come to play a significant role in supervizing how public resources are distributed, and in all three countries their enhanced role in this regard can be attributed in part to specific and unique factors.[63]

However, it is one thing to oppose extending legal controls to cover the whole terrain of social justice: it is another thing to limit the reach of legal accountability to such an extent that public authorities enjoy almost unfettered discretion when it comes to the substance of resource allocation decisions, as is currently the case in the UK. The fact that courts need to respect the primacy of political decision-making and the limits of their technical expertise does not necessarily mean that judges should defer to the political and bureaucratic decisions in the field of resource allocation in each and every case.

After all, courts are regularly asked to determine other types of disputes relating to our 'shared social life' (to return to Walzer's phrase) which affect existing resource allocation arrangements and have the potential to alter public sector priorities: this is particularly true when it comes to the provisions of tort law, anti-discrimination legislation, and the right of access to the courts protected by art 6 ECHR and the

---

[60] C Harlow, 'Public Law and Popular Justice' *Modern Law Review* (2002) 65(1): 1–18.

[61] For analysis of how public bodies in response to an adverse judicial review judgment often aim at 'proofing' future decisions against legal attack rather than modifying their policies and practices, see S Halliday, 'The Influence of Judicial Review on Bureaucratic Decision-Making' *Public Law* [2000] 110–122.

[62] For discussion of the questionable impact of the wide-ranging socio-economic case law of the Brazilian courts and how it has enabled middle-class litigants to gain greater access to communal health resources, see O Ferraz, 'Harming the Poor through Social Rights Litigation: Lessons from Brazil' *South Texas Law. Review* (2011) 89(7): 1643–68.

[63] For an overview, see M Langford (ed.) *Social Rights Jurisprudence: Emerging Trends in International and Comparative Law* (Cambridge: Cambridge University Press, 2008).

common law.[64] In other words, in performing their 'corrective' role, courts often adjudicate disputes in a manner that affects the distribution of resources: no clear demarcation line exists between corrective and distributive justice, and legal adjudication regularly blends elements of the latter in with the former.

Similarly, the fact that resource allocation decisions often have a polycentric dimension does not make them intrinsically unsuitable for judicial determination. As Jeff King has persuasively argued, polycentricity is a problem that arises across a wide range of legal issues, with tort and tax cases again serving as examples.[65] Insofar as it presents a challenge to the legitimacy of judicial decision-making, it does so in respect of particular factual scenarios where good reasons exist to be concerned about the impact on unrepresented parties. However, this type of situation is not unique to resource allocation decision-making: for example, a case like *McDonald* is arguably no more polycentric than many breach of duty claims brought against public authorities in tort.

Furthermore, while there are pressing reasons to oppose judicial intervention in the 'macro' realm of budgetary policy, the situation is different with more 'micro' disputes where the financial and resource implications at issue are relatively predictable and containable. Individual decisions can of course establish precedents that are applicable in other cases: however, in many cases, the specific nature of the facts at issue will limit the extent to which they can have a destabilizing effect on other resource allocation decisions, and the courts can use the flexible nature of the judicial review process to minimize any negative fall-out from a particular decision.[66] *McDonald* again serves as a good example: the specific nature of its facts is likely to limit its precedential value, and the same would probably be true had the outcome gone the other way.

In other words, good reasons exist to be cautious about extending the reach of legal accountability too far into the realm of social justice.[67] However, the boundary between corrective and distributive justice is porous. A clear distinction cannot always be made between resource allocation decisions and other types of public decision-making which are subject to close scrutiny by the courts. Furthermore, the various reasons why courts should defer to public authority decisions involving the distribution of resources do not apply with equal force in every situation.

As a result, the assumption that courts should avoid interfering with how public resources are distributed should be seen as more of a rule of thumb than a hard and fast requirement. However, English public law by and large treats the substance of public authority resource allocation decisions as a judicial no-go zone. In so doing,

---

[64] For examples of three cases from the fields of tort law, gender equality law and public law respectively that illustrate this point, see *Phelps v Hillingdon LBC* [2000] 3 WLR 776; Case C 127/92, *Enderby v Frenchay HA* [1993] ECR I-5535; and *R v Lord Chancellor ex p Witham* [1997] 2 All ER 779.

[65] See J King, 'The Pervasiveness of Polycentricity' *Public Law* [2008] 101–24.

[66] For further analysis on this point, see J King, *Judging Social Rights* (Oxford: Oxford University Press, 2012).

[67] Jeff King has described this as the 'risky enterprise' argument: See King *Judging Social Rights*, p.8.

it may unduly truncate the reach of legal accountability, especially when it comes to resource allocations decisions which have a grave effect on individual wellbeing.

F. The case for change

Resource allocation decisions can have a profound impact on individual lives, as graphically illustrated by the facts of *McDonald*, *FL* and other cases discussed previously. In particular, they can result in individuals being deprived of forms of social support which are essential for the maintenance of a dignified and autonomous existence. However, the 'light touch' standard of review applied under administrative law and the limited scope of existing human rights guarantees mean that such decisions will usually not be subject to close scrutiny by courts and tribunals, even though fundamental human interests are at stake.

The limited reach of legal accountability in this context means that public authorities can make life-transforming decisions without having to worry much about the 'judge over the shoulder', except when it comes to questions of compliance with procedure. It also means that public authorities in general are under no legal obligation to give due weight to human dignity or individual autonomy when it comes to the substance of resource allocation decisions, except in those exceptional circumstances when Convention rights come into play. There is no UK equivalent of the concept of the *Sozialstaat* in German public law, or the principle of social solidarity in French law, which helps to give a normative steer to administrative decision-making in those states.[68] Anthony Lester once referred to the 'ethical aimlessness' that characterized the common law before the emergence of modern rule of law and human rights standards:[69] a similar 'ethical aimlessness' still persists in English public law when it comes to the substance of resource allocation decisions.

This has consequences. For example, it means that public authorities can in certain circumstances deny all but the most minimal forms of social support to particular groups of people in need, as is done currently as part of the 'deliberate policy of destitution'[70] through which individuals whose claims for asylum have been definitively rejected are currently 'encouraged' to leave the UK by being forced into a state of extreme poverty,[71] without having to worry over-much about

---

[68] For a sample of the German jurisprudence, see the *Hartz IV* decision of the German Constitutional court, discussed further below: BVerfG, 1 BvL 1/09, 9.2.2010, Absatz-Nr. (1–220). For a sample of the French jurisprudence, see the Constitutional Council decision in the *Pensions* case, Decision No 2010-617 DC of 9 November 2010, paras 7–9.

[69] A Lester, 'English Judges as Lawmakers' *Public Law* [1993] 269.

[70] Joint Committee on Human Rights, *The Treatment of Asylum Seekers, Tenth Report of Session 2006/07, Vol. 1—Report*, accessible online at <http://www.publications.parliament.uk/pa/jt200607/jtselect/jtrights/81/81i.pdf> (accessed 10 July 2012) p.110.

[71] For detailed analysis of the human impact of this policy, see P Aspinall and C Watters, *Refugees and Asylum Seekers: A Review from an Equality And Human Rights Perspective*, Equality and Human Rights Commission, Research Report 52 (London: 2010), 57–74; I. Pinter, *'I Don't Feel Human': Examples of Destitution Among Young Refugees and Migrants* (London: The Children's Society, 2012).

judicial scrutiny.[72] It also creates a situation where procedural errors may expose a resource allocation to legal challenge, while a disregard of individual needs when it comes to the substance of the decision will rarely lead to judicial intervention. This risks skewing the focus of public authority resource allocation decision-making towards procedural compliance, and away from the substance of the issues at hand.

Furthermore, it could be argued that the limited role of legal accountability in this context is difficult to reconcile with the internal logic that has driven the expansion of legal accountability over the last few decades. As discussed above, the legal process is increasingly expected to play a key role in protecting individual rights and preventing abuse of state power. However, when it comes to protecting access to the basic socio-economic necessities that make it possible to enjoy a dignified and autonomous existence, the role of legal accountability is largely confined to ensuring that public authorities follow proper procedure: public law ceases to play an active role in protecting individual dignity in this context, and imposes few if any controls on the substance of public authority decision-making.

In this respect, it is instructive to look again at the approach adopted by the Supreme Court in *McDonald* and *KM*. In both cases, the court subjected the process by which the respondent local authorities determined the social care needs of the appellants to close scrutiny. However, it adopted a hands-off approach to the question as to whether these decisions were rational and adequately respectful of human dignity. In other words, the approach applied by the court was protective of the individuals' entitlement to fair process, but not of their entitlement to a dignified existence. This represents a triumph of form over substance: it places technical issues of procedural compliance at the heart of the legal analysis, and relegates the substantive core of the dispute at issue to the margins.

Furthermore, when the court in *McDonald*, *KM* and *FL* scrutinized the rationality of the resource allocation decisions at issue, it effectively concluded that the respondent local authorities had acted rationally because the decisions they reached were in accordance with established administrative practice.[73] This approach comes close to hollowing out rationality review: the reasonableness of a public authority's decision becomes assessed by how it has adhered to its own internal procedures.

It should be emphasised that the argument being made here is not that cases like *McDonald*, *KM* and *FL* were necessarily wrongly decided. The problem is that the local authorities in these cases are winning almost by default: the reasoning underlying the substance of their resource allocation decisions is not being subject to meaningful review, even though fundamental human interests are at stake.

The current state of the law therefore fails to provide much protection to individuals whose dignity and autonomy are put at risk by resource allocation decisions

---

[72] Lord Phillips in *R (K) v Lambeth LBC* [2003] EWCA Civ 1150 concluded that this policy did not violate Article 3 ECHR, on the grounds that 'failed' asylum seekers choosing to remain in the UK were voluntarily accepting a denial of welfare and housing support.

[73] In *McDonald*, Lord Walker placed heavy reliance on the evidence presented by the Head of Assessment at the respondent local authority's Adult Social Care Department: see paras 30–31.

by public authorities. This would perhaps not matter so much if the political process enabled public authorities to be adequately held to account for the substance of their resource distribution decisions. However, the political accountability of the executive to the legislature, and the democratic accountability of the legislature to the electorate, has limited reach in this context. Central, devolved and local governments can of course be held democratically accountable via the ballot box for their socio-economic decision-making and how it affects the population at large. However, the daily operation of the welfare state is often a complex and impenetrable process, and there is not much political capital to be gained by elected politicians and other opinion-formers by probing deeply into how the system treats marginalized individuals and groups.[74]

As a consequence, decisions of public authorities to grant or withhold social support often take place in something resembling an accountability-free vacuum. Furthermore, discrimination against particular minority groups and neglect of their specific needs remains a persistent problem, which is accentuated by the reality that those in most need of state support are often those last able to access the political system and press for change. Often, the most destitute include groups such as asylum-seekers, who have no political participation rights at all. It can therefore be argued that the normal democratic reasons why courts should defer to the distributive choices of public authorities apply with much less force in such situations.

In general, the limited role played by legal accountability mechanisms in reviewing the substance of resource allocation decisions that touch on fundamental human interest is difficult to defend. The minimal extent to which legal accountability mechanisms play a role in controlling the substance of resource allocation decisions provides little protection for key human interests, which political and democratic accountability mechanisms also struggle to vindicate. This helps to create an accountability 'grey zone', where public authorities enjoy almost unfettered discretion when it comes to the substance of resource allocation decisions.[75]

A good case can therefore be made that courts should play a greater role in holding public authorities to account for how the substance of their resource allocation decisions impacts upon the lives of individuals, especially when such decisions expose individuals to a risk of destitution, deprive them of support essential to maintain a dignified existence, or otherwise have a grave impact on their wellbeing. At present, the reach of legal accountability is unduly restrictive: the desire to keep law free of any entanglement with social justice has limited its ability to protect individuals against the abuse of state power.

---

[74] Overlapping areas of responsibility also generate uncertainty as to who is responsible for what, as illustrated by cases such as *R (on the application of Buckinghamshire CC) v Kingston upon Thames RLBC* [2010] EWHC 1703 (Admin).

[75] It also serves an example of how law can facilitate what Scott Veitch has described as 'the dispersal and disavowal of responsibility' for human suffering. S Veitch *Law and Irresponsibility: On the Legitimation of Human Suffering* (London: Routledge-Cavendish, 2007).

G. The uncertain way forward

The manner in which public law is detached from social justice has prompted increasing academic criticism in recent years.[76] It has also prompted a search for alternative modes of legal regulation, which might enable courts to play an enhanced role in reviewing resource allocation decisions without departing from their appropriate role and function. In particular, there has been a recent upsurge of interest in the question of whether socio-economic rights should be made legally enforceable.

Socio-economic rights protect the 'preconditions of an autonomous life' in a similar manner to their civil and political counterparts.[77] Many scholars have begun to argue that these rights can be made legally enforceable in a manner that respects the necessary limitations of the judicial role.[78] Furthermore, these rights are increasingly protected through law across the democratic world, with administrative and constitutional courts in France, Germany, Finland and other European countries exercising substantial review powers in the area of resource allocation in addition to the well-known examples of South Africa, Brazil, Colombia and India.[79] As Kim Lane Scheppele has argued, the idea of enforceable socio-economic rights now seems to be 'too powerful to ignore'.[80]

If the Westminster Parliament did choose to make socio-economic rights legally enforceable by the courts, this could be achieved through the introduction of a new Bill of Rights, through amendment of the existing provisions of the HRA 1998, or by an alternative statutory route. [81] If socio-economic rights were to be made enforceable through law in this way, it would represent a 'big bang' solution to the problem of the current status quo. An enforceable set of socio-economic rights would provide a new layer of legal protection for individuals. It could also provide a clear statement of the normative values that should guide public authority resource allocation decisions,[82] and perhaps even help to encourage the growth

---

[76] See eg. the analysis in E Palmer *Judicial Review, Socio-economic Rights and the Human Rights Act* (Oxford: Hart Publishing, 2007).

[77] K Moller, 'Two Conceptions of Positive Liberty: Towards an Autonomy-Based Theory of Constitutional Rights' *Oxford Journal of Legal Studies* (2009) 29(4): 757–86, 782.

[78] See eg. King, *Judging Social Rights*; C Fabre *Social Rights Under the Constitution: Government and the Decent Life* (Oxford: Oxford University Press, 2000); P O'Connell *Vindicating Socio-economic Rights: International Standards and Comparative Experiences* (Oxford: Routledge, 2012).

[79] See M Baderin and R McCorquodale (eds) *Economic, Social and Cultural Rights in Action* (Oxford: Oxford University Press, 2007); M.Langford (ed.) *Social Rights Jurisprudence: Emerging Trends in International and Comparative Law* (Cambridge: Cambridge University Press, 2008).

[80] K Scheppele, 'A Realpolitik Defense of Social Rights' *University of Texas Law Review* (2004) 82(7): 1921–61.

[81] S Fredman, 'New Horizons: Incorporating Socio-economic Rights in a British Bill of Rights' *Public Law* [2010] 297.

[82] Cowan and McDermont have suggested that the HRA 1998 translates 'a set of ideals into concrete form not just about *what* we expect in terms of obligations owed as a society—healthcare, a home, education, etc—but also a *set of values* as to how these services should be delivered': D. Cowan and M. McDermont, 'Obscuring the Public Function: A social housing case study' (2008) *Current Legal Problems* 159–90. This set of values is lacking at present when it comes to the relationship between concepts of social justice and the delivery of public services.

of a new constitutional culture of justification, deliberation and participation as suggested by Sandra Fredman and others.[83] Depending upon its contents, it could also radically transform the role of legal accountability mechanisms in the UK: for the first time, they would be expected to play a role in ensuring public authorities give effect to the particular vision of social justice that would be set out in the new charter of socio-economic rights.

However, at the time of writing, it is unlikely that any of these aspirations will become a reality in the short to medium term. In 2008, the Northern Irish Human Rights Commission recommended the inclusion of legally enforceable socio-economic rights in a future Bill of Rights for Northern Ireland. In the same year, the Joint Committee on Human Rights recommended in its report on a Bill of Rights that the courts could be given a role in reviewing the reasonableness of political decisions that impacted on the enjoyment of socio-economic rights.[84] However, neither proposal gained much parliamentary traction, and at present there is little, if any, political appetite for making socio-economic rights enforceable through the courts. The role of the courts in protecting Convention rights under the HRA 1998 remains controversial, and a further extension of judicial power is not likely to attract much support in the current political climate. As a result, it appears that no comprehensive 'big bang' solution to the current unsatisfactory state of the law will be forthcoming from the legislature any time soon.

Reform of the status quo might come about in other ways. In particular, there are elements of the case law relating to the HRA 1998 and administrative law that could play a role in plugging some of the accountability gaps that currently exist when it comes to the substance of resource allocation decisions. For example, the Court of Appeal's suggestion in *Rogers* that state action which endangered the right to life would be subject to 'rigorous scrutiny' could be confirmed and extended to cover other vital human interests.[85] Similarly, Convention rights are designed to protect fundamental human interests, and both Strasbourg and domestic jurisprudence has made it clear that a failure by the state to provide basic needs may fall foul of its provisions. As demonstrated by the *Bernard*, *Adam* and *MK* decisions referred to above, there is potential for the existing arts 3 and 8 case law on this point to be expanded, especially in situations where state responsibility for the plight of the individual is clearly engaged and the 'treatment' in question can be reasonably described as 'degrading'.[86]

However, if such case law is going to evolve, a clear steer will have to be provided by the higher courts. In *McDonald*, the majority of the Supreme Court gave little encouragement to the notion that existing administrative law or the HRA 1998

---

[83] S Fredman *Human Rights Transformed: Positive Rights and Positive Duties* (Oxford: Oxford University Press, 2008).

[84] Joint Committee on Human Rights, Session 2007–08, 29th Report, *A Bill of Rights for the UK?*, HL 165-I/HC 150-I, 10 August 2008, pp 43–56.

[85] In her dissent in *McDonald*, Baroness Hale applied a version of this approach in interpreting the relevant statutory framework in line with the assumption that the respondent local authority had to give particular weight to the importance of respecting the human dignity of the appellant.

[86] C O'Cinneide, 'A Modest Proposal' *European Human Rights Law Review* [2008] 5: 583–605.

contained the seeds for a more expansive approach than that applied by the majority. The court closely scrutinized how the respondent local authority had adhered to the relevant statutory guidelines, but was reluctant to review the substance of the decision in any detail. Taken together with the subsequent decision in *KW*, it is clear that the Supreme Court is choosing to subject public authority resource allocation to intensive scrutiny on the procedural side of the fence, but not on the substantive side.

It remains to be seen how the legal situation will develop over the next few years. The judgment in *KM* has established that the manner in which local authorities arrived at community care funding decisions which have a grave effect on individuals will be subject to 'intensive scrutiny': over time, this approach may carry over to the substance of such decisions. The ongoing debate about the enforceability of socio-economic rights may also influence developments, as may the provisions of the EU Charter of Fundamental Rights, which confers a degree of legal protection upon certain fundamental social rights.[87]

However, for now, the senior judiciary appears to be reluctant to leave the safe ground of procedural analysis and to apply heightened scrutiny to the substance of resource allocation decisions. This may reflect concerns about the democratic legitimacy of any judicial move to occupy new terrain in the socio-economic field. It may also reflect an embedded reluctance to delve too deeply into the complex realm of resource allocation, and a fear that courts might become bogged down in adjudicating multiple claims relating to housing, community care, and social welfare.

As a result, the status quo may persist for some time. Lack of political appetite for change, concerns about judicial over-reach and the fear of unanticipated consequences are likely to combine together to prevent any substantial adjustment of the existing legal position. However, this will leave a flawed and unsatisfactory legal situation in place. The reach of legal accountability is artificially truncated when it comes to the substance of resource allocation decisions that concern basic human needs: this prevents courts playing a modest but useful role in ensuring that public authorities treat vulnerable individuals in accordance with the 'standards of civilised society'.[88]

H. Conclusion

The courts cannot become a forum where every single resource allocation decision is fought out in detail through a long, complex and expensive litigation process. Courts also cannot venture too far into the realm of political and/or expert-bureaucratic decision-making: as discussed previously, they lack the

---

[87] D Ashiagbor, 'Economic and Social Rights in the European Charter of Fundamental Rights' *European Human Rights Law Review* [2004] 63–72.

[88] *McDonald v Royal Borough of Kensington and Chelsea* [2011] UKSC 33, Baroness Hale, para.79, citing Lord Lloyd in *Barry*, paras. 598F.

democratic legitimacy or the technical expertise to become social engineers. These limitations must inevitably be reflected in a cautious approach to extending legal accountability into the terrain of social justice.

However, this does not mean that courts cannot play a useful role in ensuring that resource allocation decisions meet basic needs and respect the entitlement of all humans to a dignified existence. At present, public authorities can make life-changing decisions to grant or deny access to social support without having to worry overmuch about judicial scrutiny of the substance of their decisions. However, a good case can be made that such decisions should be subject to heightened review by the courts when fundamental human interests are on the line. This would complement the functioning of the democratic process, not displace it. It would also be workable, on the basis that permission to apply for judicial review would only be available for cases whose facts disclosed the existence of a sufficiently grave situation. Finally, it would ensure some degree of protection for basic socio-economic rights which currently lack any real legal status within the UK's constitutional order.

At present, the desire to keep law free of any entanglement with social justice has limited the reach of legal accountability mechanisms. However, it is time to re-think the relationship between public law regulation and resource allocation in the social welfare context. Legal accountability has come to play an important role in regulating public administration: it is time its remit was extended to help ensure that public authorities comply with the basic requirements of social justice.

Index